# Research Methods for the Behavioral and Social Sciences

# Research Methods for the Behavioral and Social Sciences

By

**Bart L. Weathington**

**Christopher J. L. Cunningham**

**David J. Pittenger**

JOHN WILEY & SONS, INC.

*Library of Congress Cataloging-in-Publication Data:*

Weathington, Bart L.
  Research methods for the behavioral and social sciences / by Bart L. Weathington,
Christopher J. L. Cunningham, David J. Pittenger.
       p.   cm.
  Includes bibliographical references and index.
  ISBN 978-0-470-45803-7 (cloth)
  1.   Psychology—Research—Methodology. 2.   Social sciences—Research—Methodology. I.
Cunningham, Christopher J. L. II. Pittenger, David J. III. Title.
  BF76.5.W43   2010
  150.72—dc22
                                                                    2009041473

ISBN 9780470458037

Printed in the United States of America

10 9 8 7 6 5 4 3 2 1

To Jeanie, Alex, Rebecca, Mom, and Dad for literally everything.

—Bart L. Weathington

To God, my wife Lori, my family, and my students and colleagues—thank you for spending time with me on the journey.

—Christopher J. L. Cunningham

To my wife, Denise, who has, by example, taught me to enjoy the moment and to worry less about the future, which I cannot control.

—David J. Pittenger

# Contents

# Preface

The pursuit of knowledge requires no justification.

—David J. Pittenger

Ditto.

—Bart L. Weathington & Christopher J. L. Cunningham

## Philosophy for Writing This Book

For those of us who teach research methods, one of the most gratifying experiences is watching students develop a passion for conducting research and an understanding of the practical value of systematic information gathering and decision making. These students discover that they can convert their natural curiosity about behavior into testable hypotheses. Moreover, they learn that studying research methodology is not arcane and irrelevant. Indeed, they come to appreciate the fundamental value and importance of empirical research. Because the vitality of science depends on the passion to learn more about behavior, it is our belief that a course in research methods is one of the most important courses that any student can take. Therefore, we wrote a book that we hoped would be attractive to students and convey to them our enthusiasm for research. To reach those goals, we strove to incorporate several features in our book.

## Style

We wanted the book to be inviting and easily accessible for the reader. Therefore, we gladly used and active narrator voice to make the textbook as engaging and interesting as possible. There is a clear and conversational style to the text, but that does not reflect lack of rigor in the material. Throughout the text, we provide comprehensive accounts of scientists' best ideas and research methods.

## Examples

Another strategy we used was to select familiar and contemporary examples. We based many of our examples on well-known social phenomena and on research that examines interesting topics. Our goal in selecting these examples was to illustrate important topics covered in the chapter and to show how researchers use research tools to answer complex and important questions.

## Assumptions

Those familiar with parametric statistics know that they come with many mathematical strings attached. If the researcher cannot ensure that the data and the design of the data collection methods meet these basic assumptions, then the inferences derived from the statistical analysis may be suspect. In some cases, the statistic is extremely robust to violations of its assumptions. Other statistics fail to withstand even minor deviations from the requirements.

An assumption we made in writing this book is that that the reader using this book will have completed at least a general Introduction to Statistics course. Consequently, a certain level of statistical knowledge is assumed, especially the more basic concepts such as measures of central tendency, measures of dispersion, or standard scores. Nonetheless, many students seem to forget much after completing the final exam of their statistics course. This unfortunate phenomenon may mean that a single course in statistics is not enough to develop in students a sufficiently stalwart schema to ensure more efficient and durable encoding and retrieval of material. Therefore, this text does review critical statistical concepts as they relate to specific methodological techniques. Additionally, we included an appendix that can act as a statistics review.

A text should challenge students beyond their current ability. If education is not to extend the grasp of our students, then what is an education for? Thus, while we labored to write as clearly as we could, we also labored to ensure that we challenge students to extend beyond the bounds of their comfort and present to them the tools needed to understand contemporary behavioral research. In doing so, we hope that the instructor recognizes that he or she is not bound to teach every chapter or every topic in each chapter. This is a fairly thick book, and we hope that both student and instructor will recognize that it is a resource from which to draw information.

## Integration of Research Methods and Statistical Concepts

It has been our common experience that many students begin a research methods course with only a vague notion of how the statistics they had studied in the prerequisite statistics course are related to research design. Over time, we found ourselves teaching concepts related to statistical analysis along with traditional concepts related to research methods. Indeed, a careful review of statistical techniques requires discussion of research methodology. Similarly, discussions of research design require a review of statistical principles.

Therefore, in writing this book, we wanted to ensure that students receive a comprehensive and detailed review of the best techniques for studying behavior and social phenomena. Consequently, where appropriate our chapters provide a comprehensive review of research methods and the statistical concepts that support them. The review of the statistical principles, while comprehensive, is conceptual and nontechnical. Students who have completed a course in statistics will find these sections to be a useful review of important topics. Students who have not studied statistics will find these sections a suitable and readable introduction to these topics.

For example, the review of sampling procedures examines the different methods researchers use to create representative samples and demonstrates how the Central Limit Theorem allows one to make valid inferences using sample statistics. Other topics receive recurring attention throughout the book, including the important concept of statistical power. The goal is to show students that they can control power by adjusting sample size and by gaining control over specific types of variance—increasing variance due to the independent variable and decreasing variance due to random or sampling error.

## Order of Chapters

We arranged the sequence of chapters to both match the steps in conducting research and to aid readers in learning how to design and implement a research project. Consequently, the first few chapters present background information, ethics, and an overview of various research methods. Subsequent chapters review such topics as bibliographic research and methods for generating samples. The next set of chapters reviews how to create reliable and valid measurement instruments. Thus, there are separate chapters on creating tests and using correlation statistics to evaluate the reliability and validity of any measurement. The lessons learned in these chapters set the stage for all types of psychological research.

The subsequent chapters examine the issues and steps common to all single-factor and multifactor studies, as well as single-subject and nonexperimental methods. Relatively early in the text is a chapter on how to prepare a paper that follows the editorial guidelines of the American Psychological Association. In most texts it is common to reserve this chapter for the end of the book. However, it has been our experience that waiting until the end of a course to talk about the most common form of final outcome (i.e., a written report) is simply too late for this material to take root. A concrete understanding of what the finished project should look like aids student researchers in learning about and planning a research project.

In writing this text, one of our goals was to allow instructors the flexibility to rearrange the order of the chapters without a loss of continuity. Ultimately the goal of a research methods course is to produce both informed consumers of existing research and informed producers of new or refined knowledge. We believe that the order of chapters aids in the completion of this goal, but some instructors may find that a different order of chapters better fits their style.

# Pedagogy

Each chapter uses multiple methods to present the material, including clearly written text, familiar and interesting examples, and visual illustrations to help the reader understand complex and abstract concepts. The specific pedagogical features include:

- **Research in Action:** Each chapter includes case studies and critical thinking exercises. The goal of these exercises is to help the reader apply critical concepts to a research scenario.
- **Knowledge Check:** Each chapter contains several Knowledge Check questions, which consist of a series of questions that require the reader to apply the material to objective problems. These questions require more than rote memorization because they ask the reader to apply the material. Answers to these questions are provided in Appendix C.
- **Multiple Presentations of Concepts:** Throughout the book, the reader will find a combination of text, pictures, and examples to illustrate various concepts.
- **Glossary:** Each chapter contains definitions of important terms.
- **Statistical Review and Integration:** Appendix A is a statistics review designed to help students remember and understand basic statistical concepts. Additionally, many chapters have a section that deals with the statistics underlying the topics covered in that chapter.
- **Statistical tables:** Appendix B contains a comprehensive list of commonly used statistical tables.

# Supplementary Materials

No textbook is complete without ancillary materials to aid the instructor in introducing course material to students. This is especially important for a text on research methods. Accordingly, a full set of **PowerPoint slides**, a **Test Bank**, and an **instructor's manual** are available to instructors through this book's website on Wiley's Higher Education site at www.wiley.com. Of particular note is the inclusion of a **Research Journal** within the instructor's manual that provides examples of journal articles that supplement the material presented in this book. We would like to thank the journal *Modern Psychological Studies*, and particularly its current editor Dr. David Ross, for allowing us to incorporate published articles as applied examples of research methods in practice.

# Acknowledgments

Although we are the authors of the book, we cannot claim that what you will read is our work alone. Many people have had a hand in helping in the preparation of this text and in providing us with the training and resources that have allowed us to become researchers and professors. These people have earned our deepest admiration and continued thanks. Any errors, of course, are our own.

We are especially grateful to our editor at Wiley, Patricia Rossi, who has provided us with extensive feedback and guidance while still giving us the flexibility to produce a book we are proud to call our own. Countless professionals working at John Wiley & Sons, Inc., also deserve our sincere thanks. Specifically, we want to thank Katie DeChants and Kim Nir for their valued time and assistance in developing a professional publication.

Many reviewers read and commented on preliminary drafts of this book. The job of a reviewer is to scold the author for making mistakes and to offer praise only when deserved. The reviewers did their job well. Their comments were often humbling because we had failed to describe something as clearly and accurately as possible. Similarly, their comments flattered us when they found parts of the book that they liked. Consequently, the book you are about to read very much reflects their supportive criticism.

# Part I

# Overview of the Research Process

# Chapter 1
## Research and the Social Sciences

## CHAPTER OBJECTIVES

**Introduction**
**Why Is Understanding Research Methods So Important?**
**The Role of Science in Everyday Life**
**The Scientific Method**
**Brief History of the Science of Behavior**
**Bacon's Legacy**
**Other Important Historical Figures**
**Assumptions of Science**
**Requirements for Scientific Research**
**Research in Action: The Case of Facilitated Communication**

The whole of science is nothing more than a refinement of everyday thinking.
—**Albert Einstein**

## Introduction

Welcome to one of the most critical courses in the curriculum for any degree. A basic understanding of research is especially important in the social sciences. Understanding something as complex as social interactions or human behaviors and cognitions is not easy. Without an empirical, scientific approach to the development of a body of knowledge, our understanding of people will be incomplete and rife with error. Having a solid understanding and appreciation of research methods will help you to fully connect with the field you are preparing yourself for at this very moment. Each of us, your authors, is passionate about research for very different reasons. The three of us are psychologists, but our interests and research overlap with many other areas. As you read this text, an understanding of who we are and where we came from may help you to better place the techniques and concepts related to research methods in context with your own career goals. So you can have some idea of where we are coming from in future chapters, here are brief bios for you to consider:

# Bart Weathington

I became an academic and "researcher" in a nontraditional way. Growing up I was always fascinated by science (due in part to some very good teachers along the way). I was also very interested in understanding why people behave the way they do. My dad spent most of his career as an industrial engineer helping to streamline processes and improve industrial efficiency. I knew very early that engineering was not for me, but discussions with my dad about what he did for a living instilled in me an understanding that the most important component of any project is the people involved. I went through seven majors in college before figuring out that psychology was, for me, the best combination of my interests. I lucked into a course on psychology applied to business in my junior year and from that time on I knew that was what I wanted to do. However, I was much more interested in applying knowledge than in creating it.

I went to graduate school with the intention of becoming a consultant upon graduation. I wanted to help organizations solve real-world problems and help individuals maximize their potential. Little did I know that the best way I would find to do this would be to combine teaching, consulting, and research. I discovered that the best way to apply knowledge is to have an understanding of how it was learned in the first place. Understanding research methods is the key to this process. I began my career as a consultant who did a little teaching and research on the side. Now I am a teacher and researcher who consults a little on the side. It is my firm belief (and I hope you will take the same understanding away from this text) that understanding how knowledge is identified, created, and refined (i.e., research methods) will help you make better decisions in the future—whether you become a researcher yourself or if you never conduct your own research study outside of a classroom setting. Being an informed consumer of research is as important as being an informed researcher.

# Chris Cunningham

Psychology is in my family, but that's not why I became an Industrial-Organizational (I-O) psychologist. My dad was (and still is) an extremely busy child-and-school psychologist, and my mom is a professor of education at a local college. Thinking about thinking and behavior was probably our favorite pastime and also the source of many dinner-table discussions. This didn't translate into career goals until the summer between my freshman and sophomore years in college. That summer I lived by Lake Champlain in northern Vermont working as a temporary employee in a variety of roles (think ticket sales and light construction). The work was boring and tedious and I spent a lot of time thinking seriously about what kind of work would actually interest and motivate me for the long haul. Ultimately I decided to major in psychology, but this merely left me with the inevitable question, "Now what do I do?" Over the next two summers, I worked as a child-care counselor and psychiatric intern at a residential treatment facility and hospital in Pennsylvania. Although extremely important, this type of work was not personally rewarding. Pouring my heart and soul into providing therapy and assistance to patients, watching them "finish" treatment, and then watching them be readmitted weeks later in worse shape than before really bothered me.

I began to wonder whether there was another way for me to have a positive impact on peoples' lives without working in a clinical setting. Remembering my temporary worker experiences and other jobs I had held, I decided to prepare myself for graduate school in Industrial-Organizational psychology. I wanted to figure out a way to improve people's lives through their work environments. To move toward this goal, I began to focus heavily in graduate school on occupational health and safety issues. The one constant through all of this was my passionate desire to understand something and make things better.

(*Continued*)

These interests can be satisfied only with good research, and I learned the skills and techniques for this from my psychology training as an undergraduate and graduate student. This drive to learn something new every day and share that with other people is what gets me out of bed every morning. Having an understanding and appreciation of proper research methods and statistical analyses has allowed me to respond to a wide variety of challenges in my academic and consulting work and I sincerely believe these skills form the core of any social science career.

## David Pittenger

I fell in love with psychology in high school when I took a general psychology course. When I entered college I decided to be a psychology major. More specifically, I wanted to be a clinical psychologist. I imagined that I would sit in my office, listen to clients tell me their problems, and then dispense helpful advice. All I needed to do was learn how to do therapy—or so I thought. During my first term at college, I took three courses: a freshman orientation seminar, an introduction to philosophy, and an introduction to psychology. From the first day, the psychology instructor emphasized that psychology is a science and that we would learn how psychologists use the scientific method to understand human behavior. What a shock! I had taken biology, chemistry, and physics in high school. These were sciences—how could anyone confuse psychology with a science? What really startled me was when the instructor told us about the major. After the introductory course, we would have to take a course in statistics and then another course in research methods. Then, in our senior year, we would have to conduct a scientific study related to psychology. Math was never my favorite subject, and I had planned to dodge college-level mathematics as artfully as I could. I began to doubt my decision to major in psychology. Was all this science stuff really for me? Was I in the right major? I wanted to help people. Why did I have to suffer through courses in statistics and research methods? Then something interesting happened. My philosophy course surveyed great ideas in western thought. During the middle of the semester, I realized that my philosophy instructor talked about the same topics as my psychology instructor. For example, in my philosophy course we read sections from Wittgenstein's essay on the meaning of words. In the psychology course we learned how psychologists study children's language development. I recognized then that psychologists study many of the same questions that have confronted the great thinkers throughout history.

When I began graduate school, I still wanted to be a clinical psychologist and hoped to learn how the science of psychology guided therapists to new and effective treatments. By then I was not surprised to learn that my coursework included statistics and research methods. Even the courses in clinical psychology emphasized how psychologists use research to determine the effectiveness of different therapies. When I finished my master's degree, I worked in a residential psychiatric hospital as a counselor. I was a member of a treatment team and offered group and individual therapy under the direction of the ward's psychiatrist. Although I enjoyed my job, I noticed that something was missing. How did we know that our therapy worked? Our clients got better; but did their improvement reflect our efforts, or did they just get better? Other questions nagged at me. Why, for example, do people continue to do something that they have agreed is self-destructive? Why was a specific treatment useful for one client but not another? When I shared my questions with a former professor, his response was, "David, you are asking questions like an experimental psychologist. You want to understand what causes behavior. Go back to graduate school and follow your interests." I did. I returned to graduate school, where I studied the foundations of psychology—learning, memory, and the physiological basis of behavior—and I am now a professor of psychology teaching the courses that I once dreaded.

## Why Is Understanding Research Methods So Important?

Although there are differences across specialty fields in the social and behavioral sciences, there are three core types of information that anyone specializing in these areas must know. The first is basic statistics. The second is to understand the proper methods for developing and evaluating psychological tests and surveys researchers use to measure human thought and behavior. The third is how to conduct and interpret high-quality research. In this book, we will help you with the third type of information. Mixed in the chapters we will also remind you of important statistics that might help you along the way. We will also provide you with the basic information needed to begin the test development and evaluation process. If you feel you need a refresher in basic statistics, a review is included in Appendix A.

Why are these three core topics so important? Think about it— researching, analyzing, and reporting are the skills from your education that will help you find a job, keep a job, and make a contribution to society. You can think big thoughts and theorize all day long, but without these three skills, these great ideas will never translate to credible and applicable science. We do not want your good ideas to be restricted by the boundaries of your mind. This is why we all sincerely hope that you are not dreading this course or fearing something nonspecific about science or research. There is nothing scary here; just a systematic approach to learning, understanding, and questioning that will benefit you no matter what you decide to do with your degree once you graduate. There are many ways to study human behaviors and cognitions, but most prefer to use the scientific method in some way, shape, or form. Statistical description and analysis techniques provide structure to these methods, and good test development and utilization provide the conduit through which good research is conducted. In other words, to become a proficient social scientist you must learn to work with the tools of the trade: the scientific method and its attachments, statistics, and tests and assessments.

## The Role of Science in Everyday Life

### Thought-Starters

What are some examples of science in your life?

Have you "researched" anything today?

What are some big decisions or questions you are currently considering?

H. G. Wells, the nineteenth-century author, predicted that "statistical thinking will one day be as necessary for effective citizenship as the ability to read and write" (as cited by Campbell, 1974). We strongly believe this prediction has come true. Although you may not plan to become a researcher, obtaining and using an advanced degree in any field of the social sciences (and in many areas of life in general) will force you to confront issues that can be addressed only with the aid of scientific research. Consider the following example issues:

What effect does child care have on child development?

What are the best ways to prevent drug abuse?

Are treatment programs for drug and alcohol abuse effective?

Will a specific test accurately predict how well a person will do on a job?

Will this new drug cure multiple sclerosis?

What is the best way to present new information to a large group of people?

These are clear and direct questions that anyone could ask. Will you send your children to day care? If you do, what will you look for in the program? As a parent, what should you do to discourage your children from using illegal drugs? If you have a management position, should you use personality tests to predict who will be a good employee? These are the types of questions you will face when you start to apply your social sciences training to the real world. Knowledge of the scientific method can be invaluable where the rubber meets the road.

Take, for example, the classic legal case of *Daubert v. Merrell Dow Pharmaceuticals, Inc.* (1993). In this case, the Supreme Court ruled that judges, not jury members, must determine the merits and scientific validity of testimony given by expert witnesses. In response to the court's decision, the Federal Judicial Center developed the book *Reference Manual on Scientific Evidence* (1994) to help judges and lawyers understand the principles of research methods and statistics. As the authors of the book noted, "no longer can judges . . . rely on their common sense and experience in evaluating the testimony of many experts. . . . The challenge the justice system faces is to adapt its process to enable the participants to deal with this kind of evidence fairly and efficiently and to render informed decisions" (p. 1). As H. G. Wells predicted, the knowledge of the scientific method is now a vital part of our government and judicial system and therefore our everyday lives.

Apart from knowledge of proper research procedures, there may also be cases where you will have to directly collect and analyze data for your own purposes. Many psychology and sociology majors, for example, want to work in some form of counseling or social service agency. Effective clinical psychology and counseling processes closely follow the scientific method. Giving a psychological test and interviewing a client are forms of data collection. A psychological test is a specialized statistical tool. To understand the results of the test, you will need to understand basic statistical principles. Many clinical psychologists must also conduct outcomes assessment research to evaluate the effectiveness of the treatment they provide (Ogles, Lambert, & Masters, 1996). Taken a step further, those who pay for mental health therapy (e.g., often insurance companies) want to be sure that the cost of such therapy is justified (i.e., that the therapy actually works). For this reason, mental health providers routinely need to collect, analyze, and report data that demonstrate the effectiveness of their therapies.

You are not alone if you fear statistics and research methods. Many people seem to detest anything related to mathematics and statistics because they do not understand the relevance or importance of these topics to their own lives. We hope that by the time you finish this text you will know that the relevance has been there all the time—understanding how to do good research and work with statistics will be skills you can use for the rest of your life.

## The Scientific Method

The scientific method is really the most critical concept in this course for you to remember and understand. Knowing each of the steps in this process and how they are managed will allow you to conduct the highest-quality research possible. Sometimes the most difficult challenge for students in courses such as these is figuring out how to remember the core elements of a topic so that they can then (hopefully) attach some meaning to these elements and retain this knowledge in their long-term memory. Perhaps the easiest way to remember the scientific method from start to finish is to learn the mnemonic *HOMER* (Lakin, Giesler, Morris, & Vosmik, 2007):

1. *Hypothesize*
2. *Operationalize*
3. *Measure*
4. *Evaluate*
5. *Replicate, revise, report*

These are the core steps to the scientific method and they should sound vaguely familiar from middle school and high school science and various introductory social science courses you may have taken. The rest of this text focuses on ensuring you will finish with a working knowledge of all five components.

## Brief History of the Science of Behavior

Science is a way of thinking about and explaining the world around us. The scientific method consists of the process used for collecting, analyzing, and drawing conclusions from data. Research methods and statistics are complementary techniques that we use to acquire information and reach reasonable conclusions. When we speak of research methods, we refer to procedures for collecting information. When we speak of statistics, we refer to procedures for organizing, summarizing, and making inferences from the data.

Before we get into the real meat of this course, a little history lesson is necessary. It will be relatively painless, we promise. To understand where you are and where you are going, we think it is helpful to first tell you where social science has been and how it has developed. As formalized fields of study, the social sciences are technically young. However, as German psychologist Hermann Ebbinghaus (1850–1909) wrote, "psychology has a long past, but only a short history" (1910, p. 9). How can this be? Well, we know that the Greek philosophers wrote extensively about many familiar topics, including learning, language, memory, and dreams. Although many writers and great thinkers wrote about how they thought the mind works, none conducted anything that we would call an experiment. The problem is that the mental events are difficult to observe and measure. Consequently, many philosophers believed that we could not observe or measure mental events in the same way that we observe or measure physical objects.

This perception exists even today and has resulted in the social sciences being labeled as the "soft" sciences, a term that suggests that other sciences such as chemistry and physics (the so-called "hard" sciences) are more accurate or empirically valid. Interestingly, essentially identical methods are utilized across all of these scientific fields (Hedges, 1987). It is the subject matter that sets the social sciences apart. Properly designed and implemented research in the social sciences can be as valid and replicable as any other research. Historically, though, before this research could be conducted, a profound shift in studying human social interaction and behavior had to occur.

Although Greek philosophers had a profound effect on the generations of scholars who followed them, it was not until the questioning of these ancient authorities that the scientific revolution occurred. During this revolution, seventeenth-century scientists decided that there was more to learn about nature than the ancient philosophers had described in their writings. One of the more articulate spokespersons for the new scientific revolution was Sir Francis Bacon. Much of the scientific method as we know it today evolved to overcome and protect us from several basic human biases or "idols" that Bacon (1620/1994) outlined in his seminal book on this topic.

Interestingly, Sir Francis Bacon (1561–1626) was not a scientist, but rather a British politician. He was interested, however, in the developments of empirical science and became one of its strongest proponents. In 1620, he published a book on the scientific method titled *Novum Organum* ("the new instrument"). Bacon saw the scientific method as a better path to good answers. Like many of his contemporaries, Bacon distrusted the wholesale belief in everything that the ancient philosophers had to say. He (Bacon, 1620/1994) wrote, "For the ancients . . . out of a few examples and particulars, with the addition of common notions and perhaps some portion of the most popular received opinions, they flew to the most general conclusions or principles of the sciences . . . through intermediate propositions, they extracted and proved inferior conclusions" (p. 127). In essence, Bacon accused the earlier philosophers of making hasty generalizations that have little or no merit. He also argued that to comprehend the physical world, we must use the scientific method to ask and answer questions.

Bacon's most important and lasting contribution to the history of science may be his discussion of common human biases that can cause us to make irrational decisions or ignore important information. According to Bacon, there are four main human biases that hinder our ability to think clearly. He referred to each of these biases as the **Idols of the Tribe**, **Cave**, **Marketplace**, and **Theatre.** Bacon's observations were as insightful in their own time (early 1600s) as they are now. Indeed, we continue to rely on the scientific method, statistics, critical thinking, and analysis skills to overcome the obstacles to learning that each of these idols creates.

### Idols of the Tribe

The first source of bias described by Bacon was our human tendency to rely on intuition and common sense to reach conclusions. Bacon (1620/1994) suggested that:

> The Idols of the Tribe *lie deep in human nature itself and . . . it is wrongly asserted that the human sense is the measure of all things. It is rather the case that all our perceptions . . . are reflections of man [sic]* not of the universe, and the human understanding is like an uneven mirror that cannot reflect truly the rays from objects, but distorts and corrupts the nature of things by mingling its own nature with it. (p. 56)

Bacon recognized that many people have a tendency to believe that what they see and how they interpret events is accurate, and that their common sense is well informed and infallible. This tendency leads us to selectively perceive events around us, trust our first impressions, and then uncritically use those impressions to make decisions.

A common example of the Idols of the Tribe is a **self-fulfilling prophecy.** A self-fulfilling prophecy occurs when we believe something is true and our beliefs then influence the way we perceive and react to specific events to confirm our beliefs (Baron, Graziano, & Stangor, 1991). In most cases, we are unaware of how our attitudes affect our behavior. Moreover, when we believe something to be true, we tend to remember events that agree with our beliefs and forget or ignore events that disagree with our beliefs. At the heart of the problem is that our preconceived ideas have considerable influence on how we interpret and react to different situations.

Many researchers (e.g., Nisbett & Ross, 1980; Rosnow & Rosenthal, 1997) have examined the shortcomings of human decision making. The consensus among researchers is that humans tend to rely too much on intuition and common sense to make decisions. Another example of the Idols of the Tribe is the **gambler's fallacy.** If a person tosses a coin three times in a row and gets heads each time, most people believe that the fourth toss of the coin *must* be tails. Some people will argue, ''It makes *good common sense* that you cannot have four heads tossed in a row!'' However, the probability that the coin will land heads on the next toss is fixed at 50% (unless the coin is weighted). Many people make this error because they trust their intuition and preconceived beliefs about probability; that is a sure way to lose a lot of money at the gambling tables. In summary, the Idols of the Tribe refers to the human tendency to depend too much on common sense and to the tendency to make consistent errors in logical reasoning. *Why do you think this is a problem for science to avoid?*

## Idols of the Cave

This second source of bias is formed from the effect of our exposure to culture, common practice, and education on our processing of information. According to Bacon (1620/1994), our life experiences shape how we look at things. Although our experiences are valuable, there are important sources of limitations. As Bacon (1620/1994) described them, "The *Idols of the Cave* arise from the individual's particular nature, both of mind and body, and come also from education, habits and by chance. Though there are many different kinds, we cite those which call for the greatest caution, and which do most to pollute clear understanding" (p. 61).

The problem with personal experience is that it is personal, unique to you. Chances are that your background and our backgrounds are very different. Who is to say which of us has a more *valid* or accurate worldview? Each of us has experienced different important events in our lives. These events shape our beliefs and perceptions and affect how we perceive things. Although these beliefs and perceptions make us unique, we need to recognize their effect on our decision making and reasoning. Karl Popper (1902–1994), a famous philosopher, provided an interesting example of depending too much on personal experience. Early in his career, Popper worked with the psychotherapist, Alfred Adler, who had developed a comprehensive theory of personality development based on his clinical experiences. Popper (1963) described the following episode:

> Once . . . I reported to him [Adler] a case which to me did not seem particularly Adlerian, but he found no difficulty in analyzing in terms of his theory of inferiority feelings, although he had not even seen the child. Slightly shocked, I asked him how he could be so sure. "Because of my thousand fold experience," he replied; whereupon I could not help saying: "And with this new case, I suppose, your experience has become thousand-and-one fold." (p. 35)

The problem relevant to our discussion is Adler's use of personal experience. That Adler was a professional psychoanalyst does not mean that his experiences are automatically valid. A moment's thought will reveal the limitation of personal experience. Adler was a therapist and treated people suffering various psychological problems. His patients were hardly representative of the general population, and, therefore, not the foundation for a comprehensive theory of personality development that describes all people. The Idols of the Cave refers to the fact that we too often depend on our personal experiences to determine why things happen as they do. As we will soon see, we must do more than merely rely on personal experience to develop scientific explanations. *Why might this be a problem for scientific research?*

## Idols of the Marketplace

The third bias that Bacon examined involves our use of language. Turning to Bacon (1620/1994), we read, "The *Idols of the Market-place* [sic] are the most troublesome of all; these are idols that have crept into the understanding through the alliance of words and names" (p. 64). Bacon recognized that our use of words shapes how we think about things. Consider an example related to day care for children. Scarr, Phillips, and McCartney (1990) noted that during the 1950s and 1960s, developmental psychologists who studied the effect of child care examined the effects of *maternal absence* or *maternal deprivation*. Clearly, these emotionally charged phrases create a negative bias against women who choose to pursue a career while their children are infants and toddlers. Why use these phrases as if the mother deprived her children of food and water? What about the father's absence? If children suffer *maternal deprivation,* why don't they suffer *paternal deprivation* as well? Could it be that fathers are guilt-free because societal norms allow men to work outside the home? Furthermore, the words *absence* and *deprivation* evoke images of children warehoused in dangerous day-care centers. Scarr and her colleagues argued that these terms grew out of "fantasies about child development . . . mother-infant attachment . . . and the role of early experience for later development" (p. 255). These terms fell out of favor during the 1970s, when the rights of women to pursue a career became popular. Researchers then began to examine the benefits of day care. Thus, the Idols of the Marketplace reflect the power of language over our thought processes. *How could this be a limitation to good science?*

## Idols of the Theatre

The last of Bacon's idols represents the effects of our education. Here we find Bacon (1620/1994) complaining that many of the things we learn may mislead us. "The *Idols of the Theatre,* on the other hand, are not innate, nor are they secretly insulated into the understanding, but are imposed and received entirely from the fictitious tales in theories, and from wrong-headed laws of demonstration" (p. 66). In other words, the Idols of the Theatre are illustrated any time we accept an explanation without critically evaluating it first. In many cases, we automatically accept certain explanations because we learned them from someone we trust or see as an authority figure. Countless "scientific" theories have enjoyed this kind of dubious honor, including the now-debunked notions that the earth is the center of the universe and the world is flat. Apart from these seemingly ancient ideas, commonly accepted notions are all around us. Perhaps the best illustration of this is in Kohn's (1990) book on popular beliefs, in which he describes various common beliefs and their fallacy, including "No pain, no gain," "Competition builds character," "Like father, like son," and "Playing hard to get makes one more attractive."

A classic example of this bias can be found in Garcia's (1980) research on taste aversion. His experiments on taste aversion revealed that several well-established principles of classical conditioning were not accurate. Unfortunately, many psychologists did not accept Garcia's conclusions because the results contradicted the prevailing theories of classical conditioning. Garcia found it difficult to publish his papers in scholarly journals, and many reviewers ridiculed his work. In retrospect, Garcia's research has had a monumental effect on our understanding of classical conditioning principles. The defining characteristic of the Idols of the Theatre is our tendency to accept the truth of a statement without criticism. The best defense against this source of bias is simply to always think critically about what someone is asking you to believe. *Why can this be a problem?*

## Bacon's Legacy

Bacon's primary legacy is that he clearly identified the obstacles to critical thinking as they apply to science even today. Although the scientific method has been around for 400 years, the effects of his idols remain. Each of us can fall prey to the idols. Studying Bacon will help you understand why researchers use specific tactics when conducting their research. Researchers use research methods and statistics to overcome many forms of bias. By studying Bacon, you will learn that you can never become complacent with your knowledge. The lesson we can learn from Bacon is that the Idols of the Tribe, Cave, Marketplace, and Theatre are always present, and we guard against these biases whenever we utilize the scientific method to study and explain the behavior of people. Take some time to review Table 1.1 and think of examples of Bacon's idols.

## Other Important Historical Figures

The goal of this text is not to provide you with a history of science or a comprehensive listing of individuals who have influenced scientific thought. However, a brief review of two additional individuals (Gustav T. Fechner and John B. Watson) will help to illustrate the development of

## Table 1.1 Review of Bacon's Idols

| | |
|---|---|
| *Idols of the Tribe* | Biases due to overreliance on common sense and the tendency to make errors in logical reasoning. |
| *Idols of the Cave* | Biases due to dependence on personal experience to explain why things occur the way they do. |
| *Idols of the Marketplace* | Biases due to how we use specific words to describe things. |
| *Idols of the Theatre* | Biases due to uncritical acceptance of explanations that people in authority tell us are true. |

current views of research methods. Many other individuals could be listed and discussed here. It is no coincidence that both Fechner and Watson were picked for this discussion. Both contributed directly to the development of experimental psychology as a scientific field of study. Considering that all of the authors of this text are psychologists, this could be viewed as an example of one of Bacon's idols at work. Which of the idols do you think fits best in explaining this?

On October 22, 1850, *Gustav T. Fechner* (1801–1887) invented experimental psychology by discovering a way to measure mental events. All science relies on measurement, which is nothing more than assigning numbers to observations. All sciences have specific methods for measuring the phenomena they study. However, before October 22, 1850, psychologists had no objective method for measuring mental events. Fechner studied physics and human perception. In his research, he observed that there was not a one-to-one relation between the intensity of a stimulus and our perception of the stimulus. For example, imagine a friend asks you to hold out your hand and close your eyes. If your friend puts a pencil on your hand, you will notice its weight. Now imagine your friend putting this textbook on your hand. You will feel the weight of the book. What if your friend then places the same pencil on top of the book? You will probably not be able to detect the additional weight. Why are you able to feel the weight of the pencil in one situation but not the other?

Fechner reasoned that by studying the relation between changes in the intensity of a stimulus (a physical event) and changes in a person's perception (a mental event) he could study how the mind works. He then proceeded to conduct a series of famous experiments that we now recognize as the start of *psychophysics*. Fechner's experiments may not sound like the most exciting thing that you learned today. Nevertheless, his work is very important because it caused people to recognize that it is possible to study mental events using empirical techniques. Soon after Fechner published his work, other researchers began to study psychological processes. For instance, upon reading Fechner's book, Hermann Ebbinghaus began to conduct his famous research on memory. It did not take long until the science of psychology became common practice.

*John B. Watson* (1878–1958) is another important person in the history of psychology. In 1913, Watson wrote an influential paper titled "Psychology as the Behaviorist Views It." The paper began with the proclamation, "Psychology as the behaviorist views it is a purely objective experimental branch of natural science. Its theoretical goal is the prediction and control of behavior" (p. 158). This statement seems obvious now, but the historical relevance of Watson's paper is that he wrote his paper at a critical moment in the history of psychology, and his comments about the purpose of psychology did much to shape how psychologists now study psychological processes (Murray, 1983).

At the start of the twentieth century, psychology was a young science, and psychologists were searching for the best methods to conduct scientific research. At the time, many psychologists used a procedure known as

**introspection.** *Introspection* means to examine or look within. Whenever you think about your own thinking and mental events, you are using a form of introspection. Try this experiment in introspection: What reactions do you have when you read the word *mother*? Although introspection can be revealing, it has several shortcomings. Take a moment to think of a few.

Perhaps the most troubling question is, *How do we know that the self-report is accurate?* When you are asked to introspect about something, will you report everything that occurs to you? Is it possible that thinking of your mother evokes a painful memory that you do not want to share? How complete is your report? Although you may report things of which you are aware, could there be reactions that you did not recognize as important and worthy to share with others? Is it possible that there are unconscious mental processes that you do not directly experience? Psychologists' use of introspection troubled Watson because there is no way to verify the accuracy of an introspective report. The problem with introspection is that only one person can *experience or observe* your mental events—you. In science, researchers want to examine phenomena that others can see when they use the same procedures.

There are other problems with introspection. To what extent does your introspection influence the mental events you wish to study? Does thinking about your thinking affect your thinking? Are you confused? Try another thought experiment. Can you read and introspect about the process of reading at the same time? If you are like us, reading for content while introspecting is impossible. As soon as we start examining the process of reading, we are no longer reading. When we read for content, we cannot introspect. What are some other problems with introspection? Can you ask an infant to introspect? Can children ages 7 or 8 provide objective observations of their mental events? What about a person with depression or schizophrenia; will their introspections be accurate? If introspection requires objective and knowledgeable self-analysis, then we cannot use introspection to study children, people with severe psychological disorders, or animals. Watson (1913) rejected introspection as a research tool and recommended that psychologists study behavior exclusively. He believed that by focusing on behavior, psychologists could engage in the objective study of all living creatures. For Watson, if you can observe the behavior, then you can conduct scientific research.

Watson's legacy to psychology is that he focused our attention on behavior. Watson has had a lasting impact on all research involving the study of behavior and social interaction. Many researchers today subscribe to the perspective of **methodological behaviorism**, a philosophical stance evolving from Watson's beliefs. Methodological behaviorism suggests that researchers should study overt and observable behaviors as the primary focus of their research. Researchers use observable behaviors to make inferences about the emotional, cognitive, and other mental processes that occur within a person. As you will learn in this and other courses, behavior is the focal point of research in the social sciences. A developmental psychologist examining the memory of infants will conduct experiments that examine the infants' behavior. A social psychologist examining altruism examines behavior. A clinical psychologist who studies depression also examines behavior. A criminologist may look at the behavior of prisoners. An economist may look at the behavior of rational or irrational investors. Following Fechner's and Watson's lead, we use the observable behavior of individuals to make inferences about various mental or cognitive events.

## Assumptions of Science

Underlying everything we have discussed so far are two core assumptions that can be found built into any good research study. All sciences make the same basic assumptions about their subject matter. Social scientists take these assumptions to be true and use them to justify their use of the scientific method to study behavior.

### Behavior Is Determined

Our first assumption is quite possibly the most important. We believe that behaviors are caused or triggered by specific factors. This perspective is known as **determinism** and someone who believes this (that all behaviors have a knowable set of causes) can be referred to as a *determinist*. You will learn that almost all researchers are determinists of one form or another. Sigmund Freud (1856–1939), for example, was a *psychical* determinist because he believed that human behavior reflected a series of unconscious drives and motivations. He believed that there are no accidents of behavior—everything we do reveals something about our character and unconscious drives.

By contrast, B. F. Skinner (1904–1990) was an *environmental* determinist because he believed that an individual's interaction with the environment produces changes in behavior. Other researchers are *biological* determinists because they believe that biological processes control many behaviors. Finally, some researchers are *sociocultural* determinists because they believe that cultural traditions, customs, and regulations control people's lives. When you examine different fields of study, such as human development, social behavior, abnormal behavior, or psychophysiology, you will find that researchers in each area conduct research to find the things that determine behavior. Regardless of their perspective, each type of determinist believes that by observing behavior and the surrounding conditions we can infer the causes of the behavior.

Some people object to determinism and suggest that human behavior is subject to **free will.** The principle of free will states that a person's soul or mind controls how he or she acts. Many religious faiths and philosophy theories suggest that humans are special because we have a spirit and self-awareness that guides us through life. These religions also teach us that we have the freedom to choose between the good and virtuous, or the evil and sinister. Thus, at first glance it appears that there is quite a contrast between determinism and free will. Belief in determinism holds that we can explain observable behaviors by looking for and examining material causes. By contrast, belief in free will holds that each person is unique and that we cannot use the scientific method to understand human behavior.

It is not helpful to pit determinism versus free will. If you are willing to accept that people share some basic characteristics, then you will find that the scientific method does a good job of finding the causes of those common behaviors. Science does not have all the answers to important questions. Science, religion, philosophy, literature, and the arts are all different ways of knowing and experiencing our world. Each answers a unique set of questions using a different perspective. As Gould (1999) noted, science and religion are two ways of knowing. Both are equally important, yet both answer different questions. Taking a scientific perspective allows us to understand how things work, and when studying human behavior this means trying to discover why people do what they do. Religion helps us to examine our values and discover how we should behave. For many people, science and religion are not competing forces, but rather complementary methods for addressing different issues of importance. In the same vein, determinism and free will can be viewed as complementary and not always competing views.

## We Can Measure the Critical Variables

A second assumption of science is that we can directly or indirectly observe the important causes of behavior. All sciences rest on a foundation of measurement. Fechner's insights allowed psychology to become a science because he realized that we could use a person's behavior to make inferences about mental events. Physicists, chemists, and other scientists routinely use observable events to make inferences about the existence of things that they cannot directly observe. For example, no one has seen gravity, only its effects. Nevertheless, physicists can use the motion of the planets and stars to infer that there is gravity and to describe its effects. We as social scientists often study behavioral events and situations to make inferences about interpersonal and intrapersonal events that we do not fully understand and perhaps cannot directly observe.

# Requirements for Scientific Research

Now it is time to focus on specific elements of research that when combined allow us to ''be scientific'' when doing research.

## Empirical Analysis

**Empirical analysis** involves the gathering of data by observation and experimentation with the goal of learning something. One important characteristic of empirical analysis is that it involves **measurement**, or the converting of observations into numbers. There are many different types of measurement, but just about all can be grouped as either self- or other-observation, in which we use our own senses or someone else uses his or her own senses to collect information on how we interact with our environments.

Empirical methods are not the only way to gain insight into challenging questions. Within the social sciences, just about everything we "know" has come from scientists' efforts to observe and experience the phenomena of interest. Contrast this method with other ways of knowing. Mathematicians, for example, do not use empirical analysis, but instead discover new ideas using deduction and formal proofs. Here is an example of the difference between the empirical method of knowing and the mathematical way of knowing. Imagine that you have 10 quarters in your hand and toss them in the air. What is the probability of obtaining 0, 1, 2, 3, . . . or 10 heads? There are two ways of finding the answer. The first method is empirical. You would toss the 10 coins, count the heads, and then repeat these steps several thousand times until you had enough samples to make a relatively accurate conclusion about the probability of each outcome. You will eventually come to the correct answer, if you are willing to spend the hours of drudgery tossing and counting coins.

The second method uses deductive logic and analytical techniques. If you know enough about probability theory and your way around mathematical proofs, you can derive an equation that gives you the correct answer. There is nothing wrong with either method, although most people find the mathematical solution more elegant and convenient. There are many times, however, when the analytical method does not work and the empirical method is the only alternative. We can use mathematics to solve the coin problem because we know several critical things to be true, such as the fact that each coin has a 50% chance of landing heads. From these facts, we can derive additional truths. Thus, the deductive method works well when we have the necessary information before us to solve a problem. *In many cases we do not have this information.* Consequently, we must go about gathering data so that we can answer the question. In other words, empirical and deductive methods both have strengths and weaknesses.

The following is an example that illustrates the potential weakness of sole reliance on deductive logic:

1. All psychologists are human.
2. We are all psychologists.
3. Therefore, we must all be human.

Although extremely simple, this example illustrates a categorical syllogism that contains two premises (Statements 1 and 2) and a conclusion (Statement 3). In deductive logic, if we accept the premises and use the appropriate rules of logic, then the conclusion is true. Now consider the deduction:

1. All unicorns are purple.

2. Annie is a unicorn.

3. Therefore, Annie is purple.

The conclusion about Annie's color is logically consistent if we accept the premises. This example illustrates a potential problem with finding answers by deductive logic or pure reason. If we accept the premises of an argument, then we must accept the truth of logically consistent conclusions. In the example of the unicorn, the conclusion is valid although it has no bearing in truth—unless you can find a living purple unicorn. Sir Francis Bacon and many others recognized that deductive logic can lead to erroneous conclusions based on a false or unproven premise. Consequently, scientists who utilize empirical methods attempt to verify the truth of premises with gathered data. In other words, if we can obtain observable evidence that unicorns exist and are purple, *then* we can conclude that Annie is purple.

## Public Verification

**Public verification** is another important feature of empirical research. Using the empirical method requires us to rely on our senses when gathering data. If we design our research so that it can be publicly verified, then we are measuring things in a way that others can replicate with similar results. Therefore, public verification implies that anyone who uses the same procedure should be able to observe the same general outcome. Watson (1913) emphasized this requirement of good science when he called for all psychologists to drop introspection and adopt the study of behavior. Studying your own mind is fine, but this pretty much ensures you will be the only researcher who can experience your thoughts and make your observations. In other words, your mental events would not be subject to public verification. Your behavior and actions, however, are things that can be observed by anyone. Using a video camera, we can record your interactions with friends and family members and any researcher can share those observations. We can also attach sensors to your body and monitor your heart rate, the sweat on your palms, and the electrical activity of your brain. We can give you a personality test as a way to measure how you perceive yourself. In each case, we have collected public information that others can verify. Public verification also means that anyone with the appropriate equipment can repeat an experiment. This facet of public verification is extremely important. Our ability to repeat or replicate experiments gives us greater confidence in the general applicability of our results. The more times we can repeat an experiment and obtain similar results, the more likely we are to agree that an effect we observed is real and not just a fluke, due to chance.

## Systematic Observation

**Systematic observation** refers to the way we go about collecting information. Whenever we collect data, we want to make our observations under specific conditions, as we attempt to rule out alternative explanations for the outcomes we might be observing. Imagine that a psychotherapist claims that a new form of therapy helps depressed people. Although this claim sounds great, we need to determine its truth. We can do this using systematic observation. For example, we should determine whether the treatment produces better results than could be achieved with no treatment or a placebo treatment. To do this study, we could subject a large sample of depressed people to one of three conditions: no treatment, a **placebo** treatment, and the new therapy.

In this example, the systematic observation comes into play as we measure differences in our participants' levels of depression under each of the three different treatment conditions. Another way that we can use systematic observation is to compare the new therapy to other current psychotherapies being used by other clinicians. For this type of research, we want to determine whether the therapy is in some way better than other forms of therapy. Yet another way to use systematic observation is to determine whether the therapy works better with some people than others. Thus, we would conduct studies comparing the differences among men and women; children, adults, and the elderly; or people who are or are not taking antidepressant medication.

The overarching goal of systematic observation is to examine a particular phenomenon under as many relevant situations as possible. We continue to repeat our observations and experiments to determine which conditions consistently produce the effect and what other possible factors aside from the treatment might influence the phenomenon. Unfortunately, many people do not recognize the necessity of systematic observation, tending instead to accept testimonials and/or personal opinions without question. **Testimonials** are not a form of systematic observation, although they are often treated as such. Testimonials are nothing more than an example of Bacon's Idols of the Theatre. When people make a claim like this, we are supposed to believe what they say. Testimonials are also an example of the Idols of the Cave because they reflect personal experience. Watch any infomercial on television and you will hear many happy customers share their personal experiences with the product: "My life was really going nowhere fast until I enrolled in Research Methods. Now I'm 'the king of the world!'" Good researchers shy away from putting too much emphasis or weight on testimonial claims that are neither systematic nor objective. *How does this help them conduct better research?*

## Control of the Environment

In all forms of research, we attempt to exercise **control of the environment** in some way. We do this to ensure that the conditions in which we make our observations are consistent and can be replicated by other researchers who might wish to verify our findings. Researchers have the greatest level of control when they conduct research in a laboratory setting because they can control many or all external environmental conditions. This control helps to reduce the number of possible factors that might influence a participant's behavior, thoughts, or feelings. There are many cases, however, in which direct control of the research environment is not possible. This is especially true when a **field study** is being conducted, but even here a true researcher will try to ensure as much as possible that the environment is the same each time he or she collects data from that sample.

## Rational Explanation

A **rational explanation** refers to the two basic assumptions of science: (1) behavior is determined and (2) behavior follows a lawful pattern that can be studied.  Rational explanations of behavior, therefore, include two essential components. The first is that the explanation refers only to causes that one can observe or confirm through public verification. The second is that the explanation makes a clear and logical link between the cause and effect. Explanations that are not rational are not scientific. Instead, these are typically called **pseudoexplanations** because although they may sound like sophisticated explanations of some phenomenon, they do not improve our understanding in any way. A pseudoexplanation is also commonly referred to as a **nominal fallacy** or a **tautological** or **circular explanation**, referring to the tendency to use the phenomenon to define itself. Thus, a pseudoexplanation is an example of the Idols of the Tribe, as it appeals to our desire for commonsense explanations.

For example, a typical early definition of a *reinforcer* was *a stimulus, produced by a behavior, that increases the probability that the individual will repeat the behavior.* This explanation is circular because there is no independent definition of the reinforcer. The definition uses the effect of reinforcement to define the property of reinforcement. Why is this technique a problem? Consider the following exchange:

QUESTION: "What is a reinforcer?"
ANSWER: "A reinforcer is anything that increases the probability of a behavior."
QUESTION: "How do we know that something is a reinforcer?"
ANSWER: "Because it increased the probability of a behavior."
QUESTION: "Why did the probability of the behavior increase?"
ANSWER: "Because we used a reinforcer."
QUESTION: "But what is a reinforcer?"

The problem with this cycle is that we have no way of defining the reinforcer without referring to the behavior it affects. In other words, this type of definition tells us nothing about why a reinforcer works. Using the definition of reinforcement does not allow us to predict what things will serve as effective reinforcers. This definition also does not explain why a reinforcer will increase the probability of reinforcement.

Fortunately, David Premack (1959, 1965) discovered that high-frequency behaviors can reinforce low-frequency behaviors (the Premack principle). The advantage of this definition is that it breaks the circular definition, defining the cause as independent from the effect. More specifically, Premack's theory states that any high-frequency voluntary behavior will reinforce a low-frequency voluntary behavior. According to this definition of reinforcement, we can take several behaviors and categorically predict which will and will not be reinforcers. Consider this example: "For Alex, playing video games is a high-frequency behavior and studying math is a low-frequency behavior. Therefore, playing video games will serve as a reinforcer for studying math." We predict that video game playing is a reinforcer because it is a high-frequency behavior. We can then verify this hypothesis with an empirical test by allowing Alex to play video games only if he spends more time studying math. If there is an increase in the amount of time spent studying math (the effect), we can then say that the reinforcement (playing video games) caused the change.

Another feature of a rational explanation is that a researcher can empirically test and determine whether an explanation is correct. What if your professor told you that there is a special energy force that affects the brains of some people and causes them to be schizophrenic? The first question you should ask is, "Where's the empirical evidence?" What if the professor told you that no known apparatus can detect the radiation? At this point, you should realize that your professor is either losing his own mind or offering you a classic pseudoexplanation. A better explanation is one that is objectively defined in a way that can be supported with observational data by you and other researchers who may wish to replicate your work. Indeed, many researchers have tested the accuracy of the Premack principle. Some have verified Premack's predictions, whereas others have not (Mazur, 1998). Using the results of these experiments, Timberlake and Allison (1974) were able to refine Premack's definition and offer a more comprehensive definition of reinforcement.

## Parsimonious Explanation

In addition to being rational, scientists strive to make explanations *parsimonious*. **Parsimony** means simplicity. If you have difficulty remembering this concept, try to link it in your mind visually to a big fat kiss and remember that that kiss represents the "Keep It Simple, Stupid!" principle. In the present context, a scientific conclusion or explanation is parsimonious if it makes relatively few assumptions, does not refer to unobservable causes, and refers to specific causes. This requirement is also known as **Occam's razor.** Consider an example from the history of psychology. For a long time, psychologists who followed Freud believed that schizophrenia resulted from severe conflict within a person's unconscious stemming from psychological abnormalities in the person's development.

Now, many psychologists believe that much of schizophrenia reflects imbalances in various neurotransmitters in the brain. This biological account of schizophrenia is more parsimonious than Freud's because of the number of assumptions and unobservable constructs that the latter theory requires. Freud's theory depends on a large number of intrapsychic processes (e.g., id, ego, and superego) as well as a host of other conditions such as the "schizophrenicgenic mother." Psychologists cannot measure these constructs objectively. By contrast, the biological theory is relatively parsimonious because its states that schizophrenia results from imbalances in specific neurotransmitters. Researchers can measure these neurotransmitters and regulate them with medication. Furthermore, regulation of these neurotransmitters corresponds with changes in a person's schizophrenic symptoms. Please realize that we are *not* saying that simplicity automatically makes a theory correct. Instead, a parsimonious theory allows for specific predictions that researchers can directly test. Its value to science is its ability to generate many ideas for specific research projects.

### Tentative Explanations

Whenever a researcher presents the results of a study, the explanation of the results is **tentative.** No single study can account for all the potential explanations of the results. You can think of any single study as a small step in a long journey. Although each step may take us closer to our goal, it may also take us in the wrong direction. Consider the previously mentioned biological theory of schizophrenia. Although the theory is useful, it is not complete. Researchers recognize that schizophrenia is a complex set of behaviors that requires careful analysis. Although the neurotransmitter theory is useful, psychologists who study schizophrenia continue to look for additional explanations for this disorder.

As you read more about psychology, you will learn that researchers are continually revising their explanations for why things work the way they do. The change occurs because each study adds new information. Some new information may confirm what we already know and so we continue to use the theory to explain the phenomenon we study. Other new information, however, may indicate that the theory cannot account for specific events and must be revised or replaced. Therefore, psychologists recognize that explanations of behavior are as good as the data they have collected. Researchers recognize that as new data are collected, they may have to revise their explanations or develop new explanations.

Now that we have reviewed the general tenets of experimental psychology, we can look at a practical application of research methods in psychology. The following example illustrates the errors that people can make when they do not use the scientific method to examine a problem. In addition, the example shows how the scientific method can resolve a serious controversy.

## Research in Action: The Case of Facilitated Communication

Autism is a distressing condition. Children with autism are withdrawn and do not show normal signs of social or cognitive development. Raising an autistic child is challenging because the child requires exceptional patience and much attention. Although there are many treatments for autism, these programs are time consuming and expensive. Several years ago, a new procedure called *facilitated communication* became popular among people who treat autism. The theory behind facilitated communication is that people who have autism have unique mental barriers blocking their normal communication (Biklen, 1990). According to Biklen, a person with autism can communicate better with the help of a trained facilitator. The person with autism uses a keyboard to type messages. The facilitator helps by holding the autistic person's hand or arm. Biklen believed that the physical contact of the facilitation helps the autistic person focus his or her thoughts and express them through the keyboard. Although the facilitator holds the client's hand or arm, they claim that they do not influence what the child types.

Facilitated communication quickly became a popular treatment for people with autism. Many therapists attended seminars where they learned to become certified facilitators. Several schools and residential facilities incorporated facilitated communication into the treatment programs for their clients. Those who used facilitated communication often gave vivid and emotional testimonials of how facilitated communication was a god-send. Parents discovered that after many agonizing years they could finally communicate with their children. Teachers discovered that their autistic students were bright and talented people. By all accounts, facilitated communication appeared to break through the barriers of autism and liberate the person within. Although facilitated communication appeared to be a phenomenal treatment for autism, several researchers were skeptical (e.g., Hudson, Melita, & Arnold, 1993; Montee, Miltenberger, & Wittrock, 1995; Moore, Donovan, & Hudson, 1993; Wheeler, Jacobson, Paglieri, & Schwartz, 1993). These skeptics began to ask critical questions regarding the claims about facilitated communication and suggested the need for controlled experiments to determine whether facilitated communication worked.

Why is skepticism important in science? Sometimes skeptics seem to be more of a nuisance than anything. Skeptics seem to ask questions for the sake of asking questions and dismiss what seems to be a good thing. Despite these characterizations, skepticism is essential in science as it helps to ensure that we are not tricked into believing in something that is not true. Why was it important to test the claims of facilitated communication, especially if the children seemed to benefit from the treatment and the parents and teachers thought that the treatment worked? How would you go about determining whether facilitated communication allowed the child to communicate through the facilitator? How would you show that it was not the facilitator typing the child's responses? Facilitated communication appeared to work and showed that people with autism were bright individuals and could interact with others.

The problem is that perception can be deceiving. Just because people with autism appeared to communicate does not mean that the treatment worked as advertised. The skeptics argued that facilitated communication needed to be tested under controlled conditions to rule out alternative explanations. When a scientist observes that a treatment works it is also necessary to ensure that that effect results from the unique characteristics of the treatment itself and not other factors. To accomplish this, Montee et al. (1995) conducted an experiment in which the facilitator and the autistic person sat at a table. On the table was a large T-shaped screen that kept the facilitator and the autistic person each from seeing what the other saw. The researcher showed both people pictures and asked the person with autism to type what he or she had seen. The facilitator then helped with the typing as he or she normally would. As an example, the researcher might show both people a photograph of a cat. We would expect that the autistic person would indicate that he or she had seen a cat or at least an animal. The real test came when each person saw a different photograph. For example, the facilitator may see a picture of a car and the person with autism may see a picture of a hamburger. Remember that the facilitator did not see the same picture that the autistic person saw and vice versa. The results of this test are critical. If the person with autism indicated that he or she saw a hamburger, a sandwich, food, or lunch, we would have evidence that the facilitated communication worked. However, if the person said that he or she saw a car, we must conclude that the person doing the typing was the facilitator, not the person with autism.

The results of these experiments were clear; the person doing the typing was the facilitator, not the person with autism. When the researcher presented different pictures, the response always corresponded with what the facilitator saw, not what the client saw. Montee et al. (1995) replicated the findings of many other studies that examined the validity of facilitated communication. These experiments used different pairs of facilitators and clients, different pictures, and different techniques for presenting the pictures. The results were the same, however. There was no convincing evidence that facilitated communication worked to help people with autism. Consequently, facilitated communication has lost favor among professionals in the field. A formal statement of the issues associated with facilitated communication as related to practicing psychologists can be found in a statement published (and available online) by the American Psychological Association (1994).

One of the most important lessons to be learned from this example is the importance of skepticism and empirical research. We cannot always take the results we receive at face value. This is, after all, the main reason for public verification and replication. At first glance, facilitated communication seemed to be a great intervention, and many people were quick to adopt the new treatment as a way of solving a longstanding problem. What would have happened if no one intervened and questioned the value of facilitated communication? How much money would people have paid for a treatment that did not work? How long would people with autism be deprived of treatment programs that really do work? Empirical skepticism determined the limitations of facilitated communication.

## Chapter Summary

This chapter introduced you to research methods by briefly examining the history of science as it relates to research methods and by offering an overview of the meaning of scientific research. The goal of this chapter was to illustrate that studying research methods is an important component of any student's education, especially students in the behavioral sciences. Researchers use the scientific method to conduct basic research to understand various behavioral phenomena. Research methods also have many practical applications. Regardless of your current or future career objectives, it is important to understand the foundations of science and research methods.

Sir Francis Bacon was an early advocate of empirical science. He believed that the scientific method would overcome several human tendencies that are obstacles to a better understanding of our world. He called these tendencies *idols* and identified four specific ones: *Idols of the Tribe* (common modes of thought that lead to irrational conclusions), *Idols of the Cave* (overreliance on personal experiences), *Idols of the Marketplace* (biases in beliefs based on the meaning and use of words), and *Idols of the Theatre* (biased thought based on tradition, habit, or deference to authority).

We credit Gustav T. Fechner as the first experimental psychologist because on October 22, 1850, he recognized that researchers could indirectly observe or make inferences about mental events by observing reactions to physical stimuli. John Watson's contribution to research was his insistence that behavior is the proper target of research and that introspection is not a useful procedure for science. The objective study of behavior allows researchers to understand behavioral and cognitive phenomena. Therefore, many researchers in the behavioral and social sciences are methodological behaviorists.

Researchers believe that they can use the scientific method to study behavioral and cognitive phenomena. They base this belief on the assumptions that the behavior they study is determined by specific causes that can be measured. Scientific research, regardless of the discipline, has several general characteristics:

1. Empirical analysis is the process of learning through observation and experimentation and through quantifying observations.
2. Public verification requires that we conduct research that can be repeated by others and specifically that the variables we examine can be observed by everyone.
3. The systematic observation criterion requires us to make our observations under various conditions or settings.
4. Control of environment refers to our ability to conduct our research under consistent conditions. When researchers explain various

phenomena, they also attempt to make their explanations rational, parsimonious, and tentative.

5.  The rational explanation means the terms are clearly defined and can be independently assessed and defined.

6.  Parsimonious explanations are specific, make few assumptions, and generate many testable ideas. Pseudoexplanations, by contrast, are circular in definition and cannot be directly or objectively assessed.

7.  Explanations are tentative. Researchers recognize that their explanations must be revised in the face of additional research.

In the final section of the chapter, we examined the case of facilitated communication. This example illustrates what can happen if we casually and uncritically accept claims about human behavior. The example also illustrates how empirical research can demonstrate the value of a therapy.

## Knowledge Check

1.  Describe an area of psychology that you find most interesting. How does the scientific method help researchers better understand this area of psychology?

2.  Psychology is not the only discipline that examines human behavior. The authors of many great novels write about the human condition and use their stories to describe why people behave as they do. Describe the difference in perspective between a psychologist and the author of a novel.

3.  Many people believe that professional athletes have moments when they are "in the zone," during which their performance is greatly enhanced. There are also times when the athlete will be "in a slump." By contrast, statisticians argue that these phases do not exist and are nothing more than random events. Which of Bacon's four idols best describes the belief that athletes are in the zone or in a slump?

4.  You want to buy a new car. A friend of yours, an auto mechanic, says, "Stay away from that car, my shop is always filled with them. I plan to send my kids through college on the work that model makes for me." How does this example relate to Bacon's Idols of the Cave?

5.  Imagine that Gustav Fechner and John Watson are alive and meet for a conversation. In what ways would they agree that psychology is a science?

6.  Describe the meaning of introspection and why Watson objected to its use in psychology.

7.  Jean Piaget was a famous psychologist who studied the cognitive and intellectual development of children. For much of his research, he asked children of different ages to solve logical problems. Can we

consider Piaget to have followed the perspective of methodological behaviorism?

8. Use the example of facilitated communication to explain why we cannot depend on testimonials to evaluate an empirical claim.

9. Using the example of facilitated communication, show how researchers used (a) empirical analysis, (b) public verification, (c) systematic observation, and (d) control of the environment to question the validity of facilitated communication.

*Use the following scenario to answer questions 10 and 11:* Imagine that your friend believes that he has psychic powers. He claims that he can often guess what another person is thinking. Two of your other friends agree and claim that there have been several times when your friend has shown his psychic abilities. Given this information, respond to the following questions:

10. Why would you want to use empirical methods to confirm your friend's psychic abilities? Why not rely on the testimonials of your friends who are being honest when they say that your friend is psychic?

11. Your friend agrees to a test. You create a list of randomly selected common words. As you concentrate on the word, your friend tries to read your mind. He fails the test and is unable to guess any of the words. To explain the failure, he says, "Well you see, it only works when there is no doubt of my ability. You doubt my ability and that creates negative energy that blocks my ability to read minds." Based on what you read in this chapter, comment on your friend's reaction.

12. According to the text, what are the essential elements of scientific research? Describe how psychologists incorporate these in their research.

13. Contentment is a mental phenomenon that we cannot directly observe; yet it is a common experience. Describe how a psychologist might measure contentment and make it an observable phenomenon.

14. A therapist claims that he has developed a new therapy to treat aggressive children. You find several children who received the new therapy but still start fights with other children. The therapist states that the therapy works only when the child really wants to change his or her behavior. Comment on the therapist's reaction.

15. Why is public verification especially important for the science of psychology?

16. In an interview, a reporter asked a government official to explain why an accused computer hacker had broken into the government's high-security computers. The official replied, "The accused has an anti-social personality." Comment on the value of this response.

17. Would science exist if there were no measurement? Defend your answer.

# Chapter Glossary for Review

**Control of environment**—A feature of empirical research. The researcher attempts to observe the phenomenon under identical conditions. Also implies that the researcher reduces the effects of distracting or nuisance conditions that will add confusion to the data.

**Determinism**—A philosophical stance that natural events and human behavior are the result of an orderly sequence of preceding events that can be predicted using fundamental scientific laws.

**Empirical analysis**—Using observation and research methods involving the gathering of data to help with identifying answers to research questions.

**Field study**—Research conducted beyond the boundaries of a laboratory, in an environment in which the phenomenon under study tends to occur or exist.

**Free will**—A philosophical stance that human behavior is independent of external causes and that humans are free to choose how they will act.

**Gambler's fallacy**—An example of the Idols of the Tribe. The fallacy is a belief that random events follow a predetermined pattern. For example, many people believe that for six tosses of a fair coin, the pattern THHTHT is more likely than TTTHHH; both are equally likely based on laws of probability.

**Idols of the Cave**—Bacon's phrase to describe the tendency to use one's personal experience as the foundation for truth or the measure of all things.

**Idols of the Marketplace**—Bacon's phrase to describe how our use of words shapes our perception of and reaction to things.

**Idols of the Theatre**—Bacon's phrase to describe the tendency to accept a theory or statement as fact and fail to question its accuracy or generality.

**Idols of the Tribe**—Bacon's concept to describe common errors in humans' thinking. These errors of thought are present, to varying extents, in all people and include overreliance on common sense and logical errors of reasoning.

**Introspection**—A process by which one attempts to analyze his or her own conscious experiences.

**Measurement**—The process of converting observations to numbers using a set of rules.

**Methodological behaviorism**—The belief that psychologists should study observable behaviors to conduct scientific research in psychology. By observing the conditions under which behavior occurs, one can then infer the causes of the behavior or the presence of mental processes that cannot be directly observed.

**Nominal fallacy**—An example of a pseudoexplanation that makes the erroneous assumption that naming a phenomenon is the same as explaining the phenomenon.

**Occam's razor**—A version of parsimony that requires that we do not create more distinctions among things than is necessary.

**Parsimonious explanation**—A requirement in science that we offer explanations that make the fewest assumptions and require reference to few or no unobservable phenomena.

**Placebo**—A false treatment condition in which participants are not exposed to any real stimulus, but rather an imaginary placeholder such as a sugar pill or glass of water. Useful as a means of creating a control group without the participant knowing he or she is not getting the real treatment.

**Pseudoexplanation**—An explanation of a phenomenon that does not really explain the phenomenon.

**Public verification**—The requirement that the subject matter of any empirical research must be observable to any person who uses the same procedures and equipment to examine the phenomenon.

**Rational explanation**—Offering a description or interpretation of a phenomenon that follows the rules of logic.

**Self-fulfilling prophecy**—An example of the Idols of the Tribe. People will act in ways that bring about the result(s) they expected in the first place.

**Systematic observation**—A process in which the researcher varies the conditions under which he or she studies a particular phenomenon.

**Tautological (circular) explanation**—A form of pseudoexplanation that involves circular definitions, which use the phenomenon to be described when trying to define its cause.

**Tentative explanation**—The recognition that all descriptions and explanations that arise from empirical research may be incomplete or inaccurate. Additional research may force us to revise our beliefs.

**Testimonial**—A statement that a person makes about the truth of a fact or a claim based on personal experience.

## Chapter References

American Psychological Association (1994). Resolution on facilitated communication. Retrieved June 3, 2008 from http://www.apa.org/about/division/cpmscientific.html#5.

Bacon, F. (1994). *Novum organum* (P. Urbach & J. Gibson, Trans.). Chicago: Open Court. (Original work published 1620).

Baron, R. M., Graziano, W., & Stangor, C. (1991). Social perception and social cognition. In R. M. Baron & W. Graziano (Eds.), *Social psychology* (pp. 108–159). Fort Worth, TX: Holt, Rinehart and Winston.

Biklen, D. (1990). Communication unbound: Autism and praxis. *Harvard Educational Review, 60,* 291–315.

Campbell, S. (1974). *Flaws and fallacies in statistical thinking*. Englewood Cliffs, NJ: Prentice-Hall.

*Dauber v. Merrell Dow Pharmaceuticals, Inc.,* 113 S. Ct. 2786 (1993).

Ebbinghaus, H. (1910). *A summary of psychology*. Leipzig: Veit.

Federal Judicial Center (1994). *Reference manual on scientific evidence*. Washington, DC: Author.

Garcia, J. (1980). Tilting at the paper mills of academe. *American Psychologist, 36*, 149–158.

Gould, S. J. (1999). *Rock of ages: Science and religion in the fullness of life*. New York: Ballantine.

Hedges, L. V. (1987). How hard is hard science, how soft is soft science? The empirical cumulativeness of research. *American Psychologist, 42*(5), 443–455.

Hudson, A., Melita, B., & Arnold, N. (1993). Assessing the validity of facilitated communication: A case study. *Journal of Autism and Developmental Disorders, 23*, 165–173.

Kohn, A. (1990). *You know what they say . . . : The truth about popular beliefs*. New York: HarperCollins.

Lakin, J. L., Giesler, R. B., Morris, K. A., & Vosmik, J. R. (2007). HOMER as an acronym for the scientific method. *Teaching of Psychology, 34*(2), 94–96.

Mazur, J. E. (1998). *Learning and behavior*. Upper Saddle River, NJ: Prentice-Hall.

Montee, B. B., Miltenberger, R. G., & Wittrock, D. (1995). An experimental analysis of facilitated communication. *Journal of Applied Behavior Analysis, 28*, 189–200.

Moore, S., Donovan, B., & Hudson, A. (1993). Facilitator-suggested conversational evaluation of facilitated communication. *Journal of Autism and Developmental Disorders, 23*, 451–551.

Murray, D. J. (1983). *A history of western psychology*. Englewood Cliffs, NJ: Prentice-Hall.

Nisbett, R. E., & Ross, L. (1980). *Human inference: Strategies and shortcomings of social judgment*. Englewood Cliffs, NJ: Prentice-Hall.

Ogles, B. M., Lambert, M. J., & Masters, K. S. (1996). *Assessing outcomes in clinical practice*. Boston: Allyn & Bacon.

Popper, K. (1963). *Science: Conjectures and refutations*. New York: Harper and Row.

Premack, D. (1959). Toward empirical behavioral laws: I. Positive reinforcement. *Psychological Review, 66*, 219–233.

Premack, D. (1965). Reinforcement theory. In D. Levine (Ed.), *Nebraska symposia on motivation* (pp. 123–180). Lincoln: University of Nebraska Press.

Rosnow, R. L., & Rosenthal, R. (1997). *People studying people: Artifacts and ethics in behavioral research*. New York: Freeman.

Scarr, S., Phillips, D., & McCartney, K. (1990). Facts, fantasies, and the future of child care in the United States. *Psychological Science, 1*, 255–264.

Timberlake, W., & Allison, J. (1974). Response deprivation: An empirical approach to instrumental performance. *Psychological Review, 81*, 146–164.

Watson, J. B. (1913). Psychology as the behaviorist views it. *Psychological Review, 20*, 158–177.

Wheeler, D. L., Jacobson, J. W., Paglieri, R. A., & Schwartz, A. A. (1993). An experimental assessment of facilitated communication. *Mental Retardation, 31*, 49–60.

# Chapter 2
## Ethics and Research

## CHAPTER OBJECTIVES

**Introduction**
**What Is Ethics?**
**Approaches to Ethical Analysis**
**Making Ethical Decisions**
**The Ethical Code of the American Psychological Association**
**Seeking Approval for Research: The Institutional Review Board**
**Milgram's Experiment Revisited**
**Research with Animals**
**Research in Action: Ethical Dilemmas**

> The essence of morality is a questioning about morality; and the decisive move of human life is to use ceaselessly all light to look for the origin of the opposition between good and evil.
>
> —Georges Bataille

## Introduction

From the moment we wake up in the morning until we return to sleep in the evening, we confront situations that require us to act in one way or another. Typically, the choices that we make have little bearing on the lives of others. The decision whether to have a second cup of coffee or trudge off to the library to study may characterize the typical "dilemmas" we face. There are, however, cases where our actions do directly affect the lives and well-being of others. These choices represent a special case of decision making because they involve moral behavior.

Anyone who conducts research must be sensitive to and mindful of moral principles and ethical reasoning. As you will learn in this chapter, researchers are serious about their responsibility to act morally. All behavioral research affects the lives of the human participants and animal subjects. Therefore, before we begin any research, we must examine with considerable care the ethical implications of our work. In other words, we must consider the justification for and the consequences of our actions.

Researchers have a personal stake in examining the moral principles that guide their work. Foremost among these principles is the belief that the researcher should do no harm. Although scientific research is important, the potential value of any given research study does not grant an automatic license to the researcher to act without regard to the welfare of others.

Aside from this basic ethical tenet, there are also practical reasons for researchers to examine the morality of their work. Most professional organizations have a set of clearly stated ethical guidelines. One of the most far-reaching codes is maintained by the American Psychological Association (APA), which represents well over 140,000 psychologists. This code is an elaborate ethical code of conduct that establishes the foundation for the moral behavior of all APA members (APA, 2002). This code is also often followed by psychologists who are not members of APA. In addition, this code has been adopted by some state psychology and other licensing boards, making violations of this code a major issue for licensed psychologists who wish to retain their licensure. Other authoritative organizations, such as the American Sociological Association and American Anthropological Association, have similar codes of conduct that require the researcher to justify his or her research. While codes vary slightly from association to association, they all have the goals of minimizing harm and ensuring the proper use of scientific knowledge. As a representative example of these codes, the APA ethical guidelines will be discussed in more depth later in this chapter. The most up-to-date guidelines for ethics within specific scientific fields can also typically be found on all professional associations' websites.

Apart from professional societies, the federal government also monitors the ethics of research by requiring that all researchers receiving federal grants to conduct research on humans or nonhuman animals must submit a proposal of their research to an **Institutional Review Board (IRB)** for approval. An IRB is a group of researchers and other professionals (e.g., lawyers, ministers, physicians) who examine the researcher's proposed methodology to ensure that the researcher will protect the basic rights of the participants in the study. Most large research universities and colleges have an IRB and require all researchers, regardless of the funding source, to obtain IRB approval for any human research. All institutions receiving federal funding must have an IRB for human research. This being the case, you will inevitably need to seek approval from your IRB to conduct research.

In this chapter, we will examine common ethical issues that arise when researchers go about the process of actually collecting data from humans or animals. First, we will examine several broad ethical principles and perspectives that are a part of any ethical decision. We will then examine the ethical principles established by the APA as they apply to research with humans and animals. Finally, we will examine an array of case studies that will allow us to examine ethical dilemmas that researchers in the social and behavioral sciences often face.

# What Is Ethics?

What does it mean to be moral or to act morally? What is ethics? Morality and ethics represent a set of interconnected principles and ways for making choices. As we progress through this chapter, we will use ethics and morality to describe how researchers make decisions about their research design. For example, we will ask, "Is this procedure moral?" or "What is the ethical thing to do in this specific study?"

Although many people use the words *morals* and *ethics* interchangeably, there is an important difference between the two. In general, **morals** are the principles or rules that define what is right and wrong. For example, you may have learned that it is wrong to lie to others and that is good to help others. By contrast, **ethics** is the process of studying moral standards and examining how we should interpret and apply them in various situations. An example of ethics is asking whether it is acceptable to lie to another person to spare them the shock and pain created by the truth or if it is acceptable to steal something to save the life of another person.

You should recognize that ethics is more than "doing the right thing." Although it is important that you behave correctly, it is also important that you understand *why* you make the decisions you do. One might even argue that your behavior is not moral unless you can justify your actions. Consequently, whenever you conduct research, you must ask yourself whether your actions are right or wrong and be able to justify your decision. Although there are many moral standards or principles, they all share four general characteristics. Understanding these characteristics will help set the stage for our review of specific moral principles and ethical deliberation.

## Moral Principles Address the Well-Being of Others

At the heart of morality is the well-being of people who are affected by our behaviors. This concern for others is an integral component of our religions, laws, and social codes. Your parents, for example, have hopefully taught you to believe that it is bad to hurt others intentionally. Consequently, you probably believe that assault, child abuse, theft, and murder are wrong because they harm others. Thus, the well-being of others is the central feature of all codes of conduct.

## Moral Principles Transcend Other Standards, Including Self-Interest

Moral principles direct us to act without regard to our personal goals and interests. For example, during the 1960s, many people in the United States protested the segregation laws practiced in many states. These people believed that they had a moral obligation to oppose laws that systematically denied other Americans their civil liberties. By participating in marches and helping with voter registration programs, these people took considerable personal risk to stand for what they believed was right.

There is nothing wrong with pursuing self-interest; it is a reasonable goal. The question arises, however, when we must choose between a morally correct behavior and personal gratification. Would you cheat on an exam or submit a plagiarized paper to get an ''A'' in a course? If you knew you would not get caught, would this change your answer to the question?

When faced with a conflict between self-interest and moral behavior, morality should lead the way. The application of this principle to research is clear. No matter how valuable the data may be to us, we cannot overlook the rights of the participants in the research and the ethical implications of our findings to society in general.

### Moral Principles Are Constants and Universals

The laws our governments make are often arbitrary and reflect many compromises among lawmakers. By contrast, moral principles are not arbitrary and do not reflect mere agreement among a few people. For example, there is no moral principle supporting the law that we drive on the right side of the road. That law represents an arbitrary and convenient standard for motorists to follow (we could change the law to require that people drive on the left side of the road). Another example of the arbitrary nature of laws is that each state has a different set of laws. In many cases, what is legal in one state may be illegal in a neighboring state. In contrast, we treat moral principles as if they are self-evident facts that apply to all people in all situations. Consequently, we follow moral principles because they reflect a universal virtue, not because some authority directs us to do so.

### Moral Principles Are Impartial

When we examine moral problems, we attempt to solve them consistently and impartially. For example, some people oppose any research that uses animals because they believe that the research harms the animal's well-being. A person who opposes animal research may begin by endorsing the moral principle that one should act to maximize happiness and minimize suffering. They may also argue that animals, like humans, can feel pain and do suffer. These observations lead some people to believe that the dividing line between humans and animals is arbitrary and irrelevant. The conclusion from this line of reasoning is that the moral principle of maximizing happiness and minimizing suffering must be impartially and equally applied to humans and animals.

### Ethics and Ethical Codes

Ethics is a process of investigation, criticism, and decision making. When we say that someone studies ethics, we mean that he or she examines how basic moral standards and the facts of a situation lead to a consistent moral conclusion. An **ethical code**, or **code of conduct**, is a set of rules established by and for a group of people. As we noted previously, the APA has an ethical code that consists of a set of rules that governs its members. Like any set of rules, parts of the ethical code of psychologists consist of regulations agreed upon through a process of compromise and consensus. Therefore, like any collection of rules created by a group of people, the APA's code of conduct is subject to criticism and revision.

Although the APA ethical code offers a useful guideline for your research, you should not treat it as the final and authoritative word on moral behavior. Remember that ethics is the process of examining moral principles and behavior. Consequently, anyone who conducts research should consider carefully the moral implications of his or her research. There may be situations where you will have to defend the morality of your study. In these situations, saying, "I was just doing what the APA code allows me to do" will not be sufficient. Instead, you will need to be prepared to answer difficult questions regarding the protection of the dignity and well-being of your research participants, as well as the value of your research for others. You may also have to justify your choice of research methodology, by proving that no other, less potentially harmful method exists or could be practically used for your research. Questions about moral behavior require you to recount the ethical deliberations you used to reach your conclusions. The following section provides you with two different perspectives on research ethics that you can use in your own ethical analysis of research.

## Approaches to Ethical Analysis

Throughout history, people have devised different approaches to determine what constitutes ethical and unethical behavior. We cannot examine all of these in this chapter. Instead, we will examine two of the more influential approaches and encourage you to enroll in a philosophy of ethics course. The two approaches that we will review are the principle of utilitarianism and the principle of rights.

### The Principle of Utilitarianism

Jeremy Bentham (1748–1832) and John Stuart Mill (1808–1873) were two philosophers who wrote a great deal about the principles of utilitarianism. The fundamental perspective of **utilitarianism** is that ethical behaviors are those where the total positive outcomes are greater than the total negative outcomes produced by one's actions (i.e., when the positive consequences of the ends help to justify the means by which those ends were achieved). For utilitarianism, the primary focus of the ethical analysis is the consequence of our behavior. As Bentham often quipped, "the . . . truth is that it is the greatest happiness of the greatest number that is the measure of right and wrong." Therefore, a behavior is morally correct if the positive consequences outweigh the negative consequences for the greatest number of people. Mill, like Bentham, agreed that we must consider the consequences of our actions but was specific about the types of consequences we should examine. According to Mill, we should select behaviors that maximize happiness while minimizing suffering. Therefore, from Mill's perspective of utilitarianism, actions that create the greatest good or happiness for the most people are morally correct behaviors.

How would we apply this principle to behavioral research? The goal of research, according to utilitarianism, should be to maximize happiness for the greatest number of beings. Consequently, from this perspective psychologists must justify a research project by satisfying two conditions. First, the researcher should be able to show that the results will produce a useful outcome that will benefit others. Therefore, if the research jeopardizes the well-being of the participants, the researcher must demonstrate that the benefits of the study outweigh the discomfort experienced by the participants. Second, the researcher must demonstrate that the specific methods employed are better than all the available options for collecting the data. In other words, the researcher must show that there is no other, more ethical method for collecting data of the same quality.

Here is an example of how we might use utilitarian reasoning in an applied experiment. In an experiment designed to test the effectiveness of a new treatment for depression, we randomly assign some people to a control condition. By definition, people in this condition will receive nothing that will improve their mood. The other people in the experiment will receive what we believe to be an effective treatment. How can we justify withholding a useful treatment from the people in the control group? We know that these individuals are distressed and we believe that the treatment would make them feel better. Furthermore, our actions prevent these people from feeling better because we purposefully withhold the treatment.

We can justify the experiment by using the utilitarian perspective if we can successfully support two arguments. First, we must show that the results of the experiment have the potential of bringing the greatest happiness to the greatest number of people. If the experiment is successful, we can say with confidence that we have a valid treatment for depression and thereby be able to treat countless people suffering from this condition. Second, we must show that this experiment is the only way to assess the effectiveness of the treatment. We would have to prove that this research design, more than any other research design, will produce the results we need to evaluate the effectiveness of the treatment. If we can make these claims, then we can conclude that the experiment is morally acceptable because we have determined that the potential happiness for many people outweighs the temporary discomfort of a few people in a control group. A third, design-based option in the present example is to use a research design in which all participants will eventually receive the depression treatment, but at different times. This can allow you to have a control group that dwindles in size over time until all participants have had the chance to benefit from the treatment.

In the social and behavioral sciences, many experiments can cause temporary distress for the participants. For example, to understand the sensation of pain, the researcher has to inflict pain. To understand aggression, it may be necessary to create situations where one person can demonstrate aggression toward another person. Although the participants may agree that the conditions of the study are unpleasant, the researcher can justify the research if the results, in the long run, improve the lives of many and if there is no other reasonable way to collect the data.

### Disadvantages of Utilitarianism

Although intuitively appealing, the utilitarian perspective on ethics suffers from several disadvantages, most of which are due to our inability to firmly define benefits and costs. For example, how are we to know the true effect of any experiment? How do we determine the relative cost of a person's discomfort or his or her happiness? Although we use these terms every day, how do we weigh or measure discomfort and happiness? What accounting system do we use to ensure that our experiments do not go into debt by creating more discomfort than happiness? What counts as a cost? What counts as a benefit? One person may think that the results are of considerable theoretical significance and thereby serve science. You, however, may think that the results are trivial and of no known practical value. Therefore, one of the essential problems with utilitarianism is that *value, discomfort,* and *happiness* are vague terms that are hard to quantify.

### Advantages of Utilitarianism

Aside from these important disadvantages, utilitarianism does offer multiple advantages to a researcher attempting to demonstrate the ethics of his or her research. One advantage is that utilitarianism offers a clear rationale for conducting research that creates temporary discomfort in participants. The researcher can justify the temporary discomfort of a few people if he or she can show that the results have a recognized value and that there is no other reasonable way to collect the data.

Another advantage of utilitarianism is that it allows us to evaluate the morality of any research project from a surface perspective. Such a perspective may allow us to recognize that there are exceptions to some moral principles. Consequently, we can use utilitarianism to find a balance between two moral principles that may seem otherwise incompatible with each other. For instance, we may believe that each participant in a study has the right to receive information concerning his or her performance in a research project. Does this mean that the researcher must reveal everything about the participant's performance? What if the participant completed an intelligence test as a part of the study; are we obligated to disclose the results of the test to the person? Using the utilitarianism perspective would allow us to balance the benefits and costs of the disclosure. Therefore, we may withhold information if we believe that sharing the results will do more harm than good. In other situations, however, our analysis of the situation may compel us to share the full test results with the participant.

## The Principle of Rights

The utilitarian perspective requires that we examine the consequences of our actions to determine whether a behavior is morally right or wrong. The perspective of rights is a completely different method of studying ethics because it requires us to recognize that the rights of other people must guide our actions. When we speak of moral rights, we mean that every person is entitled to certain privileges regardless of who they are. That is, moral rights are universal principles applied to every person equally and impartially. The philosophical foundation for this concept of universal moral rights is most often attributed to the philosopher Immanuel Kant (1724–1804).

Kant formulated the principle of the categorical imperative as a means to determine fundamental moral principles. As you will see, the categorical imperative allows us to define moral principles and to identify our duty as moral agents. For Kant, doing the "right" thing was not enough. We often do the right thing because it serves our goals. Some people give money to charity because they can use the donation as a tax deduction, to win the admiration of others, and to express pity for the less fortunate. Although giving money to a charity may be a nice thing to do, it is not automatically the morally right thing to do. According to Kant, the individual's sense of moral duty must drive his or her actions. Consequently, a true charitable act would be to donate the money in such a way that no one knows who gave the money. The categorical imperative in this case is that giving should occur without the expectation of benefit to the donor. Following Kant's categorical imperative, it is not enough to accept blindly any code of conduct as a field guide of the right and wrong things to do in research. Rather, you should examine the moral principles that guide your work as a researcher.

An essential formulation of the **categorical imperative** is, "Act in such a way that you always treat humanity, whether in your own person or in the person of any other, never simply as a means, but always at the same time as an end" (Kant, 1750/1964, p. 96). This formulation of the categorical imperative establishes that all people are equal, as are their moral rights. More specifically, this moral code requires that we respect the dignity of other people and refuse to treat them merely as a way to serve our self-interests. We must ensure that our behavior as researchers does not deny others their basic rights. The principle also requires that we avoid actions that diminish the dignity or self-worth of other people.

This formulation of the categorical imperative is a cornerstone of the APA's ethical guidelines (APA, 2002). For example, Principle E of the code requires psychologists to respect the rights and dignity of all people. Specifically, the definition of this principle includes the passage, "Psychologists respect the dignity and worth of all people, and the rights of individuals to privacy, confidentiality, and self-determination."

The ethical perspective created by the principle of rights is different from the utilitarian perspective. As noted previously, the utilitarian perspective considers only the consequences of our behavior. By contrast, the principle of rights requires that we examine the intention of our actual behaviors throughout the research process (i.e., instead of justifying the means by focusing on the outcomes, now the focus is on the means themselves). In addition, the principle does not focus on the balance of positive and negative outcomes. Rather, the principle of rights examines the universal rights each participant has and the duty we have to respect those rights at all times.

### Disadvantages of Principle of Rights

Several criticisms can be directed at a principle-of-rights approach to justifying the ethicality of research. The first is that the system has no way to balance the conflicting rights of all individuals involved in the research process. For example, the authors of this book are psychologists who believe that all people should participate in research when given informed consent and the choice not to participate. To us, helping expand the body of scientific knowledge is a moral duty. By contrast, another person may believe that scientific research is misguided and that no one should act to help researchers. Kant's categorical imperative treats these conflicting rights as equal and gives us no way to decide between them. Because this perspective does not consider the consequences of our behavior, we have no way of resolving the conflict.

A second problem with Kant's perspective is that it can sometimes be too absolute and create conditions that we find intuitively unacceptable. For example, we may believe that confidentiality is a moral right that must be accorded to all research participants. According to Kant's categorical imperative, we must never divulge what someone did or said to us as a part of our research. Imagine that I am conducting an interview as a part of my research. In response to one of the questions, a participant tells me, ''I've been having sexual relations with the little girl who lives next door.'' Application of a categorical imperative involving the absolute right to confidentiality would lead us to not report what is clearly morally unacceptable behavior. According to Kant, the consequences of maintaining confidentiality are immaterial. If we believe that confidentiality is a universal rule, then we cannot violate the participant's confidentiality. If we call the police or warn the little girl's parents, we will violate our rule and can no longer say that confidentiality is a universal moral right of all people.

### Advantages of Principle of Rights

Kant's philosophical principles make clear that all people are equal and that we cannot treat them as if they were pieces of equipment. This perspective is in keeping with our beliefs about morality and is an integral part of the APA's (2002) code of conduct. Specifically, the code of conduct recognizes that we cannot conduct research merely to serve our self-interests. Our research procedures must respect the dignity of the people who participate in our research and recognize that they have the capacity to act freely. Following this principle saves us from committing dreadful acts in the self-serving name of science.

## Making Ethical Decisions

Life is complex and often unpredictable. Consequently, there is no way that we can create a single set of rules that prescribes what you should do in every situation that you will encounter. In a similar fashion, it is unacceptable for any researcher to attempt to justify the ethicality of research by using either the utilitarian or principle-of-rights criteria. Instead, we try to formulate general standards or principles that can guide our decisions and behavior when conducting research.

Thus far, you have learned that the perspective of utilitarianism and the perspective of rights lead to different strategies for resolving ethical conundrums. In addition, each perspective has its relative advantages and disadvantages. These two perspectives can often lead to conflicting conclusions. Because research is a practical enterprise, we need to find some way to make practical decisions.

As we have already noted, ethical reasoning requires careful thought and deliberation. To examine an ethical issue, we must begin by examining the moral principles that we hold to be true. Next, we examine the specific circumstances of the situation. Using consistent and objective reasoning, we can determine how to behave.

Figure 2.1 represents the sequence of events that we use to come to an ethical decision. The moral standards are those principles that we hold to be true. This approach requires that we attempt to balance these moral standards within the circumstances of the research project. The result of this discourse is the moral decision and our course of action. As you will see, the ethical code of the APA follows this pattern to examine ethical principles.

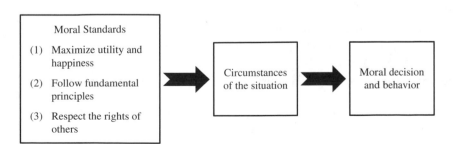

## Figure 2.1

**Ethical Decision Making**

Using fundamental moral principles and the facts of the situation, a person can come to a rational and logical decision.

# The Ethical Code of the American Psychological Association

Research on humans is a relatively new phenomenon (Resnik, 1998). Before the twentieth century, most scientists conducted research on topics unrelated to human behavior and the body. Toward the end of the nineteenth century, however, scientists began to study humans in detail. During this time, the study of people moved from purely a philosophical exercise to assert itself as an empirical science. At the same time, physicians began to use the scientific method to study various diseases and their cures. Soon, research using living people became commonplace. Unfortunately, there was no ethical code to guide researchers except their personal beliefs and conscience. The need for an ethical code for researchers studying humans became apparent in the late 1940s. It is important for us to also recognize that our perspectives on what constitutes ethical treatment of human and animal research participants has evolved with societal views over time. Thus, when we discuss historical examples of ethical and unethical research, bear in mind that some research studies that seem wrong by today's standards may have been viewed as acceptable when originally conducted.

Although this is true for some studies, it is does not hold when speaking of the war crimes conducted by the Nazis during World War II. Included in the charges filed by Allied powers at the end of the war were allegations that Nazi scientists conducted cruel experiments on Jews and other groups of people held in the concentration camps. These experiments were little more than protracted torture. As a response to these atrocities, researchers developed the Nuremberg Code (Resnik, 1998). The Nuremberg Code, listed in Box 2.1, consists of nine fundamental principles that researchers must use when conducting research with humans.

---

## Box 2.1  The Nuremberg Code of Principles Governing Research Using Humans

1. **Informed Consent:** The participant must understand what will happen to him or her in the research and then volunteer to participate.

2. **Social Value:** The results of a study should benefit society.

3. **Scientific Validity:** Only trained scientists who employ careful and well-designed studies should conduct research.

4. **No Malfeasance:** Researchers must conduct studies that are safe and minimize risk of harm to the participants.

5. **Termination:** The participant may withdraw from the study for any reason, and the researcher must stop the study if the participant is at risk of injury or death.

6. **Privacy:** The researcher must preserve the privacy/confidentiality of the participant.

*(Continued)*

7. **Vulnerable Populations:** Researchers need to use special caution to protect the rights of those who cannot act for themselves, including children, the developmentally delayed, or the mentally disabled.

8. **Fairness:** Selection of the participants for the research and assignment to treatment conditions must be fair, consistent, and equitable.

9. **Monitoring:** The researcher must continually monitor the study to ensure the safety of participants.

*Note*: The original Nuremberg Code included Principles 1–5. Principles 6–9 are more recent additions to the code (Resnik, 1998).

Unfortunately, horrible and immoral experiments on humans were not only occurring at the hands of Nazi scientists. Recently released documents from the United States Department of Energy reveal that during the 1940s and 1950s, U.S. government researchers conducted experiments on unsuspecting American citizens to determine the effects of nuclear radiation (Welsome, 1999). None of the people knew that they had been exposed to these deadly conditions. In another case, physicians at the Tuskegee Institute purposefully withheld treatment from 399 people who had contracted syphilis, for the sole purpose of studying the long-term effects of this dreadful disease (Jones, 1982). Unfortunately, these examples are not isolated cases (Resnik, 1998).

This bleak history illustrates the need to create and enforce clear ethical guidelines. The **National Research Act**, which became law in 1974 (PL–93–348), established the IRB that we described earlier. The law requires that researchers receiving federal money to conduct research with humans and animals must demonstrate that their research methods meet minimal ethical standards and that the IRB review the research proposal. As mentioned earlier, most colleges and universities now have IRB committees that review any and all research involving humans and/or animals regardless of how the research is being funded.

In the late 1960s and early 1970s, the APA created its first ethical guidelines. Since then, the APA has revised the code, with the current version published in 2002. The Ethical Principles of Psychologists and Code of Conduct establishes a set of principles that psychologist members of the APA must use to make decisions about their professional behavior. Box 2.2 lists the general ethical principles the code identifies for all psychologists.

---

**Box 2.2 The General Ethical Principles for All Members of the American Psychological Association. Based on the APA's Ethical Principles of Psychologists and Code of Conduct (2002)**

A. **Beneficence and Nonmaleficence:** Psychologists strive to benefit those with whom they work and take care to do no harm. In their professional actions, psychologists seek to safeguard the welfare and rights of those with whom they interact professionally and other affected persons, and the welfare of animal subjects of research.

*(Continued)*

*(Continued)*

B. **Fidelity and Responsibility:** Psychologists establish relationships of trust with those with whom they work. Psychologists uphold professional standards of conduct, clarify their professional roles and obligations, accept appropriate responsibility for their behavior, and seek to manage conflicts of interest that could lead to exploitation or harm.

C. **Integrity:** Psychologists seek to promote accuracy, honesty, and truthfulness in the science, teaching, and practice of psychology. In these activities psychologists do not steal, cheat, or engage in fraud, subterfuge, or intentional misrepresentation of fact.

D. **Justice:** Psychologists recognize that fairness and justice entitle all persons to access to and benefit from the contributions of psychology and to equal quality in the processes, procedures, and services being conducted by psychologists.

E. **Respect for People's Rights and Dignity:** Psychologists respect the dignity and worth of all people, and the rights of individuals to privacy, confidentiality, and self-determination.

The complete code is very long and covers many professional domains including therapy, psychological testing, psychological research, and other activities such as teaching and supervising employees. In the following sections, we will examine the basic APA ethical principles as they apply to conducting research with humans and animals.

## Seeking Approval for Research: The Institutional Review Board

In this section, we will examine how psychologists seek approval for their research and the interplay between the IRB and the ethical code of the APA. The size and complexity of an IRB will vary depending on the size of the institution and the type of research that is typically conducted there. A standard IRB is composed of researchers and other professionals who understand the legal and ethical standards that guide research. In some cases, research using specialized procedures or unique populations requires special members of the IRB. For example, the National Bioethics Advisory Commission (1998) offered specific recommendations for cases when the proposed research will use people with a mental disability (e.g., schizophrenia or a developmental disability). Specifically, the commission recommended that the IRB include at least two professionals familiar with the disability; a family member of a person with the disability or a representative of an advocacy group; and, when possible, a person with the disability. This recommendation ensures that the members of the IRB understand the nature of the disability and preserve the rights of people with the condition.

### Planning Research and Seeking IRB Approval

Researchers submit a detailed description of their research by answering a series of questions. The members of the IRB review the material and then inform the researcher whether he or she may proceed with the research. In some cases, the IRB may require minor or substantial modifications to parts of the research to protect the rights of the participants. Box 2.3 presents an example of an IRB form. The questions require the researcher to examine all aspects of his or her research. You should recognize, however, that each IRB creates its own application and review procedures.

---

## Box 2.3  An Example of an Institutional Review Board Application Form for Proposed Research Using Humans

### Proposal for Research Involving Humans

1.   Title of Project: _____

2.   Type of research: Faculty _____ Student Honors Project _____ Student Project _____ Class Project _____

3.   Starting date for the investigation: _____

4.   Name(s) of investigator(s) and campus phone number(s): _____

5.   Name of supervising faculty member and campus telephone number(s): _____

6.   Has previous research or pilot studies indicated any significant dangers or risks in the proposed procedures? Yes _____ No _____

7.   Does this research involve any active deception of the participants? Yes _____ No _____

8.   Will any information from this investigation be confidential? Yes _____ No _____
Signature of investigator(s): _____ date: _____
Signature of faculty supervisor: _____ date: _____

Respond to each of the following:

9.   Describe the general purpose of the research.

10.   Describe the procedures and tests used in the investigation.

11.   Describe how you will obtain Informed Consent or justify why you will not obtain Informed Consent. Attach a copy of the Informed Consent Contract you plan to use.

12.   Describe how you will recruit participants. Describe any special requirements of the population and any criteria for inclusion or exclusion of participants.

13.   Identify how you examined potential hazards of this research. Give references when appropriate.

14.   Describe and assess the potential hazards (physical, psychological, or legal) and estimate their likelihood and seriousness.

15.   Describe any procedures that you will employ for minimizing potential hazards and give an assessment of their potential effectiveness.

16.   Indicate how and when you will inform participants of the purpose of the research.

17.   Describe what you know about the ethical guidelines for treating humans within your discipline.

If you answered "yes" to Question #7 then provide the following information:

18a.   Explain the rationale for the deception. How and when will the participants learn of the deception?

*(Continued)*

---

*(Continued)*

18b.   Describe the expected reactions (immediate or long-term) of the participants to the deception, particularly any potential negative reactions.

If you answered "yes" to Question #8 then respond to the following:

19a.   What information obtained through this research is confidential?

19b.   Who will have access to that information?

19c.   How will you protect confidentiality?

19d.   What will happen to this information at the end of this investigation?

---

### Dignity and Competence

Two necessary facets of any research plan are that the researcher will protect the dignity and welfare of the participants and has the qualifications to use the procedures involved in the study. Qualification is important, especially when the researcher uses any sort of invasive or highly specialized techniques. Consider a couple of examples. Imagine that we wanted to conduct a study that monitored participants' physiological reactions to different conditions. Measuring physiological reactions requires electronic equipment. Therefore, we must demonstrate to the members of the IRB that our recording equipment is safe and that we know how to operate it safely. In another experiment, we may want to collect blood samples from the participants. If none of the researchers are certified to draw blood, we would have to hire a certified medical technician who can do this procedure safely, or we would need to receive the necessary training and certification.

It is for these reasons that students cannot conduct research without some form of supervision. A faculty member must verify that he or she will supervise the student. This stipulation allows students to learn how to conduct research and protects the participants from potential mistreatment.

### Voluntary Informed Consent

Voluntary **informed consent** is the hallmark of all research involving human participants. Researchers cannot coerce or force people to participate in any research. For all human research, the researcher must show that the people who participate in the study did so of their own free will. In addition, the participants must understand that they are free to withdraw from the study at any time and for any reason without penalty.

For informed consent, the researcher must offer an easy-to-understand, accurate, and complete description of the research. Specifically, the APA (2002) requires that researchers inform participants about:

1.  The purpose of the research, expected duration, and procedures
2.  Their right to decline to participate and to withdraw from the research once participation has begun

3. The foreseeable consequences of declining or withdrawing

4. Reasonably foreseeable factors that may be expected to influence their willingness to participate, such as potential risks, discomfort, or adverse effects

5. Any prospective research benefits

6. Limits of confidentiality

7. Incentives for participation

8. Whom to contact for questions about the research and their rights as participants

Box 2.4 presents a hypothetical informed consent form or letter that a student might use for his or her research. This document is a pledge from the researcher to the participant that stipulates the rights of the participant and the duties of the researcher. The participant and the researcher should each keep a copy of the signed document.

---

### Box 2.4  Example of an Informed Consent Contract

Memory for Words

Informed Consent Contract

I agree to participate voluntarily in an experiment conducted by Jane Mnemonic, ''Memory for Words.'' This research is conducted under the supervision of Dr. David J. Pittenger and has been approved by the Institutional Review Board of the University of Tennessee at Chattanooga. The researcher has explained to my satisfaction the following points:

1. My participation is voluntary. I am under no direct obligation to participate in this research. Furthermore, I understand that I may withdraw from this project at any time without penalty. If I do withdraw, the data I generated, to the extent that they may be attributed to me, will be destroyed.

2. I may receive extra credit for my Psychology 101 course for participation in this experiment. The amount of credit I receive will not reflect my skill, ability, or performance in the study.

3. All records of my behavior will remain confidential. The data for this research will be published as group averages. The researcher will not publish or share with others personally identifiable information about me without my written consent.

4. There are no inherent risks involved in participating in this research.

5. The purpose of this research is to study memory. I will be asked to listen to audiotapes of words and then recall that list.

6. The researcher will provide a complete review of the purpose of this research and expected findings at the end of my participation. In addition, the researcher will attempt to answer all reasonable questions I ask about the research.

7. Dr. Pittenger's campus telephone number is: ###-####; Ms. Mnemonic's campus telephone number is: ###-####

*(Continued)*

*(Continued)*

8. The telephone number for the university's IRB is: ###-####

| | |
|---|---|
| _____ | _____ |
| Participant's Signature | Date |
| _____ | _____ |
| Jane Mnemonic | Date |
| _____ | _____ |
| Dr. David J. Pittenger | Date |

An important consideration when drafting an informed consent form is how much information to give the participant. You do not need to fully describe your hypothesis or your research methods. Doing this may cause participants to respond in a less-than-truthful manner. Instead, you should describe the types of things you will ask them to do and the conditions to which they may be exposed in enough detail to allow them to decide whether they wish to participate in the experiment.

**Informed Consent and Minors**

Minors (people younger than 18) and people afflicted with a medical, mental, or developmental disability cannot give informed consent for themselves. To include people from these populations, you must obtain approval from their parent or legal guardian. For example, if you wanted to conduct a study that examined children's memory, you would first need to obtain the consent of the child's parents to conduct the research. You will then need to ask the child to participate in the study. As with all research, the parents and the child have the right to withdraw from the study at any time. The definition of what constitutes a "minor" for research purposes varies depending on the state and/or funding source (e.g., some federal sources of funding treat anyone under 21 years of age as a minor). Because these definitions vary, it is important for you to become familiar with the definitions relevant in the area in which you will be doing research.

Along these lines, although passive forms of consent are viewed as acceptable in some cases under the APA ethics code, we strongly urge you to consider more active or opt-in forms of consent instead, especially when conducting research with minors. Passive consent is sought when participants are by default included in a study unless a parent signs a form indicating that they will not allow such participation. This is often the case when children are asked to bring notes home from school for their parents to sign—how many of these notes actually make it home? Instead, we recommend you use an opt-in consent strategy that requires parents or legal guardians to grant full informed consent before a child is entered into any research.

## Filming or Recording Behavior

If you plan to videotape or photograph the participant's behavior, you must first obtain informed consent from the participant. In addition, you will need to explain how you will use the recording. For example, if you were studying facial expressions, you might tell the participants that you will videotape their facial reactions, but never present the tapes outside of the laboratory unless you have the written permission of the participant.

## Using College Students in Research

Many academic departments require students to participate in research or offer extra credit for participating in research. The rationale for the requirement is that participation in research is educational. If the researchers take their responsibilities seriously, they will offer each participant a detailed explanation of their research and its importance.

When you use students for your research, you need to ensure several safeguards. Each student must have a legitimate and equivalent alternative to participating in the study. For example, students may want to select between participating in an experiment, attending a guest lecture, or reading a short article related to psychology. Remember that you cannot coerce a person to participate in research. Telling them that they must be in an experiment or fail the course is coercive.

You should also assure students that their participation in any research study has no effect on the credit they will receive for the course in which they are enrolled and from which you have recruited them. In other words, if students receive extra credit for participating in a study, you cannot offer more or less credit based on their performance in the study. Similarly, you cannot penalize participants if they decide to withdraw from the study.

## When No Informed Consent Is Needed

There are special conditions when you do not need informed consent. These conditions occur where you will passively and unobtrusively observe people's behavior in natural contexts. For example, you might go to a playground and observe how the children play with each other. If you do not plan to interact with the child or alter the environment, you can collect data without asking the children for their permission to observe their play. Of course, if that playground is on school property, you should get permission from the school before making observations. Be careful with how you define "natural contexts."

State law may control recording people's actions and conversations. For example, some states make it illegal to record a telephone conversation unless both people understand that the conversation is being recorded. Therefore, you may want to consult a legal authority concerning what you can and cannot record without consent.

In other cases, you might use public domain data. Many agencies collect data that are then made available for public inspection. For example, you can go to your county's board of elections and obtain the names of registered voters, their political affiliation, and whether they voted in the previous elections. You can also review police records to determine who has been arrested, the charges, and the court's action.

Anonymous questionnaires and surveys are also typically exempt from the informed consent requirement. Therefore, if you wanted to send a questionnaire through campus mail to all students, you would not have to have the students' informed consent unless the data you collected allowed you to learn who completed the questionnaire. Even though this is often the case, we still recommend you include an informed consent form with this type of survey, but instead of requiring signed consent, you indicate that completion and return of a survey constitutes that person's consent to participate.

Although these are examples of cases where you do not need informed consent, you will still need approval from your institution's IRB. According to most institutions of higher education and the APA and other professional societies' codes of ethics, the rule is simple: *You cannot begin to collect data until the IRB approves your research proposal.* Seeking the IRB's approval ensures that your decision not to use informed consent conforms to the board members' interpretation of the ethical principles.

## Deception in Research

Deception in research means that you lie (or fail to tell the whole truth) to the participants about some important part of the research in which they are a participant. You may lead a person to believe that the other people sitting at the table are fellow students who volunteered to participate in the study. The truth may be that the other people are confederates or accomplices of the researcher and are following a script that you prepared. Use of a placebo is another type of deception because the researcher may lead participants to believe that they are actually receiving a potentially effective treatment, when it is nothing more than water or a sugar pill. There are two types of deception, **deception by omission** and **deception by commission**. Deception by omission means that you withhold important facts from the participant. Deception by commission means that you purposefully lie to or mislead the participant about an important component of the research.

Deception by omission occurs in all research to some extent, because it is impossible and impractical to tell the participants everything about the purpose and details of the research. For example, we do not describe the hypothesis we want to test, nor do we describe every aspect of the research design. If we did, the information could bias their behavior, perhaps leading them to respond in ways that they think we are seeking or that they feel are most socially desirable. We discuss these issues more in Chapter 4, when we look more carefully at threats to internal validity. Therefore, we describe the general themes of the research that will allow the potential participants to know what may happen to them during the study. For instance, we would not tell them whether they are in the placebo treatment condition. Instead, we would tell them that there is a chance that they will receive a placebo.

Deception by commission raises serious ethical concerns because the researcher is lying to the participant. Although deception by commission has many negative consequences, there are times when we must use it as a part of the research. For example, in many social psychology experiments, the researcher will create an elaborate cover story for the experiment. The cover story diverts the participant's attention from the true purpose of the study and may thereby reduce any bias in the participant's behavior.

According to the APA ethical guidelines (2002), we can use deception under special conditions. First, we must demonstrate that the participant will still obtain sufficient information about the research to offer voluntary informed consent. In the case of the placebo treatment condition, the participants should understand that the researcher will randomly assign them to either the placebo or the treatment conditions.

Second, the researcher must demonstrate to the members of the IRB that the deception is essential to collect the data. This is an example where the researcher must examine the utility of the research. In particular, the researcher must show that the deception will cause minor or no negative consequences for the participants and that the data produced by the study have legitimate scientific value.

Finally, the researcher must demonstrate that there is no other way to collect the data other than to use the deception. Your use of deception by commission must be the last resort and the only reasonable way to conduct the study.

## Confidentiality

All information/data that you collect must be confidential. Confidentiality means that the identity of your participants remains a secret. In most cases, confidentiality is easy to preserve. One way to maintain confidentiality is to use a unique but meaningless number to identify each of the participants. For example, you might use the number "2–3–47" to record the data of a person. The number is meaningless in that it does not identify the person, but does allow you to file the data. In addition, when we publish the results of the research, we typically present the data as averages across groups rather than highlighting the performance of individual people along with their names and home addresses.

Confidentiality is required by IRBs for research with human participants. It is important for you to realize, however, that confidentiality and anonymity are not the same thing. Whereas confidentiality refers to the protecting of information provided by your research participants, anonymity refers to your protection of the identities of your participants. True anonymity is rare, and is only achieved when your research collects no personally identifying information from participants. Such information could include names, personal data (such as height, weight, age, sex), and even personality characteristics. Because this type of information is so common in social science research, it is important for you to carefully consider your study design before you describe it as anonymous and confidential. In most cases, it will be sufficient and more likely for you to ensure only confidentiality.

### Informing Participants of the Results of the Research

You have a duty to explain your research to your participants. Most researchers debrief the participants at the end of the study. **Debriefing** means that you tell the participants the details of your research. If you used deception, you must describe the purpose of the research and why you used the deception. You also use the debriefing to answer the participants' questions and ensure that they understand why you conducted the research.

Debriefing does not mean that you need to tell the participant everything about the research. For example, imagine that you used a personality test as a part of your research. Can you or should you share the results of the test with the participant? In most cases, the answer is no. Only licensed clinical or assessment psychologists are qualified to interpret individual personality test results. Therefore, even though you may be able to use a personality test in research, you should not review the individual results with the participants.

In most cases, researchers do not share the individual results with others; the results remain confidential. There are two general exceptions to this rule. First, if you discover that the person committed a crime, you may need to report the facts to the police. For example, if in the course of an interview a parent indicated that he or she abused a child, you would need to report the incident. The second condition arises when the researcher discovers that the person is likely to do harm to self or others or suffers from a life-threatening illness. Fortunately, these exceptional conditions do not occur in most research projects. You should, however, be aware that there may be cases in which you could obtain information that would cause you to break the conditions of confidentiality.

## Milgram's Experiment Revisited

Any review of research ethics would be incomplete without a discussion of Milgram's (1963) classic study of obedience, which attracted much attention and generated considerable debate. To help you keep perspective on the origins of this research, you should note that it was motivated by Milgram's desire to understand how people could follow the types of orders given by the Nazis and other powerful authorities that had led to such terrible atrocities against humanity. Thus, although there are elements of the Milgram study that seem to be unethical by today's standards, we must remember also that its purpose was to understand a potentially critical human flaw (e.g., Idol of the Theatre), with the underlying hope that if we understood blind following of orders, we might be able to eventually prevent or limit such tendencies.

## Milgram's Obedience Research

Stanley Milgram (1963, 1974) conducted a series of experiments to study the conditions under which one person would obey the order to hurt another person. Milgram placed an advertisement in a local newspaper calling for people to participate in a psychology experiment. When the participants arrived at the laboratory, the researcher told them that they would take part in an experiment on learning, and that one person would be the learner and the other person would be the trainer. In fact, the learner was a member of the research team and the participant was always the trainer.

The researcher explained that the purpose of the study was to examine the effects of punishment on learning. The trainer would read a list of word pairs (e.g., *blue–box, nice–play, windy–sky, bright–night*) and then read the first word of a pair with four alternatives (e.g., *blue: sky, paint, box, boy*). The other person would then indicate which of the four words went with the first word. For each mistake, the participant trainer had to press a button that delivered an electrical shock to the learner. As a demonstration, the researcher first administered a mild shock to the trainer.

For the first part of the experiment, all went well. The trainer read the words and the learner responded correctly. After a few trials, however, the learner began to make mistakes. With each error, the trainer had to give a progressively stronger shock (15 to 450 volts in 15-volt increments). The learner, who was not really receiving the shocks, responded to the shock with a clear, albeit faked reaction from another room. He began with grunts in response to the 75-volt shock. At higher voltages, he shouted, ". . . get me out of here! I won't be in the experiment anymore! I refuse to go on!" (Milgram, 1974, p. 23). At 300 volts, the learner shouted that he would no longer respond. At 330 volts, the learner stopped responding.

If the trainer objected and wanted to stop the experiment, the researcher would say, "Please continue" or, "The experiment requires that you continue" (Milgram, 1974, p. 21). The experiment continued until the trainer refused to administer another shock or had administered the strongest possible shock. At the end of the experiment, Milgram debriefed the participants.

In his first experiment, Milgram (1963, 1974) found that 26 of the 40 trainers administered the complete range of shocks (that's more than 50% of participants!). Furthermore, he found that *all* the trainers administered shocks of 300 volts or greater! To keep this in perspective, a 300-volt shock is many times more powerful than the mild shock received by the trainer at the beginning of the experiment.

Milgram was the first psychologist to study obedience in the laboratory; thus it was anyone's guess what the participants would do. Before he conducted the experiment, Milgram (1974) had surveyed psychiatrists, college students, and middle-class adults and asked them to predict how far the typical person would go in the experiment. All three groups predicted that the typical person would stop when he or she began to administer "strong shocks" (around 135 volts).

Although it is impossible for us to evaluate the ethicality of Milgram's research in its time, for the purpose of example, what do you think would happen today if Milgram proposed this study to an IRB before conducting his research? Would the typical IRB of today's society approve the research? What would you decide if you were on the IRB? What conclusions would we reach if you followed the ethical perspectives reviewed earlier in the chapter?

### From a Utilitarian Perspective

How would we evaluate Milgram's experiment from a utilitarian perspective? Can we justify the experiment, or should we reject Milgram's proposed experiment? As you recall, the answers to these questions will arise from a cost-and-benefit analysis of the experiment. What are the costs of the experiment? How would you feel if you thought that you were hurting another person? There is no doubt that the experiment was stressful. It is also possible that the participants would become distressed to learn that they were capable of committing a horrible act.

On the other hand, there are clear benefits to conducting the experiment. Milgram's studies demonstrated that an average person could be induced to do terrible things under certain circumstances. These data are valuable to psychology because they help us understand an important behavior. Consequently, we could justify conducting the experiment given the cost/benefit analysis if we can show that the cost to the people who participate is far less than the value of the data. Furthermore, Milgram used extensive debriefing techniques to ensure that the people who participated in the experiment did not suffer long-term consequences. Hence, we could show that we have minimized the harm to the participants. Finally, we may approve the research if we can be convinced that there is no other way to collect the data. Therefore, we can conclude that as long as the researcher followed the requirements of informed consent and debriefing, we should approve the research.

We can take several tactics to use the principle of utilitarianism to reject Milgram's request. The first objection is that we cannot overlook the cost to the participants. We could argue that the emotional stress created by this experiment is not trivial. In this case, we may argue that the threat to the individual does not justify the data that will come from the experiment. Although we are still using the utility principle, we reached a different decision because we concluded that the participants' discomfort outweighs the value of the data.

Another way we can object to Milgram's experiment is to ask whether there are other ways to collect the data. Would it be possible to conduct an experiment on obedience that was not as stressful or did not require deception? If we can find alternative methods to obtain similar data, then we can conclude that parts of the experiment are unacceptable. If we find that we can create the same effect through less stressful means, then we should reject the experiment.

### From a Principle-of-Rights Perspective

How would you respond to this experiment based on your knowledge of the principle-of-rights perspective? In this case, you would not examine the cost/benefit ratio of the research. Instead, you would examine the moral principles that guide our decisions. For our purposes, we can focus on Kant's categorical imperative that requires us to determine whether the researcher respects the inherent dignity of the people who participate in the study. We have to ask whether the researcher respects the participants' dignity or treats them merely as a self-serving means of collecting data.

From the perspective of rights, deception in any form treats participants as mere opportunities to collect data and ignores their dignity. For example, someone studying grief could claim he or she needed to deceive participants by telling them that their parents have been murdered. In these situations, it may appear that the researcher has placed his or her interest in collecting data before the dignity of the participant. Thus, manipulating a person's emotions to satisfy one's scientific curiosity is unacceptable. Similarly, we could argue that the participants were not free to choose how to respond. The researcher's request to continue the shocks is a form of coercion. The researcher assumed a role of authority over the participant and consequently caused the participants to do things that they would normally avoid doing. Thus, the perspective of rights is most likely to find Milgram's experiment unacceptable.

*So, is this type of deception ethically okay?* You may be asking, "What is the right answer? Should I or should I not use deception?" We cannot give you the correct answer. You must identify that answer for yourself every time you design and carry out a study (and we hope also in every action that you take on a day-to-day basis). Ethics is a process of investigation, and you, as an intelligent and thoughtful person, must resolve the dilemma.

Part of the answer may come from examining the APA's code of conduct. You could, for example, examine the problem and determine whether the proposed research meets certain minimal qualifications. For example, you can ask: "Is there sufficient evidence of informed consent?" "Do the people really have the opportunity to stop the experiment?" "Has the researcher minimized the risks?" The answers to these questions are important for part of your ethical deliberation.

At the same time, you should examine the broader moral principles involved in your research. For example, you may find that there are some procedures that the APA ethical code treats as permissible that you find unacceptable. Thus, performing the experiment would be morally wrong from your perspective although acceptable within the APA's code of conduct.

For many years it was debated whether Milgram's experiment could ever be replicated given updates to ethics review procedures and acceptable research activities. We now know the answer thanks to Burger (2007), who worked hard with his university's IRB to modify the design of the original study to minimize the chance of harm to participants, while still allowing for the collection of useful data. Interestingly, the results of the study demonstrate that participants today obeyed the experimenter's instructions at about the same rate as in Milgram's original research (Burger, 2007). For much more insight on this modern-day replication, you should also check out a special obedience-focused issue of the APA journal, *American Psychologist*, published in January 2009 (Vol. 64, No. 1).

## Research with Animals

Although the vast majority of the research conducted by psychologists and most social scientists involves humans, animal research retains an important place in efforts to improve the quality of life for humans. For example, psychologists who study physiological processes, such as the workings of the brain, often rely on animals for their research. Because of our developing ethics codes, we are often able to test certain hypotheses only with animal subjects, rather than human participants. Although the reason to use animals is simple, the ethical rationale is not. Many people believe that subjecting animals to research of any kind is morally wrong. In this section, we will examine the general principles on both sides of the issue and review the APA's ethical position on animal research.

### The Case against Animal Research

In 1975, Peter Singer, a philosopher, published the first edition of *Animal Liberation* (1990). The book quickly became a bestseller and, for many, the authoritative statement against using animals in research. Singer used the principle of utility to establish the rights of animals as equal to humans. As Singer (1990) noted, "the basic principle of equality does not require equal or identical treatment; it requires equal consideration" (p. 2). Singer also argued that we must recognize that animals, like humans, experience pain and suffer in uncomfortable situations. Therefore, the ability to experience pain is an equally important consideration for human and animal research.

Singer (1990) coined the term **speciesism** to refer to the attitude many people use to judge the treatment of animals. According to Singer and others who share this perspective, speciesism is analogous to racism and sexism, in that each is reflected by differential treatment of members of different groups based on trivial or immaterial attributes. The color of a person's skin or a person's sex is irrelevant when we consider fundamental human rights and privileges. For example, it is racist to prohibit people from seeking an education or obtaining a job based on skin color. Being Asian, African American, Hispanic, or European has no relevance to one's ability. Therefore, denying a person a privilege based on his or her heritage is racist and unethical. From this perspective, then, the argument against speciesism is the same as the argument against racism or sexism. Because all animals, human and nonhuman, have a central nervous system and the capacity to experience pain, we cannot give special treatment to one species that we do not extend to another species. Singer (1990) refers directly to Bentham and other utilitarian philosophers to support the notion that "taking into account . . . the interests of the being, whatever those interests might be—must, according to the principle of equality, be extended to all beings, black or white, masculine or feminine, human or nonhuman" (1990, p. 5). In summary, Singer argued that the principle of utilitarianism places the well-being of nonhuman animals on the same level as humans.

### The Case for Animal Research

For most of us, this argument against animal research seems a bit extreme, and indeed there are many ways to justify animal research, especially when based on a principle of utility. For example, Steinbock (1978) acknowledged that animals can experience pain, and that experiencing pain is relevant, but noted that Singer's (1990) philosophy leads to unacceptable conclusions. She also argued that recognizing differences among species is important and that we have an obligation to defend and care for our species. Consequently, as humans we have a moral obligation to ensure the welfare of our species. Furthermore, this obligation transcends the welfare of other species.

As an example, Steinbock (1978) noted that if our home were invaded by disease-carrying rats that bit the children, we should place the welfare of the family above the rats even if we have to kill the rats. In defense of animal research, she noted that "if we can free human beings from crippling diseases, pain and death through experimentation which involves making animals suffer, and if this is the only way to achieve such results, then I think that such experimentation is justified" (p. 250).

The argument in favor of animal research is that some information cannot be obtained by other means and that the data have utility for humans. Therefore, we can justify putting animals into painful situations where the results will clearly benefit humans. Indeed, research with animals has generated many insights that have led to better understanding of human behavior. Our knowledge of how the brain works comes from, in large part, animal research. In addition, many principles of behavior that we accept with little question come from animal research. As an example, Seligman discovered the learned helplessness phenomenon when studying dogs' reactions to inescapable shock. Also, many behaviorists have conducted useful, informative, and humane research on operant conditioning using animals such as pigeons and rats.

\* \* \*

A take-home message from both sides of the animal research debate is that the well-being and comfort of all research subjects, be they animal or human, should be taken into account in the design and implementation of a research study. From a purely pragmatic perspective, the humane treatment of animals leads to better animal models that in turn enhance the applicability and interpretability of research results.

### The APA Ethical Guidelines: Animal Research

The APA ethical guidelines for animal research follow many of the same principles as the guidelines for human research. Researchers submit their research proposals to a review board that specifically evaluates research with animals. The researcher must demonstrate that the results are useful, that the researcher has no other ethical means of collecting the information, and that the subjects will experience minimal pain and suffering. Box 2.5 lists the general ethical guidelines governing research with animals.

---

**Box 2.5  Summary of the APA's Ethical Guidelines for the Treatment of Animals. Based on the APA's Ethical Principles of Psychologists and Code of Conduct (2002)**

a)   Psychologists acquire, care for, use, and dispose of animals in compliance with current federal, state, and local laws and regulations, and with professional standards.

b)   Psychologists trained in research methods and experienced in the care of laboratory animals supervise all procedures involving animals and are responsible for ensuring appropriate consideration of their comfort, health, and humane treatment.

c)   Psychologists ensure that all individuals under their supervision who are using animals have received instruction in research methods and in the care, maintenance, and handling of the species being used, to the extent appropriate to their role. (See also Standard 2.05, Delegation of Work to Others.)

d)   Psychologists make reasonable efforts to minimize the discomfort, infection, illness, and pain of animal subjects.

e)   Psychologists use a procedure subjecting animals to pain, stress, or privation only when an alternative procedure is unavailable and the goal is justified by its prospective scientific, educational, or applied value.

f)   Psychologists perform surgical procedures under appropriate anesthesia and follow techniques to avoid infection and minimize pain during and after surgery.

g)   When it is appropriate that an animal's life be terminated, psychologists proceed rapidly, with an effort to minimize pain and in accordance with accepted procedures.

---

## Research in Action: Ethical Dilemmas

The following are short scenarios describing various research practices. Read each with care and then examine the ethical issues raised by the scenario. Some of the ethical issues can be answered using the APA's ethical guidelines. Others may require additional ethical analysis.

### Another Look at Conformity

Mark wants to study conformity and use deception in his research. When the participant arrives for the study, he or she will meet the researcher and another person who appears to be another participant. In fact, the other person is Mark's associate and is a part of the experiment. The researcher says that the study requires the participants to complete several questionnaires, and then asks the participants to read and sign an informed consent contract. The informed consent says nothing about the deception. Next, Mark distributes the questionnaire and leaves the room. There are three experimental conditions. In the control group, the accomplice does nothing other than fill out the questionnaire. In another situation, the accomplice says, "Let's screw up the results and answer 'Highly Disagree' for each answer," and then laughs as he completes the questionnaire and continues to encourage the real participant to "screw up the results." For the third group, the accomplice says, "Gee, this seems like a really important research project. I'm going to answer as honestly as I can." One of the questionnaires is a legitimate test that measures how honestly a person responds.

## Knowledge Check

1. Is the deception in this experiment acceptable? What would be the arguments for and against approving the research?
2. If the research is approved, what should Mark say in his debriefing statement?

### Eavesdropping on Conversations

Sid is a psychologist and interested in dating behavior. To test one of his theories, he goes to a local college "pickup" bar. He discretely stands next to couples engaged in conversation and observes their behavior. Using a small notebook, he records the frequency of different types of comments each person makes. He also notes how often and where the couples touch each other. Finally, he records whether the two people leave the bar with each other. At no time does Sid indicate that he is a researcher listening to the conversations.

## Knowledge Check

3. Should Sid be allowed to conduct this research?
4. Should he inform the couple that he has observed them and give them the opportunity to have him destroy the data?
5. Could Sid use a tape recorder to record the couple's conversation for later analysis?
6. What could Sid do to improve the ethics of this study?

### Requiring Students to Participate in Research

Mythical University is a large state institution. The Department of Psychology requires all the graduate students to do research as a part of their training and dissertation. Most of the graduate students conduct at least one experiment each semester and use students from the campus. In addition, the faculty members conduct research. To ensure that there are sufficient numbers of students to participate in the research, the psychology faculty requires all students enrolled in Psychology 101 to participate in 10 experiments during the semester. If they miss an appointment, the students must do two additional experiments (one to replace the missed appointment and one as a penalty). Students who do more than the 10 experiments can earn extra credit for the course. Students who do not want to do any experiments may write a five-page paper as an alternative to each experiment.

## Knowledge Check

7. Is the department's policy defensible? Develop arguments in favor of and opposed to the policy.
8. What potential ethical problems does this practice create?
9. What modifications, if any, would you propose for this policy?
10. What could the department do to improve the ethics of this study?

### Questionnaire About Sex

Courtney is interested in college students' attitudes about date rape. She prepares a long questionnaire concerning different aspects of sexual behavior. Some of her questions concern the types of sexual behavior students have performed (e.g., genital–genital sex, oral sex, anal sex) as well as the frequency of each. She also asks students whether they have ever been forced/coerced to perform a sexual act they did not wish to perform or whether they ever forced/coerced another person to perform a sexual act against his or her will. She plans to ask students to come to a classroom and complete the questionnaire.

## Knowledge Check

11. Should Courtney obtain informed consent before distributing the questionnaire? Why or why not?
12. What should Courtney do if a person completing the questionnaire indicated that he raped another student?
13. Are there any precautions that Courtney needs to take when collecting the data?
14. What could Courtney do to improve the ethics of this study?

**Real-World Study of Altruism**

Richard studies altruism. For the current project, he wants to know whether the color of the person in need of help will influence a person's willingness to help. He hires two students, one white and the other black, to act as an injured person needing help. The test consists of the following situation: The actor stands next to an open car trunk, is neatly dressed, and is wearing a plaster cast that covers his entire right arm. In the car trunk is a large and bulky box. The actor stops people walking on the sidewalk and asks if they will help carry the box into a nearby house. The researcher records the proportion of people who help the white and the black actors.

## Knowledge Check

15. Does Richard need informed consent for this experiment?
16. Is Richard's use of deception defensible?
17. Should Richard debrief the people the actor asks for help? What are the consequences of debriefing and failing to debrief the people the actor stops on the street?
18. What could Richard do to improve the ethics of this study?

**Assessing Students' Depression**

Rebecca is an undergraduate student interested in the effects of academic stress on depression. She plans to administer two valid inventories several days after the start of the semester and two days before the final exams. The first test is a survey of academic and personal stress. The second test is one that many clinical psychologists use to assess severity of depression.

## Knowledge Check

19. Should Rebecca be allowed to conduct this study?
20. What should Rebecca do if she finds that one of the students is severely depressed?
21. What could Rebecca do to improve the ethics of this study?

**Use of a Control Group**

For many years, Drug X has been the drug of choice for the treatment of depression. Profit Labs has discovered a new medication, Drug Y, that researchers believe is a superior medication. Researchers for the company are in the process of designing the initial research projects to determine whether Drug Y is a superior treatment for depression. People diagnosed as severely depressed will be randomly assigned to one of three treatment conditions: Placebo Treatment, Drug X Treatment, Drug Y Treatment. The treatment phase will last for six months. A licensed clinical psychologist and a psychiatrist will evaluate each participant's condition once every 14 days.

## Knowledge Check

22. Is it appropriate to use a control group for this experiment?
23. What should we do if we find that people in the control group begin to become more depressed?
24. Midway through the experiment, the researchers find that Drug Y is much more effective than Drug X. Should they continue with the experiment for the full six months?
25. What could be done to improve the ethics of this study?

### Brain Research on Cats

Chet is a psychologist who studies the visual system using cats because their visual cortex is similar to humans'. He plans to conduct a series of experiments that will improve our knowledge of how the visual system works. These experiments require that Chet implant electrodes into the brains of the cats. In addition, the cats must be killed at the end of the experiment so that the brains can be studied in detail.

## Knowledge Check

26. Should Chet be allowed to do this research?
27. Would your opinion change if you learned that (a) Chet was doing "basic" research that had no known immediate application or that (b) Chet was finding a way to allow stroke victims to recover their sight?
28. What could Chet do to improve the ethics of this study?

## Chapter Summary

All researchers bear a responsibility to act in a moral manner. This responsibility is especially critical for psychologists because their research directly affects the lives of the people and animals that are a part of their research. This chapter reviewed basic moral principles and the process of ethics. Moral principles are the beliefs we have that help us distinguish between right and wrong. Ethics is the process of examining how we react to specific situations and make decisions on how we should act.

The four moral principles at the heart of psychological research are: (1) the concern for the welfare of other beings, (2) the belief that moral principles stand before our interests and secular laws, (3) the belief that moral principles are universal truths that do not change across time or situations, and (4) the belief that moral principles are impartial and treat everyone equally.

Two of the major philosophical systems that guide ethical analysis are the principle of utility and the principle of rights. Utilitarianism directs us to seek ways to maximize happiness and minimize discomfort. Therefore, when a researcher examines a research design, he or she must consider the consequences of conducting the study. Specifically, the researcher must show that the results of the study justify the method by demonstrating that there is no other way to collect the data, and that the importance of the data outweighs any discomfort the people or animals in the study may experience. By contrast, the principle of rights requires that the researcher focus on preserving the dignity and self-worth of the people participating in the research. Research that puts the interest of the researcher above the welfare of the participants is morally wrong.

Each researcher must resolve any moral problems created by the research design by considering basic moral principles and the specific circumstances of the particular research project. The American Psychological Association developed an ethical code of conduct to help all psychologists evaluate their professional behavior.

For any research project using humans or animals, the researcher should first receive approval from the IRB. The IRB is a committee of fellow professionals that examines the research design to ensure that the researcher preserves the participant's rights. When applying for IRB approval, the researcher must demonstrate that (1) he or she is qualified to conduct the research or is being supervised by a responsible person with the necessary qualification, (2) the participants in the study have provided voluntary informed consent to participate in the study, (3) any deception used in the research is justified in that there is no other way to collect the data and that the consequence of the deception has minimal harm to the participant, (4) the data will remain confidential, and (5) at the end of the study the researcher will provide a reasonable account of the purpose of the research to the participant.

To practice an ethical deliberation, we examined Milgram's classic experiments (and their modern replication) that examined obedience. Specifically, we examined the research from the perspective of utility and the perspective of rights.

We also reviewed our moral obligation to animals used in psychological research. Some people believe that animals should not be used in any psychological research because of the extreme suffering they experience. Others believe that animal research is justified if one can demonstrate that there is no other way to obtain the data and that the benefits of the many outweigh the suffering experienced by the animals in the study.

The "Research in Action" section presented a number of ethical dilemmas that researchers often face.

## Chapter Glossary for Review

**Categorical imperative**—An ethical perspective developed by Kant that requires that we always respect the humanity and dignity of other people and never treat others as a means to an end.

**Debriefing**—Explaining to the participants of a study why you conducted the study and the importance of the study.

**Deception by commission**—The intentional act of deceiving the participants by telling them something incorrect about the research.

**Deception by omission**—A form of deception in which the researcher withholds information about some conditions of the research from the participant.

**Ethical code** or **code of conduct**—A list of rules and guidelines that direct and guide the behaviors of members of an organization.

**Ethics**—The process of examining one's moral principles and behavior.

**Informed consent**—A requirement for all human research that ensures that the participant understands the purpose of the research, his or her rights as a participant, and the potential hazards of participating in the research.

**Institutional Review Board (IRB)**—A group of people who examine the researcher's proposed methodology to ensure that the researcher will protect the basic rights of the participants.

**Morals**—Fundamental principles that distinguish right from wrong.

**National Research Act**—A federal law (PL–93–348) that established the existence of the Institutional Review Board (IRB). The law requires that any researcher receiving federal funds to conduct research on humans must first receive IRB approval of the research.

**Speciesism**—The attitude that humans and animals have different moral rights with regard to being free of pain and suffering.

**Utilitarianism**—A perspective of ethics that requires one to examine the consequences of one's behavior and to ensure that it maximizes happiness and minimizes suffering.

## Chapter References

American Psychological Association. (2002). Ethical principles of psychologists and code of conduct. *American Psychologist, 57*, 1060–1073.

Burger, J. M. (2007). Replicating Milgram. *APS Observer 20*(11).

Jones, J. (1982). *Bad blood*. New York: Free Press.

Kant, I. (1964). *Groundwork of the metaphysics of morals* (H. J. Paton, Trans.). New York: Harper & Row. (Original work published 1750).

Milgram, S. (1963). Behavioral study of obedience. *Journal of Abnormal and Social Behavior, 7,* 371–378.

Milgram, S. (1974). *Obedience to authority: An experimental view.* New York: Harper and Row.

National Bioethics Advisory Commission (1998). *Research involving persons with mental disorders that may affect decision making capacity.* Rockville, MD: Author.

Resnik, D. B. (1998). *The ethics of science: An introduction.* New York: Routledge.

Singer, P. (1990/1975). *Animal liberation* (rev. ed.). New York: Avon.

Steinbock, B. (1978). Speciesism and the idea of equality. *Philosophy, 53,* 247–256.

Welsome, E. (1999). *The plutonium files: America's secret medical experiments in the cold war.* New York: Random House.

# Chapter 3
# The Foundations of Research

## CHAPTER OBJECTIVES

**Introduction**
**The Hypothesis in Research**
**Types of Hypotheses**
**Measurement**
**Reliability of Measurement**
**Validity of Measurement**
**Populations and Samples**
**Research in Action: Measuring Sexism**

Science knows only one commandment—contribute to science.

—Bertold Brecht

## Introduction

Psychologists look for patterns of behavior and then try to explain them. You may recall reading about the famous child psychologist, Jean Piaget (1896–1980). Piaget spent his career studying the cognitive development of children. He observed that children between the ages of 2 and 7 years (the preoperational period) think differently from children 13 and older (the formal operations period). After much careful systematic empirical observation, Piaget concluded that there are interesting similarities within these age groups and important differences among these groups. He then used these data to develop an innovative theory that revolutionized the study of child development. This chapter introduces you to many of the basic concepts that form the foundation of the research process in psychology and the social sciences. We begin by examining the research **hypothesis**.

The hypothesis is important in all research because it determines the type of data that the researcher will collect, the research methods that will be used to collect the data, and the statistical procedures that will be used to analyze the data. There are as many different strategies for collecting and analyzing data as there are forms of research hypotheses. After discussing some of the most common forms you are likely to encounter, we then turn our attention to the process of data collection from a sample of participants. In this section we delve into the issue of how samples of data can allow us to make inferences about a broader population.

# The Hypothesis in Research

What is a hypothesis? Most people believe that a hypothesis is an "educated guess." Although this is technically correct, this definition misses the full purpose and role of a research hypothesis. Therefore, we would recommend that you set that definition aside and opt instead for one that is a bit more informative: *A hypothesis is a specific prediction about the relation among two or more variables based on theory or previous research.* Yes, the first definition was shorter and easier to remember, but this second one is more accurate and actually gives you a clue about how researchers develop and use hypotheses.

### Hypotheses Come from Theory or Previous Research

Most research hypotheses do not materialize out of thin air, nor are they wild guesses. In general, hypotheses come from two general sources, existing theories and previous research. Replication serves an important role in all research. Our confidence in results of research dramatically increases as a study is repeated and shown to yield similar findings, even with slightly different methods, samples, and measurement approaches. Consider the effects of positive reinforcement on behavior. Whether the research examined humans or nonhumans, adults or children, or people with profound emotional and behavioral disorders, the results come out the same: *People repeat behaviors that are positively reinforced.* Therefore, if you want to study positive reinforcement, then your best starting point would be the large existing literature and knowledge base from these previous studies. You can use this information to help you generate a hypothesis, and when you do so you are really saying, "If the results of previous research are consistent, then when I conduct my study, I should obtain similar results." This is why we can often deduce or derive a hypothesis from an existing theory.

What is a theory? A **theory** is a broad set of general statements and claims that allows us to explain and predict various events. This definition of theory differs from the common or lay use of the word *theory*. Non-scientists often equate *theory* as interchangeable with *hypothesis* and treat both as a guess about why a situation or relationship exists. This is not what we mean by theory when conducting empirical research. For scientists, theories are based on empirical evidence and logic so that they reflect a more informed or educated statement of expectation, rather than a guess, as is the case for nonscientific use of the word.

Here is an example of a simple theory from which we can derive several hypotheses: *Aggression and violence are learned behaviors.* This theory offers one explanation for why people behave violently. We can generate several hypotheses from this simply stated theory, including the following:

- Children who watch television programs with aggressive themes will be more aggressive than children who watch television programs with nonaggressive themes.

- Children whose parents use punishment (e.g., spanking) will be more aggressive than children whose parents use other parenting techniques.
- Children taught to use conflict-resolution techniques will be less likely to be aggressive.

You can easily add your hypotheses to this list by using the theory to make predictions about the link between learning and aggression. Any hypotheses we form, however, should be based on as much existing empirical information as possible. Our ability to confirm or refute each hypothesis will help us evaluate the overall accuracy of the theory. Figure 3.1 represents the interrelation between previous research, theory, and the research hypothesis.

Figure 3.1 also illustrates that the results of a study can serve as the foundation for additional research as well as a more formal test of the theory itself. As a generality, research hypotheses designed to test the predictions of a theory represent **confirmatory research** because the researcher plans to use the data to evaluate and support or confirm the validity of an existing theory. It may also be the case (and often is) that existing theories are modified or changed based on the results of research. The process of research and theory formation is dynamic and cyclical. Existing theory should always be evaluated and, if necessary, modified based on current research. One of the many virtues of a hypothesis is that it helps protect us from the Idols of the Theatre, the uncritical acceptance of information, such as that included in theories. Bacon (1620/1994) warned us not to accept ideas or a theory merely because they sound correct or are popular, often repeated, or presented by an authority. Rather, we should determine whether we can empirically verify the hypotheses derived from the theory. Most researchers will support a theory as long as it generates interesting and empirically testable hypotheses. Researchers begin to doubt a theory when the data that are collected do not confirm its predictions or when someone offers a different theory that accounts for the same phenomenon, while also incorporating any new and unexpected findings.

# Figure 3.1

**A Diagram of the Role of Theory, Hypothesis, and Research**

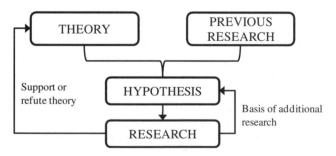

The individual research hypothesis is the product of theory, previous research, or both. For confirmatory research, the data derived from a study can influence a theory as well as serve as the guide for additional research. For exploratory research, the results of a study may inspire additional research.

Not all research is confirmatory, however. Much research in applied science is **exploratory research**. Exploratory research is not necessarily guided by theory, but rather the desire or motivation to explore an interesting phenomenon. Bacon (1994) advocated the collection of empirical data from many diverse sources and suggested that data collection should be free of preconceived notions in order to avoid the Idols of the Cave, the willingness to depend on personal experience to understand phenomena. Even when research is exploratory, systematic observation helps us to expand on our experiences by collecting a large amount of data under widely different conditions.

Many researchers share Bacon's early perspective on exploratory research. For example, in 1949, B. F. Skinner wrote a paper in which he asked the question, "Are theories necessary?" His answer was an emphatic, "No!" Indeed, Skinner argued that empirical research is valuable whether or not the researcher wants to confirm a theory. The importance of exploratory research is one that must be emphasized—the goal of any science is to examine and better understand the relationship among variables. Conducting research allows us to accumulate knowledge that in turn helps us develop new and important insights into the interesting questions we ask. While theory should be used as the basis for most research, ironically, it is often exploratory research that serves as the foundation for new theory creation.

## Hypotheses Direct Our Observations

When we prepare a hypothesis, we focus our attention on the type of information that we will study. Specifically, the hypothesis identifies the variables that we will examine and the data we will collect. In this way, a hypothesis is like a brief summary of your research game-plan. Good hypotheses help us to *operationalize* our constructs into concrete, measurable variables that can be used in developing a clear hypothesis that states how these multiple measured variables will be related. More details on "good" measurement are provided later in this chapter. A **variable** is any characteristic of a person, nonhuman subject, or research condition/environment that can take different values. Personality is an example of a person-level variable because it exists in different amounts (i.e., it varies) across different people. Similarly, biological sex is also a variable, as some people are men and others are women. We can also examine the influence of different research conditions on participants. Aspects of the research environment can often be modified, including the heat of the room, number of people sitting at a desk, or the difficulty of the task to be completed. In an experimental context, any element of the experiment that can change is considered a variable. The opposite of a variable is a **constant**, a numerical value or characteristic that, by definition, cannot change. For example, a minute always contains 60 seconds and $\pi = 3.1416 \ldots$ .

An empirical hypothesis will generally state the relation between two or more variables. Consider the hypotheses listed earlier and illustrated in

## Figure 3.2

**The Relation Between Variables Described in a Hypothesis**

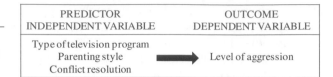

| PREDICTOR INDEPENDENT VARIABLE | OUTCOME DEPENDENT VARIABLE |
|---|---|
| Type of television program Parenting style Conflict resolution | Level of aggression |

Figure 3.2. In each case, the hypothesis states that changes in one variable correspond with changes in another variable.

Included in this example are three possible variables that have been hypothesized to predict or account for a second variable. In this example, we want to find the variables that allow us to explain or predict levels of aggression. As in most research, there are two types of variables in this example, the dependent variable and the independent variable. The **dependent variable** is the focus of the study and is the condition that the researcher wants to explain, describe, and predict. In modern usage you will sometimes see the term *response* variable or *outcome* variable used synonymously with *dependent* variable.

As an example, the first hypothesis in Figure 3.2 states that some children are more aggressive because they watch more violent television programs than children who are not aggressive. Level of aggression is the dependent variable. The other variable in the hypothesis is the explanatory or **independent variable**, the variable we expect to cause or account for a change in the dependent variable. A hypothesis explicitly describes how we expect the independent variable(s) to explain, describe, and predict the dependent variable(s).

As you will soon learn, different types of research have different types of independent variables. In some cases, the researcher can control or manipulate the levels of the independent variable. We call these **manipulated independent variables** because the researcher modifies or changes the amount or level of the independent variable, and because the variable is independent of (i.e., not affected by) other variables in the study. For example, we might conduct an experiment where the researcher has some children watch several hours of violent-themed cartoons and the other children watch several hours of nonviolent cartoons. The type of cartoon each group watches is a manipulated independent variable that was under the researcher's control.

Another type of independent variable is the **subject variable**. A subject variable is a characteristic or condition that the researcher cannot manipulate or control, but that may play an important role as an independent variable. As a rule, if a characteristic exists prior to the start of a research project, it is likely to be a subject variable. Personality, sex, intelligence, height, weight, and age are examples of these types of subject variables. Whenever people participate in a research project, they bring unique characteristics to the study. Although researchers cannot change the characteristics of the participants, they often use these characteristics as subject variables to predict meaningful dependent variables or outcomes.

Consider the content of children's television programs. We could treat this variable—content of programs—as either a manipulated independent variable or a subject variable, it just depends on the amount of control that the researcher has over the showing of these television programs. If a researcher can select the programs that children watch, then some children can be shown violent shows, while others are shown nonviolent ones. In this case, because the researcher directly controls the children's viewing experiences, this variable of program content is a manipulated independent variable. However, if a researcher decides instead to simply monitor the programs chosen by the children, then the content of television programs is a subject variable, as reflected in each child's television viewing preferences.

In summary, a good hypothesis identifies an expected relationship between at least two variables. One of these variables is the dependent variable that the researcher hopes to explain, describe, and predict. The other variable, the independent variable, is the one that the researcher uses to explain the results of the study. The independent variable will typically be either a manipulated variable or a subject variable.

## Hypotheses Describe the Relationships among Variables

Finding the orderly relationships among variables is the goal of any science. Thus, one of the most important components of a hypothesis is that it describes the relationships that we expect to observe between the variables. When we prepare a hypothesis, we use different verb phrases to describe the relation between independent and dependent variables. For example, we can state that when one variable increases, the other variable will also increase: *Children who watch more violence on television will be more likely to act aggressively*. We can also predict that an increase in one variable will lead to a decrease in the other variable: *Children who learn conflict-resolution skills will be less likely to act aggressively*.

## Hypotheses Refer to Populations

Most hypotheses are general statements about the relationships among variables in a population. The hypothesis, *Children who watch television programs with aggressive themes will be more aggressive than children who watch television programs with nonaggressive themes*, implies that the relationship between aggression and television programming is universal, applying to all children. If this hypothesis is correct, we should observe an association between aggression and television programming in data collected from any sample of children.

Populations and samples are familiar terms. We often talk about the population of the United States or the population of a city. Similarly, we often hear the word *sample* in day-to-day language. Even walking through a grocery store can present you with tasty samples of new foods and products. The companies marketing these products hope that your experience with these little samples will be enough to compel you to buy their product in the future. The meanings of population and samples are similar in research, but there are a few additional details that we need to present.

Technically, a **population** is a group of people or things that share one or more characteristics. In some cases, the definition of a population will be broad and inclusive. A social psychologist, for example, may believe that altruism is a general characteristic of all people. Therefore, he or she hopes that the results of an experiment on altruism will generalize to all people. In other cases, the population will be much more specific, as when psychologists study children within a specific age range (e.g., infants younger than 6 month of age), or people diagnosed with a specific psychological condition (e.g., depression with psychotic features).

A **sample** refers to a subset of the population. In most cases, when researchers speak of samples they mean a group of individuals or things that represent the broader population. If we assume that the sample is representative of the population, then we can assume that any conclusions we make based on data gathered from this sample will generalize to the population. Researchers define populations using empirical characteristics, or publicly verifiable characteristics. These definitions can be general (e.g., all children) or specific (e.g., only males between 8 and 12 years old). In general, we improve our ability to describe, explain, and generalize our findings regarding behaviors when we specifically define the population of interest beforehand and succeed in representatively sampling from that population when we collect data. Much more information on sampling will be presented in Chapter 7.

## Types of Hypotheses

There are four general types of research hypotheses that you are likely to see in the social sciences: (1) estimation of population characteristics, (2) correlation among variables, (3) differences among two or more populations, and (4) cause and effect. They differ in terms of the specific types of predictions that researchers are making. In some cases, researchers will examine the correlation between two variables; in other cases, the researcher will determine whether there is a meaningful difference between two groups. The type of hypothesis that a researcher uses determines the research methods that he or she will use as well as the types of conclusions the data allow.

### Estimation of Population Characteristics

The goal of this simplest form of hypothesis is to estimate the characteristics, or parameters, of a population using information or data gathered from a sample. We use special terms when we estimate and describe population parameters, including **data**, **descriptive statistics**, and **parameters**. Populations are generally too large to use for our research. Therefore, we use a representative sample of the population to estimate the population parameters. In all research, we collect data. In the majority of psychological research, these data are quantitative, though it is becoming increasingly common across most social science disciplines to also gather qualitative, or nonnumerical, data for a richer understanding of the phenomenon under study. A more in-depth discussion of qualitative research methods is presented in Chapter 17. Regardless of the type of data collected, the assumption guiding research is that the data adequately reflect the actual variables of interest.

Once the data are collected, we typically calculate descriptive statistics. A descriptive statistic is typically a number of some form that helps us to organize, summarize, and describe the data. In addition to describing the sample, we can use descriptive statistics to estimate the value of population parameters. A parameter, therefore, is a number that summarizes and describes a characteristic of a population. As a quick summary, *statistics are numbers based on direct observation and measurement and refer to the sample. Parameters are values that refer to the population. In most cases, we use statistics to estimate parameters.* If the sample is representative of the population, then we can infer that what is true of the sample is also true of the population. A common practice in research is to represent statistics using Roman letters (e.g., $A, B, C, D \ldots$ ) and to represent parameters using Greek letters (e.g., $\alpha, \beta, \gamma, \delta, \ldots$ ). By convention, we use the letter $M$ to represent the sample mean and the symbol $\mu$ (mu) to represent the population mean, the letters $SD$ to represent the sample standard deviation and the symbol $\sigma$ (sigma) to represent the population standard deviation. Although statistics are variable, in that they will change each time we collect data from a different sample, population parameters are considered to be constants.

What would this type of descriptive hypothesis look like? An example of a hypothesis pertaining to the estimation of population parameters is: *How much time does the typical 2- to 6-year-old child spend per day watching television?* In this hypothesis, we want to know the relation between a subject variable (children between the ages of two and six) and the dependent variable (time spent watching television). Another way that we can say the same thing is to write $M \approx \mu$. This expression states that the sample mean we obtain from our collected data will be approximately equivalent to the value of the overall population mean. As stated earlier, if the sample is representative of the population, then our best estimate of a population parameter is the sample statistic that we estimate from the data we collect.

## Correlation between Two Variables

Another useful form of hypothesis involves stating that there is a correlation between two variables. A correlation between variables means that these variables are linked such that as one variable changes, so does the other. This does not mean, however, that one variable causes the other. Correlation does not always indicate causation.

As an example, there is a correlation between years of education and annual income. If we collect a sample of working adults and ask them to tell us their level of education (e.g., high school, college, graduate school) and their annual income, we will find that there is a positive correlation between education and income. People with less than a high school education tend to make the lowest annual income. By contrast, people with greater levels of education tend to earn more money.

When we hypothesize about correlations, we can predict that there will be a positive, a negative, or no correlation between the two variables. A **positive correlation** means that an increase in one variable corresponds with an increase in another variable (or that a decrease in one variable corresponds to a decrease in the other). The correlation between years of education and income represents a positive correlation—an increase in years of education corresponds with an increase in annual income. By contrast, a **negative correlation** means that increases in one variable correspond with decreases in the other variable. Trick question: What is your prediction about the correlation between one's golf score and time spent practicing? There is a negative correlation between the two variables. Remember that in golf, the lower the score the better. When there is **no correlation**, there is no systematic relation between the two variables. There is no correlation, for example, between shoe size and intelligence. People with small feet are just as likely to be bright as people with big feet. Similarly, dull-witted people are equally likely to have small or large feet. Figure 3.3 presents three graphs that represent (a) a positive correlation, (b) no correlation, and (c) a negative correlation.

When we speak of a correlation between populations, we often use the parameter $\rho$ (rho) to express the size of the correlation between the two variables. When we predict that there is a positive correlation between the variables, we write $\rho > 0$. When we predict that there is a negative correlation between the variables, we write $\rho < 0$. If there is no correlation, we write $\rho = 0$. When writing or speaking of an observed correlation as a sample statistic, we typically use the Pearson product moment coefficient, $r$.

### Difference among Two or More Populations

There are many cases when we want to know whether members of separate populations are, on average, different from each other. In this situation, the independent variable may be either a manipulated independent variable or a subject variable that we use to classify the individuals as a member of separate populations. The second variable is a common dependent variable that we measure for all participants in the study. Once we have the data, we can determine whether there are meaningful and statistically significant differences among the groups. Here are two examples of this type of hypothesis:

### Example 1: Examining the Effects of Television Violence on Aggressive Behavior

We might have some children watch a television show that includes many acts of violence. Another group of children would watch a television show that includes no violence. After the children watched the television show,

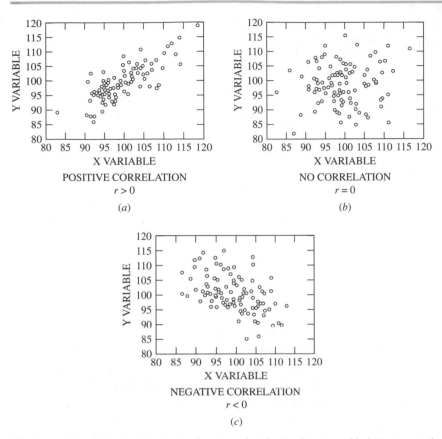

# Figure 3.3

**Three Correlations: A Positive Correlation, No Correlation, and a Negative Correlation**

The Letter $r$ Represents the Correlation for a Sample. The Greek Letter $\rho$ (rho) Represents the Correlation for the Population.

we would observe the children and look for evidence of aggressive behavior. In this case, the content of the show is a manipulated independent variable because the researcher could control whether the children in the study watched one type of show or another.

*Example 2: Determining Whether Boys Are More Aggressive Than Girls*
In this case, we can use a subject variable to create our comparison groups. The sex of the child, boy versus girl, is a subject variable because it is a condition that the researcher can measure but not control.

In both examples, we want to determine whether the typical behavior of members of one group is different from members of another group. As with the other hypotheses, we use sample statistics to make inferences about the population parameters. Therefore, when we compare two groups, we compare the difference between the sample means. If the difference between the sample means $(M_1 - M_2)$ is sufficiently large in a statistical sense, we then infer that the population means are different from each other. As an example, if you wanted to predict that the mean of one group is greater than another, you would use the statement $\mu_1 > \mu_2$. In this example, $\mu_1$ represents the mean of the first population and $\mu_2$ represents the mean of the second population.

### Cause and Effect

The last form of hypothesis is the most demanding hypothesis to test. For this hypothesis, we want to prove that changes in the independent variable cause changes in the dependent variable. Discussions of cause and effect can quickly become complicated and have been the subject of considerable philosophical analysis and debate for quite some time. It has become common in the social sciences to base determinations of cause and effect on the criteria established by John Stuart Mill (1986). Mill argued that one must show three things to infer a cause-and-effect relationship:

1. *The cause must precede the effect, temporally (X must come before Y in time order)*: This requirement recognizes that time moves in one direction, from the past to the future. Consequently, events that occur in the past can influence future events, and it is impossible for events in the future to influence events in the past.

2. *The two events in question must be correlated (X and Y must covary with each other)*: If we believe that the independent variable causes the dependent variable, then we should observe a consistent relation between the two variables. We can demonstrate the relation between the independent and dependent variables by examining the correlation between the two variables or by comparing the differences among group means. The difference between the groups is evidence that the independent variable is correlated with the dependent variable.

3. *All other possible explanations for the relationship between X and Y should be ruled out or explained*: This third criterion is difficult to achieve because it is often difficult to account for all possible explanations except for the one implied in the hypothesis.

Recognize that all the other hypotheses describe the population parameter and the general relationship among variables; they do not allow us to infer cause and effect. When we conduct research to examine cause and effect, we still examine the correlation between the variables and compare the differences among groups. Therefore, we will still need to determine whether $\mu_1 > \mu_2$. If we find that this statement is correct and the experiment meets the criteria for determining cause and effect, we can then infer that the independent variable caused the dependent variable, or IV → DV. The arrow indicates that changes in the independent variable caused changes in the dependent variable. Table 3.1 presents a summary of the four types of hypotheses. Be sure that you understand the similarities and differences among the four.

# Table 3.1  Features of the Four General Hypotheses Used in Empirical Research

| Type of Hypothesis | Purpose of Research | Mathematical Hypothesis | Written Hypothesis |
|---|---|---|---|
| *Estimate parameter* | Use sample statistics to estimate population parameters | $M \approx \mu$ | What is the average score of 5th-grade students taking a reading comprehension test? |
| *Correlation between variables* | Measure two variables to determine their correlation | $p > 0$ or $p < 0$ | There is a positive correlation between time spent studying and exam grade. |
| *Difference among populations* | Compare two or more sample groups to determine whether they are different | $\mu_1 > \mu_1$ or $\mu_1 < \mu_1$ | Men, on average, are taller than women. |
| *Cause and effect* | Determine whether the independent variable causes differences in the dependent variables | IV → DV | High levels of dopamine cause schizophrenia. |

## Knowledge Check

1. Describe the differences between a theory and a hypothesis.

2. Consider each of the following statements and determine whether they meet the criteria for a hypothesis.
   a. It is not good to spank children.
   b. Students should spend more time studying and less time playing video games.
   c. Intelligence is an inherited trait.
   d. To avoid cognitive dissonance, people will change their attitudes to match their behavior.
   e. People in an ambiguous situation will be more likely to conform with other members of a group.
   f. People with low self-esteem will not be as likely to volunteer for extra credit projects.

3. Jackie is interested in students' perception of their faculty. Her college uses a standard faculty evaluation form that asks students a series of questions regarding their performance in the course and their evaluation of the instructor's effectiveness. Jackie asks the dean if there is a relation between the students' expected course grade and instructor evaluations.
   a. Rewrite Jackie's question as a hypothesis.
   b. What is the independent variable?
   c. Is the independent variable a subject or a manipulated independent variable?
   d. What is the dependent variable?

4. Tim wants to replicate a finding first reported by Chase and Simon (1973). First, Tim finds 30 good chess players and another 30 people

who rarely play the game. For the study, he shows the participants 10 photographs of chess pieces on a chessboard. For half the pictures, the chess pieces are randomly arranged on the board. The other pictures represent the chess pieces as they would appear midway through a game. Tim shows each participant a photograph for 30 seconds. After a 10-second pause, Tim then asks the participant to recreate the arrangement of the chess pieces on a chessboard. Tim then records the accuracy of the reconstruction.

   a. What hypothesis or hypotheses do you believe that Tim can test with this research? State these in your words.

     (i) What are the independent variables?

    (ii) For each independent variable, determine whether it is a manipulated independent variable or subject variable.

    (iii) What is the dependent variable?

5. Carlos administers two tests to 500 adults (250 men and 250 women). The first test is a standard measure of empathy. The second test is a measure of the personality construct *self-monitoring*.

   a. What hypothesis or hypotheses do you believe that Carlos can test with this research? State these in your words.

     (i) What are the independent variables?

    (ii) For each independent variable, determine whether it is a manipulated independent variable or subject variable.

    (iii) What is the dependent variable?

6. Rebecca conducted a study that examined how people react to different types of feedback. Sixty people volunteered to participate in the study. During the first part of the study, Rebecca asked all the participants to solve a series of logical problems. Rebecca told a random half of the participants, *You must be really smart; you did much better than average on this test*. She told the other participants, *You must have tried hard; you did much better than average on this test*. Rebecca then gave all the participants another set of problems that contained items that could not be solved. She timed how long the participants spent on the impossible-to-solve items.

   a. What hypothesis do you believe that Rebecca tested with this research? State the hypothesis in your words.

   b. What is the independent variable?

   c. Is the independent variable a subject or a manipulated independent variable?

   d. What is the dependent variable?

## Measurement

At the heart of all research is measurement, a special form of empirical observation. Measurement allows us to record and quantify our observations in an objective and consistent manner. Therefore, measurement is a means to an end in that it allows us to answer the question, "What do we have?'' When done well, measurement can also improve the objectivity of our research efforts. Many people dismiss all of the social sciences as ''soft'' or ''inexact sciences,'' implying that psychology, sociology, and other social sciences are not as accurate or important as other more physically based sciences like physics or chemistry. This attitude misses the point because it is objectivity, not the precision of measurement, that defines the quality of any scientific endeavor. Although we strive for precision and accuracy in all measurement, our first goal is objectivity. Proper measurement can reduce various forms of bias from entering into our observations, helping us to address Bacon's Idols.

Attempting to objectively define our variables allows other researchers to choose to accept or reject our definitions. This also makes it easier for researchers to accurately replicate studies and repeat measurements. One criterion of all science is that it depends on public verification. Good measurement can help to ensure that any competent person is able to observe the same phenomenon that another researcher has observed. Can you see how public verification protects us from the Idols of the Theatre? If any person has the ability to verify a theory or replicate an existing finding, this means we do not have to rely on any singular authority to tell us what is true or false. All of us have the opportunity to collect the data and evaluate the results for ourselves.

The remainder of this chapter and part of the text discusses more basic elements of good measurement. To begin with, it is important to note that all forms of measurement share four essential features: (1) operational definitions, (2) measurement scale, (3) reliability, and (4) validity.

### Operational Definition

Measurement is the process of assigning numbers to objects, situations, or observations using a rule. An **operational definition** is the rule we use to convert our observations into numbers and our theoretical constructs into measurable variables. Consider the following questions:

1. What is the distance between Cleveland and New York?
2. How many people voted in the last presidential election?
3. What is the appearance of a light with a primary wavelength of 684 nm?
4. How large is the working memory?
5. How proficient is Martha at algebra and plane geometry?
6. How depressed is the client seeking therapy from a psychotherapist?

What does each of the questions have in common? First, each question refers to a specific construct. In the order of the questions, the constructs are:

1. Distance
2. Number or frequency

3. Appearance
4. Capacity
5. Proficiency
6. Severity

Second, we can answer each question using some form of measurement that allows the researcher to collect data relevant to each construct. To perform the measurement, we will have to define the variable and develop an appropriate measurement technique. Operational definitions define variables by stating the objective and empirical procedures for our measurement. Consequently, creating an operational definition is a critical step in any research (as you will recall from Chapter 1, it is the second step in the scientific method, HOMER). Operational definitions are different from dictionary definitions, which tend to be descriptive and imprecise. For example, a dictionary definition of *anxiety* may be, *A state of apprehension or psychic tension*. Can you see the problem with this definition? What are the observable characteristics and features of anxiety? "Apprehension" and "psychic tension" are private emotions that other people cannot directly observe. An operational definition, by contrast, refers to observable and/or measurable events that are also open to public verification. We can collect information or data from these observations or measurements and use this information to make inferences about the construct and its relationship to other constructs in our hypotheses or research model.

Take the question about the distance between Cleveland and New York. We need a clear operational definition of distance. What, specifically, do we mean by distance? How should we measure the distance? Should we draw an imaginary straight line between the city halls of the two cities and count the number of miles? Would the mode of transportation (plane, train, boat, or automobile) affect our measurement? One could measure the length of the interstate highways connecting the two cities as a measure of distance. Once we decide on the route we want to measure, what **metric** will we use? Should we record the distance in miles, kilometers, or time spent traveling? The important point to recognize is that an operational definition results in a clear statement of the type of information you will need as a researcher to test the hypotheses in your study.

Now, measuring distance is relatively straightforward, especially if you contrast this with measuring constructs that cannot be directly observed. This is the case with many constructs that you and other researchers are interested in studying. The capacity of working memory, proficiency for mathematics, and severity of depression are cognitive and emotional events that we cannot directly observe in other people. Yet, we want to use these variables to explain and predict behavior. How can we use variables that are not directly observable to explain behavior? One way is to use observable behaviors to infer the presence of events that we cannot directly see. This idea can be traced all the way back to Fechner (see Chapter 1), who realized

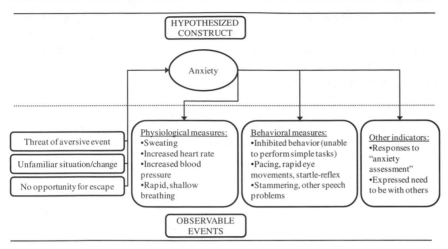

## Figure 3.4

**Depiction of the Relationship between a Hypothetical Construct, or Intervening Variable (Anxiety), and Various Observable Conditions and Reactions**

We use the hypothesized construct to help explain the link among variables. We use the observable reactions of the person to infer the presence and magnitude of the intervening construct.

that we can use a person's behavior to make inferences about their mental events. We frequently use **intervening variables** such as behaviors to describe other constructs we cannot directly measure. We also use intervening variables to explain various complicated and unobservable phenomena.

Consider the concept of anxiety as an example. Figure 3.4 presents an illustration of how we might use anxiety in a hypothesis and how we might operationally define anxiety. The illustration in Figure 3.4 consists of two parts. On the bottom are observable events that are open to public verification. For example, a researcher can create a pending threat by asking a person to give a speech on an unfamiliar topic to a group of strangers. We can also measure or directly observe many reactions. With the proper physiological recording equipment, we can objectively measure the person's physiological reactions to the pending threat. Similarly, we can watch the person to see how he or she acts in this situation, and then infer whether the person is anxious. In addition, we can design questionnaires or psychological tests to indicate the person's level of anxiety. On the top of Figure 3.4 is the hypothesized construct. We use the hypothesized construct, or intervening variable, to help explain the link between one set of variables and another. For example, we may note a positive correlation between the pending threat and specific physiological events. From this correlation, we infer that the person is anxious.

## Measurement Scale

Most people do not give much thought to the meaning of numbers. The general attitude seems to be that numbers are numbers regardless of their use. However, there are different classes, or types, of numbers. More accurately, when we measure things, we can use numbers in different ways. Furthermore, it is important to recognize the differences among the types of measurement scales. Researchers and statisticians often speak of four types of measurement scale. Each scale has unique features and presents information in a special manner. In addition, the type of scale we use will determine the type of inferences we can make from our measurement. The four types of measurement scales, in order of increasing complexity, are: (1) nominal, (2) ordinal, (3) interval, and (4) ratio.

### Nominal Scale

**Nominal scales** are the most basic form of measurement is classification. We can use nominal measurement to classify things into mutually exclusive categories based on some qualitative property. The purpose of a nominal scale is only to indicate some sort of qualitative difference among things or people. Examples of nominal scales include biological sex, religious preference, marital status, or psychiatric diagnosis. Taking religious preference a bit further, in a survey you might ask people to indicate their religious preference by selecting one of three options, such as Atheist = 1, Baptist = 2, Catholic = 3. This type of scale allows us to differentiate among people regarding their religious beliefs. The scale does not imply that one perspective is better than the others or that membership in one group represents more or less of something than membership in another group. The number of potential categories depends on the variable of interest and the characteristics of your sample. For example, depending on your sample you might need more than these three religious preferences and include variables such as Agnostic or Zoroastrian (to name only two of many other possibilities).

Nominal scales show up in many social science research projects. If you were studying child-care practices in your state, you might want to know where parents take their children during work. You could create a nominal scale definition as shown in Table 3.2. In this example, you created three types of child care. They are nominal categories to the extent that you do not wish to imply that one type of day care is better than another, only that the three types are different. Your goal will be to estimate the number of parents who select one of these options for their child or children.

Table 3.2  **Example of Operational Definitions for Nominal Scale**

| *Type of Care* | Home Care | Relative or Friend | Unlicensed Day Care |
| --- | --- | --- | --- |
| *Definition of category* | Child stays with a parent | Child stays with an unpaid relative or friend | Parent purchases child care from an unlicensed provider |

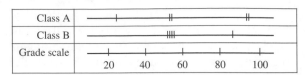

The vertical lines (|) represent the students' scores.

## Figure 3.5
**An Ordinal Scale**

### Ordinal Scale

With an **ordinal scale**, the numbers refer to a quantitative scale that is rank-ordered. In other words, whenever you rank something from highest to lowest, you are using an ordinal scale. In a horse race, for example, we rank the horse's order of finish as first, second, third, . . . , last. Movie critics use the number of stars to rate the quality of movies. A five-star rating usually means that the critic enjoyed the film and recommends it without reservation. By contrast, a one-star rating means that someone should burn all copies of the movie. We hope you recognize that, although intuitively appealing, ordinal scales are imprecise. In a horse race, a horse can win by a nose or 14 lengths. The critical feature of the ordinal scale is that there is no consistent magnitude of difference between points on the scale. Consequently, we cannot say that the difference between a 1 and a 2 is the same as the difference between a 3 and a 4. What we can assume is that $1 < 2$ and that $2 < 3$. Figure 3.5 provides an example to consider.

Imagine that two classes took the same exam. The vertical lines (|) represent the scores of individual students. In each class, one student can brag that he or she earned the highest score. Does this mean that both students did equally well? As you can see, the best score in Class A is in the 90s, whereas the highest score in Class B is in the 80s. Also, look at the difference between the first and second scores in the two classes. In Class A, the difference between the two highest scores is slight. In Class B, the difference between the two highest scores is large. The ordinal scale lacks the precision and accuracy found in other forms of measurement. There are many times, however, when the ordinal scale is the best quality scale that the researcher can use or find.

### Interval and Ratio Scales

The interval and ratio scales represent the most comprehensive type of measurement. These scales are quantitative because a one-to-one correspondence is assumed between the construct and the numbers on the measurement scale. In addition, the difference among the numbers along the scale represents equal units. These two types of measurement scale do differ with respect to the meaning of zero (0) on the scale. On an **interval scale**, the 0 is an arbitrary point selected for the sake of convenience. On a **ratio scale**, the 0 represents the absence of the construct of interest. We can use scores on a math test as an example of the difference between an **arbitrary 0** and an **absolute 0**.

A typical classroom math test covers only a small range of math skills, perhaps a student's skills with basic algebra. A student who earns a 0 on this specific test may not know much about algebra, but may know something in other aspects of math. By contrast, a comprehensive assessment of math-related knowledge or ability would have a "true 0" score that reflects a complete absence of math-related knowledge by the student. Thus, we cannot assume that a student who scores a 0 on an algebra test knows absolutely nothing about math more broadly defined. Because the test measures only a small portion of all math skills, we cannot infer that a 0 means that the student knows nothing about math. Therefore, the 0 on the math test is an arbitrary number relative to the broader construct, knowledge of math. What about two students who take the math test, one who scores an 80 and another who scores a 40? Does the student with the 80 know twice as much math as the student with the 40? Although $80 = 2 \times 40$, we cannot conclude that the student with the higher score knows twice as much math. If you look at the math knowledge scale, the difference between the two grades is minor relative to the amount of math both students know. Therefore, we would conclude that scores on the math test represent an interval scale for measuring math aptitude.

Examples of ratio scales include grams of food consumed, time spent on a task, and numbers of problems solved. As a guideline, ask yourself what the 0 on a scale actually means. If it indicates the absence of the construct being measured, then the 0 represents an absolute 0. For example, if a rat consumes 0 grams of food, we can infer that it ate nothing. In addition, eating 20 grams of food is twice as much as eating 10 grams. The same is true of time spent on a task. If a child spends 0 seconds on a task, we can assume that the child did not work on the task. In addition, 10 minutes on task is twice as long as 5 minutes on task. Table 3.3 summarizes the attributes and differences among the four scales.

## Reliability of Measurement

In terms of measurement, **reliability** refers to the consistency with which observations or measurements are made. Stated differently, assuming the construct you are measuring is not expected to change over time (e.g., general intelligence), a reliable test or measure will generally produce similar results each time we use it to assess a participant's standing on that construct. As you might guess, all researchers strive to develop and use the most reliable measurement devices available. Measures that are not reliable have very little value to researchers as they can lead to the downfall of a research project. Unfortunately, no test is perfectly reliable because **measurement error** affects all measurement techniques. For our purposes, measurement errors are random events that can increase or decrease an individual score on a given scale or assessment.

Measurement error is not the same thing as bias. Measurement error is a random variable that changes each time we use the test. In contrast, **bias**

Table 3.3 **Characteristics and Examples of the Four Measurement Scales**

| Scale | Characteristics | Examples | Mathematical Operations |
|-------|-----------------|----------|-------------------------|
| *Nominal* | Unordered and mutually exclusive categories; qualitative differences among groups | • Sex: male vs. female<br>• Psychiatric diagnosis<br>• Religious preference<br>• Political party | = vs. ≠ number of observations in each group $f(x)$ |
| *Ordinal* | Ranking or ordering of measurements | • Rank in class<br>• Level on a personality dimension (high vs. low self-esteem)<br>• Rank of quality (1 = poor, 10 = excellent) | < vs. > |
| *Interval* | Order, equal intervals, and arbitrary zero | • Temperature in Celsius<br>• Scores on most psychological tests: intelligence, personality, depression | A–B vs. B–C |
| *Ratio* | Order, equal intervals, and absolute zero | • Height, weight, age, speed<br>• Time to complete a task<br>• Number of problems solved | A/B vs. B/C |

**error** is systematic or constant, and is therefore present each time a test is used. A reliable measure can be biased. A bathroom scale, for example, may reliably report your weight although it consistently adds five pounds to your true weight. This is an example of a systematic bias that inflates your true weight every time you use this measurement device (the scale). In Classical Test Theory, an observed score is assumed to be the sum of the true score plus or minus the effects of any measurement error (random and systematic forms). In formula form, this theory can be stated as: *Observed Score = True Score ± Measurement Error ± Bias*. The ± symbol in the equation indicates that random and systematic error can add to and remove from the true score of the construct that we want to measure. For example, imagine that you administer an intelligence test to a student who has a true intelligence quotient (IQ) of 110. Due to measurement error, each time you administer the test, you may get different results.

Table 3.4 illustrates the effects of measurement error and the difference between two tests, one with higher reliability and one with lower reliability. A person completes two intelligence tests on five occasions. For both tests, there is random error. The random error is smaller for the test with the higher reliability. As you can see for both tests, measurement error raises and lowers the observed test score. Although measurement error affects both tests, the variability among the test scores is smaller for the test with higher reliability. The relation between reliability and measurement

Table 3.4  **Illustration of Reliability**

| Testing | Test with Higher Reliability | Test with Lower Reliability |
|---|---|---|
| 1 | $107 = 110 - 3$ | $118 = 110 + 8$ |
| 2 | $112 = 110 + 2$ | $105 = 110 - 5$ |
| 3 | $111 = 110 + 1$ | $107 = 110 - 3$ |
| 4 | $109 = 110 - 1$ | $111 = 110 + 1$ |
| 5 | $109 = 110 - 1$ | $109 = 110 - 1$ |
| | 110 | 110 |

error is simple: More reliable tests have less measurement error. Many factors contribute to measurement error. For the sake of simplicity, Table 3.5 lists the general classes of measurement error and several examples of each. As a researcher, your job is to determine what factors could affect the reliability of your measurement device and then design research procedures that can reduce the chances that this error will emerge. For example, if you believe that environmental distractions will corrupt the data, you will need to conduct your research in a setting where the testing conditions are consistent from subject to subject.

One of the more common methods to improve the reliability of the data is to increase the number of measurements. Carpenters have an old saying: *Measure twice, cut once.* Nothing is more frustrating than cutting a board and then finding that it is too short. To be careful, a good carpenter will double-check the necessary measurements to have greater confidence

Table 3.5  **Sources of Error that Reduce the Reliability of a Measurement Technique**

| Source of Error | Examples |
|---|---|
| *Instrument error* | • Equipment stops working<br>• Questions on a test are poorly worded<br>• Measurement scale is not precise |
| *Participant variability* | • Participant becomes fatigued or bored<br>• Participant does not understand the instructions<br>• Participant is unwilling to cooperate<br>• Participant cannot respond to some items |
| *Researcher variability* | • Researcher makes errors recording the data<br>• Researcher does not follow procedures consistently |
| *Environmental variability* | • Distractions occur in the environment, such as noise, or participant discomfort<br>• Measurement conditions are inconsistent across different participants |

before cutting a board or drilling a hole. The same (or at least similar) advice is important to remember with social science research: *Measure more than one way; interpret once with more confidence.* As an example, measures of intelligence, clinical depression, and classroom performance all usually depend on multiple measurements in order to improve reliability. As you can see in Table 3.4, an individual measurement may be a bit off the mark, but the average of several measurements will tend to hit the target.

### Determining Reliability

Reliability is commonly determined statistically using some form of correlation statistic such as Pearson's product moment coefficient ($r$). It can also be identified with the use of other statistics, such as Cohen's kappa ($\kappa$), that show the agreement or consistency between two or more scores or sets of ratings. More details on common procedures for demonstrating reliability are presented in Chapters 8 and 9.

## Validity of Measurement

**Validity** actually has less to do with elements of the measure, test, or assessment itself and more to do with the way in which a researcher uses a measure. To be more specific, validity is a property of the conclusions and interpretations that a researcher makes after studying the data collected with some measure. When people say a test is valid, what they are really saying is that a researcher using that instrument is likely to make accurate inferences based on test scores. In other words, accurate conclusions are drawn about the relationship of the construct the measure represents and other constructs that are the focus of the specific research study. When working with a measure that assesses something other than what you are interested in studying, it is common to refer to that measure as not valid. The implication is that using this measure will hinder your ability to make accurate inferences regarding the construct(s) you are trying to assess.

Figure 3.6 represents the relationship and distinction between reliability and validity in measurement. The picture represents three targets

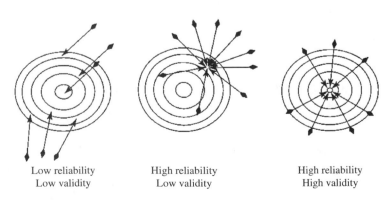

Low reliability    High reliability    High reliability
Low validity       Low validity       High validity

## Figure 3.6

**The Relationship between Reliability and Validity. The Arrows Represent Separate Measurements**

with arrows. The targets represent what we want to measure and the arrows represent the measurements we make. When the arrows are scattered across the target, as is the case in the left example, we say that the test is neither reliable nor valid. High reliability is not a guarantee of validity, however, as you can see in the middle picture. In this scenario, all the arrows hit a similar point, but this point is far away from the target construct (the bull's eye). Thus, information from this measure is consistent, but biased away from the target construct. Thus, *reliability is a necessary, but insufficient precondition for validity*. The scenario on the right illustrates a situation in which the measure is reliable and valid. All the arrows are close to each other and come close to hitting the bull's eye.

### Determining Validity

Validity is difficult to quantify because there is no single statistic or index that tells us whether something or some inference is valid. In the broadest sense, validity is a value judgment based on empirical evidence and the interpretations we want to make from the data. As Kaplan (1964) noted, validity refers to what we can accomplish using the data. From a slightly different perspective, all data are potentially valid until we attempt to interpret them. The definition of validity is fuzzy and vague because validity refers to the interpretation of the test score, not the test or measurement instrument itself.

If we gave you a test that measured your knowledge of rules of grammar, that test might contain questions about your knowledge of gerunds, dangling modifiers, relative pronouns, infinitives, subordinate conjunctions, participles, and active voice. Assuming that the test is reliable, what inferences can we draw from your score? Would it be appropriate to assume that you recognize all these terms and the associated rules of grammar? Depending on your score, such an interpretation may be correct. Can we use the test score to determine whether you are a creative writer? Probably not, regardless of your score. Good creative writing may be independent of knowledge of the formal rules of grammar. Thus, the same score from this one assessment of your knowledge of grammar can lead to valid or invalid conclusions, depending on how we choose to interpret the findings.

Researchers generally rely on several criteria to establish or demonstrate the potential validity of a measure or assessment. First, the reliability of that measure is a must. Once that is satisfied, attention then turns to identifying several additional subforms of validity that together help us to understand the full **construct validity** of a measure, or the extent to which that measure allows a researcher to make accurate inferences from observed data about the original construct. The four subforms of validity we will discuss here are: (1) face validity, (2) content validity, (3) predictive/concurrent criterion-related validity, and (4) construct validity.

**Face validity** is determined by the degree to which a participant or test-taker looks at an assessment and says to himself/herself, "This seems to clearly be an assessment of X,'' when X is the construct you are hoping to measure. Face validity is an important consideration during the test development process, because when test-takers do not believe that a measurement procedure is face valid, they may not respond honestly or fully.

As the name implies, **content validity** refers to the degree to which the measurement technique adequately samples behaviors relevant to the construct you are trying to measure. If you want to determine a person's proficiency in mathematics, you will ask the individual to solve math problems, not recite Lincoln's Gettysburg Address. In most cases, we determine the content validity of a test by having experts on the subject review the test. Therefore, you might ask several professors of mathematics whether a math test adequately assesses the student's ability to understand and apply specific mathematical concepts. Pay careful attention to the difference between face validity and content validity as they have been presented. It is very easy to confuse the two. The major difference is that face validity deals with the layperson's or test-taker's perceptions while content validity is evaluated based on the opinions of experts.

One of the important components of any good measure is that it allows us to accurately predict other behaviors or outcomes. This type of validity is referred to as **criterion-related validity** because we are trying to predict something (i.e., the criterion). In some cases, we hope that measurements that we take now will allow us to predict events later. If a test allows us to make these predictions, then we say that the test has **predictive validity**. **Concurrent validity** means that a test score correlates with other relevant behaviors or outcomes assessed at the same time as the target variable test. Predictive validity is predicated in a temporal distance between predictor and outcome. This is not the case for concurrent validity.

Look again at Figure 3.4. You can think of this picture as the model for construct validity. We say a measure has construct validity when we are able to show that it is assessing what we mean it to and when we can show that its relationships with other measured variables are in line with what you would expect based on theory. For example, in Figure 3.4, the target construct is anxiety. If we are able to show that our measure of anxiety allows us to support the theory and past research that says receiving shocks will produce anxiety and that anxiety then leads to increases in heart rate, then we are building the case for that measure's construct validity. The argument can be made that construct validity is ''true'' validity and all of the other types mentioned above (face, construct, criterion-related) are just evidence of construct validity. There are many ways to establish the construct validity of a measure, but in reality this is an ongoing challenge. It is helpful to think of construct validity in terms of a network of meaning. The technical term for this is a nomological network, but in essence it means that you establish the construct validity of a measure by linking it to other constructs that are similar and different, antecedent and consequent to the specific construct you are interested in studying.

## Populations and Samples

Previously, we noted that hypotheses help us to link our expected relationships among measured variables to relationships between constructs that exist at the population level. When we do research, we have to settle for sample-level data to test the proposed relationships that are stated in our hypotheses. Chapter 7 provides a more detailed discussion of populations and samples, but it is important to review now how we can use data collected from samples to make inferences about a population. Therefore, we need to examine the relation between target populations, sampling populations, and samples. The research hypothesis refers to variables in the population.

Because most populations are extremely large, it is impractical or impossible to truly sample from the population. Consequently, most researchers use a sample drawn from a **sampling frame** or subset of the larger target population. Ideally the sampling frame would be a complete list of every member of the population, but in reality it is usually a subset of the target population to which the researcher has or can gain access. The final sample itself is often a random selection from this sampling frame or another subsample of the population that is based on convenience. Ideally, the sample that a researcher settles on is a representative subset of individuals drawn from the sampling frame, which is hopefully a representative subset of the more general population. For example, assume that you want to study altruism. Your population may be all adults. Chances are that you will use students from your college for the research. Therefore, students at your college represent the sampling frame. The students who participate in your experiment represent the sample. Figure 3.7 represents the relation among populations, sampling frame, and samples.

The logic of sampling is deceptively simple. First, take a representative sample from the sampling frame. The representative sample should be manageable in size and share the same characteristics as the sampling population. Next, conduct the study and collect the data. Once you have analyzed the data, you can generalize from the sample to the sampling frame. If your sampling frame is representative of the population, you can then assume that what is true of the sample will be true of the population. This description of using samples to generalize about the population sounds simple and straightforward. Unfortunately, this advice is similar to saying that to build a house all you need to do is buy the right materials and follow

## Figure 3.7

**Relation between Population, Sampling Population, and the Sample**

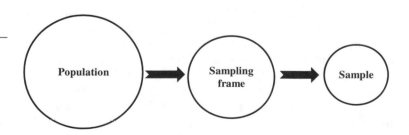

the blueprints. Although technically correct, the instructions gloss over many important points.

The fundamental question that we need to ask is, *"How do we know that the sample is representative of the population?"* We can answer that question by examining two interrelated characteristics of samples. The first characteristic of a sample is its size. The second characteristic is its ability to represent the population. How large should the sample be? We will revisit this question several times throughout this book. Research requires time, money, and energy, and each member of the sample requires these resources. Therefore, to control costs and not spend an entire lifetime on a single project, we want to keep the sample to a reasonable size. At the same time, the sample has to be large enough to adequately represent the population. If the population is very diverse on many characteristics, then the sample may need to be larger to fully reflect this diversity. A large sample, however, is not a guarantee that the sample will accurately reflect the population.

This leads us to the second characteristic of a sample, its ability to represent the population. Many popular magazines publish the results of surveys of their readers. Sometimes the editors will tout that more than 20,000 readers responded to the survey published in a previous issue. Do these results provide a good and useful source of information? Can we consider the data to be representative of the population or even the sampled population? After a moment's consideration, you should say, "No!" There are many potential problems with these data.

First, only people who read the magazine had the opportunity to respond. Second, although 20,000 is a big number, it is not an automatic protection against bias. The people who responded may represent a minority of the readership. Perhaps those who responded are also somehow qualitatively different from those who chose not to respond. As we progress through this textbook, we will examine methods researchers use to determine how large the sample should be. In some cases, we will be able to use one or two people for our research. In other cases, our sample will number in the hundreds or even thousands. Determining the size of the sample depends on what we know about the population and the type of behavior we are studying. As we begin to explore specific types of research, we will show you ways to determine the size of the sample.

Apart from the size of a sample, to be useful, samples must also actually represent the population. Because we want to generalize about the population, we need to ensure that the sample is an accurate model of the population. The **representativeness of a sample** is the consequence of the procedure the researcher uses to collect the data. We can determine whether a sample is representative of a population by examining the methods used by the researcher to collect those data. One of the most common ways to improve the representativeness of a sample during the designing phase of a study is to use **simple random sampling**. Simple random sampling means that each member of the sampling frame has an equal probability of being selected or becoming a participant. Following this

# Figure 3.8

**The Difference in Data Produced by a Convenience Sample and a Probability Sample**

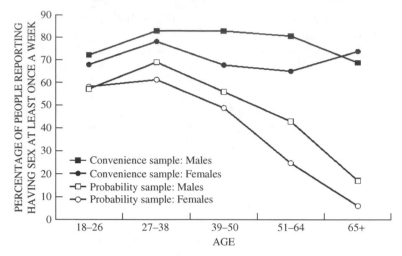

Data presented in Hyde and DeLamater (1998).

procedure, laws of probability ensure that a sample of a sufficient size will accurately reflect the overall population.

Conversely, failure to use simple random sampling can produce questionable results. Consider the following example. Hyde and DeLamater (1998) presented the results of two surveys of men's and women's sexual behavior. The first survey was administered to a sample determined by simple random probability sampling. The second survey was administered to a sample gathered via **convenience sampling**. For convenience sampling, the researcher uses members of the population that are easy (convenient) to recruit. A convenience sample is not a random sample because some people in the population have no chance of being selected. Figure 3.8 presents the results of the two studies that examined the frequency of sexual relations among adults.

Hyde and DeLamater (1998) noted that the convenience sampling represents data collected from clients of a clinic for the treatment of sexual dysfunctions and their friends. These people may not represent the typical person in the population. The other set of data represents research conducted by researchers who used random sampling of the population. We cannot trust the results of the convenience sample because the sample (people attending the clinics) is not representative of the population. By contrast, we have greater confidence in the results of the probability sample, as the results are more likely to represent the target population.

## Role of Random Sampling in Research

Many students are surprised to learn that few research studies in psychology actually use random sampling. There seems to be a general impression that all research *must* use random sampling to be valid. In some cases, this assumption is correct. In other cases, we may not need to use random sampling to conduct valid research. Our choice of whether to use random sampling depends on the type of research we conduct and the goals of the research.

## When Random Sampling Is Essential

Random sampling from the target population is essential when we want to estimate, with as much precision as possible, specific characteristics of the population. Political polling is an example of research for which random sampling is imperative. To predict who will win an election, or which policy issues are most important among registered voters, a pollster will take great pains to ensure that he or she collects a random sample from the target population. The random sample will allow the researcher to predict, for example, that "Strickland will receive 57% of the votes whereas Hollister will receive 43%, ±3 percentage points." If a true random sample of likely voters was used for this poll, then the pollster/researcher can safely predict that Strickland will receive between 54% and 60% of the vote.

Apart from politics, there are many cases when conducting research where we want to ensure we have a representative sample from the target population. For example, imagine you created a new test of depression. What scores on your test indicate normal moods; what scores represent depression? To answer these questions, you need to randomly sample from a population of depressed adults and from another population of depression-free adults. The data for the two groups will help you find which scores represent "normal" moods and which scores represent depression.

## When Random Sampling Is Not Essential

Many scientists conduct research that examines the relationships among variables. For example, what is the relationship between positive reinforcement and behavior? The answer is that people tend to repeat behaviors that are positively reinforced. Notice that we made a generalization about a population (all people) that did not estimate specific values. All we did was state that there is a lawful relationship between two variables. For this type of research, we describe the *qualitative* relationship between two variables; we do not estimate the *quantitative* values of any characteristics of the population. When we conduct research that examines the qualitative relationship among variables, we examine the general characteristics of the population. Using the current example, we assume that all people will repeat behaviors that lead to positive reinforcement, although the size of the effect may vary from person to person. In these types of situations it is not always necessary to randomly sample from the larger population because it is assumed that the phenomenon or relationship you are studying will exist for all or most people in that population anyway. The key here is that it is the variability in the population that determines whether random sampling is needed and, if so, how large the sample needs to be. We will discuss this more fully in Chapter 15.

Most researchers conduct studies using people they can easily find. They may use children in local day-care facilities or schools. They may advertise in the local newspaper for volunteers to participate in their research. They will use students enrolled in courses at a local college or university. We are taking a risk in making generalizations from a non-random sample. The students at your college or university may be radically different from students at other colleges. Children raised in the northeastern region of the country may be much different from children raised in the Deep South. People who respond to newspaper advertisements may be different from the typical person. Thus, significant cultural or geographic factors may bias the data. Although this is a legitimate concern, we must remember that researchers strive to replicate important findings. If a researcher discovers an interesting finding, then other researchers, from different parts of the country, will attempt to replicate those findings. This is why we never rely on only one study. As you will recall from earlier in this chapter, research and theory building represent a cyclical, dynamic process. The more data we have supporting a hypothesis, the more trust we have in the validity of the findings.

A good example of this replication comes from the study of obedience to authority. During the late 1960s, Milgram (1974) conducted a series of experiments designed to study the degree to which people would follow orders and give what appeared to be a powerful electrical shock to another person. Milgram repeated his experiments many times to ensure that his results were consistent. He used volunteers living in New Haven as well as other cities in Connecticut. Each time he conducted the study, he got similar results. Other researchers (Brief, Buttram, Elliott, Reizenstein, & McCline, 1995; Meeus & Raaijmakers, 1995), using different procedures and different sampling populations, have also examined obedience. The results of these studies support Milgram's original findings.

## Research in Action: Measuring Sexism

Do some people believe that women cannot be effective leaders? Schimmelpfenig and Sibicky (1997) asked this question after noting that although a substantial number of women have entered the workforce, only a few have been promoted to leadership roles. These researchers also noted that the dominant stereotype of a good leader continues to represent a masculine stereotype. Therefore, they decided to determine how people who have sexist attitudes would evaluate the leadership skills of women.

A technical issue that Schimmelpfenig and Sibicky (1997) had to overcome was how to measure sexism. They found a measure called the Modern Sexism Scale (Swim, Aikin, Hall, & Hunter, 1995) that contained a series of statements including, *Discrimination against women is no longer a problem in the United States*, and *It is easy to understand the anger of the women's groups in America.* For each question, respondents indicated their agreement or disagreement on a scale ranging from 1, which indicated *Strongly Disagree*, to 7, which indicated *Strongly Agree*. The researchers had 73 men and 83 women from their college complete the survey. Based on the Modern Sexism Scale, the researchers divided the people into two groups: High Sexism and Low Sexism.

Four weeks later, Schimmelpfenig and Sibicky (1997) asked the same people to complete another task. The cover story was that the college's administration wanted to choose a recipient for the college's annual leadership award (a real award at the college). The researchers led the people to believe that the description came from *Who's Who in American Leadership.* In addition, the researchers led half of the people to believe that the leader was a man. The other people read the same description of a woman as leader. All the participants in the study then rated the person for the following qualities: effective, competent, rational, powerful, determined, and decisive.

Figure 3.9 presents the results from Schimmelpfenig and Sibicky's (1997) study. The horizontal axis of the graph represents the various leadership qualities the participants rated. The vertical scale represents the average score the groups of participants gave the male and female leaders. Look at the effective construct at the left of the graph. Is there evidence that sexism influenced a person's rating of the leader? Participants who were not sexist (low sexism) rated the male and female leaders the same (the differences between the means are trivial). By contrast, people who were sexist (high sexism) gave the woman lower marks. This pattern of results repeats across the six leadership characteristics. Consequently, these data appear to offer tentative evidence that people who score high on the Modern Sexism Scale are more likely to evaluate men and women's leadership behavior differently, even when it is the same behavior.

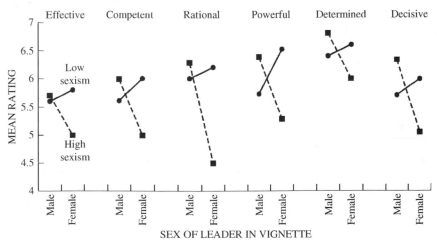

## Figure 3.9

**Interaction between Level of Sexism and Attitudes toward Leader Based on Leader's Sex**

From Schimmelpfenig and Sibicky (1997). Used with permission of the authors.

## Knowledge Check

Use the Schimmelpfenig and Sibicky (1997) study to answer the following questions.

7.  What is the population and sampling population for this research?
8.  Is random sampling a critical issue for this research?
9.  Can you identify the independent and dependent variables in this study?
10. Are the independent variables manipulated or subject variables?
11. Which scale of measurement best represents:
    a.  The raw score on the Modern Sexism Scale?
    b.  The score on the sex of the leader in the vignette?
12. Schimmelpfenig and Sibicky used an elaborate cover story for the second part of the study. How does the cover story relate to face validity?
13. Why is sexism an intervening variable?
14. What is the operational definition of sexism in this study?
15. How do the results of this study help verify that the Modern Sexism Scale does assess sexism?

## Chapter Summary

In this chapter we reviewed the foundations of all empirical research. In any scientific research project, the researcher will state a hypothesis, determine how he or she will measure the relevant variables, and then collect the necessary data. As we reviewed in this chapter, a hypothesis is more than an educated guess. The hypothesis is a statement that directs the course of the research by describing the variables to be examined, how the data are to be collected, and the relation between the variables. Some researchers develop hypotheses from specific theories in the hope of confirming the utility of the theory. In other cases, the researcher conducts exploratory research to learn more or explore interesting topics.

Most hypotheses refer to dependent and independent variables. Dependent variables refer to the focus of the study—the variable that the researcher hopes to be able to describe, predict, and explain. The independent variable is the variable that the researcher hopes will allow him or her to describe, predict, and explain the dependent variable. The independent variable may be a characteristic of the participant. Characteristics such as sex, intelligence, and personality are examples of subject variables because they are conditions that the researcher cannot manipulate. A manipulated independent variable is a type of independent variable that the researcher can control or manipulate.

There are four types of hypotheses, including descriptive, correlational, population differences, and cause and effect. For the descriptive hypothesis, the researcher hopes to collect data that will allow him or her to estimate or infer characteristics of a population. A developmental psychologist may want, for example, to describe the cognitive problems that children of a specific age can solve. When a researcher poses a correlation hypothesis, he or she predicts that changes in one variable correspond to changes in another variable. An example of a correlation hypothesis is the prediction that there is a positive correlation between the personality variables extroversion and assertiveness. The third type of hypothesis allows the researcher to predict that members of one group are different from another group. This type of hypothesis allows us to compare two or more groups. Examples of the hypothesis are, *Smokers are more anxious than nonsmokers* and *Children who attend day care are more cooperative than children who do not attend day care*. The final hypothesis refers to cause and effect. To show cause and effect, one must show (1) that the cause precedes the effect, (2) that there is a correlation between the two variables, and (3) that all other explanations have been accounted for.

All research depends on measurement. In this chapter we examined the foundations of measurement, which include operational definitions, measurement scales, reliability, and validity. Operational definitions allow us to link observable behaviors to inferred constructs. Depression, for example, is a construct that cannot be directly observed. We can operationally define depression by identifying the behaviors that we believe indicate this condition. When we operationally define a construct, we refer to a measurement scale. The measurement scale can be nominal (putting observations into categories), ordinal (ranking the construct from lower to higher), interval (a scale with a consistent scale, but no absolute 0), and ratio (a scale with a consistent scale and an absolute 0). Reliability refers to the consistency of measurement. A reliable measure is one that provides consistent answers.

Reliability is not the same thing as validity, however. To consider a test valid, we must show that data produced by the test allow us to make useful predictions. In the final section of the chapter, we reviewed populations, sampling populations, and samples. Researchers use samples to evaluate hypotheses. The hypothesis, however, refers to the population. Therefore, researchers hope that what is true of the sample will also be true of the population. Random sampling is not frequently used in behavioral research because it is difficult to gain access to the entire population. Researchers examine the qualitative relation among variables. In addition, researchers will attempt to replicate interesting findings. The more we can replicate a finding, the more confident we are in the finding.

## Chapter Glossary for Review

**Absolute 0**—A zero point on the scale that represents the absence of the construct.

**Arbitrary 0**—A zero point on the scale selected for convenience. The 0 does not represent the absence of the construct.

**Bias error**—A consistent error in measurement that reduces the validity of the test.

**Confirmatory research**—Conducting research to determine the relative merits of a theory by testing hypotheses derived from the theory.

**Constant**—A measurable characteristic that does not change or take on different values.

**Construct validity**—The ability of a test to measure the variable or construct it was designed to measure.

**Content validity**—The degree to which a test appears to be valid to experts familiar with the variables being measured.

**Convenience sampling**—A sampling technique where the researcher uses only those members of the population most easily obtained or incorporated into the research.

**Criterion-related validity**—Empirical data demonstrating the relationship between the predictor and criteria.

**Data**—The information we collect in research that is a product of measurement.

**Dependent variable**—The variable in the research that the researcher wants to explain, describe, and predict.

**Descriptive statistic** or **statistic**—A number that allows us to organize, summarize, and describe the data. Statistics refer only to samples.

**Exploratory research**—Conducting research to examine the relation among variables and to understand a particular phenomenon.

**Face validity**—The degree to which a test appears to be valid to the people taking the test.

**Hypothesis**—Any statement or prediction that describes the relation among two or more variables based on theory or previous research.

**Independent variable**—The variable that the researcher uses to explain, describe, and predict the dependent variable.

**Interval scale**—A quantitative measurement scale that uses an arbitrary 0 and consistent differences between values.

**Intervening variable**—A hypothetical variable created within a theory and used to explain the link between two or more observable behaviors.

**Manipulated independent variable**—An independent variable that the researcher can directly control or manipulate in an experiment. The researcher can assign individuals to different levels of the independent variable. Other variables in the study do not affect the independent variable.

**Measurement error**—Errors in measurement due to random and unpredictable events that reduce the accuracy and reliability of the test.

**Metric**—Refers to a standard of measurement, or the specific scale, used to make measurements.

**Negative correlation**—The description of a systematic relation between two variables—as one increases the other decreases.

**No correlation**—There is no linear relation between the two variables.

**Nominal scale**—A qualitative measurement scale that places individuals or observations into mutually exclusive categories.

**Operational definition**—A rule used to define a specific construct empirically and objectively and to determine how the researcher will measure the construct.

**Ordinal scale**—A quantitative measurement scale that ranks the observations for a particular characteristic. The differences among the numbers need not be equal.

**Parameter**—A number that summarizes or describes a characteristic of a population. Parameters refer only to populations and are estimated by statistics.

**Population**—A group of people or things that share one or more publicly verifiable characteristics.

**Positive correlation**—The description of a systematic relation between two variables—as one increases the other increases.

**Predictive/concurrent validity**—The ability of a test to accurately estimate current behavior or predict future behaviors.

**Ratio scale**—A quantitative measurement scale that uses an absolute 0.

**Reliability**—The degree to which a test produces consistent measurements of the same thing.

**Representativeness of a sample**—A condition that occurs when the sample data mirror the corresponding parameters of a population. The representativeness of a sample is the product of the sampling procedures used to create the sample.

**Sample**—A group of people or things, drawn from the population, that represents the population from which it was drawn.

**Sampling frame/population**—A subset of the population from which the researcher draws the sample. The researcher assumes that the sampled population represents the target population.

**Simple random sampling**—A method for creating samples. There is an equal chance that the researcher will select any member of the population.

**Subject variable**—A variable that represents some preexisting characteristic of the individual in the research. The researcher cannot control the subject variable but may use it to describe or predict the dependent variable.

**Theory**—A broad statement about the general causes of a phenomenon. Theories are more expansive than hypotheses and are often the source of specific hypotheses.

**Validity**—The degree to which a test measures what it is supposed to measure.

**Variable**—Any measurable characteristic that can have different values.

## Chapter References

Bacon, F. (1994). *Novum organum* (P. Urbach & J. Gibson, Trans.). Chicago: Open Court. (Original work published 1620).

Brief, A. P., Buttram, R. T., Elliott, J. D., Reizenstein, R. M., & McCline, R. L. (1995). Releasing the beast: A study of compliance with order to use race as a selection criterion. *Journal of Social Issues*, *51*, 177–193.

Chase, W. G., & Simon, H. A. (1973). Perception in chess. *Cognitive Psychology*, *4*, 55–81.

Hyde, J., & DeLamater, S. (1998). *Human sexuality*. Boston: McGraw-Hill.

Kaplan, A. (1964). *The conduct of inquiry: Methodology for behavioral science*. San Francisco: Chandler.

Meeus, W.H.J., & Raaijmakers, Q.A.W. (1995). Obedience in modern society: The Utrecht studies. *Journal of Social Issues*, *51*, 155–175.

Milgram, S. (1974). *Obedience to authority: An experimental view*. New York: Harper and Row.

Mill, J. S. (1986). *System of logic*. New York: Classworks. (Original work published 1843).

Pavlov, I. P. (1927). *Conditioned reflexes: An investigation of the physiological activity of the cerebral cortex*. London: Oxford University.

Schimmelpfenig, D. W., & Sibicky, M. E. (1997, April). Modern sexism and attitudes toward male and female leaders. Poster session presented at the annual meeting of the Southeastern Psychological Association, Atlanta, GA.

Skinner, B. F. (1949). Are theories of learning necessary? *Psychological Review*, *57*, 193–216.

Swim, J. K., Aikin, K. J., Hall, W. S., & Hunter, B. A. (1995). Sexism and racism: Old-fashioned and modern prejudices. *Journal of Personality and Social Psychology*, *68*, 199–214.

# Chapter 4
# An Overview of Empirical Methods

## CHAPTER OBJECTIVES

**Introduction**
**Internal, Statistical Conclusion, and External Validity**
**Survey of Empirical Methods**
**Intact Groups Designs and Quasi-Experimental Studies**
**Surveys**
**Correlational Studies**
**Single-Participant Research Methods**
**Meta-Analysis**
**Computers and Statistics**
**Research in Action: Effectiveness of Psychotherapy**

There are only a handful of ways to do a study properly but a thousand ways to do it wrong.

—D. L. Sackett

## Introduction

In many ways, conducting research is a creative process much like painting a picture. Using many brushes, colors, and painting techniques, the artist creates a unique piece of art. Each piece creates its own technical challenges that the artist must solve. The same is true of a researcher who must decide which research technique will produce the best data that can allow the researcher to answer the research question.

Many students seem to think that learning research methods should be like reading a cookbook. If you want to make chicken soup, find a recipe and follow the directions. If you want to conduct an experiment, find the appropriate chapter and follow the steps. Good research is not this simple. There is no such thing as the "single factor experiment recipe," nor are there five easy steps to conducting a research project. Each research project presents unique technical challenges that the researcher must solve. Selecting from a range of techniques, researchers create a **research design** that allows them to find the answer to empirical questions. Therefore, a research design is a plan for collecting data using empirical techniques. As you will learn in this chapter, there are many research techniques, each with notable merits and limitations.

As the quotation at the start of this chapter suggests, the research design process requires careful planning. As Sackett recognized, there are a lot of ways to do poor research, but only a few ways to do it well. This chapter will help you learn how researchers take an interesting hypothesis and develop a research design that produces clear and useful data.

In Chapter 3 we reviewed the concept of validity as it relates to measurement. As you learned, a measure, assessment, or test is commonly called *valid* if it measures what we want it to measure. More specifically, a measure is valid if it allows the researcher to make accurate and specific interpretations or conclusions based on its scores. We can extend this definition of validity to empirical research. Specifically, we can ask whether inferences made from the data support specific conclusions. Just as an assessment measures some constructs but not others, some research designs allow us to answer some questions but not others. We can evaluate the validity of a research project in terms of its internal validity and external validity.

## Internal, Statistical Conclusion, and External Validity

Researchers collect data to make interpretations, or inferences, about the relationships among variables. As you will learn, interpretation is one of the more critical steps in the research process because the data do not speak for themselves. Unfortunately, many people use phrases such as ''The research proves . . . '' or ''The data clearly show that . . . ''. The problem with these phrases is that research and data cannot speak for themselves. *Research* is a verb that describes the work that researchers perform, specifically the act of seeking information. Data are the pieces of information that researchers collect to help them answer a research question. Once the researchers have the data, they must interpret them. Because research requires interpretation, no data are valid or invalid until someone interprets the data. The *researchers* tell us how they *interpreted* the data. Thus, it is better to use the phrase ''Researchers tell us . . . '' or ''The researchers concluded that . . . .''

Here is an overly simplified example. What is the average Scholastic Assessment Test (SAT) score at Mythical College? Two possible answers are, ''The average SAT score of all Mythical College students is 1067'' and ''This average score indicates that students at Mythical College are better prepared for college than the typical student.'' Are these statements valid? The first statement is a straightforward answer to the question. Within the scope of the question, the answer is valid because the mean represents the typical SAT score of students at the college.

Is the second response acceptable—is the response valid? Although the data are the same, it is doubtful that you would agree with the interpretation. To verify the validity of that statement, we must first obtain the answers to several additional questions. Is an average score of 1067 better than averages for other colleges? Is the SAT test really a measure of students' preparation for college? Finally, what do we mean by *the typical student*? Is the typical student (1) anyone who graduates from high school, (2) only students who attend college, or (3) only students who complete college? Some statements about the data are valid, whereas others are not. Remember, when we say that an assessment is valid, we really mean that the *interpretation* of the scores from that assessment is valid. The same is true for interpreting the data collected in an experiment. We use validity to describe our interpretation of the data, not the data specifically. Now it is time for more information about internal and external forms of validity.

## Internal Validity

**Internal validity** refers to the cause-and-effect relationship between the independent variable (IV) and the dependent variable (DV). You should recall from Chapter 3 that we can examine the hypothesis IV → DV only under certain circumstances. Saying that an experiment is internally valid means that changes in the independent variable, which the experimenter controlled, actually caused changes in the dependent variable. By contrast, if factors other than the independent variable caused changes in the dependent variable, then we cannot conclude that the study is internally valid because the researcher has not ruled out **alternative explanations**. An alternative explanation is a reasonable explanation of the results that does not depend on the specific hypothesis, IV → DV. When we state that a study is internally valid, we have concluded that the research design has allowed us to control for and rule out alternative explanations.

## Threats to Internal Validity

There are four broad categories of factors that can threaten or limit a study's internal validity. In many cases, we can avoid these threats through good research design and attention to detail while collecting the data. Any threat to internal validity is a **confounding variable**. In general, a confounding variable is any extraneous or uncontrolled condition related to the independent variable. Specifically, a confounding variable is any variable not controlled by the researcher that is also correlated with the independent variable. Because the researcher cannot control the confounding variable, he or she cannot be sure whether the results reflect the effect of the independent variable or the effect of the confounding variable. The four major types of confounding variables that we will examine include: (1) unintentional sequence of events, (2) nonequivalent groups, (3) measurement errors, and (4) ambiguity of cause and effect.

The first threat to internal validity is the **unintended sequence of events**. As the name implies, the data may reflect a sequence of events that the researcher did not or could not control. There are cases when a researcher will want to study how a sequence of events changes behavior. A developmental psychologist, for example, may want to study changes in children's cognitive and intellectual abilities when they enter middle school. There are, however, instances when an unintentional sequence of events is the confounding variable. The following are examples of such unintentional sequences:

**Carryover effects** (also known as *testing effects*) refer to the influence of participants' earlier experiences/exposures on their present or future performance. One common example of when carryover effects are likely to emerge is when the same participants are asked to take the same assessment twice. Knowledge gained by responding to the assessment the first time may influence the participants' scores the next time they complete the same assessment. Consequently, if we used this procedure in a research project, we would not know whether the changes in participants' scores reflect the effect of the independent variable or that participants knew the answers to the questions.

**Maturation** is another example of unintended sequence of events. If the research project is *longitudinal*, spanning a long period of time, it is possible that the observed changes represent the passage of time or the maturation of the person and not a real effect of the independent variable on the dependent variable(s). For example, some depressed people will gradually improve their mental health without treatment. Consequently, the researcher must ensure that the observed improvements are greater than those that are due to the maturation effect.

**Intervening events** are related to maturation and sometimes also called *history effects*. We all live in a complex world. As time passes, you as a researcher and your participants will all be exposed to a variety of environmental factors and general life events. These can all influence your behavior in ways that are completely separate from the influence of the target independent variable in your research. For example, participants in a study could talk to each other or other people about the research, influencing future participants' behaviors. Similarly, a host of random events (e.g., accidents, natural disasters, war) could occur with dramatic influence on the behavior and cognitions of all participants. These outside factors, over which you have little control, may greatly influence your ability to draw valid inferences regarding the link between your stated independent variable and your target dependent variable.

The second broad category of threats to internal validity is the problem created by *nonequivalent groups*. The goal of an experiment is to identify differences among groups that reflect true effects of an independent variable on some dependent variable. In other words, hypothesizing that the independent variable will cause changes in the dependent variable implies that prior to exposure to the independent variable two or more groups will be identical to each other. A problem of inference arises when the two groups differ from each other due to factors other than different levels of exposure to the independent variable. Two conditions that may cause the groups to be different are mortality/attrition and the uncontrolled effects of subject variables.

**Mortality** is a rather morbid word that refers to any loss of participants from your sample of participants. Participants may drop out of a study for many reasons—they may become bored or embarrassed or move to another city. They may become sick or die. The consequence of participant mortality is that the end-differences among groups when the study is finished may represent the effect of this mortality and not the influence of the independent variable. A particular problem with subject mortality is that the people who drop out of the study may represent an important subgroup of people in the larger population. There may be important differences between those individuals that drop out of a study and those that remain.

**Subject variables** are another important source of potentially nonequivalent groups. For many research projects, the independent variable is a subject variable, some characteristic of the participant. Because the researcher does not have direct control over this variable, he or she can examine the relation between the independent and dependent variables, but cannot automatically assume a cause-and-effect relationship exists. Imagine, for example, that we compared two teaching methods, one applied to a course taught at 8:00 A.M. and the other to a section taught at 5:30 P.M. The time of day may reflect an underlying subject variable among the student participants in that those students who elected to take the early-morning section of the class may differ in some important way from those students who opted for the evening section of the course. Consequently, we will have a hard time answering our original research question, "Are the differences between the two course groups due to the impact of the teaching method or to characteristics of the students themselves?"

A third threat to internal validity includes problems created by *measurement errors*. Using an assessment or measurement instrument that is not a reliable and potentially valid measure of the independent or dependent variable raises questions about the internal validity of any cause-and-effect conclusion. Even if the assessment is valid, other problems may arise, including the following.

**Ceiling and floor effects** are important measurement errors to recognize and avoid. Sometimes a researcher may select an assessment that is not sensitive to changes in the dependent variable. As an example, imagine that a researcher wants to examine the effectiveness of a new method of teaching mathematics. At some point, the researcher is going to have to measure the participants' mathematics ability. Using an assessment that is too easy for a large number of your participants creates a *ceiling effect* because everyone will obtain a high score, and the researcher will not be able to identify meaningful differences among the participants in terms of their assessment scores. By contrast, using an assessment that is too difficult can create a *floor effect* because everyone will do poorly.

Measurement errors may also influence internal validity of a study to the extent that the assessment has *low reliability*. As discussed in more detail in Chapter 3, reliability is often conceptualized as consistency in measurement. If an assessment produces different results across multiple iterations or test administrators, then the validity of inferences based on this assessment is in question.

**Instrumentation** becomes a source of measurement error if changes are made to the actual measurement instrument over the course of an experiment. Most often this threat to internal validity is associated with malfunctioning equipment. Although modern research equipment is highly reliable, errors can occur. The operator might use the wrong settings or the equipment might fail.

Another source of measurement error is the phenomenon of **regression to the mean**. In some circumstances, the change in the participant scores from before and after exposure to an independent variable represents a normal return to the mean level of the dependent variable under study. This effect is especially likely to occur when people initially receive exceptionally high or low scores on an assessment. When tested a second time, the scores for the same people will tend to be closer to the average. For example, some people may initially receive a poor score on an assessment because they do not feel well or for other reasons unrelated to their knowledge of the material. When we measure or observe them again a few weeks later, their scores will probably be closer to normal. Consequently, these types of changes in assessment scores may reflect regression to the mean and not true effects of the independent variable.

It is important to note that extremeness in scores is often based at least in part on measurement error and its random impacts on individual participants. This being the case, if we are able to use random assignment to treatment groups, issues of regression to mean can often be avoided. The other strategy for avoiding this threat to internal validity is to ensure all measures used have demonstrated reliabilities and roughly normal distributions of scores (i.e., not demonstrating ceiling or floor effects).

The final threat to internal validity stems from our challenges in determining unambiguous *cause-and-effect relationships*. According to British philosopher John Stuart Mill (1986), before we assume cause and effect we must address three issues: (1) that the cause occurs before the effect, (2) that there is evidence for a correlation between the cause and effect, and (3) that alternative explanations for changes in the dependent variable can be ruled out. There are many cases when the method for collecting the data by itself does not allow us to address one or more of these criteria. When designing a study that is testing a causal hypothesis, therefore, we must pay attention to issues of **temporal order problem** and the possible **third variable problem**. We will review these threats to internal validity later in this chapter. For now, Table 4.1 lists the general threats to internal validity, their characteristics, and an example of each threat.

### Statistical Conclusion Validity

*Statistical conclusion validity* is associated with the use of the proper statistical or analytical methods in a given study (Shadish, Cook, & Campbell, 2002). Proper in this case refers to the use of methods that best allow a researcher to (1) demonstrate that the independent and dependent

# Table 4.1   Threats to Internal Validity

| Threat and Its Description | Examples |
| --- | --- |
| ***Unintended sequence of events:*** Changes in the dependent variable that are the results of experiences with the testing procedure (carryover effect), changes in the participant (maturation), and intervening events that may occur between phases of the experiment. | • *Carry-over effects:* Taking the same or similar tests allows the participant to practice or become more skillful at taking the test.<br>• *Maturation:* The participant grows older or changes in some way unrelated to the independent variable.<br>• *Intervening events:* The participant learns something about the experiment from another participant. |
| ***Nonequivalent groups:*** The difference among the groups is due to one or more variables related to characteristics of the participants that are unrelated to the independent variable. | • *Subject variables:* The researcher assigns the participants to different groups based on a subject variable (e.g., sex) that also influences the dependent variable.<br>• *Participant mortality:* Participants in one group are more likely to withdraw from the study. |
| ***Measurement problems:*** The measurement used to assess the independent or dependent variables does not adequately measure the variable, or it introduces additional variance to the data, thus hiding the effect of the independent variable. | • *Ceiling/floor effects:* Test may not be sensitive to differences among participants.<br>• *Measurement error and reliability:* Test may create error because of low reliability or validity.<br>• *Instrumentation:* People responsible for collecting the data change the measurement criteria for different groups.<br>• *Regression to the mean:* Participants scoring very high or low may score closer to the mean if the test is administered more than once. |
| ***Ambiguity of cause and effect:*** Inability to determine that the IV preceded the DV, or an inability to rule out a third or alternate variable that could have caused the same changes in the DV. | • *Temporal order:* When IV and DV are measured at the same point in time, it is difficult to identify whether IV is truly causing changes in the DV. IV needs to precede DV in time.<br>• *Third variable:* A relationship between an IV and a DV does not necessarily mean that another variable is the real cause of changes in the DV (e.g., TV viewing may lead to aggression, but that aggression could be caused by something altogether different). |

variable(s) covary and (2) identify the strength of this covariation or relationship. All statistical analyses are based on specific assumptions. This means there is no one-size-fits-all analysis that can be used with every set of data that a researcher may collect. This being the case, to achieve acceptable statistical conclusion validity it is the researcher's responsibility to use the best possible statistical techniques for a given analysis. It is also important for the researcher to avoid some of the most common threats to this form of validity.

### Threats to Statistical Conclusion Validity

Multiple factors can prevent a researcher from making valid inferences about the relationship between the independent and dependent variable(s) in any given study. In many ways, these threats should look rather familiar to you, as they closely parallel the threats to internal validity presented earlier in this chapter. Much more detail on these and other threats can be found in Shadish et al. (2002), among other sources.

*Low statistical power* can prevent a researcher from detecting a relationship between an independent and dependent variable. This means that a researcher may miss a relationship that is really present. There are several strategies that can be taken to boost the statistical power in a study. One common technique is to ensure that the sample of participants is large enough based on rules of sample size estimation (see Cohen, 1992, for rough examples or see your statistics book for the full skinny on this). In general, these sample size estimates are based on the size of effect that a researcher expects to observe—large expected effects require smaller sample sizes than small expected effects (i.e., it is easier to find a pitchfork than a needle in a haystack). Another power-boosting strategy is to make the differences between levels of an independent variable as large as possible. This way, if there is an effect of that variable on the dependent variable, it should be more noticeable. A third general strategy is to improve the quality of measurement by reducing error and restriction of range. Successfully doing this will improve your chances of detecting an effect if it is really there.

*Violating assumptions of statistical tests* is another major threat to statistical conclusion validity. The fix for this threat is very simple—follow the rules for your statistical tests and use the ones that are most appropriate for your particular situation. The difficulty is that this also requires researchers to have a solid working understanding of the basic underlying assumptions for basic statistical analyses (e.g., ANOVA, correlation, regression). With more advanced designs and research questions it can also be valuable to seek the advice of an expert in statistics during the design and analysis phases of a project to ensure that the assumptions for the desired statistics are being met in the actual data.

*Unreliability in measurement and setting* are two additional threats to a researcher's ability to make valid inferences from statistical analyses. Recall that the validity of an assessment tool depends, in part, on its reliability. Therefore, researchers strive to use highly reliable assessment tools. Along similar lines, if the setting in which data are collected and the administration of the study are unreliable or inconsistent, this can increase the overall amount of error present in any eventual statistical analyses. This inflated error due to unreliability can cloud a researcher's ability to make clear and accurate (valid) inferences from the results. This is one major reason why careful and systematic design and administration are so critical. The direct impact of unreliability in measurement is on the error present in the resulting statistical analyses of data that you collect. An increase in error can make it more difficult for a researcher to detect an effect of the independent variable on the dependent variable (an issue of statistical power), which can then lead to an incorrect inference being made about the data (an issue of validity).

### External Validity

**External validity** refers to the type of generalizations we can draw from the data we collect. This is commonly framed in terms of the degree to which the results we obtain can be expected to generalize to another setting, sample, or even population. The more confident we are that our sample represents the population, the greater the external validity of our interpretation of the results.

There are two types of external validity: One pertains to the **generality of findings** and the other to the **generality of conclusions**. The generality of findings refers to the link between our sample and the target population. If we assume the sample adequately represents the population, then we can generalize conclusions from the sample data to the population. The generality of conclusions refers to our ability to generalize the findings from one population to other populations. In many cases, we conduct a study using a specific group of people, but we may want to extend the results to other groups. For example, a researcher may find that a specific type of motivational strategy works well for factory workers. He or she wishes to generalize the results to the staff in managerial positions. In such a situation, we need to question whether the results found for one population will generalize to a second population.

Figure 4.1 illustrates the difference between internal and external validity. Both forms of validity come between the data and the population, indicating that validity is a process that allows us to link the sample data to the population. As you can see, external validity consists of two parts, generality of findings and generality of conclusions.

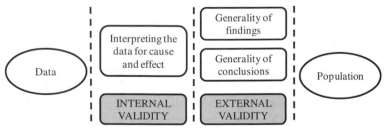

## Figure 4.1

**Difference between Internal and External Validity**

Internal validity refers to the interpretation of the data as they allow the researcher to draw a cause-and-effect relationship. External validity refers to generalizing the results to the target population.

## External Validity and the Real World

Some people complain that laboratory experiments have no bearing or relevance in "the real world." The general sentiment is that laboratory studies are contrived, unrealistic, and bogus. Furthermore, the participants in the experiments are often just college students. To make things worse, in the eyes of some, researchers conduct their experiments in clearly artificial situations, and the students participating in the experiment know that they are participating in an experiment! The primary sentiment expressed in these observations is that the results of research conducted in the laboratory have little or no relevance to the behavior of real people living in the real world. These sentiments are stereotypes that can be addressed by a sound research design. Much of what we know about behavior and social interactions comes from sound laboratory research. There is no doubt that properly designed laboratory research provides considerable external validity.

Consider the statement that the laboratory is artificial. This argument can be addressed in part by considering that reality does not stop at the door of the laboratory. The principles that govern participants' behavior do not cease to exist when an experiment begins. The laws of behavior continue to apply in the laboratory setting as much as they do on the street. Saying that behavioral social research conducted in the laboratory has little or no external validity is like saying that physics or chemistry experiments conducted in the laboratory are not valuable for explaining phenomena that occur in the broader universe. No single experiment is free from all error or bias, but there are aspects of behavior that can be observed only in the laboratory and not in the real world.

The value of the laboratory is that we can control the environment and examine how the independent and dependent variables relate to each other. To illustrate this, Anderson and Bushman (1997) offered a detailed review of how laboratory research has helped psychologists understand the nature of human aggression. They reviewed the many experiments examining aggression and showed how the results matched the results of research conducted in the real world. The point of their article was to demonstrate that many real-world studies of aggression have confirmed laboratory research.

There are many other examples where laboratory research has led researchers to discover important phenomena. A classic example comes from research conducted by Martin Seligman and his colleagues (Maier & Seligman, 1976; Overmier & Seligman, 1967; Seligman & Maier, 1967). Seligman had planned a set of experiments to examine an important theory related to classical and operant conditioning. The results of those experiments were startling. To make a long story short, what began as highly controlled laboratory research, using dogs, became the foundation for an extremely influential theory of human depression—learned helplessness theory.

The moral of this brief aside is that an experiment is not automatically trivial or invalid because the researchers conducted their work in a laboratory. Much of what we know about human behavior comes from laboratory research. Laboratory research and research conducted in natural settings are valuable and complementary tools for the researcher. As Anderson and Bushman (1997) concluded:

> The laboratory is still the best place to test causal hypotheses derived from theories. . . . . On the other hand, the real world is often the best place to observe and define new phenomena, and to create new theoretical propositions about human psychology. The real world is still the best place to devise, test, refine, and put into practice specific applications. (p. 37)

## Threats to External Validity

What are the factors that limit or reduce the external validity of a research project? Cook and Campbell (1979) identified three broad threats to external validity: (1) recruitment of participants, (2) effects of situation, and (3) effects of history.

*Recruitment of participants* is the first step researchers take when initiating a research project. In most cases, we gather these participants by simply asking people to volunteer. At many colleges, students in introductory courses receive extra credit for participating in one or more research projects. Accordingly, many researchers use college students for the sake of convenience. In some cases, this type of sampling method may limit the number and range of target populations to which we can generalize our eventual results. Consider a few examples. Imagine that a researcher wanted to study the effects of child care on a child's social and cognitive development. Because the researcher works at a large state university that has a child-care center, the researcher decides to track children from the center and a group of children from the community not in child care. The researcher works hard to ensure that both groups of children are similar in all respects except for the experience of day care. Can the researcher generalize the results of his or her study to all children at day-care centers?

We hope you see the potential threat to external validity here: How well does a college-operated day-care center represent the typical day-care facility? Do children who attend a college-operated day-care center represent the typical child who attends day care? These questions raise a potential threat to the external validity of the results. Day-care centers operated at colleges may represent the best of the best. The staff may be well educated and the facilities of good quality. Consequently, the sample from the college-operated day care may not well represent the population of typical day-care centers.

How do we overcome this threat to external validity? One way is to repeat the study in a different location or with a different sampling population. For example, many researchers have examined the effects of child care using an array of child-care settings. The child-care settings vary regarding their location, quality and training of staff, student-to-staff ratios, and other critical variables. As a whole, the research allows us to understand the effects of child care on developmental processes. Although we may question the external validity of a single study, observing similar results across an array of settings gives us greater confidence in the conclusions. Any one study may be flawed, but consistent results across a range of contexts and samples give us more confidence in our results and their external validity.

A second threat to external validity can be *effects of the research situation*. Will the results of an experiment conducted at your college generalize to a different college? What if we conducted an experiment on the motivation of employees working on an assembly line—will the results generalize to employees at the management level? Is it possible that a treatment will work in one setting because of unique circumstances that do not generalize to other situations?

Assume that you, the researcher, find that workers on an assembly line are less likely to call in sick if they received extra pay for using fewer-than-average sick days. Can we generalize these results to people who work in management—will extra money increase a manager's productivity? Notice that taking sick days and productivity are not the same. Consequently, it is possible that extra pay will impact some behaviors in some work settings but not necessarily generalize to others. However, if a similar result is found across studies that utilize participants for different situations, then researchers can more accurately conclude that results generalize across situations.

A third threat to external validity can come from the *effect of history*. Can the results of an experiment conducted 50 years ago generalize to current situations? What about an experiment conducted during a series of unique political and social conditions? Does the time during which we conduct a study affect the results and thereby compromise the external validity of the results? There are cases where the results of a study are relevant to a particular era and do not necessarily generalize to contemporary situations. In other cases, the results of older studies may still be valid today.

Consider the familiar achievement tests that most college-bound students take during their senior year of high school. Many years ago, there were large systematic differences between men and women. Women scored higher on the verbal components of the test, whereas men scored higher on the math section of the test. Some people thought that the differences represented a fundamental difference between men and women's cognitive abilities. Researchers now find that the difference between men's and women's scores on these achievement tests has declined (Hyde, 2005; Hyde & Lynn, 1988). Women now score higher than they did 50 years ago on the mathematics portions of the tests. What caused the changes in the test scores? Things have changed during the last 50 years. Women might now receive better math and science education than they would have 50 years ago because teachers are more likely to encourage women to study and excel in these subjects. Table 4.2 lists the general threats to external validity, their characteristics, and an example of each threat.

## Table 4.2  Threats to External Validity

| Threat and Its Description | Examples |
| --- | --- |
| *Recruitment of participants:* Participants in your sample do not represent the population. | • Generalizing results from one age group to another.<br>• People who volunteer in response to a newspaper recruitment ad may not represent the typical member of the population you wish to study. |
| *Effects of situation:* The environmental context for your research is unique and does not generalize or match well to other settings. | • Results of an experiment you conduct within a church setting may not generalize to a military or corporate organizational setting. |
| *Effects of history:* Unique events that only affected members of your sample limit the generalizability or applicability of your findings to other samples in other times and places. | • Results from a study you conducted ten years ago may not generalize to the present population due to changes in political, social, and economic conditions. |

## Survey of Empirical Methods

The following sections review different empirical research methods. In each section, we will give you a brief description of the method, its role in contemporary research, and its potential advantages and disadvantages. We will also add a few points about issues related to internal and external validity.

### True Experiments

We begin by reviewing the **true experiment** because it is the best technique we have as researchers to determine cause-and-effect relationships between two or more variables. The value of the true experiment is that it allows us to control for and remove potential threats to internal validity. Specifically, the true experiment allows us to ensure that the independent variable comes before the dependent variable, that the independent and dependent variables are related, and that we can account for alternative explanations. Three critical features set a true experiment apart from other research methods: (1) The independent variable is a manipulated variable under the researcher's control, (2) the researcher uses random assignment to place individuals into the different research conditions, and (3) the researcher can create one or more control conditions.

The hallmark of a true experiment is that the researcher directly controls or *manipulates the level of the independent variable.* In the other research designs, the researcher might use subject variables that he or she cannot control as the independent variable under study. By contrast, in the true experiment, the researcher can select a truly controllable or manipulable independent variable that can be applied over different experimental conditions to examine its effects on an outcome of interest.

A **qualitative independent variable** represents a variable that is measured with a nominal scale. For example, a psychologist may use different forms of psychotherapy (e.g., psychoanalytic, behavioral, family systems, and rational-emotive) to determine which is the most effective for the treatment of depression. In this example, psychotherapy is a qualitative independent variable in that the forms of treatment represent mutually exclusive types of therapy. A **quantitative independent variable** is a variable represented by an ordinal or more sophisticated type of measurement scale. For instance, the researcher may vary the time that students practice before a test. For such an experiment, time is the independent variable and measured using a ratio scale. Similarly, the researcher might vary the complexity of the task. In this situation, the researcher may have used an ordinal scale to rate the task as easy, moderately challenging, or difficult.

Whether the independent variable is qualitative or quantitative, the researcher has control over the **treatment condition** that participants experience. In the example of psychotherapies, each type of psychotherapy would represent a level of the independent variable. In an experiment that examines memory, the researcher may vary the time that people study a problem. For this experiment, time is the independent variable, and the treatment conditions might include 0 minutes, 1 minute, 5 minutes, and 10 minutes of study time. In other words, study time can itself represent a controllable independent variable (in this example, with four levels).

**Random assignment** is another necessary component of the true experiment. Random assignment occurs when each participant in an experiment has an equal chance of experiencing any one of $k$-number of possible research conditions. The value of random assignment is that it reduces alternative explanations of the results. Figure 4.2 illustrates the logic and steps of a true experiment.

In this example, the researcher begins by (we hope) randomly selecting 30 participants from the sampling population and then randomly assigning them to one of the three treatment conditions. At this point, the three groups should be similar to each other (*homogeneous*). Will they be perfectly identical? No; if we were to compare the three groups, we would find minor differences among them. If the researcher uses random assignment to form these groups, however, these differences will be trivial and should not influence the relationship between the independent and dependent variable. This is because any remaining source of difference between groups after random assignment is due to chance or random effects. Once the researcher forms the three groups, the participants in each group will experience a different level of the independent variable. The final step in the illustration is examining the differences among the groups. These differences will reflect the effects of the independent variable and random factors. In most cases, researchers use statistical techniques to determine the proportion of the difference due to the independent variable and the proportion of the difference due to random factors.

Using random assignment is an important technique to ensure the internal validity of the experiment. By randomly assigning participants to

# Figure 4.2

**A True Experiment**

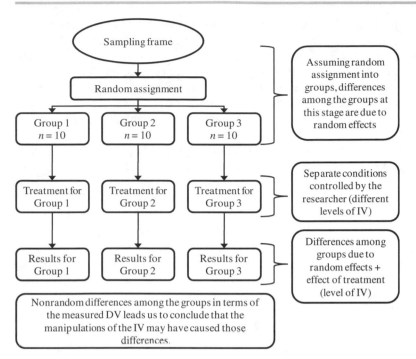

The researcher randomly assigns participants from the sampling frame to the various treatment conditions. The researcher then exposes the groups of participants to specific levels of a manipulated independent variable. In the last stage, the researcher examines the differences among the groups.

the treatment conditions, we prevent a *confound* from developing in the placement of participants to conditions. Random assignment helps us to ensure the pre-study comparability of the different treatment groups in terms of subject characteristics. Consider the following example. A researcher assigns all the women to one treatment condition and all the men to the other condition. If we find a difference between the two groups, what variable caused the difference—the sex of the participants or the level of the independent variable to which they were exposed? We cannot tell, because the sex of the people is confounded with the treatment they received. Specifically, the sex of the participants correlates with the treatment they received. Using random assignment, there should be equal proportions of men and women in both groups, causing the characteristics' treatment condition to be independent of the participant's characteristics. Therefore, we can conclude that the difference between the groups reflects the levels of the independent variable.

The final requirement of a true experiment is the *use of a control group*. **Control groups** are essential to the true experiment because they help us rule out a host of alternative explanations. In its basic form, a control group is the group of participants who experience the same treatment as the other participants except for exposure to the independent variable. Although this definition sounds simple enough, control groups can become quite sophisticated. First, there are many types of control groups. In addition, it is possible to use several control groups in a single experiment. Selecting the appropriate control condition or conditions allows the researcher to make a more convincing case that the independent variable, and not some other variable or variables, caused the differences among the groups.

The *placebo treatment* is likely to be one type of control condition you may have heard about somewhere in the past. Researchers frequently use placebos to determine the effectiveness of a drug. A placebo is a treatment condition, such as a sugar pill or a saline solution injection, which does not include the active ingredient or drug under study. In a drug study, the researcher will randomly assign some of the participants to the placebo treatment group. If the researcher finds a meaningful difference between the treatment and placebo groups, then he or she can make a convincing argument that the drug caused the difference. Placebos can also be used in non-drug-related studies, but those examples are a bit less simple to work with.

### Utility

The true experiment is one of the most important tools that researchers have to study behavior because it allows us to most clearly test cause-and-effect relationships. Although other research techniques may indicate the meaningful relation between the independent and dependent variables, only the true experiment offers an unambiguous opportunity to determine cause and effect. True experiments provide researchers with this utility because of the high level of control researchers have in the design and execution of experiments versus other widely used research methods.

### Potential Limitations

The true experiment is without equal for determining cause and effect. The true experiment does, however, have limitations. First, researchers cannot manipulate some potentially important independent variables because of ethical or practical concerns. Imagine a developmental psychologist who wants to study the effects of physical abuse on children. No one in their right mind would conduct an experiment that randomly assigns parents to a treatment condition requiring them to beat their children.

Second, it is impossible to manipulate many subject variables. For example, personality, intelligence, and sex are unique characteristics of participants that may help us understand why they do the things that they do. These characteristics are variables that researchers cannot control. Therefore, we must use other research techniques to collect and examine the data.

## Intact Groups Designs and Quasi-Experimental Studies

There are many times when it is impossible, impractical, or unethical for a researcher to manipulate the independent variable in a research study. In these cases, although we may not be able to control the independent variable, we can still study its relationship with the dependent variable. Two commonly used research methods for this purpose are the *intact groups design* and the *quasi-experimental design*. For both designs, the researcher treats a subject variable or some other existing condition as the independent variable and then works from there.

Figure 4.3 presents an example of a simple **intact groups design**. There are some important differences between this design and the true experiment.

First, the researcher does not select participants from a single population. Instead, there are several populations each defined by a different set of subject variables. For example, a clinical psychologist may want to compare scores on a new measure of depression across clients who struggle with one of several mental disorders. Perhaps one group represents people diagnosed with schizophrenia, another group represents people diagnosed with depression, and the third group represents people diagnosed with obsessive-compulsive disorder.

We cannot use random assignment to create these groups because these diagnoses already exist and cannot be manipulated by the researcher. For this reason, random assignment of people to these categories is impossible. All we can do is assume that each sample of already-diagnosed individuals adequately represents its broader sampling population. From here we can proceed as normal, collecting data and comparing scores across the different groups. As with the true experiment, we assume that differences among the groups represent random variation as well as factors associated with the subject or grouping variable. Unlike the true experiment, we cannot use these data to assume that the subject variable caused

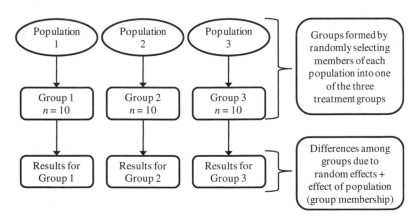

## Figure 4.3

**Intact Groups Design. In This Design, the Researcher Randomly Selects Participants from Different Sampling Populations**

The researcher then compares the differences among the groups.

## Figure 4.4

**Quasi-Experiment**

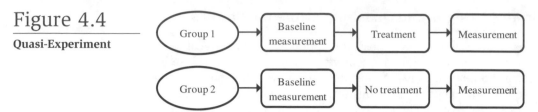

The researcher uses two preexisting groups of participants and measures each for one or more relevant dependent variables. The researcher then exposes one group to a treatment using the other group as a control condition, and then reevaluates both groups.

the differences. We can compare, however, the group averages, testing the hypothesis that the means of the three groups are not equivalent (i.e., all $\mu s$ will not be equal).

**Quasi-experimental designs** offer another alternative to a true experiment. A *quasi-experiment* is similar to a true experiment except that we cannot randomly assign participants to the treatment and control conditions. Figure 4.4 presents an example of a hypothetical quasi-experiment.

Because this is a quasi-experiment, we have not randomly assigned participants to the groups; the grouping existed before the research began. We measure both groups for the dependent variable and then expose one group to a treatment condition. After the treatment, we measure both groups again. Therefore, this study consists of a grouping variable as well as a manipulated variable. In this type of study, we call the independent variable a **quasi-independent variable** to indicate that the researcher can manipulate the variable but cannot randomly assign participants to the treatment conditions.

Consider the following example of a quasi-experiment in which a researcher wants to study the effect of a college's alcohol policy on student drinking. The researcher finds two equivalent colleges. After assessing the amount of drinking on both campuses, one college establishes a "dry-campus" policy. The introduction of the policy represents the treatment. The researcher can then return to both campuses and measure students' alcohol consumption. For this example, the researcher wants to test the hypothesis that the level of drinking at one campus will be less than the other campus, or $\mu_1 < \mu_2$.

What conclusions could the researcher reach if she found that after adoption of a "dry-campus" policy there was a radical reduction in drinking among the students? Can the researcher conclude that the introduction of the treatment caused the change? The answer to this question leads us to examining the utility and limitations of the intact groups design and quasi-experiments.

### Utility

There is no doubt that the intact groups design and the quasi-experiments are useful to researchers. Many of the variables that affect behavior are subject variables. For instance, it is common for psychologists to examine the ways men are different from women. Similarly, we can ask whether children raised by a single parent have different emotional attachments than children raised in two-parent homes. We can address these interesting topics with an intact groups design. Similarly, the quasi-experiment allows us to conduct research when random assignment of participants to treatment conditions is impossible, impractical, or unethical.

## Potential Limitations

The most important limitation of the intact groups design and the quasi-experiment is the inability to form definitive conclusions regarding cause and effect. We cannot assume cause and effect because we do not have direct control over the independent variable. In other words, these designs cannot ensure the internal validity of the link between the independent and dependent variables. There are two major threats to internal validity to review: (1) the third variable problem and (2) the temporal order problem.

The third variable problem is that some factor or condition, other than the independent variable, may affect the dependent variable. Figure 4.5 illustrates this problem.

As you can see in Figure 4.5, the third variable links to both the independent and the dependent variable. Because of this relation, we cannot be sure whether the independent variable or the third variable causes changes in the dependent variable. Assume that a researcher took a random sample of men and women and compared their verbal and writing skills. If the researcher finds that women are better writers and have better verbal skills, can he or she assume that sex causes the difference? No; other variables may account for the difference. For example, the women in this study could have taken more courses that enhance writing and verbal skills. Therefore, the number of English and other courses that require reading and writing produces the difference, not the sex of the people.

The temporal order problem is a fancy description of the classic question, Which came first, the chicken or the egg? Figure 4.6 illustrates this problem. Because we do not control the independent variable, we

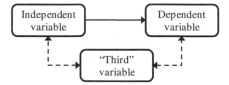

## Figure 4.5

**Third Variable Problem**

In this example, we assume that there is a direct link between the independent and dependent variables. But there may be a third variable correlated with both. The third variable is a confounding condition because it correlates with both the independent and dependent variables. The third variable prohibits us from assuming a cause-and-effect relation between the independent and dependent variables.

## Figure 4.6

**Temporal Order Problem**

This problem occurs when one uses a subject variable or measures both variables at the same time. We cannot be sure which variable produces or causes the other variable.

cannot be sure whether the independent variable caused the dependent variable or whether the opposite is true.

Imagine that you compared the self-esteem of depressed and nondepressed people, finding that people with low self-esteem are also depressed. Can you use these data to assume that low self-esteem causes depression? The problem is that in this type of research, the researcher will measure the constructs, self-esteem and depression, at the same time. Therefore, we do not know which came first, the low self-esteem or the depression.

## Surveys

Researchers use **surveys** to estimate population parameters. As you may recall from Chapter 2, we often denote this type of hypothesis as $M \approx \mu$. As an example of contemporary survey research, consider the serious problem of teen pregnancy. In the United States alone, thousands of young unmarried women become pregnant each year. The consequences of these pregnancies are staggering. According to a report by the Anne E. Casey Foundation (1999), "The combination of lost tax revenues and increased spending on public assistance, child health care, foster care, and the criminal justice system totals about $7 billion annually for births to teens" (p. 8). To understand the prevalence of teen pregnancy, we need to collect data. The Anne E. Casey Foundation's (1999) report documents the prevalence of pregnancy within each state. This report pulled together the results of health data collected by different surveys conducted by different research teams. These data are of considerable value to researchers and policymakers.

Researchers can use this type of survey data to determine future research objectives. In the present example the survey data revealed that some states have exceptionally high rates of teen pregnancy whereas others have much lower rates. What causes this difference? Additional survey research may yield an answer. A researcher may develop a questionnaire that asks teenagers about their attitudes toward premarital sex, the use of birth control, and other factors. The results of the survey may help explain why one group of young women is more likely to become pregnant than another group. In addition, policymakers may use these types of data to change a state's policies or funding for various health programs. Finding exceptionally high pregnancy rates in a state may prompt lawmakers into action to find a legislative solution.

## Utility

Surveys are extremely useful ways of obtaining information, and they give us accurate estimates of important population parameters. Surveys also allow us to collect information quickly and with minimal expense.

## Potential Limitations

Surveys suffer from several potential limitations. First, people do not always tell the truth. How would you respond if you received a questionnaire in the campus mail asking you to describe your sexual behavior or about cheating on exams? Would you be honest? Researchers who conduct surveys are aware of this problem and attempt to use techniques that produce honest results. These techniques are not always effective, however. A second problem is that what we say and what we do are often two different things. A participant's response to a survey question may not reflect the truth, but rather reflect his or her ideal view of themselves or what would be socially acceptable to say. For example, some peoples' responses to a survey might indicate that they have no sexist attitudes and that they believe that men and women should receive equal treatment. If these same individuals were observed in their day-to-day lives, we might observe very different behaviors.

# Correlational Studies

**Correlational studies** often evolve from surveys and allow researchers to test the hypothesis that two or more variables are related to one another. For a survey project, we want to estimate a population parameter. In other words, we want to know how much, how often, or how many of something exists. For a correlational study, we want to know the strength and direction of the relationship between two or more variables. Figure 4.7 presents the steps of a correlational study.

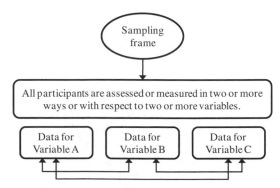

# Figure 4.7

**Correlational Design**

The researcher selects participants from the sampling population and measures two or more variables. The researcher then examines the correlation among the different variables.

In the first step, we identify a sample from our target population and then collect data on two or more variables from our participants. Typically these data are collected with assessments, often of personality and attitudes. The essential characteristic of a correlational study is that we collect two or more bits of information from each participant. In Figure 4.7 we used lines with arrows on both ends to connect the variables. This reflects the fact that in a correlational study we cannot solidly test for a cause-and-effect relationship. For example, can you assume that hours spent studying causes higher grades if you found that there is a correlation between hours spent studying and grades? No; GPA and hours studying are subject variables that the researcher does not directly control. Therefore, we cannot easily resolve the third variable or the temporal order problems.

### Utility

The correlational design is popular in behavioral and social research, especially in the study of social psychology, personality assessment, and industrial-organizational psychology. By examining the correlation among variables we may be better able to understand complex behaviors. For example, industrial/organizational psychologists examine the relation between personality and work behavior. Knowing the relation between these variables allows psychologists to predict how people will perform on the job.

### Potential Limitations

As with the intact groups design and the quasi-experimental design, the correlational design cannot support conclusions of cause and effect. Specifically, the correlational design cannot resolve the third variable problem or the sequence-of-events problem.

## Single-Participant Research Methods

When most people think about research, they have a vision of vast groups of people assigned to different treatment conditions. The researcher then combines and examines the data as a group. Although this is a popular image of psychological research, it is not completely correct. There are many cases in which a researcher will use only one or two participants as the focus of the research. Instead of examining the behavior of many people, the psychologist will examine, in detail, the behavior of one person. Single-participant research methods have a long history in the social sciences. Fechner and Ebbinghaus, two important figures in the history of psychology, conducted much groundbreaking research using single-participant designs, and their work and methods are still relevant.

Simply put, a **single-participant experiment** is conducted using isolated participants. Just as in the other types of experiments we have discussed, we measure an independent and a dependent variable with this very small "sample" (i.e., our single participant). We then try to determine whether the independent variable causes the dependent variable to change. Another feature of an experiment is that we measure the dependent variable in the presence of the independent variable as well as in its absence. We can meet these requirements using a single-participant experiment, but there are particular issues that must be considered. We consider these more fully in Chapter 14.

The **case study** may be one of the more familiar forms of single-participant methods. The essential feature of a case study is the intense review of the behavior of one person. For the most part, case studies have limited value in contemporary behavioral research and must be used with care. You probably know Sigmund Freud made extensive use of case studies to develop his theory of personality and abnormal behavior. For example, he used his famous case of Anna O. to develop his theories of hysterical disorder. Freud also used the case study methodology to show the effectiveness of psychoanalysis as a diagnostic tool and treatment technique (Freud & Breuer, 1976). Subsequent research with larger samples of participants has not supported much of Freud's theories.

There are, however, situations where a case study can help shed useful insight onto a complex problem. For example, a person known by the initials HM underwent brain surgery in the 1950s as a cure for epilepsy. Although the surgery cured HM's epilepsy, it destroyed HM's ability to create long-term memories. Many psychologists have studied HM's inability to form long-term memories and have made important discoveries about the relation between different parts of the brain and their role in memory formation (Milner, 1966; Milner, Corkin, & Teuber, 1968). The difference between Freud's and Milner's use of the case study rests in their attempts to use objective and publically verifiable empirical techniques. We will review case studies in more detail in Chapter 16.

## Utility

Single-participant experiments serve an important role in research. The real advantage of this method is that we can use sound experimental techniques to determine how to influence a person's behavior. For example, behavior modification techniques, derived from laboratory research, help children and adults with behavioral and emotional problems. Using a single-participant research design, the clinical psychologist can tailor the therapy for the particular needs of the client and then collect objective data to determine whether the treatment works. The internal validity of single-participant experiments can be quite good, depending on how well the researcher controls the independent variable and other situational variables.

Case studies also serve as important teaching tools and exemplars of basic principles. There are many times when psychologists will use a case study as a part of their work. For example, a researcher may use a case study to demonstrate the utility of a specific principle. David Premack (1959,

1965) used the behavior of several students to demonstrate the value of his theory of positive reinforcement. The single-participant experiments allowed Premack to demonstrate that his theory had practical applications as well as important theoretical applications. Within business situations, studies of single organizations have shed a great deal of light on what are considered best practices for certain challenges that other, similar organizations also might be facing.

### Potential Limitations

The problem with this research method is that we are looking at the behavior of a single person or a small group of people. The case study, for example, does not allow us to make sweeping generalizations about the population. Although we may learn much about the motivations and history of a single person, we cannot conclude that what was true for the person in the case study is true of all people.

Thus, although case studies offer interesting information, we must interpret the information with some care. What are some of the potential limitations of case studies? The following are two of the more severe problems:

1. *Verification of facts*. Many times, the person collecting the information for the case study has no way of confirming the facts that are a part of a person's history. Elizabeth Loftus (Loftus & Ketcham, 1994) provided compelling evidence that the questions people ask us can distort our memories. Therefore, a major weakness of any case study occurs when we must rely exclusively on the individual's memory for critical facts.

2. *Potential for bias in examples*. In many cases, an author will present a case study because the case fits his or her theory. Howard Gardner's book, *Leading Minds* (1995), is an example. In the book, Gardner presented an interesting theory of leadership. He then presented case studies of 10 great leaders from history (e.g., Margaret Mead, George Marshall, and Eleanor Roosevelt). Although the theory and case studies are interesting, we must ask whether they are proof of the accuracy of the theory. One problem is that Gardner may have selected people who demonstrate his theory while ignoring great leaders who do not fit his theory of leadership. Similarly, because Gardner is recounting the history of another person, he may have selected only those episodes of the person's life that fit his theory.

## Meta-Analysis

Listening to news reports of research findings can sometimes be frustrating. You may hear that a group of researchers claims that they found the cure for a terrible disease. Later, another team of researchers reports that the treatment is not effective. These experiences cause many people to think that science must be only one step removed from witchcraft. The problem is not with the scientists, but with how we look at individual research reports in isolation from the broader literature base.

No single experiment can offer definitive proof or support for a hypothesis or theorized relationship by itself. Each experiment is subject to a host of random factors that affect the results. Specifically, an experiment is a sample, and only a sample, of what you can expect in a population. Hence, there is always a chance that a single experiment or research study, no matter how well conducted, may produce misleading results. This is the reason replication and extension is such an important part of good scientific research. If a researcher reports an interesting finding, the chances are that he or she will conduct more studies to examine the effect in detail. Other researchers will join in and publish their results. How will we evaluate the accumulated collection of research findings?

Many researchers write *literature reviews* that summarize the findings of many research projects. The author reads all the relevant research and then describes what he or she believes to be the general findings. Literature reviews are important because they allow us to take a step back from the individual studies and look for the broader significance of the research. There are some problems with these types of reviews, however. Literature reviews tend to be subjective, and they are not quantitative. When the author reads the results of a study, he or she has to judge whether the results are meaningful. There are better ways to examine the outcomes of empirical research.

In 1978, Glass developed a method to more objectively analyze the outcomes of many studies. This technique, called **meta-analysis**, allows the reviewer to quantify the results of the individual studies. In other words, meta-analysis allows us to statistically analyze multiple results from multiple different studies. This type of analysis results in an overarching summary statistic that is more reliable and capable of leading to potentially more valid inferences than what you would have found in any one of the studies that were included in the meta-analytic sample. The logic of meta-analysis is rather straightforward. The more often one samples from a population of participants, settings, and measures of constructs, the greater the accuracy of the overall estimate of the observed effect or relationship. The goal of meta-analysis is, therefore, to offer a quantitatively based and objective review of the research literature.

## Utility

Since its introduction, meta-analysis has become a popular review method across many research disciplines. You will find that researchers in psychology, medicine, political science, sociology, education, and other empirical sciences use meta-analysis extensively. It is now an almost essential component of any literature review when the topics of interest have received significant attention by other researchers.

### Potential Limitations

Although meta-analysis uses objective mathematical techniques to examine the data, there remains a subjective component—selection of which studies will be included in the sample of studies used for the analysis itself. To conduct a meta-analysis, one must first determine whether the researcher used proper research methods to collect the data. The reviewer will examine the method and determine whether the data afford valid interpretations. If the reviewer finds an error in the study, he or she will exclude the results from the meta-analysis. Many people complain that this step biases the results of the meta-analysis. This is one reason for the now widely used axiom that with meta-analysis, garbage in = garbage out. Thus, meta-analyzing a bunch of questionable studies will not result in some sort of magical truth—indeed, meta-analyses depend on multiple, high-quality initial studies if they are to be of any use at all. How would you go about identifying good studies to include in a meta-analysis on a topic of your choosing?

## Computers and Statistics

Charles Babbage (1792–1871), a British mathematician who attempted to invent the first mechanical calculator, once exclaimed, "I wish to God these calculations had been [conducted] by steam." Many researchers and students who have calculated statistical tests by hand have often expressed the same sentiment.

Computers have had a profound effect on statistics and research methods by making it easier for researchers to use sophisticated statistical procedures to analyze their data. Before the advent of the computer, most researchers did not use many of the statistical procedures developed by statisticians because these tests required an overwhelming amount of calculation (Pedhazur, 1997). Although most statistical tests require simple arithmetic, the manual calculation of some statistics is impractical because of the computational burden required to complete the work. Even simple descriptive statistics, such as the standard deviation or correlation coefficient, are labor intensive because of the many repetitive calculations required to complete the work. As a generality, the greater the complexity of the statistical procedure, the greater the number of individual operations one must complete. The sample size magnifies the computational burden—the more observations you have, the more individual calculations you must perform.

The first practical computers became available in the late 1950s and early 1960s. Although these machines were huge and expensive, they gave researchers the opportunity to conduct sophisticated statistical tests. Scientists quickly embraced the computer as an essential research tool. Since the 1950s, computers have grown progressively smaller and become more sophisticated and much less expensive. The current generation of personal computers is far more sophisticated than many of the multimillion-dollar mainframe computers built in the 1970s. At the same time, statistics software has also evolved. Like the computer, these programs have become easier to use and less expensive, and provide access to many sophisticated statistical tests. The consequence of the computer revolution is that statistical techniques once considered impractical can now be calculated at the click of a mouse button. As useful as computers and computational software are, however, there are several potential problems that you must consider when using them.

## Garbage In–Garbage Out

No computer program or statistical procedure can spin gold from straw; the quality of any statistical analysis depends solely on the quality of the original data. Unfortunately, many people treat the computer and statistics as magical machines that somehow tell the truth. Computers do exactly what you tell them to do, even if it is the wrong thing. The phrase "garbage in–garbage out" means that the output of any computer program is no better than the data you ask it to analyze. Statistics packages cannot recognize when you have entered the wrong numbers or request a statistical test that does not address the hypothesis you want to test. These observations mean that we need to proceed with caution when using software packages.

## Faulty Data

The first problem to address is the accuracy of the data to analyze. Software packages treat the numbers .987 and 987 as legitimate values. That there are several orders of magnitude difference between the two numbers is of no concern for the computer. Therefore, you will need to spend a little extra time proofreading the data you have entered in the data file. Such proofreading involves more than simply looking for blank spaces in your data spreadsheet. At the very least, you should run a frequency analysis of all variables to ensure that all values you have entered conform to the expected minimum and maximum values allowable for each item and each scale. In addition, it is a good idea to check the distribution of scale scores to ensure you do not have a ceiling or floor effect present on any of your research variables.

## Selecting the Right Statistical Test

The second and far more important problem that we need to address is your knowledge of the statistical tests that the software package allows you to conduct. Most statistical software programs allow you to calculate statistics as simple as the arithmetic mean and as complicated as a multivariate analysis of covariance. Just because the computer will let you use a statistical procedure to analyze the data does not mean that it is the right statistical test to use. Consequently, we cannot emphasize strongly enough the importance that you understand the conceptual foundation of any statistical test that you calculate. Whenever you use a statistic, you should be able to justify why you selected it, show how it will help you interpret the data, and know what conclusions you can and cannot draw from its results.

Although many software packages will allow you to conduct similar statistical tests, they may have different ways of printing the final report. Two software packages may produce different reports for the analysis of the same data set and the same statistical analysis. You must practice with the computer program before you use it to analyze the data for your research. Most statistics textbooks give examples of how to calculate various statistical tests. Enter the example data into the computer program and then let the computer program analyze the data. You can then compare the program's output to the textbook example. This exercise should help you understand how the program generates the final report.

### Statistical Fishing Expeditions

Because computer software makes complex statistical tests easy to conduct, many researchers are willing to go on a "fishing expedition" with their data. These researchers conduct statistical test after statistical test in the hope of finding one that will indicate a statistically significant effect. You should select your statistical procedures as a part of your research design, and stick to that plan while analyzing the data. Exploratory analysis, also called *data mining*, of the data is acceptable only as long as it is within the framework of the original research design or if it helps generate new hypotheses for new research projects.

## Research in Action: Effectiveness of Psychotherapy

As you learned in this chapter, internal and external validity are central concepts in all research. In this section, we will review a research project that examined the effectiveness of psychotherapy.

Washing machines, tires, compact cars, and psychotherapy: Do they work—are they worth the money? *Consumer Reports* is a magazine devoted to rating the quality, safety, and economic value of different products that consumers buy. The editors take great pride in their well-deserved reputation for scrutiny, objectivity, and fairness. In 1995, the magazine published an article that examined the effectiveness of mental health treatment. We can use this research to further examine internal and external validity. To do so, we must first examine the methods the researchers used. We can begin our analysis of the study by exploring how the authors collected the data.

Each year, *Consumer Reports* sends questionnaires to its over 4 million subscribers (Kotkin, Daviet, & Gurin, 1996). In 1994, *Consumer Reports* sent

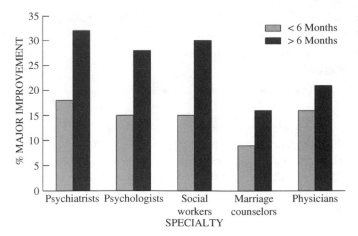

## Figure 4.8

**Percentage of Individuals Reporting a Major Improvement in Their Mental Health, Depending on the Type of Psychotherapist They Saw and the Length of Treatment**

The data are based on a figure presented by Seligman (1995).

184,000 subscribers a comprehensive survey that examined their experience with different forms of psychotherapy. Of the 184,000 subscribers contacted, 22,000 people completed the questionnaire. Of the returned questionnaires, 6,900 people indicated that they had sought professional help for emotional problems within the past three years.

Figure 4.8 presents a summary of the data. The graph presents several pieces of important information. First, the figure displays the data by the type of professional: psychiatrists, psychologists, social workers, marriage counselors, or physicians. The figure also distinguishes between people who saw the professional for less than 6 months and those who saw the professional for more than 6 months. We can treat these variables (type of provider and time in therapy) as independent variables. The dependent variable was the percentage of people who reported a "major improvement" in their condition.

The results of the survey, based on this sample, led some people to make several conclusions:

1. People benefited from psychotherapy.
2. Long-term treatment was more effective than short-term treatment.
3. Psychotherapy alone was as effective as medication and psychotherapy combined. This conclusion presumes that psychiatrists prescribed medication as a part of their treatment.
4. Mental health professionals were more effective than marriage counselors and physicians (Seligman, 1995).

Now comes the tricky part. What confidence can we have in conclusions drawn from these data? For the sake of argument, we can focus our attention on the first conclusion: *People benefited from psychotherapy.* We can rewrite the statement in several different ways:

a. People responding to the questionnaire reported being satisfied with the psychotherapy they received.

b. People receiving psychotherapy are generally satisfied with the treatment they received.

c. Psychotherapy caused people's mental health to improve.

Can you see the differences among the statements? What are the implications for these differences? Statement (a) is a report of fact. The focus of the statement is the sample of respondents. In addition, there is no particular conclusion other than a summary of the results. Now compare Statement (a) with Statement (b). Statement (b) takes a step away from the sample and makes an inference about the population. The focus of the generalization is descriptive in that it implies that because the sample of respondents expressed satisfaction we can assume that the population will express the same level of satisfaction. By contrast, Statement (c) is a dramatic shift from the first two statements. Not only does the conclusion generalize from the sample to the population, it also assumes that there is a cause-and-effect relation between psychotherapy and improved mental health.

Earlier in this chapter, we said that the data are not valid or invalid—only the researcher's interpretations. Can you use what you have learned so far to determine the types of inferences we can make from these data? Specifically, evaluate the internal and external validity of the conclusions. What type of research design does this research represent? At one level, the research is a survey. The staff of *Consumer Reports* mailed a detailed questionnaire to some of its subscribers and then reported the results of the survey. From a different perspective, you can see that we have an intact groups design because we have different groups of people receiving treatment from different providers. Can we use these data to assume a cause-and-effect relation as implied in Statement (c)?

What are the conditions necessary to assume cause and effect? Are these conditions present in the *Consumer Reports* study? The three characteristics of a true experiment are: (1) manipulated independent variable, (2) random assignment of participants to treatment conditions, and (3) control conditions.  Are these conditions present in the study? First, the researchers could not manipulate the independent variables. The people responding to the survey selected the type of therapist they saw. In addition, the researchers could not control how long the people spent in therapy. Therefore, the type of psychotherapist and the time in therapy are subject variables. In addition, the researchers could not randomly assign the people to the different categories of treatment provider or length of treatment.

Second, are there control conditions? In a true experiment, the most extreme control condition would be a group of people who receive no psychotherapy during the course of the study. We need control groups because some mental health problems improve spontaneously. Like the old saying, *Time heals all wounds*, some people may feel better as they put some distance between themselves and the situation that caused their distress. They may also find ways of coping with the problem. Thus, the purpose of a control group is to determine whether psychotherapy has a greater effect than the passage of time. Clearly, there is no control group in this study.

Because the design of the study does not meet the criteria of a true experiment, we cannot conclude with any degree of certainty that psychotherapy caused people's mental health to improve. In making this observation, we have criticized the conclusion, not the data. The specific objections we raised concern the internal validity of the interpretation. We determined that we cannot assume that the independent variable (psychotherapy) caused the dependent variable (improvement in mental health).

What about the external validity of conclusions drawn from this study? Statement (b) implies that the data are representative of the population of people who seek psychotherapy. The statement also implies that clients are generally satisfied with the treatment they receive. Strupp (1996) argued that evaluating a patient's sense of well-being is an important part of any research on the effectiveness of psychotherapy. He, like many psychotherapists, believes that research of this type should examine the client's adaptive behavior, personality structure, and sense of well-being. Therefore, the information concerning the client's evaluation of the treatment they received is an important part of the research examining psychotherapy. Consequently, the *Consumer Reports* study has the potential of telling us how people reacted to the treatment they received.

Do the data allow us to generalize from the sample to the population? Several researchers criticized the external validity of this conclusion (Brock, Green, & Reich, 1998; Brock, Green, Reich, & Evans, 1996; Jacobson & Christensen, 1996). These researchers raised several questions about who responded to the questionnaire. In an ideal world, we would prefer a random sample of all people who received psychotherapy. The current data reflect only people who received psychotherapy *and* who subscribe to *Consumer Reports*. Although we may agree that *Consumer Reports* is a good magazine, we must ask whether people who subscribe to the magazine represent the typical person seeking psychotherapy or the typical person who may require psychotherapy.

Another issue to examine is the return rate of the questionnaires. As Brock et al. (1998) noted, only a small proportion of the original sample indicated seeking help from a therapist. There may be some self-selection bias in who returned the surveys. We cannot be sure whether the data represent the population or only those satisfied with their experiences. Brock et al. argued that the sample did not represent the population and therefore does not support inferences about the population of people seeking psychotherapy.

Where does all this criticism lead us? Can we conclude that psychotherapy does not work? No; there is no information that would warrant such a reckless conclusion. Many research reports confirm the effectiveness of psychotherapy. Jacobson and Christensen (1996), for example, offered a readable account of this research. Our review of this case merely illustrates that you must interpret the *Consumer Reports* data with caution.

## Knowledge Check

1. Explain why internal and external validity refer to a researcher's interpretation of the data and not the data.

2. A researcher claims that there is a cause-and-effect relation between two variables. You believe that there is a significant threat to the internal validity. Can the researcher continue to claim that the interpretation has external validity?

3. A college instructor wants to examine the effectiveness of a new teaching method. On the first day of classes, she administers to all the students a 100-item multiple-choice test that reviews the major content areas of the course. She uses a similar test as the final exam. List the potential threats to internal validity that you believe could apply to this study.

4. A researcher believes that changes in physiological reaction (e.g., heart rate and amount of sweat on the hands) indicate when someone is lying. To test this hypothesis, he conducts a study using college students. He gives students an envelope that contains either a blank piece of paper or a $100 bill. He then tells all the students to say that they found a blank piece of paper in the envelope during a lie-detection test. Assume that the researcher finds evidence supporting the claim that one can detect a lie based on physiological reactions and that the police can use lie-detector tests in criminal investigations. What issues related to external validity does the researcher need to consider when interpreting the data?

5. Miranda found an article published in the early 1960s that examined short-term memory, but decided not to read it because it is over 40 years old. She told her friend, "Why read the paper? The results are no longer relevant today." Comment on her conclusion.

6. Describe how one's hypothesis will determine the research design that one will use.

7. How does the inclusion of one or more control groups help us determine cause and effect in a true experiment?

8. How does random assignment help ensure the internal validity of our interpretation of the data?

9. There is a strong correlation between whether a mother smokes and the health of her children. The children of mothers who smoke have more health problems than the children of mothers who do not smoke. Do these data allow us to conclude that smoking causes poor health in children?

10. The following are short descriptions of research projects. For each scenario, identify the:

(i) Independent variable(s) and the dependent variable.

(ii) Hypothesis that the researcher appears to be testing (you will have to infer this from your reading of the scenario).

(iii) Empirical method that the researcher used.

(iv) Aspects of the research design influencing our evaluation of internal validity.

(v) Aspects of the research design influencing our evaluation of external validity.

(vi) Changes you would make to the study to improve the internal and external validity.

(1) A researcher wants to determine whether there is a sex difference in altruism. To study this difference, the researcher has a male friend pose as a motorist who needs help changing a tire. The researcher counts the number of men and women who offer to help. The data suggest that men are 50 times more likely to offer help to the motorist. The researcher concludes that men are more altruistic than women.

(2) A psychologist was interested in examining the effects of a freshman seminar course. The researcher assumed that students' appreciation for the course would increase as they progressed through school. The psychologist distributed a survey to the seniors and found that the majority of the students endorsed the statement, "I enjoyed my freshman seminar." The psychologist reported to the dean that the course had succeeded at preparing students for college.

(3) A psychologist convinced a large corporation that she had a yearlong training program that increases the effectiveness of a salesperson. Impressed by the claim, the personnel director required 15 newly hired salespeople to participate in the training program. All 15 had worked for approximately 18 months as salespeople. During the year, the salespeople continued their sales work as well as spending three hours a week in the sales seminar. At the end of the year, sales for all 15 salespeople had increased a significant amount. The personnel director decided that all new salespersons would take the seminar as a part of their training.

## Chapter Summary

This chapter provided a broad overview of the research methods that behavioral researchers use to conduct their research. A research design is a plan to collect data. More specifically, the purpose of a research design is to allow the researcher to collect data that answer a research hypothesis.

Whenever we prepare to design a study, we need to consider two important forms of validity: internal validity and external validity. As you learned, internal and external validity refer to the interpretations one can make from the results of the study.

Internal validity refers to the researcher's ability to show a cause-and-effect relation between two variables, the independent and dependent variables. Cause-and-effect relations are difficult to demonstrate because of the number of threats to internal validity. Careful attention to research design can help the researcher avoid the threats to internal validity, including (1) unintentional sequence of events, (2) nonequivalent groups, (3) problems with measurement, and (4) ambiguity of cause and effect.

External validity refers to our ability to use the results to make inferences beyond the study. Specifically, we can ask how the findings generalize to the target population. We can also ask whether the results reached with one study will generalize to different populations and different applications of the variables.

There are many threats to external validity, including (1) bias in the methods used to recruit the participants for the study, (2) situational factors unique to the study, and (3) historical events that may be unique to a group of participants.

The remainder of the chapter reviewed the major research designs, including the true experiment, intact groups design and quasi-experiments, surveys and questionnaires, correlational studies, single-subject methods, and meta-analysis. The defining characteristic of a true experiment is the ability to manipulate systematically the independent variable and to randomly assign participants to the levels of the independent variable. In addition, true experiments include a control group. Participants in the control group experience the same things as the other subjects except for exposure to the independent variable.

Although true experiments are useful for inferring causality, they are sometimes impractical or impossible to perform. The intact group design and the quasi-experiment are alternatives to the true experiment. The distinguishing feature of these designs is that the researcher cannot randomly assign the participants to the different levels of the independent variable.

In our review of the quasi-experiments and intact groups design, we examined two important threats to internal validity, the third variable problem and the temporal order problem. The third variable problem is that some condition, other than the independent variable, affects both the independent and dependent variable. The temporal order problem is that the research design does not allow us to determine whether the independent variable preceded the dependent variable.

Surveys and questionnaires are useful because we can measure an interesting construct by asking participants objective questions. Correlational studies allow us to examine the relation among two or more variables. These research designs are useful for studies of personality or business administration, where we are interested in the relation between one set of behaviors and other behaviors.

As the name implies, single-subject designs allow us to study one or two people. In some single-subject designs, we can use experimental techniques to study the behavior of one person. For other situations, we examine the individual's history to create a case study.

Meta-analysis is the study of research studies. Researchers who use meta-analysis use statistical techniques to combine the results of many studies. The goal of meta-analysis is to come to some uniform conclusion about a phenomenon.

We concluded by examining the role of computers in statistical analysis. Computers are essential when conducting even moderately complex statistical tests. However, computers and statistical software are not foolproof. Misuse of the software, failure to understand the statistical tests being run, and data entry errors can lead to meaningless or even misleading results.

The "Research in Action" section used a report on the effectiveness of psychotherapy to examine how researchers can apply different research techniques to address specific empirical questions. The review of the research illustrated that the research design affects the internal and external validity of the data.

## Chapter Glossary for Review

**Alternative explanation**—Another method of explaining the results that does not depend on the independent variable.

**Carryover effects**—A form of unintentional-sequence-of-events threat to internal validity wherein the participants' experiences during one part of the research affect their performance in subsequent parts of the research.

**Case study**—An empirical research method for which the researcher examines the history and behavior of a single person. In some situations, the researcher will use case study to describe a patient's reaction to treatment.

**Ceiling and floor effects**—A form of measurement-error threat to the internal validity wherein the measurement device cannot adequately measure high-level (ceiling) or low-level (floor) performance.

**Confounding variable**—A variable related to the independent variable that the researcher cannot control and that threatens the internal validity of the cause-and-effect hypothesis, IV → DV.

**Control group**—A treatment condition in which the participants experience all aspects of the experiment except for the independent variable.

**Correlational studies**—An empirical research method for which the researcher takes two or more measurements of characteristics for each participant and then examines the correlation among the variables.

**External validity**—The degree to which we can generalize the results and conclusions reached with a sample to the population.

**Generality of conclusions**—The degree to which the conclusion reached in one population will generalize to different populations.

**Generality of findings**—The degree to which we can use the sample data to generalize about the population from which the data were drawn.

**Instrumentation**—Changes in the measurement instrument over the course of an experiment.

**Intact groups design**—A form of research for which the researcher divides participants into separate groups on the basis of one or more subject variables. The goal of the research is to determine whether there are differences among the populations represented by the groups.

**Internal validity**—The degree to which we can assume that changes in the independent variable caused changes in the dependent variable.

**Intervening events**—A form of unintentional-sequence-of-events threat to internal validity wherein the participants experience extraneous events, outside the researcher's control, that affect their behavior.

**Maturation**—A form of unintentional-sequence-of-events threat to internal validity wherein the participants grow older and consequently change their behavior.

**Meta-analysis**—A collection of statistical techniques used to combine the results of separate research projects to help one determine the relation between the independent and dependent variables.

**Mortality**—A form of nonequivalent-groups threat to internal validity wherein the participants withdraw from the research.

**Qualitative independent variable**—An independent variable best described by a nominal scale.

**Quantitative independent variable**—An independent variable described by an ordinal, interval, or ratio scale.

**Quasi-experimental design**—A form of research for which the researcher can identify an experimental group that is exposed to the variable of interest and a control that is not exposed to the variable of interest, but cannot randomly assign the participants to the two conditions.

**Quasi-independent variable**—A variable that the researcher may be able to manipulate but cannot randomly assign participants to different levels of the variable.

**Random assignment**—Each participant has an equal probability of assignment to one of the treatment conditions.

**Research design**—A procedure or plan for collecting data that will answer one or more empirical questions.

**Regression to the mean**—A form of measurement-error threat to the internal validity wherein participants who obtain exceptionally high or low scores when first tested will tend to have average scores when tested a second time.

**Reliability**—A form of measurement-error threat to the internal validity wherein measurement device produces large inconsistencies of measurement.

**Single-participant experiment**—A form of a true experiment for which the researcher examines the behavior of a small group of participants. Each participant experiences the control and treatment conditions.

**Subject variables**—A form of nonequivalent-groups threat to internal validity wherein the researcher uses a subject variable to group participants. The researcher will not be able to determine whether differences among groups reflect the independent variable or selection variable.

**Survey** or **questionnaire**—An objective method of obtaining information from members of a population. In most cases, the researcher will ask participants to answer a series of questions.

**Temporal order problem**—A threat to internal validity. Because the researcher measures two variables at the same time, or is unable to control one of the variables, there is no way to determine which is the cause and which is the effect.

**Third variable problem**—A threat to internal validity. The problem arises when a third variable correlates with both the independent and dependent variables.

**Treatment condition**—A level or setting of the independent variable. The differences among the treatment conditions may represent qualitative or quantitative differences.

**True experiment**—A form of empirical research in which the researcher randomly assigns participants to different independent groups, uses one or more control conditions, and uses a manipulated independent variable.

**Unintended sequence of events**—A category of confounding variables that threaten the internal validity of the research. The threat arises when the researcher cannot control extraneous events that occur during the research.

## Chapter References

Anderson, C. A., & Bushman, B. J. (1997). External validity of "trivial" experiments: The case of laboratory aggression. *Review of General Psychology, 1,* 19–41.

Anne E. Casey Foundation (1999). *When teens have sex: Issues and trends.* Washington, DC: Author.

Brock, T. C., Green, M. C., & Reich, D. A. (1998). New evidence of flaws in the *Consumer Reports* study of psychotherapy. *American Psychologist, 53,* 62–63.

Brock, T. C., Green, M. C., Reich, D. A., & Evans, L. M. (1996). The *Consumer Reports* study of psychotherapy: Invalid is invalid. *American Psychologist, 51,* 1083.

Cohen, J. (1992). A power primer. *Psychological Bulletin, 112,* 155–159.

Cook, T. D., & Campbell, D. T. (1979). *Quasi-experimentation: Design and analysis issues for field settings*. Chicago: Rand-McNally.

Freud, S., & Breuer, J. (1976). Studies in hysteria. In J. Strachey (Trans. and Ed.), *The complete psychological works* (Vol. 2, pp. 50–300). New York: Norton. (Original text published 1895).

Gardner, H. (1995). *Leading minds: An anatomy of leadership*. New York: Basic Books.

Glass, G. V. (1978). Integrating findings: The meta-analysis of research. *Review of Research in Education*, *5*, 351–379.

Hyde, J. S. (2005). The gender similarities hypothesis. *American Psychologist*, *60*, 581–592.

Hyde, J. S., & Lynn, M. C. (1988). Gender differences in verbal ability. *Psychological Bulletin*, *104*, 53–69.

Jacobson, N. S., & Christensen, A. (1996). Studying the effectiveness of psychotherapy: How well can clinical trials do the job? *American Psychologist*, *51*, 1031–1039.

Kotkin, M., Daviet, C., & Gurin, J. (1996). The *Consumer Reports* mental health survey. *American Psychologist*, *51*, 1080–1082.

Loftus, E., & Ketcham, K. (1994). *The myth of repressed memories: False memories and allegations of sexual abuse*. New York: St Martin's.

Maier, S. F., & Seligman, M. E. (1976). Learned helplessness: Theory and evidence. *Journal of Experimental Psychology: General*, *105*, 3–46.

Mill, J. S. (1986). *System of logic*. New York: Classworks. (Original work published 1843).

Milner, B. (1966). Amnesia following operation on the temporal lobes. In C.W.M. Witty & O. L. Zangwill (Eds.), *Amnesia* (pp. 60–93). London: Butterworth.

Milner, B., Corkin, S., & Teuber, H. L. (1968). Further analysis of hippocampal syndrome: 14-year follow-up study of H. M. *Neuropsycholgia*, *6*, 215–234.

Overmeier, J. B., & Seligman, M. E. (1967). Effect of inescapable shock upon subsequent escape and avoidance responding. *Journal of Comparative & Physiological Psychology*, *63*, 28–33.

Pedhazur, E. J. (1997). *Multiple regression in behavioral research: Explanation and prediction* (3rd ed.). Fort Worth, TX: Harcourt Brace.

Premack, D. (1959). Toward empirical behavioral laws: I. Positive reinforcement. *Psychological Review*, *66*, 219–233.

Premack, D. (1965). Reinforcement theory. In D. Levine (Ed.), *Nebraska symposia on motivation* (pp. 123–180). Lincoln: University of Nebraska Press.

Sacks, O. (1985). *The man who mistook his wife for a hat and other clinical tales*. New York: Touchstone/Simon & Schuster.

Seligman, M.E.P. (1995). The effectiveness of psychotherapy: The *Consumer Reports* study. *American Psychologist*, *50*, 965–974.

Seligman, M. E., & Maier, S. F. (1967). Failure to escape traumatic shock. *Journal of Experimental Psychology*, *74*, 1–9.

Shadish, W. R., Cook, T. D., & Campbell, D. T. (2002). *Experimental and quasi-experimental designs for generalized causal inference*. Boston: Houghton Mifflin.

Strupp, H. H. (1996). The tripartite model and the *Consumer Reports* study. *American Psychologist*, *51*, 1017–1024.

# Part II
# Nuts and Bolts of Research

# Chapter 5
# Writing the Research Report

## CHAPTER OBJECTIVES

**Introduction**
**What Do Readers Appreciate in Good Writing?**
**Elements of APA Style**
**Special Grammatical Issues**
**Academic Integrity**
**Parts of the Research Report**
**Proofreading**

> Writing is not like painting where you add. It is not what you put on the canvas that the reader sees. Writing is more like a sculpture where you remove, you eliminate in order to make the work visible. Even those pages you remove somehow remain.
>
> —**Elie Wiesel**

## Introduction

The goal of any research project is a report in which you tell others why and how you conducted the research and the implications of your findings. This does not mean you should wait to write any details down about your study until it is finished! On the contrary, writing is first and foremost a process that takes time. This is why we are taking this chapter to introduce you to the process of preparing a high-quality research report. One caveat before we dig in: Given our backgrounds and the structured nature of reports within the field of psychology, we will emphasize the guidelines of the American Psychological Association (APA), a guideline used by most of the social sciences.

In many ways, writing a research report requires you to tell a story with a clear beginning, middle, and end. You begin the report with a description of an important and at least partially unresolved question. Then you turn to details that you uncovered regarding your hypotheses and use those clues to help steer the review toward a set of logical deductions (i.e., the hypotheses). In the next part of the report, you tell the reader how you went about collecting the data for the study. Remember, good science can be repeated by others and you want others to know exactly how you tested your hypotheses. After discussing the results of the project, the last portion of this type of report is space for you to pull information together and explain how this study has answered or addressed the initial question or issue of interest.

Writing is a unique, intellectual challenge. Your goal is to influence the behavior or thinking of anyone who might choose to read what you have written. In most cases, you write to share information and persuade the reader that your interpretation of the facts is correct, or at least logical and defensible. The same is true in a good research report. At the start of your paper, you introduce the readers to the purpose of your research, and then convince them that you are asking an important and interesting question. By the end of the paper, you will have convinced the reader that your analysis and interpretation of the data were the correct ones and have answered the questions.

There is no mystery to becoming a good writer. Similarly, there are no excuses for why any intelligent person cannot write well. Writing is a craft learned and refined through practice guided by self-discipline, and by attention to detail and a willingness to seek help from others. Good writers write well because they write often. Good writers also write well because they have learned from experience and have received useful and constructive critiques of their own writing. Good writers also tend to be those people who read a great deal of what other good writers write. Reading exposes you to many styles of writing and can help you pick up good writing habits. Within the social sciences, you can learn a great deal about how to present your research findings and ideas by learning from the example set forth by other good writers in your field (yes, we're telling you that it's a good idea to read journals not just for content, but also for style and form).

Finally, good writers never work in isolation; they have others read drafts of their work, and they seek constructive or helpful criticism. Many students seem to believe that no one should read their paper until they submit it to the instructor. Nothing could be farther from the truth. In fact, all of us really hate it when we receive a "first-draft paper" from our students; they are never as good or polished as they should be. Asking someone you trust to read a draft of your paper and provide feedback *will* help you become a better writer. This can help to ensure that your work is as clear and concise as possible. For example, as we wrote this book, each of us reviewed the others' work and offered extensive comments, corrections, and constructive criticism. In addition, other social scientists read drafts of all the chapters and offered their critical comments before a final draft was submitted to the publisher. Certainly there were times when the feedback from these reviews was frustrating and less-than-positive, but overall these comments helped us to fix areas that were confusing and strengthen areas that were weak (at least we think we have succeeded in doing this).

This being the case, we hope you can see that this textbook cannot teach you how to be a good writer any more than a textbook can teach an artist how to paint like Picasso. What we can do is highlight several of the core elements and characteristics of good writing in the social sciences. Studying these characteristics will help you to critically evaluate your own writing. For this reason, we hope to achieve two things in this chapter. First, we will review general stylistic conventions that are central to good writing. Second, we will introduce you to the editorial guidelines developed by the APA, focusing on the basic details that you will need to prepare a standard research report.

## What Do Readers Appreciate in Good Writing?

Good writing, especially scientific writing, involves three essential elements: focus, organization, and integration. It may be difficult to believe, but it is *not* a requirement of scientific writing that it be dull and boring. On the contrary, there is no reason why writing or reading a scientific report must be an exercise in tedium. In truth, writing about complicated technical and theoretical issues is difficult and this is what prevents many researchers from allowing their storytelling abilities to shine through in their writing. With time, practice, attention, and multiple drafts, we are confident that anyone can prepare a research-based report that captivates the interest and attention of serious readers.

*Focus* means that there is a clear purpose for the writing and definite boundaries established for what you will and will not discuss. Some writers fall into the trap of covering too many topics. Consequently, their papers are rambling expositions of many unrelated topics. For a research report, you should focus on your research questions.

In addition to being focused, good writing is *organized*. Readers working through a well-written paper will experience a logical presentation of ideas that lead to a series of reasonable conclusions. Along the way, each paragraph leads smoothly into each subsequent paragraph—there is a sort of flow from section to section that does not disrupt the reader's attention.

Finally, with focus and organization in place, a good writer is able to *integrate* the information into a coherent message. All writing, even of research reports, requires storytelling. Your job as a writer is to bring together a series of facts and observations and show the reader with words how this puzzle fits together. Listing all the means, standard deviations, and results of the inferential statistics from your statistical analyses is not integration. Far more interesting is learning how the results of your research address your specific and well-supported and introduced hypotheses.

## Elements of APA Style

The APA developed its editorial style to promote good scientific writing and to establish a consistent format for presenting the results of research for the behavioral sciences (APA, 2009). The editorial style and format are extremely popular and used by most professional journals in education, psychology, sociology, and even some areas of business management. In this section, we will review several of the fundamental features of APA style.

**Issues of Style**

Writing a research report requires that you strive for accuracy, brevity, and clarity. You will find that writing a research report is much different from other forms of writing. We do not wish to imply that one form of writing is better than another, only that different styles serve different purposes. Consider an example from the opening pages of Mark Twain's (1876) *The Adventures of Tom Sawyer*, wherein Twain describes Aunt Polly:

> *The old lady pulled her spectacles down and looked over them about the room; then she put them up and looked under them. She seldom or never looked through them for so small a thing as a boy; they were her state pair, the pride of her heart, and were built for "style" not service—she could have seen through a pair of stove-lids just as well. (p. 9)*

In this vivid passage, Twain used metaphor and other literary devices to introduce the reader to Aunt Polly. Twain used the glasses to describe Aunt Polly's personality and her relation to Tom.

Although these and many other techniques make for good literature, they are not commonly appropriate for technical, research-based writing. In research reports, literary techniques such as ironic use of words and intentional ambiguity are distractions. These literary devices require too much inference and subjective interpretation on the part of the reader and should, therefore, be avoided unless clearly explained. Therefore, you should avoid using vague and colloquial expressions (e.g., "After *quite a long time*, the effects of the independent variable *kicked in*") and opaque jargon and euphemistic phrases (e.g., "The individual's behavior created much *collateral disruption* among *interrelated members of the domestic unit*").

Compare the passage from *Tom Sawyer* with the opening paragraph of an article by Allumbaugh and Hoyt (1999):

> *Over 2 million people die in the United States every year (U. S. Bureau of the Census, 1995). For each person who dies, there are numerous people left behind to grieve, many of whom seek help from a therapist. Loss and grief are universal human experiences. The recently bereaved represent a large at-risk population, with higher overall death and suicide rates than age-matched control participants and with an increased incidence of depression, substance abuse, and certain medical disorders. (p. 307)*

This paragraph is clear and direct. The authors presented a series of facts that make clear that they have selected an important topic. Furthermore, it does not take a vivid imagination to interpret the meaning of this paragraph. The authors made clear that the death of a person creates grief that can have severe psychological and medical consequences.

**Writing for an Audience**

You may have learned in a composition course that you should always consider your audience when writing. This advice applies to writing a research report as well. So, who is your audience? Usually it is the course instructor who has assigned you a research report. This is not a very detailed or clear understanding of your audience. As a general rule, you should think of your reader as a behavioral scientist who understands general principles in the discipline, but who may not be an expert on the topic you chose to study (yes, we are still talking about your course instructor).

Knowing your audience ahead of time should help you determine what elements of your report will require the most detailed explanation. For most research-related publications, the likely immediate audience is fellow researchers. This being the case, you can typically assume that these individuals will understand general issues in the discipline, basic research design, and statistical tests. For example, if you use a factorial ANOVA to analyze the data, you will not have to explain the difference between a main effect and an interaction. You can also assume that the reader understands the logic of conventional statistical tests. It is important to point out, however, that your research may be interesting to a secondary audience as well, especially if your findings have potential practical implications within society, families, or workplaces. For this reason, it is also important for you to provide clear and accurate discussion of the logic leading to your hypotheses and of the findings and their practical implications. If you can successfully do this, you will greatly increase your chances of making your research useful to the largest number of people.

Although most immediate readers of research reports may understand basic social science and research principles, you cannot assume that the reader knows the history and the important questions that are a part of your research as well as you do. Look again at the Allumbaugh and Hoyt (1999) paragraph from before. They have few preconceived notions concerning what the reader knows about grief or grief therapy. Although some readers may find the authors' comments obvious, we appreciated that they clearly stated that grieving can have serious mental and physical health consequences. Reading their introduction teaches you many things about the history of grief therapy and how different therapies help people overcome the emotional trauma wrought by a loved one's death.

## Value-Free Descriptions of Others

The APA has long discouraged biased descriptions of people or groups of people. Writing is considered to be "biased" when it includes any description of an irrelevant characteristic of a group of people or of a person. A bias (sexism), for example, can emerge when one draws attention to a particular sex for no particular reason. Doing so implies that there is a meaningful difference between men and women when one may not exist. Consider the word *mothering*. One connotation of the word refers to caring for others; another connotation is being overly protective. Mothering is a sexist term because both men and women have the capacity to care for others and to be overly protective. Unless the author's intent is to focus on women, better words to use here might be *parenting*, *nurturing*, or *protectiveness*. All three words are value-free, because they describe the target behavior and do not link the behavior to one sex.

There is no need to refer to a characteristic of a person or group of people unless that trait is the focus of the research. In these instances, the descriptive terms used should be objective. The best strategy is to write with words and phrases that describe the relevant characteristic of the individual's behavior, rather than the person. Therefore, it is preferable to replace the terms *fireman*, *mailman*, and *waitress* with *firefighter*, *mail carrier*, and *server*. The second set of words describes the work of the individuals in that group without implying their sex.

Writing sex-neutral sentences is not as easy as it may seem at first. There are traps you should avoid. For example, some writers use complicated combination terms such as *s/he*, *he/she*, or *him/her* to avoid sexist language. Although well-intentioned, such terms are awkward, making writing very difficult to read smoothly. Fortunately, there are two relatively simple ways you can avoid this type of lexical faux pas. First, you can convert a single noun to a plural noun (e.g., change "Each *participant* received *his* . . . " to "The *participants* received *their* . . . "). This option has the advantage of being simple to implement and does not change the meaning of the sentence. Second, you can use the singular noun and use "his or her," "he or she," or an equivalent. The only time you should use a gender-specific noun, pronoun, or adjective is when the behavior is clearly sex specific (e.g., "Each woman completed the survey soon after learning that she was pregnant").

We also extend the editorial policy regarding sexist language to the people who participate in our research or who are afflicted with a psychological or medical condition. Therefore, the APA editorial guideline recommends that we use descriptive nouns when detailing the people involved with our research. This is one reason why all the people who are involved with a study are referred to as *participants*. You can also use nouns such as *children*, *college students*, *parents*, *clients*, *individuals*, and *respondents* to refer to the participants of a study. Similarly, a diagnosis of a psychological or medical disorder describes the condition of *a* person, not *the* person. For example, people are not "schizophrenic," "autistic," or "depressive." Rather, people receive a diagnosis of schizophrenia, autism, or depression based on their cognition and behavior. Just as we avoid sexist language by describing the behavior, we are challenged to avoid biased language by describing the disability itself, rather than the person. Consequently, researchers refer to "people diagnosed with schizophrenia," "individuals with low self-esteem," or "individuals who are developmentally delayed." People are not "senior citizens" or "elderly"; they are people "over the age of 65" or "over the age of 85."

## Integrating Numbers and Text

Table 5.1 presents the general rules governing the use of numbers. Most of the rules are straightforward. A few, however, require special comment. For

## Table 5.1 General Rules for Reporting Numbers in an APA-Style Paper

- Use numbers to express values equal to or greater than 10:
  "Of the people responding, five were engaged to be married."
  "Each questionnaire contained 15 questions."

- Use numbers when the value precedes a unit of measurement:
  "The dimensions of the floor were 4.5 m $\times$ 5.2 m."

- Use numbers when the value is a part of a noun:
  "The extinction session began on Trial 5."
  "Table 1 and Figure 1 present the results of Experiment 1."

- Use words when the value begins the sentence:
  "Fourteen people refused to complete the task."

- Use numbers when the sentence contains several related numbers and at least one is equal to or greater than 10:
  "Participants received reinforcement on the first and fifth trials."
  "We used the 5th, 8th, and 15th sessions as probe trials."

- To make a number plural, add *s* or *es* as necessary. Do not use an apostrophe:
  "Skinner's perspectives became popular in the late 1960s and early 1970s."
  "Many people believe that tragedies come in threes."

- Use numbers to represent statistical results, fractions, mathematical functions, or the results of mathematical equations:
  "Of the responding participants, 63% indicated favoring Option 1."
  "We multiplied each score by 4 to equate the groups."

- If a number cannot exceed 1.00, do not use a leading 0 before the decimal point:
  "The average reaction times for the two groups were 0.85 s and 1.03 s."
  "X and Y were significantly correlated, $r(57) = -.76$, p < .05."

example, APA style recommends using the metric system and the International System of Units for reporting specific quantities. Table 5.2 includes a short list of common measures and the method of converting from traditional to metric units.

## Special Grammatical Issues

For the most part, the APA editorial guidelines follow conventional rules of grammar. Thus, what you learned in English composition courses concerning subject–verb agreement, dangling modifiers, and other elements of grammar apply to writing a research report. The APA editorial guidelines also emphasize several grammatical conventions that require extra attention.

### Active versus Passive Voice

Active and passive voice refers to the order of the subject, verb, and object of the sentence. Active voice sentences place greater emphasis on the

## Table 5.2 Common Measurement Scale and Conversion from Traditional to Metric Units

| Scale | Traditional Unit | Metric Equivalent (Abbreviation) | Conversion |
|---|---|---|---|
| Length | Foot | Meter (m) | $m = 0.3048 \times foot$ |
| | Inch | Centimeter (cm) | $cm = 2.54 \times inch$ |
| | Fraction of inch | Millimeter (mm) | $mm = .254 \times inch$ |
| | Yard | Meter (m) | $m = 0.9144 \times yard$ |
| Area | Square foot | Square meter ($m^2$) | $m^2 = .09290304 \times foot^2$ |
| | Square inch | Square millimeter ($mm^2$) | $cm^2 = 645.16 \times inch^2$ |
| Mass | Ounce | Gram (g) | $g = 28.34952 \times ounce$ |
| | Fraction of ounce | Milligram (mg) | $mg = 2.834952 \times ounce$ |
| | Pound | Kilogram (kg) | $kg = .45359237 \times pound$ |
| Volume | Cubic foot | Cubic meter ($m^3$) | $m^3 = .02831685 \times foot^3$ |
| | Cubic inch | Cubic centimeter ($cm^3$) | $cm^3 = 16.38706 \times inch^3$ |
| | Fluid ounce | Milliliter (ml) | $ml = 29.57353 \times f. ounce$ |
| | Quart | Liter (L) | $L = .9463529 \times quart$ |
| Temperature | Fahrenheit (°F) | Celsius (°C) | $°C = (°F - 32) \times 5/9$ |
| Time | Hours (h) | | $ms = 1/1000\ s$ |
| | Minutes (m) | | |
| | Seconds (s) | | |
| | Milliseconds (ms) | | |

subject, or the actor, of the sentence than the object of the sentence. In an active voice sentence the subject precedes the verb. Consequently, active voice sentences make clear who or what is responsible for the outcome. In contrast, passive voice sentences place the object before the verb. Passive voice sentences are, therefore, more difficult to interpret.

In an active voice sentence you are also able to identify yourself using personal pronouns (e.g., I or we). The goal of active voice is to make clear who did what to whom. For example, we can revise the passive voice in the following sentence: "The experiment was designed using the Solomon four-group control procedure," to be active voice: "We used the Solomon four-group control procedure for the experiment."

Examples of active voice sentences are:

"Mary(subject) caught(verb) the football(object)."

"The participants completed the questionnaire during the first phase of the study."

Examples of passive voice sentences are:

"The football(object) was caught(verb) by Mary(subject)."

"The questionnaires were completed by the participants during the first phase of the study."

The APA editorial style manual recommends using active voice for two main reasons. First, active voice sentences clearly identify who or what is responsible for the outcome. In passive voice sentences, the cause is either hidden at the end of the sentence or missing. Second, active voice sentences tend to use fewer words and are therefore easier to read and understand.

**Past and Present Tense**

The APA editorial style manual requires the past tense when referring to the work of another author and the data presented in the current report. As an example, you might write, ''Freud (1917/1957) believed . . . '' or ''Freud (1917/1957) argued . . . ,'' because Freud expressed his beliefs long before you began to write your paper. Similarly, you would use the past tense to describe the data you collected. Accordingly, you might write:

   ''The current results confirmed the hypothesis.''

or

   ''As expected, there was a significant interaction among the treatment conditions.''

When you describe an event or action that did not occur at a specific time, or if the condition remains, you may use the present perfect tense. Examples of the present perfect tense are:

   ''Since the late 1940s, psychologists have used the ANOVA and other inferential statistical techniques for their research.''

   ''Psychologists have long had an interest in the biological foundations of behavior.''

**Proper Use of Pronouns**

The APA editorial style manual emphasizes specific rules concerning the use of pronouns. Other editorial guidelines (e.g., of the Modern Language Association) do not emphasize these same conventions. Therefore, you should pay special attention to this section of your APA publication manual when writing.

**Who *versus* That**

When speaking of humans, and especially individual people, use pronouns such as *who*, *him*, or *her*. When speaking of nonhumans, use the neuter pronoun *that*. To illustrate the difference, you would write, ''The children *who* participated in the study . . . ,'' or ''The dogs *that* Pavlov studied. . . . ''

Similarly, you should write, "The psychologist *who* administered the test . . . ," because a psychologist is a person, not a thing.

### That *versus* Which

*That* and *which* are relative pronouns that have specific uses. Use *that* in clauses essential to the meaning of a sentence. In the sentence, "Much of the research that psychologists conducted in the past 30 years emphasized the social-cognitive perspective of personality," the reference to the past 30 years is essential to the meaning of the sentence and is, therefore, a restrictive clause. Use the relative pronoun *which* when the clause is not essential to the meaning of the sentence. For instance, "Gestalt therapy, which focuses on the client's emotions, became popular in the 1970s." The nonrestrictive clause adds information to the sentence, but does not change its meaning. If you can remove the clause without changing the meaning of the sentence, the clause is nonrestrictive (cf., "Gestalt therapy became popular in the 1970s"). Many people tend to use *which* and *that* indiscriminately. Consequently, Strunk and White (1979) recommended that authors go on a "which hunt" when proofreading their work.

### *Vague Pronouns*

All style guides warn against the use of vague pronouns. Unfortunately, many people continue to use the pronouns *this*, *that*, *these*, and *those* without an obvious referent. Consider the following passage:

> *Many surveys have consistently demonstrated that most people endorse the stereotype that men make better leaders than women. This may prevent women from being promoted to positions of authority. That is an example of the "glass-ceiling" phenomenon.*

What do *this* and *that* refer to in the second and third sentences? Does the second sentence mean that the results of the survey prevent women's promotions, or is it the stereotype that creates the barrier? For both sentences, the pronoun has no clear referent. Consequently, the object, or referent, in the sentences is vague. A few simple modifications can clarify these sentences:

> Several surveys of people's attitudes have consistently demonstrated that most people endorse the stereotype that men make better leaders than women. Belief in these stereotypes may cause employers to promote men, but not women, to positions of authority. This discrimination is an example of the "glass-ceiling" phenomenon.

### Commonly Misused Words

Some authors use specific words indiscriminately and incorrectly. Box 5.1 lists many of these commonly misused words and indicates their correct use. As you proofread your manuscript, look out for these problem terms; many spelling and grammar checkers built into word processors overlook these words.

# Box 5.1 Commonly Misused Words

**Affect vs. Effect**

*Affect* means to influence or to cause a change
"The independent variable affected the participants' behavior."
*Effect* represents the result or the consequence of something
"There were large treatment effects in the experimental groups."

**Among vs. Between**

Use *among* when discussing more than two people or objects
"There were minor differences among the 30 participants."
Use *between* when discussing only two people or objects
"There are minor differences between Hull's and Spence's theories."

**Amount vs. Number**

Use *amount* to refer to a general quantity
"The amount of reinforcement each participant received depended on the schedule of reinforcement."
Use *number* to refer to countable items
"The number of clients seeking treatment decreased after six months."

**Data**

*Data* is the plural form of the word *datum*. As a rule, nouns ending with "a" are plural (e.g., phenomena is the plural form of phenomenon; criteria is the plural form of criterion). "The data are consistent with the theory."

**Ensure vs. Insure vs. Assure**

*Ensure* refers to procedures that minimize the occurrence of some event
"We called all participants to ensure that they would return for the second part of the experiment."
*Insure* refers specifically to the protection against financial loss
"We instructed the clients to save 10% of their weekly income to insure against possible layoffs from the factory."
*Assure* means to convince, persuade, or to affirm a pledge
"The researcher assured the participants that the results of the study would be confidential."

**Few vs. Little**

*Few* refers to a countable quantity of objects
"Few people continue to question the importance of this theory."
*Little* refers to a general quantity
"The research attracted little attention when first published."

**Its vs. It's**

*Its* is a possessive pronoun
"The value of this theory is its ability to make novel predictions."
*It's* is a contraction of "it is." Never use contractions in technical writing.

**That vs. Which**

*That* is a relative pronoun used in clauses essential to the meaning of the sentence
"The author reviewed the evidence that supports Miller's theory."
Use *which* in clauses that are not essential to the meaning of the sentence, but provide additional information.
"The real purpose of the experiment, which the researcher did not tell the participants, was to determine the degree to which people will conform to behavior of a role model."

**Utilize vs. Use**

*Utilize* is a transitive verb that adds little to a sentence; *use* is sufficient in most cases.

**While vs. Since**

*While* refers to the simultaneous passage of time for two or more linked events
"While the participants were involved in filling out the questionnaire, the confederate began to perform various distracting behaviors."

*(Continued)*

| | |
|---|---|
| **Although vs. Because** | *Since* refers to the passage of time between the past and present<br>"Since Snyder published his paper in 1974, many researchers have become interested in the self-monitoring construct."<br><br>*Although* refers to a contradiction with a statement or fact<br>"Many people believe in extrasensory perception, although psychologists have long questioned the existence of the phenomenon."<br>Use *because* to indicate the reason for some condition or event<br>"The external validity of the experiment is questionable because the researcher did not use a random selection procedure." |

## Academic Integrity

Academic integrity means that you give complete and fair credit to the sources of the ideas you incorporate in your paper. As a rule, if you state a fact, share an observation, or report the conclusion of another writer, you need to acknowledge the origin of that idea. Following this rule allows you to avoid accusations of plagiarism. *Plagiarism* comes from a Latin word meaning to kidnap. Thus, someone who plagiarizes steals ideas from others. Most colleges have strict rules against and penalties for plagiarism. Depending on your college's academic policies, you may receive a failing grade for the assignment or the course if the instructor discovers that you have plagiarized. This issue is becoming increasingly apparent as colleges and universities increasingly make use of new software programs that automatically cross-check student work against massive electronic libraries of journal, book, and other manuscript publications from all over the world. Now is definitely the time to learn how *not* to plagiarize.

There are many forms of plagiarism. The most obvious is copying word-for-word another author's words and presenting them as yours. Other forms of plagiarism may not be as obvious, but are just as wrong. For example, presenting another person's ideas or logical arguments as yours without citing the source is also considered plagiarism. We can use the following passage to look at different forms of plagiarism.

Allumbaugh and Hoyt (1999) wrote:

> *It is commonly assumed in the psychotherapeutic community that for at least some bereaved individuals, some form of psychotherapy is useful or even necessary to assist in recovering from loss, and numerous theoretical frameworks have been proposed for psychotherapists working with bereaved clients. (p. 370)*

What if a student wrote the following sentence?

> *Many psychologists believe that some form of psychotherapy is useful and necessary to assist bereaved clients to recover from the loss. Consequently, there are many psychotherapies designed to help bereaved clients.*

This passage is an example of plagiarism for several reasons. Although the writer changed a few words and phrases, many of Allumbaugh and Hoyt's (1999) original words remain in the sentence. All the writer has done is a form of editorial recycling. Furthermore, the writer has not credited Allumbaugh and Hoyt's work. To avoid the accusation of plagiarism, the writer should write something like the following sentence:

> *According to Allumbaugh and Hoyt (1999), many psychologists believe that psycho-therapy can help some people overcome bereavement grief and have created special therapies for this condition.*

This sentence gives clear credit to the origin of the idea and is a major revision of the original text.

### Citations of Sources in the Text

From the preceding examples, you can see that the APA editorial guidelines require that you credit other people's work directly in the body of the text by listing the authors of the source and the date of publication. There are two general methods for citing a source. The first is to include the author's name in the sentence. For this procedure, list the name or names of the authors; include the date of the citation within parentheses: "Braver and Braver (1988) recommended a meta-analytic procedure for examining the data of a Solomon four-group research design."

The alternative is to treat the citation as a parenthetical statement: "Some authors (e.g., Braver & Braver, 1988) have argued that psychologists too often overlook the Solomon four-group design." Note that the ampersand (&) replaces the *and* when placing the references within parentheses. Box 5.2 presents examples of how to incorporate citations in the text.

---

### Box 5.2  Examples of Citations within the Text of a Manuscript

**Single author/single citation**
- List the author's last name followed by the date of publication.
  "Smith (1998) examined the effects of delayed reinforcement."
  "A recent study of delayed reinforcement (Smith, 1998) demonstrated . . . "

**Single author/multiple citations**
- List the author's last name followed by the dates of the individual publications
  "Smith's research (1996, 1998, 1999) demonstrates that . . . "
  "Recent research on this topic (Smith, 1996, 1998, 1999) . . . "

*(Continued)*

*(Continued)*

**Two or more authors/single citation**

- If there are two authors, list both names followed by the date of publication. Use an ampersand (&) when the citation is within the parentheses.

  ''Allumbaugh and Hoyt (1999) examined the effectiveness of . . . ''

  ''In a recent review of grief therapies (Allumbaugh & Hoyt, 1999) . . . ''

- If there are three to five names, list all the names in the first citation. On subsequent citations, list the name of the first author followed with ''et al.'' and the date.

  *First citation:* ''Gutek, Bhappu, Liao-Trouth, and Cherry (1999) examined . . . ''

  ''Recent research examining relationships (Gutek, Bhappu, Liao-Trouth, & Cherry, 1999) . . . ''

  *Subsequent citations:* ''The Gutek et al. (1999) study indicated . . . ''

  ''Several tests of this construct exist (Gutek et al., 1999).''

- If there are six or more names, list only the first name followed by ''et al.'' and the date.

**Multiple citations**

- If you include several citations from different authors in the same parentheses, list the citations alphabetically by the authors' names. Separate the citations with a semicolon.

  ''Several studies (Allen, 1980, 1981, 1985; Babcock & Wilcox, 1993; Collins & Zager, 1972) . . . ''

**Translated work**

- If the original work was translated into English, list the author's name, the date of the original publication, and the date of the translated publication.

  ''Freud (1913/1952) developed the theory of screen memory . . . ''

**Corporate author**

- List the name of the organization followed by the date of publication.

  ''Sleep disorders are a common symptom of depression (American Psychiatric Association, 1994).''

**Newspaper or magazine article with no author**

- List a short version of the title followed by the date of publication.

  ''The popular press often sensationalizes psychological research (IQ tests measure nothing, 1999).''

### Use of *et al.*

When the reference includes between three and five names, list all the names the first time you refer to the source. For subsequent references to the same source, list the name of the first author followed by the phrase ''et al.'' (which means ''and others''). If there are six or more authors in the source, list the first name followed with et al. for all references to the citation. Then in your reference section, list the first six authors followed by et al. for the remaining authors.

### Listing Dates of Citations

When you refer to a citation, you must include the date of publication. This practice helps the reader keep track of the different sources you use. The exception is if you refer to the same citation more than once within a paragraph. If you refer to the same citation more than once in a paragraph, include the date with the first citation only. For example:

> *Kohn (2000) is a critic of standardized testing commonly used in primary and secondary education. Kohn's primary concern is the emphasis on test scores rather than . . .*

> *Much of the research that Kohn (2000) cites reflects . . .*

The first paragraph begins with a citation of the date of Kohn's book. The next sentence refers to the same book, but does not include the date. In the second paragraph, however, we include the date of Kohn's book in keeping with the editorial rule.

## Additional Comments on Quotations

Ralph Waldo Emerson quipped, "I hate quotations. Tell me what you know." You should adopt the same attitude when you write a scientific research report. Researchers rarely use quotations because the focus of the research paper is on their analysis of ideas, not just on how the original authors might have expressed those ideas. Your responsibility, as the author of a paper, is to read the work of others and then synthesize that work into a concise statement that supports your argument.

That said, there are at least two instances when you can and should use quotations. First, use a quotation when it is impossible to paraphrase a passage without losing its meaning. For example, you may find that you cannot paraphrase another author's definition of a particular term or concept without altering its meaning. These instances are rare, and you should avoid the temptation of assuming that you cannot put complex ideas into your words. The more appropriate occasion for using a quotation occurs when the author's ideas and expression of those ideas is the focus of your argument. Imagine that you are writing a paper wherein you examined the effects of positive reinforcement on intrinsic motivation. As a part of your paper, you want to illustrate how another author expressed his or her opinion. You could write something like the following:

> *By contrast, some authors believe that positive reinforcement reduces intrinsic motivation. These authors typically make the unqualified claim that reinforcement has detrimental rather than beneficial effects. For example, Kohn (1993) asserted, "But the use of rewards for reading, writing, drawing, acting responsibly and generously, and so on is cause for concern. Extrinsic motivators are most dangerous when offered for something we want children to want to do" (p. 87). This sentiment is common . . .*

In this case, the quotation is evidence that supports your argument. Using the quote allows you to share with the reader Kohn's tone and sentiment regarding the effects of reinforcement. If you must use a quotation, try to keep it short. We selected only a few sentences from Kohn's book to illustrate the point we wanted to make. In addition, you should reproduce the quotation exactly as it appeared in its original form. In this example, several words are italicized because they were italicized in the original text. If we had added the italics, we would have included the following note after the italics: "[italics added]". If you drop words or sentences from the original text, replace the missing words with ellipsis points ( . . . ). If the length of the quotation is fewer than 40 words (about four lines in your word processor), include the quotation as a part of the sentence. For longer quotations, set the material off as a separate indented paragraph. As an example:

"By contrast, some authors believe that positive reinforcement reduces intrinsic motivation. These authors typically make the unqualified claim that reinforcement has detrimental rather than beneficial effects. For example, Kohn (1990) asserted,

> But not only are rewards less effective than intrinsic motivation—they actually undermine it. You started out doing something just because you found it fun. But once you were rewarded for doing it, you came to see yourself as working mostly to get the reward. Your fascination with the task mysteriously vanished [italics added] along the way and now you can't be bothered to do it unless there's some reward at stake. (p. 32)"

We indented the longer quote and separated it from the rest of the paragraph. The example also shows how you can add emphasis to the quotation to draw the reader's attention to a specific phrase in the passage. Whenever you add one of these editorial notes, place them within brackets. For example, to indicate a misspelling in the original text, use "[sic]". Bottom line: Keep your use of quotations to a minimum. Most professors do not like to read papers that read like a grocery list and are nothing more than a long collection of quotations embroidered together with a few transitional sentences from the student. Tell the reader what *you* know, how *you* would synthesize the information you have read. Your work is far more interesting to read than a string of quotations.

## Parts of the Research Report

Each research report contains the same elements, including the title page, abstract, introduction, method section, results section, discussion section, and references section. In the following pages, we will review the material that goes into each of these sections, along with several additional issues related to APA editorial style. There are several conventions for formatting a research report in APA style. Box 5.3 lists the general rules for formatting your paper. Most people now use word processors to prepare their papers and find it easy to use the program's basic setup and formatting options to prepare an APA-style paper. An example of an APA-style research report, a template to use when formatting your own work, and supplemental materials can be found in the APA manual (APA, 2009).

---

## Box 5.3  Checklist for Formatting and General Construction

- Set all margins to 1 inch.
- Left justify all text except the title of the paper and the words identifying the start of the major sections.
- Double-space everything. All the text, regardless of section, is double-spaced.
- Running heads and page numbers begin on the title page and run throughout the entire text.
- The only pages that do not have the running head and page numbers are the figures.
- Print all text in the same font and size (10 pt. or 12 pt.). Use an easy to read font (e.g., Courier or Times New Roman).
- Insert a single space after each word and punctuation mark including commas, semicolons, and periods.

---

### Title Page

The title page includes four elements: (1) the running head, (2) the title of the paper, (3) the names of the researchers, and (4) their professional affiliations. The running head, or header, is a short version of the title of the paper and appears at the upper-right corner of each page along with the page number. Most word processors allow you to include a running head or header. In addition, the program will allow you to insert the page number as a part of the header. The first line on the title page consists of the phrase "Running head:" and a short version of the title printed in CAPITAL LETTERS. Typically, the running head is an abbreviated version of the title. According to APA style guidelines, the running head cannot be more than 50 characters counting letters, spaces, and punctuation. Most titles are between 10 and 12 words. Writing a good title requires careful planning.

You can get a good impression of how to write your title by looking at the titles of the articles you use in your reference section. Your title should be a short and self-explanatory description of the research. For example, the title "A Study of Human Memory" tells the reader nothing about the purpose of the research, as it describes almost any research project on memory. By contrast, the title "A Study Showing That Writing Essays about Traumatic Events in One's Life Helps Reduce Feelings of Anxiety and Guilt among College Students Who Were Abused as Children" is very descriptive, but far too long. Examples of better titles are "Proactive Interference in the Memory of Pictures" and "Writing as a Means for Reducing Anxiety and Guilt."

Center the title horizontally on the title page. Capitalize the first letter of each major word in the title (you do not need to capitalize smaller words and articles such as *the, and, is, in, of,* and similar words). Do not use abbreviations in the title. On the line immediately following the title and centered horizontally on the page is your name. Use your full given name, rather than nicknames. The following line, also centered, contains the name of your college or university.

## Abstract

The abstract is a short (no more than 120 words) description of the research. Readers use the abstract of a research article to determine whether the article interests them and deserves their attention. Therefore, useful abstracts briefly describe the purpose of the research, the population under study, the method used to collect the data, the primary findings, and the researcher's primary conclusions. The best model for you to follow when writing your own abstract is a published abstract from the research articles you read in peer-reviewed journals.

## Introduction

The introduction to a standard APA-style manuscript begins on the third page. The objectives for writing the introduction are to capture the reader's interest and offer a compelling overview and a rationale for the research. As we noted previously, you should consider the reader to be a well-informed behavioral scientist who may or may not know much about the phenomenon that you chose to study. Consequently, your introduction must help the reader understand the phenomenon and why there is a need for more research. Although there is no set formula for writing an introduction, you can follow some useful guidelines. Figure 5.1 presents such a guide. Think of your introduction as an inverted triangle. The paper begins with a broad

## Figure 5.1

**Inverted Triangle Model of the Introduction**

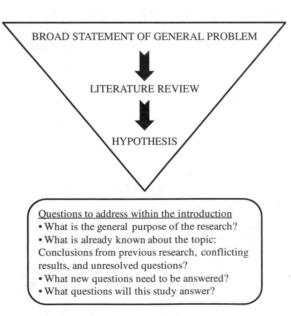

statement of the general problem. As you progress through the introduction, you should focus the text on issues directly related to your research project. In the literature review section, you can describe the findings and conclusions drawn from previous research. This portion of the introduction allows you to help the reader learn about the focus of your study and the necessity for the research. Finally, you should end the introduction with a review of the hypothesis or hypotheses that you will examine.

We can use a published article to illustrate the application of this inverted triangle. Eisenberger and Armeli (1997) conducted a set of experiments that examined the effects of positive reinforcement on intrinsic motivation. The opening sentence of their introduction was, "Over the past quarter century, the view that reward reduces task interest and creativity (Eisenberger & Cameron, 1996) has become widely accepted" (p. 652). This sentence is a broad introduction to a familiar topic in psychology. In the paragraphs that followed, Eisenberger and Armeli showed the reader that many psychologists and educators believe that positive reinforcement has many negative effects on intrinsic motivation and creativity. After establishing this fact, Eisenberger and Armeli narrowed the focus of their paper by stating, "Despite these limitations of the behavioral studies, the generally accepted conclusion that reward has inherent detrimental effects on creativity may be premature" (p. 653). This sentence makes clear that Eisenberger and Armeli do not accept the negative effects of reinforcement as a foregone conclusion. With this transition, the authors began a review of research that suggests that reinforcement does increase creativity and does not harm intrinsic motivation.

Another transitional sentence that narrowed the focus of the introduction for Eisenberger and Armeli (1997) was, "Learned industriousness theory holds that if an individual is rewarded for putting a large amount of cognitive or physical effort into an activity, the sensation of high effort acquires secondary reward properties that lessen, to some degree, effort's innate aversiveness" (p. 654). With this sentence, Eisenberger and Armeli introduced the theory of learned industriousness and summarized that the theory predicts that reinforcement will increase rather than decrease creativity. The authors then devoted several paragraphs to describing the theory and the supporting research.

In these paragraphs, the authors narrowed the scope of the paper to where they could state the purpose of the research. The concluding paragraph of the introduction was:

> In sum, the present research tested two implications of learned industriousness theory: (a) that making explicit the requirement of novel performance for obtaining a large monetary reward in one task should increase the subsequent creativity of performance in an entirely different task and (b) that a decremental effect of reward on intrinsic creative interest should occur with reward for uncreative performance, but not with reward for creative performance. (p. 655)

In 26 paragraphs, Eisenberger and Armeli led the reader through a broad introduction of the problem and a review of previous research and current theory and delivered the reader a concise statement of the purpose of the research and their predictions.

## Method Section

The method section provides the reader with a detailed description of how you collected the data for your research. The goal of writing the method section is to allow the reader to evaluate the appropriateness of your data collection techniques. This information will help the reader understand how the data relate to the research hypothesis and evaluate the internal and external validity of your conclusions. Most method sections have three subsections in which you describe (1) how you identified and obtained the sample you studied, (2) the materials, equipment, and measures you used to collect the data, and (3) the specific procedures you followed during the research.

### Participants/Subjects

The first method subsection pertains to your participants or subjects. If your population is humans, then the title of the subsection is *participants*. By contrast, if you use nonhuman animals, then the title of the section is *subjects*. Whatever its name, you will use this subsection to tell the reader the relevant details of your sample and how it was created. As you will learn in Chapter 7, sampling is a critical component of any research project. Consequently, you need to define the sampling population and the procedures for creating the sample. Similarly, you need to define the relevant characteristics of the sample. The purpose of your research usually dictates the characteristics of the sample that you should describe. At the very least, you need to indicate the number of men and women in the study as well as the average age of the participants. If your research depends on specific subject variables (e.g., ethnicity, level of education, annual household income), then you should summarize those characteristics as well.

In addition to indicating how you recruited and selected the participants, you should describe whether and how you compensated or rewarded them. Similarly, you should indicate whether and why you lost the data for any member of the original sample. Mistakes happen. Sometimes the equipment does not work, the researcher makes a mistake, or the participant does not understand the instructions or refuses to complete the study. Report errors like these if they occur. For example, you may have to write, "Of the 120 surveys distributed, 5 could not be scored due to incomplete responses," or, "The data for three participants could not be used because of a malfunctioning computer." If you used nonhuman subjects, report the relevant subject variables including the genus and species name, strain number (if appropriate), supplier or breeder of the animals, and a detailed description of the housing and handling procedures. As with human research, you should then describe additional subject variables that related to the purpose of your research.

## Materials/Measures/Apparatus

The materials or apparatus subsection includes the description of the devices you used to collect the data. As with all parts of the method section, your description of the materials must be sufficient for another researcher to repeat the research. Because the research report is a short document, you cannot describe every nuance of the materials. Rather, this section should offer the reader a short account of the materials and where you acquired them:

*Specialized apparatus:* There is no need to describe standard laboratory equipment (e.g., videotape recorders, stopwatches, or projectors) readily available to any researcher. By contrast, if the equipment is highly specialized, then you should indicate the name of the manufacturer and model number of the device.

Similarly, if you built a special apparatus for the research, you should offer a brief description of the equipment. Depending on the sophistication of the device, you may want to include a scale drawing or picture of the apparatus.

*Tests and questionnaires:* You can treat tests and questionnaires the same way you treat a piece of equipment. If you used a published test, then you should include a brief overview of the test (e.g., number of questions and measurement scale used) as well as a reference to the original source of the test. Most researchers also include a reference to research that has evaluated the reliability and validity of the test.

Although it is preferable to utilize existing and validated measures, sometimes researchers need to create their own scales to gather the necessary data for testing specific hypotheses. If you develop your own test or questionnaire for a particular study, you should make sure to describe the general nature of the questions included in the survey in this section of your manuscript. When describing the measures used in your study, it is helpful to the reader if you clearly state what a high score on each scale represents. In addition, it is common to report reliability and validity information for each scale whenever it is available (e.g., Cronbach's $\alpha$).

## Design and Procedure

The final part of the method section describes the design of your study and details the sequence of significant events all participants experienced during the study. Consequently, you should describe how you assigned participants to various conditions of the research as well as your control procedures. You should also describe the specific instructions you gave the participants. In some cases, the procedure section may indicate that you distributed a questionnaire to randomly selected classes of students after you had described the purpose of the research. In other cases, the procedure section will be long if there were a series of important stages in the research that require careful description. Remember, the goal of the method section is to provide sufficient detail so that interested readers can evaluate the quality of your data collection procedure and repeat the study if they so choose.

### Results Section

The results section presents your summary of the data and a description of the statistical tests you used to examine the data. This section, like the method section, should be based on the facts of your specific study. Specifically, you will use this section to lay before the reader the major findings of the research. You can save a more complete interpretation and evaluation of the implications of these findings for your discussion section. The outline of the results section should follow the outline you used to describe the research questions in your Introduction. Begin your results section with the general predictions (hypotheses) you made for your study. For each hypothesis, you can then provide a general description of the results followed by the specific statistical tests used to test your hypothesis.

As a side note, there is no reason why you must absolutely stick to the path implied by your introduction. If, after carefully examining your data and testing your hypotheses you find interesting patterns in the data that you did not initially expect, you may need to share these insights with readers. These serendipitous results can often reveal interesting perspectives on the phenomenon that you are studying and raise important questions for additional research. These departures from your core proposed study, however, should not cloud your clear testing of your stated hypotheses. For this reason, it is common to reserve such exploratory analyses for the discussion section.

As you prepare your results section, there are a number of editorial issues you must address, including the best way to summarize the data, the level of detail to include, and the best strategy for presenting results from specific statistical tests. By now you should have read a sufficient number of research articles to know that there are many ways to summarize data. Most researchers use a combination of narrative, simple and descriptive statistics, and graphs/figures and tables. Combining these techniques will help the reader quickly understand your primary findings and how the data relate to your research questions. The narrative is relatively straightforward. You describe in words the primary findings of the study with respect to each hypothesis. In many cases, you will find that a table or a graph will do much to augment your description of the data and help the reader visualize the results.

As a general guideline, the use of graphs/figures and tables is reserved for times when you cannot present the same information as efficiently in the narrative text. Another general guideline to keep in mind is that any graph/ figure or table should be able to stand on its own. This means that the title, labels, and descriptive notes provided with each graph/figure or table should be sufficiently detailed that a reader can examine this component

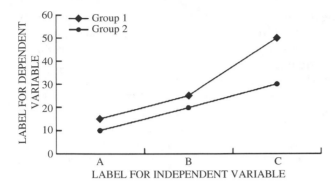

**Figure 5.2**

**Line Graph and the Essential Elements Contained in any Scientific Graph**

and understand it without having to refer back to other portions of the manuscript.

### Graphs

Most statistics textbooks have extensive reviews of how to prepare good-quality scientific graphs. Therefore, we will only highlight the essentials of a good graph. Figure 5.2 presents a prototype of a good graph. Graphs for research reports have several distinguishing features. The first significant feature is simplicity. Good graphs contain only essential visual information and are free of distracting and unessential information. For example, many popular computer programs allow you to use three-dimensional effects, fancy shading, and other features that add little information to the graph and can make the graph difficult to interpret.

Consider also Figure 5.3, which contains many unnecessary and distracting elements. Tufte (1983) called much of the unnecessary graphic elements in this graph *chartjunk*. Chartjunk refers to anything in the graph that adds nothing to the interpretation of the data.

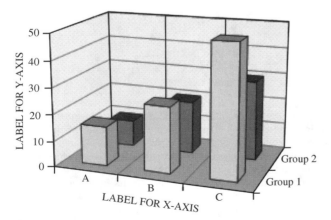

**Figure 5.3**

**Graph with Much Chartjunk**

The 3-D effect, shading, and background grid are unnecessary elements of the graph that are distracting and should not be used.

For example, the three-dimensional effect adds nothing to the display of the information. We find Figure 5.2 far easier to interpret than Figure 5.3. In general, APA-style graphs/figures should be drawn in two dimensions and be as simple as possible. Other conventions include that the vertical or Y-axis presents the dependent variable, whereas the horizontal or X-axis presents an independent variable. The lines or bars in the graph should clearly represent the pattern of the data and not be confused with distracting information. There is considerable art and science in constructing good graphs, far more than we can present here. If you want to learn more about preparing good scientific graphs, we strongly recommend that you check out Kosslyn (1994), Tufte (1983, 1990), and Wainer (1997). These authors make clear that graphs have a grammar, syntax, and style of their own.

The most commonly used graphs are bar graphs, scatter plots, and line graphs. Figure 5.4 presents an illustration of each. Use bar graphs when the independent variable represents a nominal or categorical scale. Scatter plots present the correlation between two variables. Finally, line graphs present the relation among two or more quantitative variables that are typically

# Figure 5.4

**(a) Bar Graph,**
**(b) Scatter Plot, and**
**(c) Line Graph**

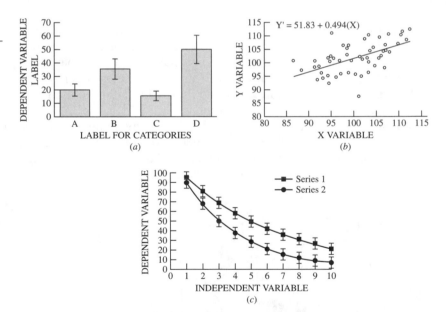

For the bar graph, the heights of the bars represent the statistic used to describe the dependent variable. The lines extending from the bars are optional and represent the standard error of the mean or some other measure of variability that helps the reader interpret the difference among the means. For the scatter plot, each dot represents the two observations recorded for each participant. The regression line drawn through the data is optional. If you include the regression line, you should also include the equation that defines its intercept and slope. For the line graph, each point on each line represents the statistic used to describe the dependent variable. The lines extending from each point are optional and represent the standard error of the mean or some other measure of variability that will help the reader interpret the difference among the groups.

continuous in nature. For scatter plots, each dot represents the two scores measured for each participant. In Figure 5.4(b), we have added a regression line to help the reader see the relation between the two variables. This addition is optional. Use the option only when you believe that it helps the reader understand the data. For the bar graph and the line graph, the data represent the descriptive statistic used to summarize the dependent variable. If the reported statistic is the mean, you can add error lines that represent the standard error of the mean. This additional information can help the reader determine which group means are statistically different from other means.

### Tables

Graphs and figures present pictures that allow us to quickly interpret the results of the data. Although graphs are useful as a research tool, there are many times when we need to present numbers. Constructing useful and easy-to-read tables is like constructing good graphs. There are some simple rules to follow that will help you present your data well; for starters we will highlight Ehrenberg's (1977) six basic features for constructing good tables.

First, round the numbers in your table to a meaningful value. In APA style, it is a convention to round most numbers to two decimal points, unless additional precision is necessary. Second, if possible, include row and column averages or totals. These summary statistics help the reader discern general trends in the data and differences among groups. A third consideration is to orient the most important data within the columns. Readers find it easier to scan a column of numbers than to scan a row of numbers. Another helpful tip is to rank the data from largest to smallest or smallest to largest, if appropriate. Ranking the data helps the reader find the extremes in the data. The fifth recommendation is to keep row-and-column spacing relatively constant. This is easy to do within most popular computer word-processing or spreadsheet programs. Remember also that all the text in your APA-style manuscript should be double-spaced. This rule generally applies to tables as well (although some journals are relaxing this thanks to the powers of current word-processing and graphics programs and their influence on current publishing techniques). Finally, use tables only when it is essential to present the quantitative data or when there is no alternative for presenting the data.

Table 5.3 presents an example of an APA-style table. The table presents the proportion of men and women who reported different forms of cheating. Each row represents the target behavior. The table includes the proportions and the result of the test for the difference between the proportions. This table allows the researcher to present much information in a concise format.

### Reporting Statistics

Once you have described the general results, you then need to present the statistical tests that justify your observations. Because your audience

## Table 5.3  APA-Style Table

**Table 1** *Proportion of different forms of cheating reported by men and women*

| Form of Cheating | Men[a] | Women[b] | Difference Between Proportions |
|---|---|---|---|
| Cheat on a test | 0.28 | 0.16 | $z = 1.75, p < .05$ |
| Plagiarize in a paper | 0.21 | 0.24 | $z = -0.32, p > .05$ |
| Copy homework | 0.38 | 0.33 | $z = 0.58, p > .05$ |

*Note.* [a]$n = 48$, [b]$n = 124$.

consists of fellow researchers, you need only indicate which statistical tests you conducted and the results of the analysis. As with all other parts of the paper, you will present the statistical results in narrative form. The general format is to indicate the statistic that you used and then describe the outcome.

Consider the following example from an experiment conducted by Eisenberger and Armeli (1997):

> *The average originality of each group's drawings is shown in Figure 1. . . . Planned comparisons revealed the large monetary reward for high divergent thought produced more creative drawings than either no reward or a small reward for high divergent thought, $t(281) = 2.57, p = .005$, and $t(281) = 2.25, p = .025$, respectively. Further, the large reward for high divergent thought produced subsequent drawings of greater originality than did the same reward for low divergent thought, $t(281) = 3.32, p = .001$. (p. 657)*

Notice how the authors stated their conclusion and then indicated the statistical test that supported their claim. Eisenberger and Armeli used a *t*-ratio for the inferential statistic. The report of the statistic included the degrees of freedom (281 in this example), the observed *t*-ratio, and the probability of the *t*-ratio being due to chance. They did not explain the meaning of the *t*-ratio as they assumed that the reader understands how to interpret this statistical test.

Another important characteristic of the Eisenberger and Armeli (1997) passage is that they chose to report the exact probability of the statistic (e.g., $p = .025$). This is a common practice among many researchers. The alternative is to establish a universal criterion for defining statistical significance and report this if the statistical test meets the criterion. For example, an author may include a sentence similar to the following early in their results section:

> "I used the criterion $\alpha = .05$ to establish statistical significance for all inferential statistics."

Later, in the results section, the writer will use $p < .05$ if the test is statistically significant. Specifically, the author would write, "$t(281) =$

## Table 5.4  Commonly Used Statistics and the Format for Presenting Them in the Text of the Results Section

| Statistics | Presentation in Text[*] |
|---|---|
| *Descriptive* | |
| Mean | $M = 25.67$ |
| Median | $Mdn = 34.56$ |
| Mode | $mode = 45.00$ |
| Standard deviation | $SD = 1.23$ |
| Standard error | $SE = 12.01$ |
| Standard error of measurement | $SEM = 0.98$ |
| | |
| *Inferential* | |
| ANOVA | $F(2,25) = 9.32, p < .05$ |
| Chi-square | $\chi^2\,(4, N = 55) = 34.10, p < .05$ |
| Mann-Whitney $U$ | $U(12,15) = 5.67, p < .05$ |
| Pearson's $r$ | $r(98) = .87, p < .05$ |
| Spearman's $r$ | $r_s(74) = -.95, p < .05$ |
| Student's $t$-ratio | $t(123) = 2.31, p < .05$ |

[*]Use italics to present the abbreviation for the statistic (as illustrated here).

$2.25, p < .05$" rather than "$t(281) = 2.25, p = .025$," even if the statistics software output indicated a $p$-value of .025.

The APA editorial guidelines encourage authors to include measures of effect size, such as $\eta^2$ or $\omega^2$, along with the results of the inferential statistic. Reporting the effect size helps the reader interpret the relation between the independent and dependent variables. Table 5.4 presents a list of commonly used descriptive and inferential statistics and the format for reporting them in the text of the results section. For the inferential statistics, the general format is to use a letter associated with the statistic (e.g., $t$ for a $t$-test ratio and $F$ for an ANOVA), the degrees of freedom, the observed statistic, and the probability of the result being due to chance. Note that you should italicize the letter representing the statistic.

## Discussion Section

During the introduction of the paper, you explain why your research questions were important. In the discussion section, you tell the reader whether your research answers the research questions, and you discuss the implications of your research for future researchers. The following passages come from the discussion section of an article written by Eisenberger and Armeli (1997). The authors began the discussion section with:

*The present findings indicate that the explicit reinforcement of novel performance for salient rewards enhances generalized creative performance without any loss of intrinsic creative interest. . . . [T]he specific requirement of novel performance in one task (generating uses for physical objects) produced greater subsequent creative performance in an entirely different task (drawing a picture) when a large reward, rather than either no reward or a small reward, was used. (p. 659)*

This passage complements the closing sentence of their introduction, wherein Eisenberger and Armeli (1997) described the purpose of their research. Moving on, the scope of the discussion broadens to review the implications of the research. Midway through the discussion section, the authors wrote:

*The results contradict the view that any increase in performance that is due to salient reward produces a countervailing decrease in intrinsic creative interest (e.g., Condry, 1977; Hennessey & Amabil, 1988). According to the overjustification hypothesis (Lepper et al., 1973), expecting reward for creative thinking would change the perceived cause of one's own performance from an interest in creativity to an interest in the reward. (p. 660)*

As you can see, the authors revisited the issues they raised in the introduction. This passage makes clear that the data do not support the consensus view regarding the deleterious effects of reinforcement. By the end of the discussion, Eisenberger and Armeli (1997) concluded:

*Texts in education and business often express the view that creative performance can be increased if course work and jobs are made more intrinsically interesting. This is a laudable goal; however, even the most interesting creative activities require long periods of difficult and unpleasant effort that is necessary for meaningful achievement. The use of periodic salient reward may provide an effective way to help individuals sustain their creative efforts when success comes slowly and with great difficulty. (p. 661)*

We have presented only a glimpse of a longer and tightly reasoned set of arguments. Nevertheless, these passages illustrate the editorial triangle illustrated in Figure 5.5. The first portion of the discussion provides a narrative review of the results as they related to the original research question. Specifically, Eisenberger and Armeli (1997) concluded that their research supported the hypothesis that positive reinforcement will enhance, not reduce, intrinsic interest and performance. Midway through the discussion section, Eisenberger and Armeli (1997) showed how their research contradicts the work of other researchers and theories concerning reinforcement. During this portion of the discussion, the authors presented arguments to convince the reader that their research and conclusions are superior to those of other studies and to show why their results do not agree with other studies.

The closing paragraph makes clear that the results of the research extend well beyond the laboratory. Eisenberger and Armeli (1997) believed that positive reinforcement has many useful applications in many settings. As we noted at the start of the chapter, reading many research articles will help you see how other authors construct their discussion sections as well as other parts of the research reports. When you read research reports, pay

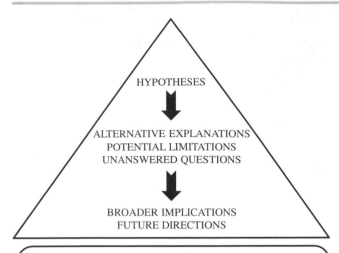

**Figure 5.5**

**Triangle Model of the Discussion**

The discussion begins by focusing on how the analysis of the data relates to the original research questions. Depending on the outcome of the study, the scope of the discussion broadens to consider alternative explanations of the data, potential limitations of the current results, and lingering questions. The discussion ends by considering the reasonable conclusions that one may draw from the research.

attention to the information the authors present in the paper. At the same time, examine how the authors present their ideas. You can learn a lot by studying the writing style of others.

## References Section

The references section identifies the source of each citation you presented in the paper. Box 5.4 presents reference style guidelines and examples for common types of sources used in APA-style papers. The APA manual provides a much more extensive treatment, and updates to common formatting are also posted on the APA main website (www.apa.org). Regardless of the type of source, the order of references is alphabetical, based on authors' last names. You should use the hanging indentation function in your word processor to ensure that the first line of each reference begins at the left margin of the page, but each subsequent line for that reference begins indented .5 inch (as with new paragraphs). The references section, as all other parts of the text, is double-spaced, and there are no extra lines between the citations.

## Box 5.4 Common Reference Section Entries for an APA-style Research Report

**Journal Articles**

*Single author:*

Flora, S. R. (1990). Undermining intrinsic interest from the standpoint of a behaviorist. *Psychological Record, 40*(2), 323–346.

Zimmerman, B. J. (1985). The development of "intrinsic" motivation: A social learning analysis. *Annals of Child Development, 2,* 117–160.

*Multiple authors:*

Balsam, D. P., & Bondy, A. S. (1983). The negative side effects of reward. *Journal of Applied Behavior Analysis, 16,* 283–296.

Hatano, G., Sigler, R. S., Richards, D. D., Inagaki, K., Stavy, R., & Wax, N. (1993). The development of biological knowledge: A multi-national study. *Cognitive Development, 8,* 47–62.

*Notes:*

- Capitalize the first letter of the first word in the title of the article and of the first word following a colon.
- Capitalize the first letter of each word in the name of the journal.
- Italicize the title of the journal, the volume number, and commas.
- If there are six or more authors, use the first author's name and "et al." even with the first citation in the text (e.g.,"Hatano et al. (1993) examined . . . ").

**Books**

*Single author:*

Amabile, T. M. (1983). *The social psychology of creativity.* New York: Springer-Verlag.

Toothaker, L. E. (1993). *Multiple comparison procedures.* Newbury Park, CA: Sage.

*Multiple authors:*

Tegano, D. W., Moran, J. D., & Sawyers, J. K. (1991). *Creativity in early childhood classrooms.* Washington, DC: National Educational Association.

*Notes:*

- Capitalize the first letter of the first word in the title of the article and of the first word following a colon.
- Italicize the title of the book.
- If the location of the publisher is not well known (e.g., Newbury Park), list the state.

**Electronic sources:**

APA published an addendum to the standard style manual in 2007, focused entirely on electronic sources (i.e., those that are available mainly through the internet). This document is freely available via the internet and includes specific guidelines for citing documents using Digital Object Identifier (DOI) codes when available, as well as proper format for citing electronic books and journal articles retrieved from online. Here are a couple of general examples:

*(Continued)*

Hopkins, S. M., & Weathington, B. L. (2006). The relationships between justice perceptions, trust, and employee attitudes in a downsized organization. *The Journal of Psychology: Interdisciplinary and Applied*, *140*(5), 477–498. doi: 10.3200/JRLP.140.5.477-498.

*Notes:*

- Include a doi if the article has one and is therefore considered final. Otherwise, report the url from which you downloaded the source.
- If the article is not final, or if its status is unclear, include the date on which you accessed it, as well as the full url for the download.

**Reprint of a classic text:**

Locke, J. (1964). *An essay concerning human understanding*. (A. D. Woozley, Ed.). Cleveland: Meridian Books. (Original work published 1690)

**Translation of a book:**

Freud, S. (1961). *Civilization and its discontents*. (J. Strachy, Trans.). New York: Norton. (Original work published 1930)

*Notes:*

- For the text citation, indicate the original and new publication dates. For example, use Locke (1690/1964) or Freud (1930/1961).

**Book chapter:**

Asher, S. R., & Hymel, S. (1981). Children's social competence in peer relations: Sociometric and behavioral assessment. In J. K. Wine & M. D. Smye (Eds.), *Social competence* (pp. 125–157). New York: Guilford Press.

*Corporate author:*

American Psychological Association (2001). *Publication manual of the American Psychological Association* (5th ed.). Washington, DC: Author.

**Magazines and Newspapers**

*Magazine:*

Lemonick, M. D. (1999, October 4). Smart genes? *Time, 154*, (11), 54–58.

*Newspaper article*

Ray, B. (1999, November 5). Domestic violence growing concern in mid-Ohio valley. *The Marietta Times*, p. A1.

*Newspaper article, no author:*

Seniors unimpressed with GOP Congress. (1999, November 4). *The Marietta Times*, p. A3.

**Other Sources**

*Computer program:*

Allen, J. D., & Pittenger, D. J. (2000). Statistics Tutor (2nd ed.) [Computer software]. New York: Wiley.

*Internet website:*

National Alliance for the Mentally Ill (November, 1999). Schizophrenia. Retrieved 11/17/1999 from National Alliance for the Mentally Ill: (http://www.nami.org/disorder/990305b.html).

### Appendix

The appendix is an optional portion of the paper and is used to present detailed information that is not appropriate for presentation in the main body of the manuscript. For example, if you created a specialized survey or questionnaire for your research, you might want to include a copy of the instrument in the appendix.

### Author Note

The author note serves several functions. It includes your mailing address and other information indicating how readers can correspond with you. You can also use the author note to acknowledge grants or fellowships that may have funded your work, and the help you received from colleagues who helped you with portions of the research. In addition, if the manuscript includes material that you have presented in other venues, you should acknowledge that presentation. For example, many authors present portions of their research at professional conferences before they attempt to publish the results in a journal. The exact location of this information usually depends on the specific journal or outlet, but in general, APA guidelines suggest that it fall here in the placement of other sections of the text.

### Tables

Unless the manuscript is a finished draft, for example, a thesis or dissertation, we do not include tables in the body of the text. Instead, each table is printed on a separate page that is included after the author note section. Be sure that you double-space the entire text of the table and make them as legible as possible. It is also a good idea to avoid too many vertical lines as they can be difficult for publishers to recreate.

### Figures

The figures section contains two parts. The first part is a listing of the figure captions or descriptions that pertain to each figure. This page contains the text for the figure caption of each figure. The individual figures are then included, one per page, following the figure captions, in the order in which the figure captions are presented. The pages containing the figures are the only pages that do not include the running head and page number. Traditional APA guidelines suggest that to identify the figure you should print on the reverse side of the figure a short version of the title, the figure number, and the word *TOP* at the top of the page. This is a good habit to practice, though as with some of the other details regarding tables, figures/ graphs, and appendices, you will need to check with each journal or publisher for any special instructions or other options.

# Proofreading

Few of us can sit down and write a perfect article on our first try (or ever, for that matter). Most authors write and revise their papers several times before they are satisfied with the work. Therefore, proofreading is an essential component of good writing. Now, for the bad news and the good news: The bad news is that proofreading is difficult. It is easy to overlook mistakes in your own writing. The good news is that there are many resources you can use to proofread and correct your work.

## Computer Programs

Most word processors have built-in spelling and grammar checkers. These are useful features, but they have many limitations. For example, spell-checking programs will identify any word as misspelled if it is not in the software's dictionary. This is a problem with many of the field-specific terms associated with any social science discipline. In addition, although this feature can help you to ensure all basic words are spelled correctly, it cannot determine whether you used the correct word in the correct way. For example, you could correctly spell *chose* when you should have written *choose*.

The same advantages and disadvantages apply to software-based grammar checkers. Grammar checkers catch obvious errors and often skip others. For example, my word processor's grammar checker quickly catches passive voice, subject–verb agreement problems, and other common errors. The program also ignores some real whoppers. Consider the following sentences:

> "The green bachelor's wife snored furiously against the winter of our discontent."

> "May grammars checker does no catch errors a frequently an I wants it too."

Our grammar checkers found no problem with either sentence, and indicated that they were easy to read. You, by contrast, should see immediately that both sentences are gibberish. The implications of this example are clear. Spelling and grammar checkers can help you as long as you recognize the limits of these tools and that there are superior methods for proofreading your work.

One very helpful, but underused, tactic is to read your paper aloud to yourself or whomever else might listen. Read it as if you were giving a speech. In most cases, you will quickly hear the faults. Missing words will become apparent, awkward phrases will stand out, and vague language will sound obscure. As you read your paper, mark and revise any awkward phrases or words. Another tactic is to ask someone else you trust to read your paper. Most colleges and universities have a writing resource center. Typically, the staff will gladly proofread your paper for clarity and style. Although they may know nothing about your topic, they can adopt the role of your intended audience. Therefore, they will point out parts of your paper that are not clear and that require refinement.

## Chapter Summary

This chapter provided an overview of the writing process for technical research reports. The guiding framework was APA style, which is the norm for all psychological and most social science publications. We worked through basic elements of APA style, including the various components of a complete research report. Also discussed were issues of integrity in reporting of research. Finally, tips were provided to improve basic proofreading abilities prior to the finalization of any research report. Embedded examples can be mimicked when producing your own research report, to ensure you are in line with appropriate reporting style.

## Chapter References

Allumbaugh, D. L., & Hoyt, W. T. (1999). Effectiveness of grief therapy: A meta-analysis. *Journal of Counseling Psychology, 46*, 370–380.

American Psychological Association (2007). *APA style guide to electronic references.* Washington, DC: Author.

American Psychological Association (2009). *Publication manual of the American Psychological Association* (6th ed.). Washington, DC: Author.

Braver, M.C.W., & Braver, S. L. (1988). Statistical treatment of the Solomon four-group design: A meta-analytic approach. *Psychological Bulletin, 104*, 150–154.

Ehrenberg, A.S.C. (1977). Rudiments of numeracy. *Journal of the Royal Statistical Society A, 140*(Pt. 3), 277–297.

Eisenberger, R., & Armeli, S. (1997). Can salient reward increase creative performance without reducing intrinsic creative interest? *Journal of Personality and Social Psychology, 72*, 652–663.

Eisenberger, R., & Cameron, J. (1996). *Detrimental effects of reward: Reality or myth? American Psychologist, 51*, 1153–1166.

Kohn, A. (1990). *You know that they say* . . . New York: Harper Collins.

Kohn, A. (1993). *Punished by rewards: The trouble with gold stars, incentive plans, A's, praise, and other bribes.* Boston: Houghton Mifflin.

Kohn, A. (2000). *The case against standardized testing: raising the scores, ruining the schools.* Portsmouth, NH: Heinemann.

Kosslyn, S. M. (1994). *Elements of graph design.* New York: Freeman.

Runyon, R. P., Coleman, K. A., & Pittenger, D. J. (2000). *Fundamentals of behavioral statistics* (9th ed.). New York: McGraw-Hill.

Strunk, W., & White, E. B. (1979). *The elements of style* (3rd ed.). New York: Macmillan.

Tufte, E. R. (1983). *The visual display of quantitative information.* Cheshire, CT: Graphics Press.

Tufte, E. R. (1990). *Envisioning information.* Cheshire, CT: Graphics Press.

Twain, M. (1986/1876). *The adventures of Huckleberry Finn.* New York: Penguin.

Wainer, H. (1997). *Visual revelations: Graphical tales of fate and deception from Napoleon Bonaparte to Ross Perot.* New York: Springer-Verlag.

# Chapter 6
# Reviewing the Literature and Forming Hypotheses

> Libraries are reservoirs of strength, grace and wit, reminders of order, calm and continuity, lakes of mental energy, neither warm nor cold, light nor dark. The pleasure they give is steady, unorgastic, reliable, deep and long-lasting. In any library in the world, I am at home, unselfconscious, still and absorbed.
>
> —Germaine Greer

## Introduction

In this chapter we will review how to use the library and other resources to find information. In addition, we will examine how researchers share information with others and how you can find information to help you design your research project. Learning these skills will help you develop ideas for your research hypotheses. The second half of the chapter will introduce you to the concept of statistical inference as well as forming and testing hypotheses.

## Bibliographic Research

To paraphrase an age-old riddle: *If a scientist conducts an experiment, but does not share the results, did the research really happen?* Progress in the sciences occurs because researchers share their work with others. As you learned in Chapter 1, almost all research evolves from previous research. You also learned that no research study by itself offers complete and final answers. At best, a good study will answer one or two questions. However, a good study will raise as many questions as it solves. Reading what others have discovered allows us to know how we should proceed with our research.

You can develop a research hypothesis by reading current research papers. As you learn more about a particular topic, you may find unanswered interesting questions that require additional research. At the same time, you may find that you have a different way of looking at a problem. This chapter will help you learn where to get the best and most current information related to contemporary research in the behavioral sciences. In the first section, we will consider three levels of bibliographic sources called *tertiary*, *secondary*, and *primary* sources. Each has a different role in your bibliographic research.

## Tertiary Bibliographic Sources

**Tertiary bibliographic sources** (also called *third-level* sources) provide the most general and nontechnical review of a topic. Almost all textbooks and articles in popular newspapers or magazines are examples of tertiary sources. The essential feature of tertiary sources is their generality and casual review of a topic. Unfortunately, the authors of these sources do not have the luxury of time and space to review the topic in detail. For example, consider an introductory psychology textbook. In a book of several hundred pages, the author(s) will probably dedicate only a few pages to attitudes and behavior, a popular topic in social psychology. If you take an advanced course in social psychology, you may find that the author of the textbook will devote a whole chapter to attitudes. You may also find whole books that exclusively examine attitudes.

Authors of general textbooks must review a nearly inexhaustible amount of information quickly and for readers not particularly familiar with the topic. Therefore, the advantage of a textbook is that it gives you a quick and easy-to-understand introduction to a topic. This advantage is also its limitation. Textbook authors review the topics already well understood and typically do not discuss current trends in research. Although authors work hard to keep their books current and accurate, several years can pass between a new discovery and its description in a textbook.

Dictionaries and encyclopedias are also tertiary sources. As with textbooks, these sources have a specific but limited function. These sources are useful to someone who wants a quick answer for a general question and does not have the time and inclination to investigate a topic at length. You should not use textbooks, dictionaries, or encyclopedias as authorities on a topic. Although they may help you understand the meaning of specific terms or psychological phenomena, they are too general to serve as the foundation of your research. When you write a research paper, you will most likely use primary and secondary sources.

## Secondary Bibliographic Sources

As you can infer from the name, **secondary bibliographic sources** stand between tertiary and primary sources. Secondary sources are more in-depth than textbooks or other tertiary sources. In general, secondary sources are comprehensive reviews and are written by an expert on the topic. There are many outlets for secondary sources. The two categories that we will review are books and literature reviews.

Each year, many researchers publish insightful and useful commentaries on different phenomena, often in the form of specialized books in a given field of interest. For example, many textbooks dealing with human behavior review Pavlov's classic conditioning experiments. Textbooks dedicated to learning may devote four or five chapters to various topics related to classical conditioning. By contrast, a secondary source book may exclusively review a single topic within classical conditioning or review the state of the art regarding current theories and trends in research.

There are limitations with secondary sources. Although secondary sources offer more focused reviews than textbooks, they are still less focused than primary sources. In addition, there remains the time lag between the publication of primary sources and their discussion in secondary sources. Although secondary sources tend to be more up-to-date than textbooks, nothing is as current as a primary resource.

A literature review shares some features with focused books and other secondary sources. There are some important differences, however. First, you will find most literature reviews published in specialized professional journals. Second, literature reviews tend to be more topic-specific. Like secondary sources, literature reviews provide a comprehensive summary of the current research. The author or authors summarize the relevant research reports and then describe the important factors or variables that explain the phenomenon.

There are several good sources of literature reviews. In most fields of study you will find journals that publish mostly literature reviews. For example, the American Psychological Association publishes the journal *Psychological Bulletin*, which includes nothing but literature reviews. Many psychologists consider *Psychology Bulletin* to be a premier journal that has a well-deserved reputation for publishing some of the best and most influential reviews of psychological research. You will also find that other journals will publish a combination of original research articles and literature reviews.

Another valuable resource is the "annual review" books published by Annual Reviews (www.annualreviews.org). These books are focused on specific fields like anthropology, economics, psychology, and sociology. Although these reviews tend to be broader than literature reviews published in scientific journals, they are a good resource to help you learn more about a specific topic.

## Primary Bibliographic Sources

**Primary bibliographic sources** are the original research reports that you will find published in research journals. A **research journal** is a special type of magazine that publishes scientific research articles. Many professional societies publish journals. For example, the American Psychological Association, the American Sociological Association, the Association for Psychological Science, the Psychonomic Society, and the Society for Research on Child Development (to name only a few professional societies) each publish one or more scholarly journals. In other cases, corporations publish scholarly journals. In all cases, the editorial board of these journals consists of prominent researchers in the field. You will find that these journals list the names and academic affiliation of the editorial board, and that the editors are well-regarded professionals working in academic or other professional institutions.

Research articles represent the greatest level of focus and detail of all the bibliographic sources. The advantage of the primary source is that there is no filtering of information. For other sources, the author must condense and remove much critical information to keep the review short and focused. Consequently, you may not learn everything about a particular experiment even when you read a secondary source. Thus, only the primary source will provide a detailed account of the research methods, the data analysis, and the complete research results.

Although primary sources contain a considerable amount of information, the reading is sometimes difficult. Professional researchers use the primary resource to communicate with other researchers. Therefore, you will find the primary source filled with pages of technical language. Don't despair! Any person who can gain entry into college can read and understand original research articles.

### Peer Review

Before moving on, we want to comment on an important characteristic of research journals and professional books, **peer review**. The goal of the peer review process is to filter out bad research and make the good research as clear and compelling as possible. Peer review is a part of the normal editing process during which experts read a manuscript to ensure that the researchers used appropriate methods to collect and analyze the data, and then made reasonable inferences from the data.

When a researcher submits a manuscript to a scientific journal, the editor will ask other researchers, who are experts in the area, to read and comment on the merits of the report. Using the reviewers' comments, the editor can reject the manuscript, require that the author revise it, or accept it for publication. If the editor accepts the manuscript for publication, it means that the reviewers and editor agreed that the study met the basic requirements for sound scientific research and that other researchers will be interested in the paper.

Although the peer review system works well, errors can and do occur. There are cases of poorly designed research or faulty conclusions finding their way into the published literature. Similarly, one editor will sometimes reject important and insightful research that another editor will publish. The peer review process involves a large subjective component that no amount of tinkering can remove. Despite its flaws, the peer review system does have a very important essential feature; it is self-correcting.

Sometimes, published articles become the center of considerable controversy. As a part of this controversy, many question whether the peer review system works. In 1998, the journal *Psychological Bulletin* published the article, "A Meta-analytic Examination of Assumed Properties of Child Sexual Abuse Using College Samples" (Rind, Tromovitch, & Bauserman, 1998). Some readers, especially several politically motivated individuals, objected to the article, arguing that its authors advocated pedophilia. (The authors made no such claim. Rather, they argued that several commonly held beliefs regarding the effects of pedophilia are not accurate and required clarification.)

In response to intense political pressure, the American Psychological Association (APA) requested that the American Association for the Advancement of Science (AAAS) conduct an independent review of the peer review process that the journal had used in evaluating the original article. The AAAS declined the request. In their letter to the APA, the AAAS noted that,

> We see no reason to second-guess the process of peer review used by the APA journal in its decision to publish the article in question. While not without its imperfections, peer review is well established as a standard mechanism for maintaining the flow of scientific information that scientists can refer to, critique, or build on *[italics added]* . . . . *Uncovering [a problem with a manuscript is] the task of those reviewing it prior to publication* [and] to the reader of the published article *[italics added]*. . . .  (Lerch, 1999)

The AAAS offered an important message in their response. Science depends on an open and free exchange of ideas. The peer review process should be a filter for faulty and flawed work but should not become a barrier that censors challenging or unpopular ideas. Furthermore, the reader has the ultimate responsibility to think critically about the information and conclusions presented in any published article. You, as the reader, must assume the responsibility to analyze and critique the ideas presented in a published article.

Errors in the published literature do not last long. If an author publishes a paper with an error, other researchers will be quick to note the mistake. In most cases, when researchers disagree with the findings printed in an article, they will conduct research to support an alternative perspective or interpretation. The researcher will then put the new results into the publication cycle. Therefore, bad ideas, poor research, and faulty inferences do not last long in the scientific community. Researchers quickly ignore and forget findings and conclusions that cannot withstand the scrutiny of systematic and direct replication. In the same vein, novel and unique results that researchers can replicate receive considerable attention in the research community.

## The Internet

Although many people find the Internet a fascinating and interesting resource, it has limitations. First, there is no peer review for the vast majority of Internet web pages. There are currently few, if any, restrictions on what one may post on a web page. In many ways, the Internet is the modern soapbox. Any person can publish his or her ideas on the Internet without fear of censorship, a constitutional right for all Americans.

The second problem with the Internet is that it is an ever-changing medium with no permanent record. Books, journals, and other print media are tangible, permanent products. There is no equivalent for web pages. This is why most guidelines for citing material from the Internet require both the address of the website and the date the material was downloaded.

Although the Internet is a wonderful resource, you should use it with care and a strong dose of skepticism. You cannot trust everything you read on the Internet. In fact, you should be careful with everything you read, regardless of its source. There are some important differences, however, between what you will find on the Internet and in professional journals. This raises the question, "How should we use the Internet?"

### Click, Check, and Double-Check

If you use the Internet, you should be aware of some things. First, search engines and subject directories are not complete and exhaustive reviews of current web pages (Brandt, 1996, 1997). Therefore, when you are searching the Internet, you should recognize that a search will be incomplete and that different search engines will produce different results. Second, you should be cautious about the material you find on the Web. As with any research project, you should not rely on one source of information. When you read something, from the Internet or some other source, you need to determine whether the information is credible. Here are a few tips you should follow as you examine a web page:

- *Check the credentials of the author.* Be skeptical of web pages that have no clearly identified author or if the author does nothing to indicate his or her credentials or professional affiliation.

- *Check how well the author annotates the web page.* If the web page contains lots of claims and conclusions but no supporting information, be suspicious. Serious authors include a bibliography with their text. The bibliography allows the reader to double-check the original sources to ensure that the author has presented the information accurately. You should use this practice for any information you use, Internet or print.

- *When in doubt, doubt.* There is an old saying about free advice—you get what you pay for. You should not rely on a web page as your primary source of information. Find corroborating evidence from other sources before you make an assertion and run the risk of embarrassing yourself with incorrect information.

- *Print a copy of the web page.* If you plan to use information from a web page, it is a good practice to print a copy of the web page. This tactic will allow you to have a permanent record of the information in case the author revises or removes the material from the Internet or if your reader wants to read the reference.

# Developing a Search Strategy

A common observation is that there are more scientists living now than at any time in history. This is especially true in the social sciences. In psychology alone, more than 4,000 people receive their Ph.D. every year. Furthermore, there are at least 1,700 journals directly and indirectly related to psychology. If we use a conservative estimate that each journal publishes 500 pages a year, then there are 850,000 psychology journal pages published each year! Additionally, it is very common for researchers to publish in journals outside their major area of expertise. Human behavior and interaction is complicated and it is becoming increasingly recognized that cross-disciplinary collaboration is needed to address many research questions. This means there is an incredible amount of information available across all of the social sciences and you will need to develop a strategy for finding articles that interest you.

## Find a Topic That Interests You

What topics do you find fascinating? Can you remember reading about an experiment in one of your courses and thinking that it was interesting? If you are looking for a research topic, it is a good idea to begin with your interests. Sometimes, when beginning a research project it is useful to sit down as a group and talk about the topic areas group members find interesting. As you and your colleagues talk, you may find that you have common questions about why people behave as they do. Another way to find interesting topics is to read textbooks. Chances are that you will find one or more interesting topics for your research.

## Read Tertiary and Secondary Sources

Once you find a topic that you find interesting, keep reading. Begin with tertiary sources; they are the easiest to read and offer the broadest coverage. Assume, for example, that you want to learn more about altruistic behavior. As you read the general sources, you may find that altruism is a broad topic and that it includes many subcomponents. While you are reading, take note of several things. Specifically, look for specialized terms, researcher's names, notable experiments, important independent and dependent variables, and recommendations for new research. This information will help you later when you begin to search the primary literature.

## Specialized Terms

Specialized words or phrases are important because they often describe specific aspects of research. If you read a chapter on altruistic behavior, you are likely to read terms such as *diffusion of responsibility*, *empathic concern*, *negative-state relief*, and *norm reciprocity*. Any one of these concepts can serve as a focal point for research on altruism. Consider *empathic concern* as an example. The phrase refers to feelings of pity for another person in distress. We can ask many empirical questions about this concept:

- Are there ways to increase and decrease the level of empathic concern that people experience, and how do these changes affect helping behavior?
- Are people more likely to feel empathic concern for people like themselves?
- Are people more likely to feel empathic concern if they feel good about themselves or are happy?

### Researchers' Names

When searching for information on a topic, why not look for people who seem to be doing the interesting research? From our reading on altruism, we have learned that Batson is a leading researcher on helping behavior. We also learned that Cialdinei, Dovidio, Schroeder, and Sibicky are other researchers who have conducted innovative studies on helping behavior. Therefore, we will want to see whether these people have done additional research on the topic.

### Notable Experiments

You will often find reference to one or more classic experiments in tertiary reviews. It is a good idea to read these articles, as they provide a historical context for the current research. If you wanted to study helping behavior, for example, you might want to read Darley and Latané's (1968) research on the diffusion of responsibility phenomenon. You may also want to find a literature review on the topic. For example, Latané and Nida (1981) reviewed the literature on the diffusion of responsibility research and found that many researchers have verified Darley and Latané's conclusion. This background reading may help you understand the purpose of more recent research.

### Talk to Your Instructors

Another good source of information is to talk with your professors about your interests. Faculty typically enjoy talking about their research. As you talk about your interests, your professor may be able to give you invaluable guidance by recommending additional readings or by helping you refine your research questions.

## Searching the Literature: The Library

Many people have the misconception that a library is simply a place that stores books. This is a gross oversimplification. A library is a place to find information. Furthermore, size does not matter; access to information is the essential service of any contemporary library. Even if the physical space of a library is small, via the Internet, interlibrary loan, and other sources it is typically possible in time to obtain any piece of published information that you desire. All you need to do is learn how to ask the right questions. Thus, the focus of this section will be to examine the resources typically found in a college library.

## Library Staff

It has been our experience that students typically overlook one of the greatest resources in the library, the professional staff. All libraries use complex storage and retrieval systems that allow librarians to store and find information efficiently. Librarians have a master of science degree in library science, which means that they know a lot about how to find information. Many librarians also have an additional master's degree in a specialized academic area. At a large university, there may be a reference librarian for each general subject matter.

## Search Tools

Most libraries now offer many computer tools to conduct professional searches. The chances are that your college subscribes to several specialized search tools such as *Proquest*©, *PsycInfo*©, *ERIC*©, and others. These specialized search tools allow you to find specific research articles quickly.

## Online Catalog

All libraries keep their bibliographic material in a well-organized system that you can use to find information quickly. Specifically, most colleges use the Library of Congress classification scheme that uses a combination of letters and numbers to classify each book, document, and other materials such as films and records. This complete set of numbers and letters is the **call number**. Each book, journal, recording, and other reference in the library has a unique call number.

Because the social sciences are a broad and interdisciplinary subject, you will find many related books spread throughout the library. For instance, librarians place books on abnormal psychology, or psychopathology, in the internal medicine section (RC) and books on animal behavior in the zoology section (QL). Therefore, you can expect to roam throughout the entire library as you search for bits of information.

Most colleges allow you to search for books using an online catalog. There are many different catalog systems, too many to describe in detail. The common feature of these systems is that you can search by the author's name, the title of the book, the topic, or a keyword. Most students find that these systems are easy to use and provide much useful information. For example, most systems will indicate whether the book you want is on the shelf or has been checked out. In some cases, you can use the program to browse through the titles on the same shelf. This is a useful feature. Because the librarians store the books in logical categories, you might find surrounding books that are interesting and related to your research topic.

### PsycInfo

There are many other databases to which your library may have access. Additionally, any computer with a connection to the Internet will have access to *Google Scholar*™. Each of these databases differs slightly in terms of content and format. However, they all have similarities, and learning to use one database will help you with using all of them. One of the most common and popular of these databases is *PsycInfo*; we will discuss it in more depth here as a proxy and example of how to use a research database.

*PsycInfo* is a comprehensive database that contains references to books and to more than 1,700 journals. Therefore, *PsycInfo* is a powerful research tool that gives you access to much of the most recent research related to psychology. Using this system, you can find research articles and literature reviews on specific topics.

Each college and university has a slightly different way of gaining access to the *PsycInfo* database. The following information will apply regardless of the system you use. Ask the reference librarian to show you how to use the resource if you have questions.

*PsycInfo* allows you to search the database using commonly used words or keywords. A **keyword** can be any term or phrase you want to use for the search. It can be a commonly used word or a technical term used by psychologists to describe a specific phenomenon. You can also use **Boolean operators** to condition your search. The two primary Boolean operators that you will use are **AND** and **OR**. For the sake of an example, assume that you are interested in learning more about eating disorders such as anorexia nervosa and bulimia and their treatment. You can use the terms *anorexia nervosa*, *bulimia*, and *treatment* as keywords.

The AND operator causes the search process to collect references that contain two or more keywords. Therefore, the AND operator is a fast way to scale down the number of references in a search. In some cases, it is useful to increase the breadth of the search and examine more rather than fewer topics. In this case, the OR operator is useful. The OR operator causes the search process to collect references that contain any combination of the key words. To summarize, AND *decreases* the number of articles included in the search, whereas OR *increases* the number of articles.

### Thesaurus

You may be wondering what keywords you should use. There are two answers to this question. First, if you followed our previous recommendations, you will read tertiary and secondary texts and note terms that the authors used to describe the phenomenon you want to study. The second answer is to use a thesaurus. For example, all of the keywords used to classify articles in *PsycInfo* are listed in the *Thesaurus of Psychological Index*

*Terms* (American Psychological Association, 2007). If you are having trouble conducting your search, such as getting too many unrelated references or not enough relevant references, you should use the thesaurus relevant to the search engine you are using to find and select alternative keywords. Using the thesaurus will help you to select the most representative articles. Each entry of the thesaurus has a brief definition of the term and a series of related terms.

### *PsycInfo* Fields

Each entry in the *PsycInfo* database consists of a number of fields. A field represents a specific type of information. There are fields for the title of the article, the author's name, and the journal that published the article. You can use several of these fields to your advantage to help make your search more productive. Consider, for example, the language field. At first glance, this field seems rather trivial until you realize that there are many foreign-language journals. When you conduct a search on a popular topic, it is common to find articles written in Russian, French, German, or Japanese. Therefore, unless you can read these languages, you should filter them out of your search. The easiest way to do this is to use the Advanced Search option and select English in the language field. You can use the same logic and other search strategies to prune your search.

### Practical Matters and *PsycInfo*

There is as much art as there is science to conducting a good search using *PsycInfo*. Much of the success in using this valuable tool comes from planning, practice, and patience. Searching through the *PsycInfo* database is like panning for gold. In some cases, you might have to use many filtering techniques to find the right set of articles. You should not expect to find five great articles in five minutes. Rather, plan to spend quality time at the computer searching for the articles you need. Thanks to the online availability of most journal articles and even some books, it is possible for researchers to quickly amass a large electronic library of materials. These collections of relevant information can be easily transported or managed using a thumb/flash drive or a free Internet-based e-mail account. We urge you to make use of the technology that is available to you, and to become comfortable with your various options for having the necessary research literature at your fingertips whenever you need it. Just be sure you abide by copyright laws when printing or sharing files.

### Selecting Articles

Once you have a list of potential articles, you need to select the articles that you will want to read in detail. The best way to make this judgment is to read the abstract for the article. All articles published in scholarly journals have an abstract that databases such as *PsycInfo* allow you to read. In most cases, the abstract is a short paragraph that describes the purpose or thesis of the article, a brief review of the author's method, and a synopsis of the major findings. Reading the abstract should allow you to determine whether you want to invest the time and energy in reading the entire article.

Reading the abstract provides a fair review of the content of the article. Depending on your interests, you may be willing to read the entire article or move on to the next abstract. If you want to find similar articles, you can use several tricks. Look at the Key Concepts and Keywords fields. These contain words and phrases that characterize this article and that may help you search for similar articles. For example, the phrases "prediction of clinical outcome" and "Treatment Outcomes" combined with "Anorexia Nervosa" may focus your search on those articles that examine the effectiveness of psychotherapies for anorexia nervosa.

## Research in Action: Does Listening to Mozart Make You Smarter?

In this section we will review an experiment conducted by Steele, Ball, and Runk (1997) as an example of how to read a journal article. Steele and his colleagues examined what has now become known as the *Mozart effect*. In essence, some people believe that listening to Mozart's music can help improve one's IQ. Steele et al. conducted an experiment to determine whether they could replicate the effect. We will begin with the introduction of the article.

Begin by reading the text in Box 6.1. The text is the introduction of the Steele et al. (1997) article.

---

### Box 6.1 Introduction from Steele, Ball, and Runk (1997) Experiment

Rauscher, Shaw, and Ky (1993) reported that 36 undergraduates increased their mean spatial reasoning scores the equivalent of 8 or 9 IQ points on portions of the Stanford-Binet Intelligence Scale: Fourth Edition (Thorndike, Hagen, & Sattler, 1986) after listening to 10 min. of Mozart's Sonata for Two Pianos in D Major, K448 (hereafter labeled the "Mozart effect"). The Mozart effect was temporary, having disappeared within 10 to 15 minutes. Rauscher, Shaw, Levine, Ky, and Wright (1994) reported further that short periods of music education in school produced both a temporary effect, immediately after music training, and a permanent increase over a school year in performance by preschool children on the Object Assembly portion of the Wechsler Preschool and Primary Scale of Intelligence–Revised (Wechsler, 1989).

The hypothesis that musical experiences of short duration can have powerful effects on IQ scores on both a short-term and long-term basis is important for both practical and theoretical reasons. However, attempts to replicate the original report by Rauscher et al. (1993) have been unsuccessful. Kenealy and Monsef (1994) were unable to produce a Mozart effect on performance using portions of the Stanford-Binet test, the Paper Folding and Cutting task and the Matrices task. Studies by Newman, Rosenbach, Burns, Latimer, Matocha, and Vogt (1995) and by Stough, Kerkin, Bates, and Mangan (1994) did not yield a Mozart effect when items from the Raven's Progressive Matrices (Raven, 1986) were the dependent measure. Carstens, Huskins, and Hounshell (1995) reported no Mozart effect when the dependent measure was the Revised Minnesota Paper Form Board Test, Form AA (Likert & Quasha, 1948).

*(Continued)*

Rauscher, Shaw, and Ky (1995) have reported a replication of the Mozart effect, using elaborations of the Stanford-Binet Paper Folding and Cutting task as the dependent measure. Further they specified that an appropriate task was one that involved not just spatial recognition but that it should incorporate spatial and temporal transformations. This observation was the basis for the dependent measure used here, a backwards digit span task. A backwards digit span task requires that a person listen to a string of digits and then reproduce them in reverse sequence. Theoretically, the backwards digit task is of interest as a spatial reasoning task because it requires rotation or transformation of the sequence (Carroll, 1993; Das, Kirby, & Jarman, 1979). Empirically, performance scores on this task correlate strongly with scores on memory for designs (Schofield & Ashman, 1986), performance with Raven's Progressive Matrices (Banken, 1985), and is a good predictor of performance with the Rod and Frame task (Haller, 1981). Right-hemisphere dysfunction reduces backwards digit span performance while left-hemisphere dysfunction reduces forward digit span performance (Rapport, Webster, & Dutra, 1994; Rudel & Denckla, 1974), although this difference does not occur in all types of disorders (Gupta, Mahto, Tandon, & Singh, 1986)

## Knowledge Check

1. What is the problem being studied?
2. What is the authors' hypothesis?
3. How was the hypothesis developed?
4. How does this study relate to the problem?
5. What type of research design did Steele et al. use?

Steele et al. (1997) provided a short and clear rationale for their study. They began by reviewing the previous research that has examined the Mozart effect and found that the results are inconsistent. In their review, they noted that several research teams did not replicate the Mozart effect when using different dependent variables. As a part of their review, Steele et al. focused on Rauscher, Shaw, and Ky's (1995) hypothesis that the Mozart effect works when the task incorporates "spatial and temporal transformations" (p. 1180). The focus of this hypothesis provides the foundation for the study. In the last paragraph of the introduction, Steele et al. made clear that they conducted the experiment to determine whether they could replicate the Mozart effect following Rauscher, Shaw, and Ky's (1993) procedures.

The next section is the method section, in which the authors described the people who participated in the study, the materials they used, and the systematic procedures they followed (see Box 6.2).

## Box 6.2  Method Section for Steele, Ball, and Runk (1997) Experiment

**Participants**

Thirty-six Euro-American upper-division university students (28 women and 8 men) from two sections of a psychology course volunteered and received course credit for their participation.

*(Continued)*

(*Continued*)

**Apparatus**

Two stimulus tapes of approximately 10 min. duration were created. One contained the Mozart Sonata for Two Pianos in D Major (K448) and the other contained the sound of a gentle rainstorm ("Spring Showers") from an environmental sounds recording. Sequences of digits were recorded on separate tapes for the digit span task. Tapes were played on a good quality portable system.

**Procedure**

The experiment took place in a room reserved for that purpose. The participant was told that the experiment concerned the effect of relaxation on recall and was instructed to sit in a large, comfortable, recliner chair. The chair faced away from the experimenter who operated the tape player that had been placed on a table by the left arm of the recliner chair.

Each participant listened in turn to the Mozart tape, the rainstorm tape, or sat quietly following the verbal instruction "to relax." The order of stimulus conditions was counterbalanced across participants using a Latin square design. Following exposure to a stimulus condition, each participant listened to three nine-digit sequences. Digits were presented on the tape at the rate of one every 2 sec. After each nine-digit sequence, the participant attempted to repeat that sequence in reverse order. The score recorded was the sum of number correct across the three sequences, the maximum score being 27. Each participant heard nine sequences of digits across the experimental session, three per stimulus condition. Digit sequences were created by a random-number generator and no sequence was repeated in a session to a participant. Three different units of digit sequences were created and assigned in a balanced fashion across participants.

The number of digits correctly recalled in reverse order was recorded for each subject for each condition. A correct recall was defined as the correct digit in the correct serial location. For example, if the original sequence was 7–5–3–1–9 and the recalled sequence was 9–1–3–4–7 then the score would be 4 correct. The Rauscher et al. prediction is that the number of digits correctly reversed in recall should be enhanced in the Mozart condition relative to both the silence and the rainstorm condition.

## Knowledge Check

6. What are the independent and dependent variables?

7. Why do you think that Steele et al. used three conditions?

8. What controls did Steele et al. use to control for confounding variables?

9. Why did Steele et al. use the backwards digit span task?

The next section of the paper is the results section, wherein Steele et al. (1997) offer a narrative account of their analysis of the data. Note how they combine the use of descriptive text, tables of descriptive statistics, and inferential statistics to describe their data (see Box 6.3).

## Box 6.3 Results Section for Steele, Ball, and Runk (1997) Experiment

Table 1 shows three descriptive measures of mean recall on the backwards digit span task. The headings under "Stimulus Condition" show mean performance as a function of the type of stimulus that

(*Continued*)

immediately preceded the recall task. There was no difference overall in mean recall as a function of the preceding stimulus condition, $F(2, 70) = 0.03$, $p = .97$. The outcomes of specific inferential contrasts were consistent with this observation, Music versus Rain, $t(35) = 0.03$, $p = .98$ and Music versus Silence $t(35) = 0.21$, $p = .83$.

The lack of differences in performance among stimulus conditions was not due to unsystematic variability. For example, a clear practice effect overall was observed $F(2, 70) = 21.92$, $p < .001$. Although serial position was completely counterbalanced in stimulus presentation, we calculated performance as a function of serial position. The headings under "Order of Task" in Table 1 give mean recall as a function of the serial position of the stimulus condition. The data indicate that mean recall was improved by additional experience in the task. This observation is confirmed by inferential tests, First versus Second $t(35) = 4.24$, $p < .001$ and Second versus Third $t(35) = 2.41$, $p = .02$.

All three stimulus conditions were administered in a single session as was done by Rauscher et al. (1993). Although the effect of music is supposed to be short-lived, it is possible that there was some carryover effect of music onto the other stimulus conditions or the reverse. Therefore we compared performances after the first stimulus condition only, when there would be no such effects. The headings under "First Stimulus" in Table 6.1 indicate recall following a stimulus condition presented first in the session. Overall there was no significant difference among treatments $F(2, 22) = 1.26$, $p = .30$. The mean recall after music is not different from that after silence, $t(11) = 0.38$, $p = .71$. Although mean recall after the rainstorm condition was lower than after music, the difference was not statistically significant, $t(11) = 1.26$, $p = .23$.

## Table 6.1  Mean Scores on Backwards Digit Span

| Condition | M | SD | n |
|---|---|---|---|
| Stimulus condition | | | |
| Music | 18.53 | 4.14 | 36 |
| Rain | 18.5 | 6.07 | 36 |
| Silence | 18.72 | 5.09 | 36 |
| Order of task | | | |
| First | 15.64 | 4.7 | 36 |
| Second | 19.14 | 4.87 | 36 |
| Third | 20.97 | 4.29 | 36 |
| First stimulus | | | |
| Music | 16.67 | 2.77 | 12 |
| Rain | 14.17 | 5.7 | 12 |
| Silence | 16.08 | 5.13 | 12 |

Note: Maximum score = 27. Number of scores in comparison $n$

## Knowledge Check

10. Did Steele et al. find evidence of the Mozart effect?
11. Why did Steele et al. also examine the "Order of Task" and "First Stimulus" effect?

The final section of the paper is the discussion section, in which the authors review the implication of their research (see Box 6.4).

## Box 6.4 Discussion Section for Steele, Ball, and Runk (1997) Experiment

Exposure for 10 min to a recording of the Mozart Sonata for Two Pianos in D Major (K448) was not followed by an enhancement in performance on a backwards digit span task, a task chosen because it required a temporally extended quasispatial solution as did the paper folding and cutting task. The lack of effect here is inconsistent with the findings of Rauscher et al. (1993, 1994, 1995) but is consistent with reports from other laboratories (Carstens et al., 1995; Kenealy & Monsef, 1994; Newman et al., 1995; Stough et al., 1994). This difference is made more puzzling by the observation that Rauscher et al. have reported large effects in their studies while both Newman et al. (1995) and Stough et al. (1994) conclude confidently that there was no Mozart effect in their experiments. One explanation for the failure of this and other experiments to obtain a Mozart effect could be related to the use of different dependent measures. But different measures cannot be the entire explanation because Kenealy and Monsef (1994) did not obtain a Mozart effect even though they used a paper folding and cutting task as did Rauscher et al. Kenealy and Monsef (1994) used silence as their control condition. Rideout and Laubach (1996) reported recently a positive effect with a paper folding and cutting task but they compared exposure to a Mozart sequence against exposure to a progressive relaxation tape only. The lack of a silence-only control condition means that one cannot state whether listening to Mozart improved performance or listening to the progressive relaxation tape reduced performance. Rauscher et al. (1993) reported a Mozart effect relative to both silence and a relaxation-tape control condition.

   There seems to be some important methodological difference between Rauscher et al.'s work and that of other experimenters that has not yet been elucidated. The nature of this difference constitutes a puzzle since the experimental design seems straightforward. Rauscher et al. (1994) emphasized the potential beneficial effects of increases in time and money allocated to music education in the grade-school curriculum. These practical considerations add to the importance of the solution of this scientific puzzle.

## Knowledge Check

12. How do the results of this experiment relate to previous research?
13. Steele et al. noted that the Rideout and Laubach (1996) study did not incorporate a silence control group. What is the relevance of that observation?
14. Have Steele et al. resolved the inconsistencies in the Mozart effect?
15. Why do you think Steele et al. commented on the requests to allocate more money to grade-school music education?

## Statistical Inference and Testing Hypotheses

Once you have reviewed the existing literature and narrowed your focus to a specific research question, it is important to consider how this information will be used. In Chapter 3 we talked about the types of research hypotheses. Now that you have done a literature review you can decide on the specific hypotheses you wish to evaluate and begin to consider the appropriate statistical techniques that will be necessary in order to test your hypotheses.

The importance of carefully establishing your hypotheses cannot be overstated. Once you have read a sufficient number of articles and other sources related to your topic of interest you will begin to feel comfortable with the general subject. At this point you will need to begin to formulate your general research question, shifting from its most general statement to a more specific question. This may require you to identify additional sources to help you specify the variables that you will study and the nature of the relationship that you expect to observe between those variables. Eventually, you will need to further boil down this specific research question into the form of a testable hypothesis, which is a mathematical representation of an expected relationship between two or more variables.

Statisticians and researchers invented inferential statistics during the early part of the twentieth century (Oakes, 1986). Over time, general rules and principles for using inferential statistics became common practice. For example, most researchers now routinely include a null and alternative hypothesis as a part of their statistical test. In this section we will examine the specific steps involved in hypothesis testing.

One important feature of all hypothesis testing is that we form the hypothesis *before* we collect or examine the data. All of us can describe the past with accuracy; predicting the future, however, is a talent. Thus, we are more impressed by and have much greater confidence in a prediction of the future that comes true. As you will see in the following steps, much of the work associated with hypothesis testing comes before we collect or analyze the data.

## State the Null and Alternative Hypotheses

The null hypothesis, $H_0$, is the mathematical statement we seek to disprove when we do a research study. More specifically, the typical null hypothesis states that the independent variable is not related to or has no effect on the dependent variable. If we find evidence through our research that there is in fact some relationship between the variables, then we can reject $H_0$ and accept instead the alternative hypothesis, $H_1$, which is typically the focus of the study. If our evidence is not strong enough to reject $H_0$, then we retain this statement of no relationship between variables. Typically, the alternative hypothesis is the central thesis of the research and states that there is a meaningful difference between the group means.

It is important to note that although it is true that the no-relation/difference hypothesis is integrally a part of the way social sciences test for relationships among variables, it is sometimes not accurate, especially outside of the experimental setting. This error in understanding has led to a great deal of controversy in the methods literature over the past few decades regarding the future of null hypothesis testing.

The null hypothesis is the hypothesis to be nullified or disproved. As conceived by Fisher it is the hypothesis that represents our current understanding of the world. If we are genuinely ignorant of any relation between two variables, then the no-relation hypothesis (hypothesis of ignorance) is correct. However, in most cases, the no-relation hypothesis is demonstrably false based on existing research and rejecting it does nothing to advance knowledge.

The implication here is that the null hypothesis can be correct only if there is no evidence to suggest that there is or should be a relationship between two or more variables. In most cases, researchers base their research on the expectation of a relationship between variables, and as such they are asserting that they expect there to be a relationship. This being the case, most social scientific researchers engage in research to collect data that they expect will support their alternative hypotheses. If these data do not reflect the expected relationship, then these researchers will revert to the null hypothesis as the next best explanation for their lack of identifying a relationship between the study variables. This is why research is theory driven. Simply disproving the null hypothesis does not mean the alternative hypothesis is true. It simply indicates there is a relation or difference among variables or groups.

The null hypothesis can be either nondirectional or directional. The nondirectional hypothesis for a two-group study will be $H_0$: $\mu_1 = \mu_2$. This version of the hypothesis states that the two population means are identical and that any observed difference between the group means is due to random events unrelated to the independent variable. By contrast, the directional null hypothesis can be either $H_0$: $\mu_1 > \mu_2$ or $H_0$: $\mu_1 < \mu_2$ The directional hypothesis predicts that one population mean is less than the other mean with the exception of the effects of random sampling error. The alternative hypothesis is always the mathematical complement of the null hypothesis. The complementary relational signs are $=$ and $\neq$, $\geq$ and $<$, and $\leq$ and $>$. As a rule, each null hypothesis has only one alternative hypothesis.

### Identify the Appropriate Statistical Test

This step may seem obvious, but is often the downfall of many students and researchers. Part of the problem is that you can apply any statistical test to any set of data. One question you could ask is, "Can I use this statistic to analyze these data?" The answer will always be "Yes" because you can use any statistical test to analyze any set of data. A better question is, "Will this statistical test allow me to answer the question I posed in my hypothesis?"

Different statistical tests provide different perspectives of the data. Some allow you to compare groups, whereas others examine the correlation between groups. Therefore, your null and alternative hypotheses will determine the type of test you use. Other factors also influence the selection of the appropriate statistical test. Many inferential statistics require that the data meet specific criteria to produce valid results. For example, the $t$-ratio for independent groups (more on this in Chapter 10) assumes that the observations for the two groups are independent, that the data are normally distributed, and that the variances of the two groups are equivalent. Failure to meet these criteria can produce spurious results.

As you plan your research, you should identify the appropriate statistical tests for analyzing the data and identify the requirements for using that test. In addition, you should identify alternative strategies for analyzing the data in the case that your data do not conform to the requirements of a specific test. There are many ways to analyze the data from a research project.

## Chapter Summary

The advance of any science depends on an exchange of information. Social scientists, like other scientists, share the results of their research in professional research journals. Because human behavior and social interaction are popular and complex topics, there is a monumental amount of information about various behavioral topics. Libraries are, therefore, important resources to help you find what researchers have discovered about psychological phenomena.

There are three classes of bibliographic source: tertiary, secondary, and primary. Tertiary sources are the most general resource, but are a useful introduction to different topics. Secondary resources are more specific and offer a more detailed review of the research that has been conducted on a specific topic. Primary resources are the original articles written by researchers.

An important component of professional research journals is peer review. Peer review means that fellow professionals review a researcher's manuscript to determine whether it is worthy of publication. In other words, peer review is a form of quality control to ensure that a journal publishes only good-quality research.

The Internet is a fascinating resource but is still in its infancy. There are few checks and balances for reviewing information posted on the Internet. Consequently, you must be cautious of information that you gather from the Internet.

We reviewed many ways that you can develop your interest in psychology and develop a research hypothesis. One of the more important resources is reading the research that has already been conducted. This background work will help you understand what psychologists know about a specific topic and what issues remain a mystery.

There are many resources you can use to locate useful information. One of the most useful resources is *PsycInfo*, a comprehensive database of primary and secondary resources. You can search the database using a search engine. These search engines use Boolean operations that allow you to find specific topics. The AND operator causes the search engine to select articles where two or more specific keywords describe the research. The OR operator allows you to conduct a broader search of related topics.

When you find an interesting research article, you will find that it is divided into several sections. The introduction offers a brief history of the research on the topic and a review of the researcher's hypotheses. In the method section, the researcher describes the techniques used to collect the data. The results section provides a detailed account of the results the researcher obtained. Finally, the discussion section includes the researcher's commentary of the meaning of the data with regard to his or her hypotheses.

In the "Research in Action" section, we reviewed a published article to illustrate how to read a research article.

The chapter ended with a discussion on forming hypotheses and the importance of selecting the appropriate statistical technique(s).

## Chapter Glossary for Review

**AND**—A Boolean operator that requires that two or more keywords be present in the citation.

**Boolean operators**—Logical terms that control the search process for keywords.

**Call number**—A combination of letters and numbers used in a library classification system to store and locate recorded information.

**Keyword**—A word or phrase used to search *PsycInfo* or other databases.

**OR**—A Boolean operator that requires that either keyword be present in the citation.

**Peer review**—Part of the editorial process for professional books and journals in which professionals in the area review a manuscript for its scientific merits.

**Primary bibliographic sources**—A class of text resource that includes original research reports.

**Research journal**—A periodic publication that contains original research articles, summaries, and commentaries. The editorial board consists of fellow researchers who have expertise on the primary topic of the journal.

**Secondary bibliographic sources**—A class of text resources that includes specialized books and articles and offers a comprehensive review of the literature for research on a specific topic.

**Tertiary bibliographic sources**—A class of text resource that includes textbooks and general reviews of a topic.

## Chapter References

American Psychological Association (2007). *Thesaurus of psychological index terms* (11th ed.). Washington, DC: Author.

Brandt, D. S. (1996). Evaluating information on the Internet. *Computers in Libraries*, *16*, 44–47.

Brandt, D. S. (1997). What flavor is your Internet search engine? *Computers in Libraries*, *17*, 47–50.

Casper, R. C., & Jabine, L. N. (1996). An eight-year follow-up: Outcome from adolescent compared to adult onset anorexia nervosa. *Journal of Youth & Adolescence*, *25*, 499–517.

Darley, J. M., & Latané, B. (1968). Bystander intervention in emergencies: Diffusion of responsibility. *Journal of Personality and Social Psychology, 10*, 202–214.

Latané, B., & Nida, S. A. (1981). Ten years of research on group size and helping. *Psychological Bulletin, 89*, 308–324.

Lerch, I. (1999, November). Reprint of letter to Dr. Richard McCarty. *Psychological Science Agenda, 12*, 2–3.

Oakes, M. (1986). *Statistical inference: A commentary for the social and behavioral sciences*. New York: John Wiley & Sons.

Rauscher, F. H., Shaw, G. L., & Ky, K. N. (1993). Music and spatial task performance. *Nature, 365*, 611.

Rauscher, F. H., Shaw, G. L., & Ky, K. N. (1995). Listening to Mozart enhances spatial-temporal reasoning: Towards a neurophysiological basis. *Neuroscience Letters, 185*, 44–47.

Rideout, B. E., & Laubach, C. M. (1996). EEE correlates of enhanced spatial performance following exposure to music. *Perceptual & Motor Skills, 82*, 427–432.

Rind, B., Tromovitch, P., & Bauserman, R. (1998). A meta-analytic examination of assumed properties of child sexual abuse using college samples. *Psychological Bulletin, 124*, 22–53.

Steele, K. M., Ball, T. N., & Runk, R. (1997). Listening to Mozart does not enhance backwards digit span performance. *Perceptual & Motor Skills, 84*, 1179–1184.

# Chapter 7
## Sampling: The First Steps in Research

> It is a capital mistake to theorize before one has data.
>
> —Sir Arthur Conan Doyle

## Introduction

Much of what we know we learn from samples. Consider some common examples. Your knowledge of the world and the decisions you make come from samples. When someone asks you whether the lunches at a restaurant are good, you use your experiences to answer the question. Your meals at the restaurant are samples. The establishment may produce thousands of meals and has served hundreds of customers since its opening. You have no way of being sure that each meal was prepared well and enjoyed. Yet, based on your experience with the restaurant, you make a single and confident conclusion, "The food here is good."

The same is true when you meet a person for the first time. Social psychologists tell us that we make long-lasting conclusions based on our first impressions of people. Think for a moment of what happens in such situations. After a mere five minutes, many people are willing to state confidently that they have formed a good impression of another person. That is, an extremely small sample of behavior creates a lasting impression of that person. Given the complexity of human behavior, this is an amazing conclusion based on such a limited sample.

As you will recall from Chapter 1, Bacon warned about the Idols of the Cave, relying too much on our personal experience for seeking truth.

Objective or scientific sampling is a way of overcoming the Idols of the Cave because it ensures that our experiences are as broad and representative as possible. Moreover, as you learned in Chapter 3, having a representative sample of the population in a study helps to ensure the external validity of the conclusions we draw from the data to other members of the population.

What are the common features of samples and sampling? First, we use samples to describe and compare things. Consider, as an example, describing someone's personality. Each of us is affected by many things, ranging from situational factors, to interactions with others, and a host of variables too numerous to list. Even for an individual, it would be impossible to observe all the things he or she would do under different situations. However, based on a representative sample of that person's behavior, we may be able to predict how he or she will react to specific situations. This observation leads us to the second feature of sampling. We use samples to help us make predictions and conclusions about other things or conditions. As the quotation at the start of this chapter suggests, our theories are the product of the data we collect. Perhaps, by extension, we can also suggest that no theory is any better than the data that inspired its creation.

How can we be sure that what we observe in the sample accurately represents the population? This is a critical question. As you learned in Chapter 3, such a question goes to the heart of external validity. If the sample is not representative of the population, then the data will be of little value to us because they do not support inferences about the population.

Therefore, the purpose of this chapter is to examine the foundations of participant samples and sampling. In the following pages, we will examine the methods researchers use to collect accurate samples of the population. In addition, we will review how statistics, based on sample data, allow us to make inferences about population parameters. Hence, we will begin with a more detailed analysis of the characteristics of samples. We assume that you have had a course in statistics and understand the foundations of descriptive statistics such as measures of central tendency (e.g., mean and median), measures of dispersion (e.g., variance and standard deviation), and $z$-scores. If you are not familiar with these statistics, or wish to brush up on your skills, you may want to review Appendix A.

## The Nature of Samples

There are several ways that we can define samples. The primary emphasis of this definition is to show that the sample is a valid representation of the population. One way to define a sample is to contrast samples with things that are not samples. We can also define samples by the methods used to create them. As you may recall from our previous discussions of validity, we cannot directly assess the external validity or the representativeness of a sample. Rather, we examine the methods used to create the sample to infer its validity. Consequently, researchers work hard to ensure that their sampling techniques produce useful data.

### Scientific Samples versus Anecdotal Evidence

What is the difference between a sample and other types of information? We can begin by considering personal experiences and anecdotal evidence and compare them to a scientific sample. Imagine a person who traveled to Paris for a short vacation and then pronounces the French to be rude and inconsiderate people. Such a conclusion is indefensible. A moment's thought will reveal that many factors bias this unflattering conclusion. Specifically, a stranger traveling abroad, spending a short time in a small portion of the country, and interacting with a minuscule proportion of the population, cannot come to a meaningful conclusion about the manners of a nation of people.

**Anecdotal evidence** and personal experience are not sampling in the technical sense of the word. Our hypothetical traveler probably did meet several rude and inconsiderate people, an experience likely to occur when traveling to any large city. Therefore, we cannot deny the person's experiences. We do deny the conclusion, however, because we do not consider the personal encounters representative of the population.

We can use the criteria of representativeness to distinguish anecdotal evidence and personal experience from scientific samples and empirical conclusions. The goal of scientific research is to identify and collect data from samples of participants that represent the population that we study. In an experimental scenario, researchers are also interested in creating treatment groups that are equivalent on all variables other than the independent variable(s) of interest. From these samples and treatment groups researchers collect data and then have to generate reasonable and valid conclusions regarding these data. When we collect the data, we use procedures that ensure that the samples will be free of bias and thereby represent the population. By contrast, anecdotal evidence is typically a haphazard collection of personal experiences that may be biased.

Unfortunately, anecdotal evidence too easily sways many people's opinions, an observation that Bacon noted when he described the Idols of the Tribe and Idols of the Cave. Social psychologists have long studied the poor decision-making processes that many people follow (Plous, 1993). A well-known phenomenon is the "person-who" effect that occurs when someone uses anecdotal evidence to discount a statistical generalization. For example, a smoker may dismiss the risk of smoking by noting that his or her father smoked two packs of cigarettes a day and lived to be 75. In this case, the person seems to ignore the larger body of evidence that people who smoke have a shorter life expectancy and an increased risk of health problems.

The problem we all must confront is the pervasive nature of anecdotal evidence and its influence on decision making. As researchers, we must remain vigilant to ensure that our data are representative of the population. Finally, you should recognize that the plural of *anecdote* is not *data*. Anecdotes, like rumors, cannot be trusted to be accurate, reliable, or valid no matter how often they are repeated.

# Probability Sampling

Before we delve into the topic of sampling any further, we must define an important term. **Random** means that each possible outcome has an equal probability of occurring and that the outcome of one event has no influence on the probability of subsequent outcomes. Imagine a balanced six-sided die. Each time you throw the die, the probability of any one side landing face-up is always 1/6. In addition, each time you throw the die, the results of the previous tosses have no effect on the current toss. That one event has no effect on other events is the principle of **independence**. Random sampling is an example of independence because selecting one object from the population will not influence the selection of other objects.

Understanding randomness is important for sampling because it allows us to link individual samples to the population. According to the **law of large numbers**, any large number of items chosen at random from a population will have, on average, the same characteristics as the population. This law is the cornerstone of probability sampling and allows us to infer that what is true of the sample is also true of the population. In this section, we will examine how we can use random events and other procedures to create samples that represent the population.

### Populations and Samples

In Chapter 3, we introduced you to the concepts of the population and the sample. As you should recall, the population consists of all the individuals or things that the researcher wants to describe. Researchers define the population by developing the criteria that determine membership in the population. Defining the population is essential as it determines the conclusions that the researcher may draw from the data (Wilkinson, 1999).

When referring to a population, many researchers refer to the **target population** or the **universe**. For example, a researcher may study the self-attributions made by people suffering depression. In this example, the target population is any adult diagnosed with depression as defined by the *Diagnostic and Statistical Manual of Mental Disorders–IV-TR* (American Psychiatric Association, 2000).

In some cases, it is impractical or impossible to draw a representative sample from the target population. Consequently, researchers will draw their sample from a smaller subset of the population called a **sampling population**. For our purposes, a sampling population consists of an accessible group of people who share the same characteristics as the target population. In most behavioral research, the sampling population consists of people who live or work near the researcher. When they report their results, researchers define the characteristics of the sampling population. Doing so allows the reader to determine whether the sampling population is representative of the target population.

Some researchers pull their study samples from an existing **subject pool**, a group of people to whom the researcher has easy access. At many colleges and universities, the academic departments maintain a subject pool of students enrolled in introductory level courses who may receive extra credit for participating in a study.

A related concept is the **sampling frame**. A sampling frame is the set of individuals within a population who can actually be reached for a specific research purpose. For example, a list of names that identifies the members of the population is a sampling frame (Babbie, 1998). If you wanted to conduct a survey of voter opinion in your community, you could obtain the list of registered voters through the local board of elections as the sampling frame. The main difference between the subject pool and the sampling frame is that people in the subject pool are willing to participate in a research project. By contrast, the sampling frame is merely the list of people who belong to a population.

Detailed descriptions of the characteristics of the population, sampling population, and sampling frame help us evaluate the external validity of inferences made from a sample. Consider, as an example, the sampling frame. How accurate and complete is the list? Does the list include all members of the sampling population, or does it systematically exclude important groups of people? What about our subject pool? Is the fact that the participants of an experiment were students enrolled in Psychology 101, Fall Term, 2003, at Mythical College important to our interpretation of the results? The answer is yes.

The connection among external validity and the sampling population, subject pool, and sampling frame is important. If any of these subgroups is not representative of the population, then it will be impossible to assume a meaningful link between the sample and the target population. For these reasons, researchers spend considerable time analyzing and describing the sources of their data. Doing so allows the researcher to establish a connection between the sample statistics and the population parameters. With these concerns in mind, we can turn our attention to the business of creating samples.

## Characteristics of Probability Sampling

There are many ways to take a representative sample from a population. We can use techniques known as simple random sampling, stratified sampling, systematic sampling, or cluster sampling, to name just a few. Although there are many types of sampling procedures, all of those mentioned above have one thing in common; they are **probability sampling** techniques. You will sometimes see the term *statistical* sampling used instead of *probability* sampling. For our purposes, we are treating these terms as interchangeable.

All probability sampling techniques share common features. First, they treat each member of the population as a potential member of a sample. This is a critical feature as it ensures that the sampling technique does not systematically exclude portions of the population from the eventual study sample, thereby biasing the results. By implication, the procedures employed in probabilistic sampling procedures are objective and

Table 7.1 **All Potential Samples of Size 2 Drawn from a Population Consisting of the Values 1 through 6**

| $S_1$ | (1,2) | $S_2$ | (1,3) | $S_3$ | (1,4) | $S_4$ | (1,5) | $S_5$ | (1,6) |
|---|---|---|---|---|---|---|---|---|---|
| $S_6$ | (2,3) | $S_7$ | (2,4) | $S_8$ | (2,5) | $S_9$ | (2,6) | $S_{10}$ | (3,4) |
| $S_{11}$ | (3,5) | $S_{12}$ | (3,6) | $S_{13}$ | (4,5) | $S_{14}$ | (4,6) | $S_{15}$ | (5,6) |

systematic. All sampling procedures create a set of rules, known as a *protocol*, for selecting members of the population. In some cases, the protocol for sampling may be minimal; in other cases the sampling protocol may be extremely elaborate. We follow the rules for creating the sample to ensure that the data are not biased.

The second feature of probability sampling is that we can determine the probability of selecting any specific sample (Cochran, 1977). This may sound a bit strange, but it is an important assumption that allows us to connect the results of the sample to the parameters of the population. Consider the following example of probability sampling.

Assume that you have a population containing the whole numbers 1 through 6. Using sampling without replacement, and with a sample size of 2, you could create the 15 potential samples listed in Table 7.1. If we use probability sampling, we can determine the probability that we will select any one of these samples. In this example, there is an equal likelihood that we will select any one of the samples. Specifically, for each sample, $p = 1/15$ or $p = .0667$. The probability ($p$) that we will select any one of these samples is approximately 6.67%.

You may object and say that we rarely know the true nature of the population, and if we did, why would we need sampling? You are correct; we rarely know the parameters of the population. This illustration shows the logic of probability sampling. For any given population, we can draw an infinite number of samples. Using mathematical techniques that we will soon review, we can estimate the probability of selecting any one of those samples. Armed with this knowledge, we can then make several interesting inferences about the population.

## Sampling Methods

There are many methods of drawing samples from the population. Each method shares a common goal: to ensure that the sample is an unbiased depiction of the population. In this section we will review several of the more frequently used sampling methods, including simple random sampling, sequential sampling, stratified sampling, and cluster sampling. This section can provide only a general introduction to sampling methods. Sampling is a science, and there are many sophisticated techniques researchers use for specific purposes (Babbie, 1998; Cochran, 1977; Salant & Dillman, 1994).

## Figure 7.1

**Random Sampling**

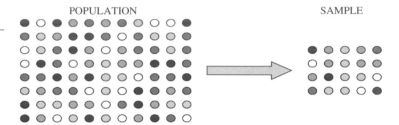

The block on the left represents the population. Each circle has an equal chance of selection. The block on the right represents the sample.

### Simple Random Sampling

**Simple random sampling** is the most basic of the sampling procedures. Simple random sampling occurs whenever each member of the population has an equal probability of selection. The steps involved in conducting a simple random sample are clear-cut. First, estimate the size of the population. Next, generate random numbers to determine which members of the population to select. In the final stage, collect the data and conduct the study.

Figure 7.1 illustrates random sampling. The block of circles on the left represents members of a population. The block of circles on the right represents a random sample of the population. In this example, there are five types of circle, each represented by a different shade. Because there is no bias in the sampling procedure, the sample should be similar to the population, and any difference between the sample and the population represents chance or random factors.

Imagine that you want to conduct a survey of student opinion at your college. The college's Institutional Review Board approved your research, and you are ready to collect the data. The first step is to determine the size of the population. This should be relatively easy. Go to the college's records office and ask the registrar for the number of students currently enrolled at the college. For the sake of the illustration, assume that there are 7,584 students enrolled at your college and that you have decided that you will create a random sample of 250 students.

For the next step, you will need 250 **random numbers**. Random numbers are a series of numbers with no order or pattern. Technically, random numbers are independent of each other. Independence means that each number has an equal chance of selection and the selection of one number has no effect on the selection of another number. Before the advent of personal computers, many researchers used a random number table created by the Rand Corporation (1955) that contains 1 million random digits. The creators of that table went to great pains to build and test a machine that produced random digits.

Many researchers now use their personal computers to generate random numbers. Different computer programs can produce a string of random numbers between specific values. In the current example, we need

Table 7.2  **Twenty Random Numbers Between 1 and 7,584 Generated Using a Spreadsheet Program and Rank Ordered from Lowest to Highest**

| 23 | 147 | 450 | 496 | 871 | 1529 | 2629 | 2660 | 2898 | 3311 |
|------|------|------|------|------|------|------|------|------|------|
| 3775 | 4020 | 4035 | 4484 | 4852 | 5565 | 5790 | 6438 | 6699 | 7558 |

250 random numbers between 1 and 7,584, inclusive. Table 7.2 presents 20 random numbers between 1 and 7,584 that we created using a spreadsheet program. Once you have generated the 250 random numbers, you could sort the entire data file in order of these numbers and select the first 250 individuals in the sorted list. If everyone cooperates with your request to complete the questionnaire, your sample will be an unbiased representation of the population.

Many computer programs generate random numbers, but most do this based on a preset random number "seed" or starting point. Researchers call these numbers *pseudorandom* numbers because of this, but in most research cases, using pseudorandom numbers is sufficient (Pashley, 1993).

## Sequential Sampling

Although simple random sampling is the gold standard of probability sampling, many researchers find it inefficient and impractical (Babbie, 1998). A suitable alternative is **sequential sampling**. For a sequential sample, we list the members of the sampling population and then select each $k$th member from the list.

The steps for sequential sampling are straightforward. First, we need to determine the **sampling interval** that identifies which members of the list to select. The sampling interval is merely:

$$\text{Sample interval} = \frac{\text{Size of population}}{\text{Desired size of sample}} \qquad (7.1)$$

In our previous example, we wanted to create a sample of 250 from a population of 7,584 students. Therefore, the sampling interval is 30 (7,584/250 = 30.336). Now all you need to do is obtain a current list of all students and then select every 30th student on the list. This procedure assumes that the list you select students from represents the entire sampling frame.

## Stratified Sampling

Stratified sampling is another variation on simple random sampling. This technique is especially useful in situations where the population contains different subgroups that the sample must include. Researchers who conduct public opinion polling, for example, want to ensure that the sample represents the population for gender, age, political affiliation, education, annual income, and a host of other variables that may affect public opinion.

# Figure 7.2

**Stratified Sampling**

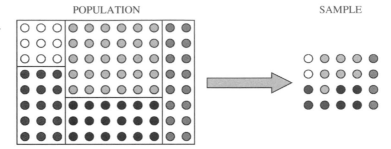

The box on the left represents a population consisting of smaller subgroups of strata. The researcher randomly selects from each stratum to create the sample. The sample will have approximately the same proportions of the subgroups as the population.

Figure 7.2 illustrates how stratified sampling works. In this example, the population contains five distinct subgroups of different sizes. The researcher wants to include a sample of each subgroup in the sample. In order not to bias the sample, the size of the subgroups in the sample should equal the relative size of the subgroups in the population.

Figure 7.2 offers a hint of how a researcher would conduct a stratified random sample. First, the researcher would identify the specific subgroups in the population and attempt to estimate their relative size. Next, the researcher can use simple random or sequential sampling within each subgroup. The result is a representative sample. If all goes well, the size of the subgroups in the sample will be the same relative size as the population.

## Cluster Sampling

Cluster sampling is a form of sampling that researchers use when it is not convenient to pull one or two people out of their environment for the research or when other methods of sampling are impractical. Researchers often use this technique when working with intact groups. An example would be a research project examining the effectiveness of different teaching techniques.

Imagine that Figure 7.3 represents students enrolled in 20 different sections of the same course. The researcher may want to know whether differences in teaching method affect students' performance in the course. It may be impractical to randomly select students and create special sections of the course. As an alternative, the researcher can select different sections at random for the research. In Figure 7.3, the researcher randomly selected five different clusters.

In other cases, the clusters may represent cities, neighborhoods, schools, or other naturally occurring clusters. The researcher can then select clusters randomly or systematically. If the researcher knows that particular clusters contain important portions of the population, he or she may then purposely select those clusters.

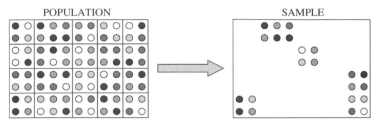

## Figure 7.3

**Cluster Sampling**

The small blocks of individuals in the left square identify separate clusters of individuals. The researcher selects several clusters for the sample.

## Nonprobability Sampling

Although probability sampling is the ideal, it is often beyond the budget, time, and personal resources of the researcher. Therefore, in many situations researchers will resort to **nonprobability sampling**. You will also see this type of sampling referred to as *judgmental* sampling since it is not statistical or based on statistical rules. These methods are convenient for the researcher, but the results of studies using samples of this sort need to be interpreted with caution. As you should recall from your reading in previous chapters, using a nonprobability sampling method may limit the inferences that you can make from the data. On the other hand, these methods can produce useful data when collected and interpreted under the right conditions (Cochran, 1977).

### Convenience Sampling

The most common type of nonprobability sampling is **convenience sampling**. In contrast to probability sampling, convenience sampling means that the researcher uses members of the population who are easy to find. Interviewing people at a shopping mall or people who walk by a particular street corner are examples of convenience sampling. In these cases, the researcher allows the individual's behavior to determine who will, and more importantly who will not, be a part of the study.

Do you see the difference between probability sampling and convenience sampling? For all forms of probability sampling, the *researcher's method* of sampling determines who will be a potential member of a sample. For convenience sampling, the *individuals' behaviors* determine whether they could become part of a study's sample. Consequently, convenience sampling can bias the results and interpretation of the data. Imagine that you wanted to conduct a survey of students at your college. Do you think you would get different results if you surveyed students lounging around the college's student union versus students studying in the library? In many ways, convenience sampling suffers the same problems as anecdotal evidence because the sample does not represent the population.

Despite these drawbacks, however, there are times when a convenience sample may be the only way to collect the data. For example, a researcher interested in studying homeless people may use people who eat at a cafeteria for the homeless. Although there may be many homeless people who do not eat at the facility, this may be the only way for the researcher to interview these people. Many good research studies have been done using a convenience sample. However, the specific results of any one particular study may be an artifact of the sample. The growth of science is dependent on a body of knowledge that builds on preexisting research. This is especially true for convenience samples, and the results of individual studies should be examined in light of existing and future research.

### Snowball Sampling

A cohort is a group of people who share a particular feature. Sometimes the members of a cohort are difficult to find and recruit for research. The members of the cohort may wish to remain anonymous, or there is no list identifying the members of the cohort. Other times the researcher may wish to access a population to which he or she would not normally have access. In such situations, the researcher may wish to use **snowball sampling**. To sample from the cohort, the researcher needs to find a member of the cohort and use him or her to find other members of the cohort. Snowball sampling has been used successfully to study human behavior in populations as diverse as gangs, employees of a specific business, and illicit drug users.

Consider, for example, the research conducted by Evelyn Hooker. In the 1940s, homosexual men and women took extraordinary precautions to keep their sexual orientation a secret. Evelyn Hooker was able to gain the trust of several homosexual men. Once they trusted her and the motives of her research, they helped Hooker recruit homosexual friends and associates for her research. Consequently, Hooker was one of the first psychologists to publish empirical research demonstrating that homosexuals and heterosexuals experience the same rates and types of mental health problems (Hooker, 1956, 1957, 1958). Without the snowball sampling technique, Hooker may never have been able to conduct this important and groundbreaking research. Her research did much to help reduce the unfounded stereotypes many people, including clinical psychologists and psychiatrists, held about homosexuality.

## Knowledge Check

1. What are the differences between anecdotal evidence and scientific sampling?
2. What are the potential problems with relying on personal experience to make decisions?
3. Describe the similarities and differences among simple random sampling, sequential sampling, stratified sampling, and cluster sampling.

4. Anne is selecting courses for next semester and must take an English literature course, but does not know which professor she should select. To solve her dilemma, she decides to ask three of her friends, who are English majors, for their recommendations.
   a. What type of sampling is Anne using?
   b. Describe the factors that may bias the information Anne receives.

5. The dean of academic affairs at a small college wants to examine the study habits of students attending the college. He randomly selects 50 students from the college and asks them to record the number of hours they work on homework each day for one week (assume that all the students participate and answer honestly). According to the results, the typical student studies an average of 3.2 hours a day.
   a. Can we conclude that the dean has a valid estimate of the students' study habits?
   b. Are there factors that can bias the results of the data?

6. Professor Smith distributes a survey to 45 students in his English Composition 101 course. Professor Jones distributes the same survey to 45 students in her Organic Chemistry 250 course.
   a. What are the factors that may bias the results of these samples?
   b. Is one sample more likely to be representative of the students at the college?

7. A national magazine publishes the results of a survey of its readers. The magazine argues that the results are valid because of the large number (e.g., 12,592) of readers who responded to the questionnaire. Do you agree that the results are valid?

8. A researcher in a large city wishes to conduct a survey and ensure that the sample includes a representative sample of each of the five major ethnic groups that live in the city. Describe how the researcher could use each probability sampling technique to create such a sample.

9. A researcher wants to examine the opinions of members of different Christian denominations (e.g., Baptist, Catholic, Episcopal, Lutheran, and Presbyterian). What might be the most cost-effective method of generating a representative sample?

10. Do you agree with the statement, "A sample of convenience is little better than anecdotal evidence"? Defend your answer.

## Central Limit Theorem

You may be wondering how we can continue to assert that a sample statistic is an unbiased estimate of the population parameter. How do we know that the mean or the standard deviation of a sample accurately estimates the mean and the standard deviation of a population (e.g., $M \approx \mu$ and $SD \approx \sigma$)? To answer that question, we need to examine an important principle in statistics known as the **Central Limit Theorem**. The Central Limit Theorem is important because it allows us to use the sample to describe the population.

The Central Limit Theorem describes the distribution of certain sample statistics from probability samples. In other words, the Central Limit Theorem describes the sampling distribution. As we noted previously, one of the characteristics of probability sampling is the ability to predict or to estimate the probability of selecting a specific sample. We can use the Central Limit Theorem and a sampling distribution to estimate the probability of obtaining, at chance, any potential sample from the population. Before we proceed, however, we need to define some terms.

A **sampling distribution** represents the result of taking many samples of a specific size from a population and plotting the frequency of a sample statistic, such as the mean, that is computed within these samples. A sampling distribution is the theoretical distribution of the potential values of a sample statistic that would occur when drawing an infinite number of equal-sized random samples from the population. We can use a thought experiment as an illustration.

Imagine that you have access to a population of college students you want to survey. You draw a random sample of 25 students, test each person, and then calculate the mean score. You can now repeat these steps to produce the mean for a second sample. Chances are that the two means from the two different samples of participants will be slightly different from each other. If you continue to collect samples from the population, you will eventually have a large collection of sample means. When you create a graph of the frequency of the values of the means, you will form the sampling distribution for the means.

Not all the sample means will be equal to each other; there will be variability among the sample means. Specifically, many of the sample means will be slightly greater or less than the population mean, and some will be much different from the sample mean. We can describe this variability using the statistical concept of **standard error ($\sigma_M$)**, or the average standard deviation of the sample distribution of the same means. Because we used random sampling to create the samples, the differences among the sample means represent random or chance factors. The Central Limit Theorem allows us to describe the shape of the sampling distribution of sample means and the amount of standard error.

The Central Limit Theorem makes several specific propositions or statements about the shape of the sampling distribution of the sample mean. The propositions are:

1. As the size of the individual samples increases, the shape of the sampling distribution of sample means will become progressively normal regardless of the shape of the population.

2. The mean of the sampling distribution of sample means ($\mu_M$) will equal the mean of the population ($\mu$), $\mu_M = \mu$.

3. The standard deviation of the sampling distribution of sample means ($\mu_M$) will equal the standard deviation of the population ($\sigma$) divided by the square root of the sample size ($\sqrt{n}$), $\sigma_M = \sigma/\sqrt{n}$.

What are the implications of these propositions? Why are they important for statistics? We will consider the answers to these questions in the following sections.

## Shape of the Sampling Distribution

One of the most interesting predictions of the Central Limit Theorem is that the shape of the sampling distribution of sample means will be normal especially as the size of each sample increases. Figure 7.4 illustrates this prediction. The top panels of the figure represent the shape of three populations: U-shaped, positively skewed, and rectangular. The lower panels represent the sampling distributions of means for sample sizes of 2, 20, and 40. Each sampling distribution represents 5,000 random samples taken from the population. As you can see, as the size of the sample increases, the distribution of means becomes progressively normal in shape.

## Mean of the Sampling Distribution: $\mu_M = \mu$

The symbol $\mu_M$ represents the theoretical mean of the sampling distribution of means. In words, the quantity represents the mean of means. As an equation,

$$\mu_M = \frac{\sum M}{N} = \frac{\text{Sum of all sample means}}{\text{Number of samples}} \qquad (7.2)$$

This equation indicates that we take the sum of all sample means drawn from the population and divide by the number of samples created. You should be clear about the difference between *sample size* and *number of samples*. Sample size, represented as $n$, refers to the number of observations in each sample. The total number of samples, represented as $N$, refers to the number of samples drawn from the population. For Equation 7.2, we assume that the sample size is constant and that $N$ is an extremely large number. As an example, look at the bottom row of graphs in Figure 7.4. Each graph represents 5,000 random samples. Therefore, $N = 5{,}000$. Each of the samples consists of 40 scores. Consequently, $n = 40$.

You should now be able to see that the sample mean is an unbiased estimate of the population mean. Although there is standard error in any sampling distribution, the error is random and nonsystematic. Therefore, any individual sample mean is equally likely to be above or below the population mean. Using these facts allows us to conclude that the sample mean is an unbiased estimate of the population mean, or that $M = \mu$.

## Standard Error of the Mean: $\sigma_M = \sigma/\sqrt{n}$

The **standard error of the mean (SEM)** is the standard deviation of the sampling distribution of sample means. The equation for *SEM* tells us that as sample size increases, the distribution of sample means will cluster closer to

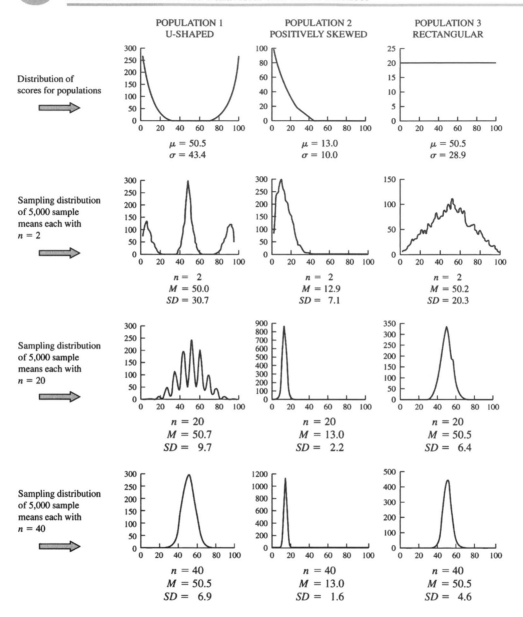

# Figure 7.4

**Central Limit Theorem**

The top panels represent the shape of the population from which the samples are drawn. The lower three rows of graphs represent the sampling distribution of the mean of samples size 2, 20, and 40. Each sampling distribution represents 5,000 random samples generated by a computer program. According to the Central Limit Theorem, the shape of the sampling distribution will become normal as sample size increases. In addition, $\mu_M = \mu$ and $\sigma_M = \sigma/\sqrt{n}$. The mean ($M$) of each sampling distribution is close to the mean of the population, and the standard deviation of each distribution ($SD$) is approximately $\sigma/\sqrt{n}$.

the population mean. As sample size increases, the sample mean will become a more accurate estimate of the population mean. In other words, the lower the SEM, the more accurate the estimate of $M$ is of the population mean.

To summarize, the Central Limit Theorem allows us to make several inferences concerning the relation between sample statistics and population parameters. First, the sample mean is an unbiased estimate of the population mean, if we use a probability sampling procedure to generate the sample. Furthermore, the sample mean becomes a better estimate of the population mean as the sample size increases. Because of these properties, researchers prefer to use the sample mean as the descriptive statistic to infer the population parameter. Second, the Central Limit Theorem allows us to determine the probability of obtaining various sample means.

## Applications of the Central Limit Theorem

In this section we will examine how we can use the Central Limit Theorem to our advantage as researchers. As you will see, we can use the Central Limit Theorem to answer two important questions, "How reliable is our sample mean?" and "How large should our sample be?" We can answer the first question by calculating the standard error of the mean and the confidence interval. Once we review these basic statistical tools, we can begin to address the second question.

We use *SEM* to describe the standard deviation of the sampling distribution of means. This value allows us to estimate the range of potential sample means drawn from a population. Figure 7.5 represents the hypothetical results of taking 20 samples at random from a population mean. Assume that the mean of the population equals 100 ($\mu = 100$), that the standard deviation of the population equals 30 ($\sigma = 30$), and that we draw 20 random samples of 9 observations each ($n = 9$). We can calculate the standard error of the mean as $\mu_M = 10.0 = 30/\sqrt{9}$.

The normal distribution in Figure 7.5 represents the hypothetical sampling distribution for sample means where $\mu_M = 100$ and $\sigma_M = 10$. The box-and-whisker plots below the graph represent the 20 individual samples. As you can see, there is variability among the individual sample means. If you look closely, almost all of the sample means fall between 80 and 120, within two standard deviations of the mean, $\pm 2\ \sigma$. Most fall between 90 and 110, within one standard deviation of the mean, $\pm 1\ \sigma$. One sample is greater than 120, but it seems to be the exception rather than the rule. This figure illustrates how we can use the sample statistics and sample size to determine the accuracy of the sample mean as an estimate of the population mean.

### Confidence Interval

You may be familiar with the concept of the confidence interval (CI). In general, a confidence interval is computed from data gathered from a

# Figure 7.5

**Illustration of the Central Limit Theorem**

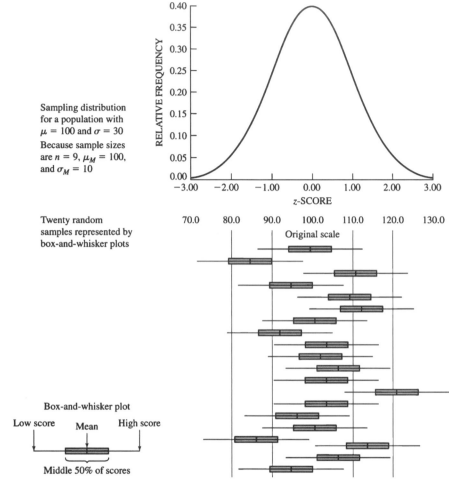

Sampling distribution for a population with $\mu = 100$ and $\sigma = 30$

Because sample sizes are $n = 9$, $\mu_M = 100$, and $\sigma_M = 10$

Twenty random samples represented by box-and-whisker plots

Box-and-whisker plot

Low score   Mean   High score

Middle 50% of scores

The modified box-and-whisker plots represent 20 random samples drawn from a population where $\mu = 100$ and $\sigma = 30$. For each plot, the long horizontal line represents the range between the lowest and highest scores. The rectangle represents the middle 50% of the sample. The vertical line within the box is the sample mean. The sample size of each sample is $n = 9$. The four long vertical lines represent the location of $\pm 1\sigma_M$ and $\pm 2\sigma_M$. For the sampling distribution of means, $\mu_M = 100$ and $\sigma_M = 10$, $10 = 30/\sqrt{9}$. Note: Typically when using a box-and-whisker plot the median and not the mean is used as the plotted measure of central tendency. However, for this example the mean was used since *SEM* deals with a sampling distribution of sample means.

sample of respondents. It provides a lower- and upper-bounded range that will include the corresponding population parameter value most of the time (often set to 95% of the time). In other words, and more importantly for our present purposes, a confidence interval is another way of evaluating the accuracy of the sample mean as an estimate of what really could be expected in the larger population. If the mean is a really accurate representation of the population parameter, then the range from the low to the high end of the confidence interval should be very narrow. Conversely, if the mean is a lousy illustration of what we should expect in the population, the range of the confidence interval should be much larger or wider.

Whenever you read or hear about a political poll, you may hear that the results are accurate to ±5 points or ±3 points. This statement reflects a confidence interval of sorts. For example, if Strickland[1] and Hollister are running for public office and a poll of registered voters shows Strickland with 60% of the popular support ±5 points, we can conclude that between 55% and 65% of the registered voters favor Strickland. Statisticians call these estimates the **point estimate** and the **interval estimate**. The point estimate refers to the use of a sample statistic to estimate the corresponding population parameter. In this example, we estimated that 60% of the voters would vote for Strickland. The interval estimate allows us to describe the accuracy of the statistic as an estimate of the population parameter.

We can also use the point and interval estimates to make inferences about the differences between population parameters. Consider two examples. First, imagine that the estimate for Strickland is 60% ±5 points and the estimate for Hollister is 40% ±5 points. There is no overlap of the interval estimates for the two candidates. Given these data, we may infer that Strickland is the clear favorite.

Now imagine a different situation. In this example, the estimate for Strickland is 52% ±5 points and the estimate for Hollister is 48% ±5 points. Because the two sample point estimates are within the interval estimate of the other sample, we would infer that the difference between 52% and 48% may represent the standard error. In other words, registered voters do not clearly favor one candidate over the other.

There are several ways to calculate the confidence interval depending on the type of data one collects. Specifically, there are confidence intervals for the proportion and for the mean. As you will see, they share common elements.

### Confidence Interval for Proportions

A proportion ($p$) is a special type of mean. In the political example regarding the Strickland–Hollister race, we might find that for Strickland, $p = 0.60$. To obtain this number, a pollster may have randomly contacted 400 registered voters who indicated that they are very likely to vote. Of these, 240 indicated that they favor Strickland. Therefore, $p = 0.60 = 240/400$. What would happen if we conducted another random sample? Assuming that people have not changed their opinion of Strickland, what range of proportions would we expect to find? To answer this question, we first need to calculate the standard error of the proportion using the following equation:

$$SE_p = \frac{\sqrt{p(1-p)}}{\sqrt{N}} \tag{7.3}$$

---

[1] As an aside, Dr. Ted Strickland was the first psychologist to be elected to the U.S. House of Representatives. He was later elected the Governor of Ohio.

For this equation, $p$ represents the proportion that we want to examine and $N$ represents the total number of people we sampled. Applying the equation to this example, we proceed with the following steps:

$$SE_p = \frac{\sqrt{(.60)(1-.600)}}{\sqrt{400}} = \frac{\sqrt{(.60)(.40)}}{20} = \frac{\sqrt{.24}}{20} = \frac{.4899}{20} = 0.0245$$

Once we have the standard error of the proportion, we can then determine the confidence interval using the equation,

$$CI = p \pm z_{(1-\alpha)/2} \qquad (7.4)$$

For this equation, $z_{(1-\alpha)/2}$ represents the $z$-score that indicates the lower and upper levels of the confidence interval. To determine the appropriate $z$-score, you will first need to determine the confidence interval that you want to use. For example, if you set $1 - \alpha = .90$, then you want to have a range that represents 90% of potential means. If you set $1 - \alpha = .95$, then you have established a 95% confidence interval. To determine the corresponding $z$-score, divide $1 - \alpha$ by 2 [e.g., $(1 - \alpha)/2$], then turn to Table B.1 of Appendix B. Looking down Column B, find the proportion that matches $(1 - \alpha)/2$ and use the corresponding $z$-score for your calculations. Table 7.3 represents the $z$-scores that correspond with different confidence intervals and the corresponding $z$-scores.

As you can see in Table 7.3, if we had selected a 95% confidence interval, the confidence interval is $.60 \pm 0.0480$. By multiplying the values by 100, we can convert the proportions to percentages—60% $\pm$ 4.8%. Therefore, if we collected additional random samples of 400 registered voters, we would expect the percentage of people supporting Strickland to range between 55.5% and 64.8%.

### Confidence Interval for Means

We can apply the same logic used in the previous section to determine the confidence interval for the arithmetic mean. You should recognize some familiar terms in Equation 7.5; $M$ represents the mean of the sample, and $SD$ $\sqrt{n}$ is the standard error of the mean. In this form of the equation, we use $SD$

## Table 7.3   Calculating the Confidence Interval for a Proportion

| Confidence interval | | | |
|---|---|---|---|
| 68% | 90% | 95% | 99% |
| $(1-\alpha)/2 = .34$ | $(1-\alpha)/2 = .45$ | $(1-\alpha)/2 = .475$ | $(1-\alpha)/2 = .495$ |
| $z_{(1-\alpha)/2}$ scores | | | |
| $z_{(1-\alpha)/2} = 1.00$ | $z_{(1-\alpha)/2} = 1.65$ | $z_{(1-\alpha)/2} = 1.96$ | $z_{(1-\alpha)/2} = 2.58$ |
| $CI = .60 \pm 1.0(0.0245)$ | $CI = .60 \pm 1.65(0.0245)$ | $CI = .60 \pm 1.96(0.0245)$ | $CI = .60 \pm 2.58(0.0245)$ |
| $CI = .60 \pm 0.0244$ | $CI = .60 \pm 0.0404$ | $CI = .60 \pm 0.0480$ | $CI = .60 \pm 0.0632$ |
| .5755–.6244 | .5595–.6404 | .5552–.6480 | .5367–.6632 |

## Table 7.4  Calculating the Confidence Interval for a Sample Mean for $df = 15$

| Confidence interval | | |
| --- | --- | --- |
| 90% | 95% | 99% |
| $(1-\alpha) = .90$ | $(1-\alpha) = .95$ | $(1-\alpha) = .99$ |
| $t_{(1-\alpha)/2}$ scores | | |
| $t_{(1-\alpha)/2} = 1.753$ | $t_{(1-\alpha)/2} = 2.131$ | $t_{(1-\alpha)/2} = 2.947$ |
| $CI = 75 \pm 1.753(1.25)$ | $CI = 75 \pm 2.131(1.25)$ | $CI = 75 \pm 2.947(1.25)$ |
| $CI = 75 \pm 2.191$ | $CI = 75 \pm 2.638$ | $CI = 75 \pm 3.684$ |
| 72.8–77.2 | 72.4–77.6 | 71.3–78.7 |

to estimate the population standard deviation. The other term in the equation, $t_{(1-\alpha)/2}$, may be new to you. This variable is similar to $z_{(1-\alpha)/2}$ in that it determines the specific values for the upper and lower limits of the confidence interval. The difference between $z_{(1-\alpha)/2}$ and $t_{(1-\alpha)/2}$ is that $z_{(1-\alpha)/2}$ represents the normal distribution, whereas $t_{(1-\alpha)/2}$ represents the sampling distribution of the mean for specific sample sizes. We can work through a problem to illustrate how to use Equation 7.5.

$$CI = M \pm t_{(1-\alpha)/2}\left(SD/\sqrt{n}\right) \qquad (7.5)$$

Assume that you create a random sample of 16 people and give each person a test. According to your calculations, $M = 75.0$ and $SD = 5.0$. What is the confidence interval for your mean? The first thing you will need to do is determine the appropriate value for $t_{(1-\alpha)/2}$. To obtain this value, turn to the appropriate table in Appendix B. In the instructions, you will see that you need to convert the sample size to the degrees of freedom ($df$) by calculating $n - 1$. For this example, the $df$ = 15 (i.e., 16 − 1). Using the value of $df$, select the appropriate value of $t$ for the equation. To find this value, use the column of numbers labeled "Level of Significance of a Two-Tailed or Nondirectional Test" and the appropriate level of $1 - \alpha$. This column of numbers represents that we want to estimate a symmetrical area about the mean of the distribution with $\alpha$ split equally between the two extreme ends of the table. For example, if we set $1 - \alpha = .95$ we find that $t_{(1-\alpha)/2} = 2.131$. Table 7.4 presents an example of these calculations.

If we had set $1 - \alpha = .95$, then the confidence interval is 72.4–77.6. Therefore, if we continue to create random samples of 16 from this population, we can expect that 95% of them will be between 72.4 and 77.6. We can also conclude that the probability of obtaining at random a sample with a mean less than 72.4 or greater than 77.6 is 5%.

### Interpreting the Confidence Interval

The confidence interval allows us to estimate the potential range of sample means that will include the population parameter $k$% of the time. Consider the 95% confidence interval, one that many researchers typically use. For the example in Figure 7.5, the 95% confidence interval extends between 80.0 and 120.0, inclusive. The confidence interval indicates that if we were to take an infinite number of samples from the population, each with a sample size of 9 (as in this example), and calculate their mean and associated confidence intervals, we would expect 95% of those confidence intervals to contain the true population value.

### Factors That Affect *SEM*

What are the factors that influence the size of the standard error? Are there ways that we can reduce the standard error and thereby increase the accuracy of the sample mean as an estimate of the population mean? According to the Central Limit Theorem, two factors influence the standard error of the mean, the standard deviation of the population ($\sigma$) and the sample size ($n$). As the standard deviation of the population decreases, the size of the *SEM* will also decrease, all else being equal.

How can you change the value of $\sigma$ if it is a constant value and parameter of the population? Technically, you cannot change $\sigma$, but you can change the way you define your population. One way to reduce $\sigma$ is to refine your definition of the population. Broad and sweeping definitions of the population tend to correspond with large variability in individual scores. As you begin to refine your definition of the population, the members of the population may tend to become more homogeneous (similar) to each other. Having a more specific definition of your population may also help you better understand the phenomenon you are studying.

Adults who suffer from depression, for example, may experience an extremely wide range of symptoms. If you defined your population as anyone who has experienced depression, your population would include about every living person. By contrast, if you defined your population as young-adult (18 to 29 years of age) women who had met the criteria for a major depressive episode lasting between one and two years, your population would probably be much more homogeneous; that is, $\sigma$ will be smaller. You may find that this more narrow definition of the population will allow you to understand depression for this population. In addition, you might be able to make more accurate statements about how depression expresses itself in different populations (e.g., men versus women; older versus younger people; short-term versus long-term depression).

As the researcher, you can directly control the size of your sample. According to the Central Limit Theorem, the sample size affects the *SEM* by $1/\sqrt{n}$. Specifically, as the sample size increases, the *SEM* will decrease. Figure 7.6 presents the relation between the *SEM* and sample size. The message presented in the graph is clear; as the sample size increases, the magnitude of the *SEM* decreases. Therefore, if you want the sample mean to accurately represent the population mean, you should maximize the sample size.

Another important message in the graph is that increasing sample size has diminishing returns. Specifically, greater increases in sample size

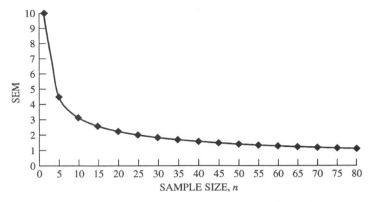

# Figure 7.6

**Size of the Standard Error of the Mean (*SEM*) as the Sample Size Increases**

As sample size increases, the size of the *SEM* decreases by $1/\sqrt{n}$.

produce minor reductions in the *SEM*. As you can see on the left side of the graph, small increases in sample size (e.g., $n = 5$ to $n = 25$) produce large drops in the *SEM*. As the sample size increases, however, the changes in *SEM* decrease. Why is this fact important?

Sampling is expensive. Selecting individuals from the population and collecting the necessary information is time consuming. In addition, recruiting and collecting data from each participant adds to the cost of the research. Therefore, it is not always practical or feasible to collect exceptionally large samples. Because of the economic impact that sample size has on the cost of the research, determining the optimal sample size of the research is an important part of any research plan. We will examine methods to determine the optimal sample size in subsequent chapters when we review specific research methods. Although these techniques vary depending on the type of research, they all depend on the propositions contained in the Central Limit Theorem.

## Sources of Bias and Error: A Reprise

The focus of this chapter has been sampling. We have examined different methods of obtaining samples that we hope are representative of the population. At different points in the chapter, we have reviewed bias and error. As a generality, *bias* refers to nonrandom and systematic factors that cause the sample mean to be different from the population mean. By contrast, *error* refers to random events that we cannot control. The goal of research design is to identify ways that we can eliminate bias and reduce error as much as possible.

Figure 7.7 presents an outline of the relation between the target population, sampling population, sampling distribution, and individual sample. Each level in the figure indicates a potential source of bias or error.

# Figure 7.7

**Potential Sources of Bias and Error when Forming Samples**

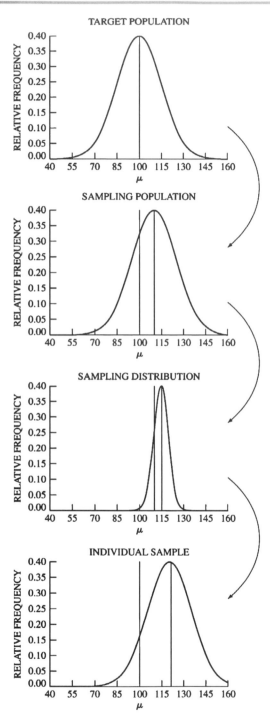

**TARGET POPULATION**

Target population: $\mu$
$\mu = 100$

Population to which we want to generalize findings

**SAMPLING POPULATION**

Nonsampling bias: $\mu' - \mu$
$\mu' = 110$

Difference between target population mean and sampling population mean
• Definition of sampling frame
• Participants decline to participate in the study
• Other forms of nonrandom bias

**SAMPLING DISTRIBUTION**

Sampling bias: $\mu_M - \mu'$
$\mu_M = 115$

Difference between sampling population mean and sampling distribution mean
• Bias in sampling method

**INDIVIDUAL SAMPLE**

Sampling error: $M - \mu_M$
$M = 120$

Difference between sampling distribution mean and sample mean
• Error is random and independent

Total error $M - \mu$
$120 - 100 = 20$

## Target Population

The target population consists of the people whom we wish to describe using our sample. The mean of the population, $\mu$, represents the typical score of individuals in the population, and differences among the individuals within the population represents the natural variation among them. We use $\sigma$ to represent the naturally occurring differences among individuals. If we draw an unbiased sample from this population, then the mean and standard deviation of the sample should estimate $\mu$ and $\sigma$, respectively.

## Sampling Population

The sampling population represents the population of individuals from which we eventually draw the sample. In Figure 7.7, the mean of the sampling population is $\mu'$. In an ideal research situation, $\mu$ and $\mu'$ will be identical because the sampling population will represent the target population. Consequently, any difference between $\mu$ and $\mu'$ represents a **nonsampling bias**. Figure 7.7 depicts a nonsampling bias because the mean of the sampling population is greater than the target population. There are several potential sources of nonsampling bias. First, our definition of the sampling population and use of a sampling frame could bias our results. As an example, imagine that a researcher wanted to examine adults who suffer from depression, a broad target population. What do you think would happen if the researcher conducted the research at a veterans' hospital? Because the veterans' hospital provides service for only current and former members of the military, it is possible that the sampling population will not accurately represent the target population. In addition, the researcher may find that the hospital's records are incomplete and inaccurate. Consequently, he or she might not be able to contact all of the hospital's current and former patients.

## Sampling Distribution

The sampling distribution represents the theoretical distribution of sample means for samples drawn from the sampling population. If the sampling procedure is truly random, then the mean of the sampling distribution will equal the mean of the sampling population, $\mu_M = \mu'$. A systematic selection bias in the sampling procedure will produce **sampling bias**.

## Individual Sample

The last step illustrated in Figure 7.7 is the creation of the individual sample. Any difference between the mean of the sample and the mean of the sampling distribution represents the standard error. The standard error, unlike the different forms of bias, is a random event. Therefore, we consider the sample mean to be equivalent to the mean of the sampling distribution.

**Total Error**

The total error is the difference between the individual sample mean and the population mean, $M - \mu$. From Figure 7.7, you can see that the total error reflects the total effects of nonsampling bias, sampling bias, and the sampling error.

**Inferences from the Sample to the Population**

At the start of the chapter, we noted that we cannot directly assess the external validity or the representativeness of a sample merely by inspecting the sample data. Because we never know the true value of $\mu$, we cannot determine what proportion of the total error reflects bias and what proportion reflects the standard error. Therefore, we need to ensure that our sampling and research methods are free of bias.

## Research in Action: Trends in HIV-Related Risk Behaviors

Human immunodeficiency virus (HIV) is a serious health risk. During 1997, HIV was the seventh leading cause of death among persons aged 15–24 in the United States (Ventura, Anderson, Martin, & Smith, 1998). The virus is bloodborne and spreads when there is an exchange of blood. Many people contract HIV while engaged in intimate contact, including sexual intercourse. Although there are many treatments for the symptoms of HIV and acquired immunodeficiency syndrome (AIDS), there is no cure for these dreadful conditions. Therefore, health experts and policymakers have worked hard to educate the public about the threat of HIV and AIDS. Part of this education has been to discourage adolescents from engaging in risky sexual behaviors (e.g., sexual relations without a condom and with multiple partners) that increase the risk of contracting HIV.

Since 1991, a division of the Centers for Disease Control (CDC) has gathered extensive data on the prevalence of risky sexual behaviors among high school–aged adolescents. To collect the data, the researchers used a two-stage cluster sampling method. First, they selected seven large-city school districts, including Boston, Chicago, Dallas, Fort Lauderdale, Jersey City, Miami, and Philadelphia. The researchers selected these cities because the spread of HIV is greatest in urban areas. In addition, these cities represent the major geographic regions of the nation. Next, the researchers randomly selected schools within these cities to conduct their survey. The survey was anonymous and contanied questions about the students' age, ethnic group, and sexual behaviors. The CDC collected data in 1991, 1993, 1995, and 1997. During these years, the return rate for the questionnaires ranged between 60% and 85% (Centers for Disease Control, 1999).

Figures 7.8 and 7.9 represent the changes in adolescent sexual behavior practices between 1991 and 1997. Specifically, Figure 7.8 represents the percentage of adolescents who had had four or more sexual

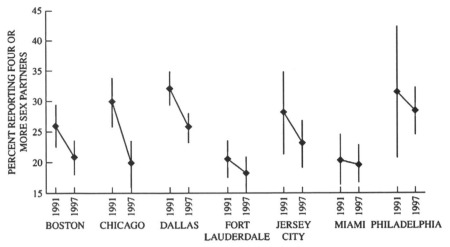

## Figure 7.8

**Percentage of Adolescents Living in Seven Metropolitan Areas Reporting Having Four or More Sex Partners During their Lifetime**

The diamonds represent the mean and the vertical lines represent the 95% confidence interval. Data based on report published by the Centers for Disease Control (1999).

partners during their lifetime. There are differences among the seven major metropolitan areas—students in some cities reported having, on average, more sexual partners than students in other cities. Using the confidence interval, you can see that there is also variability within each metropolitan area. Finally, you should see a general trend between 1991 and 1997—the percentage of adolescents reporting multiple sexual partners decreased. Furthermore, the greatest relative change appears to have occurred in Chicago and Dallas.

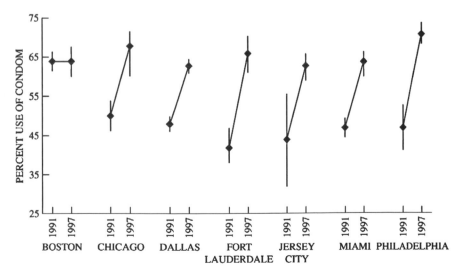

## Figure 7.9

**Percentage of Adolescents Living in Seven Metropolitan Areas Reporting they Used a Condom During a Sexual Encounter**

The diamonds represent the mean and the vertical lines represent the 95% confidence interval. Data based on report published by the Centers for Disease Control (1999).

Figure 7.9 represents the percentage of adolescents who reported using condoms during their sexual encounters. These data represent a clear trend. With the exception of Boston, each metropolitan area showed a considerable increase in condom use. In some cases, the rate of reported condom use nearly doubled.

There are important components of this example. First, you can see that basic statistical principles and sampling methods allow researchers to address an important issue of great social importance. Second, the example offers a real-life example of the application of sampling techniques. Finally, the data allow us to show how the confidence interval helps us interpret the data. Without the confidence intervals, we would not be able to say whether the differences among the means were relatively trivial or represented a stunning change.

There are some things that the statistics can and cannot tell us. It does appear that students' reported sexual behaviors have changed, and that this change represents less-risky sexual behavior. Can we conclude that educational programs and AIDS-awareness campaigns helped reduce risky sexual behaviors? Have these programs been a success? Is there anything missing—should the researchers collect additional information? If you had the opportunity to repeat this research, what would you do differently?

Are these data representative of all adolescents? What would happen if we collected similar data for rural areas or smaller cities? Is it possible that students in urban areas receive greater exposure to AIDS-awareness campaigns or are more likely to have a friend or family member contract HIV and develop AIDS?

Although there has been an increase in condom use, do we really want to say that the educational programs are a success? From one perspective, condom use among adolescents is much higher at the end of the decade than at the start. From another perspective, condom use among adolescents is still low. If 40% of the adolescents are still engaged in unprotected sexual intercourse, there is still an incredible health risk for those individuals. Adolescents who do not use condoms may well contract and spread HIV to others. From this perspective, the data are encouraging, but far from great. Recognize that the same results can afford different interpretations.

We might also question the validity of the data we collected. Were the students being honest when they completed the questionnaire? The truth is, people lie, especially about sex. Is it possible that these students say that they use condoms when they do not? Is it possible that the AIDS-awareness program taught students what to say about condom use but had no effect on their behavior?

Finally, we can ask whether we have taught adolescents the right thing. Many religious leaders and policymakers believe that adolescents should be encouraged to abstain from sexual intercourse until marriage. Some people may see the data as the results of a failed policy. Some may argue that the AIDS-awareness programs continue to encourage immoral behaviors.

Some of the questions we raised are empirical. We can collect more information to understand changes in adolescents' sexual behavior.

Researchers can conduct surveys in different parts of the country to determine whether there are differences between urban and rural areas. Similarly, researchers can collect data concerning the rates of HIV among age groups. If the students are telling the truth about their sexual behavior, then there should be a decrease in the rate of HIV.

The other questions are equally important but require different intellectual tools. Is 60% condom use high or low? To answer this question, you need to examine your priorities. If you believe that the goal of AIDS awareness is to increase condom use, then 60% is far better than 40%. If you had hoped for perfect results, the 60% rate may be encouraging, but still disappointing.

## Knowledge Check

11. What is the difference between a sampling distribution and the distribution of sample scores?

12. Assume that you were to create sampling distributions by creating random samples. Describe the factors that will affect the shape of the distribution.

13. What is the relation among $M$, $\mu$, and $\mu_M$?

14. What is the relation among $SD$, $\sigma$, and $\sigma_M$?

15. For an individual random sample:
    a. What accounts for $X - M$?
    b. What accounts for $M - \mu$?

16. For the research described in the "Research in Action" section, describe the sampling techniques that the researchers may have used to collect the data.

17. Some people are surprised to learn that some samples used to represent national trends consist of "only 500" participants. Based on what you know about sampling, why might a sample size of 500 be sufficient?

18. A researcher wants to conduct a study of people who abuse crack cocaine. Why would probability sampling be difficult to use in this situation? How could the researcher use nonprobability techniques to create a sample of this population?

19. The president of a prestigious private college reports that the average graduate of the college makes 2.5 times more money that the average graduate of other colleges. When asked about the source of the numbers, the president claims that the staff of the alumni office called a random number of the college's alumni and requested current information, including annual income. The president then says that the average income for other college graduates comes from the most recent census data that indicate the median income of college

graduates. Do you accept the president's claim that graduates of the college are more affluent than the typical college graduate?

20. A researcher believes that his or her sampling procedure may be biased. Will increasing the sample size help the researcher collect data to better represent the population?

## Chapter Summary

The primary focus of this chapter was how researchers use samples to make inferences about populations. Specifically, we examined the purpose of samples, how researchers construct useful samples, and ways to ensure that the sample represents the population.

Sampling is not a haphazard and casual method of collecting information. We examined how scientific evidence is different from personal experience and anecdotal evidence. When we depend on anecdotal evidence and personal experience, we are likely to come to the wrong conclusion. Bacon recognized this problem when he described the Idols of the Cave. Personal experience is not sufficient for understanding complex behavioral phenomenon. Rather, we need to depend on objectively constructed samples to represent the population.

Probability sampling ensures that the sample will represent the population. According to the law of large numbers, if we randomly select members of the population, the sample will share the same features as the population. Random selection means that every element of the population has an equal and independent probability of being selected. Using probability sampling, we can predict the probability of selecting different samples from the population.

When we describe sampling procedures, we make distinctions between different types of populations. The target population represents the group that we hope to describe with our research. The sampling population is the group from which we create our sample. If the sampling population is representative of the target population, then we can use the sample to make inferences about the target population. The sampling frame represents the list or resource that identifies the members of the sampling population. For all cases, the researcher creates operational definitions of the target and sampling populations.

There are several probability sampling techniques. For random sampling, each member of the population has an equal and independent probability of selection. Sequential sampling allows us to select each $k$th member from the sampling frame. Another sampling tactic is stratified sampling, in which we identify important subgroups in the population and then take random or sequential samples from each subgroup. Finally, in cluster sampling, we identify clusters of individuals and then randomly select several clusters for the research.

In some situations, nonprobability sampling procedures are the only ways of creating a sample. For convenience sampling, we allow the participants' behavior to determine whether they are included in the sample. Convenience sampling means that the participants are easy to locate. Another technique is snowball sampling, where we ask the participants to help the researcher locate or recruit additional participants for the research.

The Central Limit Theorem is a statement about the shape of a sampling distribution. The Central Limit Theorem states that for any population, the sampling distribution of means will tend to be normally distributed, especially when the sample size is large; that the mean of the sampling distribution will equal the mean of the population; and that the standard deviation of the sampling distribution will equal the standard deviation of the population divided by the square root of the sample size. The Central Limit Theorem, therefore, allows us to predict the probability of various samples.

Given the predictions of the Central Limit Theorem, we examined how the researcher can change the standard error by increasing sample size or changing $\sigma$ by redefining the population.

Creating a sample is not easy to do because there are several sources of bias and error. We examined how different factors, such as a poor-quality sampling frame, can bias our results. Similarly, we distinguished among nonsampling bias, sampling bias, and sampling error. Nonsampling bias occurs when the sampling population differs from the target population. Sampling bias occurs when we use nonprobability sampling procedures. The standard error, by contrast, represents random differences among sample means.

We ended the chapter by reviewing a comprehensive and national research study of risky sexual behavior. The example illustrated the use of various sampling procedures and demonstrated how sample data allow us to make inferences about population parameters.

## Chapter Glossary for Review

**Anecdotal evidence**—A brief and typically personal account that may not represent true events. Anecdotal evidence is often a biased and unrepresentative sample of a population.

**Central Limit Theorem**—A mathematical postulate that states that the sampling distribution of randomly generated sample means will: (1) tend to be normally distributed especially as sample size increases, (2) have a mean equal to the population mean, and (3) have a standard deviation equal to the standard deviation of the population divided by the square root of the sample size.

**Convenience sampling**—Selecting members of the population who are easy to find and study.

**Independence**—A condition that exists when each event has no effect on subsequent events.

**Interval estimate**—An estimate of the accuracy of the sample statistic as an estimate of the population parameter, specifically the potential range of sample statistics that would occur when creating additional samples.

**Law of large numbers**—Prediction that any large number of items chosen at random from the population will, on average, represent the population.

**Nonprobability sampling**—Any method of sampling that does not use random events or probability methods to create the sample.

**Nonsampling bias**—A nonrandom and systematic set of conditions that causes the mean of the sampling population to be different from the mean of the target population.

**Point estimate**—Using a sample statistic to estimate the value of the corresponding population parameter.

**Probability sampling**—A method of creating a representative sample that uses random and independent procedures for selecting individuals from the population.

**Random**—Each potential event has an equal probability of occurring, and the occurrence of one event has no influence on the probability of subsequent events.

**Random numbers**—A sequence of numbers having no pattern or sequence because there is an equal probability of selecting each number, and the selection of one number has no effect on selecting another number.

**Sampling bias**—A nonrandom and systematic set of conditions that causes the mean of the sampling distribution to be different from the mean of the sampling population.

**Sampling distribution**—A theoretical probability distribution of the potential values of a sample statistic that would occur when drawing an infinite number of equal-sized random samples from the population.

**Sampling frame**—A list or some other resource that identifies the members of the sampling population.

**Sampling interval**—The number used in sequential sampling to select members of the population for the sample.

**Sampling population**—An accessible population that shares the same characteristics as the target population and from which the researcher draws the sample.

**Sequential sampling**—A method of sampling where one selects every $k$th member from a list.

**Simple random sampling**—A method of creating a representative sample of a population. Each member of the population has an equal probability of selection, and the selection of one member has no effect on the selection of other members of the population.

**Snowball sampling**—Asking members of the sample to identify additional members of a population who could participate in the research.

**Standard error**—The random difference between a sample statistic and the corresponding population parameter.

**Standard error of the mean**—The standard deviation of the sampling distribution of means.

**Subject pool**—A group of individuals available and willing to participate in research projects.

**Target population** or **universe**—All members of a group who share one or more common characteristics defined by the researcher.

## Chapter References

American Psychiatric Association (2000). *Diagnostic and statistical manual of mental disorders* (4th ed; Text revision). Washington, DC: Author.

Babbie, E. (1998). *Survey Research Methods* (2nd ed.). Belmont, CA: Wadsworth.

Centers for Disease Control (1999). Trends in HIV-related sexual risk behaviors among high school students—selected U.S. Cities, 1991–1997. *Morbidity and Mortality Weekly Review, 48*, 440–443.

Cochran, W. G. (1977). *Sampling techniques* (3rd ed.). New York: John Wiley & Sons.

Hooker, E. (1956). A preliminary analysis of group behavior of homosexuals. *Journal of Psychology, 42*, 217–225.

Hooker, E. (1957). The adjustment of the male overt homosexual. *Journal of Projective Techniques, 21*, 18–31.

Hooker, E. (1958). Male homosexuality in the Rorschach. *Journal of Projective Techniques, 22*, 33–54.

Pashley, P. J. (1993). On generating random sequences. In G. Keren & C. Lewis (Eds.), *A Handbook for data analysis in the behavioral sciences: Methodological issues* (pp. 395–418). Hillsdale, NJ: LEA.

Plous, S. (1993). *The psychology of judgment and decision making.* Boston: McGraw-Hill.

Rand Corporation. (1955). *A million random digits with 100,000 normal deviates.* Glenco, IL: Free Press.

Salant, P., & Dillman, D. A. (1994). *How to conduct your own survey.* New York: John Wiley & Sons.

Ventura, S. J., Anderson, R. N., Martin, J. A., & Smith, B. L. (1998). Births and deaths: Preliminary data for1997. *National Vital Statistics Reports, 47*, 4.

Wilkinson, L. (1999). Statistical methods in psychological journals: Guidelines and explanations. *American Psychologist, 54*, 594–604.

# Chapter 8
## Creating and Using Assessments, Surveys, and Objective Measures

## CHAPTER OBJECTIVES

**Introduction**
**Purpose of Measurement**
**Caveat Assessor**
**Creating a Measurement Scale and Developing a Data
    Collection Strategy**
**Interviews, Questionnaires, and Attitude Surveys**
**Question Response Formats**
**Writing Good Questionnaire and Survey Items**
**Determining the Sample Size for a Survey**
**Naturalistic Observation**
**Research in Action: Analysis of Assaults**

> Psychology cannot attain the certainties and exactness of the physical sciences,
> unless it rests upon a foundation of experiment and measurement.
> —**James McKeen Cattell**

## Introduction

Measurement is at the heart of all the empirical sciences. Without objective measurement, there can be no science. This fact did not escape Cattell's (1890) attention or that of the generations of scientists who followed him. Therefore, the task of this chapter is clear; it will show you how researchers create questionnaires and surveys.

## Purpose of Measurement

There are two goals of measurement. The first is to replace the ambiguity of words and general concepts with operationally defined constructs. In our day-to-day language we often say that someone has an "extraverted personality," is a "senior citizen," or is "adept at mathematics." We may also want to know whether reinforcement will "reduce a child's intrinsic motivation." Although these phrases convey some information, they also present considerable ambiguity. What, for example, is a *senior citizen*—someone over 65, 75, or 85? Defining an age in this case clarifies our meaning of *senior* by offering an operational definition. As Wilkinson (1999) noted, the value of an operational definition is that it provides a specific method for converting observations to a specified range of potential values. Using operational definitions helps researchers achieve the goal of public verification of observation because other researchers can then use and, if necessary, critique and revise the operational definition for future work.

The second goal of measurement is standardization or consistency in measurement. Consistency of measurement allows us to compare people using a common set of procedures and scales. Standardization also implies that the numbers used in the measure have a constant meaning. For example, a score of 110 on a standardized test of a construct such as intelligence has a meaning that does not change over time, across situations, or across people.

## Caveat Assessor

There are two common misperceptions of scientific measurements. Interestingly, these two misperceptions operate in opposition to one another. On the one hand, we tend to mistrust measurement, while on the other hand we tend to put too much trust in measurement. With respect to mistrust, how many times have you read or heard something such as, "There are some things that you cannot measure," or "Some human behaviors are too complex to measure objectively"? These are common statements made by people who want to either discredit a research finding or argue that psychology cannot be a science. The problem with this type of belief is that it is inconsistent to say that you cannot objectively measure a construct that is describable with words. That we can use words to describe a specific phenomenon means that we must have the ability to recognize that phenomenon in some way. Therefore, translating those points of recognition into objective measurement cannot be too far away.

The second error associated with any measurement is due to our tendency as humans to place uncritical trust in numbers. Kaplan (1964) called this problem the **mystique of quantity**, which he defined as "an exaggerated regard for the significance of measurement, just because it is quantitative, without regard to what has been measured . . . [the] number is treated as having intrinsic scientific value" (p. 172). One consequence of the mystique of quantity is what philosophers of science call **reification**. Reification occurs when we incorrectly treat a measurement as if it represents some real thing, rather than the quantification of a more abstract construct. As Dewdney (1997) noted, because we have a word for something does not mean that this thing exists independent of the word. For perspective, the reification problem is an example of Bacon's Idol of the Marketplace, which we reviewed in Chapter 1. As you may recall, we examined how psychologists' use of phrases such as "maternal absence" influenced how they conducted and interpreted the results of their research on the effects of child care.

Consider the words *beauty*, *anxiety*, and *intelligence*, words we use routinely. For example, one might say that a painting by the famous artist Mary Cassett is "beautiful." There is nothing in the painting that is, by itself, beautiful. What does exist is Cassett's unique choice of pigmented paints and their arrangement on the canvas; nothing in the picture itself is objectively beautiful. Instead, *beauty* describes a viewer's perceptions of, and reactions to, the elements of the painting. We commonly invent words or constructs to help us make predictions and offer explanations. In most cases, we can operationally define these words for the purpose of our research. In Chapter 3, we used the example of anxiety. *Anxiety* is an abstract concept that we use to pull together different conditions and to explain various behaviors. If we have a clear operational definition of the construct, we might find that the concept helps us explain the relation among several variables.

There is nothing inherently wrong with using hypothetical terms like *intelligence*. We use these words to help us describe, predict, and explain the world. The problem arises when we forget that some of our variables are inventions, and we begin to treat them as if they are real things. Gould (1981) complained that the reification of intelligence has caused many biologists, psychologists, and sociologists to search for its genetic component much as one would search for the genetic foundation of eye color, sickle-cell anemia, Hodgkin's disease, or other heritable conditions. Many believe that such a search is a fool's errand because intelligence is not solely a biologically determined process like eye color, but rather something that develops from the interaction of a person and his or her environment and experiences.

Another serious problem that arises from the mystique of quantification and reification is that some people forget that the numbers by themselves cannot capture or express all the important characteristics associated with a particular phenomenon. No measurement, quantitative or qualitative, can represent all the important components of human behavior. Unfortunately, many people believe that a test measures the "real thing," forgetting that any test may ignore critical characteristics of an individual construct. Miles-Tapping (1996) provided a good example of this problem, when she noted an important difference in the way people who must use wheelchairs used the word *independence*. Many researchers used this word to mean that a person walks without the assistance of a cane, walker, or wheelchair. Therefore, a person who is wheelchair bound is, by that definition, not independent. By contrast, Miles-Tapping found that persons who must use a wheelchair perceive the chair as a symbol and instrument of their independence.

In summary, we need to view testing and measurement with guarded enthusiasm. With sufficient planning, analysis, and revision, social scientists can develop useful measures of the constructs that they are trying to study. We must remember, however, that although we will be able to create a measure that suits most of our needs, all measures are tentative, subject to error and bias, and forever in need of refinement.

## Creating a Measurement Scale and Developing a Data Collection Strategy

In the following sections, we will show you how to create measurement procedures for various applications including observational research, interviews, and surveys. Although each research study is unique, there is a relatively uniform process to follow when creating a sound measurement approach. We introduce the steps in this process with the following three questions that researchers must answer when designing a study and measurement strategy. Then we turn to various techniques for the gathering of data. Finally, we examine more specific information about generating the best questions to ask when gathering data.

### What Questions Are You Trying to Answer?

The best way to answer this question is to carefully review the hypothesis. If you have a well-crafted hypothesis, you should be able to use it to clearly define your independent and dependent variables. Identifying the variables is half the battle when it comes to measurement, as it helps you identify the types of phenomenon (e.g., attitudes, behaviors) you might want to assess. The more specifically you can describe the variables in your study, the better. Consider the hypothesis, "Children who participate in cooperative-learning projects will demonstrate fewer racial stereotypes and prejudicial behaviors." This is a fairly well-stated hypothesis and a good starting point for identifying an appropriate measurement strategy. From this hypothesis, we know that the independent variable is a child's participation in a co-op learning project. The dependent variable has something to do with racial stereotypes and prejudicial behaviors. All we need now is an operational definition of these latter two concepts. How will we measure a stereotype? How will you know whether a child is prejudiced?

### What Is the Most Convenient Method for Producing the Data?

Identifying observable behaviors related to the dependent variable will help determine how you will collect the data. Using the previous example, the definition of prejudicial behavior may focus on how children play with each other. Specifically, do the children from different ethnic groups play together or do they fight? In this case, you may find that an observational technique will supply the data that you need.

However, you may also want to know how the children perceive members of different ethnic groups. Because you are interested in the child's perceptions, you may want to use a questionnaire or an interview. As you will see in the following sections, each method has its relative advantages and disadvantages. Therefore, you will need to weigh these as you consider your options.

### What Is the Most Accurate Measurement Technique?

There is no such thing as a perfect measurement technique, nor is there one that is best in all research situations. Because all measurements have some form of error, you will need to consider methods that will help reduce bias and random errors. For observational research, we can use several trained observers to help ensure that we capture all the relevant information. For questionnaires, we can focus on the wording and design of the questions to ensure accurate results.

## Interviews, Questionnaires, and Attitude Surveys

There are many ways that we can ask people questions, ranging from face-to-face interviews to questionnaires sent through the mail or administered over the Internet. Although the general hypotheses should be generated before choosing the specific research technique or data-gathering procedure, it is often the case that the data collection method we choose will influence the way we ask the questions. For this reason, the questions we ask can be open-ended, allowing respondents to tell us as much or as little as they wish. Our questions can also be closed-ended, requiring a choice from among several options or a simple Yes or No response. As with all research, the selection of specific procedures represents a balancing act between the need for information and the feasibility of the procedure. What follows is a review of several common and different data collection techniques and their relative advantages and disadvantages.

### Personal Interviews

The personal interview, either face-to-face or through the telephone, is a popular and useful way to understand human attitudes and beliefs (Fontana & Frey, 1994). Personal interviews, especially face-to-face interviews, tend to encourage a high degree of cooperation by participants. In addition, people are likely to answer an interviewer's questions rather than check the ''Don't Know'' box on a questionnaire. This should not be terribly surprising—after all, it is difficult to skip or ignore a question when another person asks you a direct question. Other advantages of this method of measurement are that the interviewer can ensure that the participant understands the questions and ask follow-up questions to clarify participants' responses.

In sum, personal interviews can yield a great deal of rich information. There is no single format for the personal interview. Interviews can be highly structured or unstructured. Similarly, the interview may be limited to two people or may involve a small group. Fontana and Frey (1994) described many types of interviewing formats, each of which has a specific

Table 8.1    Review of Various Interview Methods and Their Characteristics

| Type | Characteristics | Format | Use |
|---|---|---|---|
| *Brainstorming* | Unstructured interaction among group members | No set format; interviewer asks questions to facilitate discussion | Generate ideas for a project that will be examined in detail later |
| *Case study* | Intensive study of one person's history and current situation | Unstructured and guided by interaction between interviewer and participant | Demonstration of a general principle or application of a clinical intervention; often the source of ideas for later research |
| *Focus or Delphi group* | Structured interaction between interviewer and a small group of people | Interviewer uses a script of questions, but can ask follow-up probes for additional information | Gather information regarding people's reactions to specific topics; often used for opinion gathering |
| *Formal interview* | Highly structured interaction between interviewer and participant | Interviewer follows a script with little or no room for deviation | Collection of specific information typically for a larger program of research |

role for contemporary research. These formats take place in different settings, require different roles of the interviewer, involve different numbers of people in the discussion, and use different formats for the questions. Table 8.1 presents a review of the different types of interview methods, ranging from not at all structured to highly structured.

### Potential Limitations of Interviews

Although interviews can produce rich data, this information comes at a price. Interviews are time intensive and expensive to conduct. First, you need a staff to conduct the interviews. Unless you can find a team of willing volunteers, you will need to pay staff to assist you. Second, conducting a good interview requires much practice, a bit of acting, and the ability to respond to unpredictable situations. Interviewers need to be trained in how to use the interview technique, how to answer a participant's questions, and how to react to the participant's many comments that may or may not apply to the questions asked.

Although there is no one-size-fits-all approach to good interviewing, in order to prevent experimenter and participant biases from affecting the data, it is often desirable to use at least a semi-structured interview format in which all interviewers ask the same questions, in the same order, and record responses in a structured fashion. Developing structured questions and response formats takes time and requires additional interviewer training. The benefits of doing this far outweigh the consequences, however, and it is becoming standard practice in many applied areas of research and practice linked with the social sciences. The following example illustrates some of the pitfalls common when unstructured interview processes are used.

Conducting interviews is especially difficult when there are significant racial and cultural barriers between the interviewer and the people interviewed. Consider the following example. During the 1930s, the Federal Writers' Project funded in-depth interviews of African Americans living in the southern states (Davidson & Lytle, 1992). In one case, two people independently interviewed Susan Hamlin, a former slave. During part of the first interview she said,

> Mr. Fuller [Susan's owner] was a good man and his wife's people been grand people, all good to their slaves. Seem like Mr. Fuller just git his slaves so he could be good to dem. He made all the little colored chillen love him. (p. 161)

During the second interview she said,

> . . . but our master ain't nebber want to sell his slaves. But dat didn't keep Clory [a mulatto slave owned by Mr. Fuller] frum gittin' a brutal whippin'. Dey whip' 'er untul dere wasn't a white spot on her body. Dat was de worst I ebber se a human bein' got such a beatin'. (p. 165)

Clearly, Susan told different stories about her life as a slave. In the first interview, she described the slave owner as a gentleman who treated his slaves well. The second interview tells a story about ruthless behavior. Davidson and Lytle (1992) discovered that the first interviewer was white, whereas the second interviewer was black. Clearly, Susan was distrustful of white people and unwilling to tell them of her horrible experiences.

The previous example illustrates the need to exercise caution when planning an interview. Good interviewing is not just reading the questions from a script. In many cases, the interview is successful only after the interviewer has gained the participant's trust and willingness to answer honestly. This important skill takes time and practice to cultivate. Personal interviews are useful sources of information but require considerable financial support, professional staff, and time. Consequently, researchers are most likely to use personal interview techniques only as a part of a well-funded grant.

## Self-Administered Surveys

An alternative to the personal interview is the self-administered survey. The survey is the model of simplicity; give many people a few questions and ask them to mark their answers on a sheet of paper. This technique can also be used with open-ended questions that can serve, essentially, as written interviews. More detail on response formats for these types of questions is provided later in this chapter.

The advantages to this method of data collection and measurement are obvious. First, the cost of photocopying and distributing a survey is a fraction of the cost of developing and conducting a personal interview. Second, self-administered surveys are relatively easy to distribute. We can mail the survey along with a stamped return envelope, hand them out to a class of students or some other well-defined group, or administer through an Internet link.

The real costs associated with self-administered surveys arise with respect to the quality of the data they can provide. Many people are likely to throw away surveys they receive in the mail. Therefore, survey data may be biased if the responses that are returned fail to adequately represent those of the broader population. In addition, the researcher has little control over a questionnaire once it is first administered to a participant. There is often no good way to ensure that any responses that are returned came from the person we actually intended to survey.

Although there are many potential liabilities with self-administered surveys, this method of data collection is extremely popular among behavioral researchers. In those situations where many people complete the survey this method can be a cost-effective means of obtaining data. Researchers can use a few simple techniques to maximize compliance with a survey.

### Use a Captive Audience

If one of your research goals is to maximize the number of responses from people within a certain larger group, one strategy is to try to distribute your survey within natural subgroupings of the larger group. For example, in studies that involve college students, many researchers ask students to complete a survey in the last 10 minutes of a class meeting. This is the logic behind the ever-popular Introduction to Psychology participant pools within most universities. Such large-enrollment courses provide an opportunity to gather a large amount of data quickly.

### Use Social Psychology to Your Advantage

According to Salant and Dillman (1994), there are many other strategies you can use to increase the return rate of surveys sent through the mail or hosted on the Internet. Plan to send several letters/e-mails to potential participants. The first should be an advance notice that points out that a survey will be arriving within several days. This letter should convey the importance of the research and the need for the person's response. The second mailing is the survey along with a cover letter that reiterates the importance of the research. If necessary, you can send a third and fourth letter to remind the participants to return the completed questionnaire, although there seems to be a diminishing improvement in survey returns when more than three reminders are sent.

Salant and Dillman (1994) also recommend doing what you can to enhance the distinctiveness of your communications with participants. For example, when sending mailings, use a distinctive envelope, priority mail, or some combination of the two. Although you do not want your package to look like a sweepstakes mailing, you do want it to create the impression that it contains an important document. Finally, make your cover letter as personal as possible, and convey the impression that you eagerly await the person's comments. Figure 8.1 presents examples of the types of letters a researcher might use. The first is a note to introduce the participants to the purpose of the project and tell them of the forthcoming survey. The second is a cover letter for the survey. Both letters emphasize the importance of the research and the need for a timely response from the participant.

Another successful method for increasing return rates is to give potential respondents a small token of thanks. One explanation for how this works to increase response rate comes from the social psychological phenomenon of normative reciprocity. Quite simply, if we do something nice for you, you will feel obligated to return the favor. As an example, Salant and Dillman (1994) noted that attaching a $1 bill to a questionnaire increases response rates by 5 to 8%. Larger denominations ($5 or $20) increase response rates even higher (probably not a practical option for most student research).

Finally, perhaps the easiest thing you can do as a researcher to increase response rate is to make sure you do not give your sample members an easy excuse for not completing the survey immediately. Include a sharpened pencil or a pen with the questionnaire along with a stamped return envelope and make it clear that the deadline for responses is very short.

## Question Response Formats

In addition to selecting the most appropriate method for gathering data from the potential participants in your sample, you also need to identify the right question to ask. These questions need to address the core constructs of your research and, therefore, need to extend directly from your study hypotheses or primary research questions. In general, two main types of questions are asked. The first is an **open-ended question** that asks participants to generate their own response to the question. The second is the **closed-response question** that requires the person to select a response choice from a set of options.

### Open-Ended Questions

A primary advantage of an open-ended question is that it may allow you to obtain very rich and complex data that you could not gather with a closed-response question. Consider the typical course evaluation form that most colleges use at the end of each semester. Most questions on these evaluations tend to be closed-response, asking students to rate the instructor on a five-point scale of greatness from something like Horrible to Amazing. Following these ratings, it is also common to see at least one open-ended question such as, "What do you like most about the instructor's teaching?" or, "In what ways can the instructor improve as a teacher?" Although the answers to the closed-response questions tell us what students think about our teaching in general, it is the written responses to the open-ended

**[your institution's letterhead here]**

September 23, 2010

Dear Ms. Barnas:

Good quality health care is important to everyone in this county. That is why ____ Community Hospital is looking for ways to improve its services. Hospital staff members believe that the best way to improve services is to listen to people in the community, people like you. They have asked me to help with this important research project.

You were selected to share your opinion with us about how well the hospital is doing its job. We also want you to tell us where services could be improved. You should receive the survey within the next 7 to 10 days. The packet will contain the survey, a stamped self-addressed envelope, and a pen. Completing the survey will require about 10 minutes of your time. Your answers will be completely confidential. No one will ever know how you answered these questions. The information from all the surveys will be combined and reported as a group. If you have any questions about the survey or the research, please feel free to contact me at (423) 555-1234.

Sincerely,

Joe T. Professor
Professor of Psychology
Your University, Department of Psychology

**[your institution's letterhead here]**

September 29, 2010

Dear Ms. Barnas:

Enclosed is the survey I mentioned to you in my letter from last week. Along with this survey is a return envelope and a pen. The survey should take about 10 minutes to complete and once you have finished it, please return it to me using the provided envelope. I can assure you that your answers will be completely confidential, so please be honest and thorough with your responses.

The information from all the surveys will be combined and reported in terms of overall averages and themes. The hospital will use the data from this project to find ways that it can improve services to patients living in this county. Your answers will do much to ensure that our hospital meets the future needs of the community. If you have any questions about the survey or the research, please feel free to contact me at (423) 555-1234.

Sincerely,

Joe T. Professor
Professor of Psychology
Your University, Department of Psychology
[your mailing address here]

# Figure 8.1

**An Example of the Letters that One Might Send to Participants in a Survey**

questions that are often more informative. Every semester, each of us receives comments that are sometimes flattering, sometimes humbling, but always illuminating. The written comments provide information difficult to obtain with closed-response questions.

This does not mean that open-ended questions are always the preferred question-and-response format. First, many people provide minimal or vague answers to open-ended questions, especially when they have to write out their own response. Second, written responses can be difficult to evaluate objectively. For example, how should a professor respond to the written comment, "This course is difficult and requires a lot of reading"? Is the student stating a fact or complaining about the course? Because of these ambiguities, many researchers prefer to use closed-response questions for surveys. One compromise is to ask closed-response questions and then provide room for written responses. A second approach is to use qualitative research techniques such as thematic coding to assist with the interpretation of open-ended responses (more details on these techniques are found in Chapter 17).

### Closed-Response Questions

The primary feature of the closed-response question is that the researcher supplies the response options for the person. You can use many alternative formats for a closed-response question. The following are common examples of these formats.

### Nominal Category Response
The answer options for this category represent a nominal scale. In some cases, the question will treat the options as mutually exclusive and force the person to select only one category. In other cases, the question will allow the person to select several separate categories. Table 8.2 is an example of nominal category response items.

### Forced Choice Alternatives
For these questions, we ask the participants to select a response that best represents their answer to the question. In this case, we assume that the

## Table 8.2    Example of Nominal Category Response Items

**Mutually exclusive response options:**

| Sex: | ____Female | ____Male | | |
|---|---|---|---|---|
| I am: | ____Single | ____Married | ____Divorced | ____Widowed |

**Multiple nominal response**

I use the following sources to learn about national news (please check all that apply):

| ____Newspapers | ____News magazines | ____Television news |
|---|---|---|
| ____Radio | ____Internet | |

## Table 8.3  Example of Forced Choice Alternatives

**For each of the following pairs of words, mark the word that best describes you:**
_____Liberal vs. _____Conservative
_____Shy vs. _____Outgoing
_____Leader vs. _____Follower
_____Assertive vs. _____Passive
_____Introverted vs. _____Extraverted

**Mark the statement that best describes your belief[*]**
(a)_____In the long run, people get the respect they deserve in this world,

or

(b)_____Unfortunately, an individual's worth often passes unrecognized no matter
how hard he or she tries.

[*]Item from Rotter's (1966) Internal-External locus of control scale.

alternatives represent an underlying scale that ranges between the two extremes. Table 8.3 presents examples of forced choice alternative items.

### Numerical Response Format

The numerical response format (often referred to as the Likert format) is one of the most popular options for the closed-response format questionnaire for two primary reasons. First, it offers a clear and unambiguous ordinal scale of measurement. Second, you can use the same format for many different questions. Therefore, you can combine the responses to multiple questions to yield an overall or average score. Table 8.4 presents several examples of a Likert-type response format. In its most common form, the Likert format consists of an odd number of response options reflecting a

## Table 8.4  Examples of the Likert Format

| Overall, I believe that Mayor Matthews is doing a good job. | | | | |
|---|---|---|---|---|
| 1 | 2 | 3 | 4 | 5 |
| Strongly disagree | Disagree | Neutral | Agree | Strongly agree |

| If the election were held tomorrow, I would | | | | | | |
|---|---|---|---|---|---|---|
| 1 | 2 | 3 | 4 | 5 | 6 | 7 |
| Definitely vote Democrat | | | | | | Definitely vote Republican |

| The meals prepared by the food service are | | | | | | |
|---|---|---|---|---|---|---|
| 1 | 2 | 3 | 4 | 5 | 6 | 7 |
| Consistently good | | | | | | Consistently poor |

range of negative to positive reactions to a specific item or statement. The middlemost response option in this type of scale is a neutral choice. Research on the reliability and validity of scale scores from Likert-type scales has led to the conclusion that 7 or more response options are preferred to the more commonly used 5-option response, but that at least 4 to 10 response options be provided (Chang, 1994; Preston & Colman, 2000).

### Guttman Format

A Guttman scale format, like the Likert format, represents a response continuum that ranges from one extreme to another. For this format, the researcher arranges the answer options by levels of acceptance. When the person responds, we assume he or she agrees with the statement and all the preceding statements as well. Consider the example in Table 8.5. The response alternatives are ranked in such a way that if you agree with one statement, you are likely to agree with all of the preceding statements (e.g., if you agree with option 4, then you likely agree with options 1 through 3 as well).

Although useful, the Guttman format can be difficult to prepare because you cannot rely on your own opinion to determine the best ordering of the response options. To create the scale, you should distribute the individual options to a small and representative sample of the target population, and ask the participants to identify the options that they would endorse. The order of the items for the final Guttman format represents the percent agreement for each response option—those with high levels of agreement come first, followed by options that received lower percentages of agreement and are therefore less likely or more extreme (as in the example presented in Table 8.5).

## Knowledge Check

1. Describe the "reification problem" in your words.
2. What is meant by the phrase "mystique of quantity"?
3. How are the concepts of "reification" and "mystique of quantity" related?
4. Consider the terms *intelligence*, *personality*, and *anxiety*. What are the differences between the way a researcher would use these terms and the way another person would use these terms?

## Table 8.5 Example of a Guttman Format Response Alternative

Which of the following best represents your opinion regarding abortion? Select only one option.
(1)___Abortion may be performed when the mother's life is in danger.
(2)___Abortion may be performed if the fetus has a severe disability.
(3)___Abortion may be performed in cases of rape.
(4)___Abortion may be performed as a type of family planning.
(5)___Abortion may be performed for any reason.

5. Can a science exist without measurement? Justify your opinion.

6. Describe in your words the goals and characteristics of measurement.

7. Why are operational definitions essential for creating a measurement instrument?

8. Assume that you wanted to collect data concerning students' attitudes toward minorities.
   a. What would be the relative advantages and disadvantages of using a personal interview or a self-administered questionnaire?

9. Describe in your words the similarities and differences between the Likert and Guttman formats.

10. What do you see as the differences between conducting a face-to-face interview versus a telephone interview?

11. A researcher wants to conduct a survey by posting the question on a web page. What do you see as the advantages and disadvantages of this option?

## Writing Good Questionnaire and Survey Items

The real work of preparing a good questionnaire is writing questions that sample the opinions, attitudes, beliefs, or behaviors that you want to measure. This section provides some basic guidelines for preparing survey items. Whenever possible, researchers are better off using existing scales or measures that other researchers have shown to be reliable and valid. The process of measure development is not easy and often requires multiple rounds of data collection itself. There are times, however, when no adequate measures exist, and this is when the material in this section of the chapter should be most helpful.

### Ask Single Questions or Make Single Statements

**Example:** Do you agree with the college's plan to build a new student recreation center and increase the student fee to $500 to help pay for the building?

This question has two parts, building the new student recreation center *and* increasing the student fee. Some people may agree with both statements, some may disagree with both, and others will agree with one statement but not the other. Because of the inherent ambiguity created by asking two questions in one, the question should be broken into two parts. The results will provide an unambiguous indication of student sentiment.

#### Alternatives:

1. To what extent do you agree/disagree with the college's plan to build a new student recreation center?

| Strongly disagree | Moderately disagree | Somewhat disagree | Neutral | Somewhat agree | Moderately agree | Strongly agree |
|---|---|---|---|---|---|---|
|  |  |  |  |  |  |  |

2. How willing would you be to pay $500 in student fees to help pay for a new student recreation center?

| Not at all |  |  |  |  |  | Absolutely |
|---|---|---|---|---|---|---|
|  |  |  |  |  |  |  |

### Ask Specific Questions and Avoid Vague Terms

**Example:** Do you actively support the college's decision to build a new student recreation center?

What does *actively support* mean? Although people recognize the difference between *support* and *oppose*, we have no way of determining the extent of their support. Therefore, we need to find an alternative wording that will indicate the extent to which students support this construction project.

### Alternatives:

1. I believe that the college should build a new student recreation center as soon as possible.

| Strongly disagree | Moderately disagree | Somewhat disagree | Neutral | Somewhat agree | Moderately agree | Strongly agree |
|---|---|---|---|---|---|---|
|  |  |  |  |  |  |  |

2. Which of the following building projects should be started as soon as possible? Pick one:
   ☐ An addition to the library
   ☐ A new arts and sciences building
   ☐ A new student recreation center
   ☐ Renovations to the Mary Beach and Russell residence halls

### Write Neutral Statements and Avoid a Biased Tone

**Examples:**

1. Many people believe that it is bad to spank children. Do you?

2. Do you believe that all students must complete two semesters of English composition, regardless of their writing skills?

Both questions will create a biased answer as they imply a "correct" answer. The first question makes it clear that you should agree with the majority and condemn spanking children. Similarly, the second question makes it clear that the English composition courses are not necessary for all students. By contrast, notice how the following alternatives merely ask for an opinion.

**Alternatives:**

1. Do you believe that parents should spank their children?
   ☐ Yes
   ☐ No

2. To what degree do you favor or oppose the new university policy requiring all students to complete two semesters of English composition?

| Strongly oppose | Moderately oppose | Somewhat oppose | Neutral | Somewhat favor | Moderately favor | Strongly favor |
|---|---|---|---|---|---|---|
|  |  |  |  |  |  |  |

### Ask Questions That Do Not Embarrass or Anger the Participant

**Examples:**

1. Are you still a virgin?

2. How often do you get drunk?

Highly personal questions such as these can offend some people. In addition, these questions seem to imply a moral overtone about one's sexuality and drinking habits. Research questions should be neutral in tone, and the response options should allow the individual to respond in a neutral or null manner if so desired.

**Alternatives:**

1. With how many people have you had sexual intercourse?
   ___ 0 ___ 1 ___ 2 ___ 3 ___ 4 or more

2. During the typical month, how many times do you drink until you are intoxicated?
   ___ 0 ___ 1–2 ___ 3–5 ___ 6–7 ___ 8 or more

### Whenever Possible, Use Simple Words and Concepts

**Example:** Do you believe that you received sufficient time to consider your alternatives before you were required to purchase your computer?

This question uses many formal and long words that may be difficult for some readers to understand. Good questions use simple words and sentence structure. Most word processors have a function that examines the readability of a sentence and estimates its reading level or reading score (seriously, try it). The previous question received a rating at the 12th-grade reading level. The following alternatives are easier to understand (2nd-to-5th-grade reading level).

**Alternatives:**

1. Did you feel rushed to buy the computer?

2. Did you have enough time to think about buying the computer?

### Ask Questions That the Person Can Easily Answer

**Example:** What percentage of the typical week do you spend studying?

This question asks the participant to provide an estimate and most people do not do a good job of estimating percentages. Consequently, you may not obtain useful information. As an alternative, consider asking participants to estimate the actual amount of something. You can then determine the percentages later.

**Alternative:**

1. During a typical weekday (Monday–Friday), how many hours do you do each of the following (total should = 24 hours):

   ___ = Attend classes
   ___ = Study or work on homework and class assignments
   ___ = Work at a job
   ___ = Socialize or party with friends
   ___ = Sleep
   ___ = Other activities
   _____
   24 = Total hours

### Recognize That One Question May Not Be Enough

**Example\*:** All in all, I am inclined to feel that I am a failure.

Many psychological constructs, such as opinions, attitudes, and personality, cannot be accurately measured with a single question. In these cases, it is appropriate to ask several highly related questions. The average answer to a group of questions is a more reliable measure of the person's opinion, attitude, personality, or whatever construct that you are measuring. Asking a series of related questions also creates a **priming cue** for the participant. If you ask a series of related questions, the participant will have more time to think about the issue and thereby offer a more thoughtful answer to the questions.

**Alternatives*:**

1. All in all, I am inclined to feel that I am a failure.
2. I feel that I have a number of good qualities.
3. I am able to do things as well as most other people.
4. I feel that I do not have much to be proud of.
5. On the whole, I am satisfied with myself.
6. I certainly feel useless at times.

*These items are from Rosenberg's (1965) Self-esteem Scale.

## Consider the Influence of Question Order

You should be cautious of the order of questions because each question sets the stage for how the participant will answer subsequent questions. For example, Dillman (2000) reported that 21% of college students agreed with a policy that a student should be expelled from college for plagiarism. However, 34% of another sample of students endorsed expulsion of the student if the preceding question asked whether a faculty member should be fired for plagiarism. The difference in the response rates raises the question, *which data set really represents the students' opinion*? Results like these represent what researchers call an **order effect** on participants' responses elicited by the sequencing of questions.

There is no easy solution to the order effect other than to recognize that it exists. Dillman (2000) recommended that if you suspect that the order of the questions will influence the participants' responses to critical questions, you should create several versions of the questionnaire with different sequences of questions. The alternative is to identify the order of questions in the report of the data, thus allowing the reader to understand the context in which the participants answered the questions.

## Word Questions That Reduce the Risk of a Response Set

Look at the six alternative statements in the previous section. These questions all assess a person's self-esteem. Although they measure the same thing, look at their wording. If the participant has a high level of self-esteem, then he or she will have to agree with some questions and disagree with others. If all the questions were worded in the same manner, then the person may become lazy and be tempted to give the same answer to each question without really reading the question. Researchers call this habit a **response set** (Cronbach, 1950). One way to avoid the response set is to reword the questions and statements so that half are stated in the positive (e.g., "I am a good person") and the remaining stated in the negative (e.g., "There is little to like about me"). The response scales stay the same, but before analyzing the data, responses to the reverse-coded items are reversed so that the eventual scale total score or overall mean will accurately reflect a higher level of the target variable. Whatever technique you choose, just make sure you keep notes about which items are reversed and which response scales are backwards. Otherwise, you will have some nasty surprises when it is time to code and score the data.

### Avoid Questions and Statements That Have an Obviously Correct Answer

#### Examples:

1. Women are generally not as smart as men.
2. I would not want a woman as my boss.

In some cases, being straightforward is not the best policy. Most people know that the previous statements about women are not popular. Therefore, respondents may tell you what they think you want to hear, not what they believe. One alternative is to reframe the questions to obscure the intent. For example, Swim, Aiken, Hall, and Hunter (1995) developed a test that measures sexism using subtly worded statements.

#### Alternatives:

1. Discrimination against women is no longer a problem in the United States.
2. Women often miss out on good jobs due to sexual discrimination.
3. On average, people in our society treat husbands and wives equally.

### Resources for Tests and Measurements

Why reinvent the wheel when there are many sources for information on existing, high-quality tests and measures? You can find many of these tests in published literature. Therefore, before you create your own test or scale, see whether someone has already done the hard work for you. You can use *PsycInfo*, *Mental Measures Yearbook*, or other similar research databases to search for and identify measures/tests/assessments that have been published and are already in use by other social science researchers. Often the scales and details about their development and reliability and validity can be easily found within peer-reviewed journals, highlighting yet another good reason to keep reading.

## Determining the Sample Size for a Survey

In Chapter 7, we introduced you to the Central Limit Theorem and the standard error of the mean. As you learned, we use these mathematical concepts to determine the accuracy of the sample mean as an estimate of the population mean. We can also use these concepts to determine the optimal sample size for survey-type studies. In this section, we will examine how to determine sample size for surveys in which you require the person to select one response from several options. The common example of this questionnaire is a political poll wherein you ask potential voters whom they favor in an election. We can treat the answer as a **binary response** because we want to know whether voters will vote for a candidate (Yes or No). Specifically, we want to estimate the probability ($P$) that voters will vote for a particular candidate.

Cochran (1977), in his influential text on sampling, demonstrated that Equation 8.1 allows us to estimate sample size, $n'$, given $P$ and $\alpha$. We use $\alpha$ to determine the width of the confidence interval of the mean. Also in the equation is $z_{(1-\alpha)/2}$, which represents the absolute value that defines the boundaries of $\alpha$. We reviewed how to find $z_{(1-\alpha)/2}$ in Chapter 7. Equation 8.1, therefore, allows us to estimate sample size when given specific conditions.

$$n' = \frac{\left(z^2_{\frac{1-\alpha}{2}}\right)^{(P)(1-P)}}{\alpha^2} \tag{8.1}$$

There are several steps for estimating sample size. First, we need to determine what we would consider an acceptable margin of error for our research. Smaller values of $\alpha$ will give us greater precision in our estimate. For example, if we accept $\alpha = .05$, then we are comfortable with our margin of error being $\pm 5$ percentage points. To increase the accuracy of our estimate, we could use $\alpha = .01$, which would mean that the margin of error becomes $\pm 1$ percentage points. Next, we need to select a value of $P$ that predicts what we will observe when we collect the data. If you have no way to make this prediction, you can use the conservative option by setting $P = .5$.

Table 8.6 presents the relationships among $\alpha$, $P$, and estimated sample size ($n'$). As you can see, when $P = .5$ and $\alpha = .05$, you need 384 participants in your survey to obtain a relatively reliable estimate of the population. As we reviewed in Chapter 7, the accuracy of the sample statistic depends on the method we use to create the sample. Table 8.6 also illustrates that increasing sample size will greatly increase your precision, but at a cost. For example, doubling the precision of measurement ($\alpha = .05$ to $\alpha = .025$) requires a considerable increase in sample size (384 to 2,009). It is important to note that in the present case, the required sample size follows a bell-shaped distribution, peaking in the middle at $P = .50$ and dropping off to either side. This is due to the binary nature of the outcome in the present example. One way to look at this is that respondents will be asked to either endorse a candidate or not endorse a candidate. If the results are clearly one way or the other, then a smaller sample will suffice. If there is lots of variability in the responses of people who are polled, you will want a larger sample size to increase your confidence in the quality of the resulting estimate of probability.

## Small Populations

If you are working with a small population, you can adjust your estimated sample size using Equation 8.2. You can use this equation whenever you

## Table 8.6 Relation Between $\alpha$, $P$, and Estimated Sample Size

| 95% Confidence Interval $\alpha = .05$ $z_{(1-\alpha)/2} = 1.96$ | | 97.5% Confidence Interval $\alpha = .025$ $z_{(1-\alpha)/2} = 2.24$ | | 99% Confidence Interval $\alpha = .01$ $z_{(1-\alpha)/2} = 2.58$ | |
|------|------|------|------|------|------|
| $P$ | $n'$ | $P$ | $n'$ | $P$ | $n'$ |
| .90 | 138 | .90 | 723 | .90 | 5,971 |
| .80 | 245 | .80 | 1,286 | .80 | 10,615 |
| .70 | 322 | .70 | 1,688 | .70 | 13,933 |
| .60 | 368 | .60 | 1,929 | .60 | 15,923 |
| .50 | 384 | .50 | 2,009 | .50 | 16,587 |
| .40 | 368 | .40 | 1,929 | .40 | 15,923 |
| .30 | 322 | .30 | 1,688 | .30 | 13,933 |
| .20 | 245 | .20 | 1,286 | .20 | 10,615 |
| .10 | 138 | .10 | 723 | .10 | 5,971 |

know the size of the population. If the population is small, you may find that you need fewer participants to maintain your confidence interval:

$$n^n = \frac{N(n')}{N + n'} \tag{8.2}$$

For this equation, $n'$ represents the estimated sample size from Equation 8.1 and $N$ represents the size of the population. Here is an example. Assume that you want to conduct a survey of students at your college and ask them whether they support the faculty's decision to use a plus/minus grading system. For the sake of the example, assume that you want to be accurate to within ±3 percentage points ($\alpha = .03$), that you set $P = .5$, and that there are 7,500 students at your college. Given these facts, $1 - \alpha = .97$, $(1 - \alpha)/2 = .485$, $z_{(1-\alpha)/2} = 2.17$,

$$n' = \frac{\left(\frac{z^2_{1-\alpha}}{2}\right)^{(P)(1-P)}}{\alpha^2} = \frac{\left[(2.17)^2\right](.5)(1 - .5)}{.03^2} = 1,308.03 \cong 1,308$$

$$n'' = \frac{N(n')}{N + n'} = \frac{7500(1308)}{7500 + 1308} = 1,113.74 \cong 1.113$$

Therefore, based on these formulas, you should survey at least 1,113 students to meet the objectives of your study.

The preceding example illustrates how to determine sample size for binary responses. Determining sample sizes for other response scales, such as those with Likert response formats, or those that measure quantities using ordinal, interval, or ratio scales, require a different set of procedures. We will examine these procedures in a subsequent chapter.

## Naturalistic Observation

For many types of research, there are no better tools than a pair of eyes, a sharp pencil, and a sheet of paper. Although good observational research is difficult to conduct, it can produce a wealth of useful information. With proper planning and work, one can conduct observational research that includes systematic manipulation of independent variables and the recording of dependent variables all in a natural setting. In other words, one can conduct experiments and produce data that have clear external validity. This section provides you with a brief introduction to observational methods of measurement. Additional details on these techniques are provided in Chapter 16, when we discuss qualitative methods in more depth.

Observational techniques go by many names, including "Field Studies," "Naturalistic Observation," or "Natural Experiment." The essential feature of this research technique is that we watch and record the individual's ongoing behaviors. Here are three examples of how one might use observational techniques.

### An Experiment in Anxiety

Many developmental psychologists study separation anxiety, the emotional reaction that children have when separated from their parents (e.g., Ainsworth & Bell, 1970; Ainsworth, Blehar, Waters, & Wall, 1978). To study separation anxiety, a researcher may invite parents to bring their toddlers to the department's laboratory. The researcher can then observe the children's reaction to different situations through a two-way mirror or with a hidden video camera. In this type of research, the researcher is able to control many of the different variables such as the child's age and the test situation. One can easily use naturalistic observation in a true experiment.

### Watching the Bully on the Playground

Many psychologists and educators study bullying behavior (e.g., Pepler & Craig, 1995). A popular method of studying bullying is to watch children's play during school recess. As in the previous example, the researcher finds some inconspicuous place where he or she can observe the children's play. As with all observational research, the person collecting the data will watch for and record the duration, frequency, or intensity of specific behaviors.

### Who Said What to Whom?

In some cases, the target behavior will be what people say to each other. For this type of research, we make a record of what people say in a conversation. DePaulo and Kashy (1998) conducted an interesting example of this type of research by asking participants to keep a daily journal of the lies they told their friends, family, and associates. Using an objective scoring procedure, research assistants who did not know the hypotheses being tested read and scored the episodes described in the journals. DePaulo and Kashy found that the participants did not lie often to friends, but occasionally told "white lies" to protect their friends' feelings. By contrast, the participants were more willing to tell self-serving lies to casual acquaintances and strangers.

### What to Observe

The steps we take to create a survey are the same steps we can follow to develop a strategy for observing and recording behavior. First, we need to decide what behaviors we want to observe. Unless you are observing the behavior of slugs, most creatures engage in many behaviors, too many to observe in a single study. Therefore, we need to identify a manageable set of behaviors that we can observe and document. As with all research, we select variables that correspond to the hypothesis we want to test.

Once we select the variables we want to measure, we need to ensure that there is a clear operational definition of the behaviors to be monitored. Some variables may be easy to define and measure rather objectively. For example, we can count the number of cigarettes smoked in an hour, the time spent watching television and the name of the shows selected, or the number of four-letter curses. Other behaviors are not as easily defined. For example, what do we mean by an aggressive act? Is a tackle in a football game an aggressive act or part of playing a game? If one person accidentally hurts another, is the behavior aggressive? What about verbal threats; will you include these in your definition of aggression?

Consider children's social behavior. Assume that a researcher wanted to study how children react when they are the new member of a group. The focus of the study is to determine how a child behaves when he or she is the new member of a group. Will the child immediately join the group, or will he or she be cautious and watch the other children from afar? As a part of the study, the researcher may observe the child's play and use definitions of play such as those presented in Table 8.7.

### Strategies for Collecting Quantitative Observational Data

Once you have defined the behaviors to observe, you will need to select the type of data to collect. As a generality, there are three types of quantitative observational recording techniques: frequency recording, duration recording, and interval recording. As with all aspects of research, selection of the

Table 8.7  **Examples of Definitions for Behaviors That Could be Observed**

| | |
|---|---|
| Unoccupied | Child is not engaged in play or other specific activity. |
| Solitary play | Child is playing alone with toys and is not seeking interaction with others. |
| Interactive play | Child is playing with one or more children. There is an exchange of toys, play activities, and cooperation among the children. |

recording technique depends on the definition of the variable and the research hypothesis.

### Frequency Recording

As the name implies, for frequency recording we count the number of times that a behavior occurs during a specified interval. Most researchers use frequency recording to count discrete behaviors that generally have a fixed duration. Therefore, we can count the number of times one student interrupts another student, the number of times a child offers to share a toy, or the number of cigarettes a person smokes. Other behaviors, such as studying, reading a book, napping, and watching television are behaviors better measured using other recording techniques because they are ongoing behaviors that may occur infrequently, but last for an extended period of time.

### Duration Recording

Duration recording focuses on the amount of time a person spends engaged in one behavior. This method is useful for measuring ongoing behavior that may last for an unpredictable amount of time. A researcher may use duration recording to monitor a child's behavior during a stranger-situation study. Specifically, the researcher could time how quickly the child stopped playing and returned to the parent when the stranger entered the room, how long the child stayed close to the parent, and how long it took for the child to return to playing with the toys.

### Interval Recording

For interval recording, the researcher observes one or more individuals for a fixed period of time. The researcher then divides the session into intervals of equal lengths. The interval length is short enough that the individual can engage in only one behavior during the interval (e.g., 15 s). During each interval, the researcher indicates the presence or absence of the relevant behavior. In most cases, there may be a pause or delay between intervals. Although this technique is often recommended to researchers, it has also been the target of criticism (Altmann, 1974; Murphy & Goodall, 1980; Tyler, 1979). Altmann concluded that the method has no general value for behavioral research because it does not accurately measure the frequency or the duration of behavior. She also criticized interval recording because the method cannot adequately indicate the proportion of time the individual engages in a behavior.

### Special Considerations for Observational Research

As with all research procedures, there are special controls that you should consider to collect accurate, reliable, and valid data. The essential question to ask is, "Who is collecting the data and do they know what they are doing?" The reliability of the data depends on the vigilance of the person observing and recording the data. The most common method to ensure that the data are reliable is to have two or more observers record the data and then report the average of the observations.

Before you aggregate the data, however, you need to ensure that the observers agree with each other by determining the **interrater reliability**. The interrater reliability is a statistical index that represents how well the records from multiple observers match. If the interrater reliability is high, we can place greater confidence in the data and proceed with their analysis. If the interrater reliability is low, analysis of the data may not be useful because the measurement error is too great. Low interrater reliability can indicate that the observers need to be better trained, that the definitions need to be clarified, that the recording procedure needs to be revised, or that some combination of these solutions may need to be used. There are many ways to assess interrater reliability. The following sections examine the more popular options.

### Coefficient Kappa

One of the more popular methods of determining interrater agreement is Cohen's kappa, $\kappa$. Researchers use $\kappa$ to assess interrater reliability when the data represent a nominal or an ordinal scale. As an example, consider the data presented in Table 8.8. In this example, two raters independently observed the same person and counted the number of times one of three behaviors occurred. The numbers in the table represent their assessments. Look down Column A of the table. The numbers are 15, 2, and 1. These numbers represent agreements and disagreements. Raters 1 and 2 agreed 15 times on the occurrence of Behavior A, but disagreed on the classification of three other behaviors. The numbers along the diagonal of the table represent agreements; the numbers in the other cells represent disagreements. Cohen's $\kappa$ allows us to determine the level of agreement among the raters. To calculate $\kappa$, we use the following equation:

$$\kappa = \frac{P_A - P_C}{1 - P_C}, \quad \text{where} \quad P_A = \frac{\sum O_{ii}}{T} \quad \text{and} \quad P_C = \frac{\sum R_i C_i}{T^2} \qquad (8.3)$$

In this equation, $P_A$ represents the proportion of agreement between the raters. To determine $P_A$, we add the observed agreements, $O_{ii}$, and divide by the total number of observations, $T$. The second component of $\kappa$ is $P_C$, which estimates the number of agreements that would have happened by chance.

## Table 8.8  Example of Data from Two Independent Raters who Classified the Same People or Behaviors into One of Three Categories

| | | Rater 1 Category | | | |
| | | A | B | C | Row totals $\Sigma$ |
|---|---|---|---|---|---|
| **Rater 2 Category** | A | 15 | 1 | 1 | $R_1 = 17$ |
| | B | 2 | 21 | 2 | $R_2 = 25$ |
| | C | 1 | 1 | 16 | $R_3 = 18$ |
| **Column totals** | $\Sigma$ | $C_1 = 18$ | $C_2 = 23$ | $C_3 = 19$ | $T = 60$ |

**Procedure for Calculating Coefficient Kappa, $\kappa$:**

$$P_A = \frac{\sum O_{ii}}{T} = \frac{15 + 21 + 16}{60} = \frac{52}{60} = .8667$$

$$P_C = \frac{\sum R_i C_i}{T^2} = \frac{(18 \times 17) + (23 \times 25) + (19 \times 18)}{60^2} = \frac{1223}{3600} = .3397$$

$$\kappa = \frac{P_A - P_C}{1 - P_C} = \frac{.8667 - .3397}{1 - .3397} = \frac{.5270}{.6603} = .7981 \cong .80$$

Interpreting $\kappa$ is straightforward, the larger the better. Values of $\kappa$ can range between 0, which represents no interrater reliability, and 1.0, which represents perfect interrater reliability. Most researchers strive to have $\kappa$ be greater than .75. When $\kappa < .50$, there is too much disagreement among the judges to produce useful information. Table 8.9 lists general guidelines for interpreting the size of $\kappa$.

In some situations, there may be more than two observers. Although the calculations are more cumbersome, we can still calculate $\kappa$ to determine the interrater agreement among the observers. Another technique that is perhaps more commonly used with more than two raters is to calculate a Pearson correlation coefficient, $r$, to establish the relationship between multiple sets of ratings. Researchers use this statistic specifically when observations are collected on an interval or a ratio scale. Therefore, the statistic might be used for determining the reliability of frequency and duration measures. Chapter 9 is devoted to this important statistic, so much

## Table 8.9  General Guidelines for Interpreting the Size of $k$

| Value of $k$ | Level of agreement |
|---|---|
| $<.20$ | Poor |
| $.21-.40$ | Fair |
| $.41-.60$ | Moderate |
| $.61-.80$ | Good |
| $.81-1.00$ | Excellent |

From Altman (1991).

more detail is provided there. In brief, though, we interpret the $r$ as we do $\kappa$. As with $\kappa$, the absolute values of $r$ can range between 0 and 1, with larger values representing greater levels of interrater agreement. If you are interested in learning more about the use of $r$ for establishing interrater agreement, one place to start is a recent review of this approach by Brown & Hauenstein (2005).

Another technique for indicating agreement between multiple raters is to calculate an Intraclass Correlation Coefficient (ICC) that reflects the overall similarity of a set of multiple ratings of the same target person or object. There are several ICC forms that are more or less appropriate, depending on your specific research situation. Thus, a full examination of this technique is beyond the scope of the present book, but we recommend that you review work including Bliese (2000) and other more recent statistics books for assistance in this area.

## Improving Interrater Reliability

There are a number of things that you can do to maximize the reliability and validity of observational data. One of the most important is to keep the rater from knowing your hypothesis.

If the raters know what you expect to find in the study, they may be tempted to score their observations in favor of your expectations. Another is to train the observers. Barkhof et al. (1997) provided an example of the need for training to ensure reliable data. The researchers examined the ability of five novice researchers and five expert researchers to read magnetic resonance images (MRIs) and rate the lesions of patients with multiple sclerosis (MS). Lesions are scar tissue in the central nervous system and appear as white spots on the MRI. As you might guess, the interrater agreement for the novice researchers was low compared to the experts (novice $\kappa = .37$ vs. expert $\kappa = .65$). After intensive training, the interrater reliability of the novices and experts improved (novice $\kappa = .65$ vs. expert $\kappa = .74$).

Observing behavior is not easy work. It can be difficult to do well for long uninterrupted periods. Therefore, researchers who do this type of work limit their observation time to short periods or work in shifts with other observers. Altmann (1974) described her experiences observing primate behavior and the difficulty of remaining alert during the observation session. She wrote that, "even with two observers, one 15-minute sample per hour was near the upper limit of our capacity when obtaining an accurate record" (p. 246). The implication of this is that observational sessions should be relatively short (e.g., less than 15 minutes) and punctuated with ample rest. Fortunately, video cameras make the task of observing behavior easier. Cameras do not get tired or bored, and they record all the behaviors that occur. Furthermore, the researcher has access to a permanent and rich source of information of all behaviors. Therefore, the researcher can review and score the behaviors at his or her convenience and at a pace that is not exhausting.

Another important feature of the video camera is that it is easy to hide. Hiding the video camera helps to ensure that the people being observed act naturally. If you wanted to study bullying behavior among children, using a hidden camera will record more natural behavior than having an adult researcher obviously watching the children. As you learned in Chapter 2, however, there are significant ethical issues that the researcher must confront before conducting this type of research.

### Participant Observation Research

A variant of naturalistic observation is participant observer research. There is an important difference between naturalistic observation and participant observation. For the most part, the observer in naturalistic observation is not an immediate part of the ongoing behavior as he or she attempts to record the data unbeknownst to the individuals being observed. By contrast, the participant observer joins the group to study the group's behavior.

Participant observation does allow one to study a group of people, especially if their behavior is covert or underground. This technique is especially popular among anthropologists and sociologists who study small social groups. There are several notable examples of participant observation that psychologists have used to their advantage. For example, Robert Cialdini (1984), a social psychologist, wanted to learn more about how salespeople persuade others to buy various products. As Cialdini described it, "when I wanted to learn about the compliance tactics of encyclopedia (or vacuum-cleaner, or portrait-photography, or dance-lesson) sales organizations, I would answer a newspaper ad for sales trainees and have them teach me their methods" (p. xiii). Cialdini used what he learned in the field as the basis for his laboratory research on social influence.

The participant observation technique has some serious risks, however. An infamous example is Laud Humphreys's (1970) research for his book *Tearoom Trade*. Humphreys wanted to study the men who engaged in homosexual acts in public places. To study these men, Humphreys began to hang out at public restrooms, known as "tearooms" among homosexuals, and acted as a lookout while the men had their sexual encounters. He then secretly followed the men to their homes and later interviewed them. Many commentators have criticized Humphreys's tactics because they violated the men's right to privacy. Therefore, conducting participant research cannot be entered into lightly. Participant research can also be dangerous. Many groups of people wish to remain closed to outsiders and react poorly to a stranger in their midst. For example, Thompson (1985), studying the Hell's Angels, received a severe beating from the members of the gang he had attempted to join.

## Research in Action: Analysis of Assaults

Acquaintance rape, or date rape, is an unfortunate experience that too many people encounter. Although this behavior has been examined for many

## Table 8.10   Examples of Questions Larimer et al. (1999) Used to Examine the Prevalence of Unwanted Sexual Encounters and the Use of Alcohol During Unwanted Sexual Encounters

(1) In the past year, have you been in a situation where your partner became so sexually aroused that you felt it was useless to stop them even though you did not want to have sexual intercourse?

(2) In the past year, have you had sexual intercourse with someone with whom you didn't really want to because you felt pressured by their continual arguments?

(3) In the past year, have you been in a situation where someone used some degree of physical force (twisting your arm, holding you down, etc.) to get you to have sexual intercourse with them when you didn't want to, whether or not intercourse actually occurred?

(4) In the past year, have you had someone attempt sexual intercourse with you by giving you alcohol or other drugs, but intercourse did not occur?

(5) In the past year, have you had sexual intercourse when you didn't want to because a person gave you alcohol or other drugs?

*Items based on the Sexual Experiences Survey (Koss & Oros,1982) as revised by Larimer et al. (1999).*

(1) Has drinking ever gotten you into sexual situations which you later regretted?

(2) Because you had been drinking, have you ever had sex when you really didn't want to?

(3) Because you had been drinking, have you ever had sex with someone you wouldn't ordinarily have sex with?

(4) Have you ever been pressured or forced to have sex with someone because you were too drunk to prevent it?

(5) Have you ever pressured or forced someone to have sex with you after you had been drinking?

*Items based on the Young Adult Alcohol Problem Severity Test (Wood, Johnson, & Sher, 1992) as presented by Larimer et al. (1999).*

years, Larimer, Lydum, Anderson, and Turner (1999) believed that much of the research was biased against men. Larimer and her colleagues noted that for many of the previous studies, the researchers examined women's experiences exclusively or used sex-biased survey techniques. Therefore, Larimer et al. attempted to document the prevalence of unwanted sexual encounters experienced by men and women and the role that alcohol consumption played in these encounters.

Larimer et al. (1999) asked participants to complete a series of questionnaires that examined the prevalence of unwanted sexual encounters and the use of alcohol. All of the questionnaires were scales developed and published by other researchers. Table 8.10 presents a portion of two of the scales examining unwanted sexual experiences and the relation between alcohol consumption and unwanted sexual encounters. For their first questionnaire, Larimer et al. revised the *Sexual Experiences Survey* (Koss & Oros, 1982) to ensure that questions were not sex-biased. Larimer et al. used 296 (165 males, 131 females) students who were new members of fraternities and sororities at a large West Coast public university. The majority of the students were freshmen and sophomores.

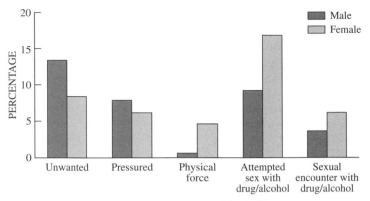

Graph based on data presented by Larimer et al. (1999).

**Figure 8.2**

**Percentage of Participants Reporting Various Types of Unwanted Sexual Encounters**

Figure 8.2 presents the results for the *Sexual Experiences Survey*. One notable feature of these data is the percentage of men reporting that they had experienced unwanted sexual encounters or had felt pressured into a sexual encounter. Also apparent in the data is that women reported higher percentages of some form of coercion (physical force or alcohol/drug use) to engage in sexual intercourse. These data are important. First, the data support previous research by replicating the finding that women often experience some forms of coercion during an unwanted sexual encounter. Second, the data suggest that both men and women experience unwanted sexual encounters. These data are interesting as they conflict with the stereotype that men are always the perpetrators and women are victims of these situations.

Figure 8.3 presents the percentage of participants who had sexual encounters related to their drinking behavior. The data make clear that nearly half of the men and women in the study later regretted a sexual encounter related to their drinking.

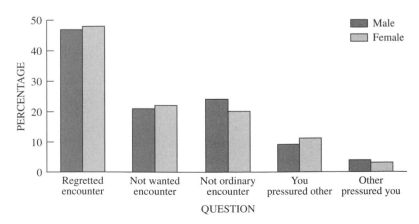

**Figure 8.3**

**Percentage of Participants Reporting Various Types of Unwanted Sexual Encounters Related to Drinking**

Graph based on data presented by Larimer et al. (1999).

# Figure 8.4

**Mean Number of Alcoholic Drinks Consumed Per Day During Past Three Months For Men and Women Who Had or Had Not Experienced an Unwanted Sexual Encounter**

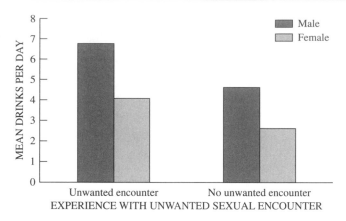

Graph based on data presented by Larimer et al. (1999).

Finally, Figure 8.4 presents the mean number of alcoholic drinks consumed per day during the previous three months. Two interesting trends appear in these data. First, men claim to consume more drinks per day than do women. Second, participants who reported an unwanted sexual encounter appear to drink more than those who had not experienced an unwanted sexual encounter. The data led Larimer et al. (1999) to conclude that men and women experience unwanted sexual intercourse. Their data also implicate alcohol as a major contributor to sexual victimization of both men and women. Because sexual coercion and unwanted sexual intercourse can have a dramatic impact on one's emotional well-being, it is essential that researchers better understand this phenomenon. As Larimer and her colleagues concluded, "further empirical study of the emotional consequences of these events and the context surrounding them for both genders is warranted" (p. 307).

Before we embrace the data too quickly, we need to examine several features of the study. To their credit, Larimer et al. (1999) recognized and described many of the problems with their research and called for additional and more refined studies. We can begin by examining the population and the sample.

The sampling population consisted of students who had joined a Greek-letter society. Although fraternities and sororities are popular on many college campuses, their membership may not be representative of the student population. Greek-letter organizations may be attractive to only a segment of the contemporary college student body. Similarly, the life experiences of students living in a fraternity or sorority may be different from life in a residence hall. For example, most Greek-letter organizations sponsor intensive training programs that sensitize their members to the dangers of alcohol abuse and sexual coercion. Thus, we cannot be sure that life in a fraternity or sorority is representative of the typical college student.

A related problem is the age of the participants when they completed the survey. Most of the participants were freshmen or sophomores.

Consequently, these students may not have had sufficient time living at college to experience the types of sexual encounters experienced by older students. If the sample had included a broader cross-section of all students, we could examine the relation between the age of student and the risk of assault. We can raise other questions about the sampling population. Are the experiences of students at large state universities similar to those of smaller colleges? Are students who attend West Coast institutions representative of students attending college in other parts of the country? Future research on this topic should attempt to sample from a broader range of students. The sample would include a greater representation of all segments of the typical college population. There is no reason that we must limit our analysis to college students. Although the data may not be as easy to obtain, it would still be informative to examine the experiences of young adults not enrolled in college. We can also question whether the sample is sufficiently large. Although 296 participants is a large sample, it may not be sufficiently large to detect small differences between men's and women's behavior or events that do not occur frequently. Consequently, those who wish to replicate this study should consider a larger sample size.

Finally, we can ask whether the wording of the questions produces the answers we need. For example, do men and women "regret" unwanted sexual relations for the same reasons? Similarly, is the phrase "pressured or forced" as clear as it can be? The phrase seems to require considerable interpretation on the part of the participant. Larimer et al. (1999) studied an interesting and important topic. Moreover, they reported findings that challenge several preconceived beliefs. Their research also demonstrates that one can examine interesting topics using questionnaire methods. At the same time, this research confirms a theme that recurs throughout this book—no individual study is complete by itself. The Larimer et al. study is one of many studies that examine the relation between date rape and alcohol and will surely not be the last such report. In fact, as of the time this chapter was written, Larimer et al. had been cited in more than 40 additional published studies.

## Knowledge Check

12. Why is it necessary to pretest a questionnaire before using it in a research project?

13. Can a researcher use closed-response questions in a face-to-face interview?

14. A researcher developed a series of open-ended and closed-response questions. What are three ways the researcher could collect the data? What are the relative advantages and disadvantages of each?

15. Describe in your words the advantages and disadvantages of open-ended and closed-response questions.

16. Imagine that you are planning to conduct a survey and need to estimate the number of participants you need to include in your sample. You decide that for most of the questions $P = .50$ and that $\alpha = .02$. How many participants will you need in the sample if your population consisted of:
    a.  1,000 people?
    b.  5,000 people?
    c.  25,000 people?
    d.  50,000 people?

17. Dr. Blume has trained observers to use frequency recording to record the behavior of 12 schizophrenic clients. According to the analysis of the data $\kappa = .47$, do you think the observers are sufficiently trained to allow Dr. Blume to proceed with the research?

18. Imagine that you have been hired to assess the content of children's television shows. You are to determine how often the different children's shows depict aggressive acts versus altruistic acts.
    a.  How would go about selecting the children's shows to watch?
    b.  How would you define aggressive acts?
    c.  How would you define altruistic acts?
    d.  Which measurement technique (frequency, duration, or interval recording) would you use and why?

19. Assume that you used two trained observers to watch the episodes from various children's shows. The observers were to watch a segment, typically 20 to 30 seconds long, and classify the behavior as aggressive, altruistic, or other. The following table presents the data. How well do the raters agree with each other?

|         |            | Rater 1        |            |        |
|---------|------------|----------------|------------|--------|
|         |            | **Aggressive** | **Altruistic** | **Other** |
|         | **Aggressive** | 121        | 13         | 57     |
| **Rater 2** | **Altruistic** | 3      | 67         | 45     |
|         | **Other**  | 12             | 10         | 93     |

20. As a researcher, what ethical responsibilities do you have when conducting personal interviews or self-administered questionnaires?

21. If you were going to use a hidden video camera to record the behavior of a group of people, what ethical issues would you need to resolve?

## Chapter Summary

All the sciences depend on objective measurement, and psychology is no exception. Although the primary focus of this chapter was creating and using questionnaires, the concepts reviewed in this chapter apply to any situation wherein the researcher must collect data. Many people do not understand the uses and limitations of measurement. Two common errors include reification of the measurement and denial of the measurement. Reification is an example of mystique of quantity and occurs when people infer too much meaning from a single measurement. In contrast, some people dismiss many psychological tests, believing that the underlying construct cannot be measured. We create psychological tests to help us describe and explain the phenomenon that we are studying.

Creating an appropriate test or measure of the dependent variable depends on the hypothesis we wish to test, the conditions of our research, and the accuracy of various techniques. Several of the more common ways of collecting information include personal interviews and self-administered surveys. Personal interviews, while time consuming and expensive to conduct, can provide valuable forms of information. By contrast, self-administered surveys are inexpensive and can produce much valuable information.

For much of the chapter, we reviewed techniques to create questions and scales to collect data. The goal of these techniques is to prepare simple and objective questions that the participants will answer honestly. When we plan any research project, it is important to determine the optimal sample size for the research. Therefore, we reviewed one method for estimating sample size. This technique allows us to predict, and thereby control, the accuracy of the population estimates. Observational techniques are also common in behavioral research. Two of the more commonly used methods for observational research are frequency recording and duration recording. These research techniques, like the questionnaire, require clear operational definitions of the behavior we wish to observe and attention to the procedures for collecting the data.

Whenever we use a measurement technique, we need to assess its reliability or consistency in measurement. We reviewed how the coefficient kappa allows us to evaluate the interrater reliability among two or more raters. In the "Research in Action" section, we examined how researchers used a survey method to evaluate the interrelation between alcohol abuse and date rape. We used this research to illustrate how the researchers selected a series of questionnaires to measure the relevant dependent variables. The example also allowed us to practice a critique of the data.

## Chapter Glossary for Review

**Binary response**—A response that has only two answers, such as Yes or No.

**Closed-response question**—A question that the participants answer by selecting from among alternative statements provided by the researcher.

**Interrater reliability**—A descriptive statistic that indicates the degree to which two or more observers agree on the classification of a behavior or an object.

**Mystique of quantity**—An uncritical trust in the meaning and importance of the numbers produced by measurement.

**Open-ended question**—A question that requires the participants to state or write their answer to the question.

**Order effect**—The effect of asking a sequence of questions on how the participant answers subsequent questions.

**Priming cue**—Questions that cause the participant to think about a topic and to more thoughtfully respond to subsequent questions.

**Reification**—To treat an abstract construct as if it has material existence independent of the words.

**Response set**—Tendency to give the same answer to all questions regardless of the true answer.

## Chapter References

Ainsworth, M.D.S., & Bell, S. M. (1970). Attachment, exploration, and separation: Illustrated by the behavior of one-year-olds in a strange situation. *Child Development, 41,* 49–67.

Ainsworth, M.D.S., Blehar, M. C., Waters, E., & Wall, S. (1978). *Patterns of attachment.* Hillsdale, NJ: Erlbaum.

Altman, D. G. (1991). *Practical statistics for medical research.* Boca Raton, FL: Chapman & Hall.

Altmann, J. (1974). Observational study of behavior: Sampling methods. *Behaviour, 49,* 227–267.

Barkhof, F., Filippi, M., vanWaesberghe, J. H., Molyneux, P., Rovaris, M., Lycklama a' Nijeholt, G., et al. (1997). Improving interobserver variation in reporting gadolinium-enhanced MRI lesion in multiple sclerosis. *Neurology, 49,* 1682–1688.

Barnette, J. J. (2000). Effects of stem and Likert response option reversals on survey internal consistency: If you feel the need, there is a better alternative to using those negatively worded stems. *Educational and Psychological Measurement, 60,* 361–370.

Bliese, P. D. (2000). Within-group agreement, non-independence, and reliability: Implications for data aggregation and analysis. In K. J. Klein & S.W.J. Kozlowski (Eds.), *Multilevel theory, research, and methods in organizations: Foundations, extensions, and new directions* (pp. 349–380). San Francisco: Jossey-Bass.

Brown, R. J., & Hauenstein, N. M. A. (2005). Interrater agreement reconsidered: An alternative to the $r_{wg}$ indices. *Organizational Research Methods, 8*(2), 165–184.

Cattell, J. M. (1890). Mental tests and measurements. *Mind, 15,* 373–381.

Chang, L. (1994). A psychometric evaluation of 4-point and 6-point Likert-type scales in relation reliability and validity. *Applied Psychological Measurement, 18,* 205–215.

Cialdini, R. B. (1984). *Influence: The psychology of persuasion.* New York: Quill.

Cochran, W. G. (1977). *Sampling techniques.* New York: John Wiley & Sons.

Cronbach, L. J. (1950). Further evidence on response sets and test design. *Educational and Psychological Measurement, 10,* 3–31.

Davidson, J. W., & Lytle, M. H. (1992). *After the fact: The art of historical detection* (3rd. ed.). New York: McGraw-Hill.

DePaulo, B. M., & Kashy, D. A. (1998). Everyday lies in close and casual relationships. *Journal of Personality and Social Psychology*, 74, 63–79.

Dewdney, A. K. (1997). *Yes, we have no neutrons: An eye-opening tour through the twists and turns of bad science*. New York: John Wiley & Sons.

Dillman, D. A. (2000). *Mail and Internet surveys: The tailored design method* (2nd ed.). New York: John Wiley & Sons.

Fontana, A., & Frey, J. H. (1994). Interviewing: The art of science. In N. S. Denzin & Y. S. Lincoln (Eds.), *Handbook of qualitative research* (pp. 75–103). Thousand Oaks, CA: Sage.

Gould, S. J. (1981). *The mismeasure of man*. New York: W. W. Norton.

Humphreys, L. (1970). *Tearoom trade: Impersonal sex in public places*. Chicago: Aldine.

Kaplan, A. (1964). *The conduct of inquiry: Methodology for behavioral science*. San Francisco: Chandler.

Koss, M. P., & Oros, C. J. (1982). Sexual experiences survey: A research instrument investigating sexual aggression and victimization. *Journal of Consulting and Clinical Psychology*, 50, 455–457.

Lando, H. A. (1976). On being sane in insane places: A supplemental report. *Professional Psychology: Research & Practice*, 7, 47–52.

Larimer, M. E., Lydum, A. R., Anderson, B. K., & Turner, A. P. (1999). Male and female recipients of unwanted sexual contact in a college students sample: Prevalence rates, alcohol use, and depression symptoms. *Sex Roles*, 40, 295–308.

Miles-Tapping, C. (1996). Power wheelchairs and independent life styles. *Canadian Journal of Rehabilitation*, 10, 137–145.

Murphy, G., & Goodall, E. (1980). Measurement error in direct observation: A comparison of common recording methods. *Behaviour Research & Therapy*, 18, 147–150.

Pepler, D. J., & Craig, W. M. (1995). A peek behind the fence: Naturalistic observation of aggressive children with remote audiovisual recording. *Developmental Psychology*, 31, 548–553.

Preston, C. C., & Colman, A. M. (2000). Optimal number of response categories in rating scales: Reliability, validity, discriminating power, and respondent preferences. *Acta Psychologica*, 104, 1–15.

Robinson, J. P., Shaver, P. R., & Wrightsman, L. S. (1991). *Measures of personality and social psychological attitudes: Volume 1 in measures of social psychological attitudes series*. San Diego: Academic Press.

Rosenberg, M. (1965). *Society and the adolescent self-image*. Princeton, NJ: Princeton University Press.

Rosenhan, D. L. (1973). On being sane in insane places. *Science*, 179, 250–258.

Rotter, J. B. (1966). Generalized expectancies for internal versus external control of reinforcement. *Psychological Monographs*, 80 (1, Whole No. 609).

Salant, P., & Dillman, D. A. (1994). *How to conduct your own survey*. New York: John Wiley & Sons.

Swim, J. K., Aiken, K. J., Hall, W. S., & Hunter, B. A. (1995). Sexism and racism: Old-fashioned and modern prejudices. *Journal of Personality and Social Psychology*, 68, 199–214.

Thompson, H. (1985). *Hell's angels*. New York: Ballantine.

Tyler, S. (1979). Time-sampling: A matter of convention. *Animal Behaviour, 27*, 801–810.

Wilkinson, L. (1999). Statistical methods in psychological journals: Guidelines and explanations. *American Psychologist, 54*, 594–604.

Wood, M. D., Johnson, T. J., & Sher, K. J. (March, 1992). *Characteristics of frequent drinking game participants in college: An exploratory study*. Poster session presented at the annual meeting of the Research Society on Alcoholism, San Diego, CA.

# Chapter 9
# A Model for Research Design

## CHAPTER OBJECTIVES

> To call in the statistician after the experiment is done may be no more than asking him to perform a postmortem examination: He may be able to say what the experiment died of.
>
> **—Sir Ronald A. Fisher**

## Introduction

The art of good science is turning an interesting question into a productive research design. A research design refers to the methods used to collect data that will decisively answer an empirical question. Consequently, a good research design must do three things. First, it must be efficient. The design should produce the best-quality data for the least amount of time, effort, and money. Second, the design must eliminate factors that bias the results. Finally, the research design should produce useful data that clearly address the research question and account for alternative explanations. In this chapter we will examine the details of good research design for projects that incorporate two levels of the independent variable. Using this format, we can review the principles of design that we can apply to all research.

## A Model for Research Design

A common myth is that the researcher is an introverted, white-lab-coat-wearing, dispassionate, and objective umpire of the data who "calls 'em as I sees 'em." Unfortunately, there are too many examples in the history of science to treat this statement as anything but fantasy. Many biologists, chemists, physicists, and psychologists have lost their objectivity and allowed their preconceived beliefs to cloud their judgment and interpretation of the data. As you learned in Chapter 1, the four idols that Bacon described 400 years ago continue to affect how people make decisions. In many cases, these idols or perspectives lead us to the wrong conclusion and prevent us from considering alternative perspectives. Consequently, the purpose of any research design is to protect researchers from lapses in objectivity and the bias inherent in personal judgment.

In any research dealing with people we have an additional source of bias: the people who participate in our research. Participants in our research come to us with their own anxieties, biases, and awareness that they are participating in a psychological study. Rarely do we have any idea what this means to them or how this affects their behavior in the study. Being a good social science researcher requires knowledge of human behavior and research design in order to conduct useful scientific studies.

We could easily fill this book with examples of the factors that can bias the results of a research project. A more efficient and useful alternative, however, is to use a model that highlights the phases of research that are most sensitive to different forms of bias. Figure 9.1 illustrates the potential sources of bias arising from the interaction among the elements of researcher, design of the study, and participants. Many of the ideas presented in this illustration come from the work of Rosnow and Rosenthal (1997) and Hyde (1991).

### Purpose of Research

The first encounter we have with personal bias is typically with ourselves, the researchers. Most research ideas come from a researcher's theoretical orientation and personal experience. In Chapter 1 we reviewed the reactions that psychologists had when Garcia (1980) attempted to publish his research on taste aversion. Garcia faced much opposition because the results of his research did not fit other psychologists' theories of classical conditioning. The prevailing theories of classical conditioning biased the type of experiments that researchers did and did not conduct.

The researcher's orientation can have considerable influence on how he or she will view a problem. Consider a group of psychologists who want to study depression. A psychologist with a cognitive perspective will examine the participant's attributions regarding his or her ability to control life's events. A physiological psychologist may focus on the level or imbalance of various neurotransmitters. Finally, a psychologist with a psychodynamic perspective will explore unresolved psychological conflicts. Although each

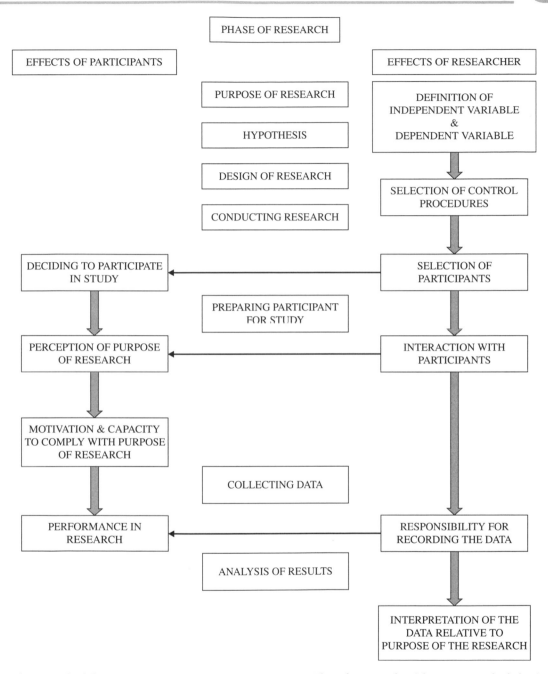

The column on the left represents the behavior of the participants. The column on the right represents the behavior of the researcher. The central column represents the general stages of research. The horizontal lines represent instances where the participants' and researchers' behavior interact. Based in part on Rosnow and Rosenthal (1997) and Hyde (1991).

## Figure 9.1

**Illustration of Potential Sources of Bias Arising from the Interaction Among the Researcher, the Design of the Study, and the People Participating in the Research**

psychologist will say that they are studying the same thing (why a person is depressed), the variables that they will tend to consider in their study are radically different.

Perhaps the best way to avoid the bias of preconceived beliefs is to remain open to alternative explanations and ideas. No one has yet cornered the market on good ideas and explanations for human behavior. Therefore, as a researcher, be willing to examine alternative explanations until the data clearly indicate that you need to move on to a different perspective. One way to practice this openness in your own research is to read widely, stretching even beyond the bounds of your particular subfield of study to search for research in other disciplines that may be somehow related to your own interests. You will be surprised at what you can find.

## Design of Research

After identifying the purpose and the hypothesis, the next step presented in Figure 9.1 is the design phase, during which the researcher develops controls for potential confounding variables. As we reviewed in Chapter 4, confounding variables are conditions that reduce the internal validity of the study. A confounding variable is an uncontrolled condition that creates a plausible alternative hypothesis for the results of the study. As we progress through this book, we will examine different research designs that help reduce or eliminate the effects of well-known confounding effects.

## Selection of Participants

When the researcher begins to select participants for the study, the opportunities for bias increase dramatically. In Chapter 7, you learned how to develop a representative sample of the population. As you learned, the need to ensure that your selection procedure will yield a representative sample of the population is a critical factor in determining the eventual generalizability or external validity of your research. Critics of social science research often find fault with the sampling procedures researchers use. Some critics have argued that researchers too often use college students for behavioral research (e.g., Rosnow & Rosenthal, 1997). Joining this argument are the complaints that many classic research studies relied on male-dominated (e.g., Hyde, 1991) and Caucasian samples (Samuda, 1975). We cannot brush off these concerns as trivial. Therefore, it is important that you clearly define the target population you wish to study and ensure that your sampling population is a fair representative of that population.

## Volunteer Participants

Related to our selection of participants is the question of who chooses to participate in our research. Do people who volunteer to participate in our research represent the typical person? The answer is probably no. Remember the objections raised in Chapter 4 about the *Consumer Reports* study of the effectiveness of psychotherapy? The central objection to that report was that the analyses were based only on data provided by people who voluntarily returned the survey. Unfortunately, not everyone who was given a survey returned it. Because we do not know why some of these people responded and others did not, we cannot be totally sure that the results are representative of the population we want to describe.

## Preparing the Participant for the Study

Have you ever been driving on the interstate and seen a police car turn onto the road behind you? What do you do? If you are like us, you first make sure you are not speeding. We become self-conscious of driving while we can see the patrol car. The same type of self-conscious reaction occurs in people who participate in a research project; they know (or perhaps dread) that a researcher is scrutinizing everything they do.

In Figure 9.1 you can see that there is a link between the researcher's interaction with the participants and the participants' perception of the purpose of the research. This link indicates that the researcher's behavior influences how each participant behaves during the study. Specifically, the participants' ideas about the purpose of the research may cause them to do what they think the researcher wants them to do. We can review this interaction between the researcher's behavior and participants' perceptions using a classic example.

The **Hawthorne effect** is an example of how the researcher's behavior and the participants' perceptions of the research may affect the reactions of those participants. The name of this phenomenon is linked to the workplace in which this research occurred: the Hawthorne plant of the Western Electric Company during the late 1920s and early 1930s. The researchers in this series of studies wanted to find ways to improve assembly-line productivity by varying working conditions. Much to their surprise, the researchers found that almost any change, even returning to the original working conditions, improved productivity (Sundstorm, McIntyre, Halfhill, & Richards, 2000). There are many possible explanations for this outcome, but most come back to the participants' awareness of being the target of researchers' attention during the research process. Performance increased when changes were tried, possibly due to participants' expectations that their performance was being watched closely and might lead to termination of employment or some other negative consequence. Thus, despite what participants may or may not have been told by the researchers, it is possible they believed their performance in the study would have an impact on future job performance evaluations and employment.

The Hawthorne plant episode is a frequently told story, with many different versions. The history of what happened at the Hawthorne plant is murky at best. Nevertheless, many writers use the Hawthorne episode to illustrate how a person's behavior changes when he or she knows that someone is watching. The lesson from this version of the story is that we need to ensure that our research design and our behavior as the researcher do not create a **demand characteristic** among the participants that could contaminate the results of the study. A demand characteristic is any condition created by the design of the study that leads the participants to infer the purpose of the research. The participants' misperception of the purpose of the research may cause them to act differently than they normally would, thereby biasing the results.

Another version of the Hawthorne story is that the researchers inadvertently created a confounding variable in their study. During the study, the workers' pay reflected their productivity; the more components they made, the more money they earned. Therefore, the workers' behavior reflected a well-known behavioral and economic principle: people work harder for valued rewards such as compensation (Parsons, 1974). The take-home message is to emphasize the need to pay attention to the design and implementation phases of the study to rule out alternative explanations of the results.

The Hawthorne effect and demand characteristics are more than historical episodes and interesting phenomena described in textbooks; they are real threats to the quality or internal validity of any research project. If we study history to avoid making the same mistakes, then we should heed the lesson learned from the Hawthorne studies when we design our research projects.

### Recording and Analyzing the Results

> **HAMLET:** *Do you see yonder cloud that's almost in shape of a camel?*
> **POLONIUS:** *By the mass, and 'tis like a camel, indeed.*
> **HAMLET:** *Methinks it is like a weasel.*
> **POLONIUS:** *It is backed like a weasel.*
> **HAMLET:** *Or like a whale?*
> **POLONIUS:** *Very like a whale.*
>
> *—Shakespeare* (1604)

Polonius is quick to see what Hamlet claims to see in the random formation of clouds. A single cloud quickly becomes a camel, a weasel, and then a whale all upon Hamlet's suggestion. Clearly, Polonius is a sycophant who readily agrees with everything Hamlet says. Are researchers like Polonius? Do they allow their research hypothesis to influence their perception? What about participants?

Do researchers see what they want to see when observing a person's behavior? The answer is yes. If we believe something to be true, we tend to interpret things within that context and act in ways that bring about the expected result. Psychologists call this phenomenon the **self-fulfilling prophecy**. One of the classic examples of the self-fulfilling prophecy is the Pygmalion-in-the-classroom effect (Rosenthal, 1994; Rosenthal & Jacobson, 1968). To demonstrate the effects of the self-fulfilling prophecy, researchers told grade-school teachers that several of the students were "late bloomers" and would soon begin to excel in school. However, the late bloomers were actually randomly selected students. Nevertheless, many of these students had moderate increases in their IQ scores by the end of the year. This increase in IQ may have been due to the way the teachers interacted with the students. Because they expected the students to blossom academically, the teachers may have given the late bloomers extra attention, support, and encouragement during the year.

In general, we refer to the self-fulfilling prophecy in research as **experimenter bias** or **experimenter effect**. Thus, this effect or bias is in reference to the researcher's treatment of the participant. If the person collecting the data knows the research hypothesis, he or she may treat the participants in the groups differently, thus affecting the participants' behavior and confounding the results.

Even after the data are collected, what will convince us as researchers that the data truly support or refute our hypothesis? Can we look at the data and shout, "Eureka, we have solved the problem!"? Data typically do not really "speak for themselves." Analyzing data is an interpretative process and therefore prone to a host of personal and subjective biases. Consequently, we tend to rely on statistical analysis and objective reasoning to reduce further opportunities for subjective inference and unsubstantiated conclusions. However, see Chapter 17 for more on alternative approaches to sense-making when data are more qualitative by nature.

Some of the answers to the research challenges identified thus far will come in the following pages and the other chapters of this book. Each research project is unique, however, and no single source can offer a fixed set of rules that covers every potential experiment and the design problems that will arise. The preferable alternative is to work through the framework illustrated in Figure 9.1 and use it to consider potential problems and suitable improvements for each research project.

To help us to explain and you to understand these principles, we want to use two research projects as examples. These examples will help us illustrate the many choices and design questions that researchers must resolve. Although the examples are from published empirical studies, we have simplified their designs a bit to better fit the purpose of our review.

## Sex Differences and Memory for Emotional Events

Do men and women differ when asked to recall emotionally significant events in their lives? Are men or women more likely to focus on the positive events in their lives? Who is more likely to ignore negative events, men or women? Seidlitz and Diener (1998) addressed these and other questions in a study.

## Changing Attitudes by Writing Essays

Imagine that someone asked you to write an essay that supported a 5% increase in your college's tuition. Would completing this request change your attitude regarding hikes in tuition? Will the task strengthen your beliefs or cause you to switch your opinion? The inspiration for these questions comes from work by Stalder and Baron (1998).

## What Is the Independent Variable?

It is critical to ensure that we define all of our terms as clearly as possible. Consider the research examining sex differences for memory of emotional events. The independent variable is sex—men versus women. Technically, sex is a subject variable because the researcher cannot actually manipulate it or randomly assign participants to be either male or female. Nevertheless, the researcher can use the variable to predict the dependent variable. We use the word *sex* when the biological distinction is the predominant characteristic differentiating groups. We use the word *gender* to refer to men and women as members of social groups or to traits associated with each sex.

Seidlitz and Diener (1998) treated their study as one that examined sex differences. What could be simpler, right? The questions do ask about sex differences, but is this the only way we can look at the problem? Many researchers study gender role, which refers to one's sexual identity. One theory is that gender-role identity is a continuous scale with masculinity and femininity on opposite ends of the scale. Accordingly, although there are only two sexes, there are many levels of gender identity.

Using gender role rather than sex is an interesting alternative for our research question. Bem (1974, 1977) developed a scale that assesses one's gender-role identity. Using this scale, we can identify men and women who have varying degrees of masculine or feminine traits. We could then determine whether people with feminine traits have different recall rates for emotional events than people with masculine traits.

The main goal of this example was to illustrate that there may be many ways to define an independent variable in a study. In this example, either definition of the independent variable (sex or gender role) is acceptable, but each represents a different research project. For the present example, we will focus on sex differences and compare men and women.

### What Type of Independent Variable?

The type of independent variable can also have profound effects on the design of the research project as well as the conclusions we can draw from the data. There are several ways we can classify independent variables.

*Subject versus Manipulated*
For the study examining the recall of emotional life events, sex is a subject variable because the condition existed before the person's participation in the study. In addition, it is impossible for the researcher to randomly assign people to be men or women. By contrast, the study examining the effects of

essay writing on attitude change uses a manipulated independent variable because the researcher can decide what type of essay each participant will write.

The difference in the type of independent variable is important because it determines the control we have over alternative explanations. If we use a manipulated variable, we can create one or more control conditions for our experiment. Consider the essay-writing project. What control groups could we create, and what function would they serve? The simplest control would be to have a group of people who do not write an essay; they just tell us what they think about a 5% tuition increase. This control will help us determine whether writing the essay had any effect on the students' attitudes. Will this single control group account for other alternative explanations?

What would happen if we asked students to write an essay on a topic unrelated to tuition? This control has the advantage that it makes the two groups comparable with the exception of the critical component, the topic of the essay. People in both groups will write an essay and experience all the things involved in writing. The only difference is that one group of people will write an essay to support an unpopular idea.

Is it also possible that people will justify the increase in tuition by saying nice things about the college? The change in opinion may reflect positive feelings about the college, not taking a disagreeable stand. If you agree with our argument, you might have a group of people who write an essay describing the good things about their college. The other group of people would write an essay supporting the tuition hike.

Can you think of other control conditions? With some time and thought you might be able to find better examples than ours. The purpose of this discussion was to reiterate the importance of defining the meaning of the independent variable. The exercise will help ensure that you measure the variable correctly and consider alternative definitions of the variable. In addition, the exercise will help you design control conditions that will allow you to account for alternative explanations.

### Between-Subjects versus Within-Subjects Variables

We can also classify independent variables as being either a between-subjects or a within-subjects variable. Figure 9.2 illustrates the difference between the two types of variable. The distinguishing feature is the number of times we test the individual.

For a **between-subjects variable**, we test the individual under only one treatment or research condition. By contrast, for a **within-subjects variable**, we test the same person under two or more research conditions. Sometimes, researchers will call a within-subjects variable a **repeated-measures variable**. For example, a person's sex is a between-subjects variable; it does not make sense to test the same person once as a male and then again as a female. An independent variable is also a between-subjects variable if we randomly assign participants to experience only one treatment condition.

# Figure 9.2

**Illustration of the Difference between a Between-Subjects Variable and a Within-Subjects Variable**

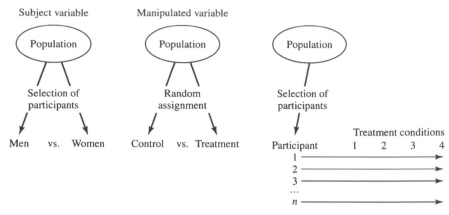

For the between-subjects variable, the researcher assesses the participant's behavior under one level of the independent variable. For the within-subjects variable, the researcher assesses each participant under multiple treatment conditions.

If we observe the behavior of a participant under different research conditions, that variable is a within-subjects variable. Time can be a within-subjects variable if we test or observe our participants' behavior on different occasions. For example, we may test our participants before and after some important event. Similarly, we may also test the same person under different levels of the independent variable. We call these variables within-subjects variables because we compare the same person's performance under different conditions or at different times.

Recognize the difference between between-subjects and within-subjects variables, because they require special considerations for research design as well as statistical analysis. For now, we will focus on between-subjects designs. We will review within-subjects research designs in a later chapter.

## What Is the Dependent Variable?

As with the independent variable, we will need to create an operational definition of the dependent variable. We can use the two studies to examine how we will define the appropriate dependent variable. How will we evaluate the emotional memories of men and women? How will we determine whether we have changed people's attitudes toward tuition increases? As you should recall from Chapter 3, we are revisiting the concepts of operational definitions, measurement, and validity.

For the study examining sex differences and memory, we could ask people to describe the happiest or saddest moments in their lives. We could then rate the emotional content contained in the statement. For instance, we might give the statement, "I remember when Mom and Dad gave me a puppy for Christmas" a low score. By contrast, we might give a high score to the statement "I can remember when we bought my first car. I was thrilled, excited, and felt like I was on top of the world. For the next couple of days. . . ."

Another tactic would be to ask people to describe within a three-minute period the significant emotional events that have happened in their lives. Using this information, we would then count the number of positive and negative events recalled. This tactic would allow us to look at the number and quality of memories listed. For example, do men and women differ in the types of events they recall as positive and negative?

Can you think of other ways to measure one's memory for emotional events? There are many different ways that we can measure the same dependent variable. Whatever method you select, you will need to examine the following characteristics of your measure.

## Reliability and Validity

Reliability refers to the *consistency* in a measurement, whereas validity refers to the *legitimacy* of the measure. The downfall of many research projects comes from selecting tests or measurement techniques that were unreliable, invalid, or both. There are many ways to ensure the reliability and validity of a measure. One is to use good techniques that other researchers also use. As you read research reports on a specific topic, you will begin to find that researchers examining a common topic tend to use similar tests. Although this is not an ideal method of guaranteeing reliability and validity, it is a good start. Researchers also study the reliability and validity of tests. You can easily find published research that evaluates the efficiency of specific testing procedures. It is important to note that reliability and validity apply equally to both the independent and dependent variables.

## Objective Recording of the Data

It is important that you use consistent and systematic measurement procedures that do not bias the results. Examining the validity of the recording method is one way to remove or reduce potential bias. Other procedural techniques help reduce potential bias in our recording. One of the most useful methods for reducing experimenter bias is to use what researchers call the single- and double-blind procedures. In this case, *blind* means that specific people involved in the research do not know the purpose of the study or the relevant independent variables that the participant experienced. Almost all researchers use some form of **single-blind** and many use a **double-blind** procedure.

The single-blind procedure indicates that the person participating in the research does not know the specifics of the researcher's hypothesis. The goal of the single-blind procedure is to reduce any demand characteristics that may result from the participants' knowledge of the researcher's hypothesis. In a true experiment, for example, the participants would not know whether they were in one of the treatment conditions or in a control group. If the single-blind approach is successful, the participants' behavior will reflect natural reactions to the research conditions.

How did the researchers use single-blind techniques in the study of sex differences and the study of attitude change? In the sex-differences study, the participants knew that the researchers were examining memory for emotional events. What the participants did not know was why the researchers were collecting the data or how the data would be analyzed. Similarly, in the attitude-change study, the participants did not know the hypothesized effect of essay writing until the researcher debriefed them.

Some research projects require additional controls to reduce the risk of experimenter bias. The double-blind procedure means that neither the person participating in the study nor the person collecting or scoring the data knows the researcher's hypothesis and the treatment the participant received. Consider the sex-differences study for recall of emotional events. If we decide to evaluate the content of the individual's memory, then the person scoring the comments must not know the hypothesis and the sex of the participant writing the essay.

### Using a Placebo

A placebo is a common technique used to create a single-blind procedure. For example, in most drug studies, some people receive a placebo treatment. The people participating in these studies understand that the researcher is examining the effectiveness of a drug. What they do not know is whether the pill is the real drug or a tablet that does not have the active ingredient being studied. This control procedure ensures that the participants' reactions are not affected by their knowledge of whether they received the drug.

A control group is an example of both a single-blind and placebo treatment. Previously, we examined different types of control conditions for the essay-writing and attitude-change experiment. One recommendation was to ask students to write an essay unrelated to increases in tuition. This control is a type of placebo in that it requires the participants to engage in the same type of behavior, writing an essay. Using this control condition helps us ensure that the topic of the essay, not its production, is the essential factor for attitude change.

### Cover Story/Deception

A cover story is another way to exercise a single-blind procedure. A cover story misleads the participants about the true purpose of the research. Graziano and Bryant (1998) examined how men perceived pictures of women when they received bogus information about changes in their heart rate. The researchers predicted that men would rate women as more attractive if they had been led to believe that their heart rates increased while looking at pictures of the women.

How did Graziano and Bryant (1998) create this cover story? When each participant arrived for the study, the researcher took him to a small room filled with physiological recording devices and attached a sensor to his finger. The researcher then told the participant,

> Most of our research is conducted over at the Medical School Building. We have all sorts of electronic wizardry and soundproof chambers over there. Right now, there are several experiments being conducted and our facilities are overcrowded. Because of this situation, we are doing this experiment here and are forced to use a fairly crude but adequate measure of heart rate and other physiological measures. . . . Here, we are recording the heart rate the way they used to do it 30 years ago. These sensors measure your pulse rate. . . . This machine gives us signals on your pulse and thus your heart rate. . . . Unfortunately, this recording method makes it necessary to have audible sounds. . . . Just try to ignore the heart sounds. I will present 10 slides to you at regular intervals and my assistant will record your heart rate along with other physiological measures. (p. 254)

This cover story offered a plausible account for the conditions surrounding the experiment. To be sure that the cover story worked, Graziano and Bryant (1998) conducted a **manipulation check**. A manipulation check is merely a test to determine whether the cover story or deception worked. In this case, Graziano and Bryant asked the participants at the end of the study whether they had any suspicions about the purpose of the research. Only 3 of the 103 volunteers expressed any suspicion that the researchers had faked the heart-rate sounds, evidence that the cover story worked.

Cover stories can be extremely effective. Their use often raises ethical concerns, however. As you learned in Chapter 2, all participants have the right to know the relevant details of a project so that they can make an informed decision on whether they will participate in the research. Therefore, if you plan to use deception or a cover story in your research, you will need to ensure that the deception does not deny a person's ability to know the true potential risks or threats of participating in the study. In addition, if you use a cover story, you must fully explain to the participants the deception and its purpose at the end of the research, typically with a debriefing statement.

## Are There Any Confounding Variables?

Each research project runs the risk of confounding. What are the potential confounding variables in the studies that we are examining? For example, the study examining the sex differences for memory of emotional events may create a confound depending on how we collect the data. What would happen if we asked 20 women and 20 men to create a list of their positive memories and then create a second list of their negative memories? Is it possible that the order of the lists will affect the data? Writing about their positive memories first may influence the participants' ability to remember negative events.

Any time we expose a participant to a sequence of events (typically when involving a within-subjects type of independent variable) there is a threat of a **carryover effect**. The carryover effect refers to the effect that previous experiences have on subsequent behavior. As an example, if we use the same test on two occasions, the participants may remember the questions and their answers, and this memory may bias the results. Using the same test twice may also give the participants cues about the purpose of the research.

As a second example, another potential confound may be that women are more verbal than men and use more words to describe their memories. We could ask that people limit their comments to three to five words, or we could wait until we collect the data to determine whether one group is wordier than the other. What if the women in our study were happier than the men; will the difference bias our data? Again, the participants' mood during the study could influence how well they recall positive and negative events. To account for this confounding variable, we can use any number of scales that assess a person's mood. The data from the measure of mood will help us determine whether there are significant differences between women's and men's mood at the time of the study.

## Knowledge Check

1. Answer these items after reading each of the short descriptions of research projects that follow.
   a. Identify the independent variable(s) and the dependent variable.
   b. What is the hypothesis that the researcher appears to be testing (you will have to infer this from your reading of the scenario)?
   c. Identify the empirical method that the researcher used.
   d. What aspects of the research design would influence our evaluation of the internal validity of the research?
   e. What aspects of the research design would influence our evaluation of the external validity of the research?
   f. What changes would you make to the study to improve the internal and external validity of the study?
      (i.) A researcher wants to test the effects of a counseling program on assertiveness behavior. For the first part of the study, students completed a test that measured their assertiveness. Those students who received the lowest scores received the counseling. Two months later, the researcher retested the participants. All participants showed a marked improvement in assertiveness. The researcher concludes that the counseling is a success.
      (ii.) An instructor wants to demonstrate to her students the value of elaborated rehearsal. She randomly divides the class into three groups. She tells the students in the first group that they are in the control group and do not need to read the next chapter in the textbook. She tells the students in the second group to read the next chapter in the textbook as if they were preparing for an exam. For the third group, she tells the students to write a letter

to their mother explaining the material presented in the chapter. The following week, all students complete a test of the material covered in the assigned chapter. On average, students who wrote the essay score 10% higher than the other groups.

(iii.) A researcher wanted to evaluate the effectiveness of a lie detector procedure. Fifty students enrolled in an introductory psychology class volunteered to participate for extra credit in the course. The researcher gave each participant an envelope that contained a $100 bill and instructed the participant to lie about the contents of the envelope during a lie detection investigation. The researcher told the participants that they could keep the money if they passed the lie detection test. After evaluating the results of the lie detector test, the researcher claimed that he could detect 80% of the participants as liars. Using these results, the researcher concluded that lie detectors are effective at detecting deception.

(iv.) A researcher wishes to examine the effect of pornography on aggression. She asks 30 men to watch a 15-minute segment of a sexually explicit videotape. After viewing the film, the researcher leads the men to believe that they will now participate in a second experiment wherein they will deliver electrical shocks to another person. The dependent variable was the length of the shocks that the men delivered. The average length of the shocks was 2.46 seconds. Using these data, the researcher claims that watching pornography increases level of aggression.

## What Are the Research Hypotheses?

Preparing the research hypothesis is an integral part of preparing a research design. Indeed, the format of the research hypothesis shapes the design of the research and the statistical analysis of the data. When we write a hypothesis, we want to be sure that it clearly states the expected relationship between the independent and dependent variables and the type of results we expect to obtain. For the memory of emotional events and essay-writing examples, we are interested in the differences between two groups. Therefore, we will frame each hypothesis as a statement of the relationship between the different treatment groups.

### Directional versus Nondirectional Hypothesis

A research hypothesis describes the relationship among population parameters. There are, however, different ways that we can write the hypothesis. The major difference is whether we use a **directional hypothesis** or a **nondirectional hypothesis**. In a directional hypothesis we predict the specific relationship between the two groups using either a greater-than or less-than type of prediction. Examples of directional hypotheses include

"Women are more likely to remember positive emotional events than men" and "People are more likely to agree with an unpopular opinion after writing an essay supporting that opinion." Both predictions use words to indicate that the behavior of one group would be greater than the behavior of the other group.

In contrast, a nondirectional hypothesis predicts that there will be differences between groups but does not specify the type of difference that will occur. We can rewrite the previous hypotheses as "Men and women will differ in their recall of positive emotional events," and "Writing an essay supporting an unpopular topic will affect a person's opinion of the topic." We have retained the emphasis on the relationship and expected differences between the groups, but we have not indicated which group will be greater than the other.

Which type of hypothesis should you use? There is no clear answer to this question, but plenty of opinions. Some researchers believe that if you are able to form a clear prediction about the direction of the results, then you should, thereby stating a directional hypothesis. The justification for this tactic is that if you are confident in your prediction based on existing research and/or theory, then you should expect only one form of outcome.

The justification for the nondirectional hypothesis, however, is that we, as researchers, should examine all results regardless of the direction of the outcome. From this perspective, we would say that any evidence of a statistically significant difference between the groups is important and worthy of our analysis.

Both directional and nondirectional hypotheses have their place in the social sciences. In many ways, selecting between directional and non-directional hypotheses is much like resolving an ethical dilemma. Specifically, the researcher needs to examine his or her philosophical stance on hypothesis testing and then develop a rationale for selecting one type of hypothesis. If you believe that it is imperative to test that $\mu_1 > \mu_2$, then you should use a directional hypothesis. By contrast, if you believe that it is essential to explore the differences between $\mu_1$ and $\mu_2$, then use a non-directional hypothesis, $\mu_1 \neq \mu_2$ (Jones & Tukey, 2000).

## Mathematical Hypotheses

In the previous section, we used words to state each hypothesis. In this section, you will learn that it is often easier and more concise to convert a well-written hypothesis into a series of mathematical or logical statements. These mathematical statements then help us interpret the results of the study.

At one level, the hypothesis refers to the relationship between the independent and dependent variables in your study. For example, our hypothesis might imply that one's sex affects the memory of emotional events or that writing essays forms attitudes. The hypothesis also refers to the parameters of the populations. According to what you learned in Chapter 7, the sample data should be representative of the target population, and we can use the sample data to generalize about the population. Consequently, the hypothesis describes what we believe to be true of the target populations.

When we prepare the **mathematical hypothesis**, we write two complementary hypotheses, the *null* hypothesis and the *alternative* hypothesis. In its basic form, the null hypothesis implies that there is no relationship between the independent and dependent variables, by indicating that the separate treatment groups will be equivalent in terms of the data associated with the dependent variable. The alternative hypothesis, by contrast, implies that there is a relationship between the independent and dependent variables, and, by implication, that the groups will be different from each other.

We can use the sex-differences study example to illustrate the null and alternative hypotheses. For the null hypothesis, we would say that one's sex is independent of memory for emotional events. As a mathematical statement, we can write the null hypothesis for this study as $H_0$: $\mu_M = \mu_F$. A translation of the equation is "The population mean of men's recall of positive emotional events equals the population mean of women's recall of positive events." The alternative hypothesis in this case is $H_1$: $\mu_M \neq \mu_F$. In writing the alternative hypothesis, we replace the equals ($=$) with not equals ($\neq$). Table 9.1 presents examples of the null and alternative hypotheses for directional and nondirectional hypotheses.

There are several important points in Table 9.1. First, we use $H_0$ and $H_1$ to refer to the null and alternative hypotheses, respectively. This practice is a convention that has evolved among statisticians and researchers. Second, and more importantly, in the alternative hypothesis, the equality sign ($>$, $<$, or $\neq$) matches the adjective in the research hypothesis (greater than, less than, not equal to). We use the complementary equality sign in the null hypothesis. For example, $=$ and $\neq$ are complementary signs as are the signs $\geq$ and $<$. Finally, the null hypothesis always implies that there is no relationship between the independent and dependent variables, whereas

**Table 9.1** Examples of Null and Alternative Hypotheses for Directional and Nondirectional Hypotheses Using a Two-Group Design

| Hypothesis | Directional Hypothesis | | Nondirectional Hypothesis |
| | Greater than | Less than | |
| --- | --- | --- | --- |
| Research hypothesis | "Men will remember more positive emotional events than women" | "Men will remember fewer positive emotional events than women" | "Men and women will differ in their recall of positive emotional events" |
| Null hypothesis | $H_0$: $\mu_M \leq \mu_F$ | $H_0$: $\mu_M \geq \mu_F$ | $H_0$: $\mu_M = \mu_F$ |
| Alternative hypothesis | $H_1$: $\mu_M > \mu_F$ | $H_1$: $\mu_M < \mu_F$ | $H_0$: $\mu_M \neq \mu_F$ |

the alternative hypothesis implies that there is a meaningful relationship between these variables.

## Evaluating Hypotheses

You may be wondering why we use the null and alternative hypotheses. It seems rather odd that we would use two hypotheses when one would seem to be enough. The practice of using null and alternative hypotheses has evolved during the past century as a way to make inferences about sample data. We can use the example of the differences between men and women's recall of life events to illustrate the reasoning behind null hypothesis testing.

When conducting empirical research, the researcher's primary responsibility is to provide evidence to support his or her claim about the relationship between the variables described in the research hypothesis. The research hypothesis and alternative hypothesis are the same thing, and the researcher must collect data that will convince us of the accuracy of his or her predictions. Therefore, we begin with the null hypothesis as a "true" or default statement that explains the linkage between your independent and dependent variable. The researcher is then required to provide evidence that is sufficiently strong to convince us that a different explanation is more accurate, that the null hypothesis is in fact "false." In the sex-difference study, the null hypothesis states that there is no meaningful difference between men and women. To reject this statement, the researcher must present data to convince us that the alternative hypothesis, not the null hypothesis, is the more accurate description of the relationship between sex and the recall of emotional life events. We require the researcher to demonstrate that there is a sizable or meaningful difference between men's and women's recall of emotional events before we are willing to accept the alternative hypothesis as accurate.

The decision to reject the null hypothesis is an inferential decision; the researcher uses sample data to draw inferences about the relationship as it would be expected to occur at the level of the population. There are two important characteristics of an inference. First, whenever we make an inference, we use the experience created by samples to describe the population. Second, whenever we make an inference, we must assume that there is a probability that we are wrong. As you know, the sample mean is an unbiased estimate of the population mean. The important word is *estimate*. There is always a probability that your inference will be wrong. By implication, then, all hypothesis testing is conditional or based on probabilities.

We use the data to determine whether to reject the null hypothesis. Look at Table 9.1. We use $\mu$ to describe the two populations. If we find that the sample means, drawn at random from the populations, are sufficiently different, we will reject the null hypothesis in favor of its alternative. Will we make mistakes when evaluating the null hypothesis? Yes.

There are two mistakes we can make when judging the null hypothesis. In the first case, we can be misled by the data and reject a true null hypothesis.

Researchers call this error a **Type I error**. We prefer to think of this as a "false alarm." Consider the following example to illustrate this type of inferential mistake. Assume that we give one group of patients suffering from depression a placebo drug treatment and a second group a drug we think will decrease symptoms of depression. For this experiment our alternative hypothesis would be that $\mu_1 \neq \mu_2$. If in actuality the drug did not have an effect, then a Type I error would occur if we decided that the two groups were not equal to each other. This decision represents a Type I error because both groups of participants actually received a noneffective treatment, yet we concluded that $\mu_1 \neq \mu_2$ and supported our incorrect alternative hypothesis. The Type I error occurred because of random events. It is possible there is a difference between the groups that reflects nothing besides the effects of chance.

A second type of inferential error is a **Type II error**. We like to think of this type of error as a "miss." A Type II error occurs when a null hypothesis is incorrect, but we fail to recognize it as false. For example, it is true that the average height of adult men is greater than the average height of adult women. Therefore the null hypothesis that $\mu_{Men} = \mu_{Women}$ (where $\mu$ represents average height) is a false statement. Imagine that you measure the heights of 10 adult women and 10 adult men and find that the average heights are equal. Because the average heights are equal, you decide not to reject the statement $\mu_{Men} = \mu_{Women}$. This decision would reflect a Type II error, because there is a real difference between the heights of men and women that you were simply unable to detect with your data. The Type II error occurred due to random error that you selected men and women whose average heights happened to be equal.

The Type I and Type II errors describe the decisions concerning the null hypothesis, not the decisions regarding the alternative hypothesis. A Type I error means that we rejected a true null hypothesis; a Type II error means that we failed to reject a false null hypothesis. Table 9.2 presents an illustration of Type I and Type II errors.

The Greek letters, $\alpha$ and $\beta$, are probability estimates; $\boldsymbol{\alpha}$ represents the probability of committing a Type I error, and $\boldsymbol{\beta}$ represents the probability of committing a Type II error. The probability of a Type I error is under the direct control of the researcher because he or she can determine the criterion for deciding to reject the null hypothesis. Therefore, if the researcher wants to

## Table 9.2   Illustration of Type I and Type II Errors

| Researcher's decision | Population parameters ("Reality") | |
| --- | --- | --- |
| | $\mu_1 = \mu_2$<br>$H_0$ is correct | $\mu_1 \neq \mu_2$<br>$H_0$ is false |
| Reject $H_0$ and accept $H_1$ | Type I error<br>$\alpha$ | Correct decision<br>$1 - \beta$ |
| Do not reject $H_0$ | Correct decision<br>$1 - \alpha$ | Type II error<br>$\beta$ |

be conservative and lower the risk of committing a Type I error, he or she can use a small value of $\alpha$. Therefore, $\alpha$ is often referred to as the **significance level** (or **criterion**) for a study as it determines the requirement for rejecting the null hypothesis.

The value of $\beta$ is more difficult to determine. As we will discuss in more detail later in this chapter, sample size, the difference between groups, and $\alpha$ all contribute to the size of $\beta$. Consequently, researchers can influence the probability of a Type II error by carefully planning their research. When designing their studies, researchers attempt to minimize $\beta$ to ensure that they will correctly detect and reject false null hypotheses.

Generally, decreasing $\alpha$ will increase $\beta$. As you lower the risk of committing a Type I error you increase the risk of committing a Type II error. Consequently, all research designs must attempt to balance the relative risk of these two errors. With careful planning, you can design your research in such a way as to reduce the risk of committing a Type I and a Type II error, but you will never be able to eliminate both errors.

In many ways, evaluating the null hypothesis is like the decision a jury must make in a criminal case. According to American legal theory, every person accused of a crime is innocent until proven guilty. The presumption of innocence is the legal equivalent of the null hypothesis. The prosecution must provide ample evidence to persuade the members of the jury to reject this assumption in favor of the most supported alternative explanation. In criminal cases, the jury must find the defendant guilty beyond a reasonable doubt. A guilty verdict means that there is ample and compelling evidence to reject the presumption of innocence. Does a "not guilty" decision prove the defendant's innocence? No, a verdict of not guilty means that there is insufficient evidence to convict the defendant; it does not prove innocence. Similarly, we can never really accept the null hypothesis or assuredly prove the alternative hypothesis. To accept means to prove true. Because we use inferential reasoning in hypothesis testing, we can never prove a hypothesis true beyond a doubt. The only decisions we can make regarding the null hypothesis are to reject or not to reject the null hypothesis.

How are Type I and Type II errors related to a jury's verdict? A Type I error is the same as convicting an innocent person. Finding an innocent person guilty is similar to a Type I error because we incorrectly reject a true null hypothesis. Similarly, a Type II error is the same as setting a criminal free. A Type II error occurs because we fail to be sufficiently convinced that the null hypothesis is wrong just as a jury may not be convinced that the defendant is guilty.

## Evaluating Hypotheses: Practical Matters

Our decision of whether to reject the null hypothesis depends on the context in which we interpret the data. When we look at the data, we need to answer one question: Is there sufficient evidence to reject the null hypothesis as a false statement? One way to answer this question is to examine the relative difference between the groups. In this section, we will examine the concept of effect size, one of the primary factors in determining whether to reject the null hypothesis.

## Effect Size

Imagine that we collect data for two groups. The mean of the first group is $M_1 = 100$; the mean of the second group is $M_2 = 105$. What can we say about the difference between the two means other than they are different from each other? What could cause the difference between the two means? Is the difference trivial or meaningful? One way to answer this important question is to examine the **effect size** of the difference between the groups.

Equation 9.1 presents how to determine the effect size for the difference between two groups. Specifically, the effect size allows us to evaluate the relative difference between two sample means:

$$d_2 = \frac{M_1 - M_2}{\sqrt{\dfrac{VAR_1 + VAR_2}{2}}} \tag{9.1}$$

For the equation, $d_2$ is the effect size for the difference between two sample means, $M_1$ and $M_2$ represent the sample means, and $VAR_1$ and $VAR_2$ represent the sample variances. We assume that the two variances are equivalent ($VAR_1 \approx VAR_2$) and that the sample sizes are the same ($n_1 = n_2$). The effect size is nothing more than a simple ratio. It is the ratio of the differences between the means to the variability of scores on the dependent variable within the treatment groups. The larger the absolute value of $d_2$, the greater the relative difference between the two treatment group means. Figure 9.3 illustrates three examples of effect size for a two-group comparison. Each curve represents the distribution of scores. For all the data sets, the standard deviation of the samples is 10.0. The pairs of means in each panel are: (a) $M_1 = 100$, $M_2 = 102$; (b) $M_1 = 100$, $M_2 = 105$; and (c) $M_1 = 100$, $M_2 = 108$. With all else being constant, as the difference between group means increases, the effect size increases. In his influential book on statistics, Cohen (1988) described the three general guidelines for estimating effect sizes shown in Figure 9.3 as (a) small, (b) moderate, and (c) large.

As you might guess, the size of $d_2$ has a lot to do with our interpretation of the null hypothesis. The larger the size of $d_2$, the stronger the relation between the independent and dependent variables. Therefore, when we design any research project, we need to find ways to increase the effect size as much as possible.

## Factors That Influence Effect Size

Two general factors influence effect size: the between-groups variance and the within-groups variance. There are many things that we can do to control these sources of variance and therefore improve the quality of our results.

# Figure 9.3

**Illustration of Effect Size with $d_2 = 0.20$, 0.50, and 0.80**

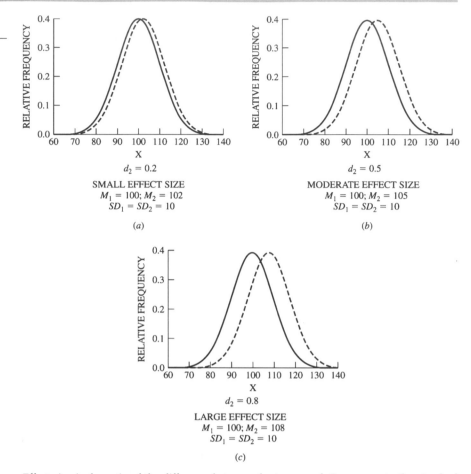

Effect size is the ratio of the difference between the two population means to the standard deviation of the groups.

Figure 9.4 depicts the two types of variance. The difference between the two group means represents the between-groups variance. The variability of scores within both groups represents the within-groups variance.

## Between-Groups Variance

The **between-groups variance** represents the difference among the group means. This variance represents the true difference between the population means plus the effect of random sampling or measurement errors. There are several ways that you can increase the difference between the population means. First, if you are using a manipulated independent variable, you will want to use levels of the independent variable that you believe create the greatest possible effect. For example, to increase the effect of the independent variable in the attitude-change study, you could tell the students that they must include five specific arguments in favor of the tuition increase. In

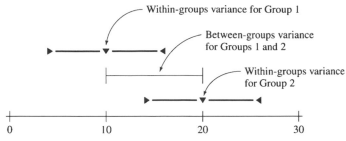

The between-groups variance represents the difference between the two group means. The within-groups variance represents the differences between individual observed scores and the group mean.

addition, you could give the students general facts (e.g., the hard-working faculty receive low salaries, the student union needs a new roof, and the price of library books increased by 18%) to help them write their essays. The goal of these tactics is to increase the effect that writing the essay has on a student's opinion.

For a subject variable, you will want to be sure that the two groups are as different as possible. In the sex-differences study, our use of sex as an independent variable does not easily lend itself to further modification because there are only two sexes. There are, however, subject variables that have differing levels. In these cases, we would want to define the sampling populations to maximize the differences between the groups. Consider a few examples. Imagine that you are interested in the introversion-extroversion personality dimension and its relation to other variables. When defining the populations, you would want to select participants who are clearly introverted or clearly extroverted. In another study, you may want to examine the effects of alcohol consumption on memory. For such a study you might want to select adults who abstain from drinking, those who are moderate social drinkers, and those who have had a long history of alcohol abuse. You should use these tactics with caution, however, as some procedures may produce spurious results. One such tactic to avoid is the median split, discussed next.

## Avoid Median Splits

Some researchers use a technique called a **median split** to create two (or more) intact groups for further comparison. This technique creates intact groups by using the score of an otherwise-continuous measure of some variable to group people. For example, if you wanted to compare the relationship between gender and recall of emotional memories across masculine and feminine individuals, you could administer the Bem Sex-Role Inventory (Bem, 1974, 1977) to students currently enrolled in the introductory psychology course and split the students into two groups based on the median of their scores. You would then label people on one side of the median as masculine and people on the other side of the median as feminine. Although this may sound like a good idea, it really is not a smart move.

A moment's thought should reveal to you the problems with the median split procedure. First, this technique results in a loss of potentially valuable information. The median split converts scores measured on an interval or more continuous form of response scale to a less informative ordinal or even nominal scale (depending on how you use it). Losing this continuous information will limit your ability to demonstrate the relationship between your independent and dependent variables.

Second, most measures of subject variables are normally distributed, and the majority of scores are close to the median. Consequently, a small difference between two scores (e.g., 99 and 101) can put people into radically different groups, even if those two groups are not necessarily different in any meaningful way. In sum, median splits can make it difficult to detect differences between groups and thereby lead to bogus conclusions (Bissonnette, Ickes, Bernstein, & Knowles, 1990; Maxwell & Delaney, 1993).

All of this said, median splits are usually not a good idea, so if you use a subject variable to classify people, ensure that it naturally places people into discrete groups. A better technique may be to utilize correlational analysis techniques. For example, you could examine the correlation between gender-role identity and number of positive or negative emotions recalled. Using this tactic would mean that you do not have to exclude people from your study. Rather, you would create a large representative sample and then examine the correlation between the subject variables and the dependent variable.

### Within-Groups Variance

The **within-groups variance** represents the difference among individuals within each condition. As Figure 9.4 illustrates, the variability among scores within a group represents the within-groups variance. Two factors contribute to the within-groups variance. The first is the natural variation within the population you are studying. As an example, look at all the students in your class; their heights and weights are different. These differences represent the natural variation that occurs for these two subject variables.

The second factor that affects within-groups variance is measurement error. Because no test is perfectly reliable, each test score includes some amount of error. Highly reliable tests contribute little measurement error; tests with lower reliability contribute more measurement error. These facts allow us to find ways to reduce the within-groups variance.

#### Homogeneous Samples

Whenever possible, try to use participants who are similar to one another. Researchers prefer to use **homogeneous** rather than **heterogeneous samples** because it allows them to limit irrelevant variability within groups. In other words, while a homogeneous sample refers to a condition wherein all the participants are similar to each other, a heterogeneous sample refers to a condition wherein there is considerable variability among the members of the sample.

There are several ways to increase the homogeneity of a sample. For example, in animal studies, researchers use animals that come from the same litter or are raised in highly controlled breeding environments. In many cases, researchers are able to use animals that are virtually identical to each other on almost all characteristics. We can do much the same with human research by selecting participants with similar subject characteristics. The important thing is to find the relevant characteristics. In studies of developmental psychology, age is an obvious grouping characteristic. Therefore, rather than lumping children into one large group (e.g., pre-adolescent) it may be better to create several smaller age groups (e.g., 5–7, 8–10, and 11–13). The goal of the researcher then is to identify the relevant subject variables and use these to create homogeneous groups.

### Reliable Measures

You can also decrease the within-groups variance by increasing the reliability of the measurement procedures. Measurement error is a random variable that increases some scores and decreases other scores. Therefore, anything you can do to increase the reliability of a test will help you detect any meaningful difference between the groups.

## Research in Action: Sex Differences and Memory for Emotional Events

We can begin with the questions regarding sex differences and the recall of emotional events. Seidlitz and Diener (1998) used students enrolled in an introductory psychology course at a large state university. The participants first completed a portion of the Satisfaction with Life Scale (Diener, Emmons, Larsen, & Griffin, 1985). This assessment consists of a series of 11-point bipolar items that ask respondents to indicate their general mood. Figure 9.5 presents several items from the inventory.

Once the participants completed the Satisfaction with Life Scale, they listed as many positive or negative life events as they could within three

Mark the number that best describes you.

Extremely happy — (0) (1) (2) (3) (4) (5) (6) (7) (8) (9) (10) — Extremely unhappy

Ecstatic — (0) (1) (2) (3) (4) (5) (6) (7) (8) (9) (10) — Utterly depressed

From Diener, Emmons, Larsen, & Griffin (1985).

# Figure 9.5

**From the Satisfaction with Life Scale**

Table 9.3 Observed Scores for the Number of Recalled Positive and Negative Life Events and Score on the Satisfaction with Life Scale

| | Number of Positive and Negative Life Events Recalled | | | | | | | | Satisfaction with Life Scale | | | |
| | Positive Events | | | | Negative Events | | | | | | | |
| | Women | | Men | | Women | | Men | | Women | | Men | |
|---|---|---|---|---|---|---|---|---|---|---|---|---|
| | 13 | 13 | 12 | 9 | 9 | 11 | 7 | 6 | 4 | 7 | 5 | 7 |
| | 8 | 11 | 10 | 10 | 5 | 10 | 6 | 7 | 7 | 3 | 7 | 5 |
| | 7 | 11 | 7 | 10 | 4 | 8 | 3 | 4 | 6 | 4 | 5 | 8 |
| | 9 | 14 | 9 | 6 | 6 | 8 | 6 | 3 | 9 | 2 | 3 | 4 |
| | 10 | 10 | 6 | 7 | 7 | 7 | 8 | 4 | 7 | 6 | 9 | 2 |
| | 10 | 12 | 10 | 8 | 7 | 7 | 7 | 8 | 7 | 8 | 2 | 6 |
| | 7 | 12 | 8 | 7 | 4 | 9 | 5 | 6 | 9 | 6 | 6 | 6 |
| | | 10 | | 7 | | 6 | | 3 | | 7 | | 5 |
| $n$ | 15 | | 15 | | 15 | | 15 | | 15 | | 15 | |
| $M$ | 10.47 | | 8.40 | | 7.20 | | 5.53 | | 6.13 | | 5.33 | |
| $VAR$ | 4.55 | | 3.11 | | 4.17 | | 3.12 | | 4.27 | | 4.10 | |
| $SD$ | 2.13 | | 1.76 | | 2.04 | | 1.77 | | 2.07 | | 2.02 | |

minutes. The researcher asked the participants to use a short phrase (three to five words) to describe each event. After completing the first list, participants created a second list of the opposite emotion. The researcher randomly determined the order in which the participants listed the positive and negative life events. A research assistant, who did not know the purpose of the study, counted the number of responses for each participant and scored the Satisfaction with Life Scale. Table 9.3 presents the hypothetical data for the study.

## Research in Action: Changing Attitudes by Writing Essays

For this experiment, the researcher randomly assigned 20 participants to one of two groups. The participants in the control group completed an attitude survey that contained a series of questions regarding their attitudes toward tuition increases. Scores for this scale can range from 0 (complete disagreement) to 4 (complete agreement).

The participants in the essay group wrote a persuasive essay supporting an increase in the college's tuition. Students writing the essay were free to form their own arguments and had 30 minutes to complete the essay. These participants then completed the same tuition-increase attitude scale. Table 9.4 presents the hypothetical data for the two groups.

## Table 9.4  Total Attitude Toward Tuition Increase Score for the Control and Essay-Writing Groups

|  | Control |  | Essay |  |
|---|---|---|---|---|
|  | 8 | 7 | 13 | 14 |
|  | 15 | 10 | 8 | 16 |
|  | 9 | 11 | 11 | 12 |
|  | 10 | 9 | 12 | 14 |
|  | 8 | 8 | 17 | 13 |
| $n$ | 10 |  | 10 |  |
| $M$ | 9.50 |  | 13.00 |  |
| $VAR$ | 5.17 |  | 6.44 |  |
| $SD$ | 2.27 |  | 2.54 |  |

## Knowledge Check

Use the data for each of the above two "Research in Action" studies to complete the following tasks.

2. Select a research hypothesis that best fits the purpose of the research. Describe the hypothesis in words and prepare the corresponding $H_0$ and $H_1$.

3. Calculate the effect size for each set of data. What inferences can you draw about the data given this statistic? For each data set, what factors contribute to the between-groups variance and the within-groups variance?

4. For each data set, describe the implications of committing a Type I or a Type II error.

## Chapter Summary

The primary theme of this chapter was designing a research project that reduces the effects of unwanted sources of error and bias. Because research is a uniquely human enterprise, there are many opportunities for the researcher's behavior to bias the participants' behavior as well as the researcher's interpretation of the data. Thus, we examined the sequence of events for the research process from defining the purpose of the study to the final interpretation of the data to examine where and how bias can enter the research process. The first source of potential bias is the effect that volunteer participants may introduce to the study. People who volunteer for a research project may not represent the typical person we hope to describe in our population.

Once we begin a study, there is a risk of the participants responding to an unintended demand characteristic. Most people know that they are participating in a research project and may want to modify their behavior to match what they believe to be the purpose of the research. A classic example of a demand characteristic is the Hawthorne effect.

A related source of bias is the researcher's expectations. If the persons interacting with the participants or recording the participants' behavior know the hypothesis under study and the treatment that the participants received, their knowledge may create subtle and not-so-subtle forms of bias. The researcher may bias the results by inadvertently treating the participants differently or interpret the behavior of the participant to be in keeping with the research hypothesis.

We then examined how the researcher can define the independent and dependent variables. The independent variable may be either a subject variable or a manipulated variable. The critical difference between the two variables is whether the researcher can randomly assign participants to different levels of the variable. If the researcher can randomly assign participants to different levels of the independent variable, then it is a manipulated variable.

The independent variable may also be characterized as either a between-subjects variable or a within-subjects variable. For a between-subjects variable, we compare and contrast different groups of people against each other. For a within-subjects variable, we observe the same person's behavior under several conditions.

There are several ways that the researcher can reduce the effects of the demand characteristic and experimenter bias. These techniques fall under the general heading of a blind. A single-blind study means that the participant does not know the researcher's hypothesis or the specific treatment condition to which he or she has been assigned. In addition, the researcher may use a placebo or a cover story to control what the participants believe about the purpose of the study and the treatment they receive. In a double-blind study, both the participant and the person collecting the data are unaware of the research hypothesis being tested and the participant's treatment condition.

A critical component of any research project is converting the research hypothesis into a mathematical hypothesis. The research hypothesis is a general description or prediction of the relation between the variables in the study. The mathematical hypothesis is a specific statement regarding the pattern of results that the study should produce. A mathematical hypothesis may be either general, as occurs in the nondirectional hypothesis, or specific, as occurs in the directional hypothesis.

Mathematical hypotheses contain two parts: a null hypothesis and an alternative hypothesis. The null hypothesis states that there is no meaningful relation between the variables in the study. The alternative hypothesis is the mathematical equivalent of the research hypothesis. The goal of the researcher is to collect data to allow him or her to reject the null hypothesis and accept the alternative hypothesis.

When evaluating the null and alternative hypotheses, a researcher can make one of two errors. The first error, a Type I error, occurs when the researcher rejects the null hypothesis as false when the null hypothesis is correct. The second error, a Type II error, occurs when the researcher fails to reject a false null hypothesis. The researcher can directly control the risk of committing a Type I error by establishing a criterion called the significance level, or $\alpha$. The size of $\alpha$ determines the probability that the researcher will commit a Type I error if the null hypothesis is a correct statement. The researcher can also influence $1 - \beta$, the probability of correctly rejecting a false null hypothesis.

The effect size is a statistic that reflects the relative difference between two groups and is a statistic that can help us understand how to increase the chances that we will successfully reject a false null hypothesis.

One way to increase the likelihood of rejecting a false null hypothesis is to increase the between-groups variance. The between-groups variance reflects the difference between the group means. If the independent variable does influence the between-groups variance, then selecting levels of the independent variable that create the greatest possible effect can increase the chance for rejecting a false null hypothesis.

The researcher can also attempt to reduce the within-groups variance. The within-groups variance represents the variability among scores within each treatment condition. If there is much heterogeneity of variance, then it will be more difficult to detect a statistically significant difference among the groups. If the researcher can make the data more homogeneous, then the within-groups variance will decrease and the researcher will be better able to detect differences among the groups.

In the final section of the chapter, we reviewed examples of two contemporary research projects. These studies demonstrated the application of good research design and demonstrated how one can collect useful data.

## Chapter Glossary for Review

**Alpha ($\alpha$)**—The probability of committing a Type I error. The level of $\alpha$ is under direct control of the researcher.

**Beta ($\beta$)**—The probability of committing a Type II error. The size of $\beta$ reflects many factors, including the design of the research, sample size, and level of $\beta$ selected.

**Between-groups variance**—The difference or variance among group means. The difference reflects differences among the population means and the effects of sampling error.

**Between-subjects variable**—A form of independent variable for which the researcher tests the participant on one occasion or under one level of the independent variable.

**Carryover effect**—A form of bias in which the effect of the participant's previous experiences in a study influences his or her performance.

**Demand characteristic**—Any unintended condition created by the design of a study that leads the participants to misinterpret the purpose of the research and respond accordingly.

**Directional hypothesis**—A research hypothesis that the researcher uses to predict the relation among groups using either a greater-than or a less-than prediction.

**Double blind**—A control procedure where the person interacting with the participants and recording the data does not know the hypothesis of the research or the relevant details of the independent variable the participant experienced. In addition, the participant does not know the details of the project or the level of independent variable.

**Effect size**—A standardized index of the different between-groups means or the relation between two variables.

**Experimenter bias** or **effect**—When the experimenter's expectancies and knowledge of the anticipated results alters the way he or she treats the participants in the different research conditions or alters his or her objectivity when recording the data.

**Hawthorne effect**—Used to describe any situation wherein the participants' assumptions about the purpose of the research bias their performance.

**Heterogeneous sample**—A sample for which the members are dissimilar to each other regarding one or more relevant variables.

**Homogeneous sample**—A sample for which all the members are similar to one another on one or more relevant variables.

**Manipulation check**—Any procedure that a researcher uses to ensure that the participants in the study accepted the cover story as the explanation for the purpose of the research.

**Mathematical hypothesis**—A statement that describes the relation between population parameters using relational symbols (e.g., $=$, $\neq$, $<$, $>$, $\leq$, and $\geq$). The null and alternative hypotheses use complementary relations (e.g., $=$ vs. $\neq$, $\geq$ vs. $<$, or $\leq$ vs. $>$).

**Median split**—A technique for creating two intact groups by first administering a test of a subject variable and then dividing the participants into two groups based on the median score.

**Nondirectional hypothesis**—A research hypothesis that the researcher uses to predict a general difference among groups.

**Self-fulfilling prophecy**—Within the research context, the tendency for a researcher to treat the participants differently based on preconceived ideas about the participants or the treatment condition that the participants receive.

**Significance level** or **criterion**—The level of $\alpha$ the researcher selects to determine whether to reject the null hypothesis.

**Single blind**—Any procedure used to prevent the participants from knowing the researcher's hypothesis or the treatment condition received.

**Type I error**—When the null hypothesis is correct and the researcher treats it as false.

**Type II error**—When the null hypothesis is false and the researcher does not reject it.

**Within-groups variance**—The variability among scores within a group. This variability represents the natural variability among the members of the population and measurement error.

**Within-subjects variable** or **repeated-measures variable**—A form of independent variable for which the researcher tests the same participant on more than one occasion or under more than one level of the independent variable.

## Chapter References

Bem, S. L. (1974). The measurement of psychological androgyny. *Journal of Consulting and Clinical Psychology, 42*, 155–162.

Bem, S. L. (1977). On the utility of alternate procedures for assessing psychological androgyny. *Journal of Consulting and Clinical Psychology, 45*, 196–205.

Bissonnette, V., Ickes, W., Bernstein, I. H., & Knowles, E. (1990). Personality moderating variables: A warning about statistical artifact and a comparison of analytic techniques. *Journal of Personality, 58*, 567–587.

Cohen, J. (1988). *Statistical power analysis for the behavioral sciences* (2nd ed.). Hillsdale, NJ: LEA.

Diener, E., Emmons, R. A., Larsen, R. A., & Griffin, S. (1985). The Satisfaction with Life Scale. *Journal of Personality Assessment, 49*, 71–75.

Garcia, J. (1980). Tilting at the paper mills of academe. *American Psychologist, 36*, 149–158.

Graziano, W. G., & Bryant, W.H.M. (1998). Self-monitoring and the self-attribution of positive emotions. *Journal of Personality and Social Psychology, 74*, 250–261.

Hyde, J. S. (1991). *Half the human experience: The psychology of women* (4th ed.). Lexington, MA: Heath.

Jones, L. V., & Tukey, J. W. (2000). A sensible formulation of the significance test. *Psychological Methods, 5*, 411–414.

Maxwell, S. E., & Delaney, H. D. (1993). Bivariate median splits and spurious statistical significance. *Psychological Bulletin, 113*, 181–190.

Parsons, H. M. (1974). What happened at Hawthorne? *Science, 183*, 922–932.

Rosenthal, R. (1994). Interpersonal expectancy effects: A 30-year perspective. *Current Directions in Psychological Science, 5*, 176–179.

Rosenthal, R., & Jacobson, L. (1968). *Pygmalion in the classroom*. New York: Holt, Reinhart & Winston.

Rosnow, R. L., & Rosenthal, R. (1997). *People studying people: Artifacts in behavioral research*. New York: Freeman.

Samuda, R. J. (1975). *Psychological testing of American minorities: Issues and consequences*. New York: Harper & Row.

Seidlitz, L., & Diener, E. (1998). Sex differences in the recall of affective experiences. *Journal of Personality and Social Psychology, 74*, 262–271.

Shakespeare, W. (1604). *The Tragedy of Hamlet, Prince of Denmark, Act 3, Scene 2*. New York: Washington Square.

Stalder, D. R., & Baron, R. S. (1998). Attritional complexity as a moderator of dissonance-produced attitude change. *Journal of Personality and Social Psychology, 75*, 449–455.

Sundstorm, E., McIntyre, M., Halfhill, T., & Richards, H. (2000). Work groups from the Hawthorne studies to work teams of the 1990s and beyond. *Group Dynamics, 4*, 44–67.

# Part III

# Common Research Designs

# Chapter 10
## Correlational Research

## CHAPTER OBJECTIVES

**Introduction**
**Conceptual Review of Correlation**
**Pearson's *r***
**Interpreting the Correlation Coefficient**
**Factors That Corrupt a Correlation Coefficient**
**Sample Size and the Correlation Coefficient**
**Applications of the Correlation Coefficient**
**Regression Analysis**
**Introduction to Mediation and Moderation**
**Regression to the Mean**
**Research in Action: Searching Short-Term Memory**
**Statistics behind the Research**

Give a researcher three weapons—correlation, regression, and a pen—and he or she will use all three.

**—Anonymous**

## Introduction

Correlational research allows us to study the relationship between two or more variables. Finding a correlation between two variables can help us in many ways. We can use the correlation to make predictions about one variable using another variable. This prediction might help us explain the dependent variable using the independent variable. For instance, a psychologist might use a personality test to predict how someone will respond in specific situations. Similarly, an employer may use an aptitude test to determine whether applicants have the skills necessary to perform a job. As you will learn in this chapter, studying the correlations between variables is a powerful tool for understanding various behavioral phenomena.

In this chapter, we will review several of the more common applications of correlation statistics. We will examine the Pearson product-moment correlation ($r$) and regression analysis. Although these are not the only statistical tools for analyzing the relation among variables, they are among the most frequently used analytical techniques in the behavioral sciences.

The primary focus of the chapter will be to examine how to use and interpret these statistics. The final section of this chapter illustrates how to calculate these statistical tests.

As a brief preview of what you are about to read, you should understand that there is a distinction between correlation research methods and correlational statistics. When we speak of the *method*, we are describing how we go about gathering the data. The most general account of the correlational method is that the researcher gathers two or more bits of information about participants in the study. In some cases, the researcher may gather the information during one session. For instance, a psychologist may examine the participants' self-esteem and attitudes toward minority groups by asking the participants to complete several questionnaires.

In other situations, the researcher will want to determine whether one variable will predict another variable. For this type of study, the researcher will collect data on two or more occasions. As an example, a researcher could administer a math aptitude test to a group of students at the start of the school year. At the end of the school year, the researcher could give the students a math achievement test. The researcher may hope to find that there is a correlation between the aptitude test and the achievement test. Using this information, teachers could use the aptitude test to predict which students may need extra help with math and which students would benefit from a more challenging review of math. In correlation research, the researcher often examines the relation among subject variables and does not necessarily place the participants into different research conditions, as is the case for a true experiment. A researcher uses correlational research to determine whether two or more variables are interrelated.

A researcher can use correlation statistics for any data set regardless of the method of collecting the data. A researcher may conduct a true experiment, a quasi-experiment, or a correlational study and then turn to correlation statistics to examine the relation between the variables. As you will learn throughout this book, there are many ways that the researcher can examine the relation among the many variables examined in a study. In this chapter, we will focus our attention on the correlation coefficient.

## Conceptual Review of Correlation

Although there are many ways to determine the correlation between two variables, all **correlation coefficients** share features. First, the correlation examines two or more sets of measurements taken from the same individual. Second, the correlation coefficient is a descriptive statistic that describes the **linear relation** between two variables. A linear relation refers to a pattern of data best described by a straight line. In addition, correlation coefficients range between −1.0 and +1.0.

Figure 10.1 presents six scatter plots representing correlations that are: $r = +1.0, r = .80, r = .50, r = 0, r = −.50$, and $r = −1.0$. As the value of the correlation becomes closer to +1.0 or  1.0, the data are more likely to

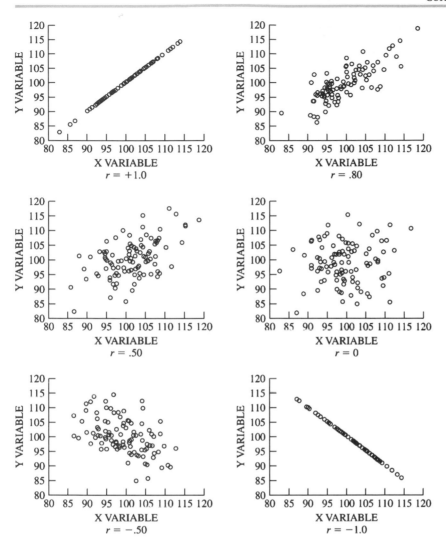

## Figure 10.1

**Scatter Plots for Six
Pairs of Data**

The correlations are: $r = 1.0$, $r = .80$, $r = .50$, $r = 0$, $r = -.50$, and $r = -1.0$.

fall on a straight line. A **positive correlation**, $r > 0$, indicates that increases in one variable correspond to increases in the other variable (or that a decrease in one corresponds to a decrease in the other). A **negative correlation**, $r < 0$, indicates that increases in one variable correspond to decreases in the other variable (or that the two variables move in opposite directions).

Finally, a correlation coefficient, regardless of its size, is not by itself evidence of a cause-and effect relationship. Extending from Chapter 3, we cannot infer a causal relation from a correlational research design because we cannot easily control for the third variable problem or resolve the temporal order problem (see Chapter 3). Thus, a correlation between two variables, regardless of the size of the correlation, is not evidence of a cause-and-effect relation.

## Pearson's $r$

Pearson popularized one of the most commonly used correlation coefficients. The full name for the statistic is the *Pearson product-moment correlation coefficient*, but most researchers refer to it as Pearson's $r$. We can use the definitional equation, presented in Equation 10.1, to examine how the statistic summarizes the data:

$$r = \frac{\sum ZxZy}{N} \tag{10.1}$$

First, we convert each observed score to a $z$-score and then determine the cross products by multiplying the pairs of $z$-scores. The sum of the cross products $(z_x z_y)$ divided by the number of pairs $(N)$ is the correlation coefficient. The advantage of using $z$-scores is that they convert the data to a common scale. The mean and standard deviation of $z$-scores are always $M = 0.00$ and $SD = 1.00$ (see Appendix A for a detailed description of this process). Because the $z$-score converts the data to the same scale, we can examine the correlation between any two variables regardless of their means and standard deviations.

## Interpreting the Correlation Coefficient

The correlation coefficient is a descriptive statistic that indicates the degree to which changes in one variable correspond with changes in a second variable. As you have already learned, the correlation coefficient can range between $-1.0$ and $+1.0$. In this section we will examine how to interpret the size of the correlation coefficient.

### Magnitude and Sign of $r$

There are two important pieces of information contained in the correlation coefficient: its sign and its magnitude. The sign of the coefficient indicates whether there is a positive or a negative relation between the variables. Many people misinterpret the sign of the correlation and believe that positive correlations are somehow better than negative correlations. Nothing could be farther from the truth. A negative correlation indicates only that there is an inverse relationship between the two variables: As one variable increases the other decreases. An example of a negative correlation is the relationship between one's score for a round of golf and time spent practicing. In golf, the goal is to get as low a score as possible. Hence, we can predict that the more a person practices, the lower his or her score is likely to be.

Perhaps a better way to look at and interpret the correlation coefficient is to examine its absolute value. When the absolute value of $r$ is zero (i.e., $|r| = 0$), there is no linear relationship between the two variables. By contrast, when $|r| = 1.0$, there is a perfect linear relationship between the variables. Cohen (1988) suggested that correlations fall into three general categories, small ($|r| = .20-.29$), medium ($|r| = .30-.49$), or large ($|r| = .50-1.00$).

You should use Cohen's (1988) size criteria with caution. These guidelines were developed to facilitate description of general behavioral research. You may find that researchers working in different areas have different guidelines for the magnitude of a correlation coefficient. For example, when examining the correlation between two conventional tests of intelligence, you may find that researchers will dismiss any correlation less than .90 because considerable research indicates that measures of intelligence tend to be highly correlated. In contrast, another researcher may consider a correlation of .40 between a standardized aptitude test and academic performance (e.g., GPA) to be large. Academic performance reflects many factors (intelligence, motivation, and academic major, to list a few), and it may be impossible to expect that a single variable will accurately predict something as complex as grades.

## Coefficients of Determination and Nondetermination

Another way to describe and examine the correlation coefficient is to square its value. The statistic $r^2$ is also known as the **coefficient of determination**. The coefficient of determination indicates the proportion of variance shared by the two variables that you have correlated. If, for example, the correlation between two variables is $r = .82$, then $r^2 = .67$. Therefore, we can conclude that if we know $X$, then the linear relationship between these two variables allows us to account for 67% of the variability in the $Y$ variable.

We can also calculate the **coefficient of nondetermination**, which is simply $1.00 - r^2$. For the current example, $1.00 - r^2 = .33$. The coefficient of nondetermination is an estimate of the proportion of unshared or unexplained variance between two variables. Thus, when $1.00 - r^2 = .33$, this means that 33% of the variability in $Y$ cannot be explained by our knowledge of $X$.

Figure 10.2 presents a conceptual illustration of the meaning of $r^2$ and $1.00 - r^2$. Imagine that the circles represent the $X$ and $Y$ variables. When $r = 0$, there is no overlap between the two circles. As the magnitude of the correlation increases, the amount of overlap increases. The overlap of the two circles represents the coefficient of determination between two variables and the unshaded areas represent the coefficient of nondetermination.

## Causality

A large correlation coefficient, positive or negative, is not evidence in itself of a cause-and-effect relationship. The problem is that when we use the correlation coefficient, there is no direct way to resolve the temporal order

# Figure 10.2

**Illustration of the Coefficient of Determination, $r^2$**

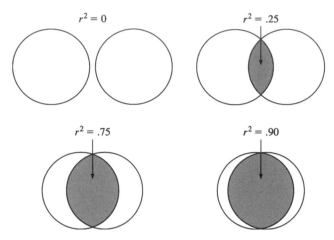

Each pair of circles represents two variables, $X$ and $Y$. The amount of overlap indicates the magnitude of the correlation between the two variables, or the amount of explained variance.

problem or the third variable problem. Recall from Chapter 3 that the temporal order criterion for cause and effect requires the cause to occur before the effect. In much correlational research we collect the data for both variables without being able to control temporal order. As an example, a researcher may examine the correlation between levels of anxiety and smoking behavior. To collect the data, the researcher asks the participants to estimate the number of cigarettes they smoke each day and to complete a standard measure of anxiety. Because the researcher collected the data at the same time, we cannot be sure whether the anxiety brings about smoking or whether smoking creates anxiety.

The third variable problem refers to a third, and unmeasured, variable that may influence the two measured variables. As an example, a researcher may find that there is a positive correlation between the amount of time a child watches television and his or her aggressiveness with other children. Although we cannot deny the correlation between the two variables, we cannot assume that watching television causes aggressiveness. It is possible that the contributing factor to both variables is the level of parental supervision. Parents who spend little time with their children may allow them to watch more television and may not teach their children to control their aggressive behaviors. By contrast, parents who spend much time with their children may limit television watching and teach their children to cooperate with others.

## Factors That Corrupt a Correlation Coefficient

If you are planning to conduct a correlational study, you need to be aware of several factors that can corrupt the magnitude of $r$, causing it to be artificially high or low. These factors include nonlinearity of the data, truncated range, extreme populations, outliers, and multiple populations. In this section we will examine how these factors affect the size of the correlation coefficient, how to detect their effects in the data, and how to avoid these problems.

## Nonlinearity

A primary assumption of the correlation coefficient is that a straight line best represents the relationship between the two variables. Knowing the correlation coefficient allows us to draw a straight line through the scatter plot that describes the relation between the variables. A **curvilinear relationship** would be characterized by a curved line that better describes the relationship between the two variables. Consider Figure 10.3 as an example. Clearly, there is a systematic connection between $X$ and $Y$, but the relationship is far from a straight line. The relationship between $X$ and $Y$ in this case is U-shaped. Using Pearson's $r$, the correlation between the variables is $r = .14$, which suggests a small linear relation between the two variables.

From one perspective, the correlation coefficient is correct; a straight line cannot strongly explain the relation between the variables. However, if we did not draw a scatter plot of the data, we would have assumed that there is a small or trivial relation between the two variables. Looking at Figure 10.3 it appears that there is a strong nonlinear relation between the $X$ and $Y$ variables. Consequently, we need to use different statistical tools to analyze the data. Fortunately, many computer statistics programs can quickly and efficiently perform the analyses necessary to appropriately analyze these data.

Therefore, a nonlinear relationship between two variables is not a problem unless you fail to recognize its existence. Finding a curved rather than a linear pattern in your scatter plot may lead to useful insights about the phenomenon that you are studying. That curvilinear relationships exist demonstrates that you cannot rush the data through a simple-minded

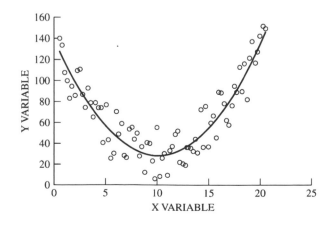

## Figure 10.3

**Illustration of Data Where a Curved Line Represents the Relation between the $X$ and $Y$ Variables**

computer analysis. A carefully planned research design implies a careful statistical analysis of the data as well.

### Truncated Range

The **truncated range** problem refers to a form of bias created by poor sampling techniques. A representative sample is one in which the characteristics of the sample match the parameters of the broader population. A truncated range occurs when the variance of the sample is much smaller than the variance of the population. Figure 10.4 represents what happens to the correlation coefficient when we have a truncated range.

Assume that the entire scatter plot in Figure 10.4 represents what would happen if you created a true representative sample of the population. For all the data, the correlation is $r = .71$, a strong linear relationship. What would happen if your selection procedure created bias and you selected only those people who have scores on the $X$ variable of 15 or greater? The smaller $x-y$ axis within the graph represents this biased sample. For those data, the correlation is $r = .10$, a small correlation that does not well represent the true correlation between the variables.

The problem is that the correlation coefficient represents the shared variance of the two variables. If your sampling procedure restricts the variance of the data, then the correlation statistic generated from these data cannot provide an accurate estimate of the true relationship in the population. The best solution to this potential problem is to avoid it by following proper sampling procedures when designing your study, to ensure that your sample will capture the natural range of potential scores for both variables in the population.

## Figure 10.4

**Illustration of the Effects of Truncating the Range of Scores on the Correlation Coefficient**

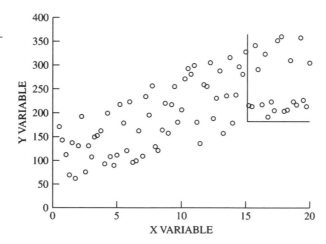

The correlation for the entire data set is $r = .71$. However, if the sample included only those scores with values of $X > 15$, as is represented by the smaller graph, the correlation would be low, closer to $r = .10$.

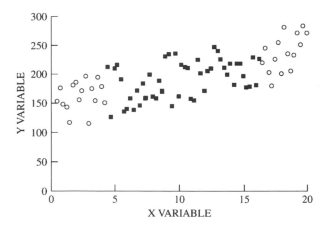

The correlation coefficient for the data represented as circles is $r = .83$. However, the correlation for all the data is $r = .69$.

## Extreme Populations

Another problem due to nonrepresentative sampling that can affect your correlation coefficient is selecting groups that represent extreme ends of the score distribution for one variable. Consider Figure 10.5 as an example of this problem. In this figure, there are two subsets of data, one represented by circles and the other by squares. If we examine only the circle data, the correlation is $r = .83$. By contrast, if we examine all the data presented in the scatter plot, the correlation is lower, $r = .69$. In general, analyzing data from the extreme ends of the variables tends to inflate the correlation coefficient.

## Outliers or Extreme Scores

As with any statistical test, outliers or extreme individual scores can also affect the value of the correlation coefficient. Hence, it is important that you review your data to ensure that you have accurately recorded all the data. Drawing a scatter plot can help you see a score or scores that stand apart from the rest of the data.

## Multiple Populations

Another problem that can create artificially high or low correlation coefficients occurs when the sample contains data from two populations, for which the relationship between your two variables of interest may be very different. In Figure 10.6, there are two populations, one represented by squares and the other represented by circles. If we ignore the two populations, the correlation of the entire data set is $r = .58$. The correlations for the separate groups are higher than for the combined data. For the squares alone, the correlation is $r = .79$; for the circles alone the correlation is $r = .82$. The important lesson is that planning is essential to good research.

## Figure 10.6

**Illustration of the Effect of Having Two Populations within One Data Set**

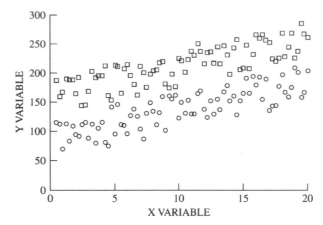

The correlation for the entire data is $r = .58$. The correlation for the data represented by circles is $r = .82$. The correlation for the data represented by the squares is .79.

As you analyze the data, determine whether there are relevant subject variables that may help you better describe the data.

## Sample Size and the Correlation Coefficient

The correlation coefficient is a descriptive statistic. It is also considered to be an unbiased estimate of the population parameter, $\rho$ (rho), the correlation between populations. Thus, as we use the sample mean, $M$, to estimate the population mean, $\mu$, we can use $r$ to estimate $\rho$. As you learned in Chapter 7, the confidence interval about any estimate of a population parameter is a function of the sample size. As sample size increases, the confidence interval decreases. Smaller confidence intervals imply that the sample statistic more closely estimates the corresponding population parameter.

Determining the confidence interval for the correlation coefficient is complicated because the sampling distribution for the correlation co-efficient is not symmetrical. The skew of the sampling distribution for $r$ increases when it moves toward $-1.00$ or $+1.00$. A section at the end of this chapter includes the formula for determining the confidence interval for Pearson's $r$. Although we will not examine those calculations here, we can use them to help guide us in determining the relation between sample size and width of the confidence interval.

Table 10.1 presents the confidence intervals for population correlations ranging between $\rho = .20$ and $\rho = .90$. For each correlation, the table presents the 95% confidence interval for specific sample sizes. We can use an example to illustrate how the table works.

Imagine that you plan to conduct a study to examine the correlation between two variables and believe that the correlation will be moderate, say $\rho = .40$. According to Table 10.1, if you collect data from 50 participants, you would predict that 95% of the sample correlations would range

Table 10.1 **Estimated 95% Confidence Intervals for Different Correlation Coefficients and Sample Sizes**

| N | $\rho = .20$ $r_{low} - r_{high}$ | $\rho = .40$ $r_{low} - r_{high}$ | $\rho = .60$ $r_{low} - r_{high}$ | $\rho = .80$ $r_{low} - r_{high}$ | $\rho = .90$ $r_{low} - r_{high}$ |
|---|---|---|---|---|---|
| 50 | −.08−.45 | .14−.61 | .39−.75 | .67−.88 | .83−.94 |
| 100 | .00−.38 | .22−.55 | .46−.71 | .72−.86 | .85−.93 |
| 150 | .04−.35 | .26−.53 | .49−.69 | .73−.85 | .86−.93 |
| 200 | .06−.33 | .28−.51 | .50−.68 | .74−.84 | .87−.92 |
| 250 | .08−.32 | .29−.50 | .51−.67 | .75−.84 | .87−.92 |
| 300 | .09−.31 | .30−.49 | .52−.67 | .76−.84 | .88−.92 |
| 350 | .10−.30 | .31−.48 | .53−.66 | .76−.83 | .88−.92 |
| 400 | .10−.29 | .31−.48 | .53−.66 | .76−.83 | .88−.92 |
| 450 | .11−.29 | .32−.47 | .54−.66 | .76−.83 | .88−.92 |
| 500 | .11−.28 | .32−.47 | .54−.65 | .77−.83 | .88−.92 |
| 600 | .12−.28 | .33−.47 | .55−.65 | .77−.83 | .88−.91 |
| 700 | .13−.27 | .34−.46 | .55−.65 | .77−.83 | .88−.91 |
| 800 | .13−.27 | .34−.46 | .55−.64 | .77−.82 | .89−.91 |
| 900 | .14−.26 | .34−.45 | .56−.64 | .78−.82 | .89−.91 |
| 1000 | .14−.26 | .35−.45 | .56−.64 | .78−.82 | .89−.91 |
| 2000 | .16−.24 | .36−.44 | .57−.63 | .78−.82 | .89−.91 |

*Note:* The sampling distribution of the correlation coefficient is not symmetrical, especially when the sample size is small. Therefore, the confidence intervals will not be symmetrical around $\rho$.

between $r = .14$ and $r = .61$, a wide range of values. What would happen if you increased your sample size? As you would expect, the width of the 95% confidence interval will decrease. Using 450 participants, for example, the 95% confidence interval is $r = .32$ to $r = .47$. Samples larger than 450 produce marginal reductions in the width of the confidence interval. If you could reasonably expect to have a higher population correlation, then you may not require as many participants to estimate accurately the correlation coefficient.

## Knowledge Check

1. Explain in your words how we can examine the correlation between two variables even when the means and standard deviations of the two variables are radically different.

2. Why does a correlation of −.75 represent a stronger relation between two variables than a correlation of +.60?

3. An instructor distributes a questionnaire to students asking them to estimate the number of hours they study each week and their current GPA. According to the data, the correlation between the two variables is +.93. Can we use these data to show students that studying causes improved grades?

4.  Paula conducted a correlational study using 100 pairs of scores and found that $r = .10$. This correlation is far less than she expected. Describe in your words what could have caused this small correlation.

5.  Devin is the director of admissions of a prestigious liberal arts college. He has learned that there is a new aptitude test designed to predict students' college academic performance. To test the value of the new test, he plans to randomly select 500 students currently enrolled at the college and pay them to take the test. He will then examine the correlation between the students' test scores and their current GPA. Do you believe that Devin has created a research design that will allow him to evaluate the correlation between test scores and academic performance?

## Applications of the Correlation Coefficient

Like most statistical tests, the correlation coefficient has many applications. In the following sections, we will see how we can use the correlation coefficient to examine the reliability and validity of tests and other measures that we create.

### Using Correlation to Determine Reliability

In Chapter 8, you learned how to use coefficient kappa ($\kappa$) to determine the interrater reliability for nominal and ordinal scales. As you might guess, we can use Pearson's $r$ to determine the reliability of a test that uses an interval or ratio scale. The comparison between $\kappa$ and $r$ is straightforward; the closer either statistic is to 1.00, the greater the reliability of the test or measurement device. In this section we will examine the many ways that we can use the correlation coefficient to examine the reliability of a test.

#### Test–Retest Reliability

One of the most common measures of reliability is test–retest reliability. To determine test–retest reliability, the researcher will administer the same test, or similar versions of the test, on two occasions. The correlation coefficient between the two scores indicates the stability of the measure over time. We can use test–retest reliability information to determine the degree to which random events that we do not want to measure affect the test scores. If the test–retest reliability is 0, we must conclude that the test scores are not stable over time and are subject to considerable fluctuation. By contrast, if the test–retest reliability is 1.00, we can conclude that the test measures the construct consistently and is unaffected by random events. This type of reliability information is most useful when measuring constructs that are not expected to change over time (e.g., general intelligence).

## Interrater Reliability

In the previous chapter we showed you how to use coefficient $\kappa$ to determine interrater reliability when there are two or more observers and they are using either a nominal or an ordinal scale. In this section we will see how we can use the correlation coefficient to calculate the interrater reliability among observers if the measurement scale is interval or ratio. For interrater reliability, the pairs of scores represent the scores given by the two observers. Specifically, $X_1$ would represent the score assigned by the first rater, and $X_2$ would represent the score assigned by the second rater. As with Cohen's $\kappa$, the larger the correlation coefficient, the greater the interrater agreement. If the interrater reliability is sufficiently large, then you can average the ratings of the two reviewers as the final observation. If the interrater reliability is very small, then it may be necessary to bring the raters together to work out a more consistent set of ratings.

## Internal Consistency Reliability

Internal consistency reliability is similar to interrater reliability. The only difference is that we are looking at the correlation among items or measurements within a test rather than the correlation between observers' ratings. **Internal consistency**, like interrater reliability, refers to the degree to which items in a test agree with one another. If a test has high internal consistency, then each test item produces the same or similar score for each person taking the test. Remember that internal consistency refers to how items in a test correlate among each other, not to the variability among test scores. For our purposes, internal consistency is a way of determining the reliability of a test. If the internal consistency is low, then the test may not be measuring the variable we want to measure. Therefore, researchers strive to ensure high levels of internal consistency.

A common measure of internal consistency is Cronbach's (1951) coefficient alpha, $r_\alpha$, or more often simply designated as $\alpha$. This statistic is a special type of correlation coefficient that represents the correlation among all the items in the test. In other words, $\alpha$ is another way to determine interrater agreement, specifically, the level of agreement among questions or items in a test. Coefficient alpha can range from 0, which represents no internal consistency, to 1.00, which represents perfect agreement among all the items in the test. The "Statistics behind the Research" section at the end of this chapter shows how to calculate this statistic.

For our purposes, the primary concern with this statistic is how we should interpret coefficient alpha. Unfortunately, many people misinterpret the meaning of $\alpha$ (Cortina, 1993; Schmitt, 1996). Some people make the mistake of assuming that a large value of $\alpha$ means that all the questions measure the same construct. This interpretation is not necessarily correct, as Cortina and Schmitt have demonstrated. Thus, you should be careful when you read about or use $\alpha$. Keep your interpretation of $\alpha$ straight; it indicates the extent to which items within a test, or a part of a test, correlate with each other—nothing more, nothing less. The question of whether all items in a test measure the same question is better answered using other statistical methods, such as factor analysis.

**Improving Test Reliability**

There are several things that you can do to improve the reliability of a test or measurement technique. One of the more simple methods is to increase the number of items or measurements. All other things being equal, the longer the test or the more times you measure something, the more reliable your resulting score will be. Imagine that a researcher wants to time how long it takes people to solve an anagram. During a preliminary experiment, the researcher asks participants to solve two anagrams (i.e., convert *rdow* and *kcab* to *word* and *back*). The researcher timed how long it took each participant to solve each anagram. Using these data, the researcher then determined the internal consistency of the measure by calculating the correlation coefficient between times required to solve the two anagrams. According to the results, the internal consistency is $r = .50$. The researcher can use the Spearman-Brown formula presented in Equation 10.2 to estimate the increase in reliability that will occur if he or she used more anagrams.

$$r' = \frac{P(r)}{1 + (P - 1)r} \tag{10.2}$$

In this equation, $r$ is the original measure of internal consistency and $r'$ is the estimated internal consistency for a test with more items or measurements. The $P$ in the equation represents the number of times the test is lengthened or shortened. For example, if $P = 2$, then the test will be twice as long. When $P = 0.50$, the test length is cut in half. What would happen if the researcher decided to require the participants to solve 10 rather than 2 anagrams? In this case, $P = 5$ because the new measure will have five times the number of measurements. According to Equation 10.2,

$$r' = \frac{5(.50)}{1 + (5 - 1).50}$$

$$r' = \frac{2.5}{1 + (4).50}$$

$$r' = \frac{2.5}{3}$$

$$r' = .83$$

Collecting more data from each participant will increase the reliability of the measure. At a basic level this is because the average of 10 measurements will be a more reliable estimate of an individual's standing on a construct than the average of only 2 measurements. Therefore, the researcher can use the average time to solve 10 anagrams as the dependent variable for the study.

More is not always better, though. Collecting more data comes at a cost. In some cases, doubling the length of a test may not be practical. For example, converting a 20-item test to a 40-item test may make the test boring and tedious. Consequently, participants may want to rush through the test, not taking the time to answer each question accurately or honestly. In this case, you will need to consider finding a more reliable test or include more participants in your study.

Apart from lengthening a scale or adding additional observations, you can also increase the reliability of a measure by using more accurate and sensitive measurement techniques. For example, if you are measuring the time it takes participants to complete a task, you will find that using a stopwatch that is accurate to within 1/100 second is more reliable than a watch that is accurate to within one second. Increases in precision correspond to increases in reliability. The development of personal computing technology has also helped researchers increase the accuracy and reliability of their measurement techniques, by allowing researchers to program a computer to control the experiment and data collection. The speed and consistency of the computer often allows the researcher to improve the reliability of the data collection procedures.

## Using Correlation to Determine Validity

Reliability is a necessary but not sufficient requirement for validity. To determine that a test is valid, we need data that demonstrate that the test measures what we intended it to measure. We can turn to the correlation coefficient as one way to demonstrate the validity of a test. To demonstrate validity, we would want to show that the test scores of our target measure correlate well with some measures that we would expect and do not correlate with other measures that should not be related. In other words, researchers hope to show that their tests demonstrate evidence of convergent and discriminant validity (Campbell & Fiske, 1959). A high correlation between two measures of similar constructs is evidence of **convergent validity**. A low correlation between two measures of different constructs is evidence for **discriminant validity**.

Figure 10.7 illustrates an example of convergent validity and discriminant validity. For convergent validity, we would expect large correlations between the new test of depression and other tests of depression. By contrast, the new test of depression should not correlate with schizophrenia or anxiety as these are different psychiatric conditions. Evidence of convergent validity and discriminant validity indicates that the instrument measures what the author of the test intended the test to measure.

Imagine that a psychologist wants to develop a new test for depression. The advantage of such a test is that it is faster and less expensive than an assessment interview conducted by a psychologist or psychiatrist. To test the validity of the instrument, the researcher could first administer the new test to a large group of people. A clinical psychologist or psychiatrist would then independently evaluate these individuals. If the test is valid, the test

## Figure 10.7

**Illustration of Convergent and Discriminant Validity**

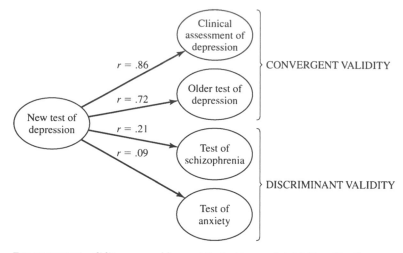

For convergent validity, we would expect the test to correlate highly with other measures of the same construct. Discriminant validity indicates that the test does not correlate well with measures of other constructs. Convergent and discriminant validity is evidence that the test measures the identified construct and not other constructs.

scores for depression should correlate with a professional's rating of the person's emotional state. At the same time, we would expect that the depression test scores should not correlate with the presence of other mental health conditions.

Another component of validity assessment is **criterion-related validity**. For criterion-related validity, we hope to show that there is a correlation between the test score and some important outcome or criterion. Specifically, researchers use criterion validity to demonstrate that one can use a test to make predictions about a person's behavior. Two forms of criterion validity are **concurrent validity** and **predictive validity**. Concurrent validity means that we can use the test to predict some condition or characteristic behavior of the person that currently exists. Predictive validity means that we can use the test to predict the person's behavior or condition in the future.

As an example, a math achievement test should be able to measure a student's current skills at mathematics. Large correlations between the test score and current math grades, for example, would be evidence of concurrent validity for the math achievement test. By contrast, an aptitude test attempts to predict whether a person will be successful at a specific task. To determine the predictive validity of an art aptitude test, we may administer the test to students to determine whether scores on the test predict success in an art class.

The utility of a test also partially determines its validity. Utility refers to the extent to which the test produces useful information that allows us to understand a specific behavior. The implication of this definition is that the use and interpretation of a test determines its validity. This is important to remember, as it means that validity is not a property of the test itself, but rather of the inferences or conclusions we make based on the data from that test. Because of this, our interpretation of test results may be valid in one situation and not valid in another. Therefore, the validity of a test is much like the internal and external validity of a research project. Again, validity is not a characteristic inherent in the test scores or the data; validity is a characteristic of the interpretations we draw from the data. You can find comprehensive reviews of this issue in the work of Cronbach (1988) and Messick (1980, 1988, 1989).

## Regression Analysis

The correlation coefficient, whether it is positive or negative, indicates the presence of a linear relation between the two variables. We can use this relation to make predictions about one variable using the other. For example, in general, the longer you stay in school, the higher your annual income. As you will soon see, we can use the correlation coefficient to convert general statements like this into a specific mathematical equation. This equation defines a straight line that best describes the linear relation between the two variables. Using this equation, we can then make specific empirical predictions.

Whenever we have two variables, $X$ and $Y$, we can use Equation 10.3 to define a straight line:

$$Y' = a + b(X) \qquad (10.3)$$

In this equation, $X$ represents the variable that we want to use to predict levels of $Y$. In regression analysis, we use $Y'$ (pronounced "Y-prime") or $\hat{Y}$ (pronounced "Y-hat") to represent the predicted scores along the regression line. Do not confuse $Y'$ and $Y$; $Y$ represents the original scores and $Y'$ represents the scores predicted by the regression equation. In most cases, $Y$ and $Y'$ will not be the same. The other components of the equation, $a$ and $b$, are constants that define the line. Specifically, $a$ is the **intercept** and $b$ is the **slope** of the line. The intercept ($a$) represents the value of $Y'$ when $X = 0$. The slope of the line indicates how much $Y'$ changes as $X$ changes. Equation 8.4 represents a conceptual formula for determining the slope in a line. The $b$ coefficient represents a ratio of the changes in $Y$ that correspond with changes in $X$.

Figure 10.8 will help you see how we use Equation 10.4 to create a straight line in a simple graph. Figure 10.8 is a graph with four regression lines. For each graph, the intercept is 50, but the slopes are different. We can describe the slope as

$$b = \frac{\text{Change in } Y}{\text{Change in } X} \qquad (10.4)$$

For example, when $b = 5$, for every one-point increase in $X$ there is a five-point increase in $Y$. By contrast, when the slope is $b = -5$, every

# Figure 10.8

**Illustrations of Four Regression Lines with the Same Intercept ($a = 50$) and Different Slopes: $b = 5$, $b = 2$, $b = 0$, and $b = -5$**

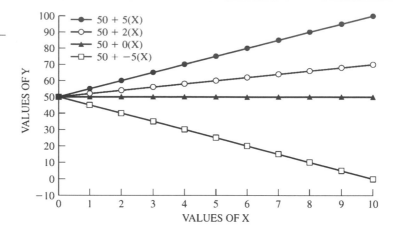

increase in $X$ corresponds to a five-point decrease in $Y$. When the slope is 0, the line is horizontal; there are no changes in $Y$ that correspond with changes in $X$.

## Characteristics of a Regression Line

The regression line has several important features we need to review. First, the regression line shares much in common with the arithmetic mean. One property of the mean is that the sum of the differences between the mean and each score in the sample is always 0. Specifically, $\Sigma(X - M) = 0$. The mean represents the balance point of the small and large scores in the sample. The regression line does the same thing; it represents the predictive equation that guarantees the smallest total discrepancy between the predicted $Y'$ and observed $Y$. In other words, with so-called least-squares regression the sum of the differences between each value of $Y$ and its predicted value, $Y'$, is always 0; that is, $\Sigma(Y - Y') = 0$. The regression line represents a special type of average. Consequently, many people also call the regression line the *line of best fit*.

## Interpreting the Regression Equation

Unless there is a perfect correlation ($r = \pm 1.00$) between the two variables, the regression line represents only an estimate of the values of $Y$. Therefore, we need a statistic that will indicate the accuracy of $Y'$. As you may recall, the standard deviation is a descriptive statistic that allows us to describe how far scores typically differ from the mean. We can do the same thing for $Y'$ using a statistic called the **standard error of estimate**. The standard error of estimate reflects the standard deviation of observed scores around the predicted scores captured by the regression line. Using the standard error of estimate, we can then determine the confidence interval for $Y'$. This confidence interval is similar to the one reviewed in Chapter 7 in that it allows us to estimate the range of potential scores for a specific value of $Y'$.

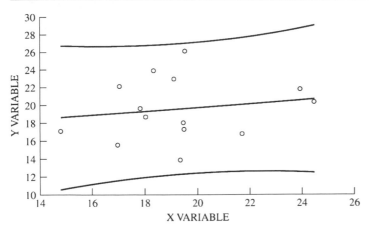

## Figure 10.9

**Scatter Plot of the Correlation between Two Variables**

The line in the center of the data represents the regression line. The outer curved lines represent the upper and lower limits for the 95% confidence interval.

The section at the end of the chapter shows how to calculate the standard error of estimate for $Y'$.

Figure 10.9 presents the original scores, the regression line, and the 95% confidence interval about the regression line. The figure makes clear that values of $X$ much less than or much greater than $M_X$ create a broader confidence interval than values of $X$ close to $M_X$.

## Introduction to Mediation and Moderation

Taking our discussion of correlation and regression to the next level, it is important to realize that the simple relationship between any two variables may be impacted by one or more additional variables. These variables can be either moderator or mediator variables depending on their relationships. According to Baron and Kenny (1986) a variable is a mediator to the extent that it accounts (partially or completely) for the relationship between the two other variables. Moderators specify when certain effects will hold (i.e., interactions), whereas mediators speak to how or why such effects occur.

Put another way, mediator variables explain how or why a relationship occurs. A third variable represents the mechanism through which the independent variable is able to influence the dependent variable of interest. Alternatively, moderation explains when a relationship occurs. A moderator is a third variable that affects the correlation between two other variables. In other words, the statistical relationship between two variables changes as a function of the moderator variable. Figure 10.10 presents a graphical representation of mediation and moderation.

In order to test for mediation, it is necessary to demonstrate that (1) both the independent and mediating variables are related to the dependent variable; (2) the independent variable is related to the mediating variable; and (3) the relationship between the independent variable and

## Figure 10.10

**A Graphical Example of Mediation and Moderation**

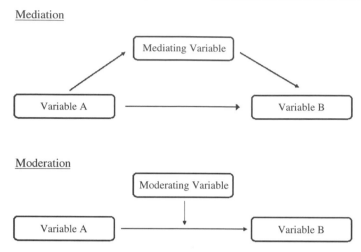

the dependent variable becomes nonsignificant or is reduced significantly when controlling for the mediating variable (Baron & Kenny, 1986; Cohen, Cohen, West, & Aiken, 2003). Moderation can be assessed using either moderated regression analysis or structural equation modeling (see Aiken & West, 1991; Cohen, Cohen, West, & Aiken, 2003). These analysis techniques are more advanced than what you may have been exposed to yet, but you can speak with your professors if you think your research interests might require these types of analytical considerations.

## Regression to the Mean

In Chapter 4 we told you that **regression to the mean** is a potential threat to the internal validity of a study. You may also recall a promise to explain the phenomenon in this chapter. We saved the explanation of the regression-toward-the-mean phenomenon because of its relation to measurement of constructs and the reliability of our measurements.

Sir Francis Galton (1889) first recognized the regression-toward-the-mean phenomenon when he was studying various inherited traits such as height. Galton noted that tall parents tend to have taller-than-average children, but not as tall as the parents. Similarly, the children of short parents tend to be taller than their parents, but shorter than average.

We can summarize the regression toward the mean phenomenon with a few simple generalizations. When the correlation is less than 1.00, the relative difference between $X$ and its mean [e.g., $(X - M_X)$] will be greater than the difference between the predicted score, $Y'$, and the mean of $Y$ [e.g., $(Y' - M_Y)$]. Consider the example of heights of parents and the heights of their children. The expression $(X - M_X)$ represents the difference between the parents' height and the average heights of parents. The expression $(Y' - M_Y)$ represents the difference between the children's height and the average height of the other children. What Galton observed was that exceptionally

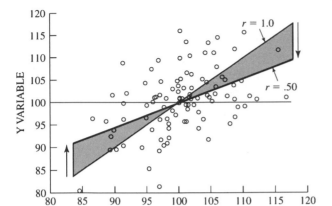

# Figure 10.11

**Illustration of Regression Toward the Mean**

The scatter plot represents $r = .50$. The bold line represents the regression line for the data. The other line represents the regression line had the correlation been $r = 1.00$. The shaded area represents the regression toward the mean. According to the regression-to-the-mean phenomenon, $|Y' - Y|$ is less than $|X - M_X|$.

tall or short parents tended to have taller- or shorter-than-average children, but that the children tended to be closer to the average height than their parents.

Mathematically, regression toward the mean states that $|(X - M_X)| > |(Y' - M_Y)|$. In addition, the amount of regression-toward-the-mean effect increases as the difference between $X$ and $M_X$ increases. Finally, the regression-toward-the-mean phenomenon is greatest when $r = 0$ and absent when $r = 1.00$. Stated from a different perspective, as the correlation between $X$ and $Y$ moves closer to 0, predicted values of $Y'$ are closer to $M_Y$. When $r = 0$, all predicted scores equal the mean of the $Y$ variable. Specifically, $Y' = M_Y$.

Figure 10.11 presents an illustration of regression toward the mean. The scatter plot represents a correlation of $r = .50$. The regression line for these data is $Y' = 45.0 + .55(X)$. The other line in the graph represents the regression line had the correlation been $r = 1.00$. The shaded area between the two regression lines represents regression toward the mean. The arrows at either end of the regression lines indicate the direction of the regression. This graph clearly shows that a value of $X$ above or below $M_X$ predicts scores of $Y'$ relatively closer to $M_Y$ when $r = .50$. When $r = 0$, then all values of $Y'$ equal the mean of $Y$.

Here is another example of regression toward the mean. Let's say you have two pairs of 50 random numbers ranging between 0 and 100. Think of these pairs of numbers as if they were scores on two psychology exams that we gave, one on Monday and the other on Friday. The first set of numbers represents Test 1; the second set represents scores for Test 2. Table 10.2 presents the highest 10 and the lowest 10 scores for Test 1. Next to each Test 1 score is the score for Test 2. The regression to the mean effect is dramatic. Almost every high score on Test 1 has a lower Test 2

Table 10.2   **Example of Regression to the Mean**

| | High Scores for Test 1 | | | Low Scores for Test 1 | | |
|---|---|---|---|---|---|---|
| | Test 1 | Test 2 | $T_2 - T_1$ | Test 1 | Test 2 | $T_2 - T_1$ |
| | 95 | 33 | −62 | 21 | 15 | −6 |
| | 95 | 92 | −3 | 21 | 48 | 27 |
| | 94 | 27 | −67 | 21 | 17 | −4 |
| | 91 | 42 | −49 | 18 | 3 | −15 |
| | 89 | 21 | −68 | 16 | 23 | 7 |
| | 87 | 81 | −6 | 13 | 21 | 8 |
| | 84 | 91 | 7 | 12 | 98 | 86 |
| | 80 | 8 | −72 | 10 | 49 | 39 |
| | 79 | 20 | −59 | 5 | 81 | 76 |
| | 78 | 26 | −52 | 4 | 94 | 90 |
| $M$ | 87.2 | 44.1 | −43.1 | 14.1 | 44.9 | 30.8 |

score. Similarly, almost every low Test 1 score has a higher Test 2 score. There is a clear regression to the mean. The amount of regression toward the mean is large in this example because we used random numbers where the correlation between the two variables is $r = 0$.

This example of regression toward the mean has practical applications for designing research projects. Imagine that we wanted to test the effectiveness of a new method to reduce people's fear of public speaking. We begin the research by selecting people who are extremely anxious giving a speech. Next, we offer these people a workshop to help reduce their anxiety. After completing the workshop, we repeat our evaluation of the participants' anxiety while giving a speech.

Is a large drop in anxiety scores evidence of the effectiveness of the workshop? Not necessarily. The drop in anxiety scores could reflect regression toward the mean and nothing more. For this reason, regression toward the mean is a potential confounding variable that raises serious questions about the internal validity of the conclusion that the workshop eases people's fear of public speaking.

How would we control for regression toward the mean? One method is to have two groups: an experimental group and a control group. Participants in the experimental group would complete the workshop, whereas the control group would not. When we subsequently evaluate both groups, we would expect the experimental group to evidence greater improvement than the control group. According to the regression-toward-the-mean effect, participants in both groups should show some improvement. If the public speaking workshop is truly effective, then the participants in the experimental group should evidence greater average improvement.

## Research in Action: Searching Short-Term Memory

During the mid to late 1960s, Saul Sternberg (1966) conducted a series of revolutionary experiments that examined how short-term memory works. You probably learned in your introductory psychology course that short-term memory can hold approximately $7 \pm 2$ chunks of information. Once we have information in short-term memory, how do we use the information? Sternberg wanted to know how we search through information stored in short-term memory. As an example, what are the last two digits of your social security number? How did you come to the answer? Did you automatically recall the last two numbers, or did you have to recite the entire number until you came to the end?

To answer these questions, Sternberg (1966) conducted an experiment. Figure 10.12 presents the sequence of events for the experiment. For each trial, Sternberg presented his participants a set of randomly selected letters to memorize. The number of letters ranged between 1 and 6 and changed on each trial. After the participants had sufficient time to study the letters, Sternberg presented a single letter and asked the participants to indicate whether the probe letter belonged in the just-memorized set of letters. For a random half of the trials, the probe letter was a letter contained in the memorized set; for the other trials, the probe letter was not in the set.

Sternberg (1966) timed how long it took participants to determine whether the probe letter belonged in the memorized set. Because these mental processes are fast, Sternberg measured the reaction time in milliseconds (1 millisecond = .001 of a second). This experiment allowed Sternberg to determine whether the size of the memorized set affected the time to answer the question. To ensure high reliability in the data, Sternberg tested each participant many times in each condition and then calculated the average response across all participants.

Before we look at the results that Sternberg obtained, we should review several of the potential outcomes for the experiment. Figure 10.13 presents three potential outcomes, each representing a different type of search strategy for short-term memory.

The first potential pattern represents a parallel search, represented by Figure 10.13(a). There is no correlation between the size of the memory set and the reaction time. According to this hypothesis, we search through short-term memory at the same rate regardless of the size of the memory set.

| Trial | Researcher presents 1 to 6 random letters set to be memorized | Researcher presents probe letter | Participant responds |
|---|---|---|---|
| 1 | E Q H D | J ⟶ Scan short-term memory ⟶ No | |
| 2 | L S K J T | K ⟶ Scan short-term memory ⟶ Yes | |
| | | Timer starts ⟶ Timer stops | |

## Figure 10.12

**Sequence of Events Sternberg (1966) Used to Study Short-Term Memory**

# Figure 10.13

**Illustration of Potential Outcomes for Sternberg's (1966) Experiment**

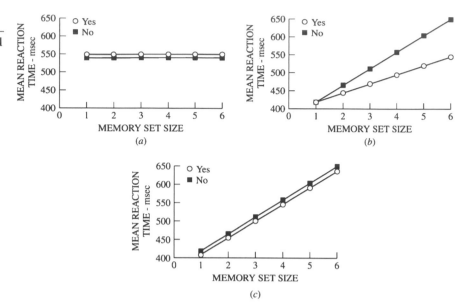

Because there is no correlation between the two variables, the regression lines are flat.

The next graph predicts that there is a positive correlation between the size of the memory set and the reaction time. An additional prediction is that the search is longer when the probe letter is not a member of the memory set. The logic of this prediction is that one must compare each letter of the memory set with the probe letter. For the negative trials, the person must search through the entire set before saying "No." By contrast, the person can say "Yes" as soon as the probe letter matches a letter in the memory set and stop the search. As Figure 10.13(b) shows, the slope of the regression line for the "No" answers is steeper than the line for the "Yes" answers.

The final graph predicts that there is a positive correlation between memory set size and reaction time, but no difference between positive and negative trials. Figure 10.13(c) indicates that as the memory set becomes longer, the reaction time is also longer, but that there are no differences in the intercepts or slopes of the two regression lines.

When we first read about this experiment, we were sure that the second prediction would be correct, as presented in Figure 10.13(b). The logic was compelling and seemed like common sense. Why would anyone want to do this experiment—the results seemed so obvious? Fortunately, Sternberg was not lulled into trusting what seemed to be an obvious answer.

Figure 10.14 presents an example of the data that Sternberg's experiment generated. There are two important features of these data. First, as the size of the memory set increases, the reaction time also increases. Second, the pattern for "Yes" trials and "No" trials is the same. Both sets of data appear to follow the same linear trend. The results did not confirm what

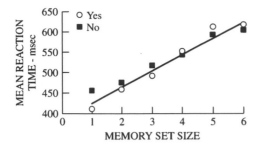

## Figure 10.14

**Example of Results Produced by Sternberg (1966) on the Time Required to Search Short-Term Memory**

seemed to be the obvious and commonsense outcome. Instead, the data confirmed the exhaustive serial search strategy. Even more impressive is that other researchers replicated the results using different tasks and populations (Searleman & Hermann, 1994).

There are lessons we can take from this example. First, do not trust commonsense explanations of the data without empirical verification. The data, not our beliefs, should guide our understanding of psychological processes. Second, we can use the concept of correlation and regression analysis in many different research applications.

## Statistics behind the Research

In this section we will examine the statistical procedures reviewed in this chapter. We will examine Pearson's product-moment correlation coefficient, regression analysis, the standard error of estimate, the confidence interval of $r$, and coefficient alpha ($\alpha$). In addition, we will introduce you to the Spearman rank-order correlation coefficient. Spearman's correlation is a useful alternative to Pearson's coefficient when an interval or ratio scale does not represent the data.

### Pearson Product-Moment Correlation Coefficient

This section provides a quick review of the calculation formula for the correlation coefficient. Although Equation 10.1 presented the definitional equation for $r$, it can be tedious to use. Therefore, if you must calculate the correlation manually, you should use the following equation:

$$r = \frac{\sum XY - \frac{(\sum X)(\sum Y)}{N}}{\sqrt{\left(\sum X^2 - \frac{(\sum X)^2}{N}\right)\left(\sum Y^2 - \frac{(\sum Y)^2}{N}\right)}} \tag{10.5}$$

### Worked Example

Assume that a student repeated Sternberg's (1966) experiment. Table 10.3 presents the data the student collected. The dependent variable represents

## Table 10.3  Data Replicating Sternberg's (1966) Experiment

| | Memory set size $X$ | $X^2$ | Reaction time $Y$ | $Y^2$ | $XY$ |
|---|---|---|---|---|---|
| Probe letter | 1 | 1 | 41 | 1681 | 41 |
| (in set) | 2 | 4 | 45 | 2025 | 90 |
| | 3 | 9 | 49 | 2401 | 147 |
| | 4 | 16 | 56 | 3136 | 224 |
| | 5 | 25 | 62 | 3844 | 310 |
| | 6 | 36 | 62 | 3844 | 372 |
| Probe letter | 1 | 1 | 45 | 2025 | 45 |
| (not in set) | 2 | 4 | 46 | 2116 | 92 |
| | 3 | 9 | 51 | 2601 | 153 |
| | 4 | 16 | 55 | 3025 | 220 |
| | 5 | 25 | 60 | 3600 | 300 |
| | 6 | 36 | 61 | 3721 | 366 |
| | $\Sigma X = 42$ | $\Sigma X^2 = 182$ | $\Sigma Y = 633$ | $\Sigma Y^2 = 34019$ | $\Sigma XY = 2360$ |

the average time, measured to the nearest 1/100 of a second, the participants required to make a correct response for each condition. For example, it took participants, on average, 0.41 seconds to indicate that the probe letter was in the set. The student chose to multiply all scores by 100 to remove the decimal points. We will use the data in Table 10.3 to calculate the correlation between memory set and reaction time for both conditions. As you can see in Table 10.4, the correlation between the variables is $r = .97$.

### Additional Tests

Once you calculate the correlation coefficient, there are additional tests that you can conduct. The selection of what additional tests to run is dependent on your hypotheses and the purpose of the research. A good place to start, however, is with the confidence interval of $r$ and regression analysis.

### *Confidence Interval of r*

This statistic allows one to determine the confidence interval for the correlation coefficient $r$. For this example, we will assume that

95% confidence interval: $r = .97$, $N = 12$, $\alpha = .05$

*Step 1:* Convert $r$ to a $z$-score using the table located in Appendix B. For this example, the table indicates that when $r = .97$, $z_r = 2.092$.

*Step 2:* Determine the lower and upper bounds of the confidence interval using the equations

$$z_L = z_r - \frac{z_{(1-\alpha)/2}}{\sqrt{n-3}} \qquad z_U = z_r + \frac{z_{(1-\alpha)/2}}{\sqrt{n-3}}$$

# Table 10.4 Worked Example of Pearson's Correlation Coefficient

$$r = \frac{\sum XY - \frac{(\sum X)(\sum Y)}{N}}{\sqrt{\left(\sum X^2 - \frac{(\sum X)^2}{N}\right)\left(\sum Y^2 - \frac{(\sum Y)^2}{N}\right)}}$$

$$r = \frac{2360 - \frac{(42)(633)}{12}}{\sqrt{\left(182 - \frac{(42)^2}{12}\right)\left(34019 - \frac{(633)^2}{12}\right)}}$$

$$r = \frac{2360 - 2215.5}{\sqrt{(182 - 147)(34019 - 33390.75)}}$$

$$r = \frac{144.5}{\sqrt{(35)(628.24)}}$$

$$r = \frac{144.5}{148.2860}$$

$$r = .9745$$

$z_{(1-\alpha)/2}$ represents the z-score associated with the confidence interval you wish to create, and $z_L$ and $z_U$ represent the lower and upper bounds of the confidence interval. For the 95% confidence $\alpha = .05$, therefore, $z_{(1-\alpha)/2} = 1.96$:

$$z_L = 2.092 - \frac{1.96}{\sqrt{12 - 3}} \qquad z_U = 2.092 + \frac{1.96}{\sqrt{12 - 3}}$$

$$z_L = 1.4387 \qquad z_U = 2.7453$$

*Step 3:* Determine the upper and lower bounds of the confidence interval using the equations

$$r_L = \frac{e^{2 \times z_L} - 1}{e^{2 \times z_L} + 1} \qquad r_U = \frac{e^{2 \times z_U} - 1}{e^{2 \times z_U} + 1}$$

For these equations, $e$ is the constant 2.71828:

$$r_L = \frac{2.71828^{2 \times 1.4387} - 1}{2.71828^{2 \times 1.4387} + 1} \qquad r_U = \frac{2.71828^{2 \times 2.7453} - 1}{2.71828^{2 \times 2.7453} + 1}$$

$$r_L = \frac{2.71828^{2.8774} - 1}{2.71828^{2.8774} + 1} \qquad r_U = \frac{2.71828^{5.4906} - 1}{2.71828^{5.4906} + 1}$$

$$r_L = \frac{17.7680 - 1}{17.7680 + 1} \qquad r_U = \frac{242.4017 - 1}{242.4017 + 1}$$

$$r_L = .89 \qquad r_U = .99$$

Therefore, the student concludes that the 95% confidence interval for the correlation coefficient is .89–.99.

### Regression Analysis

Upon calculating the correlation coefficient, one can determine the equation that defines the linear relation between $X$ and $Y$. The linear equation has a slope ($b_Y$) and an intercept ($a_Y$):

**Slope:**

$$b_Y = r\left(\frac{s_Y}{s_X}\right) \tag{10.6}$$

**Intercept:**

$$a_Y = M_Y - b_Y(M_X) \tag{10.7}$$

**Regression Equation:**

$$Y' = a_Y + b_Y(X) \tag{10.8}$$

---

## Example

$$r = .97, \quad M_X = 3.5, \quad M_Y = 52.75, \quad s_X = 1.7078, \quad s_Y = 7.2356$$

*Step 1:* Calculate the slope:

$$b_Y = r\left(\frac{s_Y}{s_X}\right)$$

$$b_Y = .97\left(\frac{7.2356}{1.7078}\right)$$

$$b_Y = .97(4.2368)$$

$$b_Y = 4.1097$$

*Step 2:* Calculate the intercept:

$$a_Y = M_Y - b_Y(M_X)$$

$$a_Y = 52.75 - 4.1097(3.5)$$

$$a_Y = 52.75 - 14.3840$$

$$a_Y = 38.366$$

*Step 3:* Using the results of Steps 1 and 2, create the regression equation:

$$Y' = a_Y + b_Y(X)$$

$$Y' = a38.366 + 4.1097(X)$$

---

We can use this equation to create a series of predicted scores. Table 10.5 presents the predicted reaction time scores using the regression equation.

# Table 10.5  Predicted Reaction Time Scores Using the Data Presented in Table 10.3 and the Regression Equation, $Y' = 38.366 + 4.1097(X)$

| X | $Y' = 38.366 + 4.1097 (X)$ |
|---|---|
| 1 | 42.4757 |
| 2 | 46.5854 |
| 3 | 50.6951 |
| 4 | 54.8048 |
| 5 | 58.9145 |
| 6 | 63.0242 |

## Standard Error of Estimate

The regression line is an estimate of probable values of Y given X. The accuracy of the prediction depends on the value of the correlation between the two variables. In addition, the variances of the two variables affect the range of potential scores for the estimate. The standard error of estimate allows us to predict the range of potential scores given the regression equation:

$$Y_T = Y' \pm s_{estY} \sqrt{1 + \frac{1}{N} + \frac{(X - M_X)^2}{\sum x^2 - \frac{(\sum x)^2}{N}}}$$

where

$$s_{estY} = s_Y \sqrt{\frac{N(1 - r^2)}{N - 2}} \qquad (10.9)$$

Using the data in Table 10.3,

$$r = .97, \quad M_X = 3.5, \quad M_Y = 52.75, \quad s_X = 1.7078, \quad s_Y = 7.2356, \quad N = 12$$

*Step 1:* Calculate the standard error of the estimate:

$$s_{estY} = s_Y \sqrt{\frac{N(1 - r^2)}{N - 2}}$$

$$s_{estY} = 7.2536 \sqrt{\frac{12(1 - .97^2)}{12 - 2}}$$

$$s_{estY} = 7.2536 \sqrt{\frac{12(1 - .9409)}{10}}$$

$$s_{estY} = 7.2536 \sqrt{\frac{12(0.0591)}{10}}$$

$$s_{estY} = 1.9317$$

*Step 2:* Apply the standard estimate to a specific predicted score of Y. Assume that X = 4.0. Using the regression equation, we calculate $Y' = 54.8048$.

*Step 3:* Complete the calculations:

$$Y_T = Y' \pm s_{estY} \sqrt{1 + \frac{1}{N} + \frac{(X - M_X)^2}{\sum x^2 - \frac{(\sum X)^2}{N}}}$$

$$Y_T = 54.8048 \pm 1.9317 \sqrt{1 + \frac{1}{12} + \frac{(4 - 3.5)^2}{182 - \frac{(42)^2}{12}}}$$

$$Y_T = 54.8048 \pm 1.9317\sqrt{1.0904}$$

$$Y_T = 54.8048 \pm 2.0171$$

Therefore $Y_T$ equals $52.7877 - 56.8219$.

### Spearman Rank-Order Correlation Coefficient

The Spearman rank-order correlation coefficient, or Spearman's $r_S$, is an alternative to the Pearson product-moment correlation coefficient that researchers use when the data are ranked (e.g., using an ordinal scale) or when the data are skewed. As with the conventional correlation coefficient, the values of $r_S$ can range between $-1.00$ and $+1.00$. Correlations close to 0 represent no linear relation between the two variables. Correlations close to $\pm 1.00$ represent large linear relations:

$$r_S = 1 - \frac{6 \sum D_i^2}{n(n^2 - 1)} \tag{10.10}$$

Assume that a researcher wanted to examine the correlation between two variables $X$ and $Y$.

*Step 1:* Convert the individual scores for X and Y to ranks.

**Original Scores:**

$X$   {90, 85, 80, 75, 71, 73, 72, 64, 66, 50}
$Y$   {3.1, 3.5, 3.55, 3, 2.5, 2.1, 2.4, 1.9, 1.1, 1.2}

Rank scores and assign rank from lowest to highest:

| $X$ | { 50 | 64 | 66 | 71 | 72 | 73 | 75 | 80 | 85 | 90 } |
|---|---|---|---|---|---|---|---|---|---|---|
| **Rank$_X$** | { 1 | 2 | 3 | 4 | 5 | 6 | 7 | 8 | 9 | 10 } |

| $Y$ | { 1.1 | 1.2 | 1.9 | 2.1 | 2.4 | 2.5 | 3 | 3.1 | 3.5 | 3.55 } |
|---|---|---|---|---|---|---|---|---|---|---|
| **Rank$_Y$** | { 1 | 2 | 3 | 4 | 5 | 6 | 7 | 8 | 9 | 10 } |

*Step 2:* Determine the difference between ranks for the paired data and then square the differences (see Table 10.6).

# Table 10.6  Worked Example for Spearman Rank-Order Correlation Coefficient

| Participant | X | Rank$_X$ | Y | Rank$_Y$ | $D = (Rank_X - Rank_Y)$ | $D^2$ |
|---|---|---|---|---|---|---|
| A | 90 | 10 | 3.10 | 8 | 2 | 4 |
| B | 85 | 9 | 3.50 | 9 | 0 | 0 |
| C | 80 | 8 | 3.55 | 10 | −2 | 4 |
| D | 75 | 7 | 3.00 | 7 | 0 | 0 |
| E | 71 | 4 | 2.50 | 6 | −2 | 4 |
| F | 73 | 6 | 2.10 | 4 | 2 | 4 |
| G | 72 | 5 | 2.40 | 5 | 0 | 0 |
| H | 64 | 2 | 1.90 | 3 | −1 | 1 |
| I | 66 | 3 | 1.10 | 1 | 2 | 4 |
| J | 50 | 1 | 1.20 | 2 | −1 | 1 |
| | | | | | | $\Sigma D^2 = 22$ |

*Step 3:* Complete the calculations:

$$r_S = 1 - \frac{6 \sum D_i^2}{n(n^2 - 1)}$$

$$r_S = 1 - \frac{6(22)}{10(10^2 - 1)}$$

$$r_S = 1 - \frac{132}{990}$$

$$r_S = 1 - .1333$$

$$r_S = .8667$$

## Confidence Interval for $r_S$

The sampling distribution of $r_S$ is similar to the sampling distribution of the Pearson product-moment correlation coefficient, $r$. Consequently, you can use the same procedures for determining the CI of $r_S$ as you did for $r$.

## Coefficient Alpha

**Coefficient alpha** is a special form of the correlation coefficient that allows one to determine the internal consistency of items in a test. The value of coefficient alpha ranges between 0 and 1.00. Higher values of coefficient alpha indicate more consistency among the individual test items. Table 10.7 presents hypothetical data for a 10-item test administered to 8 people.
    The equation for coefficient alpha is

$$r_\alpha = \left(\frac{I}{I-1}\right)\left(1 - \frac{\sum s_i^2}{s_T^2}\right) \qquad (10.11)$$

*Step 1:* Determine the variance for each item treating each person's score on the item as an observation. For Item 1,

# Table 10.7  Worked Example of Coefficient Alpha $r_\alpha$

| Test Item | A | B | C | D | E | F | G | H | $\Sigma I$ | $\Sigma I^2$ | $s^2_i$ |
|-----------|---|---|---|---|---|---|---|---|------|------|--------|
| | | | | **Person** | | | | | | **Item Variance** | |
| 1 | 5 | 2 | 4 | 3 | 4 | 2 | 6 | 5 | 31 | 135 | 1.8594 |
| 2 | 3 | 3 | 5 | 2 | 5 | 3 | 5 | 4 | 30 | 122 | 1.1875 |
| 3 | 4 | 4 | 4 | 4 | 4 | 2 | 4 | 5 | 31 | 125 | 0.6094 |
| 4 | 6 | 2 | 5 | 3 | 6 | 3 | 6 | 5 | 36 | 180 | 2.2500 |
| 5 | 3 | 4 | 3 | 3 | 4 | 4 | 5 | 6 | 32 | 136 | 1.0000 |
| 6 | 4 | 3 | 4 | 4 | 3 | 1 | 6 | 5 | 30 | 128 | 1.9375 |
| 7 | 6 | 5 | 3 | 4 | 5 | 3 | 5 | 4 | 35 | 161 | 0.9844 |
| 8 | 7 | 3 | 4 | 3 | 4 | 2 | 6 | 5 | 34 | 164 | 2.4375 |
| 9 | 4 | 4 | 5 | 2 | 6 | 3 | 5 | 6 | 35 | 167 | 1.7344 |
| 10 | 5 | 5 | 4 | 3 | 5 | 4 | 3 | 5 | 34 | 150 | 0.6875 |
| $\Sigma X$ | 47 | 35 | 41 | 31 | 46 | 27 | 51 | 50 | | | $\Sigma s^2_i = 14.6875$ |
| $(\Sigma X)^2$ | 2209 | 1225 | 1681 | 961 | 2116 | 729 | 2601 | 2500 | | | |

$$s_i^2 = \frac{\sum I_i^i - \frac{\left(\sum I_i\right)^2}{N}}{N}$$

$$1.8594 = \frac{135 - \frac{(31)^2}{8}}{8}$$

The $i$ in the equation refers to each item in the test, $N$ represents the number of people taking the test, and $i$ represents the number of test items.

*Step 2:* Add the variance for each item:

$$\sum s_I^2 = 1.8594 + 1.1875 + 0.6094 + \ldots + .6875 = 14.6875$$

*Step 3:* Determine the variance among test scores for each person taking the test:

$$s_T^2 = \frac{\sum\sum X^2 - \frac{\sum\left(\sum X\right)^2}{N}}{N}$$

$$\sum\left(\sum X\right) = 328 = 47 + 35 + 41 + \ldots + 51 + 50$$

$$\sum\sum X^2 = 14022 = 2209 + 1225 + 1681 + \ldots + 2601 + 2500$$

$$s_T^2 = 71.75 = \frac{14022 - \frac{(328)^2}{8}}{8}$$

*Step 4:* Complete the calculations:

$$r_\alpha = \left(\frac{10}{10-1}\right)\left(1 - \frac{14.6875}{71.75}\right)$$

$$r_\alpha = (1.111)(1 - .2047)$$

$$r_\alpha = .8837$$

For this example, we can conclude that the internal consistency of the test is high.

## Knowledge Check

6. Why might the test–retest reliability of peoples' weight be greater than the test–retest reliability of their personality?

7. In what ways are coefficient $\kappa$ and $r$ similar to each other?

8. What does coefficient alpha, $r_\alpha$, represent?

9. Imagine that a researcher found that $r_\alpha = .34$. What conclusions could you draw from this statistic?

10. What are some ways to increase the reliability of a test?

11. Explain in your words the importance of convergent and discriminant validity for examining the validity of a test.

12. Imagine that we randomly selected 25 students who scored extremely well on a math achievement test. We then administer a similar math achievement test to these students. What predictions can you make about the second set of scores?

## Chapter Summary

The correlation coefficient is a descriptive statistic that indicates the degree to which changes in one variable relate to changes in a second variable. Specifically, the correlation describes a linear relation between two variables. The size of the correlation coefficient ranges between $-1.00$ and $+1.00$. When the correlation coefficient is 0, then there is no meaningful linear relation between the two variables. Correlation coefficients closer to $-1.00$ or $+1.00$ represent strong linear relations between the two variables.

Pearson's correlation coefficient is the most commonly used statistic to examine the relation between two variables. The statistic works by examining the sum of the standard score cross-products ($\Sigma z_X z_Y$) of the two data sets. Using the standard scores ($z$-score) allows us to compare two variables even when the means and standard deviations of the two groups are extremely different.

The absolute value of the correlation coefficient indicates the strength of the relation between the two variables. One way to describe the size of the correlation coefficient is to use the coefficient of determination, $r^2$, which indicates the proportion of variance in one variable that the other variable can predict.

There are several errors that people often make when interpreting the size of the correlation coefficient. One common error is to use the correlation coefficient as evidence of cause and effect. Correlational research designs do not allow the researcher to control the independent variables or randomly assign participants to different levels of the independent variable. Therefore, we cannot resolve the ambiguity of cause and effect created by the third variable problem or the temporal order problem.

It is also possible to have an exceptionally low correlation because of a curvilinear relation between the two variables or because the sampling procedures did not adequately draw a representative sample from the population. These sampling errors can create a truncated range in the variances of the variables, extreme groups or outliers, and multiple unrecognized populations.

As with other descriptive statistics, we can use the concept of the standard error and the confidence interval to estimate sample size. For the correlation coefficient, the sample size needs to be large ($N = 500$) if the researcher believes that the correlation coefficient for the population is small. If the correlation is larger, however, the researcher may be able to use a smaller sample size.

The correlation coefficient has many applications for researchers. We examined how the correlation coefficient can help the researcher determine the test–retest reliability of a test or the internal consistency between two observers. A special version of the correlation coefficient, known as coefficient alpha $r_\alpha$, allows researchers to examine the internal consistency of test items. A high coefficient alpha indicates that the questions in the test are highly interrelated. Knowing the test–retest reliability or the coefficient alpha can allow the researcher to adjust the length of a test to enhance its reliability. For example, making a test longer can improve the reliability of an instrument. This increased reliability will decrease measurement error of the dependent variable.

The correlation coefficient also allows us to examine the validity of a test. By correlating a test with tests that measure the same construct, we can determine the test's convergent validity. Tests that measure the same construct should produce high correlations. By contrast, tests that measure different constructs should not correlate with each other. Researchers call this discriminant validity.

We can use regression analysis to make a formal statement about the relation between the two variables. The regression line allows us to describe the specific linear relation between $X$ and $Y$. We can also calculate a confidence interval about the regression line. Knowing the position of the regression line allows us to describe the regression-to-the-mean phenomenon. If an observed value of $X$ is greater than the mean, then the predicted value of $Y'$ will be closer to the mean of $Y$.

In the "Research in Action" section, we showed how Sternberg's study of short-term memory can be analyzed using regression statistics.

# Chapter Glossary for Review

**Coefficient alpha** $(r_\alpha)$—A common measure of internal consistency. The magnitude of $r_\alpha$ indicates whether the participants' responses to the individual test items correlate highly with each other, thus indicating internal agreement among the questions.

**Coefficient of determination** $(r^2)$—A descriptive statistic that indicates the percentage of shared variance between two variables.

**Coefficient of nondetermination** $(1-r^2)$—A descriptive statistic that indicates the percentage of unshared variance between two variables.

**Concurrent validity**—A form of criterion-related validity that indicates that the test scores correlate with the current behaviors of the individuals.

**Convergent validity**—An index of the validity of a test that requires that different methods of measuring the same construct correlate with each other.

**Correlation coefficient**—A descriptive statistic that describes the linear relation between two variables. The statistic can range between $r = -1.0$ and $r = +1.0$ and indicates the degree to which changes in one variable correspond with changes in the other variable.

**Criterion-related validity**—An index of the validity of a test that requires that the test score predict an individual's performance under specific conditions.

**Curvilinear relationship**—A systematic relation between two variables that is described by a curved rather than a straight line.

**Discriminant validity**—An index of the validity of a test that requires that measures of different constructs should not correlate with each other.

**Intercept** $(a)$—The value of $Y'$ when $X = 0$.

**Internal consistency**—A measure of the degree to which questions in a test agree or correlate with each other.

**Linear relation**—The correlation between two variables best described as a straight line.

**Negative correlation**—When $r < 0$, increases in one variable correspond with decreases in the other variable.

**Positive correlation**—When $r > 0$, increases in one variable correspond with increases in the other variable.

**Predictive validity**—A form of criterion-related validity that indicates that the test scores afford accurate predictions concerning future behavior of the individual.

**Regression to the mean**—A phenomenon in regression analysis where $|(X - M_X)| > |(Y' - M_Y)|$.

**Slope** $(b)$—The change in $Y'$ that occurs when $X$ increases by one unit.

**Standard error of estimate**—The standard deviation of predicted scores about $Y$.

**Truncated range**—A condition that occurs when the range of observed scores for both variables is smaller than the range of potential scores. This condition tends to reduce the size of the correlation coefficient.

## Chapter References

Aiken, L. S., & West, S. G. (1991). *Multiple regression: Testing and interpreting interactions*. Newbury Park, CA: Sage Publications.

Baron, R. M., & Kenny, D. A. (1986). The moderator-mediator variable distinction in social psychological research: Conceptual, strategic, and statistical considerations. *Journal of Personality and Social Psychology, 51*, 1173–1182.

Campbell, D. T., & Fiske, D. W. (1959). Convergent and discriminant validation by the multitrait-multimethod matrix. *Psychological Bulletin, 56*, 81–105.

Chaiken, S., & Maheswaran, D. (1992). *Heuristic processing can bias systematic processing: The effect of source credibility, argument ambiguity, and task importance on attitude judgment*. Unpublished manuscript, New York University, New York, NY.

Cohen, J. (1988). *Statistical power analysis for the behavioral sciences* (2nd ed.). Hillsdale, NJ: LEA.

Cohen, J., Cohen, P., West, S. G., & Aiken, L. S. (2003). *Applied multiple regression/correlation analysis for the behavioral sciences* (3rd ed.). Mahwah, NJ: Erlbaum.

Cortina, J. M. (1993). What is coefficient alpha? An examination of theory and applications. *Journal of Applied Psychology, 78*, 98–104.

Cronbach, L. J. (1951). Coefficient alpha and the internal structure of tests. *Psychometrika, 16*, 297–334.

Cronbach, L. J. (1988). Five perspectives on the validity argument. In H. Wainer & H. I. Braun (Eds.), *Test validity* (pp. 63–79). Hillsdale, NJ: Erlbaum.

Galton, F. (1889). *Natural inheritance*. London: Macmillan.

Messick, S. (1980). Test validity and the ethics of assessment. *American Psychologist, 35*, 1012–1027.

Messick, S. (1988). The once and future issues of validity: Assessing the meaning and consequences of measurement. In H. Wainer & H. I. Braun (Eds.), *Test validity* (pp. 80–95). Hillsdale, NJ: Erlbaum.

Messick, S. (1989). Validity. In R. L. Linn (Ed.), *Educational measurement* (3rd ed.). New York: American Council on Education/Macmillan.

Schmitt, N. (1996). Uses and abuses of coefficient alpha. *Psychological Assessment, 8*, 350–353.

Searleman, A., & Hermann, D. (1994). *Memory from a broader perspective*. New York: McGraw-Hill.

Sternberg, S. (1966). High-speed scanning in human memory. *Science, 153*, 652–654.

# Chapter 11
## Between-Subjects Designs

Statistics is no substitute for judgment.

—Henry Clay

## Introduction

In Chapter 9 we examined ways to design a research project that allows us to collect data relevant to the research hypothesis. Once we collect the data, we must begin the process of analysis and interpretation. Chapter 10 introduced you to correlational research and evaluating the linear relationship among variables. In many cases, however, we are interested in group differences in addition to or instead of linear relationships.

Accordingly, in the first part of this chapter we will review the logic of inferential statistics and how they allow us to evaluate group differences. As a part of this review, we will examine the types of inferences these statistics do and do not allow us to make. Inferential statistics are important to all the behavioral sciences. Unfortunately, some researchers abuse, misapply, and misinterpret these tools. Because statistical analysis forms the basis of decision making, you need to understand what conclusions, or inferences, you can and cannot draw from these statistical tests.

Take heed of Clay's comment about statistics and judgments. Statistics are wonderful tools for helping us find patterns and trends in the data. They also help us solve problems and come to decisive conclusions. However, statistical inference requires careful consideration. Statistics may help us make judgments, but they do not, cannot, and should not replace our ability to make rational decisions.

In another section of this chapter we will review how inferential statistics help us solve other important questions. For example, many researchers ask, "How many participants do I need in my research?" This is an important question because the sample size affects the accuracy of the results and conclusions of our research.

Throughout this chapter we will use the two-group experiment for our examples in this chapter, not because it is the most popular form of research design, but because it is a good way to describe the important topics in this chapter. We will review more complex research designs in subsequent chapters. Fortunately, the principles you mastered in Chapters 9 and 10, and the ones you will learn in this chapter, apply to all good research designs and inferential statistics.

## Student's *t*-Ratio for Independent Groups

One of the most important advances in modern inferential statistics was the development of Student's sampling distributions and the inferential statistics using those distributions. This statistic, known as **Student's *t* -ratio**, is a commonly used statistical procedure in the social and behavioral sciences and as such it often sets the standard for using inferential statistics. Once you master the principles used for this inferential statistic, you will be better able to use and understand other inferential statistics. The "Statistics behind the Research" section at the end of this chapter presents the *t*-ratio and its alternatives in more detail.

The *t*-ratio gets its name because it is a ratio of two measures of variability. Specifically, it is the ratio of the difference between two group means relative to the variability within groups. Equation 11.1 presents a conceptual formula for Student's *t*-ratio.

$$t = \frac{\text{Difference between group means}}{\text{Standard error of the difference between group means}} \quad (11.1)$$

The numerator of the equation represents the difference between the two group means. The difference between these two means reflects the effect of the independent variable and the effects of random error on both of the study groups. Because the *t*-ratio compares the difference between two means, the *t*-ratio can be a negative value when $M_1 < M_2$, a positive value when $M_1 > M_2$, or 0 when $M_1 = M_2$.

The denominator in this ratio is the **standard error of the difference between means**, which allows us to estimate the variability of scores within both treatment groups. Recall that the within-groups variability represents normal differences among individuals in the population and sampling error. In this way, the standard error of the difference between means is similar to the standard error of the mean, as we have discussed in previous chapters. Therefore, we can use what we have learned about the standard error of the mean and apply it to the standard error of the difference between means.

According to the central limit theorem, the distribution of sample means is normally distributed with a standard deviation of

$$s_M = \frac{SD}{\sqrt{n}}$$

The same occurs when we examine the difference between means drawn from separate populations. Imagine that we have two populations, such that $\mu_1 = 5.0$, $\sigma_1 = 1.0$ and $\mu_2 = 5.0$, $\sigma_2 = 1.0$. We draw a random sample of $n = 2$ from each population. For the first sample, the scores might be 3 and 5. For the second sample, the scores could be 4 and 6. Therefore, $M_1 = 4$ and $M_2 = 5$. The difference between the means is $M_1 - M_2 = -1$. If we continue this sampling procedure infinitely, we can create a sampling distribution of the difference between the means.

What would this sampling distribution look like? Figure 11.1 presents an illustration of what would happen. The sampling distribution at the bottom of the figure represents the distribution of the difference between means, $M_1 - M_2$. Because the null hypothesis states that $\mu_1 = \mu_2$, we predict that the mean of the sampling distribution will be $\mu_{\mu_1 - \mu_2} = 0$ and that

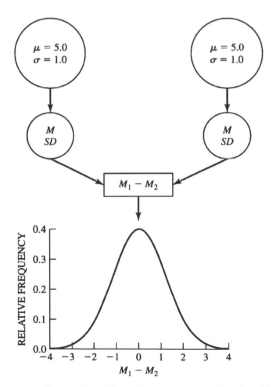

## Figure 11.1

**Standard Error of the Difference between Means**

$H_0: \mu_1 = \mu_2$. The two population means are the same. Thus $H_0$ is a true statement.

Assume that we use random sampling to create the individual samples. Therefore, $M$ is an unbiased estimate of $\mu$ and any difference between $M$ and $\mu$ is the result of sampling error.

Because the two population means are the same, $\mu_1 = \mu_2$, the typical difference between the sample means will be $M_1 - M_2 = 0$. Differences between the means reflect sampling error.

According to the null hypothesis, $\mu_1 = \mu_2$. Therefore, if we were to create an infinite number of sample pairs, the difference between the pairs would fall into the sampling distribution at the bottom of the figure. The mean of the sampling distribution will be 0 and the standard deviation will equal $\sigma_{\mu_2 - \mu_2} = \sqrt{\frac{\sigma_1^2}{n_1} + \frac{\sigma_2^2}{n_2}}$.

values above and below 0 represent random sampling error. According to the Central Limit Theorem, we can predict that the distribution of the difference between means will be symmetrical and bell-shaped.

We use the term $\sigma_{M_1-M_2}$ to represent the standard error of the difference between means. When we calculate the $t$-ratio, we use the variances of the two samples to estimate $\sigma_{M_1-M_2}$. Specifically, $SD_{M_1-M_2}$ is an unbiased estimate of $\sigma_{M_1-M_2}$, just as the $SD$ is an unbiased estimate of the population standard deviation, $\sigma$.

Many statisticians refer to $SD_{M_1-M_2}$ as the **error term** because we use it to estimate the random error that occurs when we take random samples from the population. Thus, sampling error and random error are synonymous and estimated by $SD_{M_1-M_2}$. Using this information, we can turn our attention to hypothesis testing.

What does the $t$-ratio tell us? Using Equation 11.1, you can conclude that the larger the absolute value of the $t$-ratio, the greater the relative difference between the means. The magnitude of the $t$-ratio, therefore, allows us to determine whether to reject the null hypothesis. The typical two-group nondirectional null hypothesis states that $H_0$: $\mu_1 = \mu_2$. Consequently, we predict that the average difference between the means of samples drawn from the two populations will be 0. Sampling error may cause the difference between some sample means to be greater or less than 0. However, if a $t$-ratio is sufficiently large, we can use its magnitude to reject the null hypothesis. The question before us is what we mean by *sufficiently large*.

## Review of Hypothesis Testing

How do we decide whether to reject the null hypothesis? We use estimates of probability. Imagine that your friend claims to be able to toss a coin and cause it to land heads-up at will. To test your friend's skill, you ask that he or she toss a coin 10 times in a row. If your friend produces only 5 heads out of 10 tosses, you probably will not be impressed because your friend seems to be tossing heads at random. However, if your friend can toss 10 heads in a row, you may be impressed because the probability of a run of 10 heads is less than 1 in 1,000. Could your friend have been lucky and tossed 10 heads by chance?

Yes, assuming that the probability of heads is .5. The reason for this is that when there are 10 coin tosses, the probability of having all 10 land heads-up $p = .5^{10} = .000977$. This probability is small enough that you decide that the 10 heads must represent a unique skill (either that, or a weighted or two-headed coin). We use the same reasoning when we evaluate the $t$-ratio. We ask, "If the null hypothesis is a true statement, what is the probability of obtaining a $t$-ratio that differs from some critical value?" If the probability is sufficiently small, we can infer that the null hypothesis is a false statement.

As you learned in Chapter 9, we use $\alpha$ to represent the probability of committing a Type I error (a false alarm, or rejection of the null hypothesis

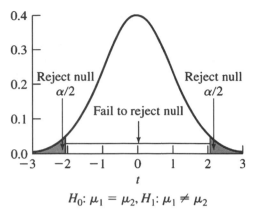

Figure 11.2

**Hypothetical Sampling Distribution of the $t$-Ratio and Testing the Null Hypothesis $H_0$: $\mu_1 = \mu_2$, a Non-directional Test**

$$H_0: \mu_1 = \mu_2, H_1: \mu_1 \neq \mu_2$$

The shaded areas represent the criterion for rejecting the null hypothesis. If the $t$-ratio falls in the shaded area, we reject $H_0$ in favor of $H_1$. If the $t$-ratio falls in the clear area, we fail to reject the null hypothesis.

when it is actually correct). Most researchers use $\alpha$ to establish the criterion for determining when to reject the null hypothesis and set $\alpha = .05$. The $\alpha$-level indicates that if the null hypothesis is correct, there is a 5% probability of committing a Type I error (rejecting $H_0$ when we should not). In some cases, the researcher may want to be more cautious and will set $\alpha = .01$, thus lowering the risk of a Type I error to 1%.

Figure 11.2 represents an example of a sampling distribution for a $t$-ratio where the nondirectional null hypothesis is $H_0$: $\mu_1 = \mu_2$. Using this sampling distribution, we can determine the probability of obtaining any specific $t$-ratio and thereby determine whether to reject the null hypothesis. You should recognize that the null hypothesis in Figure 11.2 is a non-directional hypothesis and that the alternative hypothesis is $H_1$: $\mu_1 \neq \mu_2$. In this case, we will reject the null hypothesis if the $t$-ratio is considerably less than or considerably greater than 0. As you can see, the tail ends of this figure are shaded and marked "Reject null $\alpha/2$." If the null hypothesis is correct, then the probability that the $t$-ratio will fall within either shaded area is equal to $\alpha$. Because the null hypothesis is nondirectional, we divide $\alpha$ equally between the two ends of the sampling distribution.

To illustrate, we will use an example study we discussed in Chapter 9, where we wanted to compare men's and women's recall of emotional events. In that example, we asked the question, "Do men and women differ when asked to recall emotionally significant events in their lives?" This is a nondirectional hypothesis because we want to determine whether there is a difference between the two groups. In this example, the null hypothesis is that men and women will recall approximately the same number of positive emotional events. If the null hypothesis is correct, the $t$-ratio for the difference between means should be close to 0, and any difference from 0 would represent the effect of random events.

Assume we decide to set $\alpha = .05$. According to Figure 11.2, the probability of obtaining a $t$-ratio in the upper shaded area is $p = .05/2 =$

# Figure 11.3

**(a) Hypothetical Sampling Distribution of a *t*-Ratio and Testing the Null Hypothesis H₀: $\mu_1 \geq \mu_2$ (b) Hypothetical Sampling Distribution of a *t*-Ratio and Testing the Null Hypothesis, H₀: $\mu_1 \leq \mu_2$**

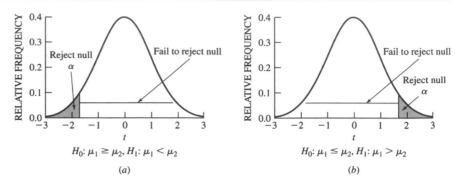

(a)               (b)

The shaded areas represent the criterion for rejecting the null hypothesis. If the *t*-ratio falls in the shaded area, we reject $H_0$ in favor of $H_1$. If the *t*-ratio falls in the clear area, we fail to reject the null hypothesis.

.025 or 2.5%. Similarly, the probability of obtaining a *t*-ratio in the lower shaded area is also $p = .025$. Added together, the two shaded areas comprise .05 or 5% of the distribution. If a *t*-ratio falls within either shaded area, we reject the null hypothesis because the probability of such a *t*-ratio is so low that we are willing to infer that null hypothesis is incorrect. In this situation, we then, by default, accept the alternative hypothesis in place of the null hypothesis. In contrast, if the *t*-ratio falls in the clear area between the two shaded areas of our distribution, we do not reject the null hypothesis.

Figure 11.3 presents how we would proceed if we used a directional hypothesis. Because the directional hypothesis predicts the relation between the means (using < or >), we place the entire $\alpha$ region on the side of the sampling distribution representing the hypothesized difference between the means. Specifically, Figure 11.3(a) represents the test we create using the null hypothesis, $H_0$: $\mu_1 \geq \mu_2$; Figure 11.3(b) represents the test created using the null hypothesis, $H_0$: $\mu_1 \leq \mu_2$.

## Testing Statistical Hypotheses

Statisticians and researchers invented inferential statistics during the early part of the twentieth century (Oakes, 1986). Over time, general rules and principles for using inferential statistics became common practice. For example, most researchers now routinely include a null and alternative hypothesis as a part of their statistical test. We discussed forming hypotheses in some detail in Chapter 3. With the information in this section we build on that material and examine the specific steps involved in hypothesis testing.

One important feature of all hypothesis testing is that we form the hypothesis before we collect or examine the data. In fact, in most social science research, the design of the research actually flows from the stated hypotheses. All of us can describe the past with accuracy; predicting the future, however, is a talent. Thus, we are more impressed by and have much greater confidence in a prediction of the future that comes true after a solid research design yields good data. As you will see in the following steps, much of the work associated with hypothesis testing comes before we collect or analyze the data.

## Steps for Hypothesis Testing

### *State the Null and Alternative Hypotheses*
As you learned earlier in this book, the null hypothesis, $H_0$, is the mathematical statement we want to disprove. More specifically, the typical null hypothesis states that there is no relation between the independent and dependent variables or that groups are equal. If we can reject the null hypothesis, then we can accept the alternative hypothesis, the focus of the study. Typically, the alternative hypothesis is the central thesis of the research and states that there is a meaningful difference between the group means.

The null hypothesis can be either nondirectional or directional. The nondirectional hypothesis for a two-group study will be $H_0: \mu_1 = \mu_2$. This version of the hypothesis states that the two population means are identical and that any observed difference between the group means is due to random events unrelated to the independent variable. In contrast, the directional null hypothesis can be either $H_0: \mu_1 \geq \mu_2$ or $H_0: \mu_1 \leq \mu_2$. The directional hypothesis predicts that one population mean is less than the other mean with the exception of the effects of random sampling error.

The alternative hypothesis (often denoted $H_1$) is always the mathematical complement of the null hypothesis. The complementary relational signs are $=$ versus $\neq$, $\geq$ versus $<$, and $\leq$ versus $>$. As a rule, each null hypothesis has only one alternative hypothesis.

### *Identify the Appropriate Statistical Test*
This step may seem obvious, but it is often the downfall of many students and researchers. Part of the problem is that you can often apply any number of statistical tests to any set of data. One question you could ask is "Can I use this statistic to analyze these data?" The answer will typically be "Yes" because you can often use a variety of statistical tests to analyze any set of data. A better question is "Will this statistical test allow me to answer the question I posed in my hypothesis?" Different statistical tests lead to different information from a set of data. For example, some allow you to compare groups whereas others examine the correlation between groups.

Therefore, your null and alternative hypotheses will largely determine the type of test you use. Other factors also influence the selection of the appropriate statistical test. Many inferential statistics require that the data meet specific criteria to produce valid results. For example, the $t$-ratio for independent groups assumes that the observations for the two groups are independent, that the data are normally distributed, and that the variances of the two groups be equivalent. Failure to meet these criteria can produce spurious results. As you plan your research, you should identify the appropriate statistical tests for analyzing the data and identify the requirements for using that test. In addition, you should identify alternative strategies for analyzing the data in the case that your data do not conform to the requirements of a specific test.

There are many ways to analyze the data from a research project. Consider the study described in Chapter 9, where the researchers wanted to compare the number of positive and negative memories that men and women recall. The researchers could use Student's $t$-ratio for independent groups to analyze the data. If, for some reason, the data do not conform to the requirements of the statistic, there are alternative statistical tests. For example, if the variances of the two groups are not equivalent, the researchers could use a special form of $t$-ratio that corrects for the inequality of variances. Similarly, the researchers could use the Mann-Whitney $U$-test, another alternative to the t-ratio. The "Statistics behind the Research" section at the end of the chapter includes an example of some alternatives.

### Determine the Appropriate Significance Level

Determining the appropriate significance level is another important step. As you learned in the previous chapter, researchers want to avoid making a Type I error. We can control the probability of committing a Type I error by selecting a suitable criterion. Because $\alpha$ represents the probability of committing a Type I error and is determined by the researcher, you have direct control over the probability of committing a Type I error. Recall that the probability of a Type I error and a Type II error are inversely related—as you reduce the risk of a Type I error, you increase the risk of a Type II error. Consequently, you should plan your research with care to ensure that the risk of both errors is at a tolerable level.

Many researchers have fallen into the habit of automatically setting $\alpha$ = .05 or $\alpha$ = .01 and then continuing on with their typical analysis of the data. There is nothing magical about these criteria for $\alpha$, but their use is common practice. Selecting the $\alpha$-level should not be reflexive. Instead, selecting $\alpha$ should be a deliberative process that examines the consequence of committing a Type I or a Type II error.

In many ways, selecting the $\alpha$-level takes us back to the utilitarian principles of ethics because the process forces us to examine the consequences of our actions. Ask yourself, "What is the cost of committing a Type I versus a Type II error?" For the American legal system, the proposition is that sending an innocent person to jail (a Type I error) is far worse than letting a guilty person back on the streets (a Type II error). Therefore, the legal criterion for finding guilt, "beyond a reasonable doubt," is equivalent to setting $\alpha$ to a small value, say $\alpha$ = .0001.

Rudner (1953) argued that researchers must make value judgments when deciding whether to reject the null hypothesis. He asserted that

> *[because] no scientific hypothesis is ever completely verified, in accepting a hypothesis the scientist must make the decision that the evidence is* sufficiently *strong or that the probability is* sufficiently *high to warrant the acceptance of the hypothesis. . . .* How sure

we need to be before we accept a hypothesis will depend on how serious a mistake would be. (*p. 350*)

Rudner recognized two important components of hypothesis tests. First, inferential statistics depend on samples and probabilities. Consequently, whenever we make a statistical decision, we must recognize the legitimate risk of committing a Type I or Type II error. Second, either error may have grave consequences depending on the purpose of the research. Therefore, as researchers we must examine the utility of our research results and the consequences of our statistical decisions.

For some experiments, committing a Type I error can have serious negative consequences. Will we, for example, use the results to justify an expensive program of research or to alter the treatment that patients currently receive? If the statistical conclusion represents a Type I error, we may end up spending money on a potentially pointless set of experiments or begin to use an ineffective treatment.

In other cases, committing a Type II error is the more serious mistake. A Type II error may cause the researcher to ignore an important relation between two variables or disregard a potentially useful treatment. For many researchers who conduct basic research, a Type II error is the more serious error because it means that they have overlooked a potentially interesting finding.

Because both Type I and Type II errors involve potentially unpleasant consequences, we should design our research to minimize the risk of both errors. Reaching a balance between the two errors is not always easy, but it is possible with careful planning. We will return to this important topic later in the chapter. Once you determine the significance level that you wish to use, you can proceed with the analysis of the data. Using the results of your data analysis, you can then determine whether you have sufficient evidence to support your original research hypothesis.

### Determine the Significance Level for the t-Ratio

We use Table B.3 of Appendix B to determine the critical value of the *t*-ratio required to reject the null hypothesis. As you learned previously, the table consists of a series of rows and columns. Each column represents the probability level we want to use for our hypothesis. Each row represents the degrees of freedom for the data. For the independent-groups *t*-ratio, the degrees of freedom are

$$df = (n_1 - 1)(n_2 - 1) \tag{11.2}$$

To determine the critical value of *t*, known as $t_{critical}$, we need to determine the level of $\alpha$, whether we wish to conduct a directional or a nondirectional test, and the degrees of freedom for the test. As an example, assume that we set $\alpha = .05$ and decide to use a nondirectional test, and that the degrees of freedom are 16. Given these facts, we see that $t_{critical} = 2.120$. What would have happened if we had decided to conduct a directional test? For $df = 16$ and $\alpha = .05$, one-tailed, $t_{critical} = 1.746$.

We can use the data for men's and women's recall of positive emotional events as an illustration of the steps for hypothesis testing (see Box 11.1). For the sake of illustration, we will assume that our hypothesis in this case is nondirectional.

## Box 11.1 Example of Steps Used in Hypothesis Testing

*Null Hypothesis:* $H_0$: $\mu_1 = \mu_2$. The average performance of the participants in the two groups is equivalent.

*Alternative Hypothesis:* $H_1$: $\mu_1 \neq \mu_2$. The average performance of the participants in the two groups is not equivalent.

*Statistical Test:* We will use the $t$-ratio because we wish to compare the difference between two independent groups.

*Significance Level:* $\alpha = .05$, two-tailed, $df = 28 = (15 - 1) + (15 - 1)$ $t_{\text{critical}}$ (28) $= \pm 2.048$.

**Number of positive events recalled**

| Women | Men |
|---|---|
| $n_1 = 15$ | $n_2 = 15$ |
| $\sum X_1 = 157$ | $\sum X_2 = 126$ |
| $\sum X_1^2 = 1707$ | $\sum X_2^2 = 1102$ |
| $M_1 = 10.47$ | $M_2 = 8.40$ |

$$t = \frac{M_1 - M_2}{\sqrt{\dfrac{\sum X_1^2 - \dfrac{(\sum X_1)^2}{n_1} + \sum X_2^2 - \dfrac{(\sum X_2)^2}{n_2}}{n_1 + n_2 - 2} \left(\dfrac{1}{n_1} + \dfrac{1}{n_2}\right)}}$$

$$t = \frac{10.47 - 8.40}{\sqrt{\dfrac{1707 - \dfrac{(157)^2}{15} + 1102 - \dfrac{(126)^2}{15}}{15 + 15 - 2} \left(\dfrac{1}{15} + \dfrac{1}{15}\right)}}$$

$$t = 2.89$$

Because the absolute value of the obtained $t$-ratio exceeds the critical value ($t_{\text{observed}} > t_{\text{critical}}$; $2.89 > 2.048$), we can reject $H_0$. If the null hypothesis were true, the probability of selecting at random two samples that differ this much or more is less than 5 times in 100 or $p < .05$.

If you used a computer program to calculate the statistic, you may have obtained output that looks something like this:

$$t(28) = 2.89, \quad p \text{ one-tailed} = .0035, \quad p \text{ two-tailed} = .007$$

Whenever the probability level of the statistic ($p$) is less than the $\alpha$-level that you establish before running your analyses, you can reject the null hypothesis. In this example, the probability associated with this $t$-ratio is $p = .007$ for the two-tailed or nondirectional test. Because $p < \alpha$, you can reject $H_0$.

## Interpreting the $t$-Ratio

Once we calculate the $t$-ratio and its probability, we can determine whether to reject $H_0$. Although we have completed one important task, there are still many opportunities to further analyze the results of our research. In this section we will examine several of the errors that many people make when interpreting the results. We will also examine the conclusions that inferential statistics afford and several statistical procedures that can enhance our interpretation of the data.

### *Statistically Significant*

Whenever the obtained $p$-value is less than the set $\alpha$ in a study, it is common to see researchers state that they found statistically significant results. This means that they feel they have sufficient statistical evidence to reject the null hypothesis. Unfortunately, many people equate "statistical significance" with "importance." Because this is clearly not the case, some researchers like to make the distinction between **statistical significance** and **clinical** or **practical significance.** Whereas statistical significance means that one has reason to reject the null hypothesis in favor of the alternative hypothesis, practical significance implies that the results have real implications for the target population (e.g., they may justify a specific intervention; Moyé, 2000). In other words, if our evaluation of the effectiveness of a new smoking-cessation intervention yielded practically significant findings, we would consider the size and direction of the observed effect to conclude that the intervention's benefits (or consequences) justify the cost of the treatment (or point toward a need to discontinue the treatment).

Under some circumstances it is possible to obtain statistical significance when the effect size is trivial (e.g., when $d_2 = .1$ or less, as discussed in Chapter 9). For example, we can claim that there is a statistically significant difference between men's and women's scores on math achievement tests, although $d_2$ is within the trivial effect size range. The difference between most men's and women's math skills is of little practical significance, especially for anything less than the most complex levels of mathematics. Therefore, when you hear that the results of a study are statistically significant, do not automatically assume that the results are of practical or clinical significance unless the researcher has compelling evidence to make such a claim.

### *Omega Squared* $(\hat{\omega}^2)$

The presence of statistical significance does not automatically confer "importance" on a finding. Given a sufficiently large sample size, any difference, however trivial, can be statistically significant. One way to clarify the importance of a statistically significant $t$-ratio is to determine the extent to which variations in the independent variable account for variations in the dependent variable. Apart from effect size indicators such as $d_2$, one of the more popular measures of association is $\hat{\omega}^2$ (**omega**

**squared**). In a study with two groups we can calculate $\hat{\omega}^2$ by

$$\hat{\omega}^2 = \frac{t^2 - 1}{t^2 + n_1 + n_2 - 1} \qquad (11.3)$$

Omega squared is an index of the degree to which the variance in one variable accounts for the variance in another variable. Omega squared can have positive and negative values. Specifically, when the absolute value of $t < 1.00$, $\hat{\omega}^2$ will be negative. For practical purposes, negative values of $\hat{\omega}^2$ have little meaning. Consequently, most researchers calculate $\hat{\omega}^2$ only when the $t$-ratio is statistically significant.

We can apply the equation for $\hat{\omega}^2$ to the sex-differences data. From that example, we know that $t = 2.89$, $n_1 = 15$, and $n_2 = 15$. Therefore,

$$\hat{\omega}^2 = \frac{(2.89)^2 - 1}{(2.89)^2 + 15 + 15 - 1}$$

$$\hat{\omega}^2 = \frac{8.3521 - 1}{8.3521 + 29}$$

$$\hat{\omega}^2 = \frac{7.3521}{37.3521}$$

$$\hat{\omega}^2 = .1968$$

We may interpret $\hat{\omega}^2$ to mean that the independent variable accounts for approximately 20% of the variance in the dependent variable. In some research contexts, accounting for 20% of the variance is a tremendous event and reflects a real advance in the science. In other contexts, 20% is barely worth considering. Consequently, you must use your knowledge of other findings in a specific area and your critical judgment to evaluate the importance of this type of effect size indicator.

It is important for us to note that you cannot judge the magnitude of an effect by merely looking at the value of the $t$-ratio or the smallness of the obtained $p$-value. For example, imagine that you found a $t$-ratio of $-3.17$ with 70 participants in each group. The difference is clearly statistically significant. Under these conditions, the probability for $t = -3.17$ is $p = .00052$. However,

$$\hat{\omega}^2 = \frac{(-3.17)^2 - 1}{(-3.17)^2 + 70 + 70 - 1}$$

$$\hat{\omega}^2 = .061$$

Neither the size of the $t$-ratio nor the size of the $p$-value can indicate the "importance" of the data. The $t$-ratio indicates only whether there is sufficient evidence to reject the null hypothesis. You must use other statistics such as $\hat{\omega}^2$ or $d_2$ to further evaluate the results of the study. Then you must evaluate the findings within a broader context and existing literature before you draw your final conclusions and inferences.

## Reporting the *t*-Ratio

Many researchers in the behavioral sciences use the *Publication Manual of the American Psychological Association* (2009) as the editorial guideline when preparing their manuscripts for publication. The recommended format for reporting the results of the *t*-ratio is

$$t(df) = t_{\text{observed}}, \, p = p, \text{ or as } t(df) = t_{\text{observed}}, \, p < \alpha$$

As an example, in the results section of your research manuscript you could write something like this:

> *Figure 1 presents the average number of positive memories recalled by women and men. An independent groups t-ratio confirmed that the women recalled more positive memories than the men, t(28) = 2.89, p < .05, $\hat{\omega}^2$ = .20.*

# Knowledge Check

1. A researcher conducts a study comparing the behavior of two groups. According to the results, the means of the two groups are $M_1 = 98$ and $M_2 = 107$.
   a. What are potential explanations for the difference between the means?
   b. Can the researcher use the difference between the means to conclude that the independent variable has a statistically significant effect on the dependent variable?
   c. How will changes in the standard error of the difference between means influence our interpretation of the difference between the two means?

2. Using the previous example, could we potentially reject the null hypothesis if it took the form $H_0: \mu_1 \leq \mu_2$? What if the null hypothesis were $H_0: \mu_1 \geq \mu_2$?

3. Why should the researcher state the null and alternative hypotheses before collecting and analyzing the data?

4. What are the factors that will determine your selection of an inferential statistic?

5. A researcher is determining the significance level of a statistical test. According to Rudner, why is this selection a value judgment? What are the consequences of selecting the significance level?

6. A researcher finds that the difference between two groups is statistically significant. Under what conditions can the researcher assume that there is a cause-and-effect relation between the independent and dependent variables?

## Common Errors in the Interpretation of $p$

Many researchers criticize the use of statistical hypothesis testing. Much of the complaint is that some people misuse or misinterpret the results of an inferential statistic. The following is a list of the more common errors. For the most part, the greatest controversy surrounds the interpretation of the established and observed probability levels ($\alpha$ and $p$) associated with inferential statistics.

### Change $\alpha$ after Analyzing the Data

Imagine that a researcher set $\alpha = .05$ before collecting the data. After analyzing the data, the researcher finds that $p = .003$. Should he or she be able to revise $\alpha$ to $\alpha = .005$ to make the data look "more significant"? What if the researcher had set $\alpha = .01$ but the analysis of the data revealed $p = .03$? Can the researcher revise $\alpha$ to $\alpha = .05$ to say that there are statistically significant results? Shine (1980) argued that the answer to both questions is an emphatic *no!* The first problem with this type of revision is that it is unethical. Researchers should set $\alpha$ before analyzing their data and stick with that decision. The reason for this is that changing this probability level after the fact nullifies your ability to lock-in the chance of a Type I error. If you choose to modify this after the fact, you are in effect ignoring the risk of a Type I error and opening yourself up to criticism for fishing through the data looking for whatever might appear to be interesting or significant, even if it was only that way because of chance.

The second reason that you should not change your interpretative standards after beginning an analysis is that the $p$-level is not a substitute for $\alpha$. Although the complete mathematical logic behind this is beyond the scope of this text, you need to understand that $p$ only estimates the probability of obtaining at least the observed results, if the null hypothesis is true. Because we estimate $p$ using sample statistics and because the null hypothesis may be false, we cannot work backward and use our observed $p$ to revise $\alpha$.

### Assume That $p$ Indicates That the Results Are Due to Chance

Carver (1978) calls this error the "odds-against-chance" error. Some researchers interpret $p$ to indicate the probability that the difference between the means is due to chance. For instance, a researcher may find that for a specific $t$-ratio $p = .023$ and conclude that the probability that the results were due to chance is 2.3% or less. This interpretation is incorrect because we begin our statistical test with an $H_0$ that states that any and all observed differences between our study groups are due to chance, and therefore the probability of identifying a difference by chance is 1.00. Because we do not know the real parameters of the populations, we cannot predict the probability that the results are due to chance. The $p$-value merely indicates the probability of obtaining a specific or more extreme difference if $H_0$ was in fact true. In other words, if your results are associated with a $p <$ .05, you can feel confident that the observed difference is not due to chance, because if it were, it would happen only less than 5% of the time.

A related error in the interpretation of the $p$-value is to assume that $p$ establishes the probability that we will commit a Type I error. If you found that $p = .023$, you could not conclude that the probability of committing a Type I error is 2.3%. The value of $\alpha$ determines the probability of a Type I error, a probability that you as the researcher will set. As a rule, you should interpret the $p$-value to mean

> *If $H_0$ is a true statement, the probability of obtaining results like these or more extreme is p. If the value of p is small enough, I am willing to reject $H_0$ in favor of the alternative hypothesis. The probability of committing a Type I error is $\alpha$.*

## Assume the Size of $p$ Indicates the Validity of the Results

Some researchers assume that the $p$-value indicates the probability that the research or alternative hypothesis is true. Again, the probability of the statistic does not allow us to determine the accuracy or truth of the alternative hypothesis. The ability to determine the validity of the research hypothesis is an extremely complicated issue. In general, the $p$-value cannot confirm the validity of the research hypothesis. The only function of the $p$-value is to determine whether there is sufficient evidence to reject $H_0$.

Some researchers infer that a small value of $p$ indicates the degree to which there is a meaningful relation between the independent and dependent variables. For example, if $p = .001$, the researcher may conclude that the independent variable has a large and important effect on the dependent variable, or claim that the data are "highly significant." This inference is not true, and worse, it is misleading to those who read the results of such research. Only effect size estimates such as $\hat{\omega}^2$ appropriately indicate the strength of the relationship between the independent and dependent variables in a study.

## Assume That $p$ Establishes the Probability That the Results Can Be Replicated

Some people assume that $(1 - p)$ indicates the probability that the experiment will yield the same result if repeated. If, for example, $p = 0.23$, a researcher may assume that the probability of replicating the experiment and rejecting $H_0$ is $1 - .023 = 0.977$. This is a false statement because the probability of correctly rejecting $H_0$ is not related to the value of $p$. The ability to replicate a given finding depends on the difference between the means, the number of participants, the amount of measurement error, and the level of $\alpha$. It is possible to have a small level of $p$ (i.e., $p = .001$) and a low probability that the results can be directly replicated.

As an aside, there is some work currently underway to develop a statistic that can tell us our probability of replicating the findings from a given study. This work is only recently being presented in some cutting-edge journals in psychology, but if you are interested you may wish to check out Killeen (2005).

You are probably wondering whether you can draw any meaningful conclusion at all from a statistically significant $t$-ratio. If you obtain a statistically significant $t$-ratio at $p < \alpha$, you may conclude that there is a statistically significant difference between the mean scores on the dependent variable measure that you used in the two groups you are studying. In addition, if your comparison is part of a true experiment designed to test causality, you may also be able to conclude that the independent variable affects the dependent variable. You may also conclude the probability of a Type I error is $\alpha$.

## The Power of a Test

Putting $\alpha$ and Type I errors aside for a minute, you may recall that a Type II error (i.e., a miss) occurs when we fail to reject the null hypothesis and it is false. Researchers want to avoid Type II errors for obvious reasons. We conduct research because we want to discover interesting facts and relationships between and among variables. If our statistical tools overlook these important findings, we will have wasted much time and energy. Therefore, researchers strive to increase the power of their statistical test when they conduct research.

In Chapter 9, we reviewed several tactics that we can use to ensure that the data we collect will allow us to correctly reject the null hypothesis in favor of the alternative hypothesis. In this section we will revisit those design tactics and show how they can increase the statistical power of an analysis.

For any statistical test, $\beta$ defines the probability of making a Type II error. The **power of a statistic**, which we represent as $1 - \beta$, is the probability of correctly rejecting a false null hypothesis. The four factors that influence statistical power are: (1) difference between the populations means, $\mu_1 - \mu_2$; (2) sample size, $n$; (3) variability in the population, $\sigma^2$; and (4) alpha ($\alpha$) level and directionality (directional versus nondirectional) of the test.

### Difference between Population Means ($\mu_1 - \mu_2$)

If the null hypothesis is false, there will be two sampling distributions similar to the ones presented in Figure 11.4(a). Each sampling distribution represents sample means drawn from separate populations. The sampling distribution for the null hypothesis is a distribution of sample means for which $\mu_1 - \mu_2 = 0$. The shaded area at the upper end of the scale represents the critical region for $\alpha = .05$ using a directional test. According to the null hypothesis, there is a 5 % probability that the difference between any pair of means will be in the critical area. The second distribution is a sampling

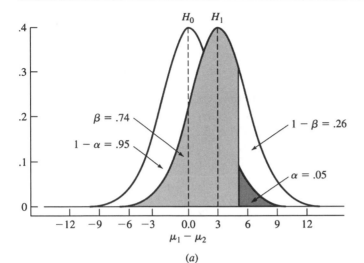

# Figure 11.4

**The Effect on Statistical Power of $\mu_1 - \mu_2$**

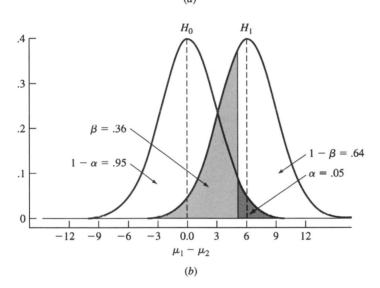

In the upper figure, the difference is 3.0. The difference in the lower figure is 6.0. For both pairs of distributions, the shaded areas represent the probabilities of committing a Type I error ($\alpha$) and a Type II error ($\beta$). The power of the statistic is $1 - \beta$. The lower figure represents greater power.

distribution of means that would occur if we draw samples of a specific size from two populations for which $\mu_1 - \mu_2 = 3$.

As you can see, the two distributions overlap, but not perfectly. What do the different areas represent? The area shaded in light gray represents $\beta$, the probability of a Type II error. Although the two population means are different, it is possible to select sample means whose differences will be less than the critical region. Those samples will not be sufficiently different to allow us to reject the null hypothesis. In this example, 74% ($\beta = .74$) of the curve is in the lightly shaded area. Thus, the probability of committing a

Type II error is 74%, whereas the probability of rejecting the null hypothesis is 26% $(1 - \beta = .26)$. Therefore, the power of this statistic is 26%. Although the population means are different from each other, the chance that we will be able to discover this difference using sample statistics is only slightly better than 1 in 4.

Figure 11.4(b) presents a different set of conditions. Now the difference between the population means is much greater $(\mu_1 - \mu_2 = 6.0)$. Notice the differences between Figure 11.4(a) and 11.4(b). There is less overlap of the two curves. Because there is less overlap, the area representing $\beta$ is smaller. Specifically, the probability of a Type II error is now 36%, whereas the probability of correctly rejecting the null hypothesis is 64%. The conclusion to draw from this example is that power increases as the difference between the two population means increases.

Intuitively this should make sense—a larger, more noticeable difference between groups should be more easily identified than a smaller difference. In Chapter 9, we reviewed tactics for increasing the differences between two study populations. The most direct method is to select levels of the independent variable that create the greatest possible difference in the dependent variable measures between the two groups. All else being equal, making the two populations as different as possible from each other will increase the statistical power of the study. There are other ways that we can increase power that we will consider next.

### Sample Size

Sample size is an important consideration because it influences how well a sample statistic will estimate the corresponding population parameter and the power of a statistical test. As sample size increases, the standard error of the mean decreases. Figure 11.5(a) presents the sampling distributions that would occur if one selected samples from two populations using small samples. Figure 11.5(b) shows the two distributions obtained when we use a larger sample size. The Central Limit Theorem explains the difference in the shape of the two sampling distributions.

As a rule, as sample size increases the standard error of the mean decreases. Consequently, the degree of overlap of the two sampling distributions decreases and the corresponding power increases. Again, intuitively this should make sense, because as the degree of potential overlap between two groups decreases, any real difference between those two groups should be more noticeable and easily identified. Although it is true that increasing sample size will increase your power to detect an effect if it is present, you also need to be aware of the costs associated with this design strategy.

Although increasing the sample size sounds easy (you just need to collect more data), the downside is that collecting data takes time and money. From the cost of purchasing materials to the time you must take out of your schedule, collecting data from each subject adds to the total cost of the research. In some cases, such as administering a set of questionnaires to

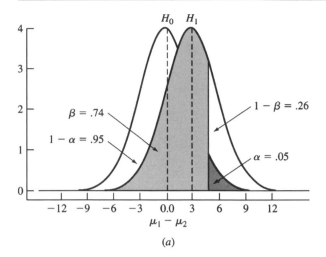

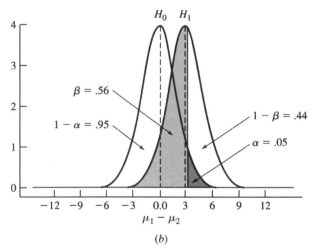

## Figure 11.5

**The Effect on Statistical Power Resulting from Changes in Sample Size or Changes in Population Variance**

For both distributions, the shaded areas represent the probability of committing a Type I error ($\alpha$) and a Type II error ($\beta$). The power of the statistics is $1 - \beta$. The lower graph represents the greater statistical power.

students in their classes, there will be a minimal cost for collecting more data. In other cases (e.g., face-to-face interviews), collecting the data from one subject will be time consuming and expensive. Therefore, you should consider all your options for increasing power before you jump to the conclusion that you need to run more participants through your study.

### Variability

If the population from which you draw the sample has considerable variability in general, the sampling distribution associated with your outcome or dependent variable scores will also have considerable variance.

We can use Figure 11.5 again to represent the effects of population variance on statistical power. The distributions in Figure 11.5(a) represent what would occur when the variance in the population is large. Consequently, there is considerable overlap of the two distributions and the power is small. Reducing the amount of variability in the population will produce a result similar to the one depicted in Figure 11.5(b).

Because the magnitude of $\sigma$ (the population standard deviation) decreased, the overlap depicted in Figure 11.5(b) decreased and the statistical power increased. The main takeaway point from all of this is that anything you can do to reduce sampling error will improve your ability to detect a statistically significant difference between the means.

Apart from making it easier to detect differences between groups, as you may recall from Chapter 9, there are also several ways that we can decrease the variability of scores within groups. For example, we can use homogeneous samples. If the participants in the individual groups are similar to each other, it is easier to detect differences among the group means. Similarly, as we use more reliable and accurate measurement techniques, the variability within the groups will tend to decrease. This in turn will help to minimize the spread of the data within each group, having the same effect that we described in the previous paragraph.

### Alpha ($\alpha$)

Alpha ($\alpha$) sets the probability of a Type I error. The smaller the $\alpha$, the lower the probability of a Type I error. Unfortunately, lowering the $\alpha$-level will decrease the power of the statistical test. As the probability of the Type I error decreases, the probability of the Type II error increases. Look at Figure 11.6 for an illustration.

Figure 11.6(a) has $\alpha = .05$; Figure 11.6(b) has $\alpha = .10$. All other aspects of the graphs are identical. Note the differences between the statistical powers for the two conditions. When $\alpha = .10$, the power is $1 - \beta = .39$. Lowering the $\alpha$ to .05 decreases the power to $1 - \beta = .26$. All things being equal, the probability of a Type I error increases as $\alpha$ decreases. Another way to say the same thing is that as $\alpha$ increases, power also increases. Think about this conceptually and it may make more sense—if you make it more difficult to identify an effect as statistically significant (linked to how low you set your $\alpha$-level), then you will also make it harder to detect an effect when it is really there (i.e., you will reduce your statistical power). The obverse also holds true.

Your selection of a directional and nondirectional test based on your hypotheses will also influence statistical power. In general, a directional test is more powerful than a nondirectional test. The difference lies with where we place the critical region for rejection. Consider a $t$-ratio with $df = 15$ and $\alpha = .05$. When we use the directional test, we place the critical region at one end of the distribution. In this example, $t_{critical}$ for the directional test is 1.753. When we conduct a nondirectional test, we split the critical regions between the two extreme ends. Consequently, the $t$-ratio required to reject

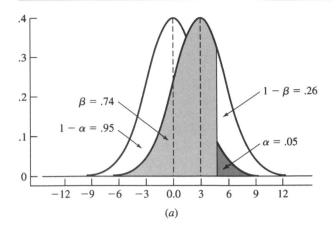

# Figure 11.6

**The Effect on Statistical Power Caused by Changes in α**

$\beta = .74$

$1 - \beta = .26$

$1 - \alpha = .95$

$\alpha = .05$

(a)

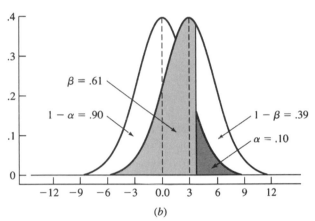

$\beta = .61$

$1 - \alpha = .90$

$1 - \beta = .39$

$\alpha = .10$

(b)

For both graphs, the difference between the means is 3.0. For the distributions in (a), $\alpha = .05$. For the distributions in (b), $\alpha$ is larger ($\alpha = .10$) and the power is greater. For both graphs, the probability of committing a Type I error ($\alpha$) and a Type II error ($\beta$) are represented by shaded areas. The power of the statistic is $1 - \beta$.

the null is larger than it would be for a comparable directional test. For the nondirectional test where $df = 15$, $t_{critical} = 2.131$.

## Estimating Sample Size

You know that sample size can be an important factor in ensuring sufficient statistical power, but you also know that going after too many participants might leave you broke and exhausted. How many participants should you include in your sample? We can use effect size estimates such as $d_2$ to estimate the number of participants we will need for a two-group study such as those examined in this chapter.

Look at Tables B.5.1 and B.5.2 of Appendix B, which provide power estimates for two sample $t$-ratios. Along the leftmost column are sample sizes ($n$), the number of participants in each group. The columns represent values of $t_{critical}$, the critical $t$-ratio needed to reject the null hypothesis, and four levels of effect size, $d_2$. There are two versions of the table, one for directional tests and the other for nondirectional tests. To use the table, select an effect size that you believe represents your research. Then determine the sample size you will need for a specific level of power. Some researchers believe that a statistical power of $1 - \beta = .80$ is an adequate level for most research. Others may want their power to be higher or lower depending on the importance of avoiding a Type II error and identifying an effect, along with the potential implications of making a Type I error.

Here is an example. You want to replicate the sex differences for the emotional memories study that we discussed earlier at your own college or university. How many participants will you need to replicate the effect? What would happen if you used a directional versus a nondirectional test to compare the differences?

For this example, assume that $\alpha = .05$, two-tailed, and that the effect size for this phenomenon is medium, $d_2 \approx .50$. According to Table B.5.2, you will need approximately 60 participants in each group to have your power set at $1 - \beta = .79$ for a nondirectional test. If you used a directional test, you would require approximately 50 participants in each group to have the power of approximately $1 - \beta = .82$. What would happen if you decided to collect data from 100 students and used a directional test? In that case, $1 - \beta = .98$. The larger sample size means that you will have a 98% chance of rejecting the null hypothesis if the null hypothesis is false.

## Caveat Emptor: Sample Size

Please remember that increasing sample size should not be the only thing you do to increase the power of a statistical test. The decision to increase sample size should come only after you have examined the design of your research. As you learned in Chapter 9 and again here, you can increase power by increasing the reliability of the tests you use to measure the dependent variable, ensuring homogeneity of variance among the participants and increasing the difference between the two groups.

## Knowledge Check

7. Assume that a researcher conducted a two-group study and found that $t(18) = 2.7$, $p < .01$. Determine whether the following statements are correct or incorrect and defend your answer.
    a.  The researcher has disproved the null hypothesis, $H_0$: $\mu_1 = \mu_2$.
    b.  The researcher has determined the probability that $H_0$ is true.
    c.  The researcher has proved the research hypothesis is correct.
    d.  The researcher can determine the probability that $H_1$ is correct.

e.  The researcher can be confident that there is an extremely high probability that he or she could replicate the findings by conducting the same experiment.

f.  The probability of the data given the null hypothesis is $p < .01$.

8. Mark and Mary each conducted an experiment studying the relation between the same independent and dependent variables. Mark used 20 participants in each group and found a statistically significant effect using $p = .045$. Mary used 100 participants in each group and found a statistically significant effect using $p = .045$.

   a.  Of the two experiments, which appears to have the greater power?

   b.  How would you account for the differences in power between the two experiments?

9. Khalil wants to conduct an experiment and believes that the effect size for the variables selected is small, $d_2 \approx .20$. How many participants should he place into each group to have statistical power of .80 for a two-sample $t$-ratio with $\alpha = .05$—two-tailed? What would be the required sample size if Khalil used $\alpha = .05$—one-tailed?

10. Khalil wants to find ways to improve the power of his study. What factors, other than increasing the number of participants in each group, should he consider in the design of his experiment that could increase power?

## Research in Action: Word Meaning and Memory

A psychology major decided to study the effect of word meaning on long-term memory. The student believed that people are more likely to recall related rather than random words. In addition, the student expected participants in the related word condition to recall words that were not in the original list. Finally, the student expected that participants would recite the list of related words faster than the participants who had memorized the unrelated words. The student decided to treat all tests as nondirectional.

To conduct the research, the student created two lists of 20 words each. The related-word list consisted of names of common plants (e.g., corn, oak, rose, etc.). The second list consisted of randomly selected words of relatively the same length and familiarity as the words in the related-word list (e.g., book, arm, pipe, etc.). The student then randomly assigned 24 participants to either the related-word or random-word condition. The researcher told all the participants that they were participating in a study of memory, and that they would recite the list 72 hours later. Each participant then had five minutes to memorize the words in their list.

When the participants returned for the test, the researcher asked them to speak into a microphone. Later, another student, who did not know the hypotheses, scored the tape recording. The variables measured were (1) the

## Table 11.1  Data for Free Recall of Related and Random Words

| | Number of words correctly recalled | | Number of new words accidentally recalled | | Seconds to complete list | |
|---|---|---|---|---|---|---|
| | Related | Random | Related | Random | Related | Random |
| $\sum X$ | 185 | 143 | 20 | 9 | 163.6 | 199.9 |
| $\sum X^2$ | 2963 | 1787 | 40 | 13 | 2289.6 | 3519.2 |
| $n$ | 12 | 12 | 12 | 12 | 12 | 12 |
| $M$ | 15.42 | 11.92 | 1.67 | 0.75 | 13.63 | 16.66 |
| $VAR$ | 10.0833 | 7.5379 | 0.6061 | 0.5682 | 5.3824 | 17.1990 |
| $SD$ | 3.1754 | 2.7455 | 0.7785 | 0.7538 | 2.3200 | 4.1472 |

number of words correctly recalled, (2) the number of words recalled that were not in the original list, and (3) the time it took the participant to complete the recitation. Table 11.1 presents the data for the experiment.

We can begin by preparing the null and alternative hypotheses for each test, as is presented in Box 11.2. The student decided to use a nondirectional hypothesis for each hypothesis and to set $\alpha = .05$.

---

### Box 11.2 Statistical Test for Word Meaning and Memory Study

*Null Hypothesis:*
For each dependent variable:

$H_0$: $\mu_1 = \mu_2$ — The performance of the related words group ($\mu_1$) will be equal to the performance for the random words list ($\mu_2$)

*Alternative Hypothesis:*
For each dependent variable:

$H_0$: $\mu_1 = \mu_2$ — The performance of the related words group ($\mu_1$) will not be equal to the performance for the random words list ($\mu_2$)

*Statistical Test:*
For each dependent variable:

We will use the t-ratio because we estimate $\sigma_{M_1 - M_2}$

*Significance Level:*
All tests:

$\alpha = .05$, two-tailed

*Sampling Distribution:*
The $t$-distribution with $df = (12 - 1) + (12 - 1) = 22$. $t_{\text{critical}}$ (22) = 2.179

*Critical Region for Rejecting $H_0$ :*
$t$-tests:

$|t_{\text{observed}}| \geq |2.179|$ If $t_{\text{observed}}$ is less than $-2.179$ or greater than $2.179$ we can reject $H_0$.

---

Table 11.2 lists the results of each statistical test.

With the calculations out of the way, the student can now prepare the results section of the manuscript. Figure 11.7 is an example of what the student could write for the results section.

# Table 11.2   Statistical Analysis for the Data Presented in Table 11.1

## Number of words correctly recalled

$$t = \frac{15.42 - 11.92}{\sqrt{\frac{\left[2963 - \frac{(185)^2}{12}\right] + \left[1787 - \frac{(143)^2}{12}\right]}{12 + 12 - 2}\left(\frac{1}{12} + \frac{1}{12}\right)}}$$

$$df = (12 - 1) + (12 - 1)$$
$$|t_{\text{ observed}}| > |t_{\text{ critical}}|$$
$$|2.88| > |2.179|$$

$t = 2.88 \quad df = 22 \quad$ **Reject** $H_0$

$$\hat{\omega}^2 = \frac{2.88^2 - 1}{2.88^2 + 12 + 12 - 1} \qquad \hat{\omega}^2 = .24$$

## Number of new words accidentally recalled

$$t = \frac{1.67 - 0.75}{\sqrt{\frac{\left[40 - \frac{(20)^2}{12}\right] + \left[13 - \frac{(9)^2}{12}\right]}{12 + 12 - 2}\left(\frac{1}{12} + \frac{1}{12}\right)}}$$

$$df = (12 - 1) + (12 - 1)$$
$$|t_{\text{ observed}}| > |t_{\text{ critical}}|$$
$$|2.94| > |2.179|$$

$t = 2.94 \quad df = 22 \quad$ **Reject** $H_0$

$$\hat{\omega}^2 = \frac{2.94^2 - 1}{2.94^2 + 12 + 12 - 1} \qquad \hat{\omega}^2 = .24$$

## Time to complete list

$$t = \frac{13.63 - 16.66}{\sqrt{\frac{\left[2289.6 - \frac{(163.6)^2}{12}\right] + \left[3519.2 - \frac{(199.9)^2}{12}\right]}{12 + 12 - 2}\left(\frac{1}{12} + \frac{1}{12}\right)}}$$

$$|t_{\text{ observed}}| > |t_{\text{ critical}}|$$
$$|-2.21| > |2.179|$$

$t = -2.21 \quad df = 22 \quad$ **Reject** $H_0$

$$\hat{\omega}^2 = \frac{2.21^2 - 1}{2.21^2 + 12 + 12 - 1} \qquad \hat{\omega}^2 = .14$$

## Statistics behind the Research

In this section we will review in more depth several statistical tests that allow us to compare the differences in dependent variable scores or measures between two independent groups. The phrase *independent groups* means that there is no specific correlation between the two groups. One way to ensure the independence of the groups is to randomly assign the participants to the two research conditions, as is done in a true experiment. We can also assume independence of the groups if we use an intact-groups design and ensure that our selection of participants for one group has no influence on the selection of participants in the other group.

     The three tests that we will examine are Student's *t*-ratio for independent groups, the Welch *t*-ratio, and the Mann-Whitney *U*-test. The Student's *t*-ratio is an inferential statistic that allows us to determine whether the difference between two sample means is statistically significant.

## Figure 11.7  Example of the Results Section and a Table of Data

Word Meaning 7

Results

Table 1 presents the means and standard deviations for the three dependent measures. Participants in the Related-Words group recalled more words than participants in the Random-Words group, $t$ (22) = 2.88, $p < 0.05$, $\omega^2 = .23$. In addition, participants in the Related-Words group recalled more words that were not part of the original list, $t$ (22) = 2.94, $p < .05$, $\omega^2 = .24$. Finally, the difference in the time required to recite the list was also statistically significant, $t$ (22) = 2.21, $p < .05$, $\omega^2 = .14$.

Word Meaning 15

Table 1

*Means and Standard Deviations for Number of Words Correctly Recalled, Number of New Words Correctly Recalled, Number of New Words Recalled, and Time to Recite List*

|  | Related Word List | Random |
|---|---|---|
| **Number of Words Correctly Recalled** | | |
| *M* | 15.42 | 11.92 |
| *SD* | 3.18 | 0.75 |
| **Number of New Words Accidentally Recalled** | | |
| *M* | 1.67 | 0.75 |
| *SD* | 0.78 | 0.75 |
| **Time to Complete List, in Seconds** | | |
| *M* | 13.63 | 16.66 |
| *SD* | 2.32 | 4.15 |

In an actual manuscript, all of the text would be double spaced.

Researchers use the test when the dependent variable represents an interval or ratio scale of measurement. The other tests are alternatives that we use when the data do not meet the mathematical assumptions of the statistic.

### Student's $t$-Ratio for Independent Groups

The complete equation for Student's $t$-ratio is

$$t = \frac{M_1 - M_2}{\sqrt{\frac{\sum X_1^2 - \frac{(\sum X_1)^2}{n_1} + \sum X_2^2 - \frac{(\sum X_2)^2}{n_2}}{n_1 + n_2 - 2} \left( \frac{1}{n_1} + \frac{1}{n_2} \right)}} \tag{11.4}$$

The degrees of freedom are calculated as

$$df = (n_1 - 1) + (n_2 - 1) \tag{11.5}$$

### Assumptions of the Test

For the test to work properly, the data must meet several assumptions. The assumptions are independence of groups, normal distribution of the data, and homogeneity of variance.

**Independence of groups.** The first assumption is that the groups are independent of each other. Chapter 14 reviews procedures for analyzing the data when this assumption is not met and there is a correlation between the groups.

**Normal distribution of the data.** A second assumption is that the data are normally distributed. The Mann-Whitney $U$-test is an alternative to the $t$-ratio that researchers can use when the data are not normally distributed. Other types of statistical corrections may also be appropriate. Related to this assumption is that the data represent interval or ratio data. If the dependent variable represents a count or ordinal scale, the Mann-Whitney $U$-test is often the preferred alternative test.

**Homogeneity of variance.** The third assumption refers to homogeneity of variance ($\sigma_1^2 = \sigma_2^2$). As a generality, if the larger variance is 3.0 times greater than the smaller variance, then we should not assume homogeneity of variance, and we should use the Welch $t$-test or the Mann-Whitney $U$-test as an alternative. Other corrections are also available.

### Forming the Hypothesis

The purpose of the t-ratio is to determine whether there is a meaningful difference between the two group means. To conduct the statistical test, you may select either a directional or a nondirectional test.

| Nondirectional or two-tailed test | Directional or one-tailed test |
|---|---|
| $H_0 : \mu_1 = \mu_2$ <br> $H_1 : \mu_1 \neq \mu_2$ | $H_0 : \mu_1 \geq \mu_2$  or  $H_0 : \mu_1 \leq \mu_2$ <br> $H_1 : \mu_1 < \mu_2$  or  $H_1 : \mu_1 > \mu_2$ |

### Sampling Distribution

To determine $t_{critical}$, establish the level of $\alpha$ and type of hypothesis, and calculate the degrees of freedom. Use Table B.3 in Appendix B to find the degrees of freedom (rows) and appropriate $\alpha$ level (columns). For an example, refer to the following chart.

| Nondirectional or two-tailed test | Directional or one-tailed test |
|---|---|
| $\alpha = .05, \quad df = 15$ <br> $H_0 : \mu_1 = \mu_2$ <br> $t_{critical} = 2.131$ | $\alpha = .05, \quad df = 15$ <br> $H_0 : \mu_1 \geq \mu_2 \quad H_0 : \mu_1 \leq \mu_2$ <br> $t_{critical} = -1.753 \quad t_{critical} = 1.753$ |

If you use a directional hypothesis, then you must convert the sign of $t_{critical}$ to conform to the test.

---

### Example

A student decided to repeat the Seidlitz and Diener (1998) study that examined the difference between men's and women's recall of emotional events. The student asked randomly selected men and women to describe in two or three words positive or happy events that occurred in their lives. Another student, who did not know whether the author of the comments was male or female, counted the number of episodes recalled. Table 11.3 presents the data.

*(Continued)*

*(Continued)*

## Table 11.3   Hypothetical Data for a Replication of the Seidlitz and Diener (1998) Study

| 1 Males | | 2 Females | |
|---|---|---|---|
| 6 | 7 | 8 | 11 |
| 12 | 10 | 10 | 11 |
| 9 | 10 | 12 | 12 |
| 10 | 9 | 9 | 12 |
| 8 | 8 | 10 | 14 |

| | | |
|---|---|---|
| $n_1 = 10$ | $n_2 = 10$ | $df = (10-1) + (10-1) = 18$ |
| $\sum X_1 = 89$ | $\sum X_2 = 109$ | $df = 18$ |
| $\sum X_1^2 = 819$ | $\sum X_2^2 = 1215$ | $t_{critical} = 1.734$ |
| $M_1 = 8.9$ | $M_2 = 10.9$ | |
| $SD_1 = 1.7288$ | $SD_2 = 1.7288$ | |

The student decided to test the hypothesis that women will recall more positive events than men (as Seidlitz & Diener, 1998, had found) and decided to set $\alpha = .05$. Accordingly, $H_0$: $\mu_W \leq \mu_M$ and $H_1$: $\mu_W > \mu_M$. Using Table B.3 of Appendix B, we find that $t_{critical} = 1.734$. The value of $t_{critical}$ is positive because the researcher wants to show specifically that $\mu_W > \mu_M$.

$$t = \frac{10.9 - 8.9}{\sqrt{\frac{819 - \frac{(89)^2}{10} + 1215 - \frac{(109)^2}{10}}{10 + 10 - 2} \left(\frac{1}{10} + \frac{1}{10}\right)}}$$

$$t = \frac{2.0}{\sqrt{\frac{26.90 + 26.90}{18}(.2)}}$$

$$t = \frac{2.0}{.7732}$$

$$t = 2.5867$$

Because $t_{observed}$ exceeds $t_{critical}$, we can reject the null hypothesis and conclude that there is a statistically significant difference between men's and women's recall of positive emotional events and that women recall more such events than do men.

### Additional Tests

**Confidence interval of the difference between means (SED).** This statistic allows you to estimate the confidence interval for potential mean differences given sample statistics:

$$SED = \sqrt{\frac{\sum X_1^2 - \frac{(\sum X_1)^2}{n_1} + \sum X_2^2 - \frac{(\sum X_2)^2}{n_2}}{n_1 + n_2 - 2}} \qquad (11.6)$$

$$CI = (M_1 - M_2) \pm t_{critical}(SED) \qquad (11.7)$$

For this equation, $t_{critical}$ represents the value for the two-tailed or non-directional test using the degrees of freedom, $df = (n_1 - 1) + (n_2 - 1)$. In this example, $df = 18$ and $t_{critical} = 2.101$. Using the data from the previous example,

$$SED = 0.7732$$

$$CI = 2.0 \pm 2.101\,(0.7732)$$

$$CI = 2.0 \pm 1.6245$$

95% confidence interval: 0.3765 to 2.0 to 3.6245

The confidence interval allows us to conclude that if we repeated the study under identical conditions, there is a 95% probability that the difference between additional sample means will fall between 0.3765 and 3.64. In other words, there is compelling evidence that there is a difference between the two group means. The span of the confidence interval also gives us some indication of the precision of our estimate.

**Omega squared ($\hat{\omega}^2$)**   This statistic is a measure of association that estimates the degree to which the independent variable shares common variance with the dependent variable. The larger the value of $\hat{\omega}^2$, the greater the relation between the variables.

$$\hat{\omega}^2 = \frac{t^2 - 1}{t^2 + n_1 + n_2 - 1}$$

$$\hat{\omega}^2 = \frac{-2.5867^2 - 1}{-2.5867^2 + 10 + 10 - 1}$$

$$\hat{\omega}^2 = \frac{5.6910}{25.6910}$$

$$\hat{\omega}^2 = 0.2215$$

For this example, we can conclude that the independent variable accounts for approximately 22% of the variance in the dependent variable.

**Effect size ($d_2$)**   Effect size is an index of the relative difference between the means. The index is similar to a $z$-score in that statistics converts the difference between the means into standard deviation units. The equation for $d_2$ is presented as Equation 11.8. Box 11.3 presents Cohen's (1988) guide for evaluating effect sizes. Use this equation only when the

### Box 11.3 Cohen's (1988) Guidelines for Evaluating Effect Sizes

| | | |
|---|---|---|
| Small effect size | $d_2 = .20$ | Generally these differences are small and difficult to detect without large sample sizes. Some researchers believe that when $d_2 \leq 0.10$, the effect is trivial. |
| Medium effect size | $d_2 = .50$ | A medium effect is sufficiently large to be seen by the naked eye when graphed. |
| Large effect size | $d_2 = .80$ | A large effect size is easily seen and requires few subjects to detect the effect. |

sample sizes of your two groups are equal (when $n_1 = n_2$). Do not use this equation when $n_1 \neq n_2$

$$d_2 = \frac{|\mu_1 - \mu_2|}{\sigma}, \sigma = \frac{SD_1 + SD_2}{2}$$

$$d_2 = \frac{|8.9 - 10.9|}{1.7288}$$

$$d_2 = \frac{2.0}{1.7288}$$ 

$$d_2 = 1.1218$$

(11.8)

### Welch t-Ratio for Independent Groups

This inferential statistic allows us to determine whether the difference between two sample means is statistically significant. Use this test when there are large differences between the variances of two groups. As a generality, when $SD^2_{larger}/SD^2_{smaller} > 3.00$, the Welch $t$-ratio is a more accurate test. Although Student's $t$-ratio is generally robust against violations of the homogeneity of variance requirement, the test will produce spurious results when the difference between the variances is large and when the sample sizes are unequal:

$$\hat{t} = \frac{M_1 - M_2}{\sqrt{\left[\frac{1}{n_1}\left(\frac{\sum X_1^2 - \left[(\sum X_1)^2/n_1\right]}{n_1 - 1}\right)\right] + \left[\frac{1}{n_2}\left(\frac{\sum X_2^2 - \left[(\sum X_2)^2/n_2\right]}{n_2-1}\right)\right]}}$$

(11.9)

$$df' = \frac{\left[\frac{1}{n_1}\left(\frac{\sum X_1^2 - \left[(\sum X_1)^2/n_1\right]}{n_1 - 1}\right) + \frac{1}{n_2}\left(\frac{\sum X_2^2 - \left[(\sum X_2)^2/n_2\right]}{n_2 - 1}\right)\right]^2}{\frac{\frac{1}{n_1}\left(\frac{\sum X_1^2 - \left[(\sum X_1)^2/n_1\right]}{n_1 - 1}\right)^2}{n_1-1} + \frac{\frac{1}{n_2}\left(\frac{\sum X_2^2 - \left[(\sum X_2)^2/n_2\right]}{n_2-1}\right)^2}{n_2-1}}$$

(11.10)

## Table 11.4 Hypothetical Data Representing Independent Groups with Unequal Variance and Sample Sizes

| A | | B | |
|---|---|---|---|
| 3 | 2 | 1 | 6 |
| 2 | 3 | 3 | |
| 2 | 2 | 3 | |
| 1 | 1 | 3 | |
| 2 | 2 | 3 | |

| | | |
|---|---|---|
| $n_1 = 10$ | $n_2 = 6$ | Note lack of homogeneity of variance: |
| $\sum X_1 = 20$ | $\sum X_2 = 19$ | $2.5667/0.4445 = \mathbf{5.77}$ |
| $\sum X_1^2 = 44$ | $\sum X_2^2 = 73$ | |
| $M_1 = 2.0$ | $M_2 = 3.1667$ | |
| $VAR_1 = 0.4445$ | $VAR_2 = 2.5667$ | |
| $SD_1 = 0.6667$ | $SD_2 = 1.6021$ | |

### Sampling Distribution

To determine $t_{critical}$, establish the level of $\alpha$ and type of hypothesis, and calculate the degrees of freedom. Use Table B.3 in Appendix B to find the degrees of freedom (rows) and appropriate $\alpha$ level (columns). For example, if $\alpha = .05$, one-tailed, and $df = 15$, $t_{critical} = 1.753$. If you use a directional hypothesis, then you must convert the sign of $t_{critical}$ to conform to the test. Table 11.4 presents data for which the sample sizes and the variances of the two groups are not equal.

### Additional Test

**Confidence interval of the difference between means (SED)**    This statistic allows you to estimate the confidence interval for potential mean differences given sample statistics:

$$SED = \sqrt{\left[\frac{1}{n_1}\left(\frac{\sum X_1^2 \left[(\sum X_1)^2/n_1\right]}{n_1 - 1}\right)\right] + \left[\frac{1}{n_2}\left(\frac{\sum X_2^2 \left[(\sum X_2)^2/n_2\right]}{n_2 - 1}\right)\right]}$$

(11.11)

For the previous example, $SED = 0.6872$; $CI = (M_1 - M_2) \pm t_{critical}$ $(SED)$; $df =$ as calculated previously. For this example, $df = 6$.

$$CI = -1.1667 \pm 2.447(0.6872)$$

$$CI = -1.1667 \pm 1.6802$$

95% confidence interval $-2.8469$ to $-1.1667$ to $0.5135$

## Example

$$\hat{t} = \frac{2.00 - 3.167}{\sqrt{\left[\frac{1}{10}\left(\frac{44 - [(20)^2/10]}{10 - 1}\right)\right] + \left[\frac{1}{6}\left(\frac{73 - [(19)^2/6]}{6 - 1}\right)\right]}}}$$

$$df' = \frac{\left[\frac{1}{10}\left(\frac{44 - [(20)^2/10]}{10 - 1}\right) + \frac{1}{6}\left(\frac{73 - [(19)^2/6]}{6 - 1}\right)\right]^2}{\frac{\frac{1}{10}\left(\frac{44 - [(20)^2/10]}{10 - 1}\right)^2}{10 - 1} + \frac{1}{6}\frac{\left(\frac{\sum X_2^2 - \left[(\sum X_2)^2/n_2\right]}{6 - 1}\right)^2}{6 - 1}}$$

$$\hat{t} = \frac{2.00 - 3.167}{\sqrt{\left[\frac{1}{10}\left(\frac{4.00}{10 - 1}\right)\right] + \left[\frac{1}{6}\left(\frac{12.833}{6 - 1}\right)\right]}}}$$

$$df' = \frac{\left[\frac{1}{10}\left(\frac{4.00}{10 - 1}\right) + \frac{1}{6}\left(\frac{12.833}{6 - 1}\right)\right]^2}{\frac{\frac{1}{10}\left(\frac{4.00}{10 - 1}\right)^2}{10 - 1} + \frac{\frac{1}{6}\left(\frac{12.833}{6 - 1}\right)}{6 - 1}}$$

$$\hat{t} = \frac{-1.167}{\sqrt{(0.0444) + (0.4278)}}$$

$$df' = \frac{(0.0444 + 0.4278)^2}{\frac{(0.0444)^2}{9} + \frac{(0.4278)^2}{5}}$$

$$\hat{t} = \frac{-1.167}{0.6872}$$

$$df' = \frac{0.22297}{.0368}$$

$$\hat{t} = -1.698$$

$$df' = 6.059$$

$$df' = 6$$

According to the calculations, the adjusted degrees of freedom = 6. Using $\alpha = .05$ for a two-tailed test $t_{critical} = \pm 2.447$. Because $t_{observed}$ is less than $t_{critical}$, we do not reject $H_0$.

### Mann-Whitney U-Test

The Mann-Whitney $U$-test is another alternative to the Student's $t$-ratio for comparing two groups. Many researchers prefer to use the $U$-test when the data do not fit the assumptions of the $t$-ratio.

### Hypotheses

**Null hypothesis.** $H_0: U = U'$: The differences between the groups' ranks are due to chance.

**Alternative hypothesis.** $H_1: U \neq U'$: The differences between the groups' ranks are not random.

**Sampling distribution.** Table B.15 of Appendix B presents the critical regions for rejecting the null hypothesis. To use the table, find the

## Table 11.5 Hypothetical Example of the Use of the Mann-Whitney $U$-Test

| Experimental | | Control | |
|---|---|---|---|
| Rating | Rank | Rating | Rank |
| 66 | 1 | 72 | 5 |
| 68 | 2 | 80 | 11 |
| 81 | 12 | 69 | 3 |
| 70 | 4 | 82 | 13 |
| 73 | 6 | 83 | 14 |
| 84 | 15 | 74 | 7 |
| 76 | 8 | 85 | 16 |
| 86 | 17 | 77 | 9 |
| 78 | 10 | 91 | 19 |
| 89 | 18 | 93 | 20 |
| | $R_1 = 93$ | | $R_2 = 117$ |
| | $N_1 = 10$ | | $N_2 = 10$ |

## Example

A student conducted an experiment to examine the effectiveness of listening to classical music on creativity. To conduct the study, the student randomly assigned participants to either an experimental group or a control group. The participants in the experimental group listened to 10 minutes of Beethoven's Ninth Symphony; participants in the control group sat in quiet for 10 minutes. After the 10 minutes, all participants wrote a short story describing the first meeting of two people who will later become lovers. Two readers, who did not know the participants' treatment condition, rated the creativity of the story on a 100-point scale. Table 11.5 presents the average of the scores for each participant.

$$U = 10(10) + \frac{10(10 + 1)}{2} - 93$$

$$U = 100 + \frac{110}{2} - 93$$

$$U = 100 + 55 - 93$$

$$U = 62$$

$$U' = 10(10) + \frac{10(10 + 1)}{2} - 117$$

$$U' = 100 + \frac{110}{2} - 117$$

$$U' = 100 + 55 - 117$$

$$U' = 38$$

In this example, the values of $U$ and $U'$ are well within the critical region of 23–77; therefore we fail to reject the null hypothesis.

numbers that correspond to the sample sizes of the two groups. For example, if $N_1 = 10$ and $N_2 = 10$, and $\alpha = .05$ for a nondirectional test, then the critical range is: 23–77. If the values of $U$ and $U'$ are within the critical range, do not reject the null hypotheses. When both values are outside the critical range, reject the null hypothesis.

$$U = N_1 N_2 + \frac{N_1(N_1 + 1)}{2} - R_1 U' = N_1 N_2 + \frac{N_2(N_2 + 1)}{2} + R_2 \quad (11.12)$$

For these equations, $N$ represents the sample sizes and $R$ represents the sum of ranks for each group. To calculate $R$ for each group, rank all the data from lowest to highest. Assign the ranks and then return the observed scores and their ranks to the original groups.

## Chapter Summary

In this chapter we examined the foundation of statistical inference using two independent groups and Student's $t$-ratio. Specifically, we examined how we compare the difference between the means to the standard error of the difference between means. As you learned, the standard error of the difference between means is an estimate of the sampling error present in the data. Therefore, if the relative difference between the sample means is sufficiently large, we can assume that the difference is in excess of sampling error and represents a meaningful difference between the population means.

There are important decisions to make when conducting an inferential statistic. First, we need to determine an acceptable $\alpha$-level to control for the probability of committing a Type I error. Researchers who find the cost of a Type I error high use a lower $\alpha$-level. Although lowering the $\alpha$-level decreases the risk of a Type I error, doing so increases the risk of a Type II error. Consequently, researchers must balance the relative costs of Type I and Type II errors to determine the $\alpha$-level to select. The researcher must also determine whether to use a directional or a nondirectional test. Another important consideration is the type of test to conduct. Each statistic has a special purpose and role in evaluating hypotheses. Selecting the wrong statistical test will produce misleading information.

Once one finds a statistically significant effect, the results must be interpreted with care. You learned that indices such as omega squared and effect size allow us to describe further the relation between the independent and dependent variables and the relative difference between the sample means. As a review, we can assume cause and effect if the researcher used a true experiment. In other designs, such as an intact-groups design, we can use the $t$-ratio to examine the difference between the groups but cannot assume that the statistically significant results indicate a cause-and-effect relation between the two variables.

We also examined the meaning of the *p*-value and that researchers often misinterpret its meaning. The *p*-value indicates the probability of obtaining the observed *t*-ratio if the null hypothesis is a correct statement. If the value of *p* is less than $\alpha$, then we can reject the null hypothesis in favor of the alternative hypothesis. Other interpretations of *p* such as (1) indicating that the results are due to chance, (2) indicating the reliability of the results, or (3) indicating the "importance" of the results are incorrect interpretations.

An important component of hypothesis testing is power analysis. The aim of power analysis is decreasing the probability of committing a Type II error. Researchers can increase the power of their research by attempting to increase the difference between the population means, increasing sample size, decreasing sampling and measurement error, and decreasing the $\alpha$-level.

## Chapter Glossary for Review

**Clinical** or **practical significance**—Indicates that the results support rejecting the null hypothesis and that the results represent an effect meaningful in the context of the research.

**Error term** $(SD_{M_1-M_2})$—Estimates the random error that occurs when taking samples from the population and is an unbiased estimate of $\sigma_{\mu_1-\mu_2}$.

**Omega squared** $(\hat{\omega}^2)$—A statistical index of the degree to which the independent variable accounts for the variance in the dependent variable.

**Power of a statistic** $(1 - \beta)$—The probability that one will correctly reject $H_0$.

**Standard error of the difference between means** $(\sigma_{\mu_1-\mu_2})$—Standard deviation of the sampling distribution of the difference between means.

**Statistical significance**—Indicates that the results support rejecting the null hypothesis.

**Student's *t*-ratio**—An inferential statistic that allows us to compare the difference between two means and determine whether there is sufficient evidence to reject the null hypothesis.

## Chapter References

American Psychological Association (2009). *Publication manual of the American Psychological Association* (6th ed.). Washington, DC: Author.

Carver, R. P. (1978). The case against statistical significance testing. *Harvard Educational Review*, 48, 278–399.

Cohen, J. (1988). *Statistical power analysis for the behavioral sciences* (2nd ed.). Hillsdale, NJ: Erlbaum.

Dixon, W. J., & Massey, F. J. (1951). *Introduction to statistical analysis*. New York: McGraw-Hill.

Killeen, P. R. (2005). An alternative to null-hypothesis significance tests. *Psychological Science, 16,* 345–353.

Moyé, L. A. (2000). *Statistical reasoning in medicine: The intuitive p-value primer.* New York: Springer.

Oakes, M. (1986). *Statistical inference: A commentary for the social and behavioral sciences.* New York: John Wiley & Sons.

Pedhazur, E. J. (1997). *Multiple regression in behavioral research: Explanation and prediction* (3rd ed.) Fort Worth, TX: Harcourt Brace.

Rudner, R. (1953). The scientist qua scientist makes value judgments. *Philosophy of Science, 20,* 349–380.

Seidlitz, L., & Diener, E. (1998). Sex differences in the recall of affective experiences. *Journal of Personality and Social Psychology, 74,* 262–271.

Shine, L. C. (1980). The fallacy of replacing an a priori significance level with an a posteriori significance level. *Educational and Psychological Measurement, 40,* 331–335.

# Chapter 12
## Single-Variable Between-Subjects Research

Variance is the spice of life.

—Anonymous

## Introduction

In Chapter 11 you learned about the classic research design that consists of two groups. Although that design is a model of simplicity, it has limitations. Because psychologists study the wondrous complexity of behavior, they often want to compare or consider more than two groups. In addition, events in nature rarely order themselves into two neat categories (e.g., it happened vs. it did not happen).

Therefore, we often need research designs that can help us answer more complex questions. The focus of this chapter will be studies for which there are more than two levels or conditions for a single independent variable. We will also examine an extremely useful statistical technique known as the **analysis of variance (ANOVA)**. Since its development by Sir Ronald Fisher in the 1920s, the ANOVA has evolved into an elaborate collection of widely used statistical procedures in contemporary behavioral and social research. Therefore, this statistic, combined with a sound research design, can tell us much about the behavior we want to study. To help illustrate the value of the ANOVA approach to design and analysis, we will use several examples from the published research literature, including the following two central studies.

### Effects of Praise on Motivation and Performance

Most of us like to be praised for our work, and we strive to receive compliments for our best efforts. Although we tend to think of praise as a reward, is it possible that some compliments could have the opposite effect and decrease one's motivation? Mueller and Dweck (1998) conducted a number of experiments in which they gave school children different types of praise. *Do you think that praise for being intelligent would affect children's motivation differently than praise for working hard?*

### Spotting a Liar

Everyone has lied at one time or another. Some people tell the occasional white lie to protect the feelings of others (e.g., "Gee, I *really* like what you did with your hair!"). Some lies are dishonorable and are intended to hurt others or to protect the guilty. Ekman and O'Sullivan (1991) asked, "How good are we at detecting when someone lies to us?" Specifically, the researchers wanted to know if professionals (e.g., Secret Service agents, judges, and psychiatrists) who routinely work with potential liars could detect lies better than other people could.

## Independent Variable

In Chapter 11 we reviewed the importance of defining the characteristics of the independent variable because its selection influences the type of research we conduct, how we analyze the data, and the conclusions we can draw from the data. In this chapter we will examine the *multilevel single-variable between-subjects* research design. This cumbersome name indicates that the design allows us to examine the relation across several specific levels, or forms, of the independent variable and the dependent variable.

The design of the multilevel study includes more than two conditions or **levels** of the independent variable. In Mueller and Dweck's (1998) study, for example, the independent variable was the type of praise that the children received for completing a project. Specifically, Mueller and Dweck considered three levels of the independent variable: (a) praise for intelligence (e.g., "Very good, you must be smart"), (b) praise for effort (e.g., "Very good, you must have worked hard"), and (c) no praise (this condition was the control condition). In the Ekman and O'Sullivan (1991) study, the independent variable was the person's profession. For the Ekman and O'Sullivan study, there were seven levels or conditions to the independent variable: (1) Secret Service agents, (2) judges, (3) psychiatrists, (4) detectives, (5) college students, (6) lawyers, and (7) FBI agents.

This chapter will focus on between-subjects designs. As you will recall, the between-subjects research design is one in which we compare the behavior of separate or independent groups of participants. In a true experiment, such as the Mueller and Dweck (1998) experiment, the researcher randomly assigns participants to one of the multiple experimental conditions formed by the levels of the independent variable. In an intact-groups design, such as the Ekman and O'Sullivan (1991) study, the researcher uses an existing subject variable (e.g., occupation) to define the levels of the independent variable and the conditions in which participants are grouped.

### Advantages of a Multilevel Design

A multilevel design allows for a more refined analysis of the relation between the independent and dependent variables. Figure 12.1 presents graphs that represent the results of four hypothetical experiments. Each graph represents a unique and complex relationship between the independent and dependent variables that a research study with only two groups for comparison could not reveal. For instance, look at Figure 12.1(d), which looks like an inverted *U*. Rotton and Cohn (2001) found an inverted U-shaped relationship, similar to the one illustrated here, between temperature and the number of aggravated assaults in a large metropolitan city.

Specifically, Rotton and Cohn (2001) found that the number of assaults increased along with increases in temperature up to a certain point, after which the number of assaults decreased as the temperature continued to increase. *What would happen if a researcher conducted an experiment examining the relationship between temperature and aggression, but used*

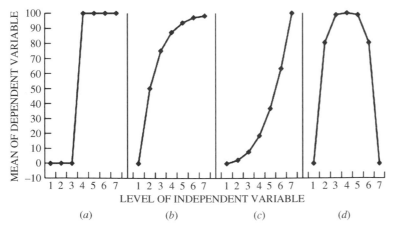

## Figure 12.1

**Hypothetical Results of Four Separate Experiments**

Each experiment represents a different relation between the independent and dependent variables. A multilevel research design will help find trends like these.

*only two temperature conditions, cold (35°F) and hot (95°F)?* According to Rotton and Cohn's data, the researcher would conclude that temperature and aggression are not related, even though we can see from Figure 12(d) that these two variables are related, just not in a linear fashion.

Another advantage of the multilevel research design is its potential to increase the statistical power of the study. This in turn can make it easier for the researcher to detect a significant effect or relationship if it is represented by the data. The increase in power occurs if the researcher can identify additional levels of the independent variable that result in less variability among the participants within the groups. Consider the Ekman and O'Sullivan (1991) study. The researchers could have compared three broad categories of professionals, including (1) detectives (Secret Service, FBI, and police detectives), (2) lawyers and judges, and (3) mental health personnel. Although this may appear to be a more simple study, it runs the risks of overlooking important differences among groups of professionals. As you will soon see, according to the results of Ekman and O'Sullivan's study, some groups of professionals are better able to detect liars than others. By grouping people from these professions together, we would overlook these important differences.

A final advantage of a multilevel design emerges when the researcher can incorporate multiple control conditions into a true experiment. By having several such control conditions, the researcher can rule out alternative explanations and thereby have greater confidence in describing the effect that the independent variable has on the dependent variable. This is valuable to researchers because it can help us to more clearly identify treatment effects when they are really present. One way to think about this is to consider the last time you tried to manage a conversation on a cell phone in a crowded room or dining hall. When everyone else in that room is talking and making noise, it is nearly impossible for you to focus in on the voices on the other end of your discussion.

That one voice over your phone represents the signal you are trying to capture. The other voices and noises in the room reflect error that obscures your ability to focus on the one signal you are trying to find and maintain. When this situation occurs, you may choose to remove yourself from the crowded space to better focus on the conversation in a quieter, more private setting. When researchers add treatment conditions to a study, it is often done for a similar reason: By separating control groups and treatment groups we can maximize our chances of identifying the signal we care about amid the noise of error that could prevent us from finding the effects we set out to study.

## Cause and Effect

Under certain circumstances, we can use the multilevel between-subjects research design to infer cause and effect between the independent and dependent variables. As a quick review, in a true experiment, the researcher randomly assigns participants to the treatment conditions, uses a manipulated independent variable, and uses control groups and procedures to account for alternative explanations of the data. Does the fact that a true experiment allows us to infer cause and effect imply that other research designs are not valuable? Absolutely not!

However, there is an important difference between true experiments and other designs in the researcher's ability to infer cause and effect from the data that are collected. Finding meaningful differences among intact groups can be helpful. Consider the research examining the ability to detect liars. What would happen if we found that one or two groups of professionals are able to detect lies? Although we could not conclude that being in a specific profession "causes" one to be a good lie detector, the results would indicate a need to engage in further research to identify how and why these groups of people are so good at detecting liars.

## Gaining Control over the Variables

One of the essential factors in determining cause and effect in any research is degree of control that the researcher has in a study over relevant variables. In general, a researcher who has greater control over the independent variable and other extraneous variables in a study will be better able to argue that there is a cause-and-effect relationship between the independent and dependent variables being studied. There are several basic strategies that a researcher can use to exercise control over the variables in a research project. We will focus on three broad issues: (1) control through research design, (2) control through research procedure, and (3) control through statistical analysis.

### Control through Research Design

Control over variables can be enhanced by properly designing a research study. Common design strategies for this purpose include random assignment of participants to treatment conditions, use of a manipulated independent variable(s), and inclusion of control groups to highlight the relationship between independent and dependent variable(s). When designing a study, researchers may also choose to incorporate additional independent variables that may help to better explain the relationship between other focal variables in a study. We discuss this use of additional variables to add control over the relationship being studied in this and the next two chapters.

The common feature of all research designs is that they are created to help researchers determine the nature and magnitude of relationships between independent and dependent variables. The many possible designs differ in terms of the control that researchers can maintain over the variables once the study begins. Of the available designs, the true experiment provides the greatest level of control for two reasons. First, the researcher can select the levels of the independent variable. By determining the levels of the independent variable, the researcher can also identify the appropriate control group conditions. Second, the researcher can use random assignment of participants to treatment conditions to minimize the influence of any participant characteristics across the various treatment groups.

### Manipulated Independent Variable as a Control

By using a manipulated independent variable, researchers can control the experiences of the groups. We can ensure that some groups of participants experience the independent variable, whereas others will not. Most importantly, we can create one or more control groups in which the independent variable is either withheld or presented at a very low level, providing us a comparison group for the other treatment groups that receive a stronger or higher level of independent variable. As you already know, having a control group allows us to determine most clearly whether the independent variable is the necessary condition for changing the dependent variable. In the Mueller and Dweck (1998) experiment, the researchers used three levels of the independent variable (praise for intelligence, praise for effort, or no praise) to determine whether the type of praise affects the child's motivation. In this study, the no-praise condition was the control group.

### Random Assignment as a Control

Using random assignment to determine which participants receive which levels of your independent variable is effectively a control procedure. This is because random assignment helps us reduce or eliminate the effect of confounding subject variables that may influence the dependent variable that we do not want to examine in the study. For example, Mueller and Dweck (1998) realized that children may differ in their general interest in any task; some children will find a task enjoyable while others will find it boring. Consequently, a child's general interest in an experimental task as well as the type of praise given by the researcher could influence that child's motivation. In their study, Mueller and Dweck reasoned that by randomly assigning the children to the three research conditions (i.e., levels of praise), each group would have approximately equal proportions of children who like, dislike, or are neutral in their liking of the experimental task.

In a quasi-experiment, we cannot randomly assign participants to the treatment conditions, but we can expose different groups of participants to different levels of the quasi-independent variable. Although we cannot randomly assign the participants to the different treatment conditions, we can attempt to design the quasi-experiment to account for alternative explanations. We will consider the design of quasi-experiments in detail in Chapter 15.

An intact-groups design affords the least amount of control over the independent variable. For example, in Ekman and O'Sullivan's (1991) lie-detection study, comparisons in lie-detecting ability were made across preexisting groups of individuals. In this study, there was no way to ensure that each of the occupational groups were equivalent beforehand (as you could if random assignment were used to place participants in each group). Although this research design does not allow us to infer cause and effect, it can indicate whether there are important variables related to the dependent variable.

## Control through Research Procedure

Once we select the design for the research, we also may need to consider techniques for controlling the influence of extraneous variables. Control through research procedure is based on the methods we use when collecting the data. Control is enhanced when the procedures we follow help us eliminate or at least reduce the influence of extraneous variables and thereby increase our ability to examine the relation between the independent and dependent variables. Remember that using a true experiment is not an automatic guarantee that you will be able to clearly identify a cause-and-effect relationship between two variables. No research design can overcome the effects of sloppy research procedure.

In Chapter 10 we examined the need for control procedures such as single- and double-blind data collection techniques. Many other control-enhancing techniques exist. The primary goal of all good research procedures is to ensure that each participant experiences the same common events in the study (to the extent possible), except for the level of the independent variable, which varies depending on their assigned treatment level/condition.

Consider some procedural issues important for Ekman and O'Sullivan's (1991) lie-detection study and Mueller and Dweck's (1998) praise-and-motivation experiment. How can we ensure that each participant in the lie-detection study sees and hears the same thing? The answer is to find a way to consistently present the liars and truth tellers. The solution identified by Ekman and O'Sullivan was to videotape college students answering questions about a film they were watching. In all cases, the models described positive feelings about a nature film they were supposedly watching. Half the models were watching a nature film and were telling the truth. The other models watched a ''gruesome'' and emotionally traumatic film. Thus, these models were lying when later recorded saying that they felt good watching the film. Ekman and O'Sullivan made the videos of the models as consistent as possible. Each film segment was approximately 60 seconds long and consisted of a head-on view of the full face and body of the truth- or lie-telling model.

How did Mueller and Dweck (1998) ensure that each child experienced the same research conditions save for the type of praise? Reading the method section of their study, you will find that the researchers employed several controls to ensure that the research conditions were nearly identical for all the children. For example, Mueller and Dweck used four female research assistants to test the children. All data collections took place in an empty classroom, free from external distractions that might have affected a child's performance or attention. In addition, each assistant followed the same data collection protocol or script when explaining the experimental task to the children. The only difference in the script was the randomly assigned presence and type of praise the assistant gave the children.

Clearly, attention to detail is a valuable asset for any researcher. That said, there is a fine line between concern for good research design and becoming obsessive-compulsive. All research projects include a nearly infinite number of factors that, if identified ahead of time, the researcher could potentially control. It is important to recognize, however, that just because we *can* exert control over a variable does not mean that we necessarily *should* in every study. The goal is to focus on extraneous variables that have a legitimate chance of influencing the dependent variable of interest, and then establishing control procedures to minimize this influence. Identifying these variables requires a combination of common sense and learning how to study the dependent variable.

There are several ways you can determine the extraneous variables that you need to control. The first is to carefully read the method section of research articles about studies that are similar to your own; doing this will allow you to benefit from the collective wisdom of a long tradition of research in a particular area of study. Another tactic is to talk with other researchers who have conducted similar research. There is often a considerable amount of "laboratory lore" involved in different types of research. For example, developmental psychologists have found ways to interact with children to ensure the child's cooperation. Many researchers consider these tricks of the trade common knowledge to those working in the field and do not describe them in the method section. Finally, you may want to consider conducting a pilot study before beginning your actual research.

A **pilot study** is a dress rehearsal for the final research project. By conducting a small-scale study with a small group of participants, you can determine (1) whether they understand your instructions, (2) whether you have effectively reduced the risk of demand characteristics and experimenter effects, and (3) whether your method of recording the data works. Armed with this information, you can make any necessary modifications to your actual study plan before beginning your full data collection.

### Control through Statistical Analysis

Control through statistical analysis depends on the mathematical techniques we use to remove or account for extraneous effects on the independent and dependent variables in a study. Statistical procedures such as ANOVA, analysis of covariance, multivariate analysis of variance, and multiple regression give researchers greater control over different sources of variance. These techniques, while useful, can be complex and require researchers to be familiar with many statistical principles that go beyond the scope of this book. It is important to note that no statistical method, no matter how advanced, can overcome a poorly designed and executed research project.

## The General Linear Model

Now that we have examined the issues surrounding the design of a multi-level single-variable between-subjects design, we can turn our attention to the logic we use to analyze the data. In this section we will examine the logic of the multilevel single-variable between-subjects research design and the statistical technique used to analyze the data. To help you understand these principles, we can use data from Mueller and Dweck's (1998) praise-and-motivation study.

For this experiment, the researchers randomly assigned 42 fifth-grade students to one of three experimental groups. The researcher asked all students to complete three problem-solving tasks. After the child solved the first set of problems, the researcher told him or her, "Wow, you did very well on these problems. You got # right. That's a really high score; you did better than 80% of the other children who try to solve these problems." For the children assigned to the Praise for Intelligence Group, the researcher then added, "You must be smart at these problems." By contrast, the researcher told the children in the Praise for Effort Group, "You must have worked hard at these problems." The children in the Control Group received no additional feedback. Notice that each child received the same comments except for the attribution regarding their good score.

During the next phase of the experiment, the researcher had the children work on a set of difficult problems and then told all of them that they had done poorly. The researcher then asked each child to rate on a 10-point scale their desire to work on the third set of problems (0 = low willingness, 10 = high willingness). Table 12.1 presents the results for this experiment. Before reviewing the results, we want to draw your attention to an important ethical issue involved in this research; the researchers deceived the children. They misled the children about their performance on the first part of the study and then rigged the second portion of the study to ensure that the children would do poorly. Mueller and Dweck (1998) recognized the ethical responsibility they had to preserve the well-being of the children. Consequently, they ensured that they received informed consent for each child participating in the study. In addition, they developed extensive debriefing procedures that ensured that the children went away from the experiment feeling proud of their efforts and participation in the study.

According to the sample means in Table 12.1, children praised for intelligence expressed the least desire to continue with the task ($M = 4.0$), whereas the children praised for effort expressed the greatest desire to continue ($M = 6.0$). The mean for the children in the control condition was intermediate between the two treatment groups ($M = 5.0$). Although we

Table 12.1  **Results for the Effects of Praise on Willingness to Continue on Task**

| No Praise (Control Group) | Praise for Intelligence | Praise for Effort |
|---|---|---|
| $n_1 = 14$ | $n_2 = 14$ | $n_3 = 14$ |
| $M_1 = 5.0$ | $M_2 = 4.0$ | $M_3 = 6.0$ |
| $SD_1 = 1.0$ | $SD_2 = 1.0$ | $SD_3 = 1.0$ |
| $VAR_1 = 1.0$ | $VAR_2 = 1.0$ | $VAR_3 = 1.0$ |

*Note:* Scores range from 0 = low willingness to 10 = high willingness.

know that there are real differences among the group means, is this difference meaningful? How much of the difference reflects the effects of the praise and how much reflects the effects of random events? We can use Equation 12.1 to help us understand the variation among the observed scores. The equation will also allow us to return to our discussion of between-groups and within-groups variance. Equation 12.1 is the **general linear model** for the data collected in a single-variable study.

$$X_{ij} = \mu = \alpha_j + \varepsilon_{ij} \qquad (12.1)$$

In this equation, $X_{ij}$ represents an observation within a specific treatment condition. The $i$ in the subscript represents the individual participant, whereas the $j$ represents the group. For example, $X_{23}$ represents the second subject in the third group. The next term, $\mu$, represents the mean for the base population. The $\alpha_j$ represents the effects for each condition on the dependent variable. For the general linear model, the value of each $\alpha_j$ may be 0, positive, or negative, depending on the effect of the level of the independent variable. Finally, $\varepsilon_{ij}$ represents random error. We assume that the error is a random variable with a mean effect of 0 and a standard deviation equal to $\sigma$, the population standard deviation. Figure 12.2 presents an illustration of how the general linear model applies to this experiment.

We begin with the sampling population. In this case, the sampling population consisted of children in the fifth grade (10- to 12-year-olds) in a public elementary school located near the researchers. From this population, we draw a sample of participants. As you learned in Chapter 7, the researchers believe that the sample is representative of the sampling population and that the sampling population is representative of the target population.

The next step in the study is the random assignment of the participants to one of the three treatment conditions. As we noted previously, using random assignment for placement of participants into groups makes it possible for the groups to be equivalent regarding subject variables. Consequently, the only thing that should differentiate the three groups is the type of feedback the children receive after completing the first task.

The final stage shown in Figure 12.2 represents the data that we collect. According to the logic of the experiment, we believe that each child's performance will reflect three things. First, $\mu$ represents the typical

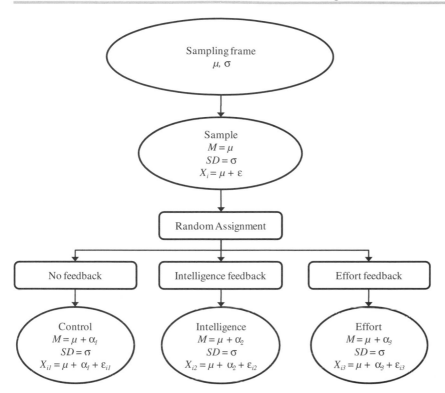

Figure 12.2

**Single-Variable Study and the General Linear Model**

After creating a random sample from the population, the mean and standard deviation of the sample should be equivalent to the corresponding population parameter. The researcher then randomly assigns the participants into one of three groups. The participants' responses ($X_{ij}$) represent the combined effects of the treatment condition ($\alpha_j$) and random events ($\varepsilon_{ij}$).

interest that fifth-grade students have in the problem-solving task. The second influence on the dependent variable is the effect of the treatment condition, $\alpha_j$. For the control group, $\alpha_1$ should equal 0 because the children in this group did not receive any praise. The researchers believe that the type of feedback will influence the participants' interest in the task. Therefore, they will predict that the values of $\alpha_j$ for the intelligence and effort groups will not equal 0. They believe that the effect of the praise will affect each child in the group. The goal of the research is to determine how the type of praise affects the children's interest in the task. The third influence is $\varepsilon_{ij}$, the random error in the equation—$\varepsilon$ represents all the random events that can influence the child's interest in the task.

Whenever we conduct a study, we want to determine what proportion of the total variance in the dependent variable is due to the independent or treatment variable and what proportion is actually due to random error. Figure 12.3 may help you better understand how we can analyze the data and use comparisons to help us make these determinations. The top three lines represent the data for each of the three groups from the Mueller and Dweck (1998) study. The $M$s represent the three group means, 4.0, 6.0, and

# Figure 12.3

**A Graphical Depiction of the Data Presented in Table 12.1**

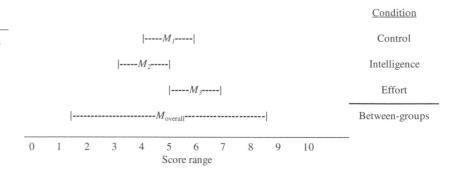

5.0, respectively. The lines surrounding the $M$s represent one standard deviation above and below the group mean. For these data, within each treatment group $SD = 1.0$. Because $VAR$ (recall that $VAR = SD^2$) is an unbiased estimate of the population variance, $\sigma^2$, we can conclude that the average within-groups variance is 1.00. The bottom line represents the variance between the three group means. Specifically, $M_{overall} = 5.0$ represents the mean of all the data. The lines surrounding $M_{overall}$ represent the variance for the three group means, $M_1$, $M_2$, and $M_3$. As you can see, the between-groups variance is greater than the within-groups variance.

The top three lines represent the praise for the no-praise control, praise-for-intelligence, and praise-for-effort treatment conditions, respectively. The $M$s represent the mean of each treatment group. The lower line represents the data for all 42 students. The $M_{overall}$ indicates the mean across all 42 participants. For each mean, the |—-| represents the limits of one standard deviation above and below the mean. The standard deviation for each group is $SD = 1.0$. The standard deviation for the three group means is $SD = 3.74$.

What affects the size of the between-groups variance? According to the general linear model, the between-groups variance represents the effect of random error, $\varepsilon_{ij}$, and the effect of the independent variable, $\alpha_j$. The question that we need to answer is whether the between-groups variance is substantively larger than the within-groups variance. If so, then we can assume that the difference we see between two treatment groups reflects the effect of the independent variable more than random error. The analysis of variance, as the name suggests, is a statistical test that allows us to compare different types of variance. For the single-independent-variable study, the ANOVA computes three types of variance.

## Components of Variance

The first form of variance is the **total variance**, which represents the variability among all the participants' scores regardless of the treatment condition they experienced. The second form of variance considered in ANOVA is the **within-groups variance**, which reflects the average amount of variability among scores for participants within each treatment group/condition. We use this measure of variability to estimate the magnitude of $\varepsilon_{ij}$. The third estimate of variance is the **between-groups variance**. Specifically, we examine the variance among the different treatment group means. The between-groups variance allows us to determine the joint effects of $\alpha_j$ and $\varepsilon_{ij}$. The primary statistic for the ANOVA is the **F-ratio**, the ratio of the between-groups variance to the within-groups variance. We use the size of the $F$-ratio to determine whether there is sufficient evidence to infer that the differences among the group means are greater than what would be due to random effects or error.

In this section we will examine the components of the ANOVA. You will likely use a computer statistics program to actually calculate your ANOVA, but you can also perform the calculations by hand using formulas that you can find in most statistics textbooks. In case you do not have such a textbook on hand, the section at the end of this chapter provides a step-by-step illustration of how to calculate the ANOVA using conventional computational equations. A convention among those who use the ANOVA is to call estimates of variance **mean squares (MS)**. The term implies that the variance of any set of numbers is the sum of squares of those numbers divided by the degrees of freedom. Therefore, whenever you read about a mean square or an *MS*, the author is describing an estimate of variance.

## Total Variance

The total variance in a set of data is nothing more than the variance of all participants in the study. As the general linear model suggests, the total variance is the sum of the effects of variance due to the independent variable, represented as $\alpha_j$, and the effects of random variation among the participants, represented as $\varepsilon_{ij}$. When we conduct an ANOVA, we **partition**, or divide, the total variance into its smaller components—the variance within-groups and the variance between-groups.

## Within-Groups Variance

The within-groups variance represents the differences among the observations caused by random error and factors not controlled by the researcher. The mean of random error is 0 and in the long run adds to or takes away nothing from the population mean. Random error is a variable and thus creates variance among the scores. Therefore, it causes individual scores to be greater than or less than the population mean. You can think of the within-groups variance as the average of the variance within each treatment group. For example, in Table 12.1 you can see that the variance in each group is 1.0. Therefore, we can conclude that the overall within-groups variance is 1.0.

When we use the ANOVA, we assume that the variances of each group are equal or homogeneous. Homogeneity of variance means that $\sigma_1 = \sigma_2 = \sigma_3 \cdots = \sigma_k$. This is an important assumption because we treat the within-groups variance as an unbiased estimate of the population variance, $\sigma^2$.

Therefore, if the variance of one group is much larger or smaller than the other group variances, our estimate of the population variance will be inaccurate. Most computer programs automatically test the homogeneity of variance assumption.

### Between-Groups Variance

The between-groups variance reflects the variability present among the means of the various treatment groups in a study. Specifically, the ANOVA determines the variance between each sample mean and the mean of the entire dataset. When we examine the differences among the sample means, we assume that some of the difference reflects random variation and that some of the variation reflects the independent variable. When we conduct this type of ANOVA, we assume that the groups are **independent**, or that the data observed in one treatment group have no influence or relation to the data observed in any of the other groups. There are a couple of general ways that we can ensure that the groups are independent for the single-variable between-subjects research.

First, in a true experiment we use random assignment to send the participants to different groups. Because the assignment of participants to research conditions is random we can conclude that the observations are independent of one another. Second, we can also conclude that the data are independent if the researcher tests each participant within only one level of the independent variable. Because the data for each group come from different people, we can assume that there is no correlation among the data from the groups.

## The *F*-Ratio

Once these three variance estimates are calculated, it is then possible to calculate an inferential statistic that helps us to determine whether the between-groups variance is sufficiently greater than the within-groups variance in a dataset to be evidence of an effect, rather than error. We call this statistic the *F*-ratio in honor of Sir Ronald Fisher, the scholar who invented the ANOVA. This statistic is nothing more than the between-groups variance divided by the within-groups variance. We can write the equation for the *F*-ratio in one of several ways:

$$F = \frac{\text{Treatment variance} + \text{Error variance}}{\text{Error variance}} \qquad (12.2.\text{a})$$

or,

$$F = \frac{\text{Between-groups variance}}{\text{Within-groups variance}} \qquad (12.2.\text{b})$$

or,

$$F = \frac{MS_{between}}{MS_{within}} \qquad (12.2.c)$$

The $F$-ratio uses the same logic as the $t$-ratio because it creates a standardized score or ratio. The $F$-ratio compares the size of the between-groups variance relative to the within-groups variance. We can use the Mueller and Dweck (1998) experiment to examine how the relation between the independent and dependent variables affects the size of the $F$-ratio.

**No Treatment Effect**

Assuming that the independent variable has no influence on the dependent variable, would all the means be equal to one another? Okay, that was a trick question: The means would probably not be precisely equal to one another because sampling (random) error will likely cause each sample mean to be slightly different from the population mean. We would expect, however, that the means would be relatively similar. More to the point, the variance between the means of the various treatment groups should equal the variance within the groups. Figure 12.4 presents an example of such a situation. For the sake of the example, we will assume that the variance within-groups is 1.0 and that the variance due to the independent variable is 0.0. Therefore,

$$F = \frac{\text{Treatment variance} + \text{Error variance}}{\text{Error variance}} = \frac{0.00 + 1.00}{1.00} = 1.00$$

In this example, the variance between-groups is equivalent to the variance within-groups. Therefore, whenever the $F$-ratio is close to 1.0, we can assume that the variance between-groups is essentially due to random

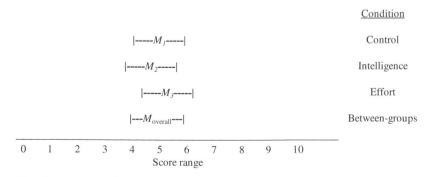

| | Condition |
|---|---|
| \|-----$M_1$-----\| | Control |
| \|-----$M_2$-----\| | Intelligence |
| \|-----$M_3$-----\| | Effort |
| \|---$M_{overall}$---\| | Between-groups |

0   1   2   3   4   5   6   7   8   9   10
Score range

## Figure 12.4

**Within-Groups Variance is 1.0 and Between-Groups Variance is 1.0**

Therefore, the ratio of the between-groups variance to the within-groups variance is $F = 1.00$. We could interpret these data to indicate that any differences between pairs of treatment group means is random or due to error, and that there is no systematic relation between the independent and dependent variables.

factors and not a meaningful treatment effect. As you can see in Figure 12.4, there is still some variance among these group means. However, because of the considerable overlap among the score distributions for these groups, we assume that the difference among the means represents chance, the effect of random error. Notice, too, that the between-groups variance is the same as the within-groups variance—when computing an *F*-ratio from these data, this would translate into a value close to 1.0.

**Treatment Effect Present**

What happens to the *F*-ratio when the levels of the independent variable correspond with changes in the dependent variable? In an experiment, the independent variable may cause the mean of your treatment groups (filled with members of your sample) to be greater or less than the mean of the population. Hence, the between-groups variance in your study will be larger than the within-groups variance. The between-groups variance increases because the treatment variance is greater than 0.0. Figure 12.5 represents what would occur if there were a statistically significant treatment effect. As you can see, the between-groups variance is now extremely large. You can also see that the variability among the three means has increased, whereas the variance within each group remains the same as it was for the example in Figure 12.4. We can represent the variance in Figure 12.5 using the following equation:

$$F = \frac{\text{Treatment variance} + \text{Error variance}}{\text{Error variance}} = \frac{13.00 + 1.00}{1.00} = 14.00$$

The increase in the treatment variance caused the *F*-ratio to be greater than 1.00. If the effect of the treatment variance is sufficiently large, we will conclude that the *F*-ratio is statistically significant and that there is a potentially meaningful difference between two or more of your treatment

# Figure 12.5

**Within-Groups Variance is 1.0 and Between-Groups Variance is 14.0**

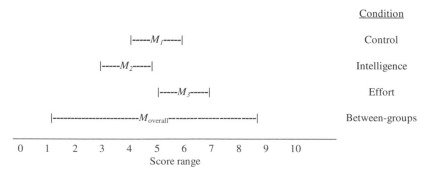

For this example, $F = 14.00$ and we can infer that the difference among the group means is greater than would be expected from random error alone. We may infer that there is a systematic relation between the independent and dependent variables.

groups. Additionally, we will infer that there is a relationship between the independent and dependent variable(s) in your study. Looking to the example in Figure 12.5, we can interpret the $F$-ratio to indicate that the variance between the groups is 14 times larger than the variance within-groups. Going a step farther, we may have statistical evidence that changes in the independent variable correspond with changes in the dependent variable.

## $H_0$ and $H_1$

The null ($H_0$) and alternative hypotheses ($H_1$) for the ANOVA are similar in form and logic to the null and alternative hypotheses used to test the $t$-ratio. Specifically, the null hypothesis specifies that there are no differences between treatment groups, implying that differences in the level of the independent variable are not associated with differences in the mean levels of the dependent variable. We write the null hypothesis as

$$H_0 : \mu_1 = \mu_2 = \mu_3 \cdots = \mu_j$$

We used a similar null hypothesis for the $t$-ratio. The only difference is that with the ANOVA we compare simultaneously more than two means. The interpretation of the null hypothesis is that all groups represent the same population and that any observed differences between the means is due to random factors or sampling error and not a potentially meaningful treatment effect.

Because the ANOVA is a general or omnibus test of variances, we do not make specific statements about how the means will be different from one another in the alternative hypothesis. Remember that the primary purpose of the ANOVA is to determine whether there are any systematic differences among the means. Because we do not specify the relation between the means in the ANOVA, we write the alternative hypothesis as

$$H_1 : \text{Not } H_0$$

or

$$H_1 : \text{All } \mu_i \text{ are not equal}$$

The alternative hypothesis for the $F$-ratio is a nondirectional hypothesis because we do not specify how the means will be different from one another, only that the between-groups variance is greater than the within-groups variance. If we can reject the null hypothesis, we must then use a special form of $t$-ratio to make specific comparisons among the treatment group means.

## *F*-Ratio Sampling Distribution

Just as Student developed a family of sampling distributions for the *t*-ratio, Fisher developed a family of sampling distributions for the *F*-ratio. The concept of the sampling distribution for the *F*-ratio is the same as that for other sampling distributions. Specifically, the sampling distribution represents the probability of various *F*-ratios when the null hypothesis is true. Two types of degrees of freedom (*df*) determine the shape of the distribution. The first *df* represents the between-groups variance. For any unbiased estimate of variance, the *df* always equal one less than the number of observations that contribute to that particular estimate of variance. For the between-groups variance, the *df* is the number of treatment groups less one. We also call this *df* the *degrees of freedom numerator* ($df_N$) because we use this to calculate the $MS_{between}$ in the numerator of the *F*-ratio.

In the ANOVA framework, the second *df* represents the within-groups variance. We also call this *df* the *degrees of freedom denominator* ($df_D$) because we use this to calculate the $MS_{within}$ in the denominator of the *F*-ratio. The critical values of the *F*-ratio for various combinations of $df_N$ and $df_D$ are presented in Appendix B. As you will see, the columns represent "Degrees of Freedom for Numerator" and the rows represent "Degrees of Freedom for Denominator." For the single-variable ANOVA, the degrees of freedom for the numerator are the **$df_{between}$** and the degrees of freedom for the denominator are the **$df_{within}$**. For degrees of freedom of $df_N = 2$ and $df_D = 39$, $F_{critical} = 3.235$.

Figure 12.6 represents the sampling distribution for the *F*-ratio when the degrees of freedom are 2 and 39. The distribution is positively skewed. Because we want to determine whether *F* is greater than 1.00, we place $\alpha$ on the right extreme of the distribution. When the *F*-ratio is 3.24, 5% of the sampling distribution is to the right of the *F*-ratio. Therefore, any observed *F*-ratio that falls in this region will allow us to reject the null hypothesis if $\alpha = .05$.

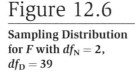

# Figure 12.6

**Sampling Distribution for *F* with $df_N = 2$, $df_D = 39$**

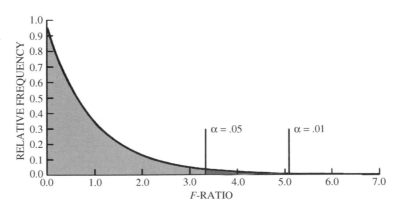

# Knowledge Check

1. Describe in your words the advantages of using a multilevel single-variable between-subjects research design.

2. Under what conditions can the researcher use the multilevel single-variable between-subjects research design to infer cause and effect?

3. What is the difference between the between-groups variance and a variance due to the independent variable?

4. Why is the mean of $\varepsilon = 0$ for all participants in a specific treatment condition?

5. For a control group used in a true experiment, why would we state that $\alpha_j = 0$?

6. Comment on the accuracy of the following statements; explain why each statement is correct or incorrect.
    a. When the $F$-ratio is statistically significant, we can infer that the size of $\varepsilon_{ij}$ is small and close to 0.
    b. All else being equal, as the size of $\varepsilon_{ij}$ increases, the probability of rejecting the null hypothesis decreases.
    c. If the $F$-ratio is less than 1.00, the variance between-groups, due to the independent variable, is less than 0.0.
    d. If the $F$-ratio is not statistically significant, we can assume that the independent variable had no effect on the dependent variable.
    e. Even in a true experiment, the researcher cannot influence the size of $\alpha_j$.
    f. For a control group in an experiment, we could write the general linear model, $X_{ij} = \mu + 0 + \varepsilon_{ij}$.
    g. It is impossible for the value of all $\alpha_j$'s to be less than 0 in the general linear model.

# Summarizing and Interpreting ANOVA Results

We can use the skills learned in Chapter 11 to determine how we will conduct an inferential statistical analysis of data similar to those summarized in Figure 12.7. Before we get there, however, you should recall that in this type of hypothesis-testing analysis, we begin by identifying the null and alternative hypotheses and proceed to determining the criterion for rejecting the null hypothesis. The following considerations must be made when engaging in an ANOVA.

## Null Hypothesis

If the null hypothesis, $H_0$: $\mu_1 = \mu_2 = \mu_3$, is true, then the average performance of the children in the three groups should be roughly equivalent. In words, this would mean that the type of praise has no influence on

## Figure 12.7

**Example of an ANOVA Summary Table**

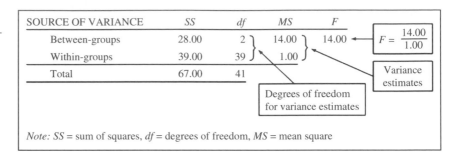

| SOURCE OF VARIANCE | SS | df | MS | F |
|---|---|---|---|---|
| Between-groups | 28.00 | 2 | 14.00 | 14.00 |
| Within-groups | 39.00 | 39 | 1.00 | |
| Total | 67.00 | 41 | | |

$$F = \frac{14.00}{1.00}$$

Variance estimates

Degrees of freedom for variance estimates

*Note:* SS = sum of squares, *df* = degrees of freedom, *MS* = mean square

the child's interest in the task. Any observed difference among the three sample means represents chance events.

### Alternative Hypothesis

If the null hypothesis is false, then we by default shift to our alternative hypothesis, $H_1$: Not $H_0$. If this is the case, then we are concluding that the average performance of the children in the three treatment groups is not equivalent. In other words, the variance among the three groups is greater than what we would expect from the within-groups variance. Therefore, we conclude that the type of praise does influence the children's interest in the task. It is important to note that a significant *F*-statistic does not by itself tell us which pairs of treatment group means are different from each other.

### Statistical Test

We will use the single-factor independent-groups ANOVA for this type of analysis because we wish to compare the difference between the three independent treatment groups (e.g., Group 1 vs. 2, 2 vs. 3, and 1 vs. 3).

### Significance Level

Using $\alpha = .05$ and the degrees of freedom, we can determine the critical value for our *F*-test. If our observed statistic is larger than this critical value, then we can infer that there is at least one statistically significant difference between pairs of treatment group means. We can find this critical value by using the following information: $\alpha = .05$, $df_N = 2$, $df_D = 39$, yielding $F_{critical}(2, 39) = 3.235$. Again, if our *F*-statistic is greater than this value, then we can conclude that there is a significant difference between the means of at least one of the pairs of treatment groups.

### Summary Table

Most statisticians report the sum of squares, degrees of freedom, mean squares, and the *F*-ratio in an **ANOVA summary table**. The summary table represents the common practice of several generations of statisticians and is now common in published research and the printouts of statistical analysis software programs. Whether you calculate the ANOVA with one of these programs or by hand, the basic format of the summary table for this type of analysis is shown in Figure 12.7.

Because our $F_{\text{observed}}$ is greater than the $F_{\text{critical}}$ ($14.00 > 3.235$), we can reject the null hypothesis and conclude that the type of praise did influence the children's motivation to continue the task (our alternative hypothesis). According to the *Publication Manual of the American Psychological Association* (2001), the recommended format for reporting the statistical results of an *F*-test is: $F(df_N, df_D) = F_{\text{observed}}$, p $= p$ or $F(df_N, df_D) = F_{\text{observed}}$, $p < \alpha$. For this example, we would report the *F*-ratio as $F(2, 39) = 14.00$, $p = .0000261$ or $F(2, 39) = 14.00$, $p < .05$. The $df_N$ refers to the numerator degrees of freedom, the degrees of freedom for the between-groups effect. The $df_D$ refers to the denominator degrees of freedom, the degrees of freedom for within-groups effect.

When we reject the null hypothesis with the results of an ANOVA, we conclude that the difference between one or more pairs of treatment group means is large enough to infer that $H_0$ is false. We accept the alternative hypothesis, $H_1$: Not $H_0$. Although the *F*-ratio allows us to take a significant step toward interpretation, we need to continue the analysis of our data to learn more about the relation between the treatment and the results.

## Effect Size and Power

All the rules you learned about interpreting the *t*-ratio apply to the interpretation of the *F*-ratio. The size of the *F*-ratio and *p* value indicates only whether we can reject the null hypothesis given the value selected for $H_0$. To evaluate the degree to which the independent variable correlates with the dependent variable, we need to convert the *F*-ratio to estimated omega squared, $\hat{\omega}^2$. The size of $\hat{\omega}^2$ indicates the degree of association between the independent and dependent variables. When we introduced you to $\hat{\omega}^2$ in Chapter 11, we told you to calculate $\hat{\omega}^2$ only if the statistic is statistically significant. The same is true for the *F*-ratio; it is good practice to calculate $\omega^2$ only after you have established that the *F*-ratio is statistically significant. For the current experiment, $\hat{\omega}^2 = .382$. Therefore, we can estimate that approximately 38% of the variance among the three treatment group means is due to the effect of the independent variable, the type of praise the participants received.

An alternative estimate for the effect size of an *F*-statistic comes from Cohen (1988). This effect size estimate, represented as *f*, provides the same type of information as *d* for the *t*-ratio. For the current example, $f = .42$ (the equations for $\hat{\omega}^2$ and *f* are presented in the final section of the chapter). According to Cohen, effect sizes for the ANOVA fall into one of three categories, as presented in Table 12.2 for the *f* estimate. The effect size for the present example experiment is what Cohen would refer to as a *large effect*.

## Table 12.2   Table of Cohen's Recommended Categories for Small, Medium, and Large Effect Sizes

| Small effect size | Medium effect size | Large effect size |
|---|---|---|
| $f = .10$ | $f = .25$ | $f = .40$ |

Effect sizes need to be interpreted with caution, especially when in the small- to medium-effect-size range. Under some circumstances, a small effect size is an extremely important finding. For example, when studying a complex social behavior in a natural environment, one has little direct control over the environment and the treatment of the participants. Furthermore, in this situation, and many others, the measurement procedures may be prone to much error. Therefore, we need always to remember to interpret effect size within a broader context. Sometimes a "small" effect size can represent a major breakthrough in a program of research (Abelson, 1985). In other cases, a "small" effect size is insignificant from a meaning standpoint and very easily forgotten.

According to Cohen (1988), effect sizes for most research in the behavioral sciences are in the small-to-moderate range (e.g., $.10 \leq f \leq .40$). Why are effect sizes so small for behavioral science research? The problem may arise from factors related to random error. First, most of the phenomena studied by behavioral scientists have multiple causes, and no single study can account for all of them. Second, there are always differences among people; even in a highly controlled laboratory experiment, each participant walks into the experiment with his or her own biases and predispositions. These experiences create differences among participants that the experimenter cannot control. Finally, measurement in the behavioral sciences inherently contains a good deal of random measurement error. This uncontrolled error can reduce the overall effect size of a research study by obscuring the effect that the researchers were seeking (i.e., the signal-to-noise metaphor). The successful researcher recognizes the presence of these inherent sources of error and attempts to improve the quality of the research procedure.

## Multiple Comparisons of the Means

When we reject the null hypothesis based on the results of an ANOVA, we can conclude only that the variance between the means of our treatment groups is greater than what we would expect due to sampling error alone. The $F$-ratio does not specify where the statistically significant differences among the groups may occur (e.g., is the significant difference between Groups 1 and 2, or Groups 1 and 3?). To determine which group means are statistically different from one another, we must return to the logic of the $t$-ratio to guide our comparisons.

You may be wondering why we would return to the $t$-ratio after conducting an ANOVA; why not conduct the $t$-ratios to begin with? The answer comes from an interesting fact related to hypothesis testing: The probability of a Type I error (i.e., a false alarm) increases depending on the number of comparisons you make using the same dataset (think back to Chapter 11). When we conduct a $t$-ratio, we assume that the groups are independent of one another. When the groups are independent, the probability of committing a Type I error is $\alpha$. The problem of inflated Type I error arises when we make **multiple comparisons** based on a single experiment with many groups. Consequently, if we were to compare three or more means from the sample experiment, the probability of committing a Type I error is greater than $\alpha$. Statisticians use Equation 12.5 to determine the probability of committing a Type I error under these conditions:

$$\alpha_e = 1 - \left(1 - \alpha_p\right)^c \qquad (12.3)$$

In this equation, $\alpha_e$ represents the **experimentwise error**, the probability of making a Type I error in any one of the potential comparisons. The other $\alpha_p$ term represents the **pairwise error**. The pairwise error represents the probability of a Type I error for a single comparison. Finally, the superscript $c$ in this equation represents the number of potential comparisons.

The size of the experimentwise error increases quickly as the number of comparisons increases. For instance, if a researcher were to conduct three $t$-ratios, the $\alpha_e$ is approximately .143. Consequently, there is a 14.3% chance that one or more of any statistically significant $t$-ratios identified from these comparisons will be false (a Type I error). Figure 12.8 helps to illustrate this problem. Assume that a researcher conducts a study with three independent groups and proceeds to compare each possible combination of mean pairs. We can also assume that the researcher set $\alpha_p = .05$ for each comparison. Because $\alpha = .05$, we assume that the probability of a Type I error (represented as $\alpha_p$) for each comparison is 5%. In this example, there are eight potential outcomes ranging from all the comparisons being statistically significant to none of the comparisons being statistically significant.

The column labeled "Probability of Outcome" represents the probability of results if the null hypothesis is a true statement for each of the comparisons. For instance, if $H_0$: $\mu = \mu$ for each of the three comparisons, then the probability that all three would be statistically significant is $p = .000125$ ($.000125 = .05 \times .05 \times .05$). In other words, the probability that we make a Type I error for each comparison is .0125%. The "Cumulative Probability" column represents the probability of obtaining one of the potential outcomes. We will focus our attention on the next-to-last line. The cumulative probability indicates the probability of obtaining one of the seven outcomes by chance, if $H_0$: $\mu = \mu$ is actually true for each comparison. For this example, the cumulative probability is $p = .143$, as predicted by Equation 12.5.

# Figure 12.8

**The Experimentwise Error Rate ($\alpha_e$) for Multiple Comparisons**

| | A vs. B | A vs. C | B vs. C | PROBABILITY OF OUTCOME | CUMULATIVE PROBABILITY | |
|---|---|---|---|---|---|---|
| **All three comparisons statistically significant** | | | | | | |
| | ☑ | ☑ | ☑ | $p = .000125 = \alpha^3$ | .000125 | |
| **At least two comparisons statistically significant** | | | | | | |
| | ☑ | ☑ | ◌ | $p = .002375 = \alpha^2(1 - \alpha)$ | | |
| | ☑ | ◌ | ☑ | $p = .002375 = \alpha^2(1 - \alpha)$ | | |
| | ◌ | ☑ | ☑ | $p = .002375 = \alpha^2(1 - \alpha)$ | .007250 | |
| **At least one comparisons statistically significant** | | | | | | |
| | ☑ | ◌ | ◌ | $p = .045125 = \alpha(1 - \alpha)^2$ | | |
| | ◌ | ☑ | ◌ | $p = .045125 = \alpha(1 - \alpha)^2$ | | |
| | ◌ | ◌ | ☑ | $p = .045125 = \alpha(1 - \alpha)^2$ | .142625 | $\alpha_e = 1 - (1 - \alpha)^c$ |
| **No comparisons statistically significant** | | | | | | |
| | ◌ | ◌ | ◌ | $p = .857375 = (1 - \alpha)^3$ | 1.000000 | |
| *Note:* ☑ Statistically significant | | | | $p = \alpha$     $p = .05$ | | |
| ◌ Not statistically significant | | | | $p = (1 - \alpha)$     $p = .95$ | | |

For this example, we assume that $H_0$: $\mu_A = \mu_B, \mu_A = \mu_C, \mu_B = \mu_C$ are true statements.

You could lower $\alpha_p$ (e.g., from .05 to .01) to keep $\alpha_e$ to an acceptable level. The problem with this tactic is that the power for the individual comparisons will be so small that few if any of the $t$-ratios will reveal statistically significant results. For example, with three potential comparisons we would have to reduce the $\alpha_p$ to approximately .01695 to maintain $\alpha_e$ at .05. We can calculate this using the equation,

$$\alpha_e = 1 - (1 - \alpha_p)^c \tag{12.4}$$

To maintain the probability of a Type I error at .05 for three comparisons, we would have to evaluate the statistical significance of each comparison at

$$\alpha_p = 1 - 3\sqrt{1 - .05} = .01695$$

Reducing $\alpha$ may reduce the risk of a Type I error, but it will increase the risk of a Type II error (a miss). If this is not acceptable in your particular situation, an alternative strategy is to use a *post-hoc* (meaning after the fact) test. Post-hoc tests are methods for comparing many sample means while controlling for inflated experimentwise comparison rates. These specialized $t$-ratios allow you to compare sample means after you conduct the ANOVA and determine which pairs of means are different from one another at a statistically significant level, all while avoiding an inflated Type I error. You will also find that most statistical packages offer a broad menu of post-hoc statistical tests. In the following subsection, we will examine one of the more popular post-hoc tests, known as **Tukey's HSD**.

# Table 12.3 Comparison of All the Differences Between All Pairs of Means Using the Tukey HSD Test

| Praise Group | M | Intelligence 4.0 | Control 5.0 | Effort 6.0 |
|---|---|---|---|---|
| Intelligence | 4.0 | — | 1.0* | 2.0* |
| Control | 5.0 | — | — | 1.0* |
| Effort | 6.0 | — | — | — |

## Tukey's HSD

Tukey (1953) developed the Honestly Significant Differences (HSD) procedure to compare all possible pairs of treatment group means after one has rejected the null hypothesis using an ANOVA. This post-hoc procedure strikes a reasonable balance between protecting against inflated Type I errors and preserving statistical power (Jaccard, Becker, & Wood, 1984). We can use the data from the Mueller and Dweck (1998) experiment to examine the use of Tukey's HSD. Table 12.3 presents a matrix of the differences between the three means from the Mueller and Dweck experiment. The asterisk (∗) indicates the statistically significant difference between means at the .05 level. If you are using a computer program to analyze the data, the program will automatically perform the necessary calculations. According to the results, all the group means are significantly different from one another. From the perspective of the purpose of the research, the HSD test confirms that children who received praise for intelligence rated the task lower than did the children in the control condition. Children in the praise-for-effort condition rated the task higher than did the children in the control condition. Therefore, it appears that the type of praise did affect the children's interest in the task.

## Estimating Sample Size

An important, if not essential, step in any research project is determining the number of participants required to provide data that will allow you to test and possibly reject the null hypothesis. This is not a trivial step; we do not want to spend our time conducting a study only to find that we cannot reject the null hypothesis due to inadequate statistical power brought on by an insufficient sample. Instead, as we design the research project we want to ensure that we do everything possible to increase the probability that we will reject a false null hypothesis. In the language of statistics, we want to increase the statistical power $(1 - \beta)$ of the study. As you should recall, one way to increase power is to increase the sample size for the research. In the following section, we will examine how to estimate the number of participants to include in a single-factor study.

Table B.13 of Appendix B presents a power estimate table that you can use to estimate the number of participants you will need for your research. Figure 12.9 presents a portion of Table A.1. The table includes the two

# Figure 12.9

**Power Table for the ANOVA**

| n | $F_c$ | .10 | .25 | .40 | .55 | $F_c$ | .10 | .25 | .40 | .55 | $F_c$ | .10 | .25 | .40 | .55 |
|---|---|---|---|---|---|---|---|---|---|---|---|---|---|---|---|
| | | | $\alpha = .05$ | $df_N = 4$ | | | | $\alpha = .05$ | $df_N = 5$ | | | | $\alpha = .05$ | $df_N = 6$ | |
| | | Effect Size, $f$ | | | | | Effect Size, $f$ | | | | | Effect Size, $f$ | | | |
| 37 | 2.422 | .17 | .77 | .99 | .99 | 2.256 | .19 | .82 | .99 | .99 | 2.135 | .20 | .85 | .99 | .99 |
| 38 | 2.420 | .18 | .78 | .99 | .99 | 2.255 | .19 | .83 | .99 | .99 | 2.134 | .21 | .87 | .99 | .99 |
| 39 | 2.419 | .18 | **.80** | .99 | .99 | 2.254 | .20 | .84 | .99 | .99 | 2.133 | .21 | .88 | .99 | .99 |
| 40 | 2.418 | .18 | .81 | .99 | .99 | 2.253 | .20 | .85 | .99 | .99 | 2.132 | .21 | .89 | .99 | .99 |
| 45 | 2.413 | .20 | .86 | .99 | .99 | 2.248 | .22 | .90 | .99 | .99 | 2.128 | .23 | .93 | .99 | .99 |

The $n$ column represents the number of observations in each treatment group. The $F_c$ column represents the critical value of $F$ for the degrees of freedom. The $f$ columns represent the four levels of effect size.

conventional alpha levels (.05 and .01). The column labeled $n$ represents the number of participants in each treatment condition, and the column marked $F_c$ represents the critical $F$-ratio required to reject $H_0$. The four other columns represent the small ($f = .10$), medium ($f = .25$), large ($f = .40$), and very large ($f = .55$) effect sizes. We can use this table to estimate the power of an experiment and to plan future research projects.

For example, assume that you want to conduct an experiment with five levels of the independent variable ($df_N = 4$) and set $\alpha = .05$. How many participants do you need to have an 80% chance of rejecting the null hypothesis? Unless you have some idea of what effect size you should expect from previous similar studies, Cohen (1988) suggests you should plan for a maximum effect size that is moderate, $f = .25$ as it reflects the power of most behavioral research. If you wish to be a bit more conservative in your estimate, you can plan using a smaller effect size estimate (e.g., $f = .10$). Similarly, if you believe that your experiment will produce a large effect size, you can increase your estimate (e.g., $f = .40$). We can use Figure 12.9 to illustrate how to use Table B.13 for the single-factor study.

For the present example, there are five groups; therefore, $df_N = 4 = 5 - 1$, and we plan to use $\alpha = .05$. How many participants will this experiment require if we assume that $f = .25$ and we want to set our power to $1 - \beta = .80$? As shown in Figure 12.9, we will need at least 39 participants in each treatment group (39 × 5 = 195 participants) to have sufficient statistical power to reject the null hypothesis.

## Research in Action: Detecting Lies

*How good are members of law enforcement at detecting when someone is lying?* Ekman and O'Sullivan (1991) asked that question by examining the ability of Secret Service agents, FBI polygraphers, police robbery detectives, judges, psychiatrists, lawyers, and college students to watch a series of videotapes and identify the liars. To conduct the study, the researchers

## Table 12.4  Summary Statistics and ANOVA Summary Table for Ekman & O'Sullivan (1991)

| SS | FBI | D | J | P | L | CS | Total |
|---|---|---|---|---|---|---|---|
| $n_1 = 10$ | $n_2 = 9$ | $n_3 = 10$ | $n_4 = 9$ | $n_5 = 10$ | $n_6 = 10$ | $n_7 = 10$ | $n = 68$ |
| $M_1 = 6.8$ | $M_2 = 5.3$ | $M_3 = 5.2$ | $M_4 = 5.1$ | $M_5 = 5.4$ | $M_6 = 5.3$ | $M_7 = 5.2$ | $M_{overall} = 5.5$ |

| Source | SS | df | MS | F |
|---|---|---|---|---|
| Between | 20.796 | 6 | 3.466 | |
| Within | 48.189 | 61 | 0.790 | 4.388 |
| Total | 68.985 | 67 | | |

$\hat{\omega}^2 = .23$, $\eta^2 = .30$

*Note:* SS = Secret Service agents, FBI = FBI agents D = detectives, J = judges, P = psychiatrists, L = lawyers, CS = college students.

developed 10 videotape presentations. Each tape consisted of a different college-aged woman in an interview. Half of the tapes presented different women lying; the other tapes were of different women telling the truth. The researchers explained to the participants that they would see 10 different women, half of whom were lying. Participants were supposed to identify who was lying. Table 12.4 presents the hypothetical results for this study. The data represent the number of correct identifications each person made. Ekman and O'Sullivan wanted to know whether members of some professions are better able to detect liars.

There are differences between this dataset and the data collected by Mueller and Dweck (1998) regarding the relationship between praise and performance. First, in Ekman and O'Sullivan's (1991) study the independent variable is a subject variable. This has no real bearing on our analysis of the data; we can continue to use the ANOVA. It will, however, change the way in which we interpret any results. Second, because we did not use random assignment of participants to the groups, we will not be able to determine unambiguously that the independent variable causes the dependent variable.

Table 12.4 presents the summary statistics and an ANOVA summary table for these data. Because the $F_{observed}$ is greater than the $F_{critical}$, we can reject the null hypothesis. Doing so allows us to assume that members of some professions are better able to detect liars than others. We will need to use Tukey's HSD to determine where the difference lies. Table 12.5 presents the matrix of mean differences and the results of Tukey's HSD test. From these data we can conclude that the Secret Service agents were better able to detect liars than members of other groups. Figure 12.10 presents the results section that one might prepare for these data. In this example, we included a graph of the data that presents the mean and the standard error of the mean. This technique helps to illustrate that the Secret Service agents performed better than the other groups of participants at detecting liars.

Table 12.5 **Matrix of Mean Differences for the Seven Groups Using the HSD to Determine the Statistical Significance of the Differences Between Pairs of Means**

| Profession | M | J 5.11 | D 5.20 | CS 5.20 | L 5.30 | FBI 5.33 | P 5.40 | SS 6.80 |
|---|---|---|---|---|---|---|---|---|
| J | 5.11 | 0.00 | 0.09 | 0.09 | 0.19 | 0.22 | 0.29 | 1.69* |
| D | 5.20 | | 0.00 | 0.00 | 0.10 | 0.13 | 0.20 | 1.60* |
| CS | 5.20 | | | 0.00 | 0.10 | 0.13 | 0.20 | 1.60* |
| L | 5.30 | | | | 0.00 | 0.03 | 0.10 | 1.50* |
| FBI | 5.33 | | | | | 0.00 | 0.07 | 1.47* |
| P | 5.40 | | | | | | 0.00 | 1.40* |
| SS | 6.80 | | | | | | | 0.00 |

*Note:* J = judges, D = detectives, CS = college students, L = lawyers, FBI = FBI agents, P = psychiatrists, SS = Secret Service agents.

## Statistics behind the Research

In this section we will examine the procedures for manually calculating the summary table for the single-factor independent-groups ANOVA and the associated statistical tests. For this example, we will use data presented in Table 12.6, which represents the results of the Ekman and O'Sullivan (1991) study.

### Assumptions of the Test

The single-variable between-groups ANOVA requires that the data meet three specific mathematical requirements. Meeting these assumptions ensures that the ANOVA will produce valid statistical interpretations of the data.

1. *Normal distribution of data.* The first assumption is that the data are normally distributed. Extreme skew in one or more of the groups may

# Figure 12.10

**Results Section Describing the Single-Factor Between-Groups Study Presented in Table 12.4**

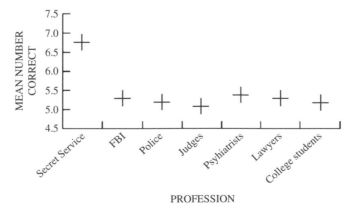

## Table 12.6 Hypothetical Data for the Ekman and O'Sullivan (1991) Study

| SS | FBI | D | J | P | L | CS | |
|---|---|---|---|---|---|---|---|
| 7 | 6 | 4 | 5 | 5 | 4 | 5 | |
| 7 | 5 | 6 | 6 | 5 | 6 | 4 | |
| 6 | 6 | 5 | 6 | 6 | 6 | 5 | |
| 7 | 4 | 4 | 7 | 5 | 4 | 6 | |
| 6 | 5 | 5 | 4 | 6 | 6 | 4 | |
| 7 | 5 | 6 | 5 | 4 | 5 | 6 | |
| 8 | 7 | 5 | 4 | 5 | 7 | 6 | |
| 7 | 4 | 6 | 4 | 5 | 6 | 5 | |
| 7 | 6 | 5 | 5 | 7 | 5 | 6 | |
| 6 | | 6 | | 6 | 4 | 5 | Totals |
| $\Sigma X_1 = 68$ | $\Sigma X_2 = 48$ | $\Sigma X_3 = 52$ | $\Sigma X_4 = 46$ | $\Sigma X_5 = 54$ | $\Sigma X_6 = 53$ | $\Sigma X_7 = 52$ | $\Sigma X = 373$ |
| $\Sigma X_1^2 = 466$ | $\Sigma X_2^2 = 264$ | $\Sigma X_3^2 = 276$ | $\Sigma X_4^2 = 244$ | $\Sigma X_5^2 = 298$ | $\Sigma X_6^2 = 291$ | $\Sigma X_7^2 = 276$ | $\Sigma X^2 = 2115$ |
| $n_1 = 10$ | $n_2 = 9$ | $n_3 = 10$ | $n_4 = 9$ | $n_5 = 10$ | $n_6 = 10$ | $n_7 = 10$ | $N = 68$ |
| $M_1 = 6.8$ | $M_2 = 5.3$ | $M_3 = 5.2$ | $M_4 = 5.1$ | $M_5 = 5.4$ | $M_6 = 5.3$ | $M_7 = 5.2$ | $M_{overall} = 5.49$ |

*Note:* SS = Secret Service agents, FBI = FBI agents, D = detectives, J = judges, P = psychiatrists, L = lawyers, CS = college students.

cause the ANOVA to produce spurious results. A quick review of the data in Table 12.6 indicates no outliers or other conditions that skew the data.

2. *Homogeneity of variance.* The second assumption is that the variances of the individual treatment conditions are relatively equal. This assumption is critical in that extremely deviant variances in one or more of the groups can produce spurious results. Coupled with this assumption is the general requirement that the sample sizes of the various treatment groups be the same. A quick review of these data suggests that the variances of the six groups are equivalent. Likewise, an equal number of participants was present in each treatment group.

3. *Independence of groups.* The final assumption is that the groups are independent. This assumption requires that there be no explicit correlation among the groups. Because the researchers used a subject variable to create the treatment groups, these groups are at least partially independent of each other. Another way to ensure independence is to use a random assignment to place participants into the different treatment groups. There are conditions when there is an explicit correlation between the groups. We will consider this research design in Chapter 14.

## Forming the Hypotheses

For the null hypothesis we assume that the independent variable and dependent variable are not related. Therefore, any observed differences

Table 12.7 **Example of Determining the Degrees of Freedom for Each Test in the Two-Variable Independent-Groups ANOVA**

| | |
|---|---|
| **Between-groups** | $df_{\text{between}} = j - 1 = 7 - 1 = 6$ |
| | $df_{\text{within}} = \Sigma(n_j - 1)$ |
| **Within-groups** | $df_{\text{within}} = (10 - 1) + (9 - 1) + (10 - 1) + (9 - 1) + (10 - 1) + (10 - 1) + (10 - 1)$ |
| | $df_{\text{within}} = 61$ |

between the group means would be due to chance or random error if the null hypothesis is true. In the present example, we can write the null hypothesis for this study as: $H_0: \mu_1 = \mu_2 = \mu_3 = \mu_4 = \mu_5 = \mu_6 = \mu_7$. In words, the null hypothesis is that the type of profession is unrelated to the ability to detect lies.

The alternative hypothesis for the F-ratio is that there is a relationship between the independent and dependent variables. Because the ANOVA compares the variance between-groups to the variance within-groups, we cannot specify which group means will be different from one another. Therefore, we write the alternative hypothesis to indicate the null hypothesis is false. Specifically, we write: $H_1$: Not $H_0$, that the ability to detect lies corresponds with the type of profession.

### Sampling Distribution

To determine whether to reject the null hypothesis we will need to determine $F_{\text{critical}}$, after we establish the level of $\alpha$ and calculate the degrees of freedom. As you learned in this chapter, the F-distribution has two degrees of freedom. The numerator degrees of freedom ($df_N$) is the degrees of freedom associated with the between-groups variance. The denominator degrees of freedom ($df_D$) is the degrees of freedom associated with the within-groups variance. Table 12.7 presents the $F_{\text{critical}}$ for the current example. The value of $F_{\text{critical}}$ allows us to determine whether to reject the null hypothesis for each observed F-ratio. When $F_{\text{observed}} \geq F_{\text{critical}}$, you can reject the null hypothesis.

We can set $\alpha = .05$, a conventional criterion of basic research that sets the probability of a Type I error to 5%. To determine $F_{\text{critical}}$, we first need to calculate the degrees of freedom for the F-distribution. Using Table B.10 of Appendix B, we can find the critical value of F-ratio needed to reject the null hypothesis. Because there is not a listing for $df_D = 61$, we can round the degrees of freedom down to 60. Therefore, $F_{\text{critical}}(6, 60) = 2.25$, $p = .05$.

### Completing the Calculations

We can now proceed with the calculation of the single-variable between-groups ANOVA. Table 12.8 presents the computational equations and a worked example for the data presented in Table 12.6. As you proceed with

## Table 12.8 Worked Example for a Single-Variable Independent-Groups ANOVA

$$SS_{between} = \sum \frac{(\Sigma x_j)^2}{n_j} - \frac{(\Sigma x_{ij})^2}{N}$$

$$SS_{between} = \frac{68^2}{10} + \frac{48^2}{9} + \frac{52^2}{10} + \frac{46^2}{9} + \frac{54^2}{10} + \frac{53^2}{10} + \frac{52^2}{10} - \frac{373^2}{68}$$

$$SS_{between} = 2066.811 - 2046.015 = 20.796$$

$$df_{between} = j - 1 = 7 - 1 = 6$$

$$MS_{between} = \frac{SS_{between}}{df_{between}} = \frac{20.796}{6} = 3.466$$

$$SS_{within} = \sum X_{ij}^2 - \sum \frac{(\Sigma x_j)^2}{n_j} = 2115 - 2066.811 = 48.189$$

$$MS_{within} = \frac{SS_{within}}{df_{within}} = \frac{48.189}{61} = 0.790$$

$$SS_{total} = \sum X_{ij}^2 - \sum \frac{(\Sigma x_{ij})^2}{N_j} = 2115 - \frac{373^2}{68} = 68.985$$

$$df_{total} = N - 1 = 68 - 1 = 67$$

$$F = \frac{SS_{between}}{MS_{within}} = \frac{3.466}{0.790} = 4.387$$

Note: $df_{total} = df_{between} + df_{within}$; $SS_{total} = SS_{between} + SS_{within}$.

your calculations, ensure that you make clear notes of your calculations. This practice will help you ensure that there are no computational errors. As a double check for your work, you should find that $df_{total} = df_{between} + df_{within}$ and that $SS_{total} = SS_{between} + SS_{within}$. Table 12.9 presents the ANOVA summary table.

### Additional Tests

**Omega squared ($\omega^2$)** is a measure of the degree of association between the independent and dependent variables:

$$\hat{\omega}^2 = \frac{df_{between}(F - 1)}{df_{between}(F - 1) + N} \tag{12.5}$$

## Table 12.9 ANOVA Summary Table for Data Present in Table 12.6

| Source | SS | df | MS | F |
|---|---|---|---|---|
| Between-groups | 20.796 | 6 | 3.466 | |
| Within-groups | 48.189 | 61 | 0.790 | 4.388 |
| Total | 68.985 | 67 | | |

$F_{critical}(6, 61) = 2.25$, $\alpha = .05$; reject $H_o$ because $F_{observed} \geq F_{critical}$

Applied to our ongoing example:

$$\hat{\omega}^2 = \frac{6(4.388 - 1)}{6(4.388 - 1) + 68} = \frac{6(3.388)}{6(3.388) + 68} = \frac{20.328}{88.328} = .2301$$

**Effect size** ($f$) is a standardized measure of the relative difference among the groups:

$$\eta^2 = \frac{df_{\text{between}}(F)}{df_{\text{between}}(F) + df_{\text{within}}} \text{ or, } \eta^2 = \frac{SS_{\text{between}}}{SS_{\text{total}}} \tag{12.6}$$

$$f = \sqrt{\frac{\eta^2}{1 - \eta^2}}$$

Applied to our ongoing example:

$$\eta^2 = \frac{20.789}{68.985} = .0301$$

$$f = \sqrt{\frac{0.301}{1 - 0.301}} = .656$$

Thus, we can conclude that the effect size is very large.

Tukey's HSD is a test used in conjunction with the ANOVA to examine the differences between means. The test protects against inflated experimentwise errors. One uses the test to compare means only if there is a significant $F$-ratio:

$$HSD = q_{\text{critical}} \sqrt{\frac{MS_{\text{within}}}{n}} \tag{12.7}$$

For this equation, HSD is the critical difference required to consider the means statistically different, $MS_{\text{within}}$ is the mean square within-groups, $n$ is the average sample size, and $q_{\text{critical}}$ is the critical value for a given $\alpha$ level for number of means and $df_{\text{within}}$. Use Table B.12 of Appendix B to find $q_{\text{critical}}$. To use Table B.12, you will need to know the number of groups in the analysis and the $df_{\text{within}}$. For this study, $j = 7$, $df_{\text{within}} = 61$, $MS_{\text{within}} = 0.790$, and $\alpha = .05$. Therefore, $q_{\text{critical}} = 4.31$.

If the number of subjects in each group is not equal, $n'$ is defined as

$$n' = \frac{j}{\Sigma\left(\frac{1}{n_j}\right)} \tag{12.8}$$

For the current example, the number of participants in each group is not the same. Therefore,

$$n' = \frac{7}{\dfrac{1}{10}+\dfrac{1}{9}+\dfrac{1}{10}+\dfrac{1}{9}+\dfrac{1}{10}+\dfrac{1}{10}+\dfrac{1}{10}} = \frac{7}{.10+.11+.10+.11+.10+.10+.10}$$

$$n' = \frac{7}{.72} = 9.72$$

$$HSD = 4.31\sqrt{\frac{0.790}{9.72}} = 4.31(0.2851) = 1.23$$

For this study, any difference between a pair of treatment group means that is 1.23 or greater can be considered statistically significant. To create the table of comparisons, order the means from lowest to highest. Then create a table of the difference between the pairs of means as was done for Table 12.5.

## Knowledge Check

7. A researcher plans to conduct a single-factor ANOVA with four independent groups. If the effect size is moderate, how many participants will the researcher require in each group to ensure an 80% chance of rejecting the null hypothesis when $\alpha = .05$?

8. Why will decreasing the within-groups variance increase the power of an ANOVA?

9. Why is the ANOVA considered an omnibus test?

10. In what ways are the $t$-ratio and $F$-ratio similar to and different from each other?

## Chapter Summary

This chapter is an extension of our previous review of single-variable between-subjects research designs. The important difference is that the design we examined in this chapter allows us to simultaneously examine many levels of the independent variable. The statistical test most often used to study the results of this research design is the analysis of variance (ANOVA).

The ANOVA is an omnibus test because it allows us to examine the effect of many different levels of the same independent variable on the dependent variable. As you learned in this chapter, the ANOVA is an extremely flexible design because we can use either quantitative or qualitative levels of the independent variable in our research. We can also use the ANOVA to analyze the data from a true experiment (for which the participants are randomly assigned to the treatment conditions) or an intact-groups design (the independent variable is a subject variable). In this chapter we revisited the themes surrounding cause and effect. Specifically, the researcher must be able to control the independent variable and account for alternative explanations to infer cause and effect. We then examined several ways that the researchers can gain control over the variables in a research project. The two that we examined are control through research design and control through research procedure.

In a true experiment, the researcher can exercise direct control over the independent variable by including control conditions and by randomly assigning the participants to the treatment conditions. Researchers exercise this type of control through the design of their study. A researcher can also exercise control over the research through good procedure. Control through procedure refers to ensuring that the experience of the participants in the different treatment conditions is identical save for the level of the independent variable.

Researchers use the general linear model to describe how the ANOVA analyzes the data. In a true experiment, for example, the participant's observed score is the total of the population mean plus the effect of the level of the independent variable plus the effects of random error. The ANOVA analyzes the variance among the scores in the study. Specifically, the ANOVA allows us to examine the within-groups and between-groups variance. The within-groups variance represents the effects of random events that influence the difference among the scores in the individual groups. The between-groups variance represents the differences among the group means. We use these variance estimates to determine the $F$-ratio.

The $F$-ratio is the between-groups variance divided by the within-groups variance. If the $F$-ratio is equal to 1.00, we must assume that the differences among the group means are due to random error. By contrast, if the $F$-ratio is statistically significant, we can assume that the differences among the means are greater than would be expected by chance if the null hypothesis were a true statement. Once we find that there is a statistically significant $F$-ratio, we can then calculate $\hat{\omega}^2$ or $\eta^2$; both indicate the proportion of the differences among the groups related to differences among the levels of the independent variable. Similarly, we can use the post-hoc tests, such as Tukey's HSD, to determine which pairs of means are different from each other. As with any research design, we can determine the power of the study. We can estimate the number of participants required in each treatment condition to ensure that we will have sufficient statistical power to reject the null hypothesis.

## Chapter Glossary for Review

**Analysis of variance**—An inferential statistical technique used to examine the difference among group means. The statistic divides the total variance among the participants into variance related to the independent variable and variance related to random error. If the ratio of the between-groups variance to the within-groups variance is sufficiently large, one may reject the null hypothesis that all group means are equal.

**ANOVA summary table**—A table that presents the sum of squares, degrees of freedom, mean square, and $F$-ratio for an analysis of variance.

**Between-groups variance**—An estimate of the variance among the individual group means.

$df_{between}$—Degrees of freedom between-groups, also presented as $df_N$.

$df_{within}$—Degrees of freedom within-groups, also presented as $df_D$.

**Effect size**—A descriptive statistic that provides a standardized measure of the relative difference among the group means. Effect sizes greater than 0 indicate a relation between the independent and dependent variables.

**Experimentwise error ($\alpha_e$)**—The probability of committing one or more Type I errors when conducting multiple $t$-ratios from a single experiment.

$f$—A measure of effect size for the analysis of variance.

**$F$-ratio**—The inferential statistic for the analysis of variance. The statistic is the between-groups variance divided by the within-groups variance. If the $F$-ratio is sufficiently large, one may reject the null hypothesis that all group means are equal.

**General linear model**—A conceptual mathematical model that describes an observed score as the sum of the population mean ($\mu$), the treatment effect for a specific level of a factor ($\alpha_j$), and random error ($\varepsilon_{ij}$). For the one-variable ANOVA, the general linear model is $Xij = \mu + \alpha_j + \varepsilon_{ij}$.

**Independent**—For a multilevel between-groups research design, independence indicates that the data collected for one group have no effect or relation to data collected in the other groups.

**Level**—The magnitude of or a condition within the independent variable. For qualitative variables, such as sex, level refers to the category for the variable (e.g., male versus female). For quantitative variables, level refers to the amount or magnitude of the independent variable.

**Mean square ($MS$)**—Another term used for an estimate of variance, especially within the context of the ANOVA.

**Multiple comparisons**—A procedure for examining pairs of means from a multilevel between-groups research design.

**Omega squared ($\hat{\omega}^2$)**—A descriptive statistic that indicates the proportion of the variance between groups that is related to the independent variable.

**Pairwise error ($\alpha_p$)**—The probability of committing a Type I error for a single $t$-ratio.

**Partition**—In statistics, refers to separating the total variance into its smaller components, the within-groups variance, and the variance due to specific variables or combinations of variables.

**Pilot study**—A rehearsal of the final research project that permits the researcher to ensure that the procedures will allow him or her to collect the data needed for the study.

**Total variance**—An estimate of the variance among all the observations collected in the study.

**Tukey's HSD**—A test used in conjunction with the ANOVA to examine the differences between means. The test protects against inflated experiment-wise errors.

**Within-groups variance**—An estimate of the average variance among scores within each group of the research.

## Chapter References

Abelson, R. P. (1985). A variance explanation paradox: When a little is a lot. *Psychological Bulletin*, *97*, 129–133.

Cohen, J. (1988). *Statistical power analysis for the behavioral sciences* (2nd ed.). Hillsdale, NJ: LEA.

Ekman, P., & O'Sullivan, M. (1991). Who can catch a liar? *American Psychologist*, *46*, 913–920.

Jaccard, J., Becker, M. A., & Wood, G. (1984). Pairwise multiple comparison procedures: A review. *Psychological Bulletin*, *96*, 589–596.

Mueller, C. M., & Dweck, C. S. (1998). Praise for intelligence can undermine children's motivation and performance. *Journal of Personality and Social Psychology*, *75*, 33–53.

Rotton, J., & Cohn, E. G. (2001). Temperature, routine activities, and domestic violence: A reanalysis. *Violence & Victims*, *16*, 203–215.

Tukey, J. W. (1953). *The problem of multiple comparisons*. Mimeographed monograph, Princeton University.

## CHAPTER OBJECTIVES

Except for the point masses of freshman physics—or the hard round spheres of the earliest models for gas molecules—few phenomena involve only a few variables.

**—Tukey, Mosteller, and Hoaglin (1991)**

## Introduction

How many times have you heard someone say something like "Television violence causes violence" and thought to yourself, "It's not that simple; there are other factors involved"? As you learn more about psychology, you will discover that most explanations of behavior include several variables. For instance, what causes one person to help others? Researchers who study altruism suggest that many variables influence helping behavior, including the number of people in the situation, the cost of helping, and the similarity between the person needing help and the helper. There are few instances where we can use a single variable to fully explain human behavior. The implication of this is that our research needs to incorporate more than one variable to understand the phenomenon that we are studying. In this chapter you will learn how to use the two-variable design and the two-factor analysis of variance (ANOVA). This research design has many advantages, including the ability to: (1) examine the effects of more than one independent variable at a time; (2) examine the interaction between the independent variables; and (3) conduct research that is an efficient use of time and effort. This chapter also sets the foundation for designs involving more than two variables or factors.

## The Logic of the Two-Variable Design

The logic of the two-variable design is similar to the single-variable design. The primary difference is that the two-variable design allows us to examine the relationship between two independent variables and a dependent variable. Specifically, the two-variable design examines how much each independent variable, by itself, influences the dependent variable. In addition, this type of design allows us to test the joint influence of the two independent variables on the dependent variable. Figure 13.1 illustrates the logic of the one- and two-variable ANOVA. As you can see, the single-variable ANOVA partitions the total variation among scores into two general components, the between-groups variation and the within-groups variation. The between-groups variation represents in part the variance caused by systematic differences among the groups. By contrast, the two-variable design further divides the between-groups variance.

Specifically, the two-factor ANOVA divides the between-groups variation into the effects due to each of the independent variables and the interaction of these variables. We can use the general linear model to examine the logic of the between-subjects two-variable ANOVA.

$$X_{ijk} = \mu + \alpha_j + \beta_k + \alpha\beta_{jk} + \varepsilon_{ijk} \qquad (13.1)$$

In this equation, $X_{ijk}$ represents an observation within a specific treatment condition. The $i$ in the subscript represents the participant in the group, the $j$

# Figure 13.1

**Single-Variable vs. Two-Variable Design**

SINGLE-VARIABLE DESIGN & ANOVA

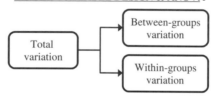

TWO-VARIABLE DESIGN & ANOVA

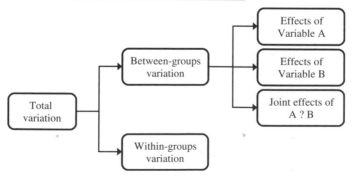

The two-variable design partitions the between-group variation into three components—effects due to Variable A, Variable B, and the joint effects of the two independent variables.

represents the level of the first independent variable, and the $k$ represents the level of the second independent variable. As in the single-variable model, $\mu$ represents the mean for the base population, and $\varepsilon_{ijk}$ represents the sampling error for each observation. The other three terms represent the effects of each independent variable and their interaction. Specifically, $\alpha_j$ represents the effects of the first independent variable, $\beta_k$ represents the effects of the second independent variable, and $\alpha\beta_{jk}$ represents the unique variation due to the interaction of the two variables.

## Advantages of the Two-Variable Design

There are several advantages of the two-variable design over the one-variable design. The two-variable design allows us to use research resources efficiently, analyze the interactive effects of two variables, and increase our statistical power.

### Increased Efficiency

What would happen if we conducted two one-variable studies rather than one two-variable study? The first study could examine the effects of three levels of the first independent variable. The second study could then examine the effect of three levels of the second independent variable. Assume for a moment that a power analysis for these experiments indicated that we need 30 participants in each treatment condition to have sufficient statistical power (e.g., $1 - \beta = .80$). Therefore, we will need 90 participants for each study, or 180 participants for both studies. By comparison, the two-variable design requires only 90 participants.

As you can see in Table 13.1, the two-variable design contains the elements of the two separate one-variable designs *and* uses fewer participants. The design retains 30 participants for each level of each treatment condition. By combining the two studies, we require half as many participants as if we attempted to conduct two separate studies. Therefore, one two-variable study is more cost effective than two one-variable studies. In addition, the two-variable design provides more information concerning the combined effects of the two independent variables.

### Analysis of the Interaction of Variables

Another advantage of the two-variable design is that it helps us understand how combinations of variables influence behavior. Because we can combine different levels of the two independent variables, we can observe their combined effect on the dependent variable, an effect that we would not be able to observe or test in a single-variable study. As you will learn, an interaction represents a unique pattern of influence on the dependent variable that cannot be explained by the independent variables separately.

# Table 13.1 Difference Between Two Single-Variable Studies and One Two-Variable Study

**Two single-variable studies**

Each study uses 30 participants in each treatment condition ($n = 30$) for a total of $N = 90$ in the whole study. Conducting both studies requires $N = 180$.

**Study 1**

|  | $a_1$ | $a_2$ | $a_3$ | Total |
|---|---|---|---|---|
|  | $n_1 = 30$ | $n_2 = 30$ | $n_3 = 30$ | $N = 90$ |

**Study 2**

|  | $b_1$ | $b_2$ | $b_3$ | Total |
|---|---|---|---|---|
|  | $n_1 = 30$ | $n_2 = 30$ | $n_3 = 30$ | $N = 90$ |

**One two-variable study**

This design combines the two studies and requires only $N = 90$

|  |  | A | | | | |
|---|---|---|---|---|---|---|
|  |  | $a_1$ | $a_2$ | $a_3$ | Total | |
| B | $b_1$ | $n_{11} = 10$ | $n_{21} = 10$ | $n_{31} = 10$ | $n_{b1} = 30$ | For each level of Variable B, |
|  | $b_2$ | $n_{12} = 10$ | $n_{22} = 10$ | $n_{32} = 10$ | $n_{b2} = 30$ | there are 30 participants. |
|  | $b_3$ | $n_{13} = 10$ | $n_{23} = 10$ | $n_{33} = 10$ | $n_{b3} = 30$ | |
|  | Total | $n_{a1} = 30$ | $n_{a2} = 30$ | $n_{a3} = 30$ | $N = 90$ | |

For each level of Variable A there are 30 participants.

Here is an example of how studying two variables can allow us to examine an interaction. Cohen, Nisbett, Bowdle, and Schwarz (1996) conducted an experiment in which they examined the reaction of white male participants who had just been insulted. When the participants arrived for the experiment, a researcher collected a sample of the participants' saliva. Next, the participants walked through a long, narrow hall. For a random half of the men, a research associate, walking in the other direction, bumped into the participant and called him an insulting name. When the participants reached the end of the hall, another researcher greeted the participant, had him complete a short task, and then collected another sample of saliva. Cohen et al. examined the change in testosterone levels in the two saliva samples. Testosterone is a hormone that has been shown to correlate with levels of arousal (especially aggression), and it is easily measured in saliva.

Figure 13.2 represents the results for the study—specifically, the average percent increase in testosterone for participants in the control and insult groups. The results seem straightforward: Insulted men produced more testosterone after the insult than men not insulted. Do these data tell the entire story? Compare Figure 13.2 with Figure 13.3. The results presented in Figure 13.3 represent the relation between changes in testosterone and two independent variables. The first independent variable is whether the participant received an insult. The second independent variable is the

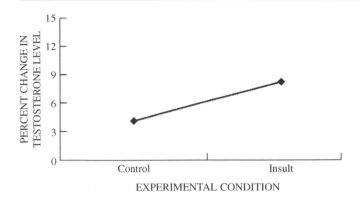

**Figure 13.2**

**Relation between Changes in Testosterone Levels and the Control and Insult Conditions**

regional background of the participants. Cohen et al. (1996) selected the participants for the study such that half of the men had lived most of their lives in the North. The other participants were men who had lived mainly in the South. The insult condition represents a manipulated independent variable because the researcher randomly assigned half the participants to the insult condition and the others to the control condition.

The regional background of the participant is a subject variable, as it reflects a characteristic of the participant that is not controlled by the researcher. Do you notice a difference between the two figures? Did men from the North respond to the insult in the same way as men from the South? Clearly, the two groups of men reacted differently to the insult condition. More specifically, in the control condition, there is no distinguishable difference between the two groups of men in terms of their levels of testosterone. The interesting difference occurs in the insult condition. From the results of this condition, you can see that in men from the North there was little reaction to the insult as indicated by the percent change in testosterone (in fact, their levels are almost equivalent to the levels found in the control group). By contrast, the change in testosterone level for the men

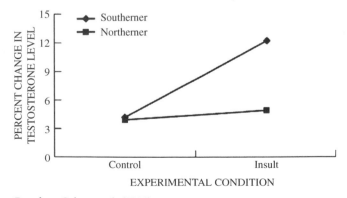

**Figure 13.3**

**Relation between Changes in Testosterone Levels and Insult Condition for Men Raised in Either Southern or Northern States**

Based on Cohen et al. (1996).

from the South shows a clear spike, as these men produced considerably more testosterone after the insult than any of the men in the other conditions. The data in Figure 13.3 represent an interaction because the men from the North and the South reacted differently to the same insult condition but showed no difference for the control condition.

Cohen et al. (1996) predicted that men who grew up in the South experience a "culture of honor" that requires them to protect their character when attacked, whereas men raised in the North experienced a different cultural norm. Because of these cultural differences, Cohen et al. predicted that men raised in the South would produce greater levels of testosterone, indicating greater levels of aggression and offense to the insult. Look again at Figure 13.2. Is it accurate to say that being insulted increases testosterone levels? Although the statement is by itself accurate, it is incomplete because it does not take into account the background of the participants. As you can see in Figure 13.3, men raised in the North did not react to the insult, whereas men raised in the South did react. Therefore, to offer a more complete and accurate account of the reaction to insult, we need to make full use of the data we have available—in this case then, we need to consider the interaction of the two independent variables (level of insult and regional background) and their influence on testosterone levels.

## Increased Statistical Power

A third advantage of the two-variable ANOVA is an increase in statistical power. In general, a two-variable or multivariable design tends to be more powerful than a single-variable design. A main reason for this is that the within-groups variance in a two-variable or multivariable design tends to be smaller than the within-groups variance in a one-variable study. Why is this true? In the one-variable design, the within-groups variance reflects the effects of sampling error and the effects of variables that the researcher has not measured. In some research situations, this unmeasured variable may be strongly associated with the dependent variable. Consequently, measuring an additional variable in a factorial design often allows the researcher to describe the data more precisely. The benefit of this tactic is that the researcher can reduce the within-groups variance in each of the treatment groups, thereby increasing the possibility of detecting a statistically significant difference between treatment groups in terms of the dependent variable.

We can use the Cohen et al. (1996) study as an example. If the researchers had performed a single-variable study examining only the effect of the insult, as presented in Figure 13.2, they would have found a statistically significant difference between the means of the two groups. The within-groups variance would be relatively large, however, because the researchers did not take into account the potential influence of participants' regional backgrounds. If we use the same data, but now conduct a two-factor ANOVA that includes regional background, the within-groups variance will decrease because we have identified another variable that systematically affects the participants' physiological reactions (i.e., testosterone level). In essence we have become more specific in our classification of participants: Instead of grouping them solely in terms of their exposure to insult, we are now also grouping them in terms of their respective regional backgrounds.

## Factorial Designs: Variables, Levels, and Cells

When researchers talk about the two-variable design, they often refer to concepts such as factorial designs, main effects, and the interaction. These terms refer to the design of the experiment and to the specific components of the general linear model of the two-variable ANOVA. Before we continue, you need to understand the meaning of these terms.

### Treatment Combinations

One of the advantages of the two-variable ANOVA is that it allows us to examine the effects of two or more independent variables and their combined effects. When we design a two-variable study, we select the number of **levels** that we want to use for each independent variable. Because we combine the two variables into one study, we create a **factorial design**. A factorial design represents a study that includes an independent group for each possible combination of levels for the multiple independent variables. In the Cohen et al. (1996) experiment, for instance, there were two levels of the insult condition (Variable A: control vs. insult) and two levels of participant background (Variable B: northerner vs. southerner). Consequently, we can say that Cohen et al. used a *2 × 2 factorial design*. This design therefore created four distinct or independent treatment groups as presented in Table 13.2.

For a $3 \times 4$ factorial design, there are 12 independent treatment conditions or **cells.** For example, the cell $a_1b_2$ represents the first level of the first independent variable (Variable A: control condition) and the second level of the second independent variable (Variable B: southerner). Hence,

Table $13.2$  **Matrix for a 2 × 2 Factorial Research Design Using Cohen et al. (1996) as an Example**

| | | Variable A Insult Condition | |
|---|---|---|---|
| **Variable B Regional Background** | | **Control** $a_1$ | **Insult** $a_2$ |
| Northern | $b_1$ | Control × Northern $a_1b_1$ | Insult × Northern $a_2b_1$ |
| Southern | $b_2$ | Control × Southern $a_1b_2$ | Insult × Southern $a_2b_2$ |

all the participants in $a_1b_2$ are men from the South assigned to the control condition.

Factorial designs can ~~vary in complexity~~ from the simple 2 × 2 design to more complex designs such as a 3 × 5 or a 4 × 6 factorial. Factorial designs can also ~~include more than two variables~~. The ~~ANOVA~~ allows researchers to ~~use any number of independent variables in a study~~. Some researchers may use three or four independent variables in one experiment. You may, for example, read in a research report that the researcher conducted a 2 × 3 × 4 ANOVA. This information implies that the researcher examined the effects of three independent variables and the interactions among all of these variables. There were two levels for the first variable, three levels of the second variable, and four levels of the third variable. If this was a fully between-subjects design, then you should also conclude that there were 24 (2 × 3 × 4 = 24) independent treatment groups, each representing a unique combination of the three variables. Thus, a distinguishing feature of all factorial designs is that they contain all possible combinations of the treatment conditions the researcher decided to use.

In this chapter we primarily focus on the two-variable model. If you need to use a more complex form of the ANOVA, such as one including three variables, you may want to review other sources such as Hayes (1981); Kirk (1982); or Winer, Brown, and Michels (1991) to learn how to conceptualize and analyze the results from more complex research designs. Because of complexities with multiple variable interactions, it is not common to see social science research that involves more than a three-way interaction (e.g., A × B × C).

## Examples of Factorial Designs

In this section we will examine how we can use the factorial design to conduct various research projects. The studies differ in the type of independent variables used and the number of levels for each variable.

### Reaction to Product Endorsements

How seriously do people take product reviews? Are readers mindful of the credibility of the reviewer? What about the evaluation of the product—do strong endorsements always lead to willingness to buy a product? Chaiken and Maheswaran (1992) conducted an interesting experiment in which they varied the credibility of the review source and the general message of the review. They asked college students to read a review of a new telephone answering machine. The researchers told half the participants that the review came from a flyer printed by the discount store K-mart (lower credibility), and half that it came from the magazine *Consumer Reports* (higher credibility). Each participant then read one of three types of review: an unambiguous strong review, an ambiguous review (the answering machine was better than some machines but not as good as others), or an unambiguous weak review. The researchers then asked the participants to rate on a 10-point scale their willingness to buy the answering machine for $50 (10 = very willing to buy).

*What type of research design did Chaiken and Maheswaran (1992) use?* Figure 13.4 illustrates the design of the experiment. Clearly, there are two independent variables. The first variable (variable or Factor A) is the credibility of the source, which has two levels, high and low. The researchers randomly assigned half the participants to the low-credibility condition and the other half to the high-credibility condition. The second variable (variable or Factor B) is the type of review the participants read. There were three levels of this variable: (1) strong review, (2) ambiguous review, and (3) weak review. The researchers randomly assigned the participants to one of the three levels of variable B. Both factors are manipulated variables because the researchers could randomly determine the type of review the participants read. Therefore the researchers used a 2 × 3 factorial design. As

## Figure 13.4

**Research Design Used by Chaiken and Maheswaran (1992)**

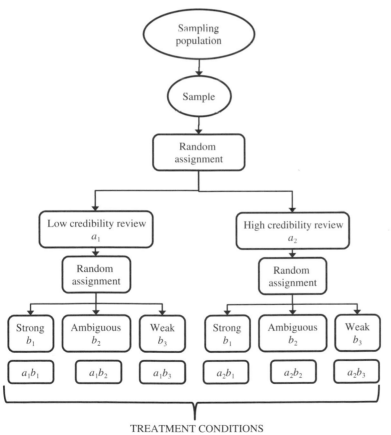

TREATMENT CONDITIONS

There are two independent variables: credibility of the review (low versus high) and conclusion of the review (strong, ambiguous, and weak). Because both variables are manipulated variables, the researcher can randomly assign participants to one of the six possible treatment combinations.

Table 13.3 **Mean Willingness to Buy the Answering Machine for the Six Treatment Conditions in the Chaiken and Maheswaran (1992) Experiment**

| Variable B<br>Level of Endorsement | | Variable A<br>Credibility of Source | | |
|---|---|---|---|---|
| | | Low<br>$a_1$ | High<br>$a_2$ | Row Means |
| Strong | $b_1$ | $M_{11} = 6.60$ | $M_{21} = 5.90$ | $M_{b1} = 6.25$ |
| Ambiguous | $b_2$ | $M_{12} = 5.40$ | $M_{22} = 8.00$ | $M_{b2} = 6.70$ |
| Weak | $b_3$ | $M_{13} = 5.10$ | $M_{23} = 3.00$ | $M_{b3} = 4.05$ |
| **Column Means** | | $M_{a1} = 5.70$ | $M_{a2} = 5.63$ | $M_{overall} = 5.67$ |

you can see in Figure 13.4, there are six separate treatment conditions representing each possible combination of the two factors.

Table 13.3 and Figure 13.5 present the results of the Chaiken and Maheswaran (1992) experiment. The data in Table 13.3 are the means for each of the six treatment conditions as well as the marginal means. *Marginal* means represent the average performance for each level of one independent variable across all levels of the other independent variable. For example, the average score for all participants who read the low-credibility review is 5.70, whereas the average scores for all participants who read the high-credibility review is 5.63. By themselves, the means lead us to conclude that the credibility of the review had little effect on the participants' evaluation of the answering machine.

However, the graph presented in Figure 13.5 reveals an interaction effect involving the two independent variables. The easy way to recognize this type of effect is to visually note that the lines in the figure are not parallel; in this case they even cross. The ambiguous review condition appears to create an especially interesting pattern of results. The participants

## Figure 13.5

**Results of the Chaiken and Maheswaran (1992) Experiment**

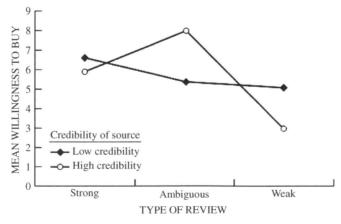

An interesting finding is the participants' willingness to buy a product that received an ambiguous rating from a highly credible source.

who read the ambiguous review from the credible source were the most willing to buy the answering machine. These results clearly illustrate an interaction because the effects of the type of review were not consistent for the source of the review. Phrased a different way, the influence of the type of review on participants' willingness to buy the answering machine was different, depending on the source of the review.

### Effects of Noise on Children Diagnosed as Hyperactive

Zentall and Shaw (1980) conducted a study to determine the effects of noise on children's ability to complete an academic task. Figure 13.6 presents the design of this study.

Specifically, the researchers selected a group of second-grade children diagnosed as hyperactive. The researchers then selected another group of children with no diagnosed learning disability. The researchers had all the children complete a grade-appropriate math test. Half the children completed the task in a quiet room, whereas the other children completed the test in a noisy room. Hopefully you are starting to realize that this study is also an illustration of a factorial design, because it is a 2 (control vs. hyperactive) × 2 (quiet vs. noisy room) between-subjects design.

## Figure 13.6

**Research Design Used by Zentall and Shaw (1980)**

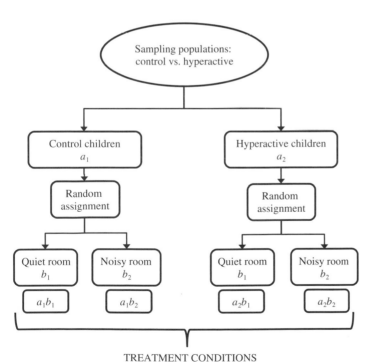

TREATMENT CONDITIONS

There are two independent variables, diagnosis of the child (control versus hyperactive) and test conditions (quiet versus noisy). The diagnosis is a subject variable. The testing condition is a manipulated variable.

# Figure 13.7

**Results of the Zentall and Shaw (1980) Study**

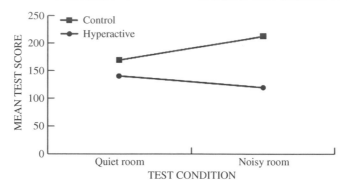

The interesting finding in this research is that the children not diagnosed as hyperactive did better in the noisy room rather than the quiet room condition. In contrast, the children diagnosed as hyperactive did better in the quiet room than the noisy room.

The first independent variable in this example is a subject variable because the presence of diagnosed learning disability is not something the researcher can manipulate. In contrast, the second independent variable is a manipulated variable because the researcher could randomly assign the students to one of the two conditions. Figure 13.7 presents the results of the Zentall and Shaw (1980) study. The most interesting and notable feature of these results is the interaction between disability and noise of testing room: Children diagnosed as hyperactive performed worse on the test when it was given in a noisy room than in a quiet room. Children in the control group, however, performed better in the noisy room than they did in the quiet room. As with the previous example, these results suggest an interaction effect of the two independent variables. In words, the influence of a child's diagnosed learning disability on his or her math test performance was different, depending on the noise level in the testing room.

## Main Effects and Interaction

The purpose of the factorial design is to examine how the two variables in the research combine and possibly interact with one another. In this section we will examine the potential outcomes for a factorial design and describe how to interpret the results. Specifically, we will examine main effects and interactions. As a brief preview, a main effect represents results wherein one or both factors separately have a statistically significant effect on the dependent variable. An interaction represents a condition where both independent variables have a joint effect on the dependent variable. For the sake of illustration, we can use hypothetical data that could have come from the study design used by Cohen et al. (1996). As a quick reminder, in this study Variable A is the insult condition (control vs. insult) and Variable B is the participant's regional background (southern vs. northern).

## Main Effects

A **main effect** refers to the effect that one independent variable has on the dependent variable holding the effect of any other independent variable(s) constant. Specifically, a main effect represents a special form of the between-groups variance of a single independent variable. In a two-variable ANOVA, there are two main effects, one for each variable. When we examine the data using an ANOVA, each main effect can be either statistically significant or not statistically significant. Consequently, there are four potential main effect results: (1) a statistically significant main effect for Variable A, (2) a statistically significant main effect for Variable B, (3) statistically significant main effects for Variables A and B, or (4) no statistically significant main effect for Variables A and B.

The statistically significant main effect represents the **additive effect** of the independent variable. An additive effect means that when we combine two variables, the effect of each variable adds a consistent effect across all treatment conditions. By contrast, the interaction indicates that there is interplay between the two variables that is more than can be explained by either variable alone. An interaction indicates a unique treatment effect that neither independent variable can explain by itself.

Figure 13.8 presents two types of main effect. In Figure 13.8(a) there is a main effect for Variable A, but not Variable B. More specifically, Figure 13.8(a) indicates that the insult condition increased the testosterone of all the participants and that there were no differences between northerners and southerners. In contrast, Figure 13.8(b) indicates that the southerners had a greater change in testosterone than the northerners, but that the insult condition had no effect on the results. There is no evidence for an interaction in either of the graphs in Figure 13.8. An easy way to recognize this is to note that the lines in these figures are parallel, indicating that the relationship between insult condition and testosterone was identical regardless of the participant's regional background.

It is also possible to have results that indicate statistically significant main effects for both independent variables, without a significant interaction. This is the situation illustrated in Figure 13.9(a). Notice that there is a statistically significant main effect for the insult condition: All the participants in the insult condition had greater increases in testosterone than all the participants in the control condition. This graph also depicts a statistically significant main effect for the participant's background: Southerners had greater increases in testosterone than northerners in the control and insult conditions. Because the lines in this graph are parallel, there is no evidence that the influence of one variable on the dependent variable depends on the other (i.e., there is no interaction present here).

Although it can be frustrating to the researchers, there are times when research produces no statistically significant findings, as illustrated in Figure 13.9(b). In this graph you can see that participants' testosterone showed a slight increase for the control and insult conditions, but there are no evident systematic differences among the four group means.

# Figure 13.8

**Two Types of Main Effect for a 2 × 2 Design**

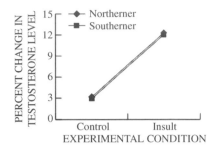

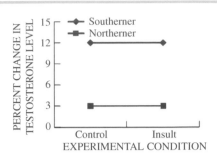

|                          | **FACTOR A** INSULT CONDITION | | |
|                          | Control | Insult | |
| **Factor B** background  | a₁ | a₂ | Row means |
| **Northerner b₁**        | 3.25 | 12.25 | 7.75 |
| **Southerner b₂**        | 3.00 | 12.00 | 7.50 |
| Column means             | 3.13 | 12.13 | 7.63 |

**Main effect for Factor A**
No main effect for Factor B
No interaction

*(a)*

|                          | **FACTOR A** INSULT CONDITION | | |
|                          | Control | Insult | |
| **Factor B** background  | a₁ | a₂ | Row means |
| **Northerner b₁**        | 3.0 | 3.0 | 3.0 |
| **Southerner b₂**        | 12.0 | 12.0 | 12.0 |
| Column means             | 7.5 | 7.5 | 7.5 |

No main effect for Factor A
**Main effect for Factor B**
No interaction

*(b)*

In (a) there is a statistically significant main effect for Variable A, insult condition—men who were insulted had larger changes in testosterone than men who were not insulted. In (b) there is evidence for a statistically significant main effect of Variable B, background—southerners had a greater increase in testosterone than northerners.

As a secondary and slightly more complex example, Figure 13.10 illustrates additive main effects for a 3 × 2 design with main effects for Variables A and B, but no interaction. For Variable A, each increase in level (e.g., $a_1$ to $a_2$ and $a_2$ to $a_3$) represents an equal change in the means. The difference between $a_1$ and $a_2$ is 20 points for both the $b_1$ and $b_2$ conditions. Similarly, the change between $a_2$ and $a_3$ is 5 points for both the $b_1$ and $b_2$ conditions. Changes in the dependent variable for all levels of Variable B are consistent across all levels of Variable A. We see this same consistency in the differences for Variable B. The average of the $b_2$ treatment condition is always 30 points greater than the $b_1$ treatment condition. This consistency across all levels of A and B means that there is no interactive effect of the two independent variables on the dependent variable in this example.

## The Interaction

An **interaction** indicates that the effect of one independent variable is not consistent across all levels of the other independent variable. In a two-variable design, there are four potential patterns of interaction. We will begin by examining the situation that arises when there is a statistically significant interaction and one statistically significant main effect.

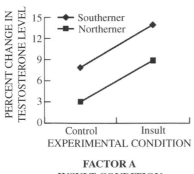

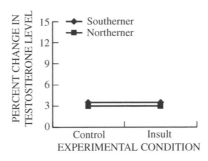

# Figure 13.9

**Two More Types of Main Effect for a 2 × 2 Design**

|  | **FACTOR A INSULT CONDITION** | | |
|---|---|---|---|
| **Factor B background** | Control $a_1$ | Insult $a_2$ | Row means |
| **Northerner $b_1$** | 3.0 | 9.0 | 6.0 |
| **Southerner $b_2$** | 8.0 | 14.0 | 11.0 |
| Column means | 5.5 | 11.5 | 6.5 |

Main effect for Factor A
Main effect for Factor B
No interaction

(a)

|  | **FACTOR A INSULT CONDITION** | | |
|---|---|---|---|
| **Factor B background** | Control $a_1$ | Insult $a_2$ | Row means |
| **Northerner $b_1$** | 3.5 | 3.5 | 3.5 |
| **Southerner $b_2$** | 3.0 | 3.0 | 3.0 |
| Column means | 3.25 | 3.25 | 3.25 |

No main effect for Factor A
No main effect for Factor B
No interaction

(b)

In (a) there are statistically significant main effects for the insult condition and the men's backgrounds. The results show that southerners had higher overall increases in testosterone and that the insult condition created greater increases in testosterone. In (b) there are no statistically significant effects.

Figure 13.11 presents two examples of statistically significant interactions. The most notable characteristic of the two graphs in Figure 13.11 is that the lines are not parallel. This is a hallmark of the interaction. The interaction represents variation among the treatment conditions that cannot be explained by the independent variables considered separately. When there is an interaction, one must examine how the two variables combine to

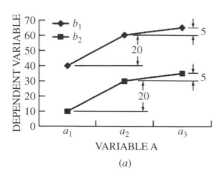

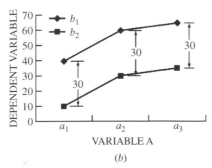

# Figure 13.10

**Additive Main Effect for a 3 × 2 ANOVA**

For this example, there are significant main effects for Variables A and B, but no interaction. For each variable, the differences among the means remain constant across all levels of the other variable.

# Figure 13.11

**Two Types of
Interaction for a 2 × 2
Design**

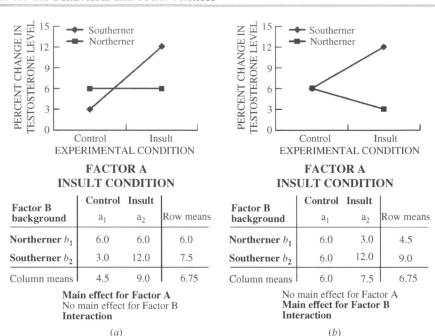

| Factor B background | FACTOR A INSULT CONDITION | | | | | |
|---|---|---|---|---|---|---|
| | Control $a_1$ | Insult $a_2$ | Row means | | | |
| Northerner $b_1$ | 6.0 | 6.0 | 6.0 | | | |
| Southerner $b_2$ | 3.0 | 12.0 | 7.5 | | | |
| Column means | 4.5 | 9.0 | 6.75 | | | |

**Main effect for Factor A**
No main effect for Factor B
**Interaction**

(a)

| Factor B background | FACTOR A INSULT CONDITION | | |
|---|---|---|---|
| | Control $a_1$ | Insult $a_2$ | Row means |
| Northerner $b_1$ | 6.0 | 3.0 | 4.5 |
| Southerner $b_2$ | 6.0 | 12.0 | 9.0 |
| Column means | 6.0 | 7.5 | 6.75 |

No main effect for Factor A
**Main effect for Factor B**
**Interaction**

(b)

In (a) there is a statistically significant interaction and significant main effect for Variable A. In (b) there is a statistically significant interaction and a significant main effect for Variable B.

produce unique results. In Figure 13.11, the insult condition, by itself, cannot account for all the differences among the four group means. Instead, it is more accurate and to the point to highlight that the effect of the insult condition interacted with participants' backgrounds. In this example, northern men showed little reaction to the insult, as measured by the level of testosterone. However, southern participants showed a considerable reaction to the same insult condition. This is evidence for an interaction of insult × regional background.

In Figure 13.11(a) there is also evidence for a statistically significant interaction of insult × regional background and a main effect for Variable A, the insult condition. This main effect indicates that, all else being equal, participants in the insult condition had greater testosterone increases than participants in the control condition. As you can see in the graph, this statement does not take into account the effect of the interaction between the insult condition and the participant's background. Looking at Figure 13.11(a) it is clear that the most important finding to highlight is that northern participants' testosterone levels did not change across the two insult conditions, but southern participants' testosterone levels did rise for southern participants who experienced the insult condition (this type of interaction is often referred to as a disordinal interaction).

Figure 13.11(b) also indicates a statistically significant interaction and main effect. In this example, the insult had opposite effects on the southern

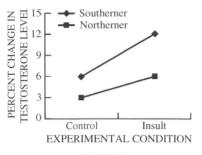
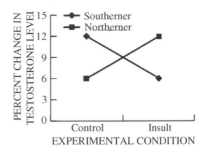

## Figure 13.12

**Two Types of Interaction for a 2 × 2 Design**

| Factor B background | FACTOR A INSULT CONDITION | | | |
|---|---|---|---|
| | Control $a_1$ | Insult $a_2$ | Row means |
| **Northerner** $b_1$ | 3.0 | 6.0 | 4.5 |
| **Southerner** $b_2$ | 6.0 | 12.0 | 9.0 |
| Column means | 4.5 | 9.0 | 6.75 |

**Main effect for Factor A**
**Main effect for Factor B**
**Interaction**

*(a)*

| Factor B background | FACTOR A INSULT CONDITION | | | |
|---|---|---|---|
| | Control $a_1$ | Insult $a_2$ | Row means |
| **Northerner** $b_1$ | 6.0 | 12.0 | 9.0 |
| **Southerner** $b_2$ | 12.0 | 6.0 | 9.0 |
| Column means | 9.0 | 9.0 | 9.0 |

**No main effect for Factor A**
**No main effect for Factor B**
**Interaction**

*(b)*

In (a) there is a statistically significant interaction and significant main effects for the Variable A and Variable B. In (b) there is a statistically significant interaction, but neither main effect is statistically significant.

and northern participants. The insult caused the southern participants' testosterone to increase but the northern participants' testosterone to decrease (this type of interaction is often referred to as an ordinal interaction, as the lines do not cross within the bounds of measurement for the variables involved).

Figure 13.12 presents the last set of potential patterns for interactions and main effects in a two-variable design. Figure 13.12(a) represents the condition where the interaction and both main effects are statistically significant. As you can see in the means, the insult condition raised the testosterone levels more than the control condition. In addition, southern men had, overall, greater increases in testosterone levels. Although both of these statements are correct, they do not fully describe all the components of the results. From the observed interaction, however, we can more completely conclude that southern participants reacted more to insults, as measured by the change in testosterone, than did northern participants.

The data presented in Figure 13.12(b) represent a scenario in which the interaction of the two independent variables is significant, but neither of the main effects is significant. Do these results mean that the independent variable had no effect on the results? No! Both independent variables influence the dependent variable, but their effects can be understood only within the context of the interaction. This is why it is so important to consider and interpret interaction effects first and then follow that with a consideration of any possible

# Figure 13.13

**Significant Interaction and Significant Main Effects for Variables A and B**

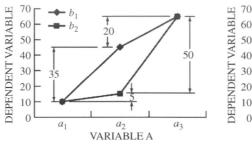

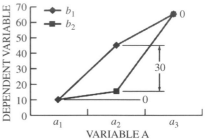

main effects in this type of design. In the present example, the main effects cancel each other because of the pattern of means.

Figure 13.13 presents another look at a significant interaction. Looking closely at the data, you can see that the changes in the dependent variable are not consistent for the different combinations of the variables. For example, the difference between $a_1b_1$ and $a_2b_1$ is 35 points, whereas the difference between $a_1b_2$ and $a_2b_2$ is 5 points. In addition, the difference between $a_1b_1$ and $a_1b_2$ is 0, whereas the difference between $a_2b_1$ and $a_2b_2$ is 30 points.

This inconsistency across treatment conditions is evidence of an interaction. You should interpret any differences among treatment group means with care when there is a statistically significant interaction. This is why you should always consider the interaction effect(s) first when reviewing the results of your ANOVA based on such data. According to the general linear model, each treatment group mean reflects the effects of each independent variable *and* their interaction. Therefore, when you see that the mean of $a_2b_1 = 45$, you must recognize that its value represents the effect of Variable A, Variable B, and the interaction of A × B. We will explore how to examine the contribution of the interaction in a subsequent section.

## Knowledge Check

Each of the following represents the cell totals and sample sizes for 2 × 2 factorial studies. For each study, determine means for the individual treatment conditions as well as the row and column means. Then prepare a graph of the means and determine whether there is evidence of main effects for variables A and B and an interaction.

1.

|  | $a_1$ | $a_2$ |  |  | $a_1$ | $a_2$ |  |
|---|---|---|---|---|---|---|---|
| $b_1$ | $\sum X_{11} = 30.00$ $n_{11} = 15$ | $\sum X_{21} = 45.00$ $n_{21} = 15$ | $\sum X_{b1} = 75.00$ $n_{b1} = 30$ | $b_1$ | $M_{11} =$ | $M_{21} =$ | $M_{b1} =$ |
| $b_2$ | $\sum X_{12} = 45.00$ $n_{12} = 15$ | $\sum X_{22} = 60.00$ $n_{22} = 15$ | $\sum X_{b2} = 105.00$ $n_{b2} = 30$ | $b_2$ | $M_{12} =$ | $M_{22} =$ | $M_{b2} =$ |
|  | $\sum X_{a1} = 75.00$ $n_{a1} = 30$ | $\sum X_{a2} = 105.00$ $n_{a2} = 30$ | $\sum X_{ijk} = 180.00$ $N = 60$ |  | $M_{a1} =$ | $M_{a2} =$ | $M_{overall} =$ |

2.

| | $a_1$ | $a_2$ | | | $a_1$ | $a_2$ | |
|---|---|---|---|---|---|---|---|
| $b_1$ | $\sum X_{11} = 100.00$ $n_{11} = 25$ | $\sum X_{21} = 150.00$ $n_{21} = 25$ | $\sum X_{b1} =$ $n_{b1} =$ | $b_1$ | $M_{11} =$ | $M_{21} =$ | $M_{b1} =$ |
| $b_2$ | $\sum X_{12} = 125.00$ $n_{12} = 25$ | $\sum X_{22} = 75.00$ $n_{22} = 25$ | $\sum X_{b2} =$ $n_{b2} =$ | $b_2$ | $M_{12} =$ | $M_{22} =$ | $M_{b2} =$ |
| | $\sum X_{a1} =$ $n_{a1} =$ | $\sum X_{a2} =$ $n_{a2} =$ | $\sum X_{ijk} =$ $N =$ | | $M_{a1} =$ | $M_{a2} =$ | $M_{overall} =$ |

3.

| | $a_1$ | $a_2$ | | | $a_1$ | $a_2$ | |
|---|---|---|---|---|---|---|---|
| $b_1$ | $\sum X_{11} = 100.00$ $n_{11} = 25$ | $\sum X_{21} = 50.00$ $n_{21} = 25$ | $\sum X_{b1} =$ $n_{b1} =$ | $b_1$ | $M_{11} =$ | $M_{21} =$ | $M_{b1} =$ |
| $b_2$ | $\sum X_{12} = 50.00$ $n_{12} = 25$ | $\sum X_{22} = 100.00$ $n_{22} = 25$ | $\sum X_{b2} =$ $n_{b2} =$ | $b_2$ | $M_{12} =$ | $M_{22} =$ | $M_{b2} =$ |
| | $\sum X_{a1} =$ $n_{a1} =$ | $\sum X_{a2} -$ $n_{a2} =$ | $\sum X_{ijk} =$ $N =$ | | $M_{a1} =$ | $M_{a2} =$ | $M_{overall} =$ |

4.

| | $a_1$ | $a_2$ | | | $a_1$ | $a_2$ | |
|---|---|---|---|---|---|---|---|
| $b_1$ | $\sum X_{11} = 125.00$ $n_{11} = 25$ | $\sum X_{21} = 225.00$ $n_{21} = 25$ | $\sum X_{b1} -$ $n_{b1} =$ | $b_1$ | $M_{11} =$ | $M_{21} =$ | $M_{b1} =$ |
| $b_2$ | $\sum X_{12} = 75.00$ $n_{12} = 25$ | $\sum X_{22} = 125.00$ $n_{22} = 25$ | $\sum X_{b2} =$ $n_{b2} =$ | $b_2$ | $M_{12} =$ | $M_{22} =$ | $M_{b2} =$ |
| | $\sum X_{a1} =$ $n_{a1} =$ | $\sum X_{a2} =$ $n_{a2} =$ | $\sum X_{ijk} =$ $N =$ | | $M_{a1} =$ | $M_{a2} =$ | $M_{overall} =$ |

5. Nisbett (1968) conducted a study to examine the relation between food taste and food consumption for obese and underweight people. Nisbett classified participants as obese or underweight by comparing their actual weight to their ideal weights. He then asked people to eat vanilla ice cream. Half the participants ate good-tasting ice cream; the others ate bitter-tasting ice cream. The dependent variable was the number of grams of ice cream consumed. The following chart presents the average amount of ice cream consumed (assume equal sample sizes).
   a. Draw a graph of the data and write a short essay describing the results.
   b. Given these results, why was it important for Nisbett to include the weight of the person as a variable in the study?

| Variable B | | Variable A Weight of Participant | | |
| | | Obese | Underweight | |
| Taste of Food | | $a_1$ | $a_2$ | Row Means |
| Good | $b_1$ | 200 | 120 | |
| Bitter | $b_2$ | 45 | 95 | |
| Column means | | | | |

6. A researcher wanted to study state-dependent learning. To examine the phenomenon, she had half the participants learn a list of 30 unrelated words while listening to a tape of Grateful Dead songs. The other participants learned the list in a quiet room. Two days later, all participants returned to the laboratory to recite the list of words. Half the participants in the music group and half the participants in the quiet group recited the list while listening to the Grateful Dead tape. The other participants recited the list in a quiet room.
   a. Draw a graph of the data and write a short essay describing the results.
   b. Could the researcher have studied the state-dependent learning phenomenon using two single-variable studies? Describe the specific advantages to using the factorial design for this research project.

| Variable B | | Variable A Learned List Condition | | |
| | | Music | Quiet | |
| Recite List Condition | | $a_1$ | $a_2$ | Row Means |
| Music | $b_1$ | 18 | 9 | |
| Quiet | $b_2$ | 11 | 15 | |
| Column means | | | | |

## Designing a Factorial Study

Designing a factorial study is relatively straightforward in that all the principles you have already learned about good research design still apply. In the following section, we will briefly review these issues as they relate to the independent and dependent variables and the necessary sample size.

## Independent Variables

We have already discussed several of the distinguishing features of the factorial design. The factorial design allows us to simultaneously examine the relation between two or more independent variables and the dependent variable. Using two or more independent variables allows us to examine how combinations of treatment conditions relate to different outcomes in the study. Of particular interest, the factorial design allows us to examine the presence of an interaction, something that we could not observe in a single-variable study. Also, we can use manipulated as well as subject variables in the study. This feature allows us to examine the relationships among a number of predictor variables and the dependent variable.

## Between-Subjects Variables

The specific research design we examine in this chapter requires that all the variables be between-subjects variables. This requirement means that we test each participant in only one treatment group or combination of treatment conditions. For examples of this, consider some of the studies we have examined so far. In the Cohen et al. (1996) study, both the insult condition and the participant background are between-subjects variables. For the insult condition, Cohen randomly assigned the participants to either the control or the insult treatment condition. Participant background is also a between-subjects variable, in that the participants grew up either in the South or the North. Each participant is therefore found in one combination treatment condition of insult and regional background. The dependent variable in this study was percent change in testosterone level, and this was used in each of the four treatment conditions.

The experiment conducted by Chaiken and Maheswaran (1992) also used between-subject variables in that the researchers randomly assigned the participants to one of six treatment conditions formed by the combinations of the two independent variables. For that experiment, both independent variables were manipulated variables, allowing the researcher to select the levels of each and then randomly assign participants to one of the conditions.

When both independent variables are between-subjects variables, we can conclude that the individual cells or treatment groups are **independent groups.** In this case, independence means that the data collected in one treatment group are not correlated with the data collected in any of the other groups. This independence of the treatment conditions helps to determine the type of statistical analysis we can use to examine the data. In a following section, we will review how to analyze the data for the two-variable between-subjects design. In the next two chapters we will discuss techniques for analyzing data from studies in which at least one of the variables is a within-subjects variable.

### Levels of the Variables

An important design consideration is the number of levels to use for each independent variable or factor. At a minimum, you must have at least two levels of each variable. You can use as many levels for both variables as you need. Consider the Chaiken and Maheswaran (1992) experiment; for their research, it made sense to have two levels of credibility of source and three levels of review endorsement. Similarly, Cohen et al. (1996) chose two levels of each variable for their study. In both cases, the questions that the researchers wished to address determined the number of levels for each independent variable. Can you think of modifications to these studies that might require more levels?

Chaiken and Maheswaran (1992) could have included a third condition for the source of the product review by including an unidentified review. The three levels of review source would then be low-credibility, high-credibility, and unidentified source. The new condition would be a type of control condition because the researcher does not identify the source of the review. Could Cohen et al. (1996) have added more levels to their study? For the participant background condition, they could have identified other regions of the country (e.g., West Coast or Rocky Mountain states) or other countries (e.g., men from Asian or African countries). In addition, Cohen et al. could have used three treatment conditions by adding a condition where the men received a compliment rather than an insult. Adding more treatment conditions may produce results that further enhance our understanding of the phenomenon we are studying. For example, if Cohen et al. (1996) had included men from the West Coast states, they could have determined whether the southerners' reaction to the insult is unique to men raised in the South. Similarly, the addition of a compliment condition (i.e., an "anti-insult") would help determine whether the increase in the testosterone occurs only in the insult condition. Such a study would be an interesting follow-up project to the original work.

In the previous chapter, you learned that adding more levels of the independent variable has the advantage of improving our understanding of the relation between the independent and dependent variables. Adding more levels of the variable can also improve the power of a study if adding treatment conditions increases homogeneity of the participants with each condition and increases the range of effect for the independent variable. These same advantages occur in the factorial design. There is a cost, however, to adding more levels of a variable in this type of design. Each level creates additional treatment groups, requiring you as the researcher to identify more participants.

Imagine that a researcher begins by planning for a $2 \times 2$ factorial design and determines that there must be at least 10 participants in each research condition. For this design, the researcher will require 40 participants to conduct the study. After thinking more about the purpose of the study, the researcher decides to switch to a $3 \times 3$ factorial design. This design will require 90 participants, more than twice as many as the $2 \times 2$

design requires. Even switching to a 2 × 3 factorial design will require 60 participants. Selecting the number of levels for each independent variable requires a balance between the intent of the research and the cost of conducting the study.

### Dependent Variables

Several characteristics of the dependent variable also require attention when conducting a factorial design. The first characteristic refers to the dependent variable's scale of measurement. In general, an ANOVA works best when the dependent variable data are measured using an interval or ratio scale. It is possible to conduct a factorial design for which the data represent a nominal ordinal scale, but in these situations a different statistical test is often required (as we discuss in Chapter 16).

## Identifying Samples and Estimating Sample Size

Apart from the variables, it is also necessary to consider the sample size of your treatment groups when planning to use an ANOVA to examine data from a factorial design. An ANOVA works best when the number of observations in each treatment group (typically denoted as $n$) is equivalent. Although minor differences in sample sizes have little effect on the validity of the ANOVA, large differences in sample sizes among the cells can cause an ANOVA to produce spurious results. Plan your study with sufficient care to ensure equal sample sizes across all treatment conditions. If circumstances beyond your control cause unequal sample sizes, you should refer to an advanced statistics textbook for recommendations for analyzing the data that you are able to collect.

When designing a factorial type study, it is common to perform a statistical power analysis to determine the number of participants necessary for each treatment group to ensure the best likelihood of detecting statistically significant effects if they are present. The steps that we follow for estimating the sample size in a factorial design are essentially the same that we use for the single-factor experiment.

First, to determine power for the two-factor ANOVA we again turn to Table B.13 in Appendix B. For this example, assume that you want to conduct a 3 × 4 factorial design. Following Cohen's (1988) recommendation, we will assume that and also that the effect size for the main effects and interaction is moderate, $f = .25$ and that we want the power of our statistic to be $1 - \beta = .80$. At this point it is important to recognize that a two-variable between-subjects ANOVA will generate three $F$-ratios: (1) for the main effect of variable A, (2) for the main effect of variable B, and (3) for the interaction of variables A and B. This being the case, you should plan your $n$ based on the smallest effect size that you expect to observe (usually the interaction of A × B).

## Table 13.4  Equations for Determining the Numerator Degrees of Freedom for a Factorial Design

| Equations | Example for a 3 × 4 Factorial Design |
|---|---|
| **Main effect for Factor A** <br> $df_A = (j - 1)$, where $j$ = # of levels of A | $df_A = (3 - 1) = 2$ |
| **Main effect for Factor B** <br> $df_B = (k - 1)$, where $k$ = # of levels of B | $df_B = (4 - 1) = 3$ |
| **Interaction for A × B** <br> $df_{A \times B} = (j - 1)(k - 1)$ | $df_{A \times B} = (3 - 1)(4 - 1) = 6$ |

The next step will be to calculate an adjusted sample size. To complete this step, you will need the degrees of freedom for the ANOVA. Table 13.4 presents the method for determining the numerator degrees of freedom for each $F$-ratio. Using these degrees of freedom, we can use Equation (13.2) to estimate power using specific sample sizes.

We will begin by examining the power of the two-factor ANOVA with 10 participants in each cell. Table 13.5 presents the application of Equation (13.2) assuming $n_{ij} = 10$, $\alpha = .05$, and $f = .25$ for each $F$-ratio.

$$n'_{effect} = \frac{jk(n_{ij} - 1)}{df_{effect} + 1} \tag{13.2}$$

According to Table 13.5, the probability of obtaining a statistically significant interaction is less than 50% ($1 - \beta \approx .45$). The probability of obtaining statistically significant main effects is also on the slim side: $1 - \beta \approx .68$ for variable A and $1 - \beta \approx .61$ for variable B. One way to increase power is to increase sample size. Table 13.6 presents the predicted power if we increase the sample size to 20. Doubling the sample size does increase the power of the interaction, but at a cost. You will need a total sample size

## Table 13.5  Estimated Power for a 3 × 4 Factorial ANOVA with $n_{ij} = 10$, $\alpha = .05$, and $f = .25$

| | $df_{effect}$ | | Adjusted $n$ | Rounded $n$ | Estimated Power |
|---|---|---|---|---|---|
| **Variable A** | 2 | $n' = \dfrac{12(10 - 1)}{2 + 1}$ | $n' = 37$ | $n' = 40$ | $1 - \beta \approx .68$ |
| **Variable B** | 3 | $n' = \dfrac{12(10 - 1)}{3 + 1}$ | $n' = 28$ | $n' = 30$ | $1 - \beta \approx .61$ |
| **Variable A × B** | 6 | $n' = \dfrac{12(10 - 1)}{6 + 1}$ | $n' = 16.429$ | $n' = 16$ | $1 - \beta \approx .45$ |

Note. The adjusted sample size has been rounded to conform to the values in the power tables. These power estimates are sufficient for general estimates of the power of the design. If you need exact power estimates, refer to Cohen (3) or software that performs such calculations.

Table 13.6  **Estimated Power for an Interaction in a 3 × 4 Factorial ANOVA with $n_{ij} = 10$, $\alpha = .05$, and $f = .25$**

|  | $df_{effect}$ | | Adjusted $n$ | Rounded $n$ | Estimated Power |
|---|---|---|---|---|---|
| **Variable A × B** | 6 | $n' = \dfrac{12(20-1)}{6+1}$ | $n' = 33.57$ | $n' = 30$ | $1 - \beta \approx .76$ |

across all treatment groups of $N = 240$ ($3 \times 4 \times 20 = 240$) participants to conduct the study. This is where you would have some important decisions to make:

- Do you have the time and energy to collect this much data?
- Are there other things that you can do to increase the effect size of the study?
- Have you used the best possible measure of the dependent variable?
- Consider the independent variables. Do you need that many treatment levels?
- Can you create greater differences among the levels of the variables?

Attending to these considerations may help you increase the power without having to use this many research participants.

## Interpreting the Interaction: Advanced Considerations

An interaction represents differences among the group means that cannot be accounted for by the main effects. Consequently, comparing treatment groups in the presence of a significant interaction requires extra caution. We can use the results of Chaiken and Maheswaran's (1992) experiment to discuss how the effects of an interaction should be described. As you will recall, the most interesting finding of the Chaiken and Maheswaran (1992) experiment was that the participants indicated that they were very willing to buy the answering machine if it received an ambiguous review from a highly credible source. If you review Table 13.3, you will see that the mean of this condition is $M_{21} = 8.00$, which is greater than the grand mean, $M = 5.67$, a difference of 2.33. How much of the difference reflects the unique combination of credibility and review endorsement? We must subtract the effects of the two main effects using Equation (13.3):

$$\Delta_{ij} = M_{ij} - M_{ai} - M_{bj} + M_{overall} \qquad (13.3)$$

In this equation, $\Delta_{ij}$ is called a **residual.** For this equation, a residual reflects the effect of the interaction after removing the influence of the main effects. Remember that an interaction reflects differences among the group means that neither main effect can explain by itself. Therefore, the residual reflects the effect of the interaction independent of the main effects. If the interaction is not statistically significant, then the residuals for all group means will be close to or equal to 0. For this example, the residual is $1.34 = 8.0 - 5.63 - 6.70 + 5.67$. The residual indicates that the mean of treatment condition $a_2b_2$ is $\Delta_{22} = 1.34$ points higher than we would expect from examining the effects of the main effects alone. Many statisticians and researchers (e.g., Tukey, Mosteller, & Hoaglin, 1991; Rosenthal & Rosnow, 1985) recommend computing the residuals for the factorial design and corresponding ANOVA as a way of interpreting the meaning of the interaction.

If there is no interaction between the two independent variables, then the residuals for each of the treatment combinations will be close to or equal to 0. As the interaction becomes more prominent, the residuals of several or all the treatment cells will become larger. Looking at the ambiguous review condition in this example, the residuals indicate that people were more likely to buy the answering machine if the review came from a high-credibility source, but less likely to buy the device if the review came from the low-credibility source. Remember that the residuals for the means represent the changes that cannot be explained by either main effect alone. Therefore, when you compare the individual cell means, you must remember that the difference will represent the interaction as well as the main effects.

Table 13.7 presents the residuals for each of the individual cells; Figure 13.4 presents a graph of the residuals. A review of Figure 13.4 indicates that the greatest effect occurred in the ambiguous-endorsement condition.

In the high-credibility condition, the participants were more likely to buy the product than would have been expected from the level of credibility or the strength of the endorsement. By contrast, in the low-credibility condition, the participants were less likely to buy the answering machine given the source and type of review. There is also an interesting pattern in the weak-endorsement condition where people were less likely to buy the answering machine after reading the high-credibility review but more willing to buy the answering machine after reading the low-credibility review. It is as if the combination of a poor review combined with a credible source makes the answering machine unappealing.

## Research in Action: Reinforcing Creativity

Eisenberger and Armeli (1997) conducted an experiment to answer the question: Does positive reinforcement influence creativity? The researchers predicted that two variables (instruction set and magnitude of reinforcement) would influence creativity. Specifically, they predicted that instructing people to be creative increases creativity. In addition,

## Table 13.7  Residuals for Means Presented in Table 13.3

| Variable B Review Type | Variable A Credibility of Source | | Row Means |
|---|---|---|---|
| | Low $a_1$ | High $a_2$ | |
| Strong $b_1$ | $M_{11} = 6.60$ $\Delta_{11} = M_{11} - M_{a1} - M_{b1} + M_{\text{overall}}$ $\Delta_{11} = 6.60 - 5.70 - 6.25 + 5.667$ $\Delta_{11} = 0.32$ | $M_{21} = 5.9$ $\Delta_{21} = M_{21} - M_{a2} - M_{b2} + M_{\text{overall}}$ $\Delta_{21} = 5.90 - 5.63 - 6.25 + 5.667$ $\Delta_{21} = -0.32$ | $M_{b1} = 6.25$ |
| Ambiguous $b_2$ | $M_{12} = 5.40$ $\Delta_{12} = M_{12} - M_{a1} - M_{b2} + M_{\text{overall}}$ $\Delta_{12} = 5.40 - 5.70 - 6.70 + 5.667$ $\Delta_{12} = -1.33$ | $M_{22} = 8.00$ $\Delta_{22} = M_{22} - M_{a2} - M_{b2} + M_{\text{overall}}$ $\Delta_{22} = 8.00 - 5.63 - 6.70 + 5.667$ $\Delta_{22} = -1.33$ | $M_{b2} = 6.70$ |
| Weak $b_3$ | $M_{13} = 5.10$ $\Delta_{13} = M_{13} - M_{a1} - M_{b3} + M_{\text{overall}}$ $\Delta_{13} = 5.10 - 5.70 - 4.05 + 5.667$ $\Delta_{13} = 1.02$ | $M_{23} = 3.00$ $\Delta_{23} = M_{23} - M_{a2} - M_{b3} + M_{\text{overall}}$ $\Delta_{23} = 3.00 - 5.63 - 4.05 + 5.667$ $\Delta_{23} = -1.02$ | $M_{b3} = 4.05$ |
| Column Means | $M_{a1} = 5.70$ | $M_{a2} = 5.63$ | $M_{overall} = 5.67$ |

Eisenberger and Armeli predicted that positive reinforcement for creativity further enhances one's creativity.

The Eisenberger and Armeli (1997) experiment consisted of two phases. During the first phase, the researchers gave fifth- and sixth-grade students common objects and asked them to describe how they might use the object. The researchers told half the students to think of common uses of the objects and told the other students to think of unusual uses for the object. Thus, the first independent variable was instruction (common uses vs. novel uses). All the children then received no reward, a small reward (18 cents), or a large reward (90 cents) for their ideas. Therefore, the second variable was the magnitude of reward (0, 18, or 90 cents).

During the second phase of the experiment, the researcher gave students a creativity test. The test consisted of a page with rows of unfilled circles. The researchers asked the children to use each circle to create a picture. Eisenberger and Armeli (1997) predicted that the creativity of the students' pictures would reflect the effect of the two variables experienced during the first phase of the experiment. The researchers used a 2 × 3 factorial design. The first variable was the initial training, instruction for use, and consisted of two levels, common versus novel. The second variable was the magnitude of reinforcement the student received for identifying the use of objects and consisted of three levels, 0, 18, or 90 cents. Table 13.8 presents the summary statistics for the experiment.

## Table 13.8  Hypothetical Results for Eisenberger and Armeli (1997) Experiment

| Variable B Magnitude of Reinforcement | | Variable A Instruction for Use | | |
|---|---|---|---|---|
| | | Common $a_1$ | Novel $a_2$ | Row Means |
| $0.00 | $b_1$ | $M_{11} = 3.90$ | $M_{21} = 4.50$ | $M_{b1} = 4.20$ |
| $0.18 | $b_2$ | $M_{12} = 6.50$ | $M_{22} = 5.90$ | $M_{b1} = 6.20$ |
| $0.90 | $b_3$ | $M_{13} = 5.40$ | $M_{23} = 10.40$ | $M_{b1} = 7.90$ |
| **Column Means** | | $M_{a1} = 5.27$ | $M_{a2} = 6.93$ | $M_{overall} = 6.10$ |

Table 13.9 presents the ANOVA summary table for the $2 \times 3$ analysis. As you can see, there is a statistically significant main effect for Variable A, instructions for use; a statistically significant main effect for Variable B, magnitude of reinforcement; and a statistically significant interaction of the two variables. Looking at the means in Table 13.8, it is apparent that children in the novel-instruction conditions earned higher creativity scores than children in the common-instruction conditions. Similarly, it appears that the magnitude of reinforcement affects creativity; children who earned more money earned higher creativity scores.

Finally, the interaction appears to predict high creativity scores for the children in the novel-instruction and 90 cent–reinforcement condition. The children in this treatment condition earned substantially higher creativity scores than would have been expected by examining the trends seen for the main effects. Box 13.1 presents an example of a results section that one might prepare for this experiment.

## Statistics behind the Research

In this section we will examine the methods used to calculate the ANOVA summary table for the two-variable between-groups ANOVA. Table 13.10

## Table 13.9  Summary Table for Data Presented in Table 13.8

| Source | SS | df | MS | F | Estimated $\omega^2$ |
|---|---|---|---|---|---|
| A | 41.667 | 1 | 41.667 | | |
| B | 137.200 | 2 | 68.600 | 8.105* | .106 |
| A×B | 86.933 | 2 | 43.567 | 13.344* | .292 |
| Within | 277.600 | 54 | 5.141 | 5.455* | .199 |
| Total | 543.400 | 59 | | | |

*$p < .05$, reject the null hypothesis that all treatment group means are equal

---

## Box 13.1  Example of Results Section for Data Presented in Table 13.9

Creativity and reward                                                                                                   5

---

    The results confirmed our prediction that rewarding unusual responses would increase creative behavior. Figure 1 presents the data for the experiment. Clearly, those children receiving large rewards for novel uses of common objects scored higher on the creativity test than children in the other conditions. This conclusion is supported with a 2 (instructions) × 3 (reward size) ANOVA of the data. There was a statistically significant main effect of instruction type, $F(1, 54) = 8.11, p < .05, \hat{\omega}^2 = .11$. The main effect for reward size was also statistically significant, $F(2, 54) = 13.34, p < .05, \hat{\omega}^2 = .29$. The interaction of the two variables was also statistically significant, $F(2, 54) = 8.45, p < .05, \hat{\omega}^2 = .20$. A Tukey HSD post hoc test indicated that the novel-use and high reward size group produced the highest creativity scores (all $ps < .05$). None of the other differences between groups was statistically significant (all $ps > .05$).

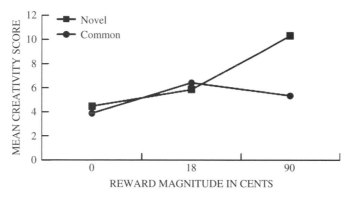

*Figure 1.* Interaction of Reward Magnitude x Instructions Predicting Creativity

---

presents the hypothetical data for the Eisenberger and Armeli (1997) experiment presented in the previous section. The table includes the data and the summary information for each treatment condition, as well as the row and column totals.

### Assumptions of the Test

The two-variable between-groups ANOVA requires that the data meet three specific mathematical requirements known as *assumptions*. Meeting these ensures that the ANOVA will produce valid statistical interpretations of the data.

### Normal Distribution of Data

The first assumption is that the data are normally distributed, or at least pretty close to looking like a bell-curve. Extreme skew in one or more of the groups may cause the ANOVA to produce spurious results. A quick review

## Table 13.10  Hypothetical Data for the Eisenberger and Armeli (1997) Experiment

| | $a_1$ | $a_2$ | |
|---|---|---|---|
| $b_1$ | $a_1b_1$<br>1  5  3    5  3<br>3  6  4    7  2<br>$\Sigma X_{11} = 39$<br>$n_{11} = 10$<br>$M_{11} = 3.90$ | $a_2b_1$<br>5  5  9    7  4<br>4  6  3    0  2<br>$\Sigma X_{21} = 10$<br>$n_{21} = 10$<br>$M_{21} = 4.50$ | $\Sigma X_{b1} = 48$<br>$n_{b1} = 20$<br>$M_{b1} = 4.20$ |
| $b_2$ | $a_1b_2$<br>5  6  6    5  8<br>8  10  6    5  6<br>$\Sigma X_{12} = 65$<br>$n_{12} = 10$<br>$M_{12} = 6.50$ | $a_2b_2$<br>6  7  2    5  5<br>12  6  8    3  5<br>$\Sigma X_{22} = 59$<br>$n_{22} = 10$<br>$M_{22} = 5.90$ | $\Sigma X_{b2} = 124$<br>$n_{b2} = 20$<br>$M_{b2} = 6.20$ |
| $b_3$ | $a_1b_3$<br>4  6  7    5  4<br>9  7  6    4  2<br>$\Sigma X_{13} = 54$<br>$n_{13} = 10$<br>$M_{13} = 5.40$ | $a_2b_3$<br>9  10  6    12  11<br>14  9  8    14  11<br>$\Sigma X_{23} = 104$<br>$n_{23} = 10$<br>$M_{23} = 10.40$ | $\Sigma X_{b3} = 158$<br>$n_{b3} = 20$<br>$M_{b3} = 7.90$ |
| | $\Sigma X_{a1} = 158$<br>$n_{a1} = 30$<br>$M_{a1} = 5.27$ | $\Sigma X_{a2} = 208$<br>$n_{a2} = 30$<br>$M_{a2} = 6.93$ | $\Sigma X_{ijk} = 366$<br>$N = 60$<br>$M_{overall} = 6.10$<br>$\Sigma X_{ijk}^2 = 2776$ |

of the data in Table 13.10 indicates that there are no outliers or other conditions that might skew the data.

### Homogeneity of Variance

The second assumption is that the variances of the individual treatment conditions be relatively equal. This is critical in that extremely deviant variances in one or more of the groups can produce spurious results. Coupled with this is the general requirement that the sample sizes are the same. Another quick review of the data suggests that the variances of the six groups are equivalent. As an aside, many computer statistics programs will conduct a test of homogeneity of variance.

### Independence of Groups

The final assumption is that the treatment groups are independent. This requires that there be no explicit correlation among the groups in your study. This is best achieved by randomly assigning participants to treatment conditions, whenever possible. There are conditions when there is an explicit correlation between the groups; we will consider this research design in the next chapter.

## Forming the Hypotheses

If the data meet the requirements of the ANOVA, we can modify our initial research hypotheses with more specific testing hypotheses. Because there are three tests in the two-variable between-subjects ANOVA, we will create a null and alternative hypothesis for each test.

### Null Hypotheses

Recall that when initially forming null hypotheses you are stating that you expect no difference between groups. In ANOVA terms this means that:

$H_0$: $F_A = 1.00$, there is no main effect for Variable A.

$H_0$: $F_B = 1.00$, there is no main effect for Variable B.

$H_0$: $F_{A \times B} = 1.00$, there is no interaction between Variables A and B.

### Alternative Hypotheses

The alternative hypotheses we initially form when developing a study state that there is a difference between treatment groups (in opposition to the null hypotheses). In ANOVA terms this means that:

$H_1$: Not $H_0$, there is a main effect for Variable A.

$H_1$: Not $H_0$, there is a main effect for Variable B.

$H_1$: Not $H_0$, there is an interaction between Variables A and B.

## Sampling Distribution

For each $F$-ratio, we will need to determine $F_{critical}$, after we establish the level of $\alpha$ and calculate the degrees of freedom. As you learned in Chapter 12, the $F$-distribution has two degrees of freedom. The numerator degrees of freedom ($df_N$ or $df_{between-groups}$) is the degrees of freedom associated with the variance between the treatment groups. The denominator degrees of freedom ($df_D$ or $df_{within-groups}$) is the degrees of freedom associated with the variance within each treatment group. Table 13.11 presents the $F_{critical}$ for each test in the current example. The value of $F_{critical}$ allows us to determine whether to reject the null hypothesis for each observed $F$-ratio. When $F_{observed} \geq F_{critical}$, you can reject the null hypothesis and by default accept the associated alternative hypothesis.

## Completing the Calculations

We can now proceed with the calculation of the two-variable independent-groups ANOVA. Table 13.12 presents the computational equations and a worked example for the data presented in Table 13.10. As you proceed with

## Table 13.11   Example of Determining the Degrees of Freedom and $F_{critical}$ for Each Test in the Two-Variable Between-Groups ANOVA

**Within**

$df_{within} = \sum (n_{jk} - 1) = (10 - 1) + \ldots (10 - 1) + (10 - 1) = 54$

**Factor A**

$df_A = (j - 1) = 2 - 1 = 1 \rightarrow F_{critical}(1, 54) = 4.02$

**Factor B**

$df_B = (k - 1) = 3 - 1 = 2 \rightarrow F_{critical}(2, 54) = 3.16$

**Interaction for A×B**

$df_{A \times B} = (j - 1)(k - 1) = (2 - 1)(3 - 1) = 2 \rightarrow F_{critical}(2, 54) = 3.16$

## Table 13.12   Worked Example for a Two-Variable Between-Groups ANOVA

$SS_A = \sum \frac{\left( \sum X_{aj} \right)^2}{n_{aj}} - \frac{\left( \sum X_{ijk} \right)^2}{N} = \frac{158^2}{30} + \frac{208^2}{30} + \frac{366^2}{30} = 41.667$

$df_A = j - 1 = 2 - 1 = 1$

$MS_A = \frac{SS_A}{df_A} = \frac{41.667}{1} = 41.667$

$SS_B = \sum \frac{\left( \sum X_{bk} \right)^2}{n_{bk}} - \frac{\left( \sum X_{ijk} \right)^2}{N} = \frac{84^2}{20} + \frac{124^2}{20} + \frac{158^2}{20} + \frac{366^2}{20} = 137.200$

$df_B = k - 1 = 3 - 1 = 2$

$MS_B = \frac{SS_B}{df_B} = \frac{137.200}{2} = 68.60$

$SS_{A \times B} = \sum \frac{\left( \sum X_{jk} \right)^2}{n_{jk}} - \frac{\left( \sum X_{ijk} \right)^2}{N} - (SS_A + SS_B)$

$SS_{A \times B} = \frac{39^2}{10} + \frac{45^2}{10} + \frac{65^2}{10} + \frac{59^2}{10} + \frac{54^2}{10} + \frac{104^2}{10} - \frac{366^2}{60} - (41.667 + 137.20) = 86.933$

$df_{A \times B} = (j - 1)(k - 1) = (2 - 1)(3 - 1) = 2$

$MS_{A \times B} = \frac{SS_{A \times B}}{df_{A \times B}} = \frac{86.933}{2} = 43.467$

$SS_{within} = \sum X_{ijk}^2 - \sum \frac{\left[ \sum (X_{jk}) \right]^2}{n_{jk}}$

$SS_{within} = 2776 - \left( \frac{39^2}{10} + \frac{45^2}{10} + \frac{65^2}{10} + \frac{59^2}{10} + \frac{54^2}{10} + \frac{104^2}{10} \right) = 277.60$

$df_{within} = \sum \left[ (n_{ij}) - 1 \right]$

$df_{within} = (10 - 1) + (10 - 1) + (10 - 1) + (10 - 1) + (10 - 1) + (10 - 1) = 54$

$MS_{within} = \frac{SS_{within}}{df_{within}} = \frac{277.60}{54} = 5.141$

$SS_{total} = \sum X_{ijk}^2 - \frac{\left[ \sum (X_{ijk}) \right]^2}{N} = 2776 - \frac{366^2}{60} = 543.400$

$df_{total} = N - 1 = 60 - 1 = 59$

$F = \frac{MS_{between}}{MS_{within}} = \frac{3.466}{0.790} = 4.388$

Note: $df_{total} = df_A + df_B + df_{A \times B} + df_{within}$; $SS_{total} = SS_A + SS_B + SS_{A \times B} + SS_{within}$.

## Table 13.13 Residuals for Means Presented in Table 13.8

| Variable B Reward | Variable A Instructions for Use | | Row Means |
| | Common $a_1$ | Novel $a_1$ | |
|---|---|---|---|
| $0.00 $b_1$ | $M_{11} = 3.90$ $\Delta_{11} = 3.90 - 5.27 - 4.20 + 6.10$ $\Delta_{11} = 0.53$ | $M_{21} = 4.50$ $\Delta_{21} = 4.50 - 6.93 - 4.20 + 6.10$ $\Delta_{21} = -0.53$ | $M_{b1} = 4.20$ |
| $0.18 $b_2$ | $M_{12} = 6.50$ $\Delta_{12} = 6.50 - 5.27 - 6.20 + 6.10$ $\Delta_{12} = 1.13$ | $M_{22} = 5.90$ $\Delta_{22} = 5.90 - 6.93 - 6.20 + 6.10$ $\Delta_{22} = -1.13$ | $M_{b2} = 6.20$ |
| $0.90 $b_3$ | $M_{13} = 5.40$ $\Delta_{13} = 5.40 - 5.27 - 7.90 + 6.10$ $\Delta_{13} = -1.67$ | $M_{23} = 10.40$ $\Delta_{23} = 10.40 - 6.93 - 7.90 + 6.10$ $\Delta_{23} = 1.67$ | $M_{b3} = 7.90$ |
| Column Means | $M_{a1} = 5.27$ | $M_{a2} = 6.93$ | $M_{overall} = 6.10$ |

your calculations, ensure that you make clear notes of your calculations. This practice will help you ensure that there are no computational errors. As a double-check for your work, you should find that $df_{total} = df_A + df_B + df_{A \times B} + df_{within}$ and that $SS_{total} = SS_A + SS_B + SS_{A \times B} + SS_{within}$. The computations presented in Table 13.12 are the foundation for the ANOVA summary table presented in Table 13.9. To calculate the $F$-ratios, divide the mean square for the effect by the mean square for the within-groups variance. For example, $F_A = 41.667/277.600 = 8.11$.

### Additional Tests

We can determine the residuals for the interaction. In Table 13.9, we see that interaction reflects the unique combination of the two variables. Of particular interest are the data for the children assigned to the largest-reward condition. Those children instructed to think of novel uses earned

## Table 13.14 Example of Calculating Omega Squared for the Interaction and Each Main Effect

Equation: $\hat{\omega}^2_{effect} = \dfrac{df_{effect}(F_{effect}-1)}{df_{effect}(F_{effect}-1)+N}$

| Variable A | Variable B | Variable C |
|---|---|---|
| $\hat{\omega}^2_A = \dfrac{1(8.105 - 1)}{1(8.105 - 1) + 60}$ | $\hat{\omega}^2_B = \dfrac{2(13.344 - 1)}{2(13.344 - 1) + 60}$ | $\hat{\omega}^2_C = \dfrac{2(8.455 - 1)}{2(8.455 - 1) + 60}$ |
| $\hat{\omega}^2_A = .106$ | $\hat{\omega}^2_B = .292$ | $\hat{\omega}^2_C = .199$ |

# Table 13.15  Example of Calculating Effect Size for the Main Effects and Interaction

**Equation:**

$$\eta^2_{effect} = \frac{df_{effect}(F)}{df_{effect}(F_{effect}) + df_{within}} \quad \text{or} \quad \eta^2_{effect} = \frac{SS_{effect}}{SS_{total}}$$

$$f_{effect} = \sqrt{\frac{\eta^2_{effect}}{1 - \eta^2_{effect}}}$$

| Variable A | Variable B | Variable C |
|---|---|---|
| $\eta^2_A = \dfrac{41.667}{543.600} = .077$ | $\eta^2_B = \dfrac{137.200}{543.600} = .252$ | $\eta^2_C = \dfrac{86.933}{543.600} = .160$ |
| $f_A = \sqrt{\dfrac{.077}{1 - .077}} = .288$ | $f_B = \sqrt{\dfrac{.252}{1 - .252}} = .580$ | $f_C = \sqrt{\dfrac{.160}{1 - .160}} = .436$ |

higher creativity scores than their counterparts instructed to think of common applications. Table 13.13 presents the residuals for the cell means.

### Omega Squared ($\hat{\omega}^2$)

Once we find that an $F$-ratio is statistically significant, we can then calculate $\hat{\omega}^2$ for the effect. As in the single-variable ANOVA, $\hat{\omega}^2$ for the two-variable ANOVA allows us to determine the proportion of the dependent variable accounted for by the particular source of variance. For the two-variable ANOVA, we can calculate $\hat{\omega}^2$ for the interaction and each main effect. Table 13.14 presents the $\hat{\omega}^2$ for this study.

### Effect Size f

We can also calculate the effect size for the interaction and each main effect. Calculating the effect size allows us to estimate the power. As you can see in Table 13.15, the effects sizes are quite large. The effect sizes are particularly large for the main effect of Variable B, the effects of reinforcement, and the interaction of Variables A and B.

## Knowledge Check

7. Imagine that a researcher conducted a single-factor ANOVA on a set of data and then reanalyzed the same data using a two-factor ANOVA. Explain how the sum of squares total and the sum of squares within would differ between the two statistical tests.

8. Is it correct to assume that when the $F$-ratio for a main effect is not statistically significant, one can assume that the variable had no influence on the dependent variable?

9. Is it correct to conclude that the mean of a treatment combination represents the effect of the interaction alone?

10. Why will a two-variable ANOVA be more powerful than a single-variable ANOVA?

# Chapter Summary

This chapter is a further extension of the between-subjects research design as we examined how we can conduct a study that includes more than one independent variable. The two-variable design allows us to simultaneously examine the effect of two variables and their interaction on the dependent variable.

The two-variable design is extremely useful to researchers because it makes better use of research resources, has greater statistical power, and allows us to examine the complex interplay between variables. This interplay between the independent variables is the interaction. The interaction is an extremely important finding in any research project because it represents an outcome that cannot be explained by either of the independent variables. The interaction indicates results beyond the simple addition of two variables.

In this chapter we reviewed the many possible outcomes for a two-factor research design. As a generality, the results can indicate that one or more main effects are statistically significant, and that the interaction is statistically significant. We also reviewed how to examine a graph and interpret the effects of the independent variables and the interaction. A large portion of the chapter reviewed the ANOVA for the two-variable design. As with the single-variable ANOVA, the two-variable ANOVA uses the $F$-ratio to determine whether there is evidence for a statistically significant effect of the independent variables and their interaction.

An important lesson to learn is that a statistically significant interaction means that the data cannot be explained simply by describing the simple effects of the independent variables. Although many researchers examine the pattern of means created by the interaction, several researchers recommend examining the residual, which indicates the effect of the interaction once the effects of the independent variables have been removed. As with other inferential statistics, we can use power tables to estimate the number of participants that we require to obtain statistically significant effects.

# Chapter Glossary for Review

**Additive effect**—In a factorial design, the effect of one variable has a consistent effect on the other variables.

**Cell**—Within a factorial design, the cell represents a unique combination of the levels of the independent variables.

**Factorial design**—A research design that uses two or more independent variables and all possible combinations of treatment levels the researcher selects.

**Independent groups**—A characteristic of the treatment conditions when both variables are between-subjects variables. If the groups are independent, we assume that there is no correlation.

**Interaction**—In a factorial design, an interaction indicates that the effects of the independent variables are not consistent across all treatment combinations. The interaction represents the differences among the sample means that neither main effect can explain.

**Level**—A unique condition or magnitude of the independent variable.

**Main effect**—Within a factorial design, refers to the primary effect that an independent variable has on the dependent variable, holding the other effects constant.

**Residual**—For a factorial experiment, the difference between the grand mean and the individual mean less the effects of the independent variables. The residual reflects the effect of the interaction.

## Chapter References

Chaiken, S., & Maheswaran, D. (1992). Heuristic processing can bias systematic processing: The effect of source credibility, argument ambiguity, and task importance on attitude judgment. Unpublished manuscript, New York University, New York, NY.

Cohen, D., Nisbett, R. E., Bowdle, B. F., & Schwarz, N. (1996). Insult, aggression, and the southern culture of honor: An "experimental ethnography." *Journal of Personality & Social Psychology, 70*, 945–960.

Cohen, J. (1988). *Statistical power analysis for the behavioral sciences* (2nd ed.). Hillsdale, NJ: LEA.

Eisenberger, R., & Armeli, S. (1997). Can salient reward increase creative performance without reducing intrinsic creative interest? *Journal of Personality & Social Psychology, 72*, 652–663.

Hayes, L. V. (1981). *Statistics*. New York: Holt, Rinehart & Winston.

Kirk, R. E. (1982). *Experimental design* (2nd ed.). Monterey, CA: Brooks/Cole.

Rosenthal, R., & Rosnow, R. L. (1985). *Contrast analysis: Focused comparisons in the analysis of variance*. New York: Cambridge.

Tukey, J. W., Mosteller, F., & Hoaglin, D. G. (1991). Concepts and examples in analysis of variance. In D. G. Hoaglin, F. Mosteller, & J. W. Tukey (Eds.), *Fundamentals of exploratory analysis of variance* (pp. 13–33). New York: John Wiley & Sons.

Winer, B. J., Brown, D. R., & Michels, K. M. (1991). *Statistical principles in experimental design* (3rd ed.). New York: McGraw-Hill.

Zentall, S. S., & Shaw, J. H. (1980). Effects of classroom noise on performance and activity of second-grade hyperactive and control children. *Journal of Educational Psychology, 72*, 830–840.

# Chapter 14
## Correlated-Groups Designs

Why speculate when you can calculate?

—Joan Baez

## Introduction

As you have learned in the previous chapters, we can be creative with our use of the independent or between-subjects design. The primary feature of the independent-groups design is its ability to examine the differences among different groups of people. Using the ANOVA, we can determine whether the variance between-groups is larger than the variance within-groups and thereby infer that there is some form of relationship between the independent and dependent variables.

This basic ANOVA framework can also be easily modified to fit other research designs. As you learned in Chapter 12, a factorial design allows us to examine the interaction between two or more variables. We can extend this capability by using ANOVA when studying the relationship between independent and dependent variables in a correlated-groups design. You will learn in this chapter that research designs such as the repeated-measures design and the matched-participants design offer you the oppor-tunity to conduct experiments that have considerable statistical power. These designs also allow the researcher to exercise greater control over the variables that influence the dependent variable. The distinguishing char-acteristic of the research designs discussed in this chapter is that there is a known or intentional correlation among the groups. In the last four research designs we examined, the treatment groups are independent. We achieve this independence by randomly assigning participants to the levels of the treatment groups.

Therefore, there should be no correlation between pairs of participants from different groups. In this chapter, we will examine research designs in which we intentionally create groups in such a way that there is a correlation among pairs of scores across the groups. The two primary design techniques that we will use for this are the **repeated-measures design** and the **matched-groups design**. Although the repeated-measures and matched-groups designs are different procedures, we are able to use the same statistical techniques to analyze the data generated by these research designs.

## Logic of the Correlated-Groups Research Design

Many factors contribute to the random variation in participants' behavior in a research project. Among the many possible factors, individual differences among participants often play a major role in the level of within-group variance that is present. If the within-group variance is too large, it will be difficult to detect differences between treatment groups due to the independent variable. If the variance between-groups is small relative to the size of the variance within-groups, then the corresponding $F$-ratio will be too small to allow us to reject the null hypothesis.

There are several design decisions we can make to reduce the within-groups variance. For example, we can try to select participants who are similar to each other, because the more homogeneous the sample, the lower the within-group variance. Another tactic is to treat significant subject variables, such as sex, as one of the independent variables in a factorial design. If the subject variable systematically contributes to the total variance, identifying it as a variable will reduce the within-groups variance. This tactic works best if the subject variable is a categorical variable (e.g., sex or marital status) or if you can cluster the participants into logical categories (e.g., age groups).

Another way to reduce the within-groups variance is to use a correlated-groups design. This procedure is an exceptionally cost-effective method for increasing statistical power. Like the factorial design, the correlated-groups design allows the researcher to reduce the within-groups variance. Figure 14.1 presents the difference between the independent-groups ANOVA and the correlated-groups research design. For the between-subjects design, the variance among the participants is part of the within-groups variation. The within-groups variation represents variance due to random error and individual differences among participants. Using a correlated-groups design and corresponding ANOVA, we can partition out the variance due to individual differences and treat it as a separate source of variance. Doing so tends to reduce the size of $MS_{\text{within}}$ and thereby increases

INDEPENDENT-GROUPS DESIGN AND ANOVA

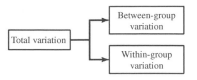

CORRELATED-GROUPS DESIGN AND ANOVA

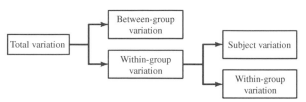

Figure 14.1

**Difference between an
Independent-Groups
and a Correlated-
Groups Research
Design**

For the between-subjects design, there is no way of identifying the variation among the participants. Therefore, the within-group variation reflects the random differences among participants and other random factors. The correlated-groups design identifies the variation among participants and separates it from the within-group variation, thereby reducing the size of the within-group variance.

the size of the *F*-ratio. Consequently, a correlated-samples design usually has greater statistical power than the equivalent between-subjects design.

While there are many types of correlated-group designs out there, two basic forms in particular are widely used. Specifically, we are talking about repeated-measures and matched-participants designs. Although these are different research procedures, both allow the researcher to exercise greater control over the variables that influence the independent variable. This increased control typically results in greater statistical power.

## Repeated-Measures Design

In the repeated-measures design, data are collected from the same participants over a series of occasions or under several different levels of the independent variable to determine whether there are systematic changes in each participant's behavior. There are two general types of repeated-measures designs.

The first type of repeated-measures design allows us to test the same participant using several levels of the same independent variable. For example, a researcher might be interested in the effectiveness of different medications for the treatment of schizophrenia. To conduct the study, the researcher uses a placebo, Drug A, and Drug B. Each participant in the study will receive each treatment to determine its effects on the symptoms associated with schizophrenia. The advantage to this procedure is that it requires fewer participants because we test each participant using each

# Figure 14.2

**Difference between an Independent-Groups and a Correlated-Groups Design**

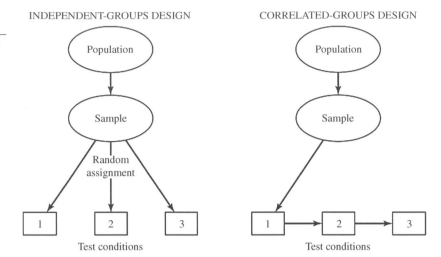

treatment rather than assigning separate groups of participants to each of the three treatment conditions. Another advantage to this design is that we can use each participant as his or her own control "group," thereby reducing the amount of variance within each treatment condition in the ANOVA (more on this later).

The second general type of repeated-measures design allows us to use time as an independent variable. For this type of research, we arrange to test or sample the participants' behavior at specific time intervals. Using this procedure we can then determine how the participants' behavior changes as a function of time. This technique is useful when time is a critical predictor variable. Thus we can use this technique when we want to observe a behavior before and after a critical event or when we want to observe changes in the behavior that occur over time.

Figure 14.2 presents an illustration of the difference between an independent-groups design and a correlated-groups design. Both designs begin with a sampling population from which we draw our sample. The difference is the number of samples we draw. For the independent-groups design, we create a separate sample for each treatment condition using random assignment. For the correlated-groups design, we create a single sample and then test each participant under each treatment condition.

## Example of a Repeated-Measures Design

As an example, imagine that we want to replicate the famous serial position effect. To conduct our study we ask four participants to listen to seven lists of seven abstract, three-syllable words. Immediately after hearing the last word of each list, the participants must repeat the list. If our results replicate the serial-position effect, words at the start and end of a list have the greatest probability of recall, whereas words toward the middle of a list have a lower probability of recall. The data in Table 14.1 and Figure 14.3 represent

Table 14.1   **Hypothetical Data for a Study of the Serial Position Effect Using Four Participants**

| Participant | Position of Word | | | | | | | Participant Means |
|---|---|---|---|---|---|---|---|---|
| | 1 | 2 | 3 | 4 | 5 | 6 | 7 | |
| 1 | 4 | 4 | 3 | 2 | 2 | 2 | 3 | 2.86 |
| 2 | 5 | 3 | 2 | 3 | 2 | 2 | 5 | 3.14 |
| 3 | 6 | 4 | 5 | 5 | 3 | 3 | 4 | 4.29 |
| 4 | 7 | 6 | 6 | 5 | 5 | 3 | 5 | 5.29 |
| Average number of words recalled | 5.5 | 4.25 | 4 | 3.75 | 3 | 2.5 | 4.25 | |

hypothetical data for such a study (this example comes from research conducted by Walker & Hulme, 1999).

There is considerable variability among the four participants in this study; some were good at recalling the words, whereas others did not do as well. If you look carefully at each participant's performance, you can see some evidence of the serial-position effect. Participants recalled the most words that came at the start or the end of the lists. The solid black line in Figure 14.3 represents the average performance of the four participants for each serial position. This line clearly illustrates the serial-position effect. As the position of the word increases, the probability that a participant will remember the word deceases up to the sixth position. Participants recall the word in the seventh position more than the word in the sixth position, as the serial-position effect predicts. What would happen if we analyzed the data from this study using a conventional independent-groups ANOVA?

Table 14.2 presents the ANOVA summary table for a conventional independent-groups ANOVA (please note, this is not the recommended

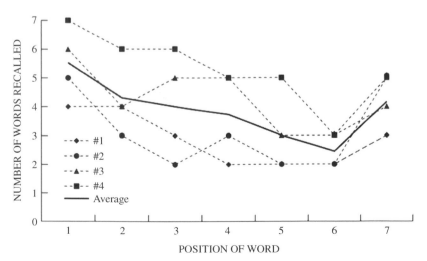

## Figure 14.3

**Number of Words Each Participant Recalled**

The solid black line represents the average performance of the four participants.

## Table 14.2 Summary Table for an Independent-Groups ANOVA Using Data in Table 14.1

|         | SS      | df | MS     | F     | p     |
|---------|---------|----|--------|-------|-------|
| Between | 22.4286 | 6  | 3.7381 | 2.166 | 0.088 |
| Within  | 36.2500 | 21 | 1.7262 |       |       |
| Total   | 58.6786 | 27 |        |       |       |

approach, but done here for illustration). For this analysis, we treated the seven word positions as if they were independent conditions each consisting of four different people. In other words, we treated the data as reflecting the responses of 28 different people who participated in the study and were randomly assigned to one of the seven conditions. The conclusion to draw from this table is that we cannot reject the null hypothesis if $\alpha = .05$.

There is a major problem with analyzing these data using an independent-groups ANOVA—the treatment groups are not independent of each other. If you reread the previous paragraph, you can see that the description of the "assumptions" had no bearing on how the researcher conducted the study. The data for all seven word positions come from the same four participants. Thus, we should assume that each participant's recall of a word in one position will influence the scores in the other positions. Participant 1 does not seem to have done well on the memory test as the scores for this person are generally low. By contrast, Participant 4 generally recalled the most words. If you look closely at the data, although there is much difference between Participants 1 and 4, both show evidence of the serial-position effect. Therefore, we should reanalyze the data using another form of the ANOVA that allows us to examine the differences among correlated groups, or groups in which the influence of the participants represents a systematic or consistent influence on their responses or outcomes.

Table 14.3 presents a summary table for a correlated-groups ANOVA. There are some differences in the summary table for an independent-groups versus a correlated-groups ANOVA. You can see that with the correlated-groups ANOVA we can reject the null hypothesis and conclude that there

## Table 14.3 Summary Table for a Correlated-Groups ANOVA Using Data in Table 14.1

|              | SS    | df | MS   | F    | p    |
|--------------|-------|----|------|------|------|
| Between      | 22.43 | 6  | 3.74 | 6.63 | 0.00 |
| Participants | 26.11 | 3  | 8.70 |      |      |
| Within       | 10.14 | 18 | 0.56 |      |      |
| Total        | 58.68 | 27 |      |      |      |

are statistically significant differences among the seven word positions, after taking into account the variability within each participant.

According to Table 14.3, the $F$-ratio increased from $F(6, 21) = 2.17$ to $F(6, 18) = 6.63$. How did this change occur? For both ANOVA summary tables the $MS_{between} = 3.74$. This number remains a constant for both forms of the ANOVA because we used $MS_{between}$ as an estimate of the variance among the seven serial position means. Because each ANOVA determines the between-group variance using the same procedures, this value will not change for the two tests. What does change for the two forms of the ANOVA is the value of $MS_{within}$.

Earlier we noted that the importance of the correlated-groups ANOVA is that it divides the variance within-groups (remember this is a reflection of error) into two components, variance due to consistent differences within participants and variance due to random error. In Table 14.3, you can see that there is a sum of squares ($SS$) for participants and a $SS$ for within-group variance. Adding $SS_{participants}$ and $SS_{within}$ in Table 14.3 equals the $SS_{within}$ of the independent-groups ANOVA reported in Table 14.2 ($36.25 = 26.11 + 10.14$). In other words, a sizable proportion of variance within each group reflects systematic differences among the participants. More concretely, some people are just better at recalling the list of words than others. When we divide the $MS_{between}$ by the revised $MS_{within}$, we obtain a much larger $F$-ratio ($6.63 = 3.7481/0.5635$).

In this way, then, the correlated-groups ANOVA allows us to detect the systematic differences among the serial position of the words that the independent-groups ANOVA could not detect. This success occurred because the correlated-groups ANOVA removes from the calculation of the $F$-ratio the variability due to consistent differences among participants. Hence, we can conclude that the correlated-groups ANOVA is more statistically powerful than the independent-groups design when there are consistent differences among the participants.

We do not need to calculate an $F$-ratio for the variance due to participants because our primary interest is the differences in the mean number of words recalled across the serial positions, not in the differences among the participants. You could, if you wanted, calculate the $F$-ratio by dividing the $MS_{participants}$ by the $MS_{within}$. The result would tell you what you had anticipated—that there are statistically significant differences among the participants. Because we want to treat the variance among participants as a nuisance variable that we control for, such findings are inconsequential.

## Advantages and Disadvantages of the Correlated-Groups Design

The primary advantage of the correlated-groups design is the increase in statistical power we obtain by identifying the systematic variance caused by consistent differences among the participants. In effect, this increase in our ability to detect differences between conditions comes from allowing each participant to serve as his or her own control condition. We do this by

Table 14.4  **Common Carryover Effects That Can Confound a Repeated-Measures Design**

| | |
|---|---|
| **Contrast** | In some cases, the change in level of the independent variable creates a contrast effect. For example, a participant switched from 50 to 25 reward points will respond differently than a participant switched from 25 to 50 points or a participant maintained at 25 points. |
| **Fatigue** | The participants become tired from or bored by repeating the same task on multiple trials. The effects of fatigue and boredom occur when the individual has little opportunity to rest between trials. |
| **Habituation/ Adaptation** | Habituation and adaptation refer to participants becoming used to the effects of the independent variable. In some cases, the participants may develop a tolerance for the independent variable. For example, a stimulus that produces fear the first time will lose its effectiveness if presented repeatedly. |
| **Learning** | The participants learn how to perform the task during the first test. Consequently, their performance on subsequent tests reflects the effect of the independent variable and the effect of learning. This form of carryover effect is prevalent whenever one uses the same test or skill-based task. |
| **Pretest Sensitization** | A pretest, given before the treatment, may alter the participant's reaction to the eventual treatment. For example, asking participants questions about racism or sexism may change how they respond to a treatment condition that causes them to confront these issues. |

testing the same participant under several treatment conditions or across time.

Another advantage of the correlated-groups design is that it requires a smaller overall number of participants because we test the same participants under more than one treatment condition. This is primarily a resource and cost advantage, but when combined with the increased statistical power, it helps to make the correlated-groups design an extremely attractive procedure depending on the research question.

Despite these general benefits, repeated measurement of the same participant can introduce unwanted effects in some cases. Can you think of some confounding variables that might arise from repeatedly testing the same participants? Consider a study for which we require the participants to complete the same test for each treatment condition. Over time, the participants' performance will change, not necessarily because of the effects of the independent variable, but because participants have more experience with the test. We use the term **carryover effect** to describe situations in which experience in one testing condition affects the participants' performance in the following conditions. Because carryover effects are typically not part of the purpose of the experiment, they can confound the interpretation of the results. Table 14.4 lists several of the more common carryover effects that can confound the interpretation of the results.

### Reducing Carryover Effects

There are several research designs that adequately address the threat of a carryover effect. The first is a between-subjects design. In many cases, this may be your only alternative to a correlated-groups design, especially if your treatment conditions are likely to lead to irreversible changes in the participants. Irreversible changes are those that cannot be undone. For example, if you were comparing methods of teaching students to multiply, you could not use a correlated-groups design. Once you expose the students to the first teaching method, they have learned something about multiplication, and there is no way of returning the student to the original state of ignorance. Because you cannot undo the effects of the teaching, you cannot directly examine the merits and effect of the second teaching method with a correlated-groups approach.

A second option is to use a technique known as the **Solomon four-group design**. This procedure is a creative use of control groups that allows you to judge the extent to which there is a carryover effect. This procedure is effective for accounting for the effects described in Table 14.4. When the changes in a participant due to an independent variable are reversible, we can shuffle the order of presentation of the levels of this variable for each participant. This shuffling of events will distribute the effects due to the sequence of events across all the participants. The goal of shuffling is to make the sequence itself a random variable that has no consistent effect on the participants' behavior.

Two other techniques for addressing carryover effects are **counterbalancing** and **Latin square designs**. A final option is to recognize that changes in the participant are an important independent variable to examine. From this perspective, an observed carryover effect is not a confounding variable, but a central focus of the research question we are asking. In the following sections we will examine each of these techniques for addressing carryover effects in more detail.

### Solomon Four-Group Design

Richard Solomon (1949) developed an extremely creative research design, presented in Table 14.5, that makes use of three control groups to account for sequence events. As Campbell and Stanley (1963) noted, the procedure is a superior research design for accounting for carryover effects.

For the Solomon design, only Group 1 and Group 3 experience the treatment condition. The difference between these groups is that Group 1 receives a pretest and a posttest; Group 3 receives only the posttest. Groups 2

## Table 14.5  The Solomon Four-Group Design

|  | Pretest | Treatment | Posttest |
|---|---|---|---|
| Group 1 | $O_1$ | →Treatment→ | $O_2$ |
| Group 2 | $O_3$ | ————————→ | $O_4$ |
| Group 3 |  | Treatment→ | $O_5$ |
| Group 4 |  |  | $O_6$ |

*Note:* $O_x$ represents an observation or test score.

# Figure 14.4

**Idealized Results of a Solomon Four-Group Design**

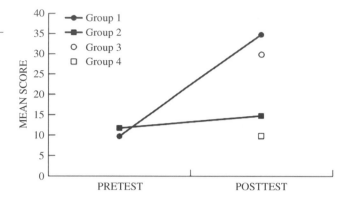

and 4 represent special control conditions that do not experience the treatment condition. Group 2 acts as a control condition for Group 1; the participants in both groups complete both the pretest and posttest, but only participants in Group 1 experience the treatment. Similarly, Group 4 acts as a control group for Group 3; the participants in both groups complete the posttest, but only participants in Group 3 receive the treatment.

Figure 14.4 presents an idealized graph of the results using data collected with a Solomon four-group design. As the graph illustrates, the participants who experienced the treatment (Groups 1 and 3) show much higher average scores than the participants in the control groups (Groups 2 and 4) for the pretest and posttest measures. There is also evidence of a carryover effect. That the posttest scores for Groups 1 and 2 are higher than the posttest scores of Groups 3 and 4 illustrates that the experience with the pretest has influenced the participants' behavior in some manner.

Solomon (1949) recommended that researchers use a simple $2 \times 2$ ANOVA factorial design to analyze the data from this type of design. Table 14.6 presents the layout of such a design. Braver and Braver (1988) noted that the Solomon four-group design is underused and frequently misinterpreted. Contrary to popular opinion, the Bravers demonstrated that the Solomon design does not require twice the number of participants

## Table 14.6  The 2 × 2 Factorial Analysis of the Solomon Four-Group Design

|  | Factor A | |
|---|---|---|
|  | Treatment | |
|  | $a_1$ Treatment | $a_2$ No Treatment |
| $b_1$ Pretest | $O_2$ | $O_4$ |
| **Factor B:** Pretesting |  |  |
| $b_2$ No Pretest | $O_5$ | $O_6$ |

even though it has more control groups. They demonstrated that the Solomon design can be a cost-effective research technique if used with the proper statistical analyses. In summary, the Solomon four-group design is a sophisticated research tool that offers considerable methodological and statistical control over carryover effects. It is a research tool often overlooked for little good reason.

## Counterbalancing

We can also reduce the presence of carryover effects by randomly changing the sequence of testing for each participant. Researchers call this shuffling procedure counterbalancing. For example, if you wanted to test the effects of three dosages of a drug on the same participants, you would shuffle the order in which each participant receives the different dosages. One participant would receive the pattern 1, 2, 3, whereas another participant may receive the pattern 3, 1, 2.

The number of potential patterns for complete or full counterbalancing is $k!$, where $k$ represents the levels of the independent variable to be tested (! represents the factorial of a number, so for example, $2! = 2 \times 1 = 2$). For three levels of the independent variable, there are 3! or $3 \times 2 \times 1 = 6$ patterns. Because there are six patterns, you will need enough participants for the study to ensure that you can use each pattern the same number of times. In other words, if there are three treatment conditions, the number of participants in the experiment must be a multiple of six to ensure equal representation of each counterbalance sequence.

## Latin Square Design

Complete counterbalancing can be expensive to conduct because of the number of participants required. Imagine conducting an experiment that used five levels of the independent variable. One would require at least $5! = 120$ participants to fill out all the sequence conditions. An alternative is to use a Latin square design. A Latin square is a collection of counterbalanced treatment sequences that ensures each treatment occurs once within each position of the sequence. The Latin square also ensures that the sequence of treatments is random, thus controlling for unwanted sequence events. Perhaps seeing how one constructs a Latin square will illustrate the value of the procedure.

Table 14.7 presents the method for generating a Latin square of any size. To use the Latin square in an experiment, randomly assign equal numbers of participants to each treatment order condition specified by the rows of the square. The Latin square is a useful design tool to overcome most carryover effects. The analysis of the data is complex, however. The analysis of data from this type of research design is beyond the scope of this textbook. Fortunately, advanced textbooks on statistics, such as those by Hayes (1981), Kirk (1982), and Winer, Brown, and Michels (1991), review the statistical procedures for the Latin square design.

## Table 14.7  Steps to Create a Latin Square for Any Number of Levels of the Independent Variable

|   | 1 | 2 | 3 | 4 | 5 |
|---|---|---|---|---|---|
| 1 |   |   |   |   |   |
| 2 |   |   |   |   |   |
| 3 |   |   |   |   |   |
| 4 |   |   |   |   |   |
| 5 |   |   |   |   |   |

**Step 1:** Create a square of $k$ rows and $k$ columns, where $k$ represents the number of levels of the independent variable. For this example, there are five levels of the independent variable.

|   | 1 | 2 | 3 | 4 | 5 |
|---|---|---|---|---|---|
| 1 | 1 | 2 | 3 | 4 | 5 |
| 2 | 2 | 3 | 4 | 5 | 1 |
| 3 | 3 | 4 | 5 | 1 | 2 |
| 4 | 4 | 5 | 1 | 2 | 3 |
| 5 | 5 | 1 | 2 | 3 | 4 |

**Step 2:** Starting with Row 1, write the numbers 1 through 5. For each subsequent row, start the line with the number of the line and then continue the sequence of numbers until you reach $k$, and then restart the numbering at 1.

|   | 4 | 1 | 5 | 3 | 2 |
|---|---|---|---|---|---|
| 1 | 4 | 1 | 5 | 3 | 2 |
| 2 | 5 | 2 | 1 | 4 | 3 |
| 3 | 1 | 3 | 2 | 5 | 4 |
| 4 | 2 | 4 | 3 | 1 | 5 |
| 5 | 3 | 5 | 4 | 2 | 1 |

**Step 3:** Using a random number table, randomly shuffle the order of the columns.

|   | 4 | 1 | 5 | 3 | 2 |
|---|---|---|---|---|---|
| 3 | 1 | 3 | 2 | 5 | 4 |
| 1 | 4 | 1 | 5 | 3 | 2 |
| 4 | 2 | 4 | 3 | 1 | 5 |
| 5 | 3 | 5 | 4 | 2 | 1 |
| 2 | 5 | 2 | 1 | 4 | 3 |

**Step 4:** Using a random number table, randomly shuffle the order of the rows. The numbers within the grid represent the Latin square. Randomly assign equal numbers of participants to each of the five sequences you generated.

### Examine the Effects of a Sequence

For some repeated-measures research, the carryover effect is not a confounding variable. Rather, the researcher may wish to treat the sequence of events as the independent variable. A classic example of this type of analysis is given by Crespi (1942), who examined the effects of changing the amount of reinforcement that rats received for running through a maze. During the first part of the experiment, rats received 64, 16, or 4 pellets of food for running through the maze. After 20 trials, Crespi changed the amount of food the rats received. The rats that had been receiving 64 pellets began to receive 16 pellets. Similarly, the rats that had received 4 pellets also began to receive 16 pellets.

The results of this experiment demonstrate a clear contrast effect. As you can see in Figure 14.5, rats switched from 64 to 16 pellets began to run slower than the rats maintained at 16 pellets. By contrast, the rats switched from 4 to 16 pellets began to run much faster than rats maintained at 16 pellets.

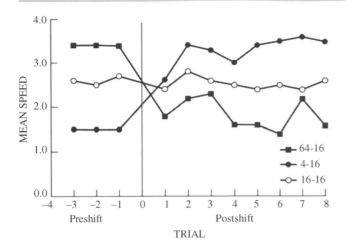

**Figure 14.5**

**Results Based on Crespi's (1942) Research on the Effect of Changing the Magnitude of Reinforcement**

For this experiment, the carryover effect is the central feature of the experiment because Crespi (1942) wanted to examine how the change in reinforcement would influence the rats' behavior.

## Knowledge Check

1. Describe in your words the meaning and purpose of the matched-groups and repeated-measures designs.

2. What are the similarities and differences between a matched-participants design and a repeated-measures design?

3. What are common carryover effects?

4. Describe in your words how the Solomon four-group design helps us contend with carryover effects.

5. In a repeated-measures research design, how does each participant act as his or her own control group?

6. Why does a correlated-groups design increase the power of the ANOVA?

7. When is the use of counterbalancing and the Latin square design necessary?

## Matched-Groups Design

The repeated-measures design allows us to examine or test each participant's behavior under more than one condition. Although this procedure has its advantages, there are some shortcomings related to the carryover effect, as we have discussed. The most serious problem arises when the treatment creates an irreversible change in the participants' behavior. In this section, we will examine another correlated-groups research design that retains the statistical power of the repeated-measures design but allows us to test each participant under only one treatment condition. Specifically, we will examine the matched-groups design.

Researchers use the matched-groups design when they believe that an important subject variable may correlate with the dependent variable. The goal of the matched-groups design is to ensure that the treatment groups are equivalent with respect to this subject variable. Therefore, each group in the study contains a separate group of participants, and for this reason we do not use a standard repeated-measures procedure. Nevertheless, the matched-groups design allows us to assume that there is a meaningful correlation among pairs of participants across the treatment conditions. This tactic allows us to identify and remove variance due to a subject variable that influences the participant's behavior.

Table 14.8 presents the steps for creating a matched-groups design. First, test each participant using a measure that correlates with the dependent variable. Second, using the test scores, rank the participants from the highest to the lowest. For the third step, cluster the participants into groups based on their rank on the test. The size of the cluster must equal the number of treatment conditions used in the study. Finally, randomly assign the participants within each cluster to one of the treatment conditions. What is the result of all this effort?

In the example presented in Table 14.8, the first participant in each group earned one of the highest three scores on the test. Similarly, the second participant in each group earned the next highest level of test scores. This pattern continues for all the participants within each group. Therefore,

## Table 14.8  Steps Used to Create a Matched-Groups Design Study

| Step 1 | | Step 2 | | Step 3 | | | | Step 4 | | |
|---|---|---|---|---|---|---|---|---|---|---|
| Pretest all participants using a measure correlated with the dependent variable. | | Rank order participants from highest to lowest based on test score. | | Group participants in clusters equal to the number of treatment groups. | | | | Randomly assign participants, by cluster, to treatment groups. | | |
| **Participant** | **Score** | **Participant** | **Score** | | | | | | **Group** | |
| | | | | | | | | **1** | **2** | **3** |
| A | 114 | A | 114 | | | | | | | |
| B | 101 | G | 111 | | | | | | | |
| C | 104 | F | 109 | **1** | A | G | F | A | F | G |
| D | 105 | I | 106 | **2** | I | D | C | C | I | D |
| E | 92 | D | 105 | **3** | H | B | E | E | H | B |
| F | 109 | C | 104 | | | | | | | |
| G | 111 | H | 103 | | | | | | | |
| H | 103 | B | 101 | | | | | | | |
| I | 106 | E | 92 | | | | | | | |

we can assume that ordered pairs of participants (e.g., the fifth participant in each group) are similar to each other inasmuch as they each received similar scores on the original test.

Some researchers call the matched-groups design a *randomized block design*. The term *block* refers to agricultural experiments conducted during the early 1900s. A block was a specific plot of land that the researcher randomly selected to receive a specific treatment. Although behavioral researchers often use both of these phrases to describe this type of design, we prefer *matched-groups design* as it emphasizes that the researcher intentionally attempts to equate the groups by measuring a specific subject variable.

We can use a hypothetical example of an experiment examining the effectiveness of several drugs on the treatment of schizophrenia. For this example, assume that the researcher will examine the effects of a placebo, Drug A, and Drug B. Because the researcher believes that the initial severity of the person's schizophrenia will influence results, the researcher first assesses the severity of symptoms for each participant. The researcher would then take the three participants with the highest scores and randomly assign them to one of the three treatment groups. Repeating this procedure for all participants ensures the equivalence among the groups with respect to initial levels of schizophrenia.

There is no reason to limit yourself to one subject variable with this type of design. In some research projects, researchers find it necessary to match participants across a number of subject variables, including age, sex, level of education, income, and other quantitative and qualitative variables that differentiate individuals and correlate with the dependent variable. A caveat is in order, however. Using more than one matching variable can greatly increase the difficulty of achieving a true balance among the participants.

The matched-groups design means that the groups are not fully independent. As you know by now, *independent* in this case means that the behavior of one group of participants has no influence on the behavior of another group of participants. In an independent-groups design, the independent groups are typically formed by random assignment of participants to different treatment groups or by randomly selecting participants from different populations, which are later compared against each other. Consequently, the behavior of one group of participants has no influence on the behavior of other groups of participants. In the matched-groups design, however, we intentionally try to create a correlation among the groups. This is why this type of design is a correlated-groups design similar to repeated-measures designs.

## Advantages and Disadvantages of the Matched-Groups Design

There is an advantage to the matched-groups design: any difference among the groups is easier to detect. As you have already learned, the correlated-groups ANOVA reduces $MS_{within}$. However, a potential disadvantage to using the matched-groups design is low statistical power. The correlated-groups ANOVA treats the scores across the treatment conditions as if they came from the same participants. The result is that the ANOVA acts as if there were fewer participants in the study. In other words, the degrees of freedom for a correlated-groups design are smaller than for the comparable independent-groups design. Review Tables 14.2 and 14.3. The degrees of freedom are (6, 21) for the independent-groups design and (6, 18) for the correlated-groups design. In general, small degrees of freedom require larger F-ratios to reject the null hypothesis. Consequently, if the matching technique does not effectively identify a significant subject variable, the statistical power of the test can be lower than a comparable between-groups design. Therefore, the advantage of a matched-groups design occurs only when your matching technique identifies a subject variable with a substantial correlation to the dependent variable.

## Yoked-Control Group

Another popular version of the matched-subjects design is the yoked-control-group design. In a **yoked-control** study, the researcher randomly pairs a control participant with a participant in the experimental group, and each experience the exact sequence of events or consequences except for the exposure of the independent variable. Researchers use the yoked-control design when the behavior of the participant affects the sequence of events in the study. Perhaps several examples of the use of a yoked-control design would be helpful.

Figure 14.6 presents an illustration of a yoked-control design. In this figure, the participants experience some sequence of events during the

## Figure 14.6

**An Illustration of a Yoked-Control Design**

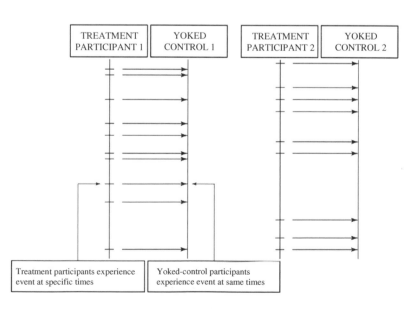

course of the experiment. As you can see, the order and pattern of events is different for the two participants in the treatment condition. The participants in the yoked-control condition each experience the same events in the same sequence and interval as their partner.

Classic examples of the yoked-control group are experiments conducted by Brady (1958) and Brady, Porter, Conrad, and Mason (1958). Brady and his associates exposed monkeys to a series of escapable shocks. Brady selected half of the monkeys to be the "executive" subject in the experimental group. These monkeys could avoid or escape an unsignaled shock by pressing a button. Paired with each executive monkey was a yoked-control monkey. The yoked-control monkey received a shock each time its executive monkey did, but the yoked-control monkey had no way to avoid or escape the shock. Brady reported that the monkeys assigned to the executive condition developed stomach ulcers, whereas the yoked-control subjects did not. From these data, Brady concluded that the responsibility of avoiding/escaping the shocks was stressful and created the ulcers.

The Brady et al. (1958) study is an important example because it contains a serious methodological error: Brady et al. did not randomly assign the participants to the experimental and yoked-control groups. It turns out that Brady et al. pretested the monkeys on a shock-avoidance task and selected the faster learners for the experimental condition and the slower learners for the yoked-control condition. Weiss (1971) recognized the problem with the procedure and repeated the experiment. For his experiment, Weiss randomly assigned rats to either the experimental group or the yoked-control condition. The results of that study were the opposite of the Brady et al. results. The rats in the yoked-control condition developed the stomach ulcers, not the rats in the executive-treatment condition. Therefore, it appears that the Brady et al. findings are the results of a methodological confound, not the effects of the treatment conditions.

In the Brady et al. (1958) and Weiss (1971) experiments, the researchers literally wired the yoked-control subjects to the same apparatus as the subjects in the experimental group. Consequently, the yoked-control subjects experienced the same series of events as their experimental pair. There are other ways to conduct a yoked-control study. For example, an experiment conducted by Eisenberger and Leonard (1980) used the yoked-control procedure to examine the effects of task complexity and positive reinforcement on the participant's persistence at a task.

For the experiment, participants in the experimental group received a list of complex anagrams to solve. The participants had to solve each anagram within an allotted time. If the participants failed to solve an anagram, they began work on the next anagram. If the participants solved the anagram, they received a reward. The researchers kept track of the solved and failed anagrams for each participant in the experimental group. The researchers then randomly paired participants in the yoked-control group with participants in the experimental group. Participants in the yoked-control group experienced the same number of successes and failures as their counterparts in the experimental group.

Eisenberger and Leonard (1980) were able to reproduce the same pattern of successes and failures by presenting the participant in the yoked-control group with a simple anagram for the success trials and an unsolvable anagram for the failure trials. Consequently, each pair of participants received the same number of rewards in exactly the same order. The only difference between the two groups was the complexity of the anagrams: Participants in the experimental groups received reinforcement for solving complex anagrams, whereas the participants in the control group received reinforcement for solving simple anagrams.

## Knowledge Check

8. How will using a matched-groups design increase the power of the ANOVA?

9. In what ways are the matched-groups design and the yoked-control design similar and different from each other?

10. Describe how a yoked-control design works and how it ensures that participants in the experimental and control groups receive the same treatment except for the independent variable.

11. How can you distinguish between an independent-groups and a correlated-groups design?

## Mixed-Model Design

As you might have guessed, we can continue to apply the logic of the ANOVA to various research applications. In this section, you will learn how to conduct a **mixed-model design**. The mixed-model design gets its name because there are two types of variables, a **between-subjects variable** and a **within-subjects variable**.

A between-subjects variable is an independent variable to which the researcher randomly assigns the participants. For each level of a between-participants variable there is a different and independent group of participants. The essential characteristic of a between-subjects variable is that participants experience only one level of the variable. Consequently, if participants are exposed to only one level of the variable, it is a between-subjects variable. If the researcher uses a subject variable (e.g., men versus women, depressed versus not depressed), then the variable is also a between-subjects variable. The term *between-subjects* refers to the fact that the ANOVA compares the differences between independent groups of different participants.

By contrast, a within-subjects variable is a correlated-samples variable. Therefore, if a factor represents a repeated-measures variable or matched-groups variable, we call it a within-subjects variable. The essential characteristic of a within-subjects variable is that we collect data from the same participant on different occasions or under different treatment conditions. We also use *within-subjects* to describe the matched-groups research design. We will examine the mixed-model design in more detail within the following "Research in Action" example.

## Research in Action: Memory for Related Words

Consider a simple experiment to demonstrate how to use a mixed-model ANOVA. A student wants to replicate a classic experiment conducted by Wickens, Born, and Allen (1963) that examined the effects of proactive interference. Proactive interference occurs when you attempt to learn new information and previously learned information interferes with the new material.

For the experiment, the researcher has the participant complete a series of trials. On each trial, the researcher presents the participant with a short list of words whose meanings are highly related (e.g., names of flowers). After seeing the words, the participant must then recall the words in the list. For the experimental and control groups, to which participants are randomly assigned, the first three trials use the same category of words. On the fourth trial, the researchers change the meaning of the words for the experimental group (e.g., names of professions), but leave the meaning of the words for the control group unchanged. Table 14.9 presents the percentage correct for the two groups across the four trials, and Figure 14.7 presents a graph of the group means.

As a quick review, we can examine the components of this experiment. First, the research does incorporate the mixed-model design. The

## Table 14.9  Hypothetical Data for an Experiment Examining Release from the Proactive Interference Effect

| **Experimental** | 1 | 82 | 53 | 48 | 63 | |
| | 2 | 92 | 51 | 39 | 60 | |
| | 3 | 63 | 41 | 10 | 52 | |
| | 4 | 75 | 57 | 51 | 72 | |
| | 5 | 78 | 49 | 43 | 77 | |
| | | $M_{11} = 78.0$ | $M_{12} = 50.2$ | $M_{13} = 38.2$ | $M_{14} = 64.8$ | $M_{a1} = 57.80$ |
| **Control** | 6 | 84 | 60 | 47 | 33 | |
| | 7 | 85 | 44 | 42 | 46 | |
| | 8 | 78 | 71 | 34 | 45 | |
| | 9 | 76 | 49 | 38 | 25 | |
| | 10 | 63 | 69 | 55 | 30 | |
| | | $M_{21} = 77.2$ | $M_{22} = 58.6$ | $M_{23} = 43.2$ | $M_{24} = 35.8$ | $M_{a2} = 53.60$ |
| | | $M_{b1} = 77.6$ | $M_{b2} = 54.4$ | $M_{b3} = 40.7$ | $M_{b4} = 50.3$ | $\bar{M} = 55.75$ |

# Figure 14.7

**Graph of the Data Presented in Table 14.9**

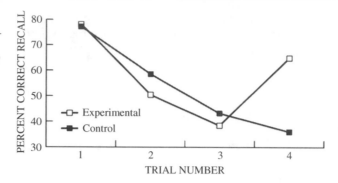

researcher randomly assigned participants to either the experimental or the control groups. Hence, the first variable is a between-subjects variable as the researcher tested the participants under one of the two conditions. The second variable is the sequence of trials. Because the researcher tested each participant on each trial, we can conclude that this sequence of trials is a within-subjects design. Specifically, the researcher assumes that there will be a correlation between the treatment groups because each participant completes the entire sequence of trials.

During the first three trials, the participants' performance in both groups decreased, as is predicted by the proactive interference phenomenon. The data for the fourth trial is interesting. The performance of the participants in the control group continued to decline. By contrast, the performance of the participants in the experimental group improved. We can use these data to demonstrate how to use a mixed-model design.

Table 14.10 presents the ANOVA summary table for the data presented in Table 14.8. There is a statistically significant interaction and main effect for the trials. The results of the interaction between trials and the experimental group indicate that the participants in the experimental group performed just like the participants in the control group until Trial 4. Switching the meaning of the words in the fourth trial undid the effects of the proactive interference.

## Table 14.10   The ANOVA Summary Table for a Mixed-Model ANOVA

| Source | SS | df | MS | F |
|---|---|---|---|---|
| A | 168.10 | 1 | 168.100 | 0.842 |
| Subjects | 1597.40 | 8 | 199.675 | |
| B | 7354.50 | 3 | 2451.500 | 30.132* |
| AB | 2174.90 | 3 | 724.967 | 8.911* |
| B × subjects | 1952.60 | 24 | 81.358 | |
| Total | 13247.50 | 39 | | |

*$p < .05$, reject $H_0$

As with the other forms of the ANOVA, we can follow the statistically significant $F$-ratio with additional tests, including post-hoc tests of the main effects and interaction and measure of effect size.

## Statistics behind the Research

In this section we will examine two versions of the correlated-groups ANOVA. The first test will examine the computational procedures for the simple one-factor correlated-groups ANOVA. The second test will examine the mixed-model design.

### Single-Factor Correlated-Groups ANOVA

To illustrate this version of the ANOVA we will return to the serial-position-effect study described at the start of the chapter. Table 14.11 presents an enhanced representation of the data. We need to know the totals for each trial ($\Sigma X_{aj}$) and for each participant ($\Sigma X_{si}$).

*Assumptions*
The three primary assumptions for this test are similar to the standard assumptions of the ANOVA. We expect that the group variances are consistent, that the distribution of errors is independent, and that the data are normally distributed. An additional assumption is that there be homogeneity of the correlations among the groups.

*Forming the Hypotheses*
As with all ANOVAs, we begin with the null hypothesis that states that the differences among the group means represent random variation. The alternative hypothesis states that the variance among the group means is greater than would be expected by chance. For this study,

> *Null hypothesis:*. The differences among the group means represent random variation.

$$H_0 : \mu_1 = \mu_2 = \mu_3 \ldots = \mu_7$$

## Table 14.11 Data to Be Analyzed Using a Single-Factor Correlated-Groups ANOVA

| | Position of Word | | | | | | | |
| --- | --- | --- | --- | --- | --- | --- | --- | --- |
| Participant | 1 | 2 | 3 | 4 | 5 | 6 | 7 | Totals |
| 1 | 4 | 4 | 3 | 2 | 2 | 2 | 3 | $\Sigma X_{s1} = 20$ |
| 2 | 5 | 3 | 2 | 3 | 2 | 2 | 5 | $\Sigma X_{s2} = 22$ |
| 3 | 6 | 4 | 5 | 5 | 3 | 3 | 4 | $\Sigma X_{s3} = 30$ |
| 4 | 7 | 6 | 6 | 5 | 5 | 3 | 5 | $\Sigma X_{s4} = 37$ |
| | $\Sigma X_{a1} = 22$ | $\Sigma X_{a2} = 17$ | $\Sigma X_{a3} = 16$ | $\Sigma X_{a4} = 15$ | $\Sigma X_{a5} = 12$ | $\Sigma X_{a6} = 10$ | $\Sigma X_{a7} = 17$ | $\Sigma X_{ij} = 109$ |
| | $M_{a1} = 5.50$ | $M_{a2} = 4.25$ | $M_{a3} = 4.00$ | $M_{a4} = 3.75$ | $M_{a5} = 3.00$ | $M_{a6} = 2.50$ | $M_{a7} = 4.25$ | $\Sigma X_{ij}^2 = 483$ |

*Alternative hypothesis:*. The variation among the group means is greater than expected by chance.

$$H_1 : \text{Not } H_0$$

### Sampling Distribution

The sampling distribution of the single-factor correlated-groups ANOVA is the conventional F-distribution. We use the $df_{\text{between}}$ and $df_{\text{within}}$ to determine $F_{\text{critical}}$ for the hypothesis testing.

### Completing the Calculations

Table 14.12 presents the steps for completing the calculations for the ANOVA summary table. For this analysis, the $F$-ratio is the variance between-groups divided by the variance within-groups. Using the following calculations, we find that $6.6338 = 3.7381/0.5635$. The degrees of freedom for the $F$-ratio are 6 and 18. Therefore, $F_{\text{critical}} (2, 18) = 2.66$ for $\alpha = .05$. Because $F_{\text{observed}} > F_{\text{critical}}$, we can reject the null hypothesis.

## Table 14.12  Steps for Creating the ANOVA Summary Table for a Single-Factor Correlated-Groups ANOVA

$$SS_{\text{between}} = \frac{\Sigma(\Sigma X_{aj})^2}{n} - \frac{(\Sigma X_{ij})^2}{nj}$$

$$SS_{\text{between}} = \frac{22^2 + 17^2 + 16^2 \cdots + 17^2}{4} - \frac{(109)^2}{4(7)} \qquad SS_{\text{between}} = 22.4286$$

$$df_{\text{between}} = j - 1 \quad df_{\text{between}} = 7 - 1 \quad df_{\text{between}} = 6$$

$$MS_{\text{between}} = \frac{SS_{\text{between}}}{df_{\text{between}}} \quad MS_{\text{between}} = \frac{22.4286}{6} \quad MS_{\text{between}} = 3.7381$$

$$SS_{\text{subjects}} = \frac{\Sigma(\Sigma X_{si})^2}{j} - \frac{(\Sigma X_{ij})^2}{nj} \quad SS_{\text{subjects}} = \frac{20^2 + 22^2 + 30^2 + 37^3}{7} - \frac{(109)^2}{4(7)}$$

$$SS_{\text{subjects}} = 26.1071$$

$$df_{\text{subjects}} = n - 1 \quad df_{\text{subjects}} = 4 - 1 \quad df_{\text{subjects}} = 3$$

$$SS_{\text{within}} = \Sigma X_{ij}^2 - \frac{\Sigma(\Sigma X_{si})^2}{j} - \frac{\Sigma(\Sigma X_{aj})^2}{n} + \frac{(\Sigma X_{ij})^2}{nj}$$

$$SS_{\text{within}} = 483 - \frac{3153}{7} - \frac{1787}{4} + \frac{11881}{28} \quad SS_{\text{within}} = 10.1429$$

$$df_{\text{within}} = (n - 1)(j - 1) \quad df_{\text{within}} = (4 - 1)(7 - 1) \quad df_{\text{within}} = 18$$

$$MS_{\text{within}} = \frac{SS_{\text{within}}}{df_{\text{within}}} \quad MS_{\text{within}} = \frac{10.1429}{18} \quad MS_{\text{within}} = 0.5635$$

$$SS_{\text{total}} \Sigma X_{ij}^2 - \frac{(\Sigma X_{ij})^2}{nj} \quad SS_{\text{total}} = 483 - \frac{(109)^2}{4(7)} \quad SS_{\text{total}} = 58.6786$$

$$df_{\text{total}} = nj - 1 \quad df_{\text{total}} = 4(7) - 1 \quad df_{\text{total}} = 27$$

*Note:* $df_{\text{total}} = df_{\text{between}} + df_{\text{subjects}} + df_{\text{within}} \qquad 27 = 6 + 3 + 18$
$SS_{\text{total}} = SS_{\text{between}} + SS_{\text{subjects}} + SS_{\text{within}} \qquad 58.6786 = 22.4286 + 26.1071 + 10.1429$

**Mixed-Model ANOVA**

To illustrate this version of the ANOVA, we will use the data presented in Table 14.9.

*Assumptions*
This test requires the same assumptions used for the single-factor correlated-groups ANOVA.

*Forming the Hypotheses*
As with all ANOVAs, we begin with the null hypothesis that states that the differences among the group means represent random variation. The primary factors of interest represent (1) the difference among the between-subjects variable, (2) the difference among the within-subjects variable, and (3) the interaction of the two variables. For this example,

> *Null hypotheses:*. There is no main effect for Factor A, the between-subjects factor. There is no main effect for Factor B, the within-subjects factor. There is no interaction between Factors A and B.

$$H_0 : F_A = 1.0$$

$$H_0 : F_B = 1.0$$

$$H_0 : F_{A \times B} = 1.0$$

> *Alternative hypotheses:*. There is a main effect for Factor A. There is a main effect for Factor B. There is an interaction for Factors A and B.

*Sampling Distribution*
The sampling distribution of the single-factor correlated-groups ANOVA is the conventional $F$-distribution. We use the $df_{effect}$ and $df_{within}$ to determine $F_{critical}$ for the hypothesis testing.

*Completing the Calculations*
Table 14.13 presents the steps for completing the calculations for the ANOVA summary table.

# Chapter Summary

In this chapter we examined another research design that allows us to increase the power of our research by identifying and removing variance due to differences among the participants. Specifically, we examined the matched-groups design and the repeated-measures design.

For the matched-groups design, the researcher identifies a subject variable that he or she believes influences the dependent variable of interest

## Table 14.13  Steps for Creating the ANOVA Summary Table

| | Participant | Trial 1 | Trial 2 | Trial 3 | Trial 4 | Participant Totals |
|---|---|---|---|---|---|---|
| **Experimental** | 1 | 82 | 53 | 48 | 63 | $\Sigma X_{s1} = 246$ |
| | 2 | 92 | 51 | 39 | 60 | $\Sigma X_{s2} = 242$ |
| | 3 | 63 | 41 | 10 | 52 | $\Sigma X_{s3} = 166$ |
| | 4 | 75 | 57 | 51 | 72 | $\Sigma X_{s4} = 255$ |
| | 5 | 78 | 49 | 43 | 77 | $\Sigma X_{s5} = 247$ |
| | | $\Sigma X_{11} = 390$ | $\Sigma X_{12} = 251$ | $\Sigma X_{13} = 191$ | $\Sigma X_{14} = 324$ | $\Sigma X_{a1} = 1156$ |
| | | $M_{11} = 78.0$ | $M_{12} = 50.2$ | $M_{13} = 38.2$ | $M_{14} = 64.8$ | $M_{a1} = 57.8$ |
| **Control** | 6 | 84 | 60 | 47 | 33 | $\Sigma X_{s6} = 224$ |
| | 7 | 85 | 44 | 42 | 46 | $\Sigma X_{s7} = 217$ |
| | 8 | 78 | 71 | 34 | 45 | $\Sigma X_{s8} = 228$ |
| | 9 | 76 | 49 | 38 | 25 | $\Sigma X_{s9} = 188$ |
| | 10 | 63 | 69 | 55 | 30 | $\Sigma X_{s10} = 217$ |
| | | $\Sigma X_{21} = 386$ | $\Sigma X_{22} = 293$ | $\Sigma X_{23} = 216$ | $\Sigma X_{24} = 179$ | $\Sigma X_{a2} = 1074$ |
| | | $M_{21} = 77.2$ | $M_{22} = 58.6$ | $M_{23} = 43.2$ | $M_{24} = 35.8$ | $M_{a2} = 53.6$ |
| | | $\Sigma X_{b1} = 776$ | $\Sigma X_{b2} = 544$ | $\Sigma X_{b3} = 407$ | $\Sigma X_{b4} = 503$ | $\Sigma X_{ijk} = 2230$ |
| | | $M_{b1} = 77.6$ | $M_{b2} = 54.4$ | $M_{b3} = 40.7$ | $M_{b4} = 50.3$ | $\bar{M} = 55.75$ |
| | | | | | | $\Sigma X_{ijk}^2 = 137570$ |

$n = 5$ :  Number of participants in each level of Factor A, the between-subjects variable
$j = 2$ :  Number of levels for Factor A
$k = 4$ :  Number of levels for Factor B

$$SS_A = \frac{\Sigma(\Sigma X_{aj})^2}{nk} - \frac{(\Sigma X_{ijk})^2}{njk} \qquad SS_A = \frac{1156^2 + 1074^2}{5(4)} - \frac{(2230)^2}{(5)(2)(4)} \qquad SS_A = 168.10$$

$$df_A = j - 1 \qquad df_A = 2 - 1 \qquad df_A = 1$$

$$MS_A \frac{SS_A}{df_A} \qquad MS_A = \frac{168.10}{1} \qquad MS_A = 168.10$$

$$SS_{subjects} = \frac{\Sigma(\Sigma X_{si})^2}{k} - \frac{\Sigma(\Sigma X_{aj})^2}{nk}$$

$$SS_{subjects} = \frac{246^2 + 242^2 + 166^2 \cdots 188^2 + 217^2}{4} - \frac{1156^2 + 1074^2}{5(4)} \qquad SS_{subjects} = 1597.40$$

$$df_{subjects} = (j - 1)(n - 1) \qquad df_{subjects} = (2 - 1)(5 - 1) \qquad df_{subjects} = 8$$

$$MS_{subjects} = \frac{SS_{subjects}}{df_{subjects}} \qquad MS_{subjects} = \frac{1597.40}{8} \qquad MS_{subjects} = 199.675$$

$$F_A = \frac{MS_A}{MS_{subjects}} \qquad F_A = \frac{168.100}{199.675} \qquad F_A = 0.842$$

$$SS_B = \frac{\Sigma(\Sigma X_{bk})^2}{nj} - \frac{(\Sigma X_{ijk})^2}{njk} \qquad SS_B = \frac{776^2 + 544^2 + 407^2 + 503^2}{5(2)} - \frac{(2230)^2}{(5)(2)(4)} \qquad SS_B = 7354.50$$

(Continued)

$$df_B = k - 1 \quad df_B = 4 - 1 \quad df_B = 3$$

$$MS_B = \frac{SS_B}{df_B} \quad MS_B = \frac{7354.50}{3} \quad MS_B = 2451.50$$

$$SS_{AB} = \frac{\Sigma(\Sigma X_{jk})^2}{n} - \frac{(\Sigma X_{ijk})^2}{njk} - SS_A - SS_B$$

$$SS_{AB} = \frac{390^2 + 251^2 + 191^2 \cdots 216^2 + 179^2}{5} - 124332.50 - 168.10 - 7354.50 \quad SS_{AB} = 2174.90$$

$$df_{AB} = (j-1)(k-1) \quad df_{AB} = (2-1)(4-1) \quad df_{AB} = 3$$

$$MS_{AB} = \frac{SS_{AB}}{df_{AB}} \quad MS_{AB} = \frac{2174.90}{3} \quad MS_{AB} = 724.967$$

$$SS_{B \times \text{subjects}} = \sum X_{ijk}^2 - \frac{\Sigma(\Sigma X_{jk})^2}{n} - \frac{\Sigma(\Sigma X_{si})^2}{k} + \frac{\Sigma(\Sigma X_{aj})^2}{nk}$$

$$SS_{B \times \text{subjects}} = 137570 - \frac{390^2 + 251^2 + 191^2 \cdots 216^2 + 179^2}{5} - \frac{246^2 + 242^2 + 166^2 \cdots 188^2 + 217^2}{4}$$

$$+ \frac{1156^2 + 1074^2}{5(4)}$$

$$SS_{B \times \text{subjects}} = 1952.60$$

$$df_{B \times \text{subjects}} = j(n-1)(k-1) \quad df_{B \times \text{subjects}} = 2(5-1)(4-1) \quad df_{B \times \text{subjects}} = 24$$

$$MS_{B \times \text{subjects}} = \frac{SS_{B \times \text{subjects}}}{df_{B \times \text{subjects}}} \quad MS_{B \times \text{subjects}} = \frac{1952.60}{24} \quad MS_{B \times \text{subjects}} = 81.358$$

$$SS_{\text{total}} = \sum X_{ijk}^2 - \frac{(\Sigma X_{ijk})^2}{N} \quad SS_{\text{total}} = 137570 - \frac{(2230)^2}{40} \quad SS_{\text{total}} = 13247.50$$

$$df_{\text{total}} = njk - 1 \quad df_{\text{total}} = (5)(2)(4) - 1 \quad df_{\text{total}} = 39$$

$$F_B = \frac{MS_B}{MS_{B \times \text{subjects}}} \quad F_B = \frac{2451.50}{81.358} \quad F_B = 30.132$$

$$F_{AB} = \frac{MS_{AB}}{MS_{B \times \text{subjects}}} \quad F_{AB} = \frac{724.967}{81.358} \quad F_{AB} = 8.911$$

---

$$df_{\text{total}} = df_A + df_{\text{subjects}} + df_B + df_{AB} + df_{B \times \text{subjects}} \qquad 39 = 1 + 8 + 3 + 3 + 24$$

$$Note: SS_{\text{total}} = SS_A + SS_{\text{subjects}} + SS_B + SS_{AB} + SS_{B \times \text{subjects}} \qquad 13247.50 = 168.10 + 1597.40 + 7354.50$$
$$+ 2174.90 + 1952.60$$

and then assigns the participants to the treatment conditions in such a way that each group has the same proportion of people who are high and low on the subject variable.

For the repeated-measures design, the researcher tests the same participants under a series of different treatment conditions. As a generality, the matched-groups and repeated-measures designs can increase the power of the statistical test because the corresponding ANOVA identifies systematic variance among the subjects and removes this variance from the common error term. Therefore, the designs make it easier to detect the differences among the various groups.

The repeated-measures design does have a potential disadvantage, however. In some cases, there may be a significant carryover effect that will bias or confound our interpretation of the data. In some cases, the carryover effect can be overcome using a Latin square design. In other cases, the carryover effect may be the focus of the study.

The ANOVA for the correlated-groups design is similar to the ANOVA for between-groups designs. The notable difference is that the ANOVA estimates the variance due to the differences among the participants. This strategy can reduce the common error term and then increase the probability that the differences among the groups will be detected.

Another version of the within-subjects design allows us to mix between-groups and within-groups variables. A between-subjects variable is one where the participants in one treatment condition are different from the participants in the other treatment conditions. A within-subjects variable is one where there is an intended correlation among the groups. This correlation occurs when we use either a matched-groups or a repeated-measures design.

## Chapter Glossary for Review

**Between-subjects variable**—An independent variable that represents different groups of participants. Each level of the variable consists of a different group of participants.

**Carryover effect**—A form of confounding variable that can occur when using a repeated measures design. Exposing the participant to one level of the independent variable can affect the participant's performance when tested under other conditions.

**Counterbalancing**—A technique to reduce the carryover or sequencing effects in a repeated-measures design. The researcher tests the participants under the identified treatment conditions; however, the order of the exposure is different. Specialized tactics for counterbalancing include Latin square designs.

**Latin square design**—A special form of counterbalancing. The procedure balances the sequence of treatment conditions such that order of treatments is balanced across all participants.

**Matched-groups design**—A form of correlated-groups research design in which the researcher matches participants for common characteristics and then assigns them to one of the treatment conditions. The procedure ensures that the groups will be similar regarding the relevant subject variables.

**Mixed-model design**—A research design that contains both a between-subjects variable and a within-subjects variable.

**Repeated-measures design**—A form of correlated-groups research design that allows the researcher to test the same participants under different treatment conditions or on different occasions.

**Solomon four-group design**—This procedure is a creative use of control groups that allows you to judge the extent to which there is a carryover effect.

**Within-subjects variable**—An independent variable that represents either a repeated-measures condition or a matched-groups design.

**Yoked-control design**—A form of control procedure for which the researcher randomly pairs participants; one member of the pair is assigned to the experimental group and the other to the control condition. The participant in the control condition experiences the exact same sequence of events as the experimental partner but does not experience the critical feature of the experiment.

## Chapter References

Brady, J. V. (1958). Ulcers in "executive" monkeys. *Scientific American*, *199*, 95–104.

Brady, J. V., Porter, R. W., Conrad, D. G., & Mason, J. W. (1958). Avoidance behavior and the development of gastroduodenal ulcers. *Journal of the Experimental Analysis of Behavior*, *1*, 69–73.

Braver, M.C.W., & Braver, S. L. (1988). Statistical treatment of the Solomon four-group design: A meta-analytic approach. *Psychological Bulletin*, *104*, 150–154.

Campbell, D. T., & Stanley, J. C. (1963). *Experimental and quasi-experimental designs for research*. Chicago: Rand McNally.

Crespi, L. P. (1942). Quantitative variation of incentive and performance in the white rat. *American Journal of Psychology*, *55*, 467–517.

Eisenberger, R., & Leonard, J. M. (1980). Effects of conceptual task difficulty on generalized persistence. *American Journal of Psychology*, *93*, 285–298.

Hayes, L. V. (1981). *Statistics*. New York: Holt, Rinehart & Winston.

Kirk, R. E. (1982). *Experimental design* (2nd ed.). Monterey, CA: Brooks/Cole.

Solomon, R. L. (1949). An extension of control group design. *Psychological Bulletin*, *46*, 137–150.

Walker, I., & Hulme, C. (1999). Concrete words are easier to recall than abstract words: Evidence for a semantic contribution to short-term serial recall. *Journal of Experimental Psychology: Learning, Memory, & Cognition*, *25*, 1256–1271.

Weiss, J. M. (1971). Effects of coping behavior with and without a feedback signal on stress pathology in rats. *Journal of Comparative & Physiological Psychology*, *77*, 22–30.

Wickens, D. D., Born, D. G., & Allen, C. K. (1963). Proactive inhibition and item similarity in short-term memory. *Journal of Verbal Learning and Verbal Behavior*, *2*, 440–445.

Winer, B. J., Brown, D. R., & Michels, K. M. (1991). *Statistical principles in experimental design* (3rd ed.) New York: McGraw-Hill.

# Part IV
## Special Research Designs

If we knew what we were doing, it wouldn't be called research.

—**Albert Einstein**

## Introduction

After a cursory study of standard research guidelines for social science research it is easy to conclude that the results of a research project can be valid only if the researcher used legions of participants randomly selected from the target population and randomly assigned to treatment conditions in a highly controlled experiment. Although it is true that much research in the behavioral sciences uses many participants whom the researcher randomly assigns to various treatment groups, it is also true that behavioral scientists conduct many fine and valid experiments using single or very small groups of participants. Similarly, many researchers conduct revealing studies for which random assignment is impossible or unethical. These alternatives to the typical true experiment offer the researchers valuable tools that allow them to address interesting, albeit complex, questions about human behavior. In this chapter we will review three important research paradigms: (1) single-participant experiments, (2) longitudinal designs, and (3) quasi-experiments.

These methods for conducting research are extremely useful tools that all behavioral researchers can use depending on their specific research questions. Used correctly, these research techniques allow one to examine the relation among variables. Furthermore, these techniques adhere to the same rigorous standards of objectivity and validity as the other research designs we have reviewed in this book. Thus, each of these paradigms offers researchers analytical tools to help them understand various behavioral phenomena.

## Single-Participant Experiments

The features that set these methods apart from other research designs are the methods used to collect and analyze the data. For instance, the single-participant experimental paradigm, as the name implies, is a collection of research techniques used to conduct controlled experiments that focus on the behavior of individuals. Whereas much behavioral research examines the average behavior of groups of participants, the single-participant research examines how the individual responds to the experimental conditions.

## Longitudinal Designs

The longitudinal design also allows us to examine from a different perspective because it allows us to track the behavior of a group of individuals across time. Longitudinal designs are a special case of the repeated-measures procedure as the researcher tracks changes in the participants' behavior. There is an important difference between longitudinal designs and repeated-measures research. In most cases, longitudinal designs use a timeframe that covers months and even years. By contrast, most repeated-measures research examines behavior over a much shorter period. So, the difference between the repeated-measures and longitudinal design is the emphasis and timeframe of the research.

In the repeated-measures design, we typically want to know how individuals perform under a series of experimental conditions that we control. We may test the same participants using several different dosages of a drug to determine its effect on a behavior. In another experiment, we may expose one group of participants to different sequences of events to find how the pattern of events affects behavior. We may also be interested in observing an individual's behavior over time.

Indeed, for a longitudinal study, the researcher is more interested in the development or emergence of behavior that occurs over time. Consider language development as an example. Developmental psychologists who study language examine the profound changes in children's use of language that emerges during early childhood. This research has allowed psychologists to chronicle how language emerges and becomes more complex as the child matures. Clinical psychologists also conduct longitudinal research to examine the long-term effects of various treatments. As an example, clinical psychologists studying alcohol and drug abuse therapies may want to follow the health of the patients over several years to understand the risk of relapses.

### Quasi-Experiments

The quasi-experiment paradigm is unique because it does not use random assignment in the same way that it is used in true experiments. Quasi-experimental methods have evolved as a way to examine behavior under conditions where meeting the requirements of a true experiment is impossible or impractical. The name *quasi-experiment* represents that the researcher may have partial control over the independent variable. For most quasi-experimental research, the researcher cannot randomly assign participants to the research conditions. However, quasi-experimental designs can yield interesting insights into human behavior.

$$*  *  *$$

There is no such thing as the best method for studying any behavioral phenomenon. As you learn more about research, you will discover that scientists use many research techniques to study the same behavioral phenomenon. Their selection of technique represents their training and perspective as well as their belief concerning the best way to conduct a specific research project. With this brief introduction, we can turn our attention to more detail about these paradigms.

## Single-Participant Experiments

As the name implies, single-participant experiments (often known as *case studies*) examine how individuals respond to changes in the independent variable. Another term you will often find used interchangeably with *single-participant research* is *small n research* (i.e., research that includes only a small number of participants). While we will use the term *single-participant* research most often during this discussion, keep in mind that the information and techniques we will discuss in this chapter are equally applicable to studies utilizing only one participant or a small group of participants.

There are many examples of famous researchers who used single-participant experiments. As an example, consider Gustav T. Fechner, whom we introduced in Chapter 1. Fechner discovered that he could study the workings of the mind by examining changes in behavior. As an important part of his work, Fechner developed a host of research methods that he described in his book *Elements of Psychophysics* (1966/1860). The research that Fechner conducted typically examined how an individual's perception of specific stimuli (lights, sounds, weights) changed in conjunction with changes in the stimulus. Not only did his work help to establish the science of psychology, modern researchers continue to use his techniques when studying topics related to sensation and perception.

Sometime between 1875 and 1878, Hermann Ebbinghaus read Fechner's book and recognized that he could adapt Fechner's research techniques to study memory (Boring, 1957). Ebbinghaus' seminal book, *On Memory* (1913/1885), included many experiments for which he was the sole participant. The results of these studies remain the standard introduction to the analysis of memory and forgetting phenomena. Similarly, Ivan Pavlov conducted many insightful experiments in classical conditioning using single-participant experiments. Those who read his original research will find that he used two or three dogs for experiments to examine specific conditioning phenomena. Edward Thorndike and B. F. Skinner also adopted the single-participant experimental procedure for their own work on operant conditioning. Indeed, Skinner, and the many behaviorists who followed his lead, developed a comprehensive collection of research techniques that they called the **experimental analysis of behavior**. The experimental analysis of behavior is a perspective of research that focuses on the pattern of behavior produced in individuals by systematic changes in the independent variable. As Skinner (1953) described it, the goal of experimental analysis of behavior is to "predict and control the behavior of an individual organism" (p. 35).

Although researchers originally used the single-participant experiment to examine basic research topics such as perception, memory, and classical and operant conditioning, researchers now use these techniques for a host of applied and basic research projects. Specifically, researchers use the single-participant experiments when they want to determine how systematic changes in the environment influence an individual's behavior. As Dermer and Hoch (1999) observed, the single-participant experiment is an invaluable tool for research in such diverse areas as audiological rehabilitation, clinical and counseling psychology, and education. A trip to the library will reveal that there are many journals dedicated to single-participant research. The journals *Behavioral Assessment, Journal of Applied Behavior Analysis, Journal of the Experimental Analysis of Behavior,* and *The Behavior Analyst* are only a few of the scholarly outlets for single-participant experiments.

Unfortunately, many researchers appear to ignore these important research techniques. Ellis (1999) speculated that single-participant designs are unfairly characterized as "too behavioral, overly simplistic or circumscribed, . . . and too difficult to do" (p. 566). Koehler and Levin (1998) echoed this sentiment in an article wherein they examined the utility of single-participant research designs.

### Reprise of Internal and External Validity

You may be suspicious of single-participant designs because of concerns for the internal and external validity of a study that is based on one, two, or four participants. This is a legitimate concern and one that requires our analysis.

**Figure 15.1**

**Hermann Grid**

As you look at the illustration, you will see faint gray squares at the intersections of the white lines. The gray images are illusions that people with normal vision see.

We can have confidence, however, in the internal and external validity of single-participant experiments as long as we remember that validity is more a function of how we collect and interpret the data than it is due to the number of participants in the study. The sample size does not determine the internal or external validity of the experiment or the data.

Consider Figure 15.1 as an example. The picture contains a series of black squares neatly arranged in rows and columns set on a white background, nothing more. Although the picture is a black-and-white image, you will perceive faint gray images at the intersections of the white rows and columns. Furthermore, if you stare at the intersection of two white lines, the gray images disappear, but you will see the gray images at the intersections in the periphery of your vision. The gray dots are an illusion in that you perceive something that does not exist. Psychologists call this figure the Hermann Grid in honor of Ludimar Hermann, the German physiologist who wrote extensively about the fascinating illusion it creates.

What does this illusion have to do with single-participant experiments? The answer is simple: everything. Reread the previous paragraph. We used unambiguous language to describe what you would experience. We did not use qualified statements such as "you are likely to see" or "chances are that you will see." Instead, our language was simple and declarative. The fact is that people with normal vision see this illusion. Experiment by showing the picture to the next 10 people you meet. Everyone will have the same experience: They will see the phantom gray dots. How many people do you have to test to conclude that the Hermann Grid produces the illusion of the phantom spots? You could expand your sample to 100 people, but the results will be consistent. Everyone will experience the illusion.

Because of all this, you do not need to show the grid to many people to be convinced that the effect is strong. From a statistical perspective, therefore, the Hermann Grid produces a powerful effect. Researchers who study the Hermann Grid and similar sensation-perception phenomena typically use only two or three participants to conduct their research.

When we speak of external validity, we are concerned about two types of generalization. First, we want to ensure that the participants used in the research represent the broader population we wish to describe. Second, we want to ensure that the phenomenon we observe will occur with samples drawn from different populations. Sample size is not the critical factor in determining external validity. Rather, the critical factor is the types of generalizations we make of the data.

When there is little variability among people, as is the case for the perception of the Hermann Grid illusion, we do not require many participants to represent the population. By contrast, when the differences among individuals in the population are large, then the sample must also be large to represent the population. Remember that the value of any research finding is the ability to replicate the finding with additional research. Our confidence in a finding increases with the ability of other researchers to replicate a particular finding, not the number of participants used in the research.

What about internal validity for the single-participant experiment? Again, the issue of internal validity does not concern itself with the number of participants. Instead, when we speak of internal validity we mean to show that one has convincing evidence that changes in the independent variable caused changes in the dependent variable. In this regard, the single-participant experiment can support conclusions of cause and effect as well as any true experiment that we have studied in this book. We can use the Hermann Grid as an example.

What are the variables that influence the illusion? You can reproduce the grid using different brightness (shades of gray) for the squares and lines. Similarly, you can use different hues (colors) for the squares and lines. You can also vary the size of the squares and the width and height of the lines separating the squares. You can even change the shape of the squares by using different geometrical shapes (e.g., triangles, squares, pentagons, circles). If you were to vary these conditions systematically, you could determine how changes in these variables influence the strength of the illusion. Specifically, you can ask the same person to look at many different versions of the Hermann Grid to examine how the distance between the squares influences the perception of the illusory gray images.

## When to Use Single-Participant Procedures

Those who routinely use single-participant procedures believe that single-participant designs are most useful when the researcher wishes to understand the changes in behavior of the individual that correspond to changes in the individual's environment (Morgan & Morgan, 2001). This definition surely covers many research situations. Some might argue that almost all psychological research should use single-participant research designs because the primary focus of psychology is the study of the behavior of the individual. Such a perspective ignores many important questions related to human behavior that may not be answered using only single-participant designs. Thus it might be helpful to examine some of the general circumstances for which a single-participant design is well suited and circumstances for which a single-participant design might not be appropriate.

The primary goal of the single-participant design is to determine how specific changes in the environment of the individual affect that participant's behavior. Consequently, single participant designs are most frequently used when a researcher wants to examine how the introduction and removal of a specific condition affects the behavior of an individual. For example, a clinical psychologist might want to determine whether exposing a person to a therapy will reduce undesirable behaviors and increase desirable behaviors. In such an example, the researcher wants to show that the therapy causes the person's behavior to change, hopefully for the better. In one of the following examples, we will review how a team of researchers used a single-participant research design to study the effectiveness of a method of treating panic attacks.

There are three design features that enhance the likelihood of a researcher conducting a successful single-participant design. First, the researcher needs to have direct control over the independent variable. Thus, the single-participant design is like a true experiment in that the researcher can control significant elements of the participant's environment and determine when to add and remove the independent variable. Second, the researcher must be able to regularly measure or observe the participant's behavior. Monitoring the participant's behavior allows the researcher to determine how changes in the independent variable correspond to changes in the dependent behavior. Third, the researcher must be able to observe the participant across a significant span of time. For many single-participant studies, the researcher will examine the participant's behavior across many days, even weeks and months.

These conditions are not always attainable, however, so there are conditions where the single-subject design is not appropriate. Most of these cases involve situations in which researchers are interested in defining a population or examining the differences between populations. For example, a researcher may be interested in the emotional development of children who attended preschool versus children who did not. For this type of research, we want to know whether there are systematic differences among the populations representing the two groups of children. In addition, the predictor variable (preschool vs. no preschool) is a variable that the researcher does not control.

## Types of Single-Participant Experiments

There are two broad categories of single-participant experiments: **baseline studies** and **discrete trial studies**. As a generality, researchers use baseline studies to examine changes in an ongoing or continuous behavior. For example, a researcher may want to examine how a specific treatment technique changes the social skills of an autistic child. The researcher would perform a baseline study to track changes in the child's behavior before, during, and after the treatment. This research would allow the researcher to determine whether the treatment influences the child's social skills.

By contrast, a discrete trial study allows us to examine how a participant reacts to specific test conditions. Consider an experiment studying the Hermann Grid. We could construct many versions of the Hermann Grid by varying the distance between the squares. On each trial, we present one of the grids and determine whether the participant perceives the illusory gray squares. This research will allow us to determine the conditions that produce the illusion.

Baseline studies examine changes in the frequency of the ongoing behaviors of an individual. Consequently, all baseline studies begin by developing operational definitions of the behaviors to be measured. We want to develop a reliable method for observing the behavior or behaviors that we want to modify. Once we decide on the appropriate behavior to observe and the data recording strategy, we can begin by establishing a baseline.

The general format of a baseline design is first to establish a baseline of the individual's behavior and then introduce the change or intervention into the individual's environment. If the intervention is effective, there should be a commensurate and consistent change in the individual's behavior. You may recognize that the single-participant design has much in common with the repeated-measures design discussed in Chapter 13. Specifically, we expose the same participant to different treatment conditions to examine how the independent variable influences the dependent variable. The baseline is, therefore, the control condition for the experiment as it represents the participant's behavior in the absence of the treatment condition.

## Establishing Cause and Effect

The rules for determining cause and effect are straightforward: Use a control condition, demonstrate that there is a relationship between the independent and dependent variables, and rule out alternative explanations. There are a number of specific techniques that we can use to achieve these goals for the single-participant experiment.

### Establish a Baseline

The first step is to establish a baseline that we can use for a frame of reference. The goal of this step is to determine the typical pattern of the behavior that we want to modify. The baseline should be a representative sample of the individual's normal behavior. For example, if we wanted to examine the effectiveness of a social skills training technique for children diagnosed with autism, we would want to examine how often the child engages in specific types of social interactions with other children. Similarly, if we wanted to examine how a tutoring program helps students master math skills, we would need to determine the child's ability to solve specific classes of math problems.

In some cases, the baseline represents a small sample of the individual's behavior. A child with autism may spend little time playing with other children. Alternatively, a child having trouble with math may be able to solve only the most simple of math problems. Because the behavior is extremely consistent, the baseline may be short. For the autistic child, we may observe his or her behavior for three or four sessions to establish the baseline. Similarly, for the student having problems with math, the baseline may consist of the scores on several short math quizzes.

If the target behavior is variable, then the baseline will need to be longer to establish a suitable pattern of the behavior. Sometimes behaviors are cyclical; the behavior increases and decreases. For such cases, the baseline will need to be longer to establish the normal pattern for the behavior. Having the longer baseline will help the researcher determine the extent to which changes in the behavior reflect the independent variable or the cyclical nature of the behavior. The baseline should contain at least three observations (Barlow & Hersen, 1984). There is no hard-and-fast rule to establish the length of the baseline, as highlighted by Sidman (1960), who advised his readers that the "... rule to follow for the criterion will depend upon the phenomenon being investigated and upon the level of experimental control that can be maintained" (p. 258). Therefore, the researcher needs to exercise common sense to determine whether the baseline is a fair and stable representation of the individual's behavior.

### Examine the Effects of the Intervention

There are a number of general techniques used in an experiment to study the effects of the intervention. The prototypes for these techniques are the **ABA** and the **ABAB** designs. Researchers call these designs **reversal designs** because the researchers use several phases in the research during which they repeatedly add and remove a treatment condition. As a generality, the "A" phase represents the baseline or no-treatment condition and the "B" represents the intervention or treatment-present condition. The goal of the reversal design is to demonstrate that as the research conditions change (A to B and B to A), there is a corresponding shift in the individual's behavior.

Figure 15.2 illustrates the results of a hypothetical ABAB design. The behavior being monitored is the amount of time a second-grade student is "on task" during a classroom assignment. During the baseline condition, the child spends relatively little time on task. At the start of the treatment condition, there is a marked increase in the on-task behavior. When the researcher removes the intervention, the on-task behavior also decreases. Finally, when the researcher reestablishes the treatment condition, the on-task behavior increases. Data such as these would lead the researcher to conclude that the treatment effectively modifies the student's behavior.

### Direct Replication

A single-participant experiment does not mean that there is only one participant in the study, merely that the researcher does not aggregate

# Figure 15.2

**Hypothetical Example of Data Produced by an ABAB Research Design**

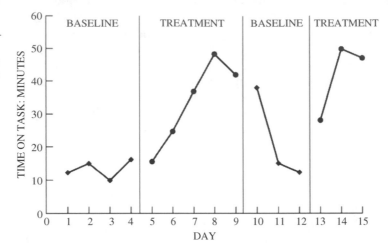

the behavior of many participants into a single index such as the arithmetic mean. Instead, the hallmark of the single-participant research design is that the researcher reports the behavior of each individual in the study. **Direct replication** means the researcher will use the same treatment procedures to examine the pattern of behavior for each of several single participants. If the treatment is effective, then there should be similar patterns of behavior change for each participant who is exposed to the treatment. Therefore, the single-participant experiment is like other true experiments in that the researcher examines the data of several individuals under highly controlled conditions. The difference, however, is that in most experiments, the researcher examines and reports the *average* performance of the participants. In contrast, the researcher using a single-participant design will report the individual behavior of each participant.

One of the benefits of the single-participant design is that researchers can use it to demonstrate the relationship between independent and dependent variables with both inter- and intra-participant replication to demonstrate the relationship between the independent and dependent variables. The intra-participant replication occurs when one uses ABAB or other reversal designs. By adding and removing the independent variable, we can establish the link between changes in the independent variable and changes in the dependent variable. As you saw in Figure 15.2, changes in the treatment condition corresponded with changes in the behavior of the student, thus replicating the effect intra-participant. If we use the same procedure on several participants, we will generate inter-participant replication. The inter-participant replication is, therefore, another way of describing direct replication.

### Potential Problems with Reversal Designs
In Chapter 13 you learned about the threats to internal validity created when using a repeated-measures design. Specifically, we must be concerned with the threats created by a carryover effect. For example, it is possible to

remove the intervention and not observe a corresponding change in the underlying behavior. For example, once a child learns to solve math problems, removal of the intervention does not cause the child to forget all that he or she learned. The child will probably continue to do well because of the good grades and other forms of positive reinforcement received for doing well on math tests. In these cases, we can use a reversal design, but the carryover effect will produce an unavoidable confounding variable.

We must also consider the ethics of removing an intervention once we show that it is effective. Why would we want to remove something that we now believe improves the individual's quality of life? In most clinical research, once the researcher finds that the treatment is effective, the researcher will begin to administer the treatment to all the participants receiving the placebo or in the baseline phase of the study. The following is a brief review of several research techniques that overcome the problems created in a reversal design.

## Multiple-Baseline Design

A suitable alternative to the reversal design is the **multiple-baseline design**. The advantage of this procedure is that it allows us to demonstrate the effectiveness of an intervention when the reversal design is not appropriate. In addition, the procedure allows us to examine the effectiveness of an intervention across behaviors, individuals, or settings.

The primary characteristic of the multiple-baseline design is that we monitor the ongoing behavior of the participants and then systematically introduce the independent variable at different times. One of the more popular of these procedures is the *multiple baseline across participants*. To use this procedure, we begin by monitoring the behavior of all the individuals in the study. Once we establish the baseline, we introduce the treatment for one of the participants while the others remain in the baseline condition. After some time has elapsed, we introduce the treatment to the second participant while keeping the remaining participants in the baseline condition. The goal of this procedure is to introduce the independent variable to each participant on a staggered basis to demonstrate that the participant's behavior changes only after the researcher introduces the independent variable.

Figure 15.3 illustrates the application of the multiple-baseline-across-participants procedure. There are three participants. For each participant, we begin to track the behavior that we want to modify. Participant 1 is the first to experience the independent variable while the other participants remain in the baseline condition. Later, we introduce the independent variable into the environment of Participant 2. Finally, we add the independent variable to the environment of Participant 3. Using this procedure, we can be sure that the introduction of the independent variable, and not some confounding variable, caused the change in the participant's behavior.

# Figure 15.3

**Multiple-Baseline-
across-Participants
Procedure**

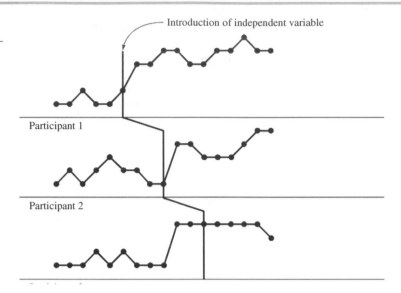

Introduction of independent variable

Participant 1

Participant 2

We can also apply the multiple-baseline procedure across situations and across behaviors. For the *multiple-baseline-across-behaviors* procedure, the researcher may identify several behaviors that he or she wants to modify with the same intervention. To use this technique, the researcher needs to ensure that the behaviors are independent of each other.

As an example, a researcher examining the effectiveness of an intervention with children diagnosed with autism may examine how the intervention works with three behaviors: (1) talking to other children, (2) participating in group activities, and (3) following instructions of the teacher. As with the multiple-baseline-across-individuals procedure, the researcher would collect baseline information for all three behaviors and then stagger the start of the intervention for each behavior. In theory, the intervention should influence the target behavior, but not the other behaviors. The specific behavior will not change until the intervention begins.

The *multiple-baseline-across-situations* procedure works in the same manner except that we identify different situations where the intervention can be applied. Assume that a teacher wants to study the effectiveness of a tutoring technique for a child's academic performance. The teacher can treat the academic subjects (e.g., math, social studies, English, and science) as separate situations. By staggering the start of the tutoring intervention for each subject, the teacher can demonstrate that the tutoring improves the child's academic work when the tutoring begins for the topic.

## Research in Action: Treatment for Panic Disorder

Because we will review three research paradigms, three "Research in Action" sections, one to illustrate the application of each paradigm, will

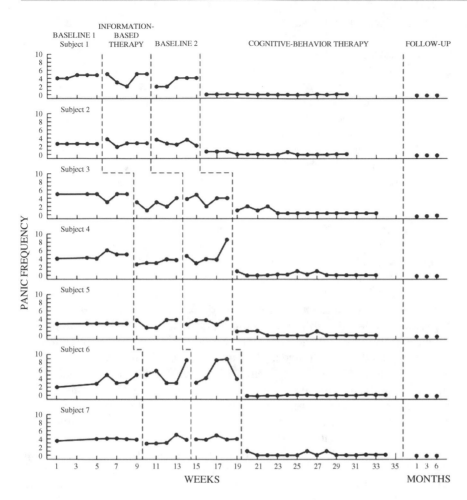

## Figure 15.4

**Multiple-Baseline-across-Participants Design**

The dependent variable is the frequency of panic attacks experienced by seven participants over a 35-week period. The vertical dashed lines represent the start of each phase of the experiment for the individual participants. During the first three phases of the experiment, the participants' panic attacks were assessed during three baseline phases. The fourth phase of the experiment included the cognitive-behavior modification treatment. The last three points represent a long-term follow-up of the patients. Data from Laberge, Gauthier, Côté, Plamondon, and Cormier (1993).

be presented in this chapter. In this section, we will examine an application of the single-participant design.

Figure 15.4 presents an example of a single-participant experiment conducted by Laberge, Gauthier, Côté, Plamondon, and Cormier (1993). The researchers wanted to demonstrate the effectiveness of cognitive-behavioral therapy for the treatment of panic disorder. The researchers examined the frequency of panic attacks of seven individuals using a multiple-baseline procedure.

This experiment also contained a slight methodological twist that helps demonstrate the effectiveness of cognitive-behavior therapy. During the first phase, the researchers monitored the frequency of panic attacks to establish a baseline. Then the researchers started a session called "information-based therapy." During this intervention the participants received detailed information about panic attacks and learned how their thinking leads to panic attacks. Laberge et al. (1993) treated this phase of the experiment as a placebo treatment as they believed that it did not include the critical components of a legitimate treatment. Following the information-based therapy phase was another baseline period during which the researchers continued to monitor the frequency of the panic attacks. The first and second baseline conditions allowed the researchers to estimate the frequency of panic attacks while the person was under observation. The second control condition was the information-based therapy session. This condition allowed the researchers to determine whether the placebo treatment had any effect on the frequency of panic attacks.

The critical part of the experiment began when Laberge et al. (1993) began to use the cognitive-behavior therapy to treat the participants for the panic attacks. The researchers staggered the start of each phase of the experiment after the initial baseline period across the individuals. By staggering the onset of the different intervention periods, the researchers demonstrated that the change in the panic attack coincided with the start of the legitimate treatment intervention, not other conditions that could have changed in the environments of the individuals. In this example, the researchers used direct replication within the multiple-baseline-across-participants procedure to demonstrate that the intervention brings about a change in the individual's behavior. The researchers also demonstrated the effectiveness of the cognitive-behavior by including the placebo treatment. There were no discernible changes in the frequency of the panic attacks during the first three phases (Baseline 1, information-based therapy, and Baseline 2) of the experiment. The panic attacks stopped, however, when the participants received the cognitive-behavior therapy. Looking at the graph it appears that the effectiveness of the intervention lasted well into the follow-up period.

One thing you may note about single-participant designs is the lack of formal statistical analysis. Many of the early pioneers of single-participant research designs believed that inferential statistical analysis was not appropriate for the analysis of individual participants and believed that the effect of the independent should be clear and unambiguous to visual inspection of the data (Morgan & Morgan, 2001). Therefore, most single-participant designs use simple graphs and basic descriptive statistics to present the data.

## Knowledge Check

1. Explain why a reversal design, such as the ABAB design, produces results that support conclusions regarding cause and effect.

2. Imagine that two researchers examined the effectiveness of a new treatment intervention for depression. One researcher used a multiple-baseline-across-participants research design to examine the effect of the treatment on 12 participants. The other researcher randomly assigned 25 participants to a placebo treatment group and another 25 participants to the treatment condition, and then compared the average level of depression between the two groups. Assume that the researchers work at the same institution and sampled from the same subject pool.

   a. Explain why the two studies are comparable with regard to internal validity.

   b. Explain why the two studies are comparable with regard to external validity.

3. Using the previous example, what are the ethical considerations that would make one research design preferable to the other research design?

4. Imagine that your professor wants to demonstrate the effectiveness of homework for helping students learn research methods. How could he or she use the multiple-baseline-across-participants or across-situations procedures to conduct the research?

## Longitudinal Designs

The primary goal of **longitudinal designs** is to examine how behavior, attitudes, or other outcomes change over time. Developmental psychologists have long used these techniques to examine the systematic changes in children's behavior. Longitudinal designs are also popular in other areas of research, such as clinical psychology where the researchers wish to study the development of different behavioral and emotional disorders or the risk of relapse after treatment.

The fundamental feature of a longitudinal design is relatively straightforward. The researcher identifies a sample of participants and then arranges to monitor their behavior, for example, over a predetermined period of time. For example, a developmental psychologist may be interested in the emotional development of children whose parents use day-care or preschool programs and children who spend most of their preschool years at home with an adult. As another example, a clinical psychologist may study the long-term effectiveness of substance-abuse treatment programs. In each case, the researcher would identify the appropriate sample of participants to study and then measure the appropriate dependent variables several times afterward. The developmental psychologist would examine the children's emotional development as they begin and progress through kindergarten and the first elementary grades. The clinical psychologist would routinely evaluate the clients for evidence of a relapse or other problems. The decision of what timeframe to use for a longitudinal study should be taken with care and take into account logistical constraints as well as the research question that you are trying to answer.

During the past two decades, psychologists have become extremely interested in longitudinal research methods due to the development and application of new statistical methods to analyze the data from these types of studies. As you will soon learn, these new statistical tests make the longitudinal research design an extremely useful research tool. Before we describe these new statistics, we should first examine the foundations of the longitudinal design.

The conventional longitudinal design requires that the researcher track one or more groups of individuals over a specified time. The groups can represent an important subject variable (e.g., sex, intelligence, parent's marital status, or other categorical condition) or a treatment condition randomly assigned by the researcher. The researcher then arranges to periodically evaluate the members of the sample.

Although the conventional longitudinal design is popular and produces useful information, it does suffer from some shortcomings. First, the data may take a long time to obtain. Often this is an unavoidable problem. Tracking the progress of a group of patients who have just completed a program of treatment may require a significant follow-up period to evaluate the long-term effectiveness of the treatment.

Another problem related to the length of this type of study is the problem of participant dropout or attrition. Over time, it is common for individuals to leave the sample when they stop participating. These people may become bored with the study, move to another city or state, or otherwise become incapable of participating in the study. This problem of attrition can play havoc with many standard statistical tests such as the ANOVA. Fortunately, alternative statistical tools can overcome the problems created by participant dropout.

There are other problems related to the longitudinal research that are more difficult to resolve. One of these problems is the **cohort effect**. The cohort effect refers to differences among groups of people that share a common characteristic. For example, a cohort may be a group of people born at the same time and who had a common experience. A cohort effect occurs when members of one group are consistently different from people in a different group who have had different experiences. Some cohort effects are the source of the *generation gap*. For example, some of our older relatives, who grew up during the big-band era, despise the rock-and-roll music that we listened to as adolescents.

There are more serious examples of a cohort effect. For example, some evidence, dubbed the "Flynn effect," indicates considerable increases in intelligence scores during the past century. According to Flynn (1998), intelligence test scores have increased 3 points, on average, each decade over the past 70 years. Children born after 2000 will have an average IQ 21 points greater than their great-great grandparents born in the 1930s. As another example, Lewinsohn, Rohde, Seeley, and Fischer (1993) reported a large cohort effect for the prevalence of depression and other psychological disorders. Lewinsohn et al. found higher rates of depression among people born in more recent decades than in the past.

The presence of a cohort effect forces us to examine the external validity of conclusions based on one cohort and generalized to others. For example, would conclusions about racial stereotypes based on research conducted during the 1920s generalize to contemporary populations?

### Cross-Sectional Sequential Designs

Many developmental psychologists study the transitions that children make as they pass through various critical phases of their lives. As an example, a psychologist may want to examine changes in the personality of children as they pass through adolescence (e.g., 8 through 15). Using a conventional longitudinal design would require eight years to collect the data for the study, a considerable test of one's patience and persistence. The **cross-sectional sequential design** is an alternative method that allows the researcher to examine developmental transitions, but over a shorter period of time.

Figure 15.5 presents the logic of the cross-sectional sequential design. The researcher can select cross-sections of the age span that he or she wants

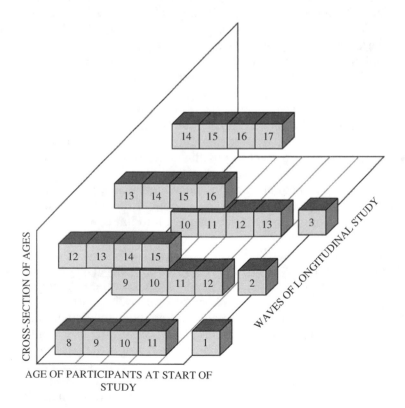

## Figure 15.5

**Cross-Sectional
Sequential Design**

CROSS-SECTION OF AGES

WAVES OF LONGITUDINAL STUDY

AGE OF PARTICIPANTS AT START OF
STUDY

to study. Starting in Year 1, for example, the researcher could select participants age 8 through 15. Over the course of the next three years, the researcher can continue to monitor the changes in these participants. By the end of the third year, the researcher will have data that indicate the differences in a wide range of ages and how those changes relate to the passage of time. The cross-sectional sequential design provides the researcher with much information.

First, the researcher can use the data to compare the differences among blocks of ages. For example, the researcher who uses the design illustrated in Figure 15.5 will have three blocks of children aged 10 through 12 and three blocks of children aged 13 through 15. Analyzing these data will indicate whether there are systematic differences between these age groups. Second, the cross-sectional sequential design allows the researcher to examine the changes observed in the children as they grow older.

### Survival Analysis

For many years, researchers used the repeated-measures ANOVA to analyze the data of longitudinal data. Although this tactic yields useful information, it does have its limitations. First, the correlated-groups ANOVA has specific mathematical requirements, or assumptions, of the data that are often difficult to achieve. Failure to meet these requirements can produce invalid $F$-ratios. Second, the longitudinal design is subject to high levels of participant attrition. Losing large numbers of participants from a longitudinal research project can wreak havoc on the data analysis, especially with ANOVA techniques. Fortunately, statisticians have developed a class of statistical tests that provide researchers an alternative method for analyzing the data generated by longitudinal designs (Greenhouse, Stangl, & Bromberg, 1989; Gruber, 1999; Lewinsohn et al., 1993; Luke & Homan, 1998; Singer & Willett, 1991; Willett & Singer, 1993). These statistical tests overcome the problems created by participants dropping out of the research and the failure of the data to meet the mathematical requirements of the ANOVA.

Survival analysis is a common and popular statistical tool in medical research where the goal is to determine the amount of time it takes for an event to occur. For example, a physician may want to know which of two surgical procedures is the best for the long-term health of patients, such as preventing a second heart attack. To collect the data, the researcher will track the patients after the surgery to determine which surgical technique is more effective at preventing a second heart attack or other significant problems. One characteristic that makes survival analysis unique is that it treats time as a dependent variable rather than an independent variable.

In the conventional longitudinal analysis, we treat time as an independent variable. We then determine whether we can use the passage of time to explain or predict some outcome. A developmental psychologist studying language development might use a child's age to predict when the child will begin to use two words to form simple sentences or when the child will begin to correctly use irregular verbs (e.g., *went* vs. *goed*). By contrast, in survival analysis, we treat the *time* between several events as the dependent variable. Perhaps an example will help illustrate how we can use survival analysis and the longitudinal design.

Stice, Killen, Hayward, and Taylor (1998) examined the onset of the binge-and-purge eating disorder in adolescent girls. The researchers began by creating a sample of 543 young women aged 13 to 17 and then used a comprehensive set of surveys and structured interviews to assess the participants' health and whether they engaged in binge eating and purging. Stice et al. then reassessed the young women each year for the next four years. As the researchers noted, the average annual attrition rate was 15%.

Using the survival analysis procedures, Stice et al. found that the risk of the onset for an eating disorder begins after 14, peaks at approximately 16, and then decreases. Other researchers have used the same techniques to examine the difference between men and women for onset of depressive disorders and also for the risk of relapse among cocaine abusers following treatment (Willett & Singer, 1993). In all these examples, the critical questions are: "How much time typically elapses between two critical events (e.g., treatment and relapse)?" and "If an event has not occurred after a specific interval, what is the probability that it will occur?"

The statistical analysis rules that underlie this approach are beyond the scope of this book and require intensive computational procedures best done by a computer. Fortunately, most professional statistical packages used by psychologists (e.g., BMDP®, SAS®, SPSS®, etc.) include survival analysis routines. The primary message that we want you to appreciate is that these statistical tests are well suited for longitudinal data you might collect within the social sciences. They correct for dwindling sample size without compromising the validity of the interpretations of the results.

## Research in Action: Onset of Bulimia

For this example of research in action, we can return to the study of the risk of bulimia among young women conducted by Stice et al. (1998). The researchers began with a sample of 543 students from three high schools in California. The average age of the women was 14.9 years and ranged from 13 to 17. At the start of the study, none of the participants showed signs of bulimia.

The researchers then reassessed the participants once a year for the subsequent three years. The assessments consisted of a structured interview conducted by trained researchers who looked for symptoms of eating disorders, especially bulimia. As with most research of this type, some of the participants did not complete the study. Approximately 10% of the original sample moved to another school, and others were absent during the assessment period or chose not to complete the remaining interviews.

Stice et al. (1998) then examined the risk of the women developing bulimia between the ages of 13 (the youngest age of the participants) through 19 (the oldest age by the end of the three years of the study). For most statistical tests, the researchers would have to throw out all the data of the participants who did not complete the study because many statistical tests such as the correlation coefficient, regression analysis, and the ANOVA require a complete record of observations for each participant. Survival analysis does not make this requirement, however, as the statistic uses the available data for each wave of measurement to determine the proportion of participants who show evidence of the syndrome.

Even though some women dropped out of the study, we can use their data to make inferences about the presence of bulimia. Consider, for example, a participant who is 16 at the start of the study and who is available for the first and second measurement sessions, but drops out before the third session. Although she dropped out of the study, she still provided the researchers with five years of data. Recall that at the start of the study, none of the participants showed evidence of bulimia. Therefore, we can assume that the young woman was symptom free when she was 13, 14, 15, and 16.

Using this information, Stice et al. (1998) were able to determine the age when the greatest proportion of women began the binge-and-purge eating pattern associated with bulimia. Because the survival analysis uses *proportions* (proportion = number of people with condition/total in current sample), the statistic is not affected by loss of participants from the sample. Figure 15.6 presents an example of the data reported by Stice et al.

As Stice et al. (1998) noted, their project was the first to examine the onset of bulimia in a population of young women. Having these data allow researchers to understand the forces associated with the onset of bulimia. Perhaps more importantly, the data can help counselors and others working with adolescents to find the optimal time to introduce prevention programs and look for risk factors that predict the onset of bulimia and other eating disorders.

## Figure 15.6

**Risk of Onset of Binge Eating**

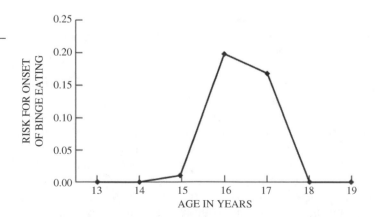

# Quasi-Experiments

In some circumstances, a true experiment is either impractical or unethical. We may not be able to randomly assign participants to different treatment conditions although we can randomly select one group of participants to receive a treatment while the other group acts as a control group. For example, a teacher may not be able to randomly assign students to different classes. However, he or she can randomly select one group to experience a new teaching method while the other class experiences a conventional course. In other cases, it is unethical to subject people to some treatment condition or fail to provide them with treatment. But fateful events occur naturally that allow us to determine how people react to specific conditions. In this section of the chapter, we will introduce you to two of the more common quasi-experimental techniques, the nonequivalent control-group design and the interrupted time series.

The term *quasi-experiment* literally means that the research resembles an experiment. In a quasi-experiment there is an independent variable and a dependent variable, and the researcher wants to determine whether introduction of the independent variable produces a change in the dependent variable. In addition, there is a control group of individuals who do not experience the independent variable. Consequently, the researcher can compare the differences in outcome between the treatment and control groups. The missing component from this research is the random assignment of participants to the treatment conditions.

The primary disadvantage of the quasi-experiment is that the lack of random assignment means that we can never fully rule out alternative explanations for the effect we observe. The primary advantage of the quasi-experiment is that we can collect useful information that will allow us to examine the effects of the independent variable on the dependent variable. The quasi-experiment is another useful tool that the researcher can select when the circumstances of the research prohibit the conventional true experiment.

## Nonequivalent Control-Group Design

The nonequivalent control-group design is a common example of the quasi-experimental design. The researcher begins with two groups created by situations beyond his or her control. For example, the researcher may study students assigned to classrooms or who attend different schools. Because the researcher cannot randomly assign the participants to the two groups, we must consider them nonequivalent. If the researcher randomly assigned the participants to the groups, then we would conclude that the groups were equivalent before the start of the experiment, and any difference between the groups would represent sampling error. In a quasi-experiment we must consider the groups to be nonequivalent because we cannot be sure whether factors unrelated to the study create systematic differences between the participants.

Although the researcher cannot randomly assign the participants to the treatment conditions, he or she can randomly determine which group will receive the treatment. The main feature of the design includes two observations for both groups. The researcher will assess both groups at the same time, introduce the intervention for the experimental group, and then observe the relevant dependent variable a second time.

Although the nonequivalent control-group design is a popular design that controls for some threats to internal validity (Campbell & Stanley, 1966), there are other threats to internal validity that it cannot directly withstand (West, Biesanz, & Pitts, 2000). The design is subject to threats due to history, regression to the mean, and instrumentation. We will review these threats in the following paragraphs.

### History

It is possible that one of the groups will experience an event or change in the environment, unrelated to the purpose of the study, which confounds the analysis and interpretation of the data. For example, a researcher may wish to study the effects of a binge-drinking campaign for college students. After finding two colleges equivalent in size and student body, the researcher randomly selects one of the colleges as the experimental group and the other as a control group. During the course of the study, the researcher cannot control for outside factors that may change one of the campuses. A student at one of the colleges may die due to binge drinking. This tragic and uncontrolled event may affect the students' attitudes toward binge drinking. The event also confounds the results as we do not know whether changes in student attitude represent the treatment program or the student's death.

### Regression to the Mean

Regression to the mean may be a confounding factor if the researcher selected the experimental and control groups using a test or measure that had low reliability. Consider again the researcher studying drinking behavior at colleges. It is possible that the time during the semester the researcher collects the data will confound the results. For example, collecting the data just before or just after midterms may cause the researcher to underestimate or overestimate the amount of drinking at the college. Any changes observed may merely reflect regression to the mean.

### Instrumentation

Another threat to the internal validity of a nonequivalent control-group design is instrumentation. During the course of the study it is possible that there will be a change in the methods or measures used to collect data from one group, but not the other. Consider the binge-drinking study. The researcher may require that the student-life staff keep track of the number of episodes or problems related to drinking. It is possible that the staff of the colleges become more selective in what they are willing to ignore and what they document. Thus, the changes in drinking patterns may reflect changes in the way the staff at one of the schools collects and reports the data.

## Interrupted Time Series Design

The interrupted time series is much like an AB design used in single-participant research. The researcher makes repeated measures of the frequency or rate of behavior in a sample of participants before and after a critical event. These data can come from many sources. As with most quasi-experiments, the researcher may not be able to control when the critical event occurs but can use its presence to examine interesting aspects of human behavior.

Hawton et al. (1999) reported the results of an interrupted time series that examined the effects of a television program on suicide attempts. The researchers learned that the medical television drama *Casualty* (a popular television show in England) would include an episode in which one of the characters dies of an overdose of the drug paracetamol. Hawton and his associates contacted the emergency rooms of 49 hospitals in England and asked them to monitor the number of cases of self-administered overdoses of paracetamol and other substances. The hospitals tracked the frequency of drug overdoses for three weeks before the episode aired and for three weeks after the broadcast.

Figure 15.7 presents the percent change in the number of reported overdoses for paracetamol after the broadcast of the episode of *Casualty*. Hawton et al. (1999) found that there was a statistically significant increase in all forms of self-administered overdoses. The cases of paracetamol overdoses were greatly elevated and continued at higher rates for two weeks. Data such as these might lead one to conclude that the television show led some of the viewers to mimic the characters in the drama.

The simple time series study suffers from the same problems of internal validity we faced with the simple AB research design. In the current example, we cannot be sure whether the television show produced the changes in drug overdoses or if other events, unrelated to the show, contributed to the effect. Therefore, researchers hope to find instances

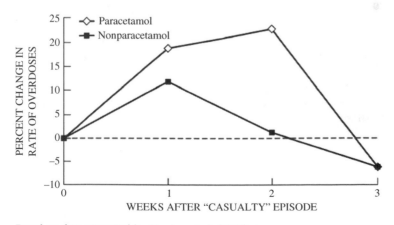

Based on data presented by Hawton et al. (1999)

## Figure 15.7

**Percent Change in the Rate of Overdoses Presented in Hospitals after a Particular Episode of the British Television Show,** *Casualty*

# Figure 15.8

**Proportion of Self-Administered Overdoses of Paracetamol that Occurred Three Weeks Before and Three Weeks After the Broadcast of an Episode of the Television Drama,** *Casualty*

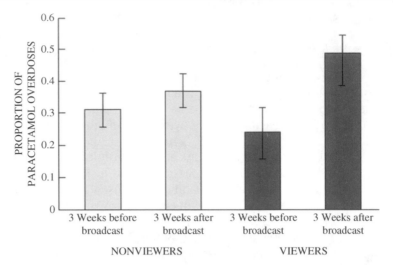

For each bar in the graph, the vertical lines represent the 95% confidence interval of the proportion. The nonviewer and viewer categories represent whether the patients watch *Casualty*, specifically the episode including the paracetamol overdosage.

where nature provides the equivalent to the controlled experiment. Can you think of some alternative design options?

One option would be to find two groups for which only one experiences the critical event. Hawton et al. (1999) were able to include this control in their research. They designed their questionnaire to include questions asking patients whether they had seen the particular episode of *Casualty*. Using this information, the researchers were able to compare the rates of self-poisonings for nonviewers and viewers of *Casualty*. The results of this analysis help to reinforce the hypothesis that the television episode contributed to the increase in drug overdoses. Figure 15.8 presents the results of this analysis. Among nonviewers of the program, there was no statistically significant difference in the proportion of paracetamol overdoses. By contrast, for the viewers of the program, there was a marked increase in paracetamol overdoses after the *Casualty* episode. Evidence such as this reinforces the conclusion that a television show may influence rates of drug overdoses.

As with the single-participant design, the creative researcher can use many variants of the interrupted time series to examine the relation between two variables. Cook and Campbell (1979) provide a comprehensive review of the more subtle and specialized methods along with a review of the statistical procedures used to study interrupted time series data.

## Research in Action: Traffic Laws and Safety

For this example of applied research, we will examine a study conducted by West, Hepworth, McCall, and Reich (1989). The researchers wanted to study the effects of a drunk-driving law that Arizona had adopted during the 1980s. In 1982, Arizona instituted a drunk-driving law that required those convicted of driving while intoxicated to receive jail sentences. The law required first-time offenders to be jailed for at least 24 hours, fined $250, and have their driver's license temporarily suspended. Those who supported the law argued that the benefit of the law would be, among other things, a decrease in traffic fatalities (West et al., 1989).

To examine the effects of the new law, West et al. (1989) reviewed the monthly police reports for the city of Phoenix, Arizona. Recognizing that there are cyclical patterns to traffic fatalities, they reviewed the records 30 months prior to the enactment of the law and 30 months after the enactment of the law. West and his colleagues also collected the same information from the El Paso police department. El Paso is a city in Texas that has much in common with Phoenix. The primary difference between the two cities is that Texas had not recently passed any drunk-driving legislation. Thus, this study combines the features of an interrupted time series and a quasi-control group.

Figure 15.9 presents the number of reported fatalities for the two cities. Two characteristics of this graph require explanation. First, both graphs contain a segment labeled "Media Coverage." These months represent the time before the enactment of the law that the Phoenix newspaper, *Arizona Republic*, reported extensively about the pending law. Second, the horizontal lines within the graph represent the average reported fatalities during the period.

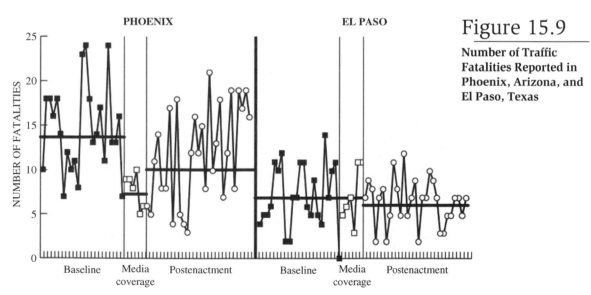

## Figure 15.9

**Number of Traffic Fatalities Reported in Phoenix, Arizona, and El Paso, Texas**

The Baseline and Media Coverage phases represent the time before the enactment of the new and stricter drunk-driving law in Arizona. The Media Coverage phase represents the time during which there was intense media coverage in a Phoenix newspaper. The horizontal lines represent the average monthly fatalities for the specific period.

Looking at the graphs, it is apparent that the new law did affect Arizona drivers. Prior to enforcement of the law, there were, on average, 14 traffic fatalities each month. During the months prior to the enforcement of the new law, when the media coverage was at its highest, the fatality rate decreased to 7 deaths per month. Over time, the rate of fatalities did increase to 10. By contrast, the number of traffic fatalities for El Paso remained relatively constant during the changes in Phoenix.

## Knowledge Check

5. In what ways are repeated-measures designs and longitudinal designs similar to and different from each other?

6. Explain how time can be a dependent variable.

7. Describe the similarities between an interrupted time series study and a multiple-baseline study.

## Chapter Summary

The research designs considered in this chapter are alternatives to the conventional experiment. Although single-participant, longitudinal, and quasi-experiments are empirical forms of analysis, they differ from the research designs considered in the earlier chapters.

The distinguishing feature of the single-participant experiment is the attention paid to the individual participant. Rather than average the responses of all the participants for subsequent statistical analysis, researchers who use single-participant research designs focus their analysis on the consistency of behavior observed across individuals. We revisited the issue of internal and external validity for the single-participant research design. Single-participant research designs can afford substantial internal validity and external validity that compares favorably to other research projects.

The typical research designs for the single-participant baseline experiment are the ABA and ABAB reversal designs and the multiple-baseline experiment. In the reversal design, the researcher observes the participant's behavior during a baseline period and then examines how additions to and removal of the intervention influence behavior. The multiple-baseline experiment allows the researcher to stagger the onset of the intervention across participants, behaviors, or situations.

Longitudinal research designs allow researchers to track changes in behavior over a long period. An alternative to the longitudinal design that avoids the cohort effect is the cross-sectional sequence procedure. This design allows the researcher to examine the differences among participants of different ages, potential cohort effects, and the effects of growing older.

One of the more recent developments in the analysis of longitudinal research is survival analysis. Survival analysis is a collection of statistical techniques that allows the researcher to examine changes in the participant's behavior over time. The statistical techniques allow researchers to overcome problems with participant dropout and other events that may make statistical tests such as the ANOVA inappropriate.

The quasi-experiment represents a method of conducting research used when the researcher cannot randomly assign participants to the treatment conditions. Two of the more popular quasi-experiments are the nonequivalent control group and the interrupted time series analysis.

## Chapter Glossary for Review

**Baseline study**—A form of single-participant research design in which the researcher monitors the changes in an ongoing behavior of the participant during changes in the participant's environment.

**Cohort effect**—A systematic difference between different cohorts due to unique experiences of the cohorts.

**Cross-sectional sequential design**—A type of longitudinal design for which the researcher selects participants that represent a cross-section of ages. The researcher then monitors the relevant variables across a number of subsequent times.

**Direct replication**—A tactic used in single-participant experiments to demonstrate that the intervention brought about changes in the behavior. Specifically, the researcher exposes several individuals to the same treatment conditions to determine whether the intervention has the same general effect on all the participants.

**Discrete trial study**—A form of single-participant research design in which the researcher assesses the participant's reaction to a specific event or stimulus.

**Experimental analysis of behavior**—A specific form of single-participant research that emphasizes the analysis of changes in an individual's behavior that result from controlled changes in the environment.

**Longitudinal design**—A procedure that allows the researcher to monitor the behavior of participants across a long period.

**Multiple-baseline design**—A research tactic used in single-participant baseline studies wherein reversal procedures (e.g., the ABAB) design is not appropriate. The researcher staggers the start of the intervention across participants, behaviors, or situations to determine whether the change in behavior occurs with the change in the environment.

**Reversal design (ABA and ABAB designs)**—A form of baseline study for which the researcher examines the participant's behavior when the intervention is added to and removed from the environment.

## Chapter References

Barlow, D. H., & Hersen, M. (1984). *Single case experimental designs: Strategies for studying behavior change* (2nd ed.). Boston: Allyn & Bacon.

Boring, E. G. (1957). *History of experimental psychology* (2nd ed.). New York: Appleton-Century-Crofts.

Campbell, D. T., & Stanley, J. C. (1966). *Experimental and quasi-experimental designs for research*. Chicago: Rand McNally.

Dermer, M. L., & Hoch, T. A. (1999). Improving descriptions of single-subject experiments in research texts written for undergraduates. *Psychological Record, 49,* 49–66.

Ebbinghaus, H. (1913). *On memory: An investigation to experimental psychology* (H. A. Ruger & C. E. Bussenius, Trans.). New York: Columbia University Press. (Original work published 1885).

Ellis, M. V. (1999). Repeated measures designs. *Counseling Psychologist, 27,* 552–578.

Fechner, G. (1966). *Elements of Psychophysics* (H. E. Adler, Trans.). New York: Holt, Rinehart & Winston. (Original work published 1860).

Flynn, J. R. (1998). IQ gains over time: Toward finding the causes. In U. Neisser (Ed.), *The rising curve: Long-term gains in IQ and related measures* (pp. 25–66). Washington, DC: American Psychological Association.

Greenhouse, J. B., Stangl, D., & Bromberg, J. (1989). An introduction to survival analysis: Statistical methods for analysis of clinical trial data. *Journal of Consulting and Clinical Psychology, 57,* 536–544.

Gruber, F. A. (1999). Tutorial: Survival analysis—A statistic for clinical, efficacy, and theoretical applications. *Journal of Speech, Language, and Hearing Research, 42,* 432–447.

Hawton, K., Simkin, S., Deeks, J. J., O'Connor, S., Keen, A., Altman, D. G., Philo, G., & Bulstrode, C. (1999). Effects of a drug overdose in a television drama on presentations to hospital for self-poisoning: Time series and questionnaire study. *British Medical Journal, 318,* 972–977.

Koehler, M. J., & Levin, J. R. (1998). Regulated randomization: A potential sharper analytical tool for the multiple-baseline design. *Psychological Methods, 3,* 206–217.

Laberge, B., Gauthier, J. G., Côté, G., Plamondon, J., & Cormier, H. J. (1993). Cognitive behavioral therapy of panic disorder with secondary major depression: A preliminary investigation. *Journal of Consulting and Clinical Psychology, 61,* 1028–1037.

Lewinsohn, P. M., Rohde, P., Seeley, J. R., & Fischer, S. A. (1993). Age-cohort changes in the lifetime occurrence of depression and other mental disorders. *Journal of Abnormal Psychology, 102,* 110–120.

Luke, D. A., & Homan, S. M. (1998). Time and change: Using survival analysis in clinical assessment and treatment evaluation. *Psychological Assessment, 10,* 360–378.

Morgan, D. L., & Morgan, R. K. (2001). Single-participant research design bringing science to managed care. *American Psychologist, 56,* 119–127.

Sidman, M. (1960). *Tactics of scientific research*. New York: Basic Books.

Singer, J. D., & Willett, J. B. (1991). Modeling the days of our lives: Using survival analysis when designing and analyzing longitudinal studies of duration and timing of events. *Psychological Bulletin, 110,* 268–290.

Skinner, B. F. (1953). Some contributions of an experimental analysis of behavior to psychology as a whole. *American Psychologist, 8,* 30–38.

Stice, E., Killen, J. D., Hayward, C., & Taylor, C. B. (1998). Age of onset for binge eating and purging during late adolescence: A 4-year analysis. *Journal of Abnormal Psychology, 4,* 671–675.

West, S. G., Biesanz, J. C., & Pitts, S. C. (2000). Causal inference and generalization in field settings. In H. T. Reis & C. M. Judd (Eds.), *Handbook of research methods in social and personality psychology* (pp. 40–84). Cambridge, UK: Cambridge University Press.

West, S. G., Hepworth, J. T., McCall, M. A., & Reich, J. W. (1989). An evaluation of Arizona's July 1982 drunk driving law: Effect on the city of Phoenix. *Journal of Applied Social Psychology, 19,* 1212–1237.

Willett, J. B., & Singer, J. D. (1993). Investigating onset, cessation, relapse, and recovery: Why you should, and how you can, use discrete-time survival analysis to examine event occurrence. *Journal of Consulting and Clinical Psychology, 61,* 952–965.

# Chapter 16
# Research with Categorical Data

The only relevant test of the validity of a hypothesis is comparison of prediction with experience.

—Milton Friedman

## Introduction

Throughout this book we have examined research projects that primarily used interval or ratio scales to measure the dependent variable. Although much behavioral research relies on interval and ratio scales, there are also many important applications of nominal and ordinal scales in contemporary research. As you will see, it is often the case that we may want to know how many people fit into specific categories. Because these research projects examine the frequency of different events, we will need a different set of research design and analysis tools to examine the data. Therefore, the focus of this chapter will be collecting and using this type of categorical data. Before we jump too far ahead, though, we should review some background information.

Nominal and ordinal scales consist of a set of mutually exclusive classes. **Mutually exclusive** means that a person or a measurement fits only one classification. For example, sex is a mutually exclusive classification system because you are either male or female. Political party is also a mutually exclusive system—most states require you to register as a Democrat, Republican, or some other political party. In contrast, a diagnosis for a psychological disorder may not be mutually exclusive to the extent that a person may have several diagnosed conditions. Because a person can receive a diagnosis of "depression" and "substance dependent," we cannot treat the individual diagnoses as mutu-ally exclusive.

The independent variable for categorical data research can represent either a nominal scale or an ordinal scale. A nominal scale is typically used to represent a construct that consists of readily identified groups. One's sex and political party are examples of nominal scales in that there is no implied order in the different scale options. An ordinal scale suggests that there is a continuum underlying the scale options. For example, most colleges use the terms *freshman*, *sophomore*, *junior*, and *senior* to identify the students' seniority from youngest to oldest. These groups are mutually exclusive in that a student can be in only one level. The groups also represent an ordinal scale in that we presume that the classification scheme represents the number of courses or credit hours the student completed (i.e., seniors are expected to have more education completed than freshmen).

The dependent variable for categorical research is typically the num-ber of people who or observations that fit within a category defined by the independent variable(s). We count the number of persons and things that occur in specific conditions. For some research projects, we may use a single variable with many classification levels. As an example, a researcher may want to count the number of reported marriages that occur each month to determine whether there is a relation between time of year and weddings. The independent variable, month, is clearly a mutually exclusive class, as a couple's wedding can occur in only 1 of the 12 months. The dependent variable is the number of weddings reported within each month.

In other research projects, the researcher may want to examine the relation among several variables. An example of a two-variable study would be examining the relation between one's political party (Democrat vs. Republican) and support for welfare reform legislation (favor legislation vs. oppose legislation), as presented in Table 16.1. Both variables, political party and attitude toward the legislation, are mutually exclusive categories. The dependent variable is the number of people within each of the four categories.

As with all research, the reliability and validity of the measurement tools are essential to the quality of the research project. The same rule applies to categorical data. Researchers who use categorical data place considerable emphasis on creating clear and useful definitions of the categories used in the research. As you recall from Chapter 8, there are many ways to prepare clear definitions of our terms and verify the reliability of those terms. Research with

Table 16.1  **Example of Categorical Research Examining Two Variables**

|  |  | **Party Affiliation** | |
|  |  | *Democrat* | *Republican* |
| **Attitude toward Legislation** | *Favor* | 103 | 98 |
|  | *Oppose* | 97 | 102 |

categorical data has two distinguishing features: the data we collect and the statistical tests we use to analyze the data.

In the previous chapters, we studied research projects that examine the average performance of people within specific treatment conditions. For categorical research the data are the frequencies, or number of people, within each condition. Because of this difference, we need to use different statistical procedures to analyze the data. Therefore, this chapter will review several common research procedures for conducting categorical research and the statistics used to analyze the data. Specifically, we will examine the $\chi^2$ statistic. Karl Pearson, the statistician who popularized the correlation coefficient $(r)$, also invented the **chi-square ($\chi^2$)** statistic. The $\chi^2$ is an inferential statistic that allows us to determine whether the number of observations within mutually exclusive classes differs significantly from hypothetical conditions.

## Goodness-of-Fit Test

The purpose of the **goodness-of-fit test** is to determine whether the frequencies of different mutually exclusive categories match or fit a hypothesized population. For an example of how this statistic works, we can examine the relation between month and rate of marriages. Imagine that a student went to the county courthouse, drew a random sample of 600 marriage licenses issued during the past year, and recorded the month of the marriage. Figure 16.1 presents the data.

For the $\chi^2$ statistic we use $O_i$ to indicate the observed frequency within each class. The symbol $T$ represents the total of all observations. Looking at the data it is clear that June stands out as a popular month for weddings, whereas January is not a popular month for exchanging vows. We can now raise the question, "Is the distribution of frequencies different from a known population?"

Table 16.2 presents the observed frequencies along with the expected frequencies. The column listed "Expected Proportions" represents data

## Figure 16.1

**Hypothetical Data of the Number of Marriages for Each Month**

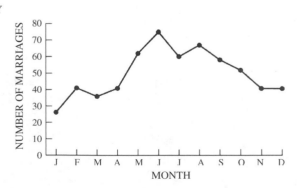

| MONTH | OBSERVED FREQUENCY |
|---|---|
| January | $O_1 = 26$ |
| February | $O_2 = 41$ |
| March | $O_3 = 36$ |
| April | $O_4 = 41$ |
| May | $O_5 = 62$ |
| June | $O_6 = 75$ |
| July | $O_7 = 60$ |
| August | $O_8 = 67$ |
| September | $O_9 = 58$ |
| October | $O_{10} = 52$ |
| November | $O_{11} = 41$ |
| December | $O_{12} = 41$ |
| TOTAL | $T = 600$ |

## Table 16.2  Extension of the Data Presented in Figure 16.1

| Month | Observed Frequency | Expected Proportions | Expected Frequency $= p \times T$ |
|---|---|---|---|
| January | $O_1 = 26$ | 0.04 | $E_1 = .04 \times 600 = 24$ |
| February | $O_2 = 41$ | 0.07 | $E_2 = .07 \times 600 = 42$ |
| March | $O_3 = 36$ | 0.06 | $E_3 = .06 \times 600 = 36$ |
| April | $O_4 = 41$ | 0.07 | $E_4 = .07 \times 600 = 42$ |
| May | $O_5 = 62$ | 0.10 | $E_5 = .10 \times 600 = 60$ |
| June | $O_6 = 75$ | 0.12 | $E_6 = .12 \times 600 = 72$ |
| July | $O_7 = 60$ | 0.10 | $E_7 = .10 \times 600 = 60$ |
| August | $O_8 = 67$ | 0.11 | $E_8 = .11 \times 600 = 66$ |
| September | $O_9 = 58$ | 0.10 | $E_9 = .10 \times 600 = 60$ |
| October | $O_{10} = 52$ | 0.09 | $E_{10} = .09 \times 600 = 54$ |
| November | $O_{11} = 41$ | 0.08 | $E_{11} = .08 \times 600 = 48$ |
| December | $O_{12} = 41$ | 0.06 | $E_{12} = .06 \times 600 = 36$ |
| **Totals** | 600 | 1.00 | 600 |

*Note*: The proportions represent data based on national data. The expected values ($E_i$) equal the hypothetical proportion ($p$) multiplied by the total number of observations ($T$).

provided by the Department of Health and Human Services (1995). According to this information, approximately 4% of marriages occur in January, whereas 12% of marriages occur in June. Using the proportions from the national sample, we can estimate how many weddings should occur within each month for our sample of 600 couples.

According to the results, we would expect 24 marriages in January and 72 marriages in June for any random sample of 600 marriages. Looking at Table 16.2, you can see that there are slight differences between the observed frequencies and the expected frequencies. For example, the student's sample had more than expected marriages in June and July and fewer than expected marriages in November. Do these differences represent random variation or are the differences statistically significant? To answer that question, we turn to the $\chi^2$ test of goodness-of-fit:

$$\chi^2 = \sum \frac{(O_i - E_i)^2}{E_i} \qquad (16.1)$$

Equation 16.1 defines the $\chi^2$ statistic. The numerator is the squared difference between the observed ($O_i$) and expected ($E_i$) scores for each category. The denominator is the expected value for the same class. If the random or chance factors created the difference between the observed and expected scores, then the $\chi^2$ will be relatively small. By contrast, $\chi^2$ will be large if there is a nonrandom difference between the observed and expected scores.

As with the other inferential statistics you have learned to use, the $\chi^2$ statistic has its own family of sampling distributions. The degrees of freedom for the $\chi^2$ statistic is one less the number of classes. Stated mathematically, the degrees of freedom for the goodness-of-fit test is

$$df = k - 1 \qquad\qquad (16.2)$$

In our example, there are 12 months, therefore the degrees of freedom are $df = 12 - 1 = 11$. Table B.14 of Appendix B lists the critical values for the $\chi^2$ statistic. As you can see, the critical value to reject the null hypothesis is 19.675. Like the ANOVA, the $\chi^2$ is a nondirectional statistic. This means that the $\chi^2$ will indicate whether the pattern of observed frequencies deviates from the expected frequencies. It does not indicate whether one particular difference is significantly greater or less than the expected value.

### Assumptions of the Goodness-of-Fit Test

The goodness-of-fit $\chi^2$ test requires the data to meet several assumptions. These assumptions include: (1) mutually exclusive categories, (2) exhaustive conditions, (3) independence of observations, and (4) sufficient sample size. We have already examined the requirement of mutually exclusive categories. In summary, each subject fits into only one category. Examples of mutually exclusive events include one's sex, political party, and marital status. It is critical to ensure that we use procedures that prohibit double counting the individuals. If we allow some people or observations to count in several categories, the results test will produce biased results. Because the couples could list only one wedding date, we can be confident there will be only one reported wedding for each couple.

The issue of an inflated $T$, or total number of observations (i.e., a very large sample size or large number of measurements), can be a serious problem for the accuracy of the $\chi^2$ test. Counting the same participant several times biases the data. Therefore, researchers who conduct categorical data research spend much time ensuring that their definitions of the categories and the procedures they use to collect the data ensure that the data conform to the mutually exclusive requirement. The exhaustive-conditions assumption indicates that there is a category available for each person in the sample. In the example illustrating the relation between marriages and months, we can consider the conditions exhaustive because the researcher included a category for each month.

What if a researcher wanted to examine the relation between political party and attitude toward a new law? To meet the exhaustive-conditions requirement, the researcher would need to include a category for each political party (Communist, Democrat, Green, Libertarian, Republican, etc.) or a category for each of the major parties and a category of "Other" party affiliation. The purpose of the exhaustive-conditions requirement is to ensure that the researcher classifies each person in the sample. Dropping people from the sample because they do not meet the classification scheme will bias the results.

The independence of observations means that the classification of subjects into one category has no effect on the other categories. To meet the

## Table 16.3    Extension of the Data Presented in Tables 16.2 and 16.3

| Month | $O$ | $E$ | $O_i - E_i$ | $(O_i - E_i)^2$ | $\frac{(O_i - E_i)^2}{E_i}$ |
|---|---|---|---|---|---|
| January | $O_1 = 26$ | $E_1 = 24$ | 2 | 4 | 0.1667 |
| February | $O_2 = 41$ | $E_2 = 42$ | −1 | 1 | 0.0238 |
| March | $O_3 = 36$ | $E_3 = 36$ | 0 | 0 | 0.0000 |
| April | $O_4 = 41$ | $E_4 = 42$ | −1 | 1 | 0.0238 |
| May | $O_5 = 62$ | $E_5 = 60$ | 2 | 4 | 0.0667 |
| June | $O_6 = 75$ | $E_6 = 72$ | 3 | 9 | 0.1250 |
| July | $O_7 = 60$ | $E_7 = 60$ | 0 | 0 | 0.0000 |
| August | $O_8 = 67$ | $E_8 = 66$ | 1 | 1 | 0.0152 |
| September | $O_9 = 58$ | $E_9 = 60$ | −2 | 4 | 0.0667 |
| October | $O_{10} = 52$ | $E_{10} = 54$ | −2 | 4 | 0.0741 |
| November | $O_{11} = 41$ | $E_{11} = 48$ | −7 | 49 | 1.0208 |
| December | $O_{12} = 41$ | $E_{12} = 36$ | 5 | 25 | 0.6944 |
| Totals | 600 | 600 | | | $\chi^2 = 2.2771$ |

*Note:* This table shows how one calculates the goodness-of-fit $\chi^2$.

independence requirement, there must be equivalent criteria for entry into each category. For this example, we can assume that the decision of one couple to wed in February had no effect on the plans of the other couples. The final requirement is that sample size be sufficiently large. The general rule is that none of the expected frequencies should be less than 5. If the expected frequencies are too small, the $\chi^2$ will be more likely to produce erroneous results.

In the current example, we can see that we have met all the requirements of the $\chi^2$ test. The groups are mutually exclusive, the conditions are exhaustive, the classification of the people is independent, and the sample size appears to be sufficiently large. Therefore, we can proceed with the test. Table 16.3 presents the $\chi^2$ test for the number of marriages by month. For these data, the null hypothesis is that the observed frequencies will equal the expected frequencies.

The value of $\chi^2_{observed}$ is less than $\chi^2_{critical} (2.28 < 19.68)$. Therefore, we cannot reject the null hypothesis. This result suggests that the distribution of marriages matches the national trends. We must conclude that we have no reason to assume that the difference between the observed and expected frequencies is anything other than chance. In this example, we used empirical data to determine the values of the expected frequencies. This tactic allowed us to determine whether the selection of wedding dates differs from national trends. There are cases in which we want to determine whether the data are evenly distributed across a set of categories.

Consider the following example. A social worker wants to know whether there is a relation between the time of year and the occurrence of depression. Using the data collected by a large metropolitan-area hospital, the social worker records the number of admissions for depression that occurred during the past five years. The researcher divides the year into the

Table 16.4 **Hypothetical Data Representing the Number of People Admitted to a Hospital for Depression During Different Seasons Over a Five-Year Interval**

| Season | $O$ | $E$ | $O_i - E_i$ | $(O_i - E_i)^2$ | $\frac{(O_i - E_i)^2}{E_i}$ |
|--------|-----|-----|-------------|-----------------|------------------------------|
| Spring | 495 | 517.5 | $-22.5$ | 506.25 | 0.9783 |
| Summer | 503 | 517.5 | $-14.5$ | 210.25 | 0.4063 |
| Autumn | 491 | 517.5 | $-26.5$ | 702.25 | 1.3570 |
| Winter | 581 | 517.5 | 63.5 | 4032.25 | 7.7918 |
| **Totals** | 2070 | 2070 | 0.0 | | $\chi^2 = 10.5334$ |

four seasons (e.g., winter = November, December, January, and February). The data are presented in Table 16.4.

The researcher may want to know whether the frequency of severe depression varies with the time of year. The simplest null hypothesis to propose is that the rate of admission for depression is equal throughout the year. Therefore, the researcher determined that the expected number of admissions in each season should be equal. In other words, the expected frequency for each season is $517.5 = 2070/4$. The remainder of the test follows the same procedures listed previously.

With $df = 3$ and $\alpha = .05$, $\chi^2_{critical} = 7.815$. Because the observed value of $\chi^2$ is greater than the critical value ($10.5334 > 7.815$), we may assume that the distribution of admissions for depression does deviate from the expected hypothesized values. By casual inspection of the data, it appears that there is an increase of admissions during winter.

## $\chi^2$ Test of Independence

We can extend the logic of $\chi^2$ to cases where we have two categorical variables. The question that we want to address in this situation is whether these variables are independent of each other. The following is an example to help illustrate how to use the $\chi^2$ **test of independence**. What are the long-term effects of childhood sexual abuse? Are children who experience this type of abuse more likely to suffer severe emotional disorders later in their life?

Gladstone, Parker, Wilhelm, Mitchell, and Austin (1999) addressed that question by conducting an extensive review of 171 women receiving treatment for a major depressive episode. Of these women, 40 reported experiencing sexual abuse as children. The researchers then examined the case history of all the women and looked for evidence of self-injurious behavior. The data in Table 16.5 represent the number of patients who attempted to commit suicide.

In this example, the $\chi^2$ test of independence allows us to examine the relationship between history of childhood sexual abuse and rates of attempted suicide. If the two variables are independent of each other, then the

## Table 16.5 Contingency Table Representing the Number of Women Reporting Childhood Sexual Abuse and One or More Suicide Attempts

| | Childhood Sexual Abuse | | |
| | Abused | Not Abused | Row Total |
| --- | --- | --- | --- |
| Attempted Suicide | 16 | 23 | 39 |
| No Suicide Attempts | 24 | 108 | 132 |
| Column Total | 40 | 131 | 171 |

rate of suicide attempts will have nothing to do with the abuse experience. By contrast, if a history of sexual abuse does affect risk of suicide, then we should observe a nonrandom pattern in the data.

As with the goodness-of-fit test, we need to determine the expected value for each cell in the table. The expected value represents the frequency within a cell that we would expect to occur given the independence of the two variables. Perhaps an example would help. According to the data presented in Table 16.5, we know that 40 women experienced childhood sexual abuse. Converting this number to a percentage, we can say that 23.39% ([40/171] × 100) of the women experienced the abuse. We also know that 39 women attempted to commit suicide. If the rate of suicide attempts and history of abuse are independent of each other, then we can conclude that 23.39% of the women who attempted suicide also have a history of abuse. We would expect that 9.12 (9.12 = 39 × .2339) women would be in the cell, "Attempted Suicide"/"Abused." We can use the following equation for determining the expected frequencies for each cell:

$$E_{ij} = \frac{R_i C_j}{T} \tag{16.3}$$

In this equation, $R_i$ and $C_j$ represent the row-and-column totals for each category, and $T$ represents the total number of observations. Therefore, $E_{ij}$ represents the expected frequency for each cell if there is no correspondence between the two variables. Table 16.6 presents the expected values for the data.

If there is no relationship between the two independent variables, then the overall difference between the observed and expected frequencies should be minimal. In this case, each expected frequency ($E_{ij}$) should equal the corresponding observed frequency ($O_{ij}$), and if it does, $\chi^2$ will equal 0. If the differences between the observed and expected frequencies are sufficiently large, we can infer that there is a relationship between the two variables and that the two variables are therefore not independent. For this example, a statistically significant $\chi^2$ would allow us to assume a correspondence between a history of childhood sexual abuse and suicide attempts.

## Table 16.6  Extension of the Data Presented in Table 16.5

| | Childhood Sexual Abuse | | |
| --- | --- | --- | --- |
| | *Abused* | *Not Abused* | *Row Total* |
| *Attempted Suicide* | $O_{11} = 16$ | $O_{12} = 23$ | $R_1 = 39$ |
| | $E_{11} = \frac{40 \times 39}{171} = 9.12$ | $E_{12} = \frac{131 \times 39}{171} = 29.88$ | |
| *No Suicide Attempts* | $O_{21} = 24$ | $O_{22} = 108$ | $R_2 = 132$ |
| | $E_{21} = \frac{40 \times 132}{171} = 30.88$ | $E_{22} = \frac{131 \times 132}{171} = 101.12$ | |
| *Column Total* | $C_1 = 40$ | $C_2 = 131$ | $T = 171$ |

This table illustrates how one calculates the expected values for each cell.

The formal mathematical statement for the $\chi^2$ test is:

$$\chi^2 = \sum_{i=1}^{r} \sum_{j=1}^{c} \frac{(O_{ij} - E_{ij})}{E_{ij}} \tag{16.4}$$

The equation is much like the goodness-of-fit test. The difference is that we need to calculate a ratio for each cell in the matrix. The number of rows, $r$, and the number of columns, $c$, determine the degrees of freedom. Specifically,

$$df = (r - 1)(c - 1) \tag{16.5}$$

For Equation 16.5, $r$ represents the number of rows, and $c$ represents the number of columns in the matrix of data. With this information, we can now proceed to our calculations. Carrying out the steps in Equation 16.4, we find

$$\chi^2 = \frac{(16 - 9.12)^2}{9.12} + \frac{(23 - 29.88)^2}{29.88} + \frac{(24 - 30.88)^2}{30.88} + \frac{(108 - 101.12)^2}{101.12} = 8.77$$

Because $\chi^2_{\text{observed}}$ is much greater than $\chi^2_{\text{critical}} (8.77 > 3.841)$, we can reject the null hypothesis. These data allow the researcher to infer that the risk of suicide attempt corresponds with the experiencing of sexual abuse as a child. Looking at the differences between the observed and expected values, you can see what should be an obvious effect: Women who experienced sexual abuse as children are more likely to attempt suicide than women who did not experience the abuse.

### Interpreting $\chi^2$

We need to interpret a statistically significant $\chi^2$ test for independence with caution. Specifically, we need to be mindful of whether a statistically significant $\chi^2$ allows us to infer cause and effect. The primary purpose of the $\chi^2$ test of independence is to determine whether the variables involved function independently from one another. If we fail to reject the null hypothesis for this test, we must conclude that we do not have evidence for the interdependence between the variables. We must then assume that the data represent the random distribution of observed scores. If we *do* reject the null hypothesis, we can then conclude that there is a correspondence between the variables and that they are not independent from each other.

Just as with the Pearson product-moment correlation, a relationship between variables in this type of analysis is also not, by itself, evidence of a cause-and-effect relationship between the independent and dependent variables. We can use the current example to illustrate this important consideration. What were the researcher's independent variables? Both variables in this example are subject variables as they represent conditions of the participants beyond the control of the researcher. The researchers could not randomly assign the participants to the different categories. These observations mean that we cannot easily rule out alternative explanations for the data we have observed.

We also need to examine how the researchers created the sample. Is the sample representative of the general population? The participants in this research were women in therapy for depression. Consequently, this sample may not represent all the women who suffered childhood abuse; some may not have sought treatment from a psychologist. Thus, we cannot automatically assume that all people who experience sexual abuse are at risk for suicide. In determining the long-term effects of childhood sexual abuse, we would need to sample from the general population and work to find those with a history of childhood sexual abuse, independent of their current treatment for a psychological disorder.

## $\chi^2$ Test of Homogeneity

Are there conditions when we can assume a cause-and-effect relationship for the $\chi^2$ test? The short answer to this question is yes, if we conduct the study using a different set of procedures. Imagine that a researcher randomly assigns equal numbers of participants to one of four psychotherapy conditions and then evaluates the clients' conditions after the treatment using three classifications: (1) no change, (2) moderate improvement, and (3) good improvement. The $\chi^2$ **test of homogeneity** allows us to determine whether the pattern of observed frequencies deviates from chance levels. If we find a statistically significant $\chi^2$, we can then assume, because of the design of the study, that a cause-and-effect relationship is present. The data in Table 16.7 represent hypothetical results for such a study.

In this example, we can treat the type of psychotherapy as a manipulated independent variable because the researcher randomly assigned the participants to one of the conditions. The second variable, the outcome measure, is the condition of the participants at the end of the study.

# Table 16.7   Hypothetical Data for an Example of a $\chi^2$ Test of Homogeneity [a]

|  | Psychotherapy Condition | | | | |
|---|---|---|---|---|---|
|  | *Control* | *Informative* | *Individual: Type A* | *Individual Type B* | *Row Total* |
| *No Change* | $O_{11} = 19$ $E_{11} = 14$ | $O_{12} = 15$ $E_{12} = 14$ | $O_{13} = 7$ $E_{13} = 14$ | $O_{14} = 15$ $E_{14} = 14$ | 56 |
| *Moderate* | $O_{21} = 21$ $E_{21} = 17$ | $O_{22} = 22$ $E_{22} = 17$ | $O_{23} = 9$ $E_{23} = 17$ | $O_{24} = 16$ $E_{24} = 17$ | 68 |
| *Good* | $O_{31} = 20$ $E_{31} = 29$ | $O_{32} = 23$ $E_{32} = 29$ | $O_{33} = 44$ $E_{33} = 29$ | $O_{34} = 29$ $E_{34} = 29$ | 116 |
| *Column Total* | 60 | 60 | 60 | 60 | 240 |

$\chi^2 = 23.46, df = (3-1)(4-1) = 6, \chi^2_{critical} = 12.592, \alpha = 0.5$; reject $H_0$ because $\chi^2 > \chi^2_{critical}$

Therefore, this study has all the hallmarks of a true experiment: (1) manipulated independent variable, (2) a control group, and (3) random assignment of participants to the treatment conditions. Data such as these could lead the researcher to conclude that the type of therapy influences the rate at which the clients' condition improves.

The procedures for calculating the $\chi^2$ are identical to those presented for the test of independence. Therefore, the only differences between the $\chi^2$ test of independence and the $\chi^2$ test of homogeneity are the methods used to create the sample and the interpretations we can draw from the test. To review, for the test of independence, we create a sample and then assess the participants for the variables in the study. In the Gladstone et al. (1999) study, the researchers created a sample of women seeking treatment and then determined the number of individuals who had attempted suicide and the number who had been sexually abused as children. By contrast, for the test for homogeneity, we create a sample of equal numbers of participants within the different levels of one variable and then assess the dependent variable using an outcome measure.

## Reporting $\chi^2$

The style guide published by the American Psychological Association (2009) recommends that we report $\chi^2$ as $\chi^2(df, N = n) = \chi^2, p < \alpha$, or in this most recent example, $\chi^2(6, N = 240) = 23.46, p < .05$. The recommended format has us report the degrees of freedom and the number of subjects used in the study. We also indicate whether the probability level associated with the statistic is greater than or less than the $\alpha$-level selected for the study.

## Assumptions of the $\chi^2$ Test

To make a valid interpretation of the $\chi^2$ test, you must ensure that the data meet three specific assumptions. These assumptions are similar to the ones associated with all forms of $\chi^2$ tests, including the goodness-of-fit test, which we already reviewed. Specifically, (1) the categories must be mutually exclusive, exhaustive, and independent; (2) the data must represent frequencies; and (3) the sample size must be sufficiently large. Regarding sample size, many authors offer general guidelines for the $\chi^2$ test of independence. For example, Siegel and Castellan (1988) noted that when either the number of rows or the number of columns is greater than two, "no more than 20% of the cells should have an expected frequency of less than 5, and no cell should have an expected frequency less than 1" (p. 199).

Some researchers have found that the $\chi^2$ test maintains the same rate of Type I errors even with severe violations of this assumption. For example, Good, Grover, and Mitchell (1970) suggested that expected values could be as low as 0.33 with no change in the probability of committing a Type I error. Although the $\chi^2$ test appears to be able to withstand the effect of small frequencies, we should not forget the issue of statistical power. As with all inferential statistics, the probability of correctly rejecting the null hypothesis increases as the sample size increases. Therefore, although $\chi^2$ may be computationally valid when the sample size is small, your power to identify a significant effect may be insufficient.

## Further Analysis of the $\chi^2$

The $\chi^2$ test allows us to determine whether to reject the null hypothesis; however, the results provide no information for determining the strength of the relationship between the independent variables. In the next two sections, you will learn how to determine the degree of correspondence between the variables and how to more closely examine the differences observed within each cell.

### Cramér's Coefficient Φ

In Chapter 8 you learned that Pearson's product-moment correlation coefficient is a statistic used to indicate the degree of association between two variables. The larger the absolute value of $r$, the greater the association between the two variables. **Cramér's coefficient($\Phi$)** (phi) serves the same purpose as $r$; it indicates the degree of association between two variables analyzed using the $\chi^2$ statistic:

$$\Phi = \sqrt{\frac{\chi^2}{T(S-1)}} \qquad (16.6)$$

Equation 16.6 presents Cramér's $\Phi$. In the equation, $T$ represents the total number of observations and $S$ represents the smaller value of number of rows or number of columns. Because the size of $\Phi$ depends on the value of $\chi^2$, we can infer that if $\chi^2$ is statistically significant, the same is true of $\Phi$.

There are important differences between $r$ and $\Phi$, however. Whereas $r$ can range between –1 and 1, $\Phi$ can have values only between 0 and 1. Nevertheless, we can use the magnitude of $\Phi$ as an index of the relation between the two variables. Another important difference between $r$ and $\Phi$ is that $r$ is a measure of the linear relation between two variables. In Chapter 8 you learned that we use $r$ when we assume that a straight line describes the relation between two variables. There are, however, instances when there are systematic relations between two variables best described by curved lines. The $\Phi$ does not assume a linear relation between the two variables. The $\Phi$ is a general statistic that allows us to estimate how one variable predicts the other variable.

We can use the data from Table 16.6 to illustrate how to calculate Cramér's $\Phi$:

$$\Phi = \sqrt{\frac{8.77}{177(2-1)}} = \sqrt{\frac{8.77}{171}} = \sqrt{0.05129} = .226$$

Therefore, we can conclude that the relationship between experiences of childhood sexual abuse and attempted suicides is of moderate strength.

### Post-Hoc Analysis of $\chi^2$

You may recall from our discussion of the analysis of variance that the ANOVA is a general test because it allows us to conclude that there is a relationship between at least two means among others in a larger set, but it does not tell us which specific treatment groups are significantly different from the others. For the ANOVA, the Tukey's HSD is a commonly used post-hoc test to compare the differences among specific means. A similar situation arises for the $\chi^2$ test. We can use the $\chi^2$ test to reject the hypothesis that the two conditions are independent of one another, but we cannot determine from the test which condition or conditions contributed to the statistically significant result.

One technique that many researchers use is to convert the differences between the observed and expected values to a statistic called the **standardized residual (e)**. The standardized residual allows us to determine the relative difference between the observed and expected frequencies. Using the standardized residual, we can then determine which cells in the data table represent statistically significant differences and which represent chance findings. Equation 16.7 presents the method of calculating $e$:

$$e_{ij} = \frac{O_{ij} - E_{ij}}{\sqrt{E_{ij}}} \tag{16.7}$$

Although Equation 16.7 provides an estimate of the standardized residual, many researchers prefer to use a more refined estimate of the residual. Equation 16.8 (Haberman, 1973; Delucchi, 1993) presents the method of calculating the variance for each cell:

$$v_{ij} = \left(1 - \frac{C_i}{T}\right)\left(1 - \frac{R_j}{T}\right) \tag{16.8}$$

Using Equations 16.7 and 16.8, we can now calculate what statisticians call the **adjusted residual** ($\hat{e}$):

$$\hat{e}_{ij} = \frac{e_{ij}}{\sqrt{v_{ij}}} \tag{16.9}$$

The advantage of calculating $\hat{e}$ is that it is normally distributed with a mean of 0 and a standard deviation of 1. Therefore, we can treat $\hat{e}$ as if it were a $z$-score. If the absolute value of $\hat{e}$ is sufficiently large, we can assume that the difference between the observed and expected values is statistically significant. For example, $z = \pm 1.96$ represents the critical value for $\alpha = .05$, two-tailed. In other words, if $\hat{e} \leq 1.96$ or $\hat{e} \geq 1.96$, we can assume that the difference between $O$ and $E$ is statistically significant at $\alpha = .05$. Table 15.8 presents the calculations for $e$, $v$, and $\hat{e}$. From this work, we can conclude that the difference between the observed and expected frequencies for each cell is statistically significant.

## Table 16.8  Extension of the Data Presented in Table 16.6

| | Childhood Sexual Abuse | | Row Total |
|---|---|---|---|
| | *Abused* | *Not Abused* | *Row Total* |
| *Attempted Suicide* | $O_{11} = 16 \quad E_{11} = 9.12$<br>$e_{11} = \dfrac{16 - 9.12}{\sqrt{9.12}}$<br>$e_{11} = 2.278$<br>$v_{11} = .766 \times .772 = .591$<br>$\hat{e}_{11} = \dfrac{2.278}{\sqrt{.591}} = 2.96$ | $O_{12} = 23 \quad E_{12} = 29.88$<br>$e_{12} = \dfrac{23 - 29.88}{\sqrt{29.88}}$<br>$e_{12} = -1.258$<br>$v_{12} = .234 \times .772 = .181$<br>$\hat{e}_{12} = \dfrac{-1.258}{\sqrt{.181}} = -2.96$ | $R_1 = 39$<br>$.772 = 1 - \dfrac{39}{171}$ |
| *No Suicide Attempts* | $O_{21} = 24 \quad E_{21} = 30.88$<br>$e_{21} = \dfrac{23 - 29.88}{\sqrt{29.88}}$<br>$e_{21} = -1.238$<br>$v_{21} = .766 \times .228 = .175$<br>$\hat{e}_{21} = \dfrac{-1.238}{\sqrt{.175}} = -2.96$ | $O_{22} = 108 \quad E_{22} = 101.12$<br>$e_{22} = \dfrac{108 - 101.12}{\sqrt{101.12}}$<br>$e_{22} = -0.684$<br>$v_{22} = .234 \times .228 = .053$<br>$\hat{e}_{22} = \dfrac{0.684}{\sqrt{.053}} = 2.96$ | $R_2 = 132$<br>$.228 = 1 - \dfrac{132}{171}$ |
| *Column Total* | $C_1 = \mathbf{40}$<br>$.766 = 1 - \dfrac{40}{171}$ | $C_2 = \mathbf{131}$<br>$.234 = 1 - \dfrac{131}{171}$ | $T = 171$ |

## McNemar Test

The McNemar test is a special form of the $\chi^2$ test that we can use to compare correlated samples. We can use the McNemar test to compare the proportion of participants who fit within a specific category before and after some event or under different conditions. The McNemar test works specifically with a 2 × 2 table, as presented in Table 16.9.

Equation 16.10 presents the basic form of the McNemar test:

$$\chi^2 = \frac{(|B - C| - 1)^2}{B + C}, df = 1 \qquad (16.10)$$

Once you calculate the $\chi^2$ test, you can use Table B of Appendix B to determine whether to reject the null hypothesis. An alternative method is to take the square root of the $\chi^2$, which produces a $z$-score. This transformation works only when the degrees of freedom of the $\chi^2$ tests are $df = 1$:

$$z = \sqrt{\chi^2} \qquad (16.11)$$

The null hypothesis of this test is that the difference between the B and C cells is due to chance. A significantly large value of $\chi^2$ indicates that the observed frequencies in the B and C cells do not represent chance factors.

We can use an example from research conducted by Cairns et al. (1989) to illustrate the utility of the McNemar test. Cairns et al. were interested in the developmental changes in aggressive tendencies of children. More specifically, they examined the number of times boys and girls described aggressive tendencies toward other boys and girls. To collect the data, research associates interviewed the children, first in the fourth grade and then again in the seventh grade. During the interviews, the researcher asked the children to describe two recent conflicts with other children. Another research associate, blind to the research questions and nature of the children responding, read and scored verbatim transcripts of the interviews. Part of the coding indicated whether the child described physical aggression toward another child. The data in Table 16.10 present an example of Cairns et al.'s results for boy participants.

In this table, the numbers represent frequency of events for two conditions. Look at the data for Grade 4. These data represent the results for the 104 boys interviewed. The question that the researchers wanted to address is the number of times the boys described physical conflicts with

## Table 16.9   Layout for a McNemar Test

| | | Condition II | |
|---|---|---|---|
| | | 1 | 2 |
| **Condition I** | 1 | A | B |
| | 2 | C | D |

# Table 16.10 Procedure for Calculating the McNemar Test

### Boys' Reports of Conflicts: Grade 4

|  | Physical Aggression | No Physical Aggression | Total |
|---|---|---|---|
| Conflict with Males | 48 | 56 | 104 |
| Conflict with Females | 26 | 78 | 104 |

$$\chi^2 = \frac{(|56 - 26| - 1)^2}{56 + 26} = \frac{(|30| - 1)}{82} = \frac{841}{82} = 10.2561$$

$$z = \sqrt{10.2561} = 3.20$$

$$\Phi = \sqrt{\frac{10.2561}{104(2-1)}} = 0.314$$

### Boys' Reports of Conflicts: Grade 7

|  | Physical Aggression | No Physical Aggression | Total |
|---|---|---|---|
| Conflict with Males | 49 | 55 | 104 |
| Conflict with Females | 12 | 92 | 104 |

$$\chi^2 = \frac{(|55 - 12| - 1)^2}{55 + 12} = \frac{(|43| - 1)}{67} = \frac{1764}{67} = 26.3284$$

$$z = \sqrt{26.3284} = 5.13$$

$$\Phi - \sqrt{\frac{26.3284}{104(2-1)}} = 0.50341$$

other boys and the number of physical conflicts with girls. According to the results, 48 of the boys reported a physical conflict with another boy. These same 104 boys reported 26 physically aggressive conflicts with girls. The research question is whether boys are more likely to be physically aggressive with boys than with girls.

According to Table B.14 of Appendix B, the critical value of $\chi^2$ for $df = 1$ and $\alpha = .05$ is $\chi^2 = 3.841$; therefore we can reject the null hypothesis for both the fourth-grade data and the seventh-grade data. We can conclude that the pattern of reported physical conflicts is not random. Specifically, these data suggest that boys are more likely to report themes of physical aggression toward other boys than toward girls and that this pattern appears to become stronger as boys grow older.

## Knowledge Check

1. Describe in your words the uses of the $\chi^2$ statistic. How are these uses of the $\chi^2$ test similar to and different from each other?

2. A student conducted a study in which three groups of rats (5 per group) were reinforced under three different schedules of

reinforcement (100%, 50%, and 25%). The number of bar-pressing responses obtained during extinction is as follows: 100%, 615; 50%, 843; 25%, 545. Criticize the use of the chi-square as the appropriate statistical technique.

3. Neil asked 50 participants to think about their earliest memory of their father and their earliest one of their mother. Then he asked them to evaluate each memory as to whether it is positive or negative. He obtained the results listed in the accompanying table.

|  | Memory of Mother | Memory of Father |
|---|---|---|
| Positive | 35 | 31 |
| Negative | 15 | 19 |

Neil plans to analyze his data using $\chi^2$. Do you think such an analysis is appropriate? Explain.

4. Bill believes that the current generation of students is much different from students in the 1960s. He asks a sample of students at his college the following question: Which of the following best describes your reason for attending college (pick only one alternative)?
   a. Develop a philosophy of life
   b. Learn more about the world around me
   c. Obtain a good-paying job
   d. Unsure of reason
   Researchers asked the same question of students at the college in 1965. Here are the results of the two surveys:

|  | 1965 | 2001 |
|---|---|---|
| Develop a philosophy of life | 15 | 8 |
| Learn more about the world around me | 53 | 48 |
| Obtain a good-paying job | 25 | 57 |
| Unsure of reason | 27 | 47 |

Is Bill justified in concluding that there is a difference between the current class of students and students in 1965?

5. Erin is the chair of a department of psychology. She sent a questionnaire to all students who graduated from the program during the past 10 years. One question asked whether the student attended a graduate program and the type of program attended. Of the students returning questionnaires, 88 indicated that they were in or had completed a Ph.D. program:

| Program | Number of Students |
|---|---|
| Clinical | 12 |
| Counseling | 23 |
| Developmental | 8 |
| Experimental | 7 |
| Industrial-Organizational | 15 |
| Physiological | 5 |
| Social | 8 |

Can Erin assume that graduates of the department equally attend each of the seven programs?

6. Jackie conducted a study in which she compared the helping behavior of passersby under two conditions. What can you conclude from the results shown in the accompanying table?

| | Condition A | Condition B |
|---|---|---|
| **Helped** | 75 | 45 |
| **Did Not Help** | 40 | 80 |

Set up this study in formal statistical terms and draw appropriate conclusions.

7. Robert wanted to determine the effects of a televised debate on voters' preferences. The day before a televised debate, Robert asked 100 randomly selected people their current preference. After the debate, Robert asked the same people to identify their candidate of choice. Use the following data to describe how voters' preference changed after watching the debate.

| | | After the Debate | |
|---|---|---|---|
| | | **Candidate A** | **Candidate B** |
| | **Candidate A** | 20 | 25 |
| **Before the Debate** | | | |
| | **Candidate B** | 30 | 25 |

## Research in Action: Long-Term Effects of Childhood Abuse

In a previous example, we saw that people sexually abused as children are more likely to attempt suicide than people not sexually abused. Mulder, Beautrais, Joyce, and Fergusson (1998) examined the effects of abuse on other emotional and behavioral problems. The researchers were concerned that most of the research that examines the effects of domestic violence used current patients for the sample. Mulder et al. believed that using a random sample of the general population would improve the external validity of the conclusions.

To conduct their research, Mulder et al. (1998) contacted a stratified (for age and sex) random sample of 1,200 registered voters from the Canterbury region of New Zealand. Of the individuals, 1,028 agreed to participate in an in-depth interview that included a review of their history and a structured interview conducted by trained clinical psychologists. One of the characteristics that they examined was dissociative symptoms, which include a disruption of normal functions including "consciousness, memory, identity, or perception" (American Psychiatric Association, 1994, p. 477). These researchers decided to measure dissociative symptoms because these symptoms are highly related to other psychiatric illnesses.

Of the people interviewed, 28 reported having been physically, but not sexually, abused as a child. An additional 43 people reported that they experienced sexual abuse as a child. Table 16.11 presents the analysis of the data. The three columns represent three classes of childhood experience, "No Abuse," "Abused," and "Abused and Sexually Assaulted." The rows represent whether the patients evidenced a high level of dissociation disorders. Using these data, we can determine whether there is a relation between the presence of dissociation disorders and childhood abuse.

For these data, $\chi^2_{observed}=17.97$ is greater than $\chi^2_{critical}$. Therefore, we can conclude that there is a relationship between the high levels of dissociation and childhood experiences. Careful inspection of the data reveals an interesting pattern. Higher levels of dissociation occur with reports of physical abuse than with sexual abuse. Mulder et al. (1998) recognized immediately that their findings conflicted with popular opinion among

Table 16.11 **Hypothetical Data Representing the Frequency of Various Psychological Disorders and the Presence or Absence of Physical Abuse**

| | History | | | |
|---|---|---|---|---|
| | No Abuse | Abused | Abused and Sexually Assaulted | Row Total |
| **High Dissociation** | $O_{11} = 56$<br>$E_{11} = 60.5107$<br>$\hat{e}_{11} = -2.28^*$ | $O_{12} = 7$<br>$E_{12} = 1.7704$<br>$\hat{e}_{12} = 4.12^*$ | $O_{13} = 2$<br>$E_{13} = 2.719$<br>$\hat{e}_{13} = 0.046^*$ | $R_1 = 65$ |
| **Low Dissociation** | $O_{21} = 901$<br>$E_{21} = 896.4893$<br>$\hat{e}_{21} = 2.27^*$ | $O_{22} = 21$<br>$E_{22} = 26.2296$<br>$\hat{e}_{22} = 4.12^*$ | $O_{23} = 41$<br>$E_{23} = 40.2811$<br>$\hat{e}_{23} = 0.46$ | $R_2 = 963$ |
| **Column Total** | $C_1 = 957$ | $C_2 = 28$ | $C_3 = 43$ | $T = 1028$ |

Notes: $*\,p < .05$
$\chi^2 = 0.3362 + 15.4478 + 0.7190 + 0.2270 + 1.22555 + 0.01280 = 17.97$
$df = (2 - 1)(3 - 1) = 2$
$\Phi = \sqrt{\frac{17.97}{1028(2-1)}} = 0.13$

clinicians and with previous research. As they noted, however, "our study is one of few, to our knowledge, that have examined this relationship in randomly selected general population samples" (p. 810). They go on to note that using a clinical population for a sampling population introduces substantial bias that may confound the relation among the variables.

These data are interesting and should lead researchers to reconsider with care the relationship between sexual abuse and subsequent psychological disorders. The data also set the stage for additional research in this area. For example, Mulder et al. (1998) made a significant contribution by attempting to use a random sample of the general population. This tactic was definitely a step in the right direction, although we should ask whether sampling from a list of registered voters is representative of the general population. We may also want to raise questions concerning the measurement and classification of the various forms of abuse. It is possible that there are other variables lurking in the background. We do not know, for example, how often people experienced episodes of sexual or physical abuse. Perhaps it is not the type of abuse but the frequency of abuse that influences the risk of dissociative symptomatology. Perhaps it is the age of the victim at which the abuse is experienced. Hopefully future research will help us to understand these tragic occurrences better so that we may prevent them.

## Knowledge Check

1. A student conducts a study of binge drinking at her college. She randomly selects 300 students who attend a small liberal arts college and asks them to complete a questionnaire that examines their drinking behavior. The results of the questionnaire allow the researcher to identify students who engage in binge drinking. One question that she wants to address is whether there is a relation between sex and binge drinking. Here are the data from the study:

|  |  | Sex | |
|---|---|---|---|
|  |  | *Male* | *Female* |
| | *Yes* | 28 | 30 |
| **Binge Drinker** | | | |
| | *No* | 98 | 144 |

   Use these data to determine whether there is a relation between sex and binge drinking.

2. A social scientist wanted to find whether there are ways to increase the return rate of questionnaires sent in the mail. She randomly selected 300 people listed as registered voters and prepared to mail them a

short questionnaire with a stamped return envelope. For a random subsample of 100 people, the researcher first sent a separate letter explaining that the recipient would receive a survey and that it was essential to return the questionnaire. Another randomly selected 100 people received a telephone call explaining the importance of compliance. The other 100 people received no presurvey contact. The following data indicate the number who returned the survey (compliance) or did not return the survey.

|  | Presurvey Contact | | |
|---|---|---|---|
|  | *Letter* | *Phone Call* | *Nothing* |
| **Compliance** | 44 | 68 | 21 |
| **No Compliance** | 56 | 32 | 79 |

a. Is there evidence that there is a relation between the type of contact and the rate of compliance?
b. Which techniques appear to be the most successful in creating compliance?

## Chapter Summary

Many research projects use a nominal scale to assess the dependent or outcome variable. These data require a different statistical method for analysis. Therefore, the purpose of this chapter was to examine the analysis of categorical data using varieties of the analyses and appropriate follow-up tests. The goodness-of-fit test is a special version of the $\chi^2$ test that allows us to determine whether the observed frequencies differ from the expected values. As with most statistical tests, the $\chi^2$ is based on specific assumptions in order for its results to be validly interpreted. Specifically, the $\chi^2$ requires that the data the categories represent be mutually exclusive categories, that the observations be independent, and that the sample size be greater than five per category.

The $\chi^2$ test of independence allows us to determine whether two groups are independent. As with the $\chi^2$ goodness-of-fit test, the test of independence compares the difference between the observed and expected frequencies. As with other statistical tests, the $\chi^2$ has a number of post-hoc tests that allow us to analyze the data further. For example, Cramér's coefficient $\Phi$ allows us to determine the extent to which one variable predicts the other variable. The adjusted standardized residual allows us to convert the difference between the observed and expected frequencies to a $z$-score.

The McNemar test is another version of the $\chi^2$ test. It allows us to observe the change in frequencies that occur when monitoring participants on two occasions or when the participants are matched.

# Chapter Glossary for Review

**Adjusted residual ($\hat{e}$)**—An enhancement of $e$ that fits the normal distribution.

**Chi-square ($\chi$)**—A form of inferential statistic used to examine the frequencies of categorical, mutually exclusive classes. The statistic determines whether the observed frequencies equal hypothesized frequencies.

**Cramér's coefficient ($\Phi$)**—A descriptive statistic used with the $\chi^2$ test of independence to quantify the degree of association between the two categorical variables.

**Goodness-of-fit test**—A version of the $\chi^2$ test that determines whether a statistically significant difference exists between observed frequencies and expected frequencies within mutually exclusive classes.

**Mutually exclusive**—A classification scheme for which a person or observation may be placed into only one of the available categories (e.g., sex, political party, and religion).

**$\chi^2$ test of homogeneity**—A version of the $\chi^2$ test that determines whether the distribution of frequencies for independent populations is independent.

**$\chi^2$ test of independence**—A version of the $\chi^2$ test that determines whether the distribution of frequencies for two categorical variables is independent.

**Standardized residual ($e$)**—A descriptive statistic that indicates the relative difference between the observed and expected scores for a single condition in the $\chi^2$ test of independence.

# Chapter References

American Psychiatric Association (1994). *Diagnostic and statistical manual of mental disorders* (4th ed.). Washington, DC: Author.

American Psychological Association (2009). *Publication manual of the American Psychological Association* (6th ed.). Washington, DC: Author.

Cairns, R. B., Cairns, B. D., Neckerman, H. J., Ferguson, L. L., et al. (1989). Growth and aggression: I. Childhood to early adolescence. *Developmental Psychology*, *25*, 320–330.

Delucchi, K. L. (1993). On the use and misuse of the chi-square. In G. Keren & C. Lewis (Eds.), *A handbook for data analysis in the behavioral sciences: Statistical issues* (pp. 295–320). Hillsdale, NJ: LEA.

Gladstone, G., Parker, G., Wilhelm, K., Mitchell, P., & Austin, M. (1999). Characteristics of depressed patients who report childhood sexual abuse. *American Journal of Psychiatry*, *156*, 431–437.

Good, I. J., Grover, T. N., & Mitchell, G. J. (1970). Exact distributions for chi-squared and for the likelihood-ratio statistic for the equiprobable multinomial distribution. *Journal of the American Statistical Association*, *32*, 535–548.

Haberman, S. J. (1973). The analysis of residuals in cross-classified tables. *Biometrics*, *29*, 205–220.

Mulder, R. T., Beautrais, A. L., Joyce, P. R., & Fergusson, D. M. (1998). Relationship between dissociation, childhood sexual abuse, childhood physical abuse, and mental illness in a general population sample. *American Journal of Psychiatry, 155*, 806–811.

Siegel, S., & Castellan, N. J. (1988). *Nonparametric statistics for the behavioral sciences* (2nd ed.). New York: McGraw-Hill.

# Chapter 17
# Qualitative and Mixed-Methods Research

## CHAPTER OBJECTIVES

Introduction
Qualitative versus Quantitative Research
Theory and Perspectives Guiding Qualitative Research
Mixing Methods: Quantitative and Qualitative Combined
Qualitative and Mixed-Methods Data Collection and Analysis
Benefits and Challenges of Mixed-Methods Research
Sources of Published Qualitative and Mixed-Methods Research
Research in Action: Gender- and Job-Based Differences
   in Work Stress

> You may have heard the world is made up of atoms and molecules, but it's really made up of stories. When you sit with an individual that's been here, you can give quantitative data a qualitative overlay.
>
> —William Turner

## Introduction

Up to this point we have discussed research methods that are primarily quantitative. In other words, they require you to collect some sort of numerical information ranging from observations of frequency and intensity of behaviors to participant responses to scale or survey questions. As we have illustrated in the preceding chapters, in many areas of the social sciences these types of quantitative observations are tremendously useful. There are times, however, when the goal of research is not so much to quantify an effect or difference between groups, but rather to more descriptively explain or qualify a phenomenon.

Our purpose in this chapter is to provide you with a slightly different set of research tools and to remind you one final time that it is your research question that should drive the method you use, not the other way around. This being the case, there will likely be times in your future career (whatever that may be) when you will want to ask a question that requires less quantification and more qualification, fewer numbers and statistics, and more detail and description. In these cases, a qualitative and/or combined qualitative and quantitative method for data collection and analysis may be useful to you. The present chapter is designed to provide you with the most basic overview possible. Many other excellent sources exist throughout most social science disciplines for more detailed treatment of all of the information presented here. If you are interested in learning more than what we can provide in this brief chapter, please begin by checking out the works we have cited in this chapter and included in the chapter references.

## Qualitative versus Quantitative Research

Whereas quantitative research is designed to empirically identify the presence and magnitude of differences between individuals and/or groups of individuals, **qualitative research** is typically more focused on sense-making in a purer sense. Quantitative research is also typically designed to test predetermined hypotheses that are formed based on existing theory (a deductive process), while qualitative research often functions to develop theory from the data that are collected (an inductive process). With these two distinctions in mind, it is also often suggested that qualitative research tends to focus more on rich description of a phenomenon than on its quantification. Thus, instead of relying on numbers, counts, and frequency-type data, qualitative research will often involve the collection and analysis of detailed observations, stories or narrative histories, sounds, pictures, or video.

Qualitative methods often bring a new or fresh perspective to existing research in fields of science that have been dominated by quantitative methods. When combined with quantitative techniques, qualitative strategies can often help researchers to more strongly support their research design choices and final inferences (Shaw, 2003). For example, in the case of healthcare-related interventions, which are implemented in highly complex environments, answering the question of why some interventions work while others fail is not easily done within a quantitative framework. Such a question can be more comprehensively addressed with the use of a qualitative or combination of qualitative and quantitative (i.e., **mixed-methods**) strategy (O'Cathain, 2009).

Despite the prevalence of qualitative methods in some social science areas (e.g., ethnography, sociology), there has not been widespread acceptance of qualitatively influenced research within psychology and other fields. The reasons for this are varied and not fully understood, although one major contributing factor has been the lack of education regarding these methods, especially within the field of psychology (Tashakkori & Teddlie, 2003; Teddlie & Tashakkori, 2003). Apart from differences in education or formal training, it has also been suggested that qualitative researchers are somehow inherently different from quantitative researchers in terms of their perspectives on research methodologies and their goals for research studies.

Although these and other reasons may be true, we also believe that these reasons do not support the continued separation of quantitative and qualitative research methods. There are many reasons for this, not the least of which being that the benefits of combining these two general approaches to research often outweigh the challenges, as we discuss later in this chapter. It is interesting to note that Corbin and Strauss (2008) suggest that the best qualitative researchers may share a set of personal characteristics that at first look seem antithetical to what is conveyed during standard quantitative method instruction. Specifically, they suggest that good qualitative researchers are those who, among other things, are: (1) interested in the humanism present in everyday life; (2) inherently curious, creative, and imaginative; (3) capable of guiding their actions in a logical fashion; (4) able to live with and appreciate ambiguity; and (5) capable of accepting themselves as a research instrument (p. 13).

Careful consideration of these characteristics outlined by Corbin and Strauss (2008), however, should make it clear to you that these are the same qualities that ensure success as a researcher in any field, using any combination of methods. The only difference that immediately emerges here is that while qualitative researchers do typically acknowledge themselves as a major part of the research instrument and process, quantitative researchers are often interested in removing themselves as much as possible from the research process so as to minimize the influence of potential sources of systematic error or bias.

## Theory and Perspectives Guiding Qualitative Research

At the heart of most qualitative research is a belief that understanding about a phenomenon can be induced from the data as they are collected. This emergent perspective on theory development has been criticized and modified many times in the recent decades, but it remains in some way, shape, or form an underlying distinguishing feature of this type of research from the more deductive, theory-based reasoning applied in most quantitative research. Perhaps the most well-known discussion of this inductivist approach to qualitative research is contained within explanations of the **grounded theory** methodology, which remains a common guiding perspective for many qualitative researchers. By definition, this orientation toward research implies that one develops the relevant theory for a study from the data as they are collected and analyzed in a qualitative fashion (Glaser & Strauss, 1967; Locke, 2001).

The primary challenge to pure or "simplistic inductivism" (Silverman, 2005) is the fact that no matter how detached a researcher may wish to be from existing theory and preconceptions, when we enter into a research situation we will have an impact on that system. In previous chapters we have referred to this impact using words such as *reactivity* or citing Bacon's Idols to remind us that when we carry preconceptions into the data collection or analysis process we may influence our findings and interpretations. All of these risks also exist in the case of qualitative research, and for this reason there is no way to ensure that the development of understanding can occur completely from the data and not from the researcher's own experience or knowledge.

Indeed, it is increasingly common to see modern qualitative research guided by some (at least loosely) preconceived hypotheses. This is also a reflection of the trend in qualitative research away from a singular model or paradigm of study toward multiple approaches to this type of research (Teddlie & Tashakkori, 2003). A primary reason for this is that just as in quantitative research, the body of scientific knowledge is cumulative and as it develops it becomes more difficult (and not desirable) to ignore it completely when initiating a research study. As we have emphasized and discussed in multiple ways in this textbook, your challenge is not to reinvent the wheel, but rather to continue the development and modification of the entire vehicle to which that wheel belongs.

## Mixing Methods: Quantitative and Qualitative Combined

In many cases, qualitative research is based on a different set of theories regarding the research process. In some forms of qualitative work the research questions emerge from the data, rather than the data being gathered to address specific hypotheses that are stated at the beginning of the study design process. In addition to a different perspective on the research process itself, qualitative research often requires a different set of data collection tools. Some of these we have already discussed, but in their quantitative forms. The following sections will detail more fully some of the most common prevailing theories and methods used in qualitative research.

Despite the differences in these two general approaches to research, there are times when it is appropriate to combine these methods. Such combination can take place during any of several stages of the research process, from identification of research questions and hypotheses, through sampling and selection of participants, through the actual collection, analysis, and interpretation of the data. In many cases these two approaches may be mixed at more than one stage of the process. Mixed-methods research can be seen as

> [t]he type of research in which a researcher or team of researchers combines elements of qualitative and quantitative research approaches (e.g., use of qualitative and quantitative viewpoints, data collection, analysis, inference techniques) for the broad purposes of breadth and depth of understanding and corroboration. (Johnson, Onwuegbuzie, & Turner, 2007, p. 123)

What does mixed-methods research look like? It really depends on how quantitative or qualitative the research is in its underlying nature. Bryman (2006) offers several insights regarding these issues in his qualitative content analysis of 232 social science articles based on mixed-methods research. In general, Bryman's findings suggest that the most common mixed-methods approaches have, to this point, included either a self-administered survey or questionnaire, or a structured or semistructured interview. The vast majority of studies in this review were also of a cross-sectional variety, meaning all data were collected concurrently at one point in time.

After coding the reasons for mixed-methods work given by the authors of the studies that Bryman (2006) reviewed, a list of the common reasons or justifications for combining quantitative and qualitative methods was generated. Because these reasons sometimes differed from what was actually practiced by the researchers and shared in the article, Bryman also coded the articles for what was actually practiced. The top five most common explanations for mixed-methods research actually demonstrated in these published articles were (adapted from p. 108):

1. *Enhancement*: building on findings from one method using evidence gathered from the other method

2. *Triangulation*: using findings from one method to verify or corroborate findings collected using the other method

3. *Completeness*: using both methods to more comprehensively examine an area or issue of interest than would be possible with one method used alone

4. *Illustration*: using qualitative data to explain quantitative findings, or vice versa

5. *Sampling*: using one method to help with the sampling of participants or cases in a targeted and focused fashion

Although Bryman's (2006) findings suggest there may be disconnect between what researchers say they are doing and what they actually accomplish when attempting mixed-methods research, a more important implication is that the combination of quantitative and qualitative methods benefits researchers in multiple ways, providing all of us with improved information and richness of detail that is not obtained when singular methods are utilized.

So, when should you consider qualitative or mixed-methods research methods? In general, when your research questions are more in line with developing understanding than identifying differences, some form of qualitative inquiry may be helpful. Perhaps the set of considerations listed in Box 17.1 will be even more useful to you when you develop your research design.

---

### Box 17.1  Qualitative or Mixed-Methods May Be a Good Idea If . . .

- . . . you are not totally sure what the question is that you are trying to answer, but you know where you might start looking for relevant information.

- . . . your goal is to study a particular phenomenon within its natural context, in detail.

- . . . other researchers who have studied this topic have relied on qualitative or mixed-methods (and you agree with this approach).

*(Continued)*

*(Continued)*

- . . . other researchers have relied on quantitative methods to study this issue (and you disagree with this approach and want to try something else).

- . . . it is feasible/practical for you to engage in qualitative inquiry given your available resources (i.e., you have a fair amount of time and interest).

- . . . you feel you will learn more about the topic using these methods than quantitative techniques alone.

- . . . you feel sufficiently comfortable with qualitative or mixed-methods research techniques to use them.

*Note*: Adapted from Silverman (2005).

## Qualitative and Mixed-Methods Data Collection and Analysis

There are numerous qualitative research techniques in use today. The one feature they all share in common is that they are designed to allow the researcher to gather a very rich and complex dataset. These methods are also designed to assist the researcher in making sense of the rich data collected. To give you a taste for what qualitative research techniques and analyses look like, we have selected a few very common ones to briefly present to you here.

### Data Collection Techniques

In many ways, the same rules for good design of quantitative research studies still apply when qualitative data are involved. There are a few areas, however, where these two general types of methods diverge. One major area has to do with sampling, in that much qualitative research is directed at a particular sample and as such may not lend itself to the use of random sampling as easily as standard quantitative studies. Instead, it is more common to see purposive and/or stratified sampling techniques utilized within qualitative studies to ensure that the phenomenon or process of interest will be observed. As an example, a qualitative researcher (likely an ethnomusicologist) interested in studying the role that music plays in the cultural expression and social functioning of a small tribe in Africa would focus on gathering observations and data from members of that tribe who perform and/or take part in musical events within that community.

#### Field Notes
A second major area of difference between typical quantitative and qualitative methods pertains to the central role of field notes. In general, **field notes** are detailed observations made by the researcher on a regular basis

throughout the research process. These types of notes often include observations made about the people and places in which data are being collected. Also included will be personal reflections on the data and research process as well as initial attempts to begin piecing together the story or puzzle that the data are hopefully going to reveal. We recommend to our students that keeping field notes is good practice for all types of research (quantitative and qualitative), but it becomes absolutely necessary for qualitative research that is based on observations within a specific context. They often provide the only reliable source of information that the researcher can later use to interpret and make sense of various participants' responses within those specific contexts.

Wolfinger (2002) indicates that the generation of field notes is in itself both a skill and an art. As such, the most effective strategy for field notes will depend on the research. From a practical perspective, he notes that there are three general considerations that may influence a researcher's field note-taking strategy:

1. The researcher's ability to take notes in the field (i.e., can observations be recorded in real time, or do they need to be summarized at the end of a period of more secretive or participant-type involvement?).

2. The degree to which the research has changed as the researcher narrows from a broad concept to more focused data collection needs (i.e., this will change the types of information the researcher can and will attend to).

3. The intended audience of this research (i.e., depending on where this work will be presented or published, different types of information may need to be emphasized).

In terms of how to actually condense and summarize your field notes, some guidance can be gleaned from Emerson, Fretz, and Shaw (1995) and from Wolfinger's (2002) extension of Emerson et al.'s work. One technique is to focus on the observations you have made during the data collection that seem most unique, special, or interesting (i.e., salient episodes). To most quantitatively trained researchers, this approach seems less than desirable primarily because the identification of such salient episodes is based on each researcher's highly subjective judgment. However, as Wolfinger points out, the identification of these special events can be guided by at least two general rules of thumb: typically that the information may "stick out" or distinguish itself (1) from the other responses collected by the researcher or (2) from what the research was expecting to observe (p. 89).

A second general technique for field note-taking and organization is to be as comprehensive or thorough as possible, describing all details that you can capture about your observations during a set time period. For this technique to be most beneficial, the notes should be generated in a systematic fashion, meaning that the researcher should follow a note-taking guide of sorts, which helps him or her provide all relevant details. As highlighted by Wolfinger (2002), such a list can include the basics of *who, what, when, where,* and *why,* expanded to fit the situation, or it can be focused on components of the observable situation, including such features as the space, actor, activity, time, goal, and feelings (for more details on these and other approaches to field-note taking, see also Lofland, Snow, Anderson, & Lofland, 2005). It is also possible to organize comprehensive field notes in some form of chronological order, which can often help researchers remember details of their observations that they may otherwise miss (Wolfinger).

One of the most difficult things for field researchers of any discipline to learn is to separate the act of information gathering from interpretation. We like to think of it in rather simple terms: When you are in the field collecting data (whether it is quantitative or qualitative by nature), you should act like a sponge—nothing more, nothing less. Then, once you are finished with the data, you can wring yourself out and attempt to make sense of what you have just learned. The reason for this is that if you are constantly allowing yourself to interpret data as you perceive it (especially when you are gathering observations), then you are more likely to confine yourself to only information that connects with your preconceived notions (also known as *tacit beliefs,* as noted by Wolfinger, 2002). If instead you allow yourself to take in all information that you possibly can, your later interpretation will be based on a more complete set of details.

### *Other Techniques*

Apart from differences in sampling and the critical role of field notes, many other qualitative or mixed-methods data collection techniques have actually already been presented in earlier portions of this textbook. Table 17.1 highlights a few of these methods, illustrating how they can be used for primarily quantitative or qualitative research means.

Obviously this is a very abbreviated summary and illustration of how similar methods can be used in both quantitative and qualitative ways. An extension of this is that these methods can also be used in mixed-methods fashion, incorporating elements of quantitative and qualitative focus to help the researcher achieve his or her aims. There are many other approaches to data collection within qualitative research, but most of these ways involve elements of the handful of techniques summarized in Table 17.1. More than anything, the distinction between quantitative and qualitative data collection is often that qualitative data involve more than finite numbers, and often include details regarding behavioral processes and contextual factors that may be linked to what the participant or respondent does or says.

### Analytical Approaches

Although we have said that qualitative research is often more about sense-making than hypothesis testing, this does not mean that you are allowed to forget everything else you have learned up to this point about appropriate analytical techniques. On the contrary, the systematic research process is at least as important in qualitative research as it is in the quantitative forms we

Table 17.1   **Application of Similar Methods for Quantitative and Qualitative Research**

| | Research Method | |
| --- | --- | --- |
| | **Quantitative Examples** | **Qualitative Examples** |
| *Behavioral Observations* | Counting frequency<br>Rating intensity | Describing process or actions<br>Highlighting perceived causes and effects |
| *Interviews* | Rating specific responses of the interviewee to specific questions for quality or accuracy | Recording and transcribing the entirety of the interview experience, including interviewer questions, interviewee responses, gaps in conversation, etc., viewing all as meaningful information and reflections of interviewees' own reality |
| *Survey* | Gathering self-ratings of agreement or satisfaction with descriptive items and scales | Eliciting writing responses to open-ended questions or comment-request boxes |
| *Case Study* | Small-*n* or single-participant study of changes in behaviors, attitudes, or other measurable variables | More in-depth review of individualized cases, with goal of providing detail regarding context and process, rather than generalizable quantified effects |

*Note:* Portions adapted from Patton (2002), Rapley (2001), Silverman (2005), and Shaw (2003).

have already discussed. The reason for this should be rather clear to you, when you remember why we strive for systematic processes of data collection and analysis in the first place. Remember Bacon's Idols? We know it has probably been a while since you read Chapter 1, but our point here is that while quantitative research can be valid only when based on good design and systematic measurement with high-quality measures, qualitative research can be only as valid as the process that the researcher follows when gathering and interpreting the data.

This being said, it is very common for qualitative researchers to view their analyses as a combination of science and art (Corbin & Strauss, 2008). This view may seem to contradict the emphasis we have placed on the scientific method throughout this textbook. In reality, though, your efforts to adhere to the basic scientific method will at times test you and require you to adapt and respond in ways that you can do effectively only if you are able to be creative and imaginative. In this way, it can be argued that all forms of research involve, at some level, a mixture of science and art.

Indeed, there may be more room for flexibility and imagination within qualitative research than in quantitative analyses because the objectives are typically rather different. More specifically, in quantitative research the objective of an analysis is typically to quantify a difference between groups, a change over time, or the existence of a measurable phenomenon. In qualitative research, the emphasis is on telling a story or piecing together a puzzle that can help to explain a particular phenomenon and its relationship to other factors in the people and environment(s) involved.

Because of this, there is often a distinction to be made regarding the role of participant responses when the data collection method involves direct communication with respondents (e.g., interviews, case studies, content analysis). This distinction pertains to whether the responses are viewed as representative of that person's external reality or internal experience. A related approach to analysis partially avoids this distinction, choosing to highlight instead the possibility that responses are really constructed narratives that capture the respondents' perceptions within a specified context (Silverman, 2005). In effect, this narrative approach to analysis of responses may enhance the realism and eventual generalizability of the qualitative researchers' conclusions as it facilitates a more comprehensive consideration of the context in which the responses were generated.

Another distinction with respect to analysis between qualitative and quantitative research is that qualitative researchers are often taught to begin their analysis of the data as soon as the first piece of information is collected (Corbin & Strauss, 2008). This is in direct contrast to most quantitative research, in which analyses are often delayed until the full set of data can be collected. There are several reasons for this rather obvious difference between these two approaches to research. A primary one is that the theory that will be used to explain findings is often derived from the data in qualitative research, whereas it is established beforehand in quantitative research, as already mentioned. This being the case, it is necessary for qualitative researchers to begin developing the explanatory framework, story, or theory immediately so that it can be as comprehensive as possible upon project completion.

While experimental methods are necessary in order to most effectively demonstrate causality, taking a qualitative perspective can aid in identifying causal mechanisms, identifying the ordering of events across time, and facilitating the interpretation of complex relationships among variables (Miles & Huberman, 1994). The rationale behind this perspective is that qualitative techniques may facilitate more complete consideration of contextual factors and potential third variables (or confounds, as discussed earlier in this textbook), making it possible to understand the true nature of the causal effect.

With respect to common mixed-methods analytical approaches, one very commonly used technique involves the coding of data into categories (Duriau, Reger, & Pfarrer, 2007). These categories can be created for the purposes of quantification or qualification, making this technique especially useful to the beginning researcher interested in mixed-methods research. The goal with **content analysis** is typically to quantify otherwise-qualitative data. Although this may sound confusing or somehow contradictory to the goal of qualitative research, it really is not. Such quantification is often done to identify the qualitative content areas that are of highest importance or greatest prevalence.

The qualitative aspect of this analytical approach comes into play during the formation of content categories. In addition, once the categories are formed and data are sorted, a new door may be opened to more discussion or data collection to try to explain the initial categorization findings. Content categories may be defined beforehand, based on existing theory and/or relevant literature, or they may be developed from the data themselves once they are collected. This latter form is often referred to as *thematic coding*, although it is common to see *content* and *thematic coding* used interchangeably.

As summarized in Duriau et al. (2007), there are multiple sets of guidelines in the literature regarding the proper steps in a content analysis. One of the most common ones is associated with Weber's (1990) discussion of the content-coding process. Table 17.2 summarizes these steps, also adapting the simplified presentation made by Duriau et al.

Thematic coding differs from other, more quantitatively oriented forms of content coding. The goal of thematic coding is typically to extract themes from a set of data. Typically these data are verbal in nature, either collected via open-ended survey or interview questions, or extracted from communication records (e.g., e-mail or Internet chat logs). Thematic coding also can be used with records of speeches or recorded dialogues between people. Conceptually, the same strategies used when extracting themes from any of these forms of data could be used with video of a person's movements or nonverbal behaviors as well, although this is not an area in which this analytical technique is typically employed.

In thematic coding, the first task of the researcher is typically to get very familiar with the data that have been collected. By reviewing the material closely and comparing one person's responses to another's, for example, the researcher will likely start to see patterns emerge in the responses. For example, when doing organizational surveys regarding employee satisfaction or morale, it is common to ask respondents to provide "any other comments" they might have regarding what is more or less satisfying to them at work. As one begins to sift through these responses it typically becomes clear that most issues will fall into a smaller subset of

## Table 17.2 Common Content Analysis Steps

(1) Define the recording unit (word, phrase, sentence, paragraph).

(2) Define the coding categories.

(3) Test the coding by applying it to a sample of your collected data.

(4) Assess the accuracy and reliability of this sample coding (perhaps using multiple coders to check for intercoder consistency).

(5) Revise the coding rules and/or instructions to improve consistency and accuracy in coding.

(6) Return to step 3 and run the cycle until you achieve sufficient consistency and accuracy in coding.

(7) Code all data.

(8) Assess overall consistency and accuracy of the codings.

*Note:* Adapted from Weber (1990), pp. 21–25 and Duriau et al. (2007), p. 19.

categories, often involving pay, supervisors/management, coworkers, work environment concerns, and aspects of the job itself. In addition, if the job is a service job, it is not uncommon to see a thread of responses all related to interactions with difficult customers.

By sorting and labeling responses into thematic categories, the qualitative research can begin to make sense of the rich information that has been provided. The goal in thematic coding is not necessarily to quantify the number of responses per category (although that is always an option), but rather to identify which categories are most prevalent and/or important to respondents and then to dig into the responses in those categories to start to make sense of whatever phenomenon is under study. As an example, consider a study by Santos, Ortiz, Morales, and Rosales (2007), in which the meaning of ethnic identity was explored, with an emphasis on how this was associated with students' adjustment to college in ethnically diverse college settings.

Although some studies regarding these issues had been performed with quantitative surveys, Santos et al. decided to lean more on qualitative semistructured interviews with each participant as their data collection strategy. The semistructured nature of these interviews means that while all students were asked the same 13 general questions, additional probe or follow-up questions were also used if necessary to elicit sufficient detail from respondents regarding the five core issues Santos et al. were interested in examining: (1) ethnic identification, (2) personal meaning of ethnicity, (3) expressions of ethnicity, (4) influences of interethnic interactions on ethnicity, and (5) sociohistorical forces that have impinged on ethnic identity.

The data from these interviews were then content analyzed to identify representative themes. To minimize the influence of the two primary researchers' experience in this area of study, they used the skills of two student assistants (the last two authors on the paper) to assist in the coding. Nevertheless, despite this precaution, Santos et al. (2007) clearly note that because they are all of Latino heritage, "bias may have unintentionally entered the data analysis process" (p. 106). The steps in their content analysis followed very closely those outlined by Weber (1990) and summarized in Table 17.2. At multiple points, the consistency among codings was checked with interrater or intercoder reliability estimates. Defined themes served as the core categories into which the interview data were separated.

From this careful approach to qualitative content analysis and thematic coding, Santos et al. (2007) identified nine themes associated with ethnic diversity and the student participants' experience on college campuses. These themes could be further grouped into positive and negative groupings. The positive themes included: sense of belonging, multicultural competence, evolving ethnic identity, interethnic connectedness, and politicized ethnicity. The negative themes were: ethnic discomfort, perceived discrimination, interethnic tension, and ethnic segregation (p. 107).

Instead of merely reporting the prevalence of these types of themes in a quantitative summary table (what would be a very nonqualitative analysis of qualitative data), Santos et al. (2007) used the qualitative data from the interviews to further describe and illustrate each of these nine themes. There is insufficient space here to represent all of this, but to give you a sense for these illustrations, Table 17.3 captures a few examples of the positive and negative themes. You will find much more detail in Santos et al.'s (2007) article.

## Benefits and Challenges of Mixed-Methods Research

In this chapter we have tried to present you with a general overview of perspectives on qualitative and mixed-methods research theory and analytical methods. In case you have not already identified our bias in this

### Table 17.3  Themes and Supporting Example Interview Responses from Santos et al. (2007)

| Themes | Illustration/Example |
| --- | --- |
| *Positive Themes* | |
| Sense of belonging | There is so much diversity [here], it helps me to feel comfortable and if people do look at me differently, I do not notice it. I do not think people look at me and say, "Look there is a Korean girl." No, it's just another . . . student. (from a Korean American participant) |
| Multicultural competence | I like the diversity, there's a good blend here . . . You don't understand how people are unless you're in contact with them and talk to them. I think being here has helped me understand the plight of different ethnic groups. |
| Interethnic connectedness | Everyone here is an [campus mascot name]. We are all the same age basically . . . so it's easy to find people that have the same interest. When people have closer interests, it's easier to accept someone into your group. There's still that common ground. (from a White participant) |
| *Negative Themes* | |
| Feelings of ethnic discomfort | I am not sure what it means to be White really. There are so many functions, like Black History Month, the Cinco de Mayo celebration, and there's not really a White celebration. I don't really see anything on this campus for my culture. I kind of feel left out. (from a White participant) |
| Perceptions of discrimination | I just feel that being an Asian minority is limiting. Like, you know. If you're supposedly going [here] there's a lot of Asians there. You might have a better GPA than another person of a different ethnic group that you hardly see at that school; they'll get in before you because of their ethnic background and race. I thought that was pretty unfair. |
| Interethnic tension | Caucasians move back a little to let you through. They do this to prevent any type of conflict between African Americans and Caucasians. I guess I can understand that [Whites] just want to avoid a conflict, but they act as though, gosh you know, [African Americans] might try and beat me up or something. |

chapter, we believe that it is rarely the case that a research study is best served by *either* qualitative or quantitative methods. In many, dare we say *most* cases, the researcher can learn the most about a phenomenon by using a combined, mixed-methods approach.

This mixing of methods can be done at the same time or sequentially, with some data collected quantitatively and other data collected qualitatively, for instance. The mixing can apply to the collection and analysis of data. Combining qualitative and quantitative methods is also a fantastic way that you as a researcher can successfully apply principles of data triangulation to ensure you are gaining the clearest possible understanding of the phenomenon you are studying. As you will recall from earlier in this text, *triangulation* refers to the process of operationalizing and measuring constructs or variables in multiple ways to converge upon a more accurate observation or assessment (Webb, Campbell, Schwartz, & Sechrest, 1966/2000). This can include multiple approaches within either quantitative or qualitative methodologies, or a combination of the two.

The mixing of these two more general forms of research has been around for quite some time, but it has recently been gaining in popularity (Teddlie & Tashakkori, 2003). Underlying most mixed-methods research efforts is the guiding philosophy that quantitative and qualitative methods are compatible and complementary (Teddlie & Tashakkori). When are mixed methods most appropriate? A mixed-methods approach is most appropriate if you think a combination of quantitative and qualitative methods will help you to answer your research questions as clearly as possible (Teddlie & Tashakkori). In a related fashion, the use of mixed methods makes it possible for you to engage in both theory testing and theory building within the same research project.

These benefits are all that most researchers need in order to at least consider the opportunities of mixed-methods research. If this is not enough, there are other more practical, yet related reasons. Although most physical sciences lend themselves to quantification of observations and measurements, researchers in the social sciences are challenged with the goal of understanding phenomena that exist within and between people. As noted throughout this text, our efforts to operationalize and quantify psychological and social constructs are always limited by the presence of error. Although we have highlighted many strategies for minimizing error through careful design and planning of research throughout this textbook, there are also elements of error that cannot be fully avoided, due to the idiosyncrasies of study participants and the situations in which research is conducted. In many of these research situations it is valuable to collect data with a variety of methods.

At times this can be done within the confines of either a quantitative or qualitative research framework, but it is often the case that a mixed-methods approach will provide more comprehensive information. This can have value for your ability to draw accurate and rational inferences from your data. It can also have positive implications for the external validity or generalizability of your findings, in that a combination of quantitative and qualitative data is likely to provide you with a clearer picture of the

## Table 17.4  Tips for Successfully Combining Quantitative and Qualitative Methods

(1)  Keep good field notes. This will be especially useful to you if/when some aspect of your quantitative analyses does not fully make sense.

(2)  When measuring specific constructs, include an opportunity for participants to provide their own description or definition of what you are trying to measure, perhaps with an open-ended response option or comment box.

(3)  Collect observations while collecting survey responses; focus on the environment and the nonverbals in the participants (similar to field notes, but perhaps more specific).

(4)  When planning for the use of multiple methods (triangulation), utilize at least one more qualitative technique such as interviews, focus groups, or textual analysis.

(5)  When developing your discussion of your findings, look for ways to encourage both quantitative and qualitative forms of follow-up research based on your findings.

phenomenon as it functions within a detailed and specific context. Assuming valid inferences are made from the data you collect, the use of mixed methods should enhance your ability to retain the transferability of inferences across situations, populations, and time periods (Teddlie & Tashakkori, 2003).

As a concluding summary statement, we thought it might be helpful to list for you in Table 17.4 a few clear examples of ways in which you can meaningfully connect quantitative and qualitative research methods into your own research.

### Challenges of Qualitative and Mixed-Methods Research

There are many challenges associated with the effort to integrate quantitative and qualitative methods. It is not as simple as deciding to do so. Bryman (2007) undertook his own mixed-methods study of these issues and found that there are several core explanations for why quantitative and qualitative methods may not "play nice" and integrate well within a particular study. Among the many reasons that emerged from his interviews with researchers were:

1.  A tendency to report only the qualitative or the quantitative data, but not both

2.  A tendency to report findings for one method, followed by findings from the other method, without any attempt at integration

3.  The perceived need to focus the presentation of results toward either a quantitatively or qualitatively focused audience

4.  A personal preference or comfort with one method over the other

5.  A research design that inhibits the integration of quantitative and qualitative data (e.g., if the quantitative structure overly limits the qualitative follow-up)

6. The pressure to publish some results as quickly as possible, which might push the researcher to lean on one method more than the other

7. Skill deficits regarding one method or the other, which might force the researcher to use one technique more

8. The tendency for some journals to favor one type of data more than the other, influencing the researchers' leanings

It is our hope that by making you aware of these common barriers to successful integration of quantitative and qualitative methods, you will be better prepared to avoid or resolve these issues when they arise in your own research.

Apart from actual barriers to the successful use of mixed methods in research, there are also lingering questions about the validity of qualitative research. Cho and Trent (2006) point out that this "attack" on validity is increasing and is in large part due to the insistence that scientific research is used to support practice, and that this science should have evidence of replicability, testable hypotheses, and objective measurement procedures, all of which are techniques foreign to most qualitative researchers (p. 319). The standard perspective on validity within qualitative research is that it is linked to the correspondence between what the researcher observed or studied and what is true in reality (Cho & Trent).

Two newer perspectives regarding the validity of qualitative research are referred to as *transactional* and *transformational* validity. Cho and Trent (2006) define transactional validity as "an interactive process between the researcher, the researched, and the collected data that is aimed at achieving a relatively higher level of accuracy and consensus by means of revisiting facts, feelings, experiences, and values or beliefs collected and interpreted" (p. 322). In many ways, the techniques used by the researcher are seen as the means to achieving high levels of this type of validity. This is similar to the use of highly reliable scales in quantitative research as being necessary to lead to valid inferences. Among the widespread techniques for enhancing this form of validity in qualitative research is **member checking**, or reviewing data/observations with the respondent to ensure the information was collected accurately and to gather further reactions from the respondent (Cho & Trent).

Evidence of transformational validity develops through the research process and is not contingent on the particular techniques used by the researcher (Cho & Trent, 2006). The real support for the transformational validity of a study comes from its influence on the actions of others (i.e., the degree to which the study motivates some sort of action or change in others; Cho & Trent). As Cho and Trent are careful to note, however, there is no way to guarantee that any set of techniques will lead to valid conclusions. Each qualitative study presents researchers with similar challenges to quantitative studies: Validity is a goal that all forms of research must strive to achieve.

# Sources of Published Qualitative and Mixed-Methods Research

This being the case, where can you turn for good examples of solid qualitative and mixed-methods research? As mentioned early in this chapter, it is still not yet very common to see much qualitative research published within psychological and some sociological outlets. In large part this is due to the lack of consistent or readily available guidance regarding how such research should be presented in writing (Bryman, 2007). This is, however, changing as researchers increasingly see the benefits. In recent years several very good examples of qualitative and mixed-methods research have been published in solid research outlets. Among the most common peer-reviewed journals publishing qualitative research are *Journal of Mixed Methods Research*, *Qualitative Research*, and *Qualitative Inquiry*.

With respect for how to go about publishing mixed-methods research, there is an increasing amount of attention paid to this issue, especially by those interested in improving education regarding these methods. If you find yourself in a position to be publishing qualitative or mixed-methods research, we strongly recommend that you first read Kidd (2002) for some practical guidance regarding qualitative research. Kidd found that there was increasing interest in reading qualitative research, but that there are not consistent guidelines or standards for evaluating it in many well-established psychology journals. This being the case, it is of the utmost importance for you to clearly, concisely, but thoroughly, describe your qualitatively oriented research so that others actually can understand you.

For mixed-methods research, Creswell and Tashakkori (2007) suggest in an editorial in the *Journal of Mixed Methods Research* that articles summarizing the results of mixed-methods research should "report both qualitative and quantitative research and include both approaches in the data collection, analysis, integration, and the inferences drawn from the results" (p. 108). Creswell and Tashakkori also summarize some core features of high-quality mixed-methods journal articles, highlighting the following features:

- Well-developed quantitative *and* qualitative components (the writing should not emphatically favor one method over the other and both components should be evident through most if not all phases of the research process).

- An effort should be made to integrate the quantitative and qualitative components, rather than treating them as separate elements (this should facilitate more complete understanding of the findings).

- The methods reported should in some way build on existing methods (i.e., authors should emphasize the contribution of their research methodology to the broader field).

We acknowledge that these are criteria for publication in one journal, but these criteria are good guiding rules for any journal in which you may hope to publish your own mixed-methods research. We hope these, combined with our earlier discussion of writing up your research, will help you effectively present all your hard work.

## Research in Action: Gender- and Job-Based Differences in Work Stress

Our final "Research in Action" section presents you with a recent example of a mixed-methods study from the field of occupational health psychology. As you might imagine, mixed-methods studies can range in the degree to which they represent more of a quantitative, qualitative, or truly balanced mix of quantitative and qualitative methods. Given the primary orientation of this textbook, we have identified an example that represents a quantitatively framed, mixed-methods consideration of occupational stress differences between men and women and across different job or occupational groups (Liu, Spector, & Shi, 2008).

This study was designed to address a large number of hypotheses, all of which were focused on possible differences between men and women, and across various occupational groupings. The general objective was to see whether the stress experience differed qualitatively across these different classifications. As Liu et al. (2008) summarize in the introduction to their article, there is substantial evidence in the published literature that suggests men and women experience stress differently. In addition, evidence compiled across many studies of occupational stress done in many different jobs, along with the objective differences in characteristics between jobs, supports the expectation that there would be differences in the experience of stress across occupations.

The experience of stress is a very difficult construct to operationalize or adequately measure. From earlier chapters in this textbook you should remember that an inability to operationalize a construct clearly really challenges the researcher's ability to eventually build support for the construct validity of any measure of that construct. This is one reason why Liu et al. (2008) decided to use a mixed-methods approach in this study: To better assess the stress experience they found it beneficial to collect both qualitative and quantitative evidence of exposure to stressors in the work environment.

How did they do this? Liu et al. (2008) surveyed a sample of university faculty and support staff. Although surveying is typically connected only with quantitative research, it is possible to utilize open-ended questions and other forms of nonconstructed responses to elicit qualitative information from respondents. In this case, the qualitative information pertained to participants' descriptions of a stressful event that occurred at work within the previous 30 days. This assessment of stress is known as the Stress Incident Record (SIR, originally developed by Keenan & Newton, 1985). In addition to these open responses, participants were asked to provide quantitative self-ratings of two stressors (interpersonal conflict and job autonomy) and several strains often associated with the experience of job-related stress (frustration, negative emotions at work, job satisfaction, turnover intentions, and physical symptoms).

Quantitative data from this study were scored following the standard guidelines for the various measures. The qualitative data collected with the Stress Incident Record (179 described stress incidents) were content analyzed. Weber's (1990) procedures (detailed earlier in this chapter) were followed for this process (Liu et al., 2008, p. 360) with three coders who were otherwise unaffiliated with the project doing the coding. After training to enhance consistency in codings, the raters independently sorted respondents' descriptions of stressful work experiences into various categories of job stressors and strains. Interrater agreement was calculated as an index of consistency in categorization of these described stressful experiences. Any discrepancies were then discussed until consensus could be reached on all collected stress incidents.

From the coding of qualitative data, Liu et al. (2008) identified five main job stressor categories: (1) organizational constraints (e.g., computer crashed), (2) workload (trying to meet a deadline), (3) interpersonal conflict (e.g., coworker accused me of not being a team player), (4) lack of job autonomy (coordinator didn't respect my efforts or decision), and (5) work mistakes (couldn't get the survey to work properly and abandoned the project). In addition to these categories of work-related stressors, five psychological strains also emerged from the coded stress incident descriptions: (1) anger, (2) frustration, (3) anxiety, (4) feeling overwhelmed, and (5) sadness. Four physical strains were also commonly described: (1) tiredness, (2) physical tension, (3) being sick, and (4) stomach problems.

Among the many results from this study, Liu et al. (2008) performed a chi-square analysis that revealed differences between men and women in terms of the types of stress incidents they reported. More specifically, Liu et al. (2008) found that women were more likely to report interpersonal conflicts, while men reported more incidents of workload and work-related mistakes as stressful. With respect to experienced strains, men and women also significantly differed in that men were more likely to report fewer psychological and physical strains than their female counterparts. Results based on the analyses with the quantitative data mirrored these findings, suggesting that women reported more depression, higher turnover intentions, and higher physical symptoms than men.

The other general set of hypotheses tested by Liu et al. (2008) involved differences in reported stress experiences and strain between occupations. In general, Liu et al. focused on the distinction between staff and faculty in this sample. In doing so, they found that based on the coded qualitative data, staff reported significantly more conflicts and more frustration than faculty. Faculty reported more anger than staff. These results were also confirmed by the analyses of the quantitative data, which revealed that staff reported higher levels of interpersonal conflict, more depression, higher turnover intentions, and higher physical symptoms than faculty.

There was also some evidence of an interactive effect of gender and job type on the reporting of stress and strain. For example, female faculty reported more incidents than did male staff, but male staff reported more stress incidents than female staff. From the quantitative data it was also revealed that gender influenced the relationship between interpersonal conflict and the strain of negative emotion. This is an interaction effect of gender and stressor on strain.

This study is interesting because in addition to the use of mixed methods for data collection and analysis, it also provides an example of the use of mixed methods for the interpretation of results. For example, Liu et al. (2008) suggested that the observed differences between men and women may be due to differences in their experiences of emotion associated with stressors. More specifically, Liu et al. propose that men may experience more intense emotional reactions to conflict and as such experience more anger when dealing with interpersonal conflict than women would. This conclusion was reached after reviewing the qualitatively analyzed stress incidents. The ability to use qualitative data for analysis and for illustration and interpretative assistance makes it invaluable to this particular study. Without this descriptive information, Liu et al. would have had a much more difficult time explaining their findings of differences between men and women.

## Knowledge Check

1. How would you explain the distinction between qualitative and quantitative research to your mother? What about mixed-methods research?

2. For each of the following general research objectives, outline a basic research plan that incorporates qualitative and quantitative methods:
   a. An evaluation of patient satisfaction with physician care during office visits.
   b. Assessing employee job satisfaction at an oil refinery.
   c. Examining the impact of work on children in families where both parents (if present) work full-time jobs.
   d. Consideration of the benefits and costs associated with religious involvement on marital satisfaction.

3. What are some of the most important pros and cons associated with using quantitative and qualitative methods? Are there any new technologies that could help you enhance these pros and minimize these cons?

4. Generate an example to fit with each of the possible reasons for doing qualitative or mixed-methods research highlighted in Box 17.1. These examples should come from your own interests in your primary field of study.

5. With a partner, locate the text (transcript) of a recent speech by some politician (easily available on the Internet) and follow the steps for content coding summarized in Table 17.2. What primary themes did you observe? Provide illustrative snippets from the transcript of the speech.

6. Read the full text of the Liu et al. (2008) article summarized in the "Research in Action" section of this chapter. What are some alternative qualitative and mixed-methods techniques that these researchers could have integrated into this study that would add something to what they already accomplished?

## Chapter Summary

There are times when the goal of research is to describe or qualify an object of study. Accordingly, this chapter began with an overview of qualitative research and a comparison of the differences between qualitative and quantitative research. Qualitative research is an inductive process that utilizes data to drive theory creation, whereas quantitative research is typically deductive in nature and is based on an existing body of knowledge. Our contention in this chapter is that both qualitative and quantitative techniques are valid and useful methodologies. The research question being addressed should drive the methodologies, not the other way around.

Mixed-methods research is growing in popularity and represents using the "best of both worlds" by combining qualitative and quantitative techniques to more fully answer a research question. Many techniques, such as interviews, used in traditional quantitative research can be adapted for qualitative purposes. Increasing training and publication outlets for qualitative research is leading to an increase in the use of alternative techniques. Whereas fields such as ethnography have used these techniques for some time, the other social sciences are just now catching up and recognizing the benefit of mixed-methods designs.

## Chapter Glossary for Review

**Content analysis**—Empirical method used to quantify qualitative information.

**Field notes**—Detailed observations made by the researcher based on observation or other qualitative methods.

**Grounded theory**—Research orientation that involves the identification and development of theory from the data as they are collected and analyzed.

**Member checking**—Reviewing data with respondents to ensure information was collected and coded accurately.

**Mixed-methods research**—Research involving the use of both quantitative and qualitative methods.

**Qualitative research**—An inductive method of conducting research typified by purposive sampling, rich descriptions, detailed observations, and exploratory hypotheses.

## Chapter References

Bryman, A. (2006). Integrating quantitative and qualitative research: How is it done? *Qualitative Research*, *6*(1), 97–113.

Bryman, A. (2007). Barriers to integrating quantitative and qualitative research. *Journal of Mixed Methods Research*, *1*(1), 8–22.

Cho, J., & Trent, A. (2006). Validity in qualitative research revisited. *Qualitative Research*, *6*(3), 319–340.

Corbin, J., & Strauss, A. (2008). *Basics of qualitative research* (3rd ed.) Los Angeles: SAGE.

Creswell, J. W., & Tashakkori, A. (2007). Editorial: Developing publishable mixed methods manuscripts. *Journal of Mixed Methods Research*, *1*(2), 107–111.

Duriau, V. J., Reger, R. K., & Pfarrer, M. D. (2007). A content analysis of the content analysis literature in organization studies: Research themes, data sources, and methodological refinements. *Organizational Research Methods*, *10*(1), 5–34.

Emerson, R. M., Fretz, R. I., & Shaw, L. L. (1995). *Writing ethnographic fieldnotes*. Chicago: University of Chicago Press.

Glaser, B. G., & Strauss, A. L. (1964). Awareness contexts and social interaction. *American Sociological Review*, *29*, 669–679.

Glaser, B. G., & Strauss, A.L. (1967). *The discovery of grounded theory: Strategies of qualitative research*. London: Wiedenfeld and Nicholson.

Johnson, R. B., Onwuegbuzie, A. J., & Turner, L. A. (2007). Toward a definition of mixed methods research. *Journal of Mixed Methods Research*, *1*(2), 112–133.

Keenan, A., & Newton, T. J. (1985). Stressful events, stressors, and psychological strains in young professional engineers. *Journal of Occupational Behavior*, *6*, 151–156.

Kidd, S. A. (2002). The role of qualitative research in psychological journals. *Psychological Methods*, *7*(1), 126–138.

Liu, C., Spector, P. E., & Shi, L. (2008). Use of both qualitative and quantitative approaches to study job stress in different gender and occupational groups. *Journal of Occupational Health Psychology*, *13*(4), 357–370.

Locke, K. (2001). *Grounded theory in management research*. Los Angeles: SAGE.

Lofland, J., Snow, D. A., Anderson, L., & Lofland, L.H. (2005). *Analyzing social settings: A guide to qualitative observation and analysis* (4th ed.). Belmont: Wadsworth.

Miles, M., & Huberman, A. (1994). *Qualitative data analysis: An expanded sourcebook*. Thousand Oaks, CA: SAGE.

O'Cathain, A. (2009). Editorial: Mixed methods research in the health sciences: A quiet revolution. *Journal of Mixed Methods Research*, *3*(1), 3–6.

Patton, M. Q. (2002). *Qualitative research and evaluation methods*. Thousand Oaks, CA: SAGE.

Rapley, T. J. (2001). The art(fulness) of open-ended interviewing: Some considerations on analysing interviews. *Qualitative Research*, *1*(3), 303–323.

Santos, S. J., Ortiz, A. M., Morales, A., & Rosales, M. (2007). The relationship between campus diversity, students' ethnic identity and college adjustment: A qualitative study. *Cultural Diversity and Ethnic Minority Psychology*, *13*(2), 104–114.

Shaw, I. (2003). Qualitative research and outcomes in health, social work and education. *Qualitative Research*, *3*(1), 57–77.

Silverman, D. (2005). *Doing qualitative research* (2nd ed.). Thousand Oaks, CA: SAGE.

Tashakkori, A., & Teddlie, C. (2003). Issues and dilemmas in teaching research methods courses in social and behavioural sciences: U.S. perspective. *International Journal of Social Research Methodology*, *6*(1), 61–77.

Teddlie, C., & Tashakkori, A. (2003). Major issues and controversies in the use of mixed methods in the social and behavioral sciences. In A. Tashakkori & C. Teddlie (Eds.), *Handbook of mixed methods in social & behavioral research* (pp. 3–50). Thousand Oaks, CA: SAGE.

Weber, R. (1990). *Basic content analysis* (2nd ed.). Thousand Oaks, CA: SAGE.

Webb, E. J., Campbell, D. T., Schwartz, R. D., & Sechrest, L. (1966/2000). *Unobtrusive measures* (rev. ed.). Thousand Oaks, CA: SAGE.

Wolfinger, N. H. (2002). On writing fieldnotes: Collection strategies and background expectancies. *Qualitative Research*, *2*(1), 85–95.

# Appendix A

## Statistics Behind the Research or, "What Was I Supposed to Remember from My Statistics Class Anyway?"

## Introduction

We assume that you have already had a course in statistics and have learned the basics of descriptive and inferential statistics. We also assume that you, like many students, appreciate the opportunity to review several of the basic concepts related to statistical procedures. Therefore, this appendix will provide you with a brief review of commonly used statistics. If you believe that you understand concepts such as measures of central tendency, measures of dispersion, and $z$-scores, then you may skip this appendix. If, however, you want a quick review of these concepts, this appendix provides an overview of the critical concepts you need to know.

Many students say they hate math and statistics, though it often seems that these strong emotions are linked more to discomfort with the topics rather than any real underlying animosity. It is true that statistics require long and tedious involvements, but thankfully for you, many of the elements of statistics that were time-consuming in the past are now handled by computers. The problem with this is that many students do not realize what calculations the computer is doing. This in turn makes it difficult for these students to accurately interpret the resulting output. Thus, while you study statistics now and in any future setting, your goal should be to understand not just how to do statistics, but also why researchers use these tools. It is also critical to be able to explain statistical information to other people. We hope that reviewing the material in this appendix will allow you to understand how to interpret and use basic statistics. This appendix should also help you handle the material presented in the other chapters of this text.

## Variables $X$, $Y$, $N$, $n$

For all equations in this book, the letters $X$, $Y$, $N$, and $n$ have a consistent meaning. In all cases, $X$ and $Y$ represent the variables. More specifically, $X$ and $Y$ represent sets of data. In correlational research, for example, we might use $X$ and $Y$ to represent the two tests we administer to participants in the study. For example, we might collect data for 10 people using two measures. In this case, we use $X$ to represent the data for the first variable and $Y$ to represent the data for the second variable. Here are two sets of data:

$$X \{18\ 10\ 11\ 13\ 8\ 11\ 6\ 10\ 3\ 10\}$$
$$Y \{18\ 17\ 13\ 6\ 6\ 7\ 4\ 9\ 3\ 10\}$$

We use the letters $N$ and $n$ to indicate the number of observations we have for a study. The distinction between $N$ and $n$ is one of scope: $N$ represents all the observations used in a study, whereas $n$ represents the number of observations in a set. For this example, we would write $N = 20$ to indicate that there are 20 individual data points. For each group there are 10 observations. Therefore, we would write $n_X = 10$ and $n_Y = 10$.

## Subscripts ($X_1$) and Superscripts ($X^2$)

Mathematicians use subscripts and superscripts to indicate types of information and indicate specific mathematical operations, respectively. Whenever you see a subscript, such as $X_1$ or $Y_1$, the subscript represents the individual score within a specific group. Using the two data sets we have already presented, we can identify the individual scores as:

| | | | |
|---|---|---|---|
| $X_1 = 18$ | $X_6 = 11$ | $Y_1 = 18$ | $Y_6 = 7$ |
| $X_2 = 10$ | $X_7 = 6$ | $Y_2 = 17$ | $Y_7 = 4$ |
| $X_3 = 11$ | $X_8 = 10$ | $Y_3 = 13$ | $Y_8 = 9$ |
| $X_4 = 13$ | $X_9 = 3$ | $Y_4 = 6$ | $Y_9 = 3$ |
| $X_5 = 8$ | $X_{10} = 10$ | $Y_5 = 6$ | $Y_{10} = 10$ |

We can also use letters in the subscripts to help identify the groups. For example, $n_X$ and $n_Y$ represent the sample sizes for the groups $X$ and $Y$. In a true experiment, we might use $X_{a1}$ and $X_{a2}$ to represent two groups of participants. The symbol $X_{a1}$ represents the first group, whereas $X_{a2}$ represents the second group. In several of the more advanced chapters in this book we introduce you to more complicated designs that may involve multiple subscripts. It will be easier for you to understand that material if you remember that we use subscripts to identify different variables and observations within sets of data.

In contrast to subscripts, a superscript, such as $X^2$ or $Y^2$, represents a mathematical operation. The most commonly used superscript in statistics is squaring, or $X^2$. Thus if $X_2 = 10$, then $X_2^2 = 100$.

## Population Parameters

In statistics, Greek letters ($\mu$, $\sigma$, $\rho$) represent population parameters. A parameter is a statistic that describes a characteristic of a population. We use Roman letters (e.g., $M$, $SD$, and $r$) to represent sample statistics. The more commonly measured population parameters and the equivalent sample statistics are:

| Measure | Population parameter | Sample statistic |
|---|---|---|
| Mean | $\mu$ | $M$ |
| Variance | $\sigma^2$ | $VAR$ |
| Standard deviation | $\sigma$ | $SD$ |
| Correlation | $\rho$ | $r$ |

## Summation, $\Sigma$

### Sum of Scores, $\Sigma X$

The Greek letter $\Sigma$ (sigma) is a mathematical symbol that tells us to find the sum of a group of numbers. Specifically, it indicates the sum of all values in a set. For example, $\Sigma X$ represents the sum of all scores in set $X$; $\Sigma Y$ represents the sum of all scores in set $Y$. For example, if

$$X \{18\ 10\ 11\ 13\ 8\ 11\ 6\ 10\ 3\ 10\}$$
$$Y \{18\ 17\ 13\ 6\ 6\ 7\ 4\ 9\ 3\ 10\}$$

then

$$\Sigma X = 18 + 10 + 11 + 13 + 8 + 11 + 6 + 10 + 3 + 10 = 100$$
$$\Sigma Y = 18 + 17 + 13 + 6 + 6 + 7 + 4 + 9 + 3 + 10 = 93$$

### Sum of Squared Scores, $\Sigma X^2$

In many cases you will see a summation sign that looks like $\Sigma X^2$ or $\Sigma Y^2$. This symbol means that you first square each score in the set and then add all the squared scores. For example,

$$\Sigma X^2 = 18^2 + 10^2 + 11^2 + 13^2 + 8^2 + 11^2 + 6^2 + 10^2 + 3^2 + 10^2$$
$$\Sigma X^2 = 324 + 100 + 121 + 169 + 64 + 121 + 36 + 100 + 9 + 100 = 1144$$
$$\Sigma Y^2 = 18^2 + 17^2 + 13^2 + 6^2 + 6^2 + 7^2 + 4^2 + 9^2 + 3^2 + 10^2$$
$$\Sigma Y^2 = 324 + 289 + 169 + 36 + 36 + 49 + 16 + 81 + 9 + 100 = 1109$$

### Sum of Scores Squared, $(\Sigma X)^2$

You will also see a summation sign that looks like $(\Sigma X)^2$ or $(\Sigma Y)^2$. These symbols call for a different set of steps than $\Sigma X^2$ and $\Sigma Y^2$. The expression $\Sigma X^2$ means that you first square each score in the set and then add all the squared scores. By contrast, the expression $(\Sigma X)^2$ means that we first add all the scores in the set and then square the total. For example,

$$\Sigma X = 100 \qquad\qquad \Sigma Y = 93$$
$$(\Sigma X)^2 = 100^2 = 10,000 \quad (\Sigma Y)^2 = 93^2 = 8649$$

### Sum of Cross Products, $\Sigma XY$

Another common summation operation is $\Sigma XY$, which we call the sum of cross products. $\Sigma XY$ is not the same thing as $(\Sigma X)(\Sigma Y)$. To calculate the cross products, we first multiply each number by its pair and then add the individual cross products. For example,

| X | | Y | | Cross product $XY$ |
|---|---|---|---|---|
| 18 | × | 18 | = | 324 |
| 10 | × | 17 | = | 170 |
| 11 | × | 13 | = | 143 |
| 13 | × | 6 | = | 78 |
| 8 | × | 6 | = | 48 |
| 11 | × | 7 | = | 77 |
| 6 | × | 4 | = | 24 |
| 10 | × | 9 | = | 90 |
| 3 | × | 3 | = | 9 |
| 10 | × | 10 | = | 100 |
| $\Sigma X = 100$ | | $\Sigma Y = 93$ | | $\Sigma XY = 1,063$ |

For these data, $(\Sigma X)(\Sigma Y) = 100 \times 93 = 9,300$, whereas $\Sigma XY = 1,063$. This important difference cannot be overlooked.

## Measures of Central Tendency

The measures of central tendency are descriptive statistics that summarize the data with a single number that represents the typical score. We use measures of central tendency because we typically believe that most scores on a scale or responses to an item cluster around the typical or most common score or response in the data set. Consequently, a measure of central tendency is a convenient tool for indicating the most typical score in a set of data. Selecting an appropriate measure of central tendency depends on the measurement scale used to represent the variable, the symmetry of the data, and the inferences to be made from the measure of central tendency. In the following subsections we will review the mode, median, and arithmetic mean.

### Mode, $M_0$

Of the many measures of central tendency, the mode is the easiest to calculate. It is also the least precise, but it still has value to us when we want to describe certain types of data (more on that later). By definition, the mode is:

$$M_0 = \text{Most frequently occurring score or scores in the data} \qquad \text{(A.1)}$$

Here is an example of how to calculate the mode using the data set $X$:

$$X \{18\ 10\ 11\ 13\ 8\ 11\ 6\ 10\ 3\ 10\}$$

**Step 1:** Rank the numbers from lowest to highest:

$$X \{3\ 6\ 8\ 10\ 10\ 10\ 11\ 11\ 13\ 18\}$$

**Step 2:** Find the most frequently occurring score:

$$M_0 = 10$$

As you can see, the mode is easy to determine and it can be a useful tool for indicating the location of a cluster of frequently occurring scores in your data set. This central tendency statistic is also useful when there are multiple *peaks* or several *common scores* in the data set. In such cases, we may describe the data as *bimodal* (two modes) or *multimodal*. The mode is most often used to describe the central tendency of data gathered with a nominal scale. The mode can also be useful when the data are discrete values that have no intermediate values, such as the number of children in a family.

### Median, *Mdn* or $Q_2$

The median is a second and slightly more precise measure of central tendency. The definition of the median is:

$Mdn$ or $Q_2$ = Score that divides a ranked data set in half, or, the midpoint

of a set of scores                                                          (A.2)

Although there is no single formula for calculating the median, there are easier and more difficult techniques. Here is a relatively straightforward example of how to calculate a median using the two example data sets from this appendix. For this example, $n_X = 10$ and $n_Y = 9$:

$$X\ \{18\ 10\ 11\ 13\ 8\ 11\ 6\ 10\ 3\ 10\}$$
$$Y\ \{18\ 17\ 4\ 6\ 6\ 13\ 7\ 9\ 10\}$$

**Step 1:** Rank the numbers from lowest to highest:

$$X\ \{3\ 6\ 8\ 10\ 10\ 10\ 11\ 11\ 13\ 18\}$$
$$Y\ \{4\ 6\ 6\ 7\ 9\ 10\ 13\ 17\ 18\}$$

**Step 2:** Add 1 to $n$ and then divide by 2:

$$\text{For } X :\ (10+1)/2 = 5.5$$
$$\text{For } Y :\ (9+1)/2 = 5$$

**Step 3:** Starting with the lowest score, count up to the value from Step 2:

$$X\ (3\ 6\ 8\ 10\ 10\ 10\ 11\ 11\ 13\ 18)$$
$$Y\ (4\ 6\ 6\ 7\ 9\ 10\ 13\ 17\ 18)$$

**Step 4:** If the midpoint falls between the two numbers, add them and divide by 2:

$$\text{For } X,\ Mdn = (10+10)/2 = 10$$
$$\text{For } Y,\ Mdn = 9.0$$

The median is a useful descriptive statistic especially for skewed or nonsymmetrically distributed sets of scores or data. The median, unlike our final central tendency statistic, the arithmetic mean, is not affected by the presence of outlying or extremely high or low scores.

## Arithmetic Mean, $M$

One of the most common measures of central tendency in the behavioral sciences is the arithmetic mean, $M$. When the data or set of scores we have collected roughly follows a normal or bell-curved shape, then this central tendency statistic is the preferred one because of its value to many of the other statistics we commonly rely on when testing our hypotheses. For the sake of definition, the mean is the sum of all observed scores divided by the number of observations in the data set. We define the arithmetic mean as:

$$M = \frac{\sum X}{n} \tag{A.3}$$

Here is an example of how to calculate the arithmetic mean using two data sets $X$ and $Y$:

$$X \{18 \ 10 \ 11 \ 13 \ 8 \ 11 \ 6 \ 10 \ 3 \ 10\}$$
$$Y \{18 \ 17 \ 4 \ 6 \ 6 \ 13 \ 7 \ 9 \ 10\}$$

**Step 1:** Calculate the sum of scores for each set:

$$\sum X = 18 + 10 + 11 + 13 + 8 + 11 + 6 + 10 + 3 + 10 = 100.0$$
$$n_X = 10$$
$$\sum Y = 18 + 17 + 4 + 6 + 6 + 13 + 7 + 9 + 10 = 90.0$$
$$n_Y = 9$$

**Step 2:** Divide the sum of scores ($\sum X$) by the sample size, $n_x$ or $n_Y$:

$$M_X = \frac{100}{10} = 10$$
$$M_Y = \frac{90}{9} = 10$$

The mean has a number of unique features. By definition, the mean is the point in the distribution that is the smallest total difference between itself and each observation. Therefore, $\sum(X - M) = 0$ and $\sum(X - M)^2 = $ minimal value (this second feature is known as the *least squares criterion*). In addition to these two properties, the arithmetic mean is also viewed as an unbiased estimate of the population mean, $\mu$. Despite these strengths, this central tendency statistic is, however, sensitive to outliers and to skewed distributions. When the data are positively skewed, the mean will be greater than the median (e.g., $M > Mdn$). When the data are negatively skewed, the mean will be less than the median (e.g., $M < Mdn$). Table A.1 provides a summary of the main measures of central tendency presented here.

## Measures of Variability

A central tendency statistic indicates only one characteristic of the data: the typical or common score in your data set. Although this is a useful bit of information, we also really need additional information to fully describe the data to other researchers and those who might be interested in our research. One of the more important characteristics of a data set is the amount of

# Table A.1   Summary of Frequently Used Measures of Central Tendency

| Statistic | Definition | Appropriate for These Scales of Measurement | Features/Properties |
|---|---|---|---|
| Mode $M_0$ | Most common score in a data set | Nominal, ordinal interval, ratio | Imprecise and potentially misleading for ordinal, interval, or ratio data |
| Median $Mdn$ | Midpoint of a ranked distribution of scores | Ordinal, interval, ratio | Good to use when extreme scores skew the distribution of data |
| Arithmetic Mean $M$ | Total of a set of scores divided by the number of scores | Interval, ratio | Commonly used measure; $\Sigma(X - M) = 0$ and $\Sigma(X - M)^2 =$ minimal value; $M$ is an unbiased estimate of $\mu$ |

variability present among those scores. Variability reflects differences be-tween data points in the data set and the typical or most common score (i.e., spread around the indicator of central tendency). For researchers to draw valid inferences from their data, it is very important to know whether the data they have collected are clustered close to the measure of central tendency or spread widely, indicating lack of consistency in responses. Much like the measures of central tendency, selecting an appropriate measure of variability depends on the measurement scale used to represent the variable, the symmetry of the data, and the inferences to be made from the measure of variability.

## Simple Range

The range is the easiest measure of variability to calculate. The definition of the range is:

$$\text{Range} = X_{\text{highest}} - X_{\text{lowest}} \qquad (A.4)$$

Like the mode, the range is easy to calculate; however, it is greatly affected by outliers. Therefore, most researchers use it only as a general descriptive tool. Here is an example of how to calculate the range:

$$X \{18\ 10\ 11\ 13\ 8\ 11\ 6\ 10\ 3\ 10\}$$
$$Y \{18\ 17\ 4\ 6\ 6\ 13\ 7\ 9\ 10\}$$

**Step 1:** Rank the scores from lowest to highest:

$$X \{3\ 6\ 8\ 10\ 10\ 10\ 11\ 11\ 13\ 18\}$$
$$Y \{4\ 6\ 6\ 7\ 9\ 10\ 13\ 17\ 18\}$$

**Step 2:** Determine the difference between the highest and lowest scores:

$$\text{Range}_X = 15.0 = 18 - 3$$
$$\text{Range}_Y = 14.0 = 18 - 4$$

### Semi-Interquartile Range

Another measure of score variability is the semi-interquartile range (*SIR*). The semi-interquartile range is half of the difference between the 75th percentile and the 25th percentile in a set of scores. This probably makes more sense when you look at the formula:

$$SIR = \frac{Q_3 - Q_1}{2}$$ 
(A.5)

In this equation, $Q_3$ represents the 75th percentile and $Q_1$ represents the 25th percentile. The 75th percentile indicates that 75% of the scores in the data set are at or below the value for $Q_3$, while 25% of the scores in the set are at or below the value of $Q_1$. To help you keep things in perspective, remember that the median (*Mdn*) is also sometimes called $Q_2$, and it represents the midpoint of a set of scores, or the value below which 50% of the scores in a set would exist in the distribution of scores. The following example illustrates how to calculate the *SIR*:

$$X \{18\ 10\ 11\ 13\ 8\ 11\ 6\ 10\ 3\ 10\}$$
$$Y \{18\ 17\ 4\ 6\ 6\ 13\ 7\ 9\ 10\}$$

**Step 1:** Rank the scores from lowest to highest:

$$X \{3\ 6\ 8\ 10\ 10\ 10\ 11\ 11\ 13\ 18\}$$
$$Y \{4\ 6\ 6\ 7\ 9\ 10\ 13\ 17\ 18\}$$

**Step 2:** Calculate the median (add 1 to the sample size and divide by 2):

For $X$, $Q_2$ or $Mdn = (10 + 1)/2 = 5.5$
For $Y$, $Q_2$ or $Mdn = (9 + 1)/2 = 5$

**Step 3:** Starting with the lowest score, count up to the value from Step 2:

$$X \{3\ 6\ 8\ 10\ 10\ 10\ 11\ 11\ 13\ 18\}$$
↑

$$Y \{4\ 6\ 6\ 7\ 9\ 10\ 13\ 17\ 18\}$$
↑

**Step 4:** Determine the midpoint of the upper and lower halves using the same procedure described in Step 2. Specifically, add 1 to the number of scores in each half and divide by 2:

Position of $Q_3$ and $Q_1$ for $X = (5 + 1)/2 = 3$
Position of $Q_3$ and $Q_1$ for $Y = (4 + 1)/2 = 2.5$

**Step 5:** Using numbers from the previous step, determine $Q_1$ and $Q_3$. If the location of $Q_1$ or $Q_3$ falls between two numbers, take the average of the two:

$X$ {3 6 8 10 10 10 11 11 13 18}

↑                    ↑

For $X$, $Q_1 = 8.0$ and $Q_3 = 11.0$

$Y$ {4 6 6 7 9 10 13 17 18}

↑                ↑

For $Y$, $Q_1 = (6 + 6)/2 = 6$ and $Q_3 = (13 + 17)/2 = 15$

**Step 6:** Calculate *SIR*:

$$SIR_X = (11 - 8)/2 = 1.5$$
$$SIR_Y = (15 - 6)/2 = 4.5$$

As with the median, extreme scores do not affect the semi-interquartile range. Therefore, researchers often use the statistic to describe a distribution of data that is skewed or somehow deviant from a normal bell-shaped form.

## Variance and Standard Deviation

The variance and standard deviation are two of the most commonly used measures of score variability. In the following table you will see that there are several ways to write the equations for these statistics. Here we are presenting a definitional and a computational form of these equations. Statisticians use the *definitional equation* to help describe and explain the purpose of these two important variability statistics. The *computational equations*, as the name implies, are equations people use when they have to calculate these statistics by hand. Even if you never perform one of these calculations yourself, understanding these formulas can help you interpret these statistics when they are generated by your favorite statistical software program.

As you can see in the following summary table, there are two forms of the variance and standard deviation equations. The first form, the sample statistic, determines the variance and standard deviation when the data are the population. The second form, the unbiased estimate of the population, allows us to estimate the population parameter using sample data. In most cases, you will use the unbiased estimate of the population form of the equations.

| Sample Statistic | Unbiased Estimate of Population Value |
|---|---|
| **Variance** | |
| *Definitional equations* (A.6) | |
| $s^2 = \dfrac{\sum (X-M)^2}{N}$ | $VAR = \dfrac{\sum (X-M)^2}{N-1}$ |

*Computational equations* (A.7)

$$s^2 = \frac{\sum X^2 - \frac{(\sum x)^2}{N}}{N} \qquad\qquad VAR = \frac{\sum X^2 - \frac{(\sum x)^2}{n}}{n-1}$$

## Standard Deviation

*Definitional equations* (A.8)

$$s = \sqrt{\frac{\sum (X-M)^2}{N}} \qquad\qquad SD = \sqrt{\frac{\sum (X-M)^2}{n-1}}$$

*Computational equations* (A.9)

$$s = \sqrt{\frac{\sum X^2 - \frac{(\sum x)^2}{N}}{N}} \qquad\qquad SD = \sqrt{\frac{\sum X^2 - \frac{(\sum x)^2}{n}}{n-1}}$$

We can examine the definitional equations for the variance and standard deviations to help understand what these statistics mean. If you look at the numerator of the equations, you will see the expression $\sum (X - M)^2$. The name of this equation is the *sum of squares*. More specifically, the sum of squares is the sum of the squared deviation scores. Deviation scores are calculated by subtracting the $M$ of a set of scores from each of the scores in the set, $(X - M)$. These scores reflect the difference between the mean and an observed score. As you can see, the larger the difference between the mean and the observed score, the greater the deviation score. Because $\sum (X - M) = 0$, we square each deviation score. Squaring the deviation scores ensures that there are no negative deviation scores. Therefore, $\sum (X - M)^2$ will always be greater than 0 unless all the scores in a data set are the same number.

Once we determine the sum of squares, we divide this number by another number, the denominator. For the unbiased estimate of the population equation, the denominator is $n - 1$. Thus, the variance is an estimate of the typical squared deviation between the scores and the mean. The final step is to calculate the square root of the variance, otherwise known as the *standard deviation*. Doing so returns the value of this variability statistic to the scale that was used to measure variable $X$ in the first place. This means that the standard deviation is an index of the typical deviation of scores within a collected data set gathered from a sample of participants.

The following is a step-by-step example of how to determine the variance and standard deviation of a set of data. We can begin by using a sample of data:

$$X \{18\ 10\ 11\ 13\ 8\ 11\ 6\ 10\ 3\ 10\}$$

**Step 1:** Calculate the sum of scores:

$$\sum X = 18 + 10 + 11 + 13 + 8 + 11 + 6 + 10 + 3 + 10 = 100$$

**Step 2:** Calculate the sum of squared scores:

$$\Sigma X^2 = 18^2 + 10^2 + 11^2 + 13^2 + 8^2 + 11^2 + 6^2 + 10^2 + 3^2 + 10^2$$
$$\Sigma X^2 = 324 + 1100 + 121 + 169 + 64 + 121 + 36 + 100 + 9 + 100 = 1144$$

**Step 3:** Complete the equations.

|  | Sample Statistic | Unbiased Estimate of Population Value |
|---|---|---|
| **Variance** | | |
| | $s^2 = \dfrac{\sum X^2 - \frac{\left(\sum x\right)^2}{N}}{N}$ | $VAR = \dfrac{\sum X^2 - \frac{\left(\sum x\right)^2}{n}}{n-1}$ |
| | $s^2 = \dfrac{1144 - \frac{(100)^2}{10}}{10} = \dfrac{144}{10} = 14.4 \text{ Variance}$ | $VAR = \dfrac{1144 - \frac{(100)^2}{10}}{10 - 1} = \dfrac{144}{9} = 16$ |
| **Standard Deviation** | | |
| | $s = \sqrt{s^2}$ | $SD = \sqrt{VAR}$ |
| | $s = \sqrt{14.4} = 3.79$ | $SD = \sqrt{16} = 4$ |

Figure A.1 presents four hypothetical distributions with population means of 50 and standard deviations of 5, 10, 15, and 20. As the standard deviation increases, the spread of data becomes much wider. For the distribution with a standard deviation of 5, the majority of the scores are close to the mean of 50, with close to 95% of these scores falling between 40 and 60. In contrast, the distribution with the standard deviation of 20 has scores spread across the entire response scale from 10 to 90. Table A.2 summarizes the frequently used measures of variability we have discussed.

## Standardized or *z*-Score

The *z*-score allows us to convert observed scores to standardized scores, which can be more easily compared with one another, even if the different scores were measured with different response scales. This ability to convert data from different measures or scales to a common scale is one major advantage of using *z*-scores. This transformation is also important when data from different groups have different means and standard deviations, as a *z*-score allows us to compare these scores. These standardized scores are also the basis for calculating correlation coefficients between two variables. Another advantage of the *z*-score is that it can help us interpret or make inferences about specific observations. If we assume that the normal distribution represents our data, we can use the *z*-score to convert observed scores to percentiles.

# Figure A.1

**Four Distributions of Data, Each with a Mean of 50 and Standard Deviation of 5, 10, 15, or 20**

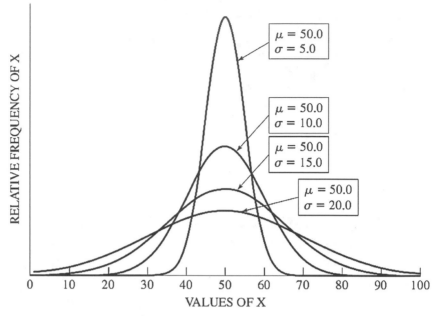

As the standard deviation increases, the spread of the scores around the mean becomes much wider.

# Table A.2   Summary of Frequently Used Measures of Variability

| Statistic | Definition | Appropriate for These Measurement Scales | Features/Properties |
|---|---|---|---|
| Range | $\text{Range} = X_{\text{highest}} - X_{\text{lowest}}$ | | |
| Semi-interquartile range, $SIR$ | $SIR = \frac{Q_3 - Q_1}{2}$ | Ordinal, interval, or ratio | Imprecise and potentially misleading when the data contain outliers |
| Variance of a sample, $s^2$ | $s^2 = \frac{\sum (X-M)^2}{N}$ | Ordinal, interval, or ratio | Good to use when extreme scores skew the distribution of data |
| Standard deviation of a sample, $s$ | $s = \sqrt{\frac{\sum (X-M)^2}{N}}$ | Interval or ratio | Used when the data represent the population of scores |
| Unbiased estimate of standard variance, $VAR$ | $VAR = \frac{\sum (X-M)^2}{N-1}$ | Interval or ratio | Used when data represent a sample, but desire is to draw inferences about the larger population (more common in behavioral and social science research) |
| Unbiased estimate of standard deviation, $SD$ | $SD = \sqrt{\frac{\sum (X-M)^2}{n-1}}$ | | |

There are two ways to calculate the $z$-score. The first method assumes that the data represent an intact group. Therefore, we use $s$ to calculate the standard deviation of the data. The equation for this version of the $z$-score is:

$$z = \frac{(X - M)}{s} \qquad \text{(A.10)}$$

In the second method, if the data are collected from a sample and used to estimate population parameters (a more common scenario in most social science research), we may use $SD$ as a less-biased estimate of the variability element of this equation. Thus, in this case, we would use the following equation to calculate the $z$-score:

$$z = \frac{(X - M)}{SD} \qquad \text{(A.11)}$$

To illustrate the use of these formulas, consider the following example. Imagine that you give 10 people two tests, Test A and Test B. We will assume that the data from these tests represent an intact group. Therefore we will calculate $s$ to determine the standard deviation. Looking at Table A.3, you can see the tests have different means and standard deviations. For Test A, $M_A = 100$ and $s_A = 75$. For Test B, $M_B = 3.0$ and $s_B = 1.0$.

Table A.3 also presents the $z$-scores for the tests. The means and standard deviations of the $z$-scores for Test A and Test B are $M = 0.0$ and

## Table A.3  Example of $z$-Scores within a Study in Which Each Person Completed Two Tests

| Person | Test A | Test A z-scores | Test B | Test B z-scores |
|---|---|---|---|---|
| A | 440 | $(440 - 500)/75 = -0.8$ | 3.4 | $(3.4 - 3.0)/1 = 0.4$ |
| B | 560 | $(560 - 500)/75 = 0.8$ | 2.4 | $(2.4 - 3.0)/1 = -0.6$ |
| C | 515 | $(515 - 500)/75 = 0.2$ | 2.8 | $(2.8 - 3.0)/1 = -0.2$ |
| D | 395 | $(395 - 500)/75 = -1.4$ | 4.2 | $(4.2 - 3.0)/1 = 1.2$ |
| E | 500 | $(500 - 500)/75 = 0.0$ | 3.0 | $(3.0 - 3.0)/1 = 0.0$ |
| F | 545 | $(545 - 500)/75 = 0.6$ | 2.6 | $(2.6 - 3.0)/1 = -0.4$ |
| G | 605 | $(605 - 500)/75 = 1.4$ | 1.2 | $(1.2 - 3.0)/1 = -1.8$ |
| H | 425 | $(425 - 500)/75 = -1.0$ | 3.6 | $(3.6 - 3.0)/1 = 0.6$ |
| I | 605 | $(605 - 500)/75 = 1.4$ | 4.8 | $(4.8 - 3.0)/1 = 1.8$ |
| J | 410 | $(410 - 500)/75 = -1.2$ | 2.0 | $(2.0 - 3.0)/1 = -1.0$ |
| $\Sigma X_A = 5000$ | | $\Sigma z_A = 0.0$ | $\Sigma X_B = 30$ | $\Sigma z_B = 0.0$ |
| $\Sigma X_A^2 = 2{,}556{,}250$ | | $\Sigma X_A^2 = 10$ | $\Sigma z_B^2 = 100$ | $\Sigma z_B^2 = 10$ |
| $M_A = 500$ | | $M_{Az} = 0.0$ | $M_B = 3.0$ | $M_{Bz} = 0.0$ |
| $s_A = 75$ | | $s_{Az} = 1.0$ | $s_B = 1.0$ | $s_{Bz} = 1.0$ |

Note: Next to each test score is the corresponding z-score, which represents the relative difference between the observed score and the group mean score.

$s = 1.0$. This is always the case for $z$-scores. Thus, when you calculate $z$-scores using $s$ for the standard deviation, then

$$\Sigma z = 0.0 \quad \Sigma z^2 = n \quad M_z = 0.0 \quad s_z = 1.0$$

When you use $SD$ to calculate $z$-scores, then

$$\Sigma z = 0.0 \quad \Sigma z^2 = n - 1 \quad M_z = 0.0 \quad s_z = 1.0$$

Once we convert the observed scores to $z$-scores, we can directly compare pairs of scores from different groups. As an example, consider Person B's scores on the two tests. Person B earned a score of 560 on the first test and a score of 2.4 on the second test. We can say that Person B scored better than average on the first test because that person's $z$-score for that test is $z = 0.80$. This score indicates that Person B scored 0.8 standard deviations above the group mean score on that test. However, Person B scored 0.6 standard deviations below the group average on the second test, as reflected by the $z$-score of $z = -0.6$.

Thus, using the $z$-score, we can quickly determine whether a person's score is above or below the mean and the relative magnitude of the difference. For example, $z$-scores of $-0.2$ and $0.1$ indicate that the scores are not too far below or above the mean. In contrast, $z$-scores of $-1.95$ or $1.64$ indicate scores far below and far above the mean.

### Determining Percentiles Using the $z$-Score

Once we have converted an observed score to a $z$-score, we can then use this $z$-score to determine a percentile for each score. A percentile is a number that represents the percentage of individuals that received the same or a lower/ higher score. For example, if you took a test and learned that you scored at the 90th percentile, then you can conclude that you did as well as or better than 90% of the people who took the test. If, however, your test score was at the 45th percentile, you should conclude that your score was lower than average, being only as high as or better than 45% of the test-takers.

Converting $z$-scores to percentiles is rather easy, especially if we use Table B.1 of Appendix B. If you look at that table, you will see that there are three columns. Column A represents the $z$-scores. Because the normal distribution is symmetrical, we can use this column to examine positive as well as negative $z$-scores. Column B of the table represents the area of the normal distribution that exists between the mean and the $z$-score. Column C represents the area of the curve beyond the $z$-score. Using this table, we can convert the $z$-score to a percentile. The following instructions show you how to convert negative and positive $z$-scores to percentiles.

### Negative $z$-Scores

If the $z$-score is negative or equal to 0 ($z \leq 0$), then use the following procedure.

**Step 1:** Convert the observed score to a $z$-score:

$$X = 440 \quad M = 500 \quad s = 75$$
$$z = (440 - 500)/75 = -0.8$$

**Step 2:** Locate the value of the $z$-score, ignoring the sign, using Column A from Table B.1 of Appendix B, and then note the value listed in Column C. This value represents the proportion of the distribution beyond the $z$-score:

$$z = 0.80 \quad \text{Proportion beyond } z\text{-score} = .2119$$

**Step 3:** Multiply the proportion beyond $z$-score by 100 and round to the nearest whole number. The resulting product is the percentile that you are seeking:

$$.2119 \times 100 = 21.19 \rightarrow 21\%$$

In this example then, we can conclude that only 21% of people taking the test will earn a score of 440 or less (remember that the original $z$-score was negative). In other words, if you gave this test to 100 people, you would expect that only 21 of them would have a score of 440 or lower. You could also conclude that 79% $(100\% - 21\%)$ of the people taking the test would have a score greater than 440.

## Positive $z$-Scores

If the $z$-score is positive $(z > 0)$, then use the following procedure.

**Step 1:** Convert the observed score to a $z$-score:

$$X = 515 \quad M = 500 \quad s = 75$$
$$z = (515 - 500)/75 = 0.20$$

**Step 2:** Locate the value of the $z$-score using Column A from Table B.1 of Appendix B, and then note the value listed in Column B. This value represents the proportion of the distribution of scores that falls between the mean and this individual $z$-score:

$$z = 0.20 \quad \text{Proportion between mean and } z\text{-score} = .0793$$

**Step 3:** Add the value found in Step 2 and .5000. This step accounts for the half of the normal curve that falls below the mean:

$$.5793 = .5000 + .0793$$

**Step 4:** Multiply the result of Step 3 by 100 and round to the nearest whole number. The product is the percentile:

$$.5793 \times 100 = 57.93 \rightarrow 58\%$$

# Figure A.2

**Normal Curve**

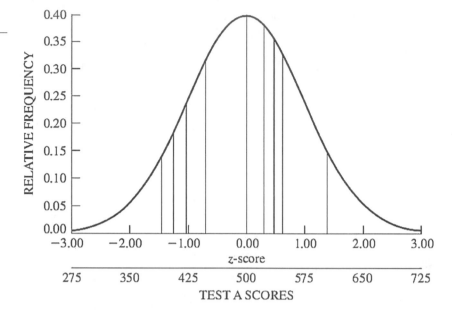

The vertical lines represent the location of values of X presented in Table A.4.

Therefore, a score of 515 represents the 58th percentile, indicating that 58% of the people taking this test would be expected to score at or below 515. What percentage of people taking the test will score greater than 515? Given the mean and standard deviation of the test, we would expect that 42% (100% − 58%) will receive a score of 515 or greater. Figure A.2 and Table A.4 illustrate how to determine the percentile score for each of the 10 scores recorded for Test A. When you convert z-scores to percentiles, it is a good idea to draw a sketch of the normal distribution and label the mean and relative location of the z-score.

## Table A.4  Complete Illustration of Converting Observed Scores to Percentiles

| X | z-Scores | Area Below z-Scores | Rounded Percentile |
|---|---|---|---|
| 395 | $(395 - 500)/75 = -1.40$ | .0808 | $.0808 \times 100 = 8$ |
| 410 | $(410 - 500)/75 = -1.20$ | .1151 | $.1151 \times 100 = 12$ |
| 425 | $(425 - 500)/75 = -1.00$ | .1587 | $.1586 \times 100 = 16$ |
| 440 | $(440 - 500)/75 = -0.80$ | .2119 | $.2119 \times 100 = 21$ |
| 500 | $(500 - 500)/75 = 0.00$ | .5000 | $.5000 \times 100 = 50$ |
| 515 | $(515 - 500)/75 = 0.20$ | $.5000 + .0793 = .5793$ | $.5793 \times 100 = 58$ |
| 545 | $(545 - 500)/75 = 0.60$ | $.5000 + .2257 = .7257$ | $.7257 \times 100 = 73$ |
| 560 | $(560 - 500)/75 = 0.80$ | $.5000 + .2881 = .7881$ | $.7881 \times 100 = 79$ |
| 605 | $(605 - 500)/75 = 1.40$ | $.5000 + .4192 = .9192$ | $.9192 \times 100 = 92$ |
| 605 | $(605 - 500)/75 = 1.40$ | $.5000 + .4192 = .9192$ | $.9192 \times 100 = 92$ |

*Note:* Areas found in Table B.1 in Appendix B.

## Knowledge Check

| $X_{A1}$ | $Z_{A1}$ | Percentile | $X_{A2}$ | $X_{A2}$ | Percentile |
|------|-------|-----------|------|--------|-----------|
| 26 | | | 11 | | |
| 23 | | | 29 | | |
| 17 | | | 17 | | |
| 29 | | | 41 | | |
| 22 | 1.200 | 88 | 27 | −1.200 | 12 |
| 19 | | | 25 | | |
| 11 | | | 5 | | |
| 20 | | | 23 | | |
| 18 | | | 19 | | |
| 15 | | | 33 | | |

Using the data in the preceding table, calculate the following:

a. $\Sigma X_{a1}$    $\Sigma X_{a2}$

b. $\Sigma_1 + \Sigma_2$

c. $(\Sigma X_{a1})^2$    $(\Sigma X_{a2})^2$

d. $Mdn_{a1}$    $Mdn_{a2}$

e. $M_{a1}$    $M_{a2}$

f. $S_{a1}^2$    $S_{a2}^2$

g. $s_{a1}$    $s_{a2}$

h. $VAR_{a1}$    $VAR_{a2}$

i. $SD_{a1}$    $SD_{a2}$

j. Using the data, and $M$ and $s$ for each group, convert each score to a z-score.

k. Using the z-scores you just calculated, determine the percentile for each score.

# Appendix B
## Statistical Tables

## CONTENTS

### Table B.1: Proportions of the Area Under the Normal Curve

**Using Table B.1**

To use Table B.1, convert the raw score to a *z*-score using the equation below (also discussed in Appendix A), where *X* is the observed score, *M* is the mean of the data, and *SD* is the standard deviation of the data:

$$z = \frac{(X - M)}{SD}$$

The *z*-score is a standard deviate that allows you to use the standard normal distribution. The normal distribution has a mean of 0.0 and a standard deviation of 1.0. The normal distribution is symmetrical. The values in Table B.1 represent the proportion of area in the standard normal curve that occurs between specific points. The table contains $z$-scores between 0.00 and 3.98. Because the normal distribution is symmetrical, the table represents $z$-scores ranging between $-3.98$ and 3.98.

Column A of the table represents the $z$-score. Column B represents the proportion of the curve between the mean and the $z$-score. Column C represents the proportion of the curve that extends from the $z$-score to $\infty$.

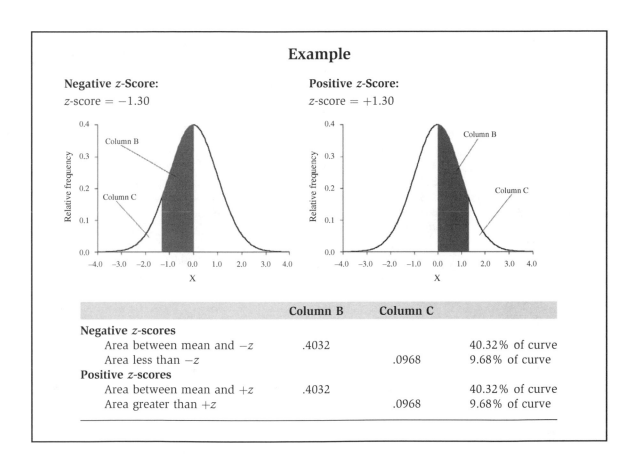

## Example

**Negative z-Score:**

$z$-score $= -1.30$

**Positive z-Score:**

$z$-score $= +1.30$

|  | Column B | Column C |  |
|---|---|---|---|
| **Negative z-scores** |  |  |  |
| Area between mean and $-z$ | .4032 |  | 40.32% of curve |
| Area less than $-z$ |  | .0968 | 9.68% of curve |
| **Positive z-scores** |  |  |  |
| Area between mean and $+z$ | .4032 |  | 40.32% of curve |
| Area greater than $+z$ |  | .0968 | 9.68% of curve |

Area **between** $-z$ and $+z$: $.4032 + .4032 = .8064$ or 80.64% of curve

Area **below** $-z$ and **above** $+z$: $.0968 + .0968 = .1936$ or 19.36% of curve

In the following examples, we add .5000 to the area between the mean and $z$-score. The .5000 represents the proportion of the curve on the complementary half of the normal curve:

Area at and **below** $+z = +1.30$: $.5000 + .4032 = .9032$ or 90.32% of curve

Area at and **above** $-z = -1.30$: $.4032 + .5000 = .9032$ or 90.32% of curve

# Table B.1

| A | B | C | A | B | C | A | B | C |
|---|---|---|---|---|---|---|---|---|
| z | Area between M and z | Area beyond z | z | Area between M and z | Area beyond z | z | Area between M and z | Area beyond z |
| 0.00 | 0.0000 | 0.5000 | 0.40 | 0.1554 | 0.3446 | 0.80 | 0.2881 | 0.2119 |
| 0.01 | 0.0040 | 0.4960 | 0.41 | 0.1591 | 0.3409 | 0.81 | 0.2910 | 0.2090 |
| 0.02 | 0.0080 | 0.4920 | 0.42 | 0.1628 | 0.3372 | 0.82 | 0.2939 | 0.2061 |
| 0.03 | 0.0120 | 0.4880 | 0.43 | 0.1664 | 0.3336 | 0.83 | 0.2967 | 0.2033 |
| 0.04 | 0.0160 | 0.4840 | 0.44 | 0.1700 | 0.3300 | 0.84 | 0.2995 | 0.2005 |
| 0.05 | 0.0199 | 0.4801 | 0.45 | 0.1736 | 0.3264 | 0.85 | 0.3023 | 0.1977 |
| 0.06 | 0.0239 | 0.4761 | 0.46 | 0.1772 | 0.3228 | 0.86 | 0.3051 | 0.1949 |
| 0.07 | 0.0279 | 0.4721 | 0.47 | 0.1808 | 0.3192 | 0.87 | 0.3078 | 0.1922 |
| 0.08 | 0.0319 | 0.4681 | 0.48 | 0.1844 | 0.3156 | 0.88 | 0.3106 | 0.1894 |
| 0.09 | 0.0359 | 0.4641 | 0.49 | 0.1879 | 0.3121 | 0.89 | 0.3133 | 0.1867 |
| 0.10 | 0.0398 | 0.4602 | 0.50 | 0.1915 | 0.3085 | 0.90 | 0.3159 | 0.1841 |
| 0.11 | 0.0438 | 0.4562 | 0.51 | 0.1950 | 0.3050 | 0.91 | 0.3186 | 0.1814 |
| 0.12 | 0.0478 | 0.4522 | 0.52 | 0.1985 | 0.3015 | 0.92 | 0.3212 | 0.1788 |
| 0.13 | 0.0517 | 0.4483 | 0.53 | 0.2019 | 0.2981 | 0.93 | 0.3238 | 0.1762 |
| 0.14 | 0.0557 | 0.4443 | 0.54 | 0.2054 | 0.2946 | 0.94 | 0.3264 | 0.1736 |
| 0.15 | 0.0596 | 0.4404 | 0.55 | 0.2088 | 0.2912 | 0.95 | 0.3289 | 0.1711 |
| 0.16 | 0.0636 | 0.4364 | 0.56 | 0.2123 | 0.2877 | 0.96 | 0.3315 | 0.1685 |
| 0.17 | 0.0675 | 0.4325 | 0.57 | 0.2157 | 0.2843 | 0.97 | 0.3340 | 0.1660 |
| 0.18 | 0.0714 | 0.4286 | 0.58 | 0.2190 | 0.2810 | 0.98 | 0.3365 | 0.1635 |
| 0.19 | 0.0753 | 0.4247 | 0.59 | 0.2224 | 0.2776 | 0.99 | 0.3389 | 0.1611 |
| 0.20 | 0.0793 | 0.4207 | 0.60 | 0.2257 | 0.2743 | 1.00 | 0.3413 | 0.1587 |
| 0.21 | 0.0832 | 0.4168 | 0.61 | 0.2291 | 0.2709 | 1.01 | 0.3438 | 0.1562 |
| 0.22 | 0.0871 | 0.4129 | 0.62 | 0.2324 | 0.2676 | 1.02 | 0.3461 | 0.1539 |
| 0.23 | 0.0910 | 0.4090 | 0.63 | 0.2357 | 0.2643 | 1.03 | 0.3485 | 0.1515 |
| 0.24 | 0.0948 | 0.4052 | 0.64 | 0.2389 | 0.2611 | 1.04 | 0.3508 | 0.1492 |
| 0.25 | 0.0987 | 0.4013 | 0.65 | 0.2422 | 0.2578 | 1.05 | 0.3531 | 0.1469 |
| 0.26 | 0.1026 | 0.3974 | 0.66 | 0.2454 | 0.2546 | 1.06 | 0.3554 | 0.1446 |
| 0.27 | 0.1064 | 0.3936 | 0.67 | 0.2486 | 0.2514 | 1.07 | 0.3577 | 0.1423 |
| 0.28 | 0.1103 | 0.3897 | 0.68 | 0.2517 | 0.2483 | 1.08 | 0.3599 | 0.1401 |
| 0.29 | 0.1141 | 0.3859 | 0.69 | 0.2549 | 0.2451 | 1.09 | 0.3621 | 0.1379 |
| 0.30 | 0.1179 | 0.3821 | 0.70 | 0.2580 | 0.2420 | 1.10 | 0.3643 | 0.1357 |
| 0.31 | 0.1217 | 0.3783 | 0.71 | 0.2611 | 0.2389 | 1.11 | 0.3665 | 0.1335 |
| 0.32 | 0.1255 | 0.3745 | 0.72 | 0.2642 | 0.2358 | 1.12 | 0.3686 | 0.1314 |
| 0.33 | 0.1293 | 0.3707 | 0.73 | 0.2673 | 0.2327 | 1.13 | 0.3708 | 0.1292 |
| 0.34 | 0.1331 | 0.3669 | 0.74 | 0.2704 | 0.2296 | 1.14 | 0.3729 | 0.1271 |
| 0.35 | 0.1368 | 0.3632 | 0.75 | 0.2734 | 0.2266 | 1.15 | 0.3749 | 0.1251 |
| 0.36 | 0.1406 | 0.3594 | 0.76 | 0.2764 | 0.2236 | 1.16 | 0.3770 | 0.1230 |
| 0.37 | 0.1443 | 0.3557 | 0.77 | 0.2794 | 0.2206 | 1.17 | 0.3790 | 0.1210 |
| 0.38 | 0.1480 | 0.3520 | 0.78 | 0.2823 | 0.2177 | 1.18 | 0.3810 | 0.1190 |
| 0.39 | 0.1517 | 0.3483 | 0.79 | 0.2852 | 0.2148 | 1.19 | 0.3830 | 0.1170 |

(Continued)

# Table B.1 (Continued)

| A | B | C | A | B | C | A | B | C |
|---|---|---|---|---|---|---|---|---|
| z | Area between M and z | Area beyond z | z | Area between M and z | Area beyond z | z | Area between M and z | Area beyond z |
| 1.20 | 0.3849 | 0.1151 | 1.60 | 0.4452 | 0.0548 | 2.00 | 0.4772 | 0.0228 |
| 1.21 | 0.3869 | 0.1131 | 1.61 | 0.4463 | 0.0537 | 2.01 | 0.4778 | 0.0222 |
| 1.22 | 0.3888 | 0.1112 | 1.62 | 0.4474 | 0.0526 | 2.02 | 0.4783 | 0.0217 |
| 1.23 | 0.3907 | 0.1093 | 1.63 | 0.4484 | 0.0516 | 2.03 | 0.4788 | 0.0212 |
| 1.24 | 0.3925 | 0.1075 | 1.64 | 0.4495 | 0.0505 | 2.04 | 0.4793 | 0.0207 |
| 1.25 | 0.3944 | 0.1056 | 1.65 | 0.4505 | 0.0495 | 2.05 | 0.4798 | 0.0202 |
| 1.26 | 0.3962 | 0.1038 | 1.66 | 0.4515 | 0.0485 | 2.06 | 0.4803 | 0.0197 |
| 1.27 | 0.3980 | 0.1020 | 1.67 | 0.4525 | 0.0475 | 2.07 | 0.4808 | 0.0192 |
| 1.28 | 0.3997 | 0.1003 | 1.68 | 0.4535 | 0.0465 | 2.08 | 0.4812 | 0.0188 |
| 1.29 | 0.4015 | 0.0985 | 1.69 | 0.4545 | 0.0455 | 2.09 | 0.4817 | 0.0183 |
| 1.30 | 0.4032 | 0.0968 | 1.70 | 0.4554 | 0.0446 | 2.10 | 0.4821 | 0.0179 |
| 1.31 | 0.4049 | 0.0951 | 1.71 | 0.4564 | 0.0436 | 2.11 | 0.4826 | 0.0174 |
| 1.32 | 0.4066 | 0.0934 | 1.72 | 0.4573 | 0.0427 | 2.12 | 0.4830 | 0.0170 |
| 1.33 | 0.4082 | 0.0918 | 1.73 | 0.4582 | 0.0418 | 2.13 | 0.4834 | 0.0166 |
| 1.34 | 0.4099 | 0.0901 | 1.74 | 0.4591 | 0.0409 | 2.14 | 0.4838 | 0.0162 |
| 1.35 | 0.4115 | 0.0885 | 1.75 | 0.4599 | 0.0401 | 2.15 | 0.4842 | 0.0158 |
| 1.36 | 0.4131 | 0.0869 | 1.76 | 0.4608 | 0.0392 | 2.16 | 0.4846 | 0.0154 |
| 1.37 | 0.4147 | 0.0853 | 1.77 | 0.4616 | 0.0384 | 2.17 | 0.4850 | 0.0150 |
| 1.38 | 0.4162 | 0.0838 | 1.78 | 0.4625 | 0.0375 | 2.18 | 0.4854 | 0.0146 |
| 1.39 | 0.4177 | 0.0823 | 1.79 | 0.4633 | 0.0367 | 2.19 | 0.4857 | 0.0143 |
| 1.40 | 0.4192 | 0.0808 | 1.80 | 0.4641 | 0.0359 | 2.20 | 0.4861 | 0.0139 |
| 1.41 | 0.4207 | 0.0793 | 1.81 | 0.4649 | 0.0351 | 2.21 | 0.4864 | 0.0136 |
| 1.42 | 0.4222 | 0.0778 | 1.82 | 0.4656 | 0.0344 | 2.22 | 0.4868 | 0.0132 |
| 1.43 | 0.4236 | 0.0764 | 1.83 | 0.4664 | 0.0336 | 2.23 | 0.4871 | 0.0129 |
| 1.44 | 0.4251 | 0.0749 | 1.84 | 0.4671 | 0.0329 | 2.24 | 0.4875 | 0.0125 |
| 1.45 | 0.4265 | 0.0735 | 1.85 | 0.4678 | 0.0322 | 2.25 | 0.4878 | 0.0122 |
| 1.46 | 0.4279 | 0.0721 | 1.86 | 0.4686 | 0.0314 | 2.26 | 0.4881 | 0.0119 |
| 1.47 | 0.4292 | 0.0708 | 1.87 | 0.4693 | 0.0307 | 2.27 | 0.4884 | 0.0116 |
| 1.48 | 0.4306 | 0.0694 | 1.88 | 0.4699 | 0.0301 | 2.28 | 0.4887 | 0.0113 |
| 1.49 | 0.4319 | 0.0681 | 1.89 | 0.4706 | 0.0294 | 2.29 | 0.4890 | 0.0110 |
| 1.50 | 0.4332 | 0.0668 | 1.90 | 0.4713 | 0.0287 | 2.30 | 0.4893 | 0.0107 |
| 1.51 | 0.4345 | 0.0655 | 1.91 | 0.4719 | 0.0281 | 2.31 | 0.4896 | 0.0104 |
| 1.52 | 0.4357 | 0.0643 | 1.92 | 0.4726 | 0.0274 | 2.32 | 0.4898 | 0.0102 |
| 1.53 | 0.4370 | 0.0630 | 1.93 | 0.4732 | 0.0268 | 2.33 | 0.4901 | 0.0099 |
| 1.54 | 0.4382 | 0.0618 | 1.94 | 0.4738 | 0.0262 | 2.34 | 0.4904 | 0.0096 |
| 1.55 | 0.4394 | 0.0606 | 1.95 | 0.4744 | 0.0256 | 2.35 | 0.4906 | 0.0094 |
| 1.56 | 0.4406 | 0.0594 | 1.96 | 0.4750 | 0.0250 | 2.36 | 0.4909 | 0.0091 |
| 1.57 | 0.4418 | 0.0582 | 1.97 | 0.4756 | 0.0244 | 2.37 | 0.4911 | 0.0089 |
| 1.58 | 0.4429 | 0.0571 | 1.98 | 0.4761 | 0.0239 | 2.38 | 0.4913 | 0.0087 |
| 1.59 | 0.4441 | 0.0559 | 1.99 | 0.4767 | 0.0233 | 2.39 | 0.4916 | 0.0084 |

*(Continued)*

# Table B.1 (Continued)

| A | B | C | A | B | C | A | B | C |
|---|---|---|---|---|---|---|---|---|
| z | Area between M and z | Area beyond z | z | Area between M and z | Area beyond z | z | Area between M and z | Area beyond z |
| 2.40 | 0.4918 | 0.0082 | 2.80 | 0.4974 | 0.0026 | 3.20 | 0.4993 | 0.0007 |
| 2.41 | 0.4920 | 0.0080 | 2.81 | 0.4975 | 0.0025 | 3.22 | 0.4994 | 0.0006 |
| 2.42 | 0.4922 | 0.0078 | 2.82 | 0.4976 | 0.0024 | 3.24 | 0.4994 | 0.0006 |
| 2.43 | 0.4925 | 0.0075 | 2.83 | 0.4977 | 0.0023 | 3.26 | 0.4994 | 0.0006 |
| 2.44 | 0.4927 | 0.0073 | 2.84 | 0.4977 | 0.0023 | 3.28 | 0.4995 | 0.0005 |
| 2.45 | 0.4929 | 0.0071 | 2.85 | 0.4978 | 0.0022 | 3.30 | 0.4995 | 0.0005 |
| 2.46 | 0.4931 | 0.0069 | 2.86 | 0.4979 | 0.0021 | 3.32 | 0.4995 | 0.0005 |
| 2.47 | 0.4932 | 0.0068 | 2.87 | 0.4979 | 0.0021 | 3.34 | 0.4996 | 0.0004 |
| 2.48 | 0.4934 | 0.0066 | 2.88 | 0.4980 | 0.0020 | 3.36 | 0.4996 | 0.0004 |
| 2.49 | 0.4936 | 0.0064 | 2.89 | 0.4981 | 0.0019 | 3.38 | 0.4996 | 0.0004 |
| 2.50 | 0.4938 | 0.0062 | 2.90 | 0.4981 | 0.0019 | 3.40 | 0.4997 | 0.0003 |
| 2.51 | 0.4940 | 0.0060 | 2.91 | 0.4982 | 0.0018 | 3.42 | 0.4997 | 0.0003 |
| 2.52 | 0.4941 | 0.0059 | 2.92 | 0.4982 | 0.0018 | 3.44 | 0.4997 | 0.0003 |
| 2.53 | 0.4943 | 0.0057 | 2.93 | 0.4983 | 0.0017 | 3.46 | 0.4997 | 0.0003 |
| 2.54 | 0.4945 | 0.0055 | 2.94 | 0.4984 | 0.0016 | 3.48 | 0.4997 | 0.0003 |
| 2.55 | 0.4946 | 0.0054 | 2.95 | 0.4984 | 0.0016 | 3.50 | 0.4998 | 0.0002 |
| 2.56 | 0.4948 | 0.0052 | 2.96 | 0.4985 | 0.0015 | 3.52 | 0.4998 | 0.0002 |
| 2.57 | 0.4949 | 0.0051 | 2.97 | 0.4985 | 0.0015 | 3.54 | 0.4998 | 0.0002 |
| 2.58 | 0.4951 | 0.0049 | 2.98 | 0.4986 | 0.0014 | 3.56 | 0.4998 | 0.0002 |
| 2.59 | 0.4952 | 0.0048 | 2.99 | 0.4986 | 0.0014 | 3.58 | 0.4998 | 0.0002 |
| 2.60 | 0.4953 | 0.0047 | 3.00 | 0.4987 | 0.0013 | 3.60 | 0.4998 | 0.0002 |
| 2.61 | 0.4955 | 0.0045 | 3.01 | 0.4987 | 0.0013 | 3.62 | 0.4999 | 0.0001 |
| 2.62 | 0.4956 | 0.0044 | 3.02 | 0.4987 | 0.0013 | 3.64 | 0.4999 | 0.0001 |
| 2.63 | 0.4957 | 0.0043 | 3.03 | 0.4988 | 0.0012 | 3.66 | 0.4999 | 0.0001 |
| 2.64 | 0.4959 | 0.0041 | 3.04 | 0.4988 | 0.0012 | 3.68 | 0.4999 | 0.0001 |
| 2.65 | 0.4960 | 0.0040 | 3.05 | 0.4989 | 0.0011 | 3.70 | 0.4999 | 0.0001 |
| 2.66 | 0.4961 | 0.0039 | 3.06 | 0.4989 | 0.0011 | 3.72 | 0.4999 | 0.0001 |
| 2.67 | 0.4962 | 0.0038 | 3.07 | 0.4989 | 0.0011 | 3.74 | 0.4999 | 0.0001 |
| 2.68 | 0.4963 | 0.0037 | 3.08 | 0.4990 | 0.0010 | 3.76 | 0.4999 | 0.0001 |
| 2.69 | 0.4964 | 0.0036 | 3.09 | 0.4990 | 0.0010 | 3.78 | 0.4999 | 0.0001 |
| 2.70 | 0.4965 | 0.0035 | 3.10 | 0.4990 | 0.0010 | 3.80 | 0.4999 | 0.0001 |
| 2.71 | 0.4966 | 0.0034 | 3.11 | 0.4991 | 0.0009 | 3.82 | 0.4999 | 0.0001 |
| 2.72 | 0.4967 | 0.0033 | 3.12 | 0.4991 | 0.0009 | 3.84 | 0.4999 | 0.0001 |
| 2.73 | 0.4968 | 0.0032 | 3.13 | 0.4991 | 0.0009 | 3.86 | 0.4999 | 0.0001 |
| 2.74 | 0.4969 | 0.0031 | 3.14 | 0.4992 | 0.0008 | 3.88 | 0.4999 | 0.0001 |
| 2.75 | 0.4970 | 0.0030 | 3.15 | 0.4992 | 0.0008 | 3.90 | 0.5000 | 0.0000 |
| 2.76 | 0.4971 | 0.0029 | 3.16 | 0.4992 | 0.0008 | 3.92 | 0.5000 | 0.0000 |
| 2.77 | 0.4972 | 0.0028 | 3.17 | 0.4992 | 0.0008 | 3.94 | 0.5000 | 0.0000 |
| 2.78 | 0.4973 | 0.0027 | 3.18 | 0.4993 | 0.0007 | 3.96 | 0.5000 | 0.0000 |
| 2.79 | 0.4974 | 0.0026 | 3.19 | 0.4993 | 0.0007 | 3.98 | 0.5000 | 0.0000 |

## Table B.2: 1,200 Two-Digit Random Numbers

### Using Table B.2

This table consists of two-digit random numbers that can range between 00 and 99 inclusive. To select a series of random numbers, select a column and row at random, and then record the numbers. You may move in any direction to generate the sequence of numbers.

---

### Example

A researcher wished to randomly assign participants to one of five treatment conditions. Recognizing that the numbers in Table B.2 range between 00 and 99, the researcher decided to use the following table to convert the random numbers to the five treatment conditions:

| Range of Random Numbers | Treatment Condition |
|---|---|
| 00–20 | 1 |
| 21–40 | 2 |
| 41–60 | 3 |
| 61–80 | 4 |
| 81–99 | 5 |

---

## Table B.2

| | 1 | 2 | 3 | 4 | 5 | 6 | 7 | 8 | 9 | 10 | 11 | 12 | 13 | 14 | 15 | 16 | 17 | 18 | 19 | 20 | 21 | 22 | 23 | 24 |
|---|---|---|---|---|---|---|---|---|---|---|---|---|---|---|---|---|---|---|---|---|---|---|---|---|
| 1 | 43 | 41 | 16 | 31 | 22 | 44 | 10 | 41 | 45 | 00 | 47 | 19 | 43 | 67 | 83 | 02 | 79 | 05 | 98 | 92 | 64 | 82 | 06 | 89 |
| 2 | 26 | 44 | 01 | 04 | 28 | 85 | 11 | 91 | 23 | 02 | 39 | 79 | 44 | 45 | 93 | 20 | 17 | 91 | 35 | 15 | 25 | 82 | 18 | 41 |
| 3 | 83 | 39 | 26 | 84 | 04 | 16 | 89 | 79 | 68 | 85 | 61 | 63 | 03 | 20 | 17 | 76 | 95 | 80 | 27 | 39 | 35 | 82 | 10 | 86 |
| 4 | 65 | 94 | 48 | 27 | 77 | 65 | 34 | 95 | 04 | 51 | 78 | 90 | 14 | 76 | 90 | 83 | 17 | 76 | 69 | 50 | 34 | 01 | 25 | 08 |
| 5 | 89 | 38 | 32 | 05 | 09 | 49 | 87 | 93 | 21 | 24 | 88 | 74 | 30 | 94 | 26 | 19 | 23 | 72 | 94 | 80 | 90 | 24 | 55 | 44 |
| 6 | 77 | 80 | 30 | 43 | 26 | 01 | 43 | 46 | 66 | 40 | 52 | 00 | 44 | 69 | 84 | 10 | 48 | 96 | 49 | 85 | 49 | 84 | 97 | 41 |
| 7 | 43 | 42 | 26 | 74 | 51 | 05 | 56 | 43 | 06 | 80 | 58 | 22 | 57 | 02 | 11 | 95 | 00 | 91 | 88 | 17 | 71 | 98 | 32 | 56 |
| 8 | 76 | 76 | 61 | 17 | 69 | 06 | 73 | 37 | 77 | 06 | 36 | 28 | 05 | 73 | 31 | 04 | 44 | 33 | 40 | 74 | 46 | 26 | 02 | 99 |
| 9 | 42 | 05 | 88 | 83 | 15 | 05 | 28 | 52 | 88 | 78 | 88 | 66 | 50 | 80 | 24 | 38 | 31 | 20 | 48 | 73 | 18 | 85 | 18 | 90 |
| 10 | 46 | 74 | 76 | 34 | 97 | 40 | 59 | 34 | 86 | 11 | 50 | 98 | 69 | 59 | 46 | 74 | 59 | 60 | 98 | 76 | 96 | 42 | 34 | 83 |
| 11 | 67 | 15 | 82 | 94 | 59 | 55 | 27 | 99 | 02 | 34 | 47 | 34 | 88 | 98 | 72 | 15 | 38 | 73 | 57 | 42 | 56 | 09 | 85 | 83 |
| 12 | 03 | 58 | 51 | 69 | 14 | 89 | 24 | 06 | 35 | 31 | 16 | 65 | 71 | 76 | 04 | 80 | 01 | 36 | 00 | 67 | 78 | 73 | 07 | 37 |
| 13 | 79 | 98 | 19 | 32 | 25 | 95 | 89 | 54 | 20 | 78 | 29 | 81 | 96 | 34 | 62 | 53 | 26 | 09 | 02 | 04 | 63 | 95 | 03 | 53 |
| 14 | 56 | 12 | 61 | 36 | 21 | 69 | 96 | 06 | 22 | 06 | 01 | 80 | 57 | 72 | 23 | 55 | 05 | 74 | 42 | 55 | 91 | 45 | 60 | 91 |
| 15 | 58 | 80 | 33 | 35 | 75 | 33 | 35 | 42 | 06 | 79 | 73 | 29 | 89 | 73 | 99 | 07 | 05 | 54 | 42 | 77 | 78 | 99 | 33 | 92 |
| 16 | 31 | 51 | 77 | 53 | 92 | 51 | 35 | 71 | 34 | 46 | 79 | 43 | 76 | 15 | 76 | 46 | 40 | 04 | 36 | 84 | 83 | 64 | 56 | 73 |
| 17 | 25 | 77 | 95 | 61 | 71 | 10 | 82 | 51 | 57 | 88 | 29 | 59 | 55 | 84 | 71 | 89 | 64 | 34 | 38 | 33 | 11 | 45 | 47 | 19 |
| 18 | 02 | 12 | 81 | 84 | 23 | 80 | 58 | 65 | 74 | 13 | 46 | 09 | 33 | 66 | 86 | 74 | 94 | 96 | 07 | 22 | 52 | 39 | 31 | 36 |
| 19 | 18 | 38 | 40 | 30 | 34 | 27 | 70 | 62 | 35 | 71 | 48 | 96 | 73 | 74 | 28 | 61 | 15 | 37 | 23 | 16 | 91 | 29 | 03 | 06 |
| 20 | 31 | 76 | 47 | 77 | 59 | 14 | 66 | 85 | 27 | 10 | 63 | 58 | 48 | 66 | 66 | 17 | 91 | 16 | 55 | 70 | 30 | 53 | 05 | 94 |
| 21 | 50 | 93 | 33 | 61 | 20 | 55 | 10 | 61 | 08 | 76 | 62 | 14 | 22 | 65 | 44 | 95 | 75 | 68 | 94 | 76 | 51 | 21 | 22 | 12 |
| 22 | 45 | 75 | 89 | 11 | 64 | 06 | 22 | 39 | 20 | 04 | 91 | 47 | 16 | 48 | 19 | 93 | 12 | 02 | 17 | 15 | 94 | 74 | 77 | 37 |
| 23 | 17 | 97 | 59 | 42 | 77 | 26 | 29 | 88 | 66 | 62 | 53 | 28 | 95 | 01 | 10 | 85 | 31 | 10 | 25 | 75 | 10 | 35 | 99 | 60 |
| 24 | 23 | 25 | 86 | 94 | 12 | 75 | 66 | 93 | 87 | 95 | 09 | 48 | 85 | 43 | 20 | 94 | 00 | 38 | 53 | 45 | 11 | 77 | 01 | 66 |
| 25 | 63 | 17 | 05 | 28 | 67 | 39 | 72 | 85 | 02 | 34 | 69 | 56 | 53 | 66 | 09 | 38 | 72 | 31 | 85 | 29 | 62 | 18 | 29 | 37 |

*(Continued)*

# Table B.2 (Continued)

| | 1 | 2 | 3 | 4 | 5 | 6 | 7 | 8 | 9 | 10 | 11 | 12 | 13 | 14 | 15 | 16 | 17 | 18 | 19 | 20 | 21 | 22 | 23 | 24 |
|---|---|---|---|---|---|---|---|---|---|---|---|---|---|---|---|---|---|---|---|---|---|---|---|---|
| 26 | 99 | 81 | 28 | 63 | 05 | 26 | 66 | 16 | 66 | 69 | 18 | 56 | 26 | 53 | 29 | 38 | 08 | 04 | 27 | 93 | 54 | 83 | 53 | 15 |
| 27 | 86 | 72 | 54 | 89 | 57 | 45 | 05 | 82 | 32 | 64 | 93 | 24 | 83 | 44 | 56 | 65 | 29 | 68 | 69 | 14 | 70 | 79 | 92 | 39 |
| 28 | 42 | 50 | 86 | 19 | 08 | 81 | 57 | 09 | 69 | 35 | 29 | 06 | 52 | 43 | 53 | 99 | 57 | 55 | 30 | 63 | 63 | 67 | 94 | 94 |
| 29 | 42 | 80 | 75 | 06 | 05 | 62 | 69 | 04 | 90 | 49 | 10 | 48 | 34 | 21 | 63 | 94 | 19 | 99 | 96 | 79 | 83 | 41 | 86 | 38 |
| 30 | 82 | 48 | 69 | 65 | 59 | 74 | 64 | 25 | 66 | 93 | 32 | 56 | 14 | 57 | 80 | 10 | 36 | 17 | 39 | 48 | 46 | 94 | 88 | 43 |
| 31 | 24 | 81 | 98 | 33 | 40 | 89 | 60 | 97 | 28 | 64 | 78 | 93 | 07 | 84 | 07 | 02 | 63 | 35 | 64 | 30 | 29 | 49 | 37 | 00 |
| 32 | 15 | 84 | 59 | 73 | 01 | 21 | 67 | 43 | 43 | 74 | 00 | 28 | 64 | 66 | 03 | 80 | 60 | 08 | 51 | 67 | 51 | 89 | 00 | 46 |
| 33 | 92 | 31 | 60 | 34 | 23 | 72 | 00 | 19 | 78 | 73 | 80 | 36 | 51 | 54 | 45 | 76 | 17 | 34 | 35 | 74 | 78 | 20 | 49 | 95 |
| 34 | 05 | 80 | 10 | 40 | 30 | 63 | 25 | 78 | 91 | 13 | 77 | 39 | 90 | 78 | 89 | 17 | 45 | 76 | 28 | 64 | 12 | 37 | 60 | 34 |
| 35 | 67 | 51 | 92 | 66 | 84 | 33 | 15 | 34 | 42 | 73 | 54 | 93 | 02 | 01 | 19 | 87 | 36 | 58 | 08 | 11 | 58 | 38 | 88 | 98 |
| 36 | 71 | 44 | 83 | 33 | 92 | 84 | 96 | 76 | 87 | 24 | 59 | 41 | 71 | 36 | 86 | 14 | 54 | 31 | 41 | 25 | 15 | 59 | 74 | 52 |
| 37 | 43 | 13 | 62 | 58 | 75 | 90 | 94 | 10 | 65 | 16 | 51 | 90 | 01 | 40 | 18 | 21 | 51 | 82 | 69 | 91 | 65 | 91 | 22 | 32 |
| 38 | 97 | 55 | 94 | 52 | 18 | 65 | 73 | 90 | 55 | 80 | 51 | 05 | 60 | 53 | 01 | 52 | 46 | 57 | 21 | 05 | 76 | 61 | 05 | 23 |
| 39 | 32 | 75 | 70 | 24 | 04 | 98 | 03 | 79 | 84 | 34 | 50 | 06 | 25 | 00 | 05 | 00 | 04 | 25 | 68 | 58 | 99 | 48 | 06 | 80 |
| 40 | 23 | 87 | 76 | 65 | 51 | 19 | 93 | 54 | 81 | 09 | 71 | 83 | 97 | 24 | 90 | 01 | 81 | 14 | 70 | 16 | 07 | 16 | 05 | 93 |
| 41 | 21 | 77 | 33 | 17 | 02 | 64 | 55 | 23 | 21 | 84 | 80 | 02 | 79 | 30 | 61 | 46 | 33 | 94 | 28 | 92 | 44 | 27 | 76 | 20 |
| 42 | 90 | 11 | 17 | 05 | 24 | 52 | 08 | 39 | 94 | 07 | 43 | 58 | 33 | 72 | 04 | 51 | 81 | 79 | 63 | 70 | 94 | 71 | 71 | 68 |
| 43 | 89 | 00 | 39 | 09 | 55 | 13 | 96 | 24 | 47 | 81 | 18 | 37 | 82 | 37 | 37 | 01 | 95 | 82 | 38 | 57 | 20 | 20 | 35 | 83 |
| 44 | 58 | 65 | 18 | 34 | 73 | 85 | 20 | 47 | 04 | 68 | 77 | 28 | 80 | 14 | 37 | 24 | 97 | 62 | 87 | 38 | 09 | 09 | 08 | 50 |
| 45 | 80 | 35 | 64 | 10 | 03 | 18 | 24 | 41 | 54 | 12 | 99 | 97 | 50 | 14 | 15 | 80 | 71 | 87 | 47 | 79 | 50 | 62 | 87 | 42 |
| 46 | 87 | 26 | 52 | 18 | 56 | 47 | 76 | 29 | 40 | 08 | 12 | 07 | 40 | 49 | 29 | 70 | 60 | 74 | 20 | 50 | 51 | 00 | 17 | 42 |
| 47 | 54 | 23 | 81 | 36 | 70 | 93 | 10 | 05 | 39 | 54 | 20 | 49 | 10 | 70 | 49 | 13 | 37 | 59 | 44 | 52 | 98 | 13 | 64 | 48 |
| 48 | 72 | 08 | 17 | 30 | 70 | 44 | 08 | 10 | 25 | 81 | 53 | 39 | 81 | 67 | 13 | 80 | 74 | 09 | 71 | 06 | 95 | 05 | 17 | 00 |
| 49 | 34 | 59 | 02 | 12 | 20 | 31 | 15 | 96 | 18 | 12 | 37 | 32 | 25 | 96 | 71 | 52 | 78 | 01 | 77 | 18 | 63 | 66 | 96 | 09 |
| 50 | 97 | 89 | 00 | 94 | 82 | 17 | 49 | 92 | 29 | 73 | 30 | 17 | 78 | 53 | 45 | 29 | 39 | 24 | 95 | 61 | 63 | 76 | 90 | 86 |

## Table B.3: Critical Values for Student's *t*-Test

### Using Table B.3

For any given *df*, the table shows the values of $t_{critical}$ corresponding to various levels of probability. The $t_{observed}$ is statistically significant at a given level when it is equal to or greater than the value shown in the table:

For the single-sample *t*-ratio, $df = N - 1$.

For the two-sample *t*-ratio, $df = (n_1 - 1) + (n_2 - 1)$.

---

## Examples

**Nondirectional Hypothesis:**

$H_0: \mu - \mu = 0$   $H_1: \mu - \mu \neq 0$   $\alpha = .05$   $df = 30$

$t_{critical} = \pm 2.042$ If $|t_{observed}| \geq |t_{critical}|$, then reject $H_0$

**Directional Hypothesis:**

$H_0: \mu - \mu = 0$   $H_1: \mu - \mu > 0$   $\alpha = .05$   $df = 30$

$t_{critical} = +1.697$ If $t_{observed} \geq t_{critical}$, then reject $H_0$

$H_0: \mu - \mu \geq 0$   $H_1: \mu - \mu < 0$   $\alpha = .05$   $df = 30$

$t_{critical} = -1.697$ If $t_{observed} \leq t_{critical}$, then reject $H_0$

# Table B.3

| | Level of Significance of a One-Tailed or Directional Test $H_0: \mu - \mu \geq 0$ or $H_0: \mu - \mu \leq 0$ | | | | | |
|---|---|---|---|---|---|---|
| | $\alpha = 0.10$ $1 - \alpha = .90$ | $\alpha = .05$ $1 - \alpha = .95$ | $\alpha = .025$ $1 - \alpha = .975$ | $\alpha = .01$ $1 - \alpha = .99$ | $\alpha = .005$ $1 - \alpha = .995$ | $\alpha = .0005$ $1 - \alpha = .9995$ |
| | Level of Significance of a Two-Tailed or Nondirectional Test $H_0: \mu - \mu = 0$ | | | | | |
| df | $\alpha = .20$ $1 - \alpha = .80$ | $\alpha = .10$ $1 - \alpha = .90$ | $\alpha = .05$ $1 - \alpha = .95$ | $\alpha = .02$ $1 - \alpha = .98$ | $\alpha = .01$ $1 - \alpha = .99$ | $\alpha = .001$ $1 - \alpha = .999$ |
| 1 | 3.078 | 6.314 | 12.706 | 31.821 | 63.656 | 636.578 |
| 2 | 1.886 | 2.920 | 4.303 | 6.965 | 9.925 | 31.600 |
| 3 | 1.638 | 2.353 | 3.182 | 4.541 | 5.841 | 12.924 |
| 4 | 1.533 | 2.132 | 2.776 | 3.747 | 4.604 | 8.610 |
| 5 | 1.476 | 2.015 | 2.571 | 3.365 | 4.032 | 6.869 |
| 6 | 1.440 | 1.943 | 2.447 | 3.143 | 3.707 | 5.959 |
| 7 | 1.415 | 1.895 | 2.365 | 2.998 | 3.499 | 5.408 |
| 8 | 1.397 | 1.860 | 2.306 | 2.896 | 3.355 | 5.041 |
| 9 | 1.383 | 1.833 | 2.262 | 2.821 | 3.250 | 4.781 |
| 10 | 1.372 | 1.812 | 2.228 | 2.764 | 3.169 | 4.587 |
| 11 | 1.363 | 1.796 | 2.201 | 2.718 | 3.106 | 4.437 |
| 12 | 1.356 | 1.782 | 2.179 | 2.681 | 3.055 | 4.318 |
| 13 | 1.350 | 1.771 | 2.160 | 2.650 | 3.012 | 4.221 |
| 14 | 1.345 | 1.761 | 2.145 | 2.624 | 2.977 | 4.140 |
| 15 | 1.341 | 1.753 | 2.131 | 2.602 | 2.947 | 4.073 |
| 16 | 1.337 | 1.746 | 2.120 | 2.583 | 2.921 | 4.015 |
| 17 | 1.333 | 1.740 | 2.110 | 2.567 | 2.898 | 3.965 |
| 18 | 1.330 | 1.734 | 2.101 | 2.552 | 2.878 | 3.922 |
| 19 | 1.328 | 1.729 | 2.093 | 2.539 | 2.861 | 3.883 |
| 20 | 1.325 | 1.725 | 2.086 | 2.528 | 2.845 | 3.850 |
| 21 | 1.323 | 1.721 | 2.080 | 2.518 | 2.831 | 3.819 |
| 22 | 1.321 | 1.717 | 2.074 | 2.508 | 2.819 | 3.792 |
| 23 | 1.319 | 1.714 | 2.069 | 2.500 | 2.807 | 3.768 |
| 24 | 1.318 | 1.711 | 2.064 | 2.492 | 2.797 | 3.745 |
| 25 | 1.316 | 1.708 | 2.060 | 2.485 | 2.787 | 3.725 |
| 26 | 1.315 | 1.706 | 2.056 | 2.479 | 2.779 | 3.707 |
| 27 | 1.314 | 1.703 | 2.052 | 2.473 | 2.771 | 3.689 |
| 28 | 1.313 | 1.701 | 2.048 | 2.467 | 2.763 | 3.674 |
| 29 | 1.311 | 1.699 | 2.045 | 2.462 | 2.756 | 3.660 |
| 30 | 1.310 | 1.697 | 2.042 | 2.457 | 2.750 | 3.646 |
| 40 | 1.303 | 1.684 | 2.021 | 2.423 | 2.704 | 3.551 |
| 50 | 1.299 | 1.676 | 2.009 | 2.403 | 2.678 | 3.496 |
| 60 | 1.296 | 1.671 | 2.000 | 2.390 | 2.660 | 3.460 |
| 70 | 1.294 | 1.667 | 1.994 | 2.381 | 2.648 | 3.435 |
| 80 | 1.292 | 1.664 | 1.990 | 2.374 | 2.639 | 3.416 |
| 90 | 1.291 | 1.662 | 1.987 | 2.368 | 2.632 | 3.402 |
| 100 | 1.290 | 1.660 | 1.984 | 2.364 | 2.626 | 3.390 |
| 150 | 1.287 | 1.655 | 1.976 | 2.351 | 2.609 | 3.357 |
| 200 | 1.286 | 1.653 | 1.972 | 2.345 | 2.601 | 3.340 |
| 500 | 1.283 | 1.648 | 1.965 | 2.334 | 2.586 | 3.310 |
| 1000 | 1.282 | 1.646 | 1.962 | 2.330 | 2.581 | 3.300 |
| $\infty$ | 1.282 | 1.645 | 1.960 | 2.326 | 2.576 | 3.290 |

## Table B.4: Power of Student's Single-Sample *t*-Ratio

### Using Table B.4

This table provides the power $(1 - \beta)$ of the single-sample *t*-ratio given effect size, sample size $(n)$, $\alpha$, and directionality of the test.

---

**Example**

A researcher plans to conduct a study for which $H_0$: is $\mu = 12.0$ using a two-tailed *t*-ratio. The researcher sets $\alpha = .05$ and believes that that the effect size is .20. Approximately how many participants should be in the sample for the power to be approximately .80? According to Table B.4, if the researcher uses 200 participants, the power will be $1 - \beta = .83$.

Note that for Cohen's *d*, an estimate of effect size:

$$d = .20 = \text{"small"} \quad d = .50 = \text{"medium"} \quad d = .80 = \text{"large"}$$

---

## Table B.4

| | | $\alpha = .05$ Two-Tailed | | | | | $\alpha = .01$ Two-Tailed | | | |
|---|---|---|---|---|---|---|---|---|---|---|
| $n$ | $t_c$ | .10 | .20 | .50 | .80 | $t_c$ | .10 | .20 | .50 | .80 |
| 5 | 2.306 | .07 | .09 | .19 | .37 | 3.355 | .02 | .03 | .07 | .16 |
| 6 | 2.228 | .07 | .09 | .22 | .44 | 3.169 | .02 | .03 | .08 | .21 |
| 7 | 2.179 | .07 | .09 | .24 | .50 | 3.055 | .02 | .03 | .10 | .25 |
| 8 | 2.145 | .07 | .10 | .27 | .57 | 2.977 | .02 | .03 | .11 | .30 |
| 9 | 2.120 | .07 | .10 | .30 | .62 | 2.921 | .02 | .03 | .13 | .35 |
| 10 | 2.101 | .07 | .10 | .33 | .67 | 2.878 | .02 | .03 | .14 | .40 |
| 11 | 2.086 | .07 | .11 | .35 | .72 | 2.845 | .02 | .03 | .16 | .45 |
| 12 | 2.074 | .07 | .11 | .38 | .76 | 2.819 | .02 | .03 | .18 | .50 |
| 13 | 2.064 | .07 | .11 | .41 | .80 | 2.797 | .02 | .04 | .19 | .54 |
| 14 | 2.056 | .07 | .12 | .44 | .83 | 2.779 | .02 | .04 | .21 | .59 |
| 15 | 2.048 | .07 | .12 | .46 | .86 | 2.763 | .02 | .04 | .23 | .63 |
| 16 | 2.042 | .07 | .12 | .49 | .88 | 2.750 | .02 | .04 | .25 | .67 |
| 17 | 2.037 | .07 | .13 | .51 | .90 | 2.738 | .02 | .04 | .27 | .71 |
| 18 | 2.032 | .07 | .13 | .54 | .92 | 2.728 | .02 | .04 | .29 | .74 |
| 19 | 2.028 | .07 | .14 | .56 | .94 | 2.719 | .02 | .05 | .31 | .78 |
| 20 | 2.024 | .08 | .14 | .59 | .95 | 2.712 | .02 | .05 | .33 | .80 |
| 21 | 2.021 | .08 | .14 | .61 | .96 | 2.704 | .02 | .05 | .35 | .83 |
| 22 | 2.018 | .08 | .15 | .63 | .97 | 2.698 | .02 | .05 | .37 | .85 |
| 23 | 2.015 | .08 | .15 | .65 | .97 | 2.692 | .02 | .05 | .39 | .87 |
| 24 | 2.013 | .08 | .16 | .67 | .98 | 2.687 | .02 | .05 | .41 | .89 |
| 25 | 2.011 | .08 | .16 | .69 | .98 | 2.682 | .02 | .06 | .43 | .91 |
| 30 | 2.002 | .08 | .18 | .78 | .99 | 2.663 | .02 | .07 | .53 | .96 |
| 40 | 1.991 | .09 | .23 | .89 | .99 | 2.640 | .03 | .09 | .70 | .99 |
| 50 | 1.984 | .10 | .28 | .95 | .99 | 2.627 | .03 | .11 | .82 | .99 |
| 60 | 1.980 | .11 | .32 | .98 | .99 | 2.618 | .04 | .14 | .90 | .99 |
| 70 | 1.977 | .13 | .37 | .99 | .99 | 2.612 | .04 | .17 | .95 | .99 |

*(Continued)*

# Table B.4  (Continued)

| n | $t_c$ | .10 | .20 | .50 | .80 | $t_c$ | .10 | .20 | .50 | .80 |
|---|---|---|---|---|---|---|---|---|---|---|
| | | $\alpha = .05$ Two-Tailed | | | | | $\alpha = .01$ Two-Tailed | | | |
| 80 | 1.975 | .14 | .42 | .99 | .99 | 2.607 | .04 | .20 | .98 | .99 |
| 90 | 1.973 | .15 | .46 | .99 | .99 | 2.604 | .05 | .23 | .99 | .99 |
| 100 | 1.972 | .16 | .50 | .99 | .99 | 2.601 | .05 | .26 | .99 | .99 |
| 150 | 1.968 | .22 | .69 | .99 | .99 | 2.592 | .08 | .43 | .99 | .99 |
| 200 | 1.966 | .28 | .82 | .99 | .99 | 2.588 | .11 | .59 | .99 | .99 |
| 250 | 1.965 | .34 | .90 | .99 | .99 | 2.586 | .15 | .72 | .99 | .99 |
| 300 | 1.964 | .39 | .95 | .99 | .99 | 2.584 | .18 | .82 | .99 | .99 |
| 350 | 1.963 | .45 | .98 | .99 | .99 | 2.583 | .22 | .89 | .99 | .99 |
| 400 | 1.963 | .51 | .99 | .99 | .99 | 2.582 | .26 | .94 | .99 | .99 |
| 500 | 1.962 | .61 | .99 | .99 | .99 | 2.581 | .35 | .98 | .99 | .99 |
| 600 | 1.962 | .69 | .99 | .99 | .99 | 2.580 | .43 | .99 | .99 | .99 |
| 700 | 1.962 | .76 | .99 | .99 | .99 | 2.579 | .51 | .99 | .99 | .99 |
| 800 | 1.961 | .82 | .99 | .99 | .99 | 2.579 | .59 | .99 | .99 | .99 |
| 900 | 1.961 | .87 | .99 | .99 | .99 | 2.579 | .66 | .99 | .99 | .99 |
| 1000 | 1.961 | .90 | .99 | .99 | .99 | 2.578 | .72 | .99 | .99 | .99 |

## Table B.5.1: Power of Student's Two-Sample $t$-Ratio, One-Tailed Tests

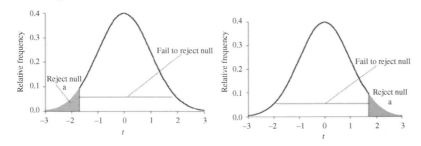

### Using Table B.5.1

This table provides the power $(1 - \beta)$ of the two-sample $t$-ratio given effect size, sample size $(n)$, and $\alpha$ when the researcher uses a directional test.

---

### Example

A researcher plans to conduct a study for which $H_0$: is $\mu_1 \leq \mu_2$ using a one-tailed $t$-ratio. The researcher sets $\alpha = .05$ and believes that the effect size is .20. Approximately how many participants should be in the sample for the power to be approximately .80? According to Table B.5.1, if the researcher uses 300 participants in each sample, the power will be $1 - \beta = .81$.

Note that for Cohen's $d$, an estimate of effect size:

$$d = .20 = \text{``small''} \quad d = .50 = \text{``medium''} \quad d = .80 = \text{``large''}$$

---

# Table B.5.1

| n | $\alpha = .05$ One-Tailed | | | | | $\alpha = .01$ One-Tailed | | | | |
|---|---|---|---|---|---|---|---|---|---|---|
| | $t_c$ | .10 | .20 | .50 | .80 | $t_c$ | .10 | .20 | .50 | .80 |
| 5 | 1.860 | .12 | .13 | .21 | .33 | 2.896 | .04 | .04 | .07 | .13 |
| 6 | 1.812 | .12 | .14 | .22 | .38 | 2.764 | .03 | .04 | .08 | .15 |
| 7 | 1.782 | .12 | .14 | .24 | .42 | 2.681 | .03 | .04 | .08 | .18 |
| 8 | 1.761 | .12 | .14 | .26 | .46 | 2.624 | .03 | .04 | .09 | .21 |
| 9 | 1.746 | .12 | .14 | .28 | .50 | 2.583 | .03 | .04 | .10 | .23 |
| 10 | 1.734 | .12 | .14 | .29 | .54 | 2.552 | .03 | .04 | .11 | .26 |
| 11 | 1.725 | .12 | .14 | .31 | .57 | 2.528 | .03 | .04 | .12 | .29 |
| 12 | 1.717 | .12 | .15 | .33 | .61 | 2.508 | .03 | .04 | .13 | .32 |
| 13 | 1.711 | .12 | .15 | .35 | .64 | 2.492 | .03 | .04 | .14 | .35 |
| 14 | 1.706 | .12 | .15 | .36 | .67 | 2.479 | .03 | .04 | .15 | .37 |
| 15 | 1.701 | .12 | .15 | .38 | .70 | 2.467 | .03 | .04 | .16 | .40 |
| 16 | 1.697 | .12 | .16 | .40 | .73 | 2.457 | .03 | .04 | .17 | .43 |
| 17 | 1.694 | .12 | .16 | .41 | .75 | 2.449 | .03 | .05 | .18 | .46 |
| 18 | 1.691 | .12 | .16 | .43 | .78 | 2.441 | .03 | .05 | .19 | .49 |
| 19 | 1.688 | .12 | .16 | .45 | .80 | 2.434 | .03 | .05 | .20 | .52 |
| 20 | 1.686 | .12 | .17 | .46 | .82 | 2.429 | .03 | .05 | .21 | .54 |
| 21 | 1.684 | .12 | .17 | .48 | .84 | 2.423 | .03 | .05 | .22 | .57 |
| 22 | 1.682 | .12 | .17 | .50 | .85 | 2.418 | .03 | .05 | .23 | .59 |
| 23 | 1.680 | .12 | .17 | .51 | .87 | 2.414 | .03 | .05 | .24 | .62 |
| 24 | 1.679 | .12 | .18 | .53 | .88 | 2.410 | .03 | .05 | .25 | .64 |
| 25 | 1.677 | .12 | .18 | .54 | .89 | 2.407 | .03 | .05 | .26 | .66 |
| 30 | 1.672 | .13 | .19 | .61 | .94 | 2.392 | .03 | .06 | .32 | .76 |
| 40 | 1.665 | .13 | .22 | .73 | .98 | 2.375 | .03 | .07 | .44 | .89 |
| 50 | 1.661 | .14 | .25 | .82 | .99 | 2.365 | .04 | .09 | .55 | .96 |
| 60 | 1.658 | .15 | .28 | .88 | .99 | 2.358 | .04 | .10 | .65 | .99 |
| 70 | 1.656 | .15 | .31 | .92 | .99 | 2.354 | .04 | .12 | .73 | .99 |
| 80 | 1.655 | .16 | .34 | .95 | .99 | 2.350 | .04 | .13 | .80 | .99 |
| 90 | 1.653 | .17 | .37 | .97 | .99 | 2.347 | .05 | .15 | .85 | .99 |
| 100 | 1.653 | .18 | .40 | .98 | .99 | 2.345 | .05 | .17 | .90 | .99 |
| 150 | 1.650 | .21 | .53 | .99 | .99 | 2.339 | .07 | .26 | .99 | .99 |
| 200 | 1.649 | .25 | .64 | .99 | .99 | 2.336 | .09 | .35 | .99 | .99 |
| 250 | 1.648 | .29 | .74 | .99 | .99 | 2.334 | .10 | .45 | .99 | .99 |
| 300 | 1.647 | .33 | .81 | .99 | .99 | 2.333 | .12 | .54 | .99 | .99 |
| 350 | 1.647 | .36 | .86 | .99 | .99 | 2.332 | .14 | .62 | .99 | .99 |
| 400 | 1.647 | .40 | .90 | .99 | .99 | 2.331 | .17 | .69 | .99 | .99 |
| 500 | 1.646 | .47 | .96 | .99 | .99 | 2.330 | .21 | .81 | .99 | .99 |
| 600 | 1.646 | .53 | .98 | .99 | .99 | 2.329 | .26 | .89 | .99 | .99 |
| 700 | 1.646 | .59 | .99 | .99 | .99 | 2.329 | .30 | .94 | .99 | .99 |
| 800 | 1.646 | .64 | .99 | .99 | .99 | 2.329 | .35 | .97 | .99 | .99 |
| 900 | 1.646 | .69 | .99 | .99 | .99 | 2.328 | .40 | .98 | .99 | .99 |
| 1000 | 1.646 | .74 | .99 | .99 | .99 | 2.328 | .45 | .99 | .99 | .99 |

## Table B.5.2: Power of Student's Two-Sample $t$-Ratio, Two-Tailed Tests

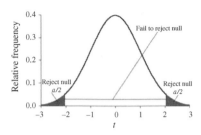

### Using Table B.5.2

This table provides the power $(1 - \beta)$ of the two-sample $t$-ratio given effect size, sample size ($n$), and $\alpha$ when the researcher uses a nondirectional test.

---

### Example

A researcher plans to conduct a study for which $H_0$: is $\mu_1 = \mu_2$ using a two-tailed $t$-ratio. The researcher sets $\alpha = .05$ and believes that the effect size is .20. Approximately how many participants should be in the sample for the power to be approximately .80? According to Table B.5.2, if the researcher uses 400 participants in each group, the power will be $1 - \beta = .82$.

Note that for Cohen's $d$, an estimate of effect size:

$$d = .20 = \text{``small''} \quad d = .50 = \text{``medium''} \quad d = .80 = \text{``large''}$$

---

## Table B.5.2

| | $\alpha = .05$ Two-Tailed | | | | | $\alpha = .01$ Two-Tailed | | | | |
|---|---|---|---|---|---|---|---|---|---|---|
| $n$ | $t_c$ | .10 | .20 | .50 | .80 | $t_c$ | .10 | .20 | .50 | .80 |
| 5 | 2.306 | .07 | .08 | .13 | .22 | 3.355 | .02 | .02 | .04 | .08 |
| 6 | 2.228 | .07 | .08 | .14 | .26 | 3.169 | .02 | .02 | .05 | .10 |
| 7 | 2.179 | .07 | .08 | .15 | .29 | 3.055 | .02 | .02 | .05 | .12 |
| 8 | 2.145 | .07 | .08 | .17 | .33 | 2.977 | .02 | .02 | .06 | .14 |
| 9 | 2.120 | .07 | .08 | .18 | .36 | 2.921 | .02 | .02 | .07 | .16 |
| 10 | 2.101 | .07 | .08 | .19 | .40 | 2.878 | .02 | .02 | .07 | .19 |
| 11 | 2.086 | .06 | .08 | .21 | .43 | 2.845 | .02 | .02 | .08 | .21 |
| 12 | 2.074 | .06 | .08 | .22 | .47 | 2.819 | .02 | .02 | .09 | .23 |
| 13 | 2.064 | .06 | .08 | .23 | .50 | 2.797 | .02 | .03 | .09 | .26 |
| 14 | 2.056 | .06 | .09 | .25 | .53 | 2.779 | .02 | .03 | .10 | .28 |
| 15 | 2.048 | .06 | .09 | .26 | .56 | 2.763 | .02 | .03 | .11 | .31 |
| 16 | 2.042 | .06 | .09 | .28 | .59 | 2.750 | .02 | .03 | .11 | .33 |
| 17 | 2.037 | .06 | .09 | .29 | .62 | 2.738 | .02 | .03 | .12 | .36 |
| 18 | 2.032 | .06 | .09 | .30 | .65 | 2.728 | .02 | .03 | .13 | .38 |

*(Continued)*

# Table B.5.2

| n | $t_c$ | .10 | .20 | .50 | .80 | $t_c$ | .10 | .20 | .50 | .80 |
|---|-------|-----|-----|-----|-----|-------|-----|-----|-----|-----|
| | | $\alpha = .05$ Two-Tailed | | | | | $\alpha = .01$ Two-Tailed | | | |
| 19 | 2.028 | .06 | .10 | .32 | .68 | 2.719 | .02 | .03 | .14 | .41 |
| 20 | 2.024 | .06 | .10 | .33 | .70 | 2.712 | .02 | .03 | .15 | .43 |
| 21 | 2.021 | .07 | .10 | .35 | .72 | 2.704 | .02 | .03 | .15 | .46 |
| 22 | 2.018 | .07 | .10 | .36 | .75 | 2.698 | .02 | .03 | .16 | .48 |
| 23 | 2.015 | .07 | .10 | .37 | .77 | 2.692 | .02 | .03 | .17 | .51 |
| 24 | 2.013 | .07 | .10 | .39 | .79 | 2.687 | .02 | .03 | .18 | .53 |
| 25 | 2.011 | .07 | .11 | .40 | .80 | 2.682 | .02 | .03 | .19 | .56 |
| 30 | 2.002 | .07 | .12 | .47 | .88 | 2.663 | .02 | .04 | .24 | .67 |
| 40 | 1.991 | .07 | .14 | .60 | .96 | 2.640 | .02 | .05 | .34 | .83 |
| 50 | 1.984 | .08 | .16 | .70 | .99 | 2.627 | .02 | .06 | .44 | .92 |
| 60 | 1.980 | .08 | .18 | .79 | .99 | 2.618 | .02 | .07 | .54 | .97 |
| 70 | 1.977 | .09 | .21 | .85 | .99 | 2.612 | .02 | .08 | .63 | .99 |
| 80 | 1.975 | .09 | .23 | .90 | .99 | 2.607 | .03 | .09 | .71 | .99 |
| 90 | 1.973 | .10 | .25 | .93 | .99 | 2.604 | .03 | .10 | .78 | .99 |
| 100 | 1.972 | .10 | .28 | .96 | .99 | 2.601 | .03 | .11 | .83 | .99 |
| 150 | 1.968 | .13 | .39 | .99 | .99 | 2.592 | .04 | .18 | .97 | .99 |
| 200 | 1.966 | .16 | .50 | .99 | .99 | 2.588 | .05 | .26 | .99 | .99 |
| 250 | 1.965 | .19 | .60 | .99 | .99 | 2.586 | .07 | .35 | .99 | .99 |
| 300 | 1.964 | .22 | .69 | .99 | .99 | 2.584 | .08 | .43 | .99 | .99 |
| 350 | 1.963 | .25 | .76 | .99 | .99 | 2.583 | .10 | .51 | .99 | .99 |
| 400 | 1.963 | .28 | .82 | .99 | .99 | 2.582 | .11 | .59 | .99 | .99 |
| 500 | 1.962 | .34 | .90 | .99 | .99 | 2.581 | .15 | .72 | .99 | .99 |
| 600 | 1.962 | .39 | .95 | .99 | .99 | 2.580 | .18 | .82 | .99 | .99 |
| 700 | 1.962 | .45 | .98 | .99 | .99 | 2.579 | .22 | .89 | .99 | .99 |
| 800 | 1.961 | .51 | .99 | .99 | .99 | 2.579 | .26 | .94 | .99 | .99 |
| 900 | 1.961 | .56 | .99 | .99 | .99 | 2.579 | .31 | .96 | .99 | .99 |
| 1000 | 1.961 | .61 | .99 | .99 | .99 | 2.578 | .35 | .98 | .99 | .99 |

## Table B.6: Critical Values for Pearson's Correlation Coefficient

### Using Table B.6

For any given *df*, this table shows the values of *r* corresponding to various levels of probability. The $r_{observed}$ is statistically significant at a given level when it is equal to or greater than the value shown in the table.

---

### Examples

**Nondirectional Hypothesis:**

$H_0$: $\rho = 0$    $H_1$: $\rho \neq 0$    $\alpha = .05$,    $df = 30$

$t_{critical} = \pm.3494$    If $|t_{observed}| \geq |t_{critical}|$, then reject $H_0$

*(Continued)*

*(Continued)*

**Directional Hypothesis:**

$H_0$: $\rho \leq 0$   $H_1$: $\rho > 0$   $\alpha = .05$   $df = 30$

$t_{critical} = +.2960$   If $|t_{observed}| \geq |t_{critical}|$, then reject $H_0$

$H_0$: $\rho \geq 0$   $H_1$: $\rho < 0$   $\alpha = .05$   $df = 30$

$t_{critical} = -.2960$   If $t_{observed} \leq t_{critical}$, then reject $H_0$

Note that the relation between the correlation coefficient and the $t$-ratio is:

$$r_c = \frac{t_c}{\sqrt{(n-2) + t_c^2}}$$

# Table B.6

| | Level of Significance of a One-Tailed or Directional Test $H_0: \rho \leq 0$ or $H_0: \rho \geq 0$ | | | | | |
|---|---|---|---|---|---|---|
| | $\alpha = 0.1$ | $\alpha = 0.05$ | $\alpha = 0.025$ | $\alpha = 0.01$ | $\alpha = 0.005$ | $\alpha = 0.0005$ |
| | Level of Significance of a Two-Tailed or Nondirectional Test $H_0: \rho = 0$ | | | | | |
| *df* | $\alpha = 0.2$ | $\alpha = 0.1$ | $\alpha = 0.05$ | $\alpha = 0.02$ | $\alpha = 0.01$ | $\alpha = 0.001$ |
| 1 | .9511 | .9877 | .9969 | .9995 | .9999 | .9999 |
| 2 | .8000 | .9000 | .9500 | .9800 | .9900 | .9990 |
| 3 | .6870 | .8054 | .8783 | .9343 | .9587 | .9911 |
| 4 | .6084 | .7293 | .8114 | .8822 | .9172 | .9741 |
| 5 | .5509 | .6694 | .7545 | .8329 | .8745 | .9509 |
| 6 | .5067 | .6215 | .7067 | .7887 | .8343 | .9249 |
| 7 | .4716 | .5822 | .6664 | .7498 | .7977 | .8983 |
| 8 | .4428 | .5494 | .6319 | .7155 | .7646 | .8721 |
| 9 | .4187 | .5214 | .6021 | .6851 | .7348 | .8470 |
| 10 | .3981 | .4973 | .5760 | .6581 | .7079 | .8233 |
| 11 | .3802 | .4762 | .5529 | .6339 | .6835 | .8010 |
| 12 | .3646 | .4575 | .5324 | .6120 | .6614 | .7800 |
| 13 | .3507 | .4409 | .5140 | .5923 | .6411 | .7604 |
| 14 | .3383 | .4259 | .4973 | .5742 | .6226 | .7419 |
| 15 | .3271 | .4124 | .4821 | .5577 | .6055 | .7247 |
| 16 | .3170 | .4000 | .4683 | .5425 | .5897 | .7084 |
| 17 | .3077 | .3887 | .4555 | .5285 | .5751 | .6932 |
| 18 | .2992 | .3783 | .4438 | .5155 | .5614 | .6788 |
| 19 | .2914 | .3687 | .4329 | .5034 | .5487 | .6652 |
| 20 | .2841 | .3598 | .4227 | .4921 | .5368 | .6524 |
| 21 | .2774 | .3515 | .4132 | .4815 | .5256 | .6402 |
| 22 | .2711 | .3438 | .4044 | .4716 | .5151 | .6287 |
| 23 | .2653 | .3365 | .3961 | .4622 | .5052 | .6178 |
| 24 | .2598 | .3297 | .3882 | .4534 | .4958 | .6074 |
| 25 | .2546 | .3233 | .3809 | .4451 | .4869 | .5974 |

*(Continued)*

# Table B.6  (Continued)

| df | Level of Significance of a One-Tailed or Directional Test $H_0: \rho \leq 0$ or $H_0: \rho \geq 0$ | | | | | |
|---|---|---|---|---|---|---|
| | $\alpha = 0.1$ | $\alpha = 0.05$ | $\alpha = 0.025$ | $\alpha = 0.01$ | $\alpha = 0.005$ | $\alpha = 0.0005$ |
| | Level of Significance of a Two-Tailed or Nondirectional Test $H_0: \rho = 0$ | | | | | |
| | $\alpha = 0.2$ | $\alpha = 0.1$ | $\alpha = 0.05$ | $\alpha = 0.02$ | $\alpha = 0.01$ | $\alpha = 0.001$ |
| 30 | .2327 | .2960 | .3494 | .4093 | .4487 | .5541 |
| 35 | .2156 | .2746 | .3246 | .3810 | .4182 | .5189 |
| 40 | .2018 | .2573 | .3044 | .3578 | .3932 | .4896 |
| 50 | .1806 | .2306 | .2732 | .3218 | .3542 | .4432 |
| 60 | .1650 | .2108 | .2500 | .2948 | .3248 | .4079 |
| 70 | .1528 | .1954 | .2319 | .2737 | .3017 | .3798 |
| 80 | .1430 | .1829 | .2172 | .2565 | .2830 | .3568 |
| 90 | .1348 | .1726 | .2050 | .2422 | .2673 | .3375 |
| 100 | .1279 | .1638 | .1946 | .2301 | .2540 | .3211 |
| 150 | .1045 | .1339 | .1593 | .1886 | .2084 | .2643 |
| 300 | .0740 | .0948 | .1129 | .1338 | .1480 | .1884 |
| 500 | .0573 | .0735 | .0875 | .1038 | .1149 | .1464 |
| 1000 | .0405 | .0520 | .0619 | .0735 | .0813 | .1038 |

## Table B.7: Critical Values for Spearman's Rank-Order Correlation Coefficient

### Using Table B.7

For any given $df$, the table shows the values of $r_S$ corresponding to various levels of probability. The $r_{S\text{-observed}}$ is statistically significant at a given level when it is equal to or greater than the value shown in the table.

---

## Examples

**Nondirectional Hypothesis:**

$H_0: \rho_s = 0$    $H_1: \rho_s \neq 0$    $\alpha = .05$        $df = 30$

$r_{critical} = \pm.350$    If $|r_{observed}| \geq |r_{critical}|$, then reject $H_0$

**Directional Hypothesis:**

$H_0: \rho_s \leq 0$    $H_1: \rho_s > 0$    $\alpha = .05$        $df = 30$

$r_{critical} = +.296$    If $r_{observed} \geq r_{critical}$, then reject $H_0$

$H_0: \rho_s \geq 0$    $H_1: \rho_s < 0$    $\alpha = .05$        $df = 30$
$r_{critical} = -.296$    If $r_{observed} \leq r_{critical}$, then reject $H_0$

*(Continued)*

*(Continued)*

When $df > 28$, we can convert the $r_S$ to a $t$-ratio and then use Table B.7 for hypothesis testing:

$$t = r_S \sqrt{\frac{N - 2}{1 - r_S^2}}$$

For example, $r_S = .60$, $N = 42$:

$$t = .60 \sqrt{\frac{42 - 2}{1 - .60^2}} \quad t = .60 \sqrt{\frac{40}{.64}} \quad t = .60 \sqrt{62.5}$$

$$t = 4.74, \ df = 40$$

If $\alpha = .05$, two-tailed,

$$t_{\text{critical}} = 1.684 \quad \text{Reject } H_0: \ \rho_S = 0$$

# Table B.7

| | Level of Significance of a One-Tailed or Directional Test $H_0: \rho_s \leq 0$ or $H_0: \rho_s \geq 0$ | | | | | |
|---|---|---|---|---|---|---|
| | $\alpha = 0.1$ | $\alpha = 0.05$ | $\alpha = 0.025$ | $\alpha = 0.01$ | $\alpha = 0.005$ | $\alpha = 0.0005$ |
| | Level of Significance of a Two-Tailed or Nondirectional Test $H_0: \rho_s = 0$ | | | | | |
| $df$ | $\alpha = 0.2$ | $\alpha = 0.1$ | $\alpha = 0.05$ | $\alpha = 0.02$ | $\alpha = 0.01$ | $\alpha = 0.001$ |
| 2 | 1.000 | 1.000 | | | | |
| 3 | .800 | .900 | 1.000 | 1.000 | | |
| 4 | .657 | .829 | .886 | .943 | 1.000 | |
| 5 | .571 | .714 | .786 | .893 | .929 | 1.000 |
| 6 | .524 | .643 | .738 | .833 | .881 | .976 |
| 7 | .483 | .600 | .700 | .783 | .833 | .933 |
| 8 | .455 | .564 | .648 | .745 | .794 | .903 |
| 9 | .427 | .536 | .618 | .709 | .755 | .873 |
| 10 | .406 | .503 | .587 | .678 | .727 | .846 |
| 11 | .385 | .484 | .560 | .648 | .703 | .824 |
| 12 | .367 | .464 | .538 | .626 | .679 | .802 |
| 13 | .354 | .446 | .521 | .604 | .654 | .779 |
| 14 | .341 | .429 | .503 | .582 | .635 | .762 |
| 15 | .328 | .414 | .485 | .566 | .615 | .748 |
| 16 | .317 | .401 | .472 | .550 | .600 | .728 |
| 17 | .309 | .391 | .460 | .535 | .584 | .712 |
| 18 | .299 | .380 | .447 | .520 | .570 | .696 |
| 19 | .292 | .370 | .435 | .508 | .556 | .681 |
| 20 | .284 | .361 | .425 | .496 | .544 | .667 |
| 21 | .278 | .353 | .415 | .486 | .532 | .654 |
| 22 | .271 | .344 | .406 | .476 | .521 | .642 |
| 23 | .265 | .337 | .398 | .466 | .511 | .630 |
| 24 | .259 | .331 | .390 | .457 | .501 | .619 |
| 25 | .255 | .324 | .382 | .448 | .491 | .608 |
| 26 | .250 | .317 | .375 | .440 | .483 | .598 |
| 27 | .245 | .312 | .368 | .433 | .475 | .589 |
| 28 | .240 | .306 | .362 | .425 | .467 | .580 |
| 29 | .236 | .301 | .356 | .418 | .459 | .571 |
| 30 | .232 | .296 | .350 | .412 | .452 | .563 |

## Table B.8: $r$ to $z$ Transformation

### Using Table B.8

This table provides the Fisher $r$ to $z$ transformation. Both positive and negative values of $r$ may be used. For specific transformations, use the following equation:

$$z_r = \frac{1}{2} \log_e \left( \frac{1 + r}{1 - r} \right)$$

**Example**

$r = .25 \rightarrow z_r = .255$

## Table B.8

| $r$ | $z_r$ | $r$ | $z_r$ | $r$ | $z_r$ | $r$ | $z_r$ |
|------|-------|------|-------|------|-------|------|-------|
| 0.00 | 0.000 | 0.25 | 0.255 | 0.50 | 0.549 | 0.75 | 0.973 |
| 0.01 | 0.010 | 0.26 | 0.266 | 0.51 | 0.563 | 0.76 | 0.996 |
| 0.02 | 0.020 | 0.27 | 0.277 | 0.52 | 0.576 | 0.77 | 1.020 |
| 0.03 | 0.030 | 0.28 | 0.288 | 0.53 | 0.590 | 0.78 | 1.045 |
| 0.04 | 0.040 | 0.29 | 0.299 | 0.54 | 0.604 | 0.79 | 1.071 |
| 0.05 | 0.050 | 0.30 | 0.310 | 0.55 | 0.618 | 0.80 | 1.099 |
| 0.06 | 0.060 | 0.31 | 0.321 | 0.56 | 0.633 | 0.81 | 1.127 |
| 0.07 | 0.070 | 0.32 | 0.332 | 0.57 | 0.648 | 0.82 | 1.157 |
| 0.08 | 0.080 | 0.33 | 0.343 | 0.58 | 0.662 | 0.83 | 1.188 |
| 0.09 | 0.090 | 0.34 | 0.354 | 0.59 | 0.678 | 0.84 | 1.221 |
| 0.10 | 0.100 | 0.35 | 0.365 | 0.60 | 0.693 | 0.85 | 1.256 |
| 0.11 | 0.110 | 0.36 | 0.377 | 0.61 | 0.709 | 0.86 | 1.293 |
| 0.12 | 0.121 | 0.37 | 0.388 | 0.62 | 0.725 | 0.87 | 1.333 |
| 0.13 | 0.131 | 0.38 | 0.400 | 0.63 | 0.741 | 0.88 | 1.376 |
| 0.14 | 0.141 | 0.39 | 0.412 | 0.64 | 0.758 | 0.89 | 1.422 |
| 0.15 | 0.151 | 0.40 | 0.424 | 0.65 | 0.775 | 0.90 | 1.472 |
| 0.16 | 0.161 | 0.41 | 0.436 | 0.66 | 0.793 | 0.91 | 1.528 |
| 0.17 | 0.172 | 0.42 | 0.448 | 0.67 | 0.811 | 0.92 | 1.589 |
| 0.18 | 0.182 | 0.43 | 0.460 | 0.68 | 0.829 | 0.93 | 1.658 |
| 0.19 | 0.192 | 0.44 | 0.472 | 0.69 | 0.848 | 0.94 | 1.738 |
| 0.20 | 0.203 | 0.45 | 0.485 | 0.70 | 0.867 | 0.95 | 1.832 |
| 0.21 | 0.213 | 0.46 | 0.497 | 0.71 | 0.887 | 0.96 | 1.946 |
| 0.22 | 0.224 | 0.47 | 0.510 | 0.72 | 0.908 | 0.97 | 2.092 |
| 0.23 | 0.234 | 0.48 | 0.523 | 0.73 | 0.929 | 0.98 | 2.298 |
| 0.24 | 0.245 | 0.49 | 0.536 | 0.74 | 0.950 | 0.99 | 2.647 |

## Table B.9: Power of Pearson's Correlation Coefficient

**Using Table B.9:**

This table provides estimates of the power $(1 - \beta)$ of the Pearson Correlation Coefficient $(r)$ given effect size, sample size $(n)$, $\alpha$, and directionality of the test.

### Example

A researcher plans to conduct a study for which $H_0$: is $\rho = 0.0$ using a two-tailed test. The researcher sets $\alpha = .05$ and believes that the effect size is .30. Approximately how many participants should be in the sample for the power to be approximately .80? According to Table B.9, if the researcher uses 90 participants, the power will be $1 - \beta = .82$.

Note that for effect sizes,

$$r = .10 = \text{"small"} \quad r = .30 = \text{"medium"} \quad r = .50 = \text{"large"}$$

## Table B.9

| | $\alpha = .05$ One-Tailed Effect Size: $r$ | | | | | | $\alpha = .05$ Two-Tailed Effect Size: $r$ | | | | |
|---|---|---|---|---|---|---|---|---|---|---|---|
| $n$ | 0.10 | 0.30 | 0.50 | 0.70 | 0.95 | $n$ | 0.10 | 0.30 | 0.50 | 0.70 | 0.95 |
| 10 | .07 | .19 | .42 | .75 | .98 | 10 | .03 | .11 | .29 | .63 | .99 |
| 11 | .07 | .21 | .46 | .80 | .99 | 11 | .03 | .12 | .33 | .69 | .99 |
| 12 | .08 | .23 | .50 | .83 | .99 | 12 | .04 | .14 | .37 | .74 | .99 |
| 13 | .08 | .24 | .54 | .87 | .99 | 13 | .04 | .15 | .40 | .78 | .99 |
| 14 | .08 | .26 | .57 | .89 | .99 | 14 | .04 | .16 | .44 | .82 | .99 |
| 15 | .09 | .27 | .60 | .91 | .99 | 15 | .04 | .17 | .47 | .85 | .99 |
| 16 | .09 | .29 | .63 | .93 | .99 | 16 | .04 | .19 | .50 | .88 | .99 |
| 17 | .09 | .31 | .66 | .94 | .99 | 17 | .05 | .20 | .53 | .90 | .99 |
| 18 | .09 | .32 | .69 | .96 | .99 | 18 | .05 | .21 | .56 | .92 | .99 |
| 19 | .10 | .33 | .71 | .96 | .99 | 19 | .05 | .22 | .59 | .93 | .99 |
| 20 | .10 | .35 | .73 | .97 | .99 | 20 | .05 | .24 | .61 | .94 | .99 |
| 21 | .10 | .36 | .75 | .98 | .99 | 21 | .05 | .25 | .64 | .95 | .99 |
| 22 | .10 | .38 | .77 | .98 | .99 | 22 | .05 | .26 | .66 | .96 | .99 |
| 23 | .11 | .39 | .79 | .98 | .99 | 23 | .06 | .27 | .69 | .97 | .99 |
| 24 | .11 | .40 | .81 | .99 | .99 | 24 | .06 | .28 | .71 | .97 | .99 |
| 25 | .11 | .42 | .82 | .99 | .99 | 25 | .06 | .30 | .73 | .98 | .99 |
| 26 | .11 | .43 | .84 | .99 | .99 | 26 | .06 | .31 | .75 | .98 | .99 |
| 27 | .12 | .44 | .85 | .99 | .99 | 27 | .06 | .32 | .76 | .98 | .99 |
| 28 | .12 | .46 | .86 | .99 | .99 | 28 | .06 | .33 | .78 | .99 | .99 |
| 29 | .12s | .47 | .88 | .99 | .99 | 29 | .06 | .34 | .80 | .99 | .99 |
| 30 | .12 | .48 | .89 | .99 | .99 | 30 | .07 | .35 | .81 | .99 | .99 |
| 31 | .12 | .49 | .89 | .99 | .99 | 31 | .07 | .37 | .83 | .99 | .99 |
| 32 | .13 | .50 | .90 | .99 | .99 | 32 | .07 | .38 | .84 | .99 | .99 |
| 33 | .13 | .52 | .91 | .99 | .99 | 33 | .07 | .39 | .85 | .99 | .99 |
| 34 | .13 | .53 | .92 | .99 | .99 | 34 | .07 | .40 | .86 | .99 | .99 |

*(Continued)*

# Table B.9 (Continued)

| n | α = .05 One-Tailed Effect Size: r | | | | | n | α = .05 Two-Tailed Effect Size: r | | | | |
|---|------|------|------|------|------|-----|------|------|------|------|------|
| | 0.10 | 0.30 | 0.50 | 0.70 | 0.95 | | 0.10 | 0.30 | 0.50 | 0.70 | 0.95 |
| 35 | .13 | .54 | .93 | .99 | .99 | 35 | .07 | .41 | .87 | .99 | .99 |
| 36 | .13 | .55 | .93 | .99 | .99 | 36 | .07 | .42 | .88 | .99 | .99 |
| 37 | .14 | .56 | .94 | .99 | .99 | 37 | .08 | .43 | .89 | .99 | .99 |
| 38 | .14 | .57 | .94 | .99 | .99 | 38 | .08 | .44 | .90 | .99 | .99 |
| 39 | .14 | .58 | .95 | .99 | .99 | 39 | .08 | .45 | .91 | .99 | .99 |
| 40 | .14 | .59 | .95 | .99 | .99 | 40 | .08 | .46 | .91 | .99 | .99 |
| 50 | .17 | .69 | .98 | .99 | .99 | 50 | .09 | .56 | .96 | .99 | .99 |
| 60 | .18 | .75 | .99 | .99 | .99 | 60 | .11 | .64 | .98 | .99 | .99 |
| 70 | .20 | .81 | .99 | .99 | .99 | 70 | .12 | .71 | .99 | .99 | .99 |
| 80 | .22 | .85 | .99 | .99 | .99 | 80 | .13 | .77 | .99 | .99 | .99 |
| 90 | .23 | .89 | .99 | .99 | .99 | 90 | .15 | .82 | .99 | .99 | .99 |
| 100 | .25 | .92 | .99 | .99 | .99 | 100 | .16 | .86 | .99 | .99 | .99 |
| 200 | .40 | .99 | .99 | .99 | .99 | 200 | .28 | .99 | .99 | .99 | .99 |
| 300 | .53 | .99 | .99 | .99 | .99 | 300 | .40 | .99 | .99 | .99 | .99 |
| 400 | .63 | .99 | .99 | .99 | .99 | 400 | .51 | .99 | .99 | .99 | .99 |
| 500 | .72 | .99 | .99 | .99 | .99 | 500 | .60 | .99 | .99 | .99 | .99 |

## Table B.10: Critical Values for the F-ratio

### Using Table B.10

This table provides the critical values required to reject the null hypothesis for the analysis of variance. Note that the bold text represents $\alpha = .01$, whereas the regular text represents $\alpha = .05$. To use the table, you will need to identify the degrees of freedom for the numerator and denominator. The numerator degrees of freedom are those used to determine the mean square for the treatment effect or interaction. The denominator degrees of freedom are those used to determine the mean square for the within-groups or error variance.

---

## Example: One-Factor ANOVA

A researcher conducts a study that produces the following ANOVA summary table:

| Source | SS | df | MS | F |
|--------|------|-----|-------|------|
| Between-groups | 28.00 | 2 | 14.00 | 3.50 |
| Within-groups | 156.00 | 39 | 4.00 | |
| Total | 184.00 | 41 | | |

(Continued)

(*Continued*)

**From the Summary Table:**

Degrees of freedom, numerator: $df_N = 2$

Degrees of freedom, denominator: $df_D = 39$

$F_{observed} = 3.50$

**From Table B.10:**

Because the exact values of the degrees of freedom for the denominator are not listed, you must interpolate between the two adjacent numbers:

$F_{critical} (2, 38) = 3.24, \alpha = .05$       $F_{critical} (2, 38) = 5.21, \alpha = .01$

$F_{critical} (2, 40) = 3.23, \alpha = .05$       $F_{critical} (2, 40) = 5.15, \alpha = .01$

Therefore,

$F_{critical} (2, 39) = 3.235, \alpha = .05$           $F_{critical} (2, 39) = 5.18, \alpha = .01$

$F_{observed} = 3.50 > F_{critical} = 3.235,$       $F_{observed} = 3.50 < F_{critical} = 5.18$

Reject $H_0$                                          Do not reject $H_0$

---

## Example: Two-Factor ANOVA

| Source | SS | df | MS | F |
|---|---|---|---|---|
| Variable A | 0.067 | 1 | 0.067 | 0.01 |
| Variable B | 80.433 | 2 | 40.217 | 6.859 |
| AB | 58.233 | 2 | 29.117 | 4.966 |
| Within-groups | 316.600 | 54 | 5.863 | |
| Total | 455.333 | 59 | | |

**From the Summary Table:**

**Critical Values:**

$\alpha = .05$                      $\alpha = .01$

$F_{critical} (1, 54) = 4.02$       $F_{critical} (1, 54) = 7.12$

$F_{critical} (2, 54) = 3.16$       $F_{critical} (2, 54) = 5.01$

| **Result** | **Statistical Decision** | |
|---|---|---|
| | ($\alpha = .05$) | ($\alpha = .01$) |
| Variable A: $df_N = 1$, $df_D = 54 \rightarrow F_{observed} = 0.01$ | Do not reject $H_0$ | Do not reject $H_0$ |
| Variable B: $df_N = 2$, $df_D = 54 \rightarrow F_{observed} = 6.86$ | Reject $H_0$ | Reject $H_0$ |
| Variable AB: $df_N = 2$, $df_D = 54 \rightarrow F_{observed} = 4.97$ | Reject $H_0$ | Do not reject $H_0$ |

## Table B.10

| | | Degrees of Freedom for Numerator | | | | | | | | | | | | | | | | | |
|---|---|---|---|---|---|---|---|---|---|---|---|---|---|---|---|---|---|---|---|---|
| | α | 1 | 2 | 3 | 4 | 5 | 6 | 7 | 8 | 9 | 10 | 11 | 12 | 13 | 14 | 15 | 30 | 50 | 100 | 1000 |
| 1 | 0.05 | 161 | 199 | 216 | 225 | 230 | 234 | 237 | 239 | 241 | 242 | 243 | 244 | 245 | 245 | 246 | 250 | 252 | 253 | 254 |
| | 0.01 | 4052 | 4999 | 5404 | 5624 | 5764 | 5859 | 5928 | 5981 | 6022 | 6056 | 6083 | 6107 | 6126 | 6143 | 6157 | 6260 | 6302 | 6334 | 6363 |
| 2 | 0.05 | 18.51 | 19.00 | 19.16 | 19.25 | 19.30 | 19.33 | 19.35 | 19.37 | 19.38 | 19.40 | 19.40 | 19.41 | 19.42 | 19.42 | 19.43 | 19.46 | 19.48 | 19.49 | 19.49 |
| | 0.01 | 98.50 | 99.00 | 99.16 | 99.25 | 99.30 | 99.33 | 99.36 | 99.38 | 99.39 | 99.40 | 99.41 | 99.42 | 99.42 | 99.43 | 99.43 | 99.47 | 99.48 | 99.49 | 99.50 |
| 3 | 0.05 | 10.13 | 9.55 | 9.28 | 9.12 | 9.01 | 8.94 | 8.89 | 8.85 | 8.81 | 8.79 | 8.76 | 8.74 | 8.73 | 8.71 | 8.70 | 8.62 | 8.58 | 8.55 | 8.53 |
| | 0.01 | 34.12 | 30.82 | 29.46 | 28.71 | 28.24 | 27.91 | 27.67 | 27.49 | 27.34 | 27.23 | 27.13 | 27.05 | 26.98 | 26.92 | 26.87 | 26.50 | 26.35 | 26.24 | 26.14 |
| 4 | 0.05 | 7.71 | 6.94 | 6.59 | 6.39 | 6.26 | 6.16 | 6.09 | 6.04 | 6.00 | 5.96 | 5.94 | 5.91 | 5.89 | 5.87 | 5.86 | 5.75 | 5.70 | 5.66 | 5.63 |
| | 0.01 | 21.20 | 18.00 | 16.69 | 15.98 | 15.52 | 15.21 | 14.98 | 14.80 | 14.66 | 14.55 | 14.45 | 14.37 | 14.31 | 14.25 | 14.20 | 13.84 | 13.69 | 13.58 | 13.47 |
| 5 | 0.05 | 6.61 | 5.79 | 5.41 | 5.19 | 5.05 | 4.95 | 4.88 | 4.82 | 4.77 | 4.74 | 4.70 | 4.68 | 4.66 | 4.64 | 4.62 | 4.50 | 4.44 | 4.41 | 4.37 |
| | 0.01 | 16.26 | 13.27 | 12.06 | 11.39 | 10.97 | 10.67 | 10.46 | 10.29 | 10.16 | 10.05 | 9.96 | 9.89 | 9.82 | 9.77 | 9.72 | 9.38 | 9.24 | 9.13 | 9.03 |
| 6 | 0.05 | 5.99 | 5.14 | 4.76 | 4.53 | 4.39 | 4.28 | 4.21 | 4.15 | 4.10 | 4.06 | 4.03 | 4.00 | 3.98 | 3.96 | 3.94 | 3.81 | 3.75 | 3.71 | 3.67 |
| | 0.01 | 13.75 | 10.92 | 9.78 | 9.15 | 8.75 | 8.47 | 8.26 | 8.10 | 7.98 | 7.87 | 7.79 | 7.72 | 7.66 | 7.60 | 7.56 | 7.23 | 7.09 | 6.99 | 6.89 |
| 7 | 0.05 | 5.59 | 4.74 | 4.35 | 4.12 | 3.97 | 3.87 | 3.79 | 3.73 | 3.68 | 3.64 | 3.60 | 3.57 | 3.55 | 3.53 | 3.51 | 3.38 | 3.32 | 3.27 | 3.23 |
| | 0.01 | 12.25 | 9.55 | 8.45 | 7.85 | 7.46 | 7.19 | 6.99 | 6.84 | 6.72 | 6.62 | 6.54 | 6.47 | 6.41 | 6.36 | 6.31 | 5.99 | 5.86 | 5.75 | 5.66 |
| 8 | 0.05 | 5.32 | 4.46 | 4.07 | 3.84 | 3.69 | 3.58 | 3.50 | 3.44 | 3.39 | 3.35 | 3.31 | 3.28 | 3.26 | 3.24 | 3.22 | 3.08 | 3.02 | 2.97 | 2.93 |
| | 0.01 | 11.26 | 8.65 | 7.59 | 7.01 | 6.63 | 6.37 | 6.18 | 6.03 | 5.91 | 5.81 | 5.73 | 5.67 | 5.61 | 5.56 | 5.52 | 5.20 | 5.07 | 4.96 | 4.87 |
| 9 | 0.05 | 5.12 | 4.26 | 3.86 | 3.63 | 3.48 | 3.37 | 3.29 | 3.23 | 3.18 | 3.14 | 3.10 | 3.07 | 3.05 | 3.03 | 3.01 | 2.86 | 2.80 | 2.76 | 2.71 |
| | 0.01 | 10.56 | 8.02 | 6.99 | 6.42 | 6.06 | 5.80 | 5.61 | 5.47 | 5.35 | 5.26 | 5.18 | 5.11 | 5.05 | 5.01 | 4.96 | 4.65 | 4.52 | 4.41 | 4.32 |
| 10 | 0.05 | 4.96 | 4.10 | 3.71 | 3.48 | 3.33 | 3.22 | 3.14 | 3.07 | 3.02 | 2.98 | 2.94 | 2.91 | 2.89 | 2.86 | 2.85 | 2.70 | 2.64 | 2.59 | 2.54 |
| | 0.01 | 10.04 | 7.56 | 6.55 | 5.99 | 5.64 | 5.39 | 5.20 | 5.06 | 4.94 | 4.85 | 4.77 | 4.71 | 4.65 | 4.60 | 4.56 | 4.25 | 4.12 | 4.01 | 3.92 |
| 11 | 0.05 | 4.84 | 3.98 | 3.59 | 3.36 | 3.20 | 3.09 | 3.01 | 2.95 | 2.90 | 2.85 | 2.82 | 2.79 | 2.76 | 2.74 | 2.72 | 2.57 | 2.51 | 2.46 | 2.41 |
| | 0.01 | 9.65 | 7.21 | 6.22 | 5.67 | 5.32 | 5.07 | 4.89 | 4.74 | 4.63 | 4.54 | 4.46 | 4.40 | 4.34 | 4.29 | 4.25 | 3.94 | 3.81 | 3.71 | 3.61 |
| 12 | 0.05 | 4.75 | 3.89 | 3.49 | 3.26 | 3.11 | 3.00 | 2.91 | 2.85 | 2.80 | 2.75 | 2.72 | 2.69 | 2.66 | 2.64 | 2.62 | 2.47 | 2.40 | 2.35 | 2.30 |
| | 0.01 | 9.33 | 6.93 | 5.95 | 5.41 | 5.06 | 4.82 | 4.64 | 4.50 | 4.39 | 4.30 | 4.22 | 4.16 | 4.10 | 4.05 | 4.01 | 3.70 | 3.57 | 3.47 | 3.37 |
| 13 | 0.05 | 4.67 | 3.81 | 3.41 | 3.18 | 3.03 | 2.92 | 2.83 | 2.77 | 2.71 | 2.67 | 2.63 | 2.60 | 2.58 | 2.55 | 2.53 | 2.38 | 2.31 | 2.26 | 2.21 |
| | 0.01 | 9.07 | 6.70 | 5.74 | 5.21 | 4.86 | 4.62 | 4.44 | 4.30 | 4.19 | 4.10 | 4.02 | 3.96 | 3.91 | 3.86 | 3.82 | 3.51 | 3.38 | 3.27 | 3.18 |
| 14 | 0.05 | 4.60 | 3.74 | 3.34 | 3.11 | 2.96 | 2.85 | 2.76 | 2.70 | 2.65 | 2.60 | 2.57 | 2.53 | 2.51 | 2.48 | 2.46 | 2.31 | 2.24 | 2.19 | 2.14 |
| | 0.01 | 8.86 | 6.51 | 5.56 | 5.04 | 4.69 | 4.46 | 4.28 | 4.14 | 4.03 | 3.94 | 3.86 | 3.80 | 3.75 | 3.70 | 3.66 | 3.35 | 3.22 | 3.11 | 3.02 |
| 15 | 0.05 | 4.54 | 3.68 | 3.29 | 3.06 | 2.90 | 2.79 | 2.71 | 2.64 | 2.59 | 2.54 | 2.51 | 2.48 | 2.45 | 2.42 | 2.40 | 2.25 | 2.18 | 2.12 | 2.07 |
| | 0.01 | 8.68 | 6.36 | 5.42 | 4.89 | 4.56 | 4.32 | 4.14 | 4.00 | 3.89 | 3.80 | 3.73 | 3.67 | 3.61 | 3.56 | 3.52 | 3.21 | 3.08 | 2.98 | 2.88 |
| 16 | 0.05 | 4.49 | 3.63 | 3.24 | 3.01 | 2.85 | 2.74 | 2.66 | 2.59 | 2.54 | 2.49 | 2.46 | 2.42 | 2.40 | 2.37 | 2.35 | 2.19 | 2.12 | 2.07 | 2.02 |
| | 0.01 | 8.53 | 6.23 | 5.29 | 4.77 | 4.44 | 4.20 | 4.03 | 3.89 | 3.78 | 3.69 | 3.62 | 3.55 | 3.50 | 3.45 | 3.41 | 3.10 | 2.97 | 2.86 | 2.76 |
| 17 | 0.05 | 4.45 | 3.59 | 3.20 | 2.96 | 2.81 | 2.70 | 2.61 | 2.55 | 2.49 | 2.45 | 2.41 | 2.38 | 2.35 | 2.33 | 2.31 | 2.15 | 2.08 | 2.02 | 1.97 |
| | 0.01 | 8.40 | 6.11 | 5.19 | 4.67 | 4.34 | 4.10 | 3.93 | 3.79 | 3.68 | 3.59 | 3.52 | 3.46 | 3.40 | 3.35 | 3.31 | 3.00 | 2.87 | 2.76 | 2.66 |
| 18 | 0.05 | 4.41 | 3.55 | 3.16 | 2.93 | 2.77 | 2.66 | 2.58 | 2.51 | 2.46 | 2.41 | 2.37 | 2.34 | 2.31 | 2.29 | 2.27 | 2.11 | 2.04 | 1.98 | 1.92 |
| | 0.01 | 8.29 | 6.01 | 5.09 | 4.58 | 4.25 | 4.01 | 3.84 | 3.71 | 3.60 | 3.51 | 3.43 | 3.37 | 3.32 | 3.27 | 3.23 | 2.92 | 2.78 | 2.68 | 2.58 |

Degrees of Freedom for Denominator

(Continued)

| df | α | | | | | | | | | | | | | | | | | | | |
|----|------|------|------|------|------|------|------|------|------|------|------|------|------|------|------|------|------|------|------|------|
| 19 | 0.05 | 1.88 | 1.94 | 2.00 | 2.07 | 2.23 | 2.26 | 2.28 | 2.31 | 2.34 | 2.38 | 2.42 | 2.48 | 2.54 | 2.63 | 2.74 | 2.90 | 3.13 | 3.52 | 4.38 |
|    | 0.01 | 2.50 | 2.60 | 2.71 | 2.84 | 3.15 | 3.19 | 3.24 | 3.30 | 3.36 | 3.43 | 3.52 | 3.63 | 3.77 | 3.94 | 4.17 | 4.50 | 5.01 | 5.93 | 8.18 |
| 20 | 0.05 | 1.85 | 1.91 | 1.97 | 2.04 | 2.20 | 2.22 | 2.25 | 2.28 | 2.31 | 2.35 | 2.39 | 2.45 | 2.51 | 2.60 | 2.71 | 2.87 | 3.10 | 3.49 | 4.35 |
|    | 0.01 | 2.43 | 2.54 | 2.64 | 2.78 | 3.09 | 3.13 | 3.18 | 3.23 | 3.29 | 3.37 | 3.46 | 3.56 | 3.70 | 3.87 | 4.10 | 4.43 | 4.94 | 5.85 | 8.10 |
| 21 | 0.05 | 1.82 | 1.88 | 1.94 | 2.01 | 2.18 | 2.20 | 2.22 | 2.25 | 2.28 | 2.32 | 2.37 | 2.42 | 2.49 | 2.57 | 2.68 | 2.84 | 3.07 | 3.47 | 4.32 |
|    | 0.01 | 2.37 | 2.48 | 2.58 | 2.72 | 3.03 | 3.07 | 3.12 | 3.17 | 3.24 | 3.31 | 3.40 | 3.51 | 3.64 | 3.81 | 4.04 | 4.37 | 4.87 | 5.78 | 8.02 |
| 22 | 0.05 | 1.79 | 1.85 | 1.91 | 1.98 | 2.15 | 2.17 | 2.20 | 2.23 | 2.26 | 2.30 | 2.34 | 2.40 | 2.46 | 2.55 | 2.66 | 2.82 | 3.05 | 3.44 | 4.30 |
|    | 0.01 | 2.32 | 2.42 | 2.53 | 2.67 | 2.98 | 3.02 | 3.07 | 3.12 | 3.18 | 3.26 | 3.35 | 3.45 | 3.59 | 3.76 | 3.99 | 4.31 | 4.82 | 5.72 | 7.95 |
| 23 | 0.05 | 1.76 | 1.82 | 1.88 | 1.96 | 2.13 | 2.15 | 2.18 | 2.20 | 2.24 | 2.27 | 2.32 | 2.37 | 2.44 | 2.53 | 2.64 | 2.80 | 3.03 | 3.42 | 4.28 |
|    | 0.01 | 2.27 | 2.37 | 2.48 | 2.62 | 2.93 | 2.97 | 3.02 | 3.07 | 3.14 | 3.21 | 3.30 | 3.41 | 3.54 | 3.71 | 3.94 | 4.26 | 4.76 | 5.66 | 7.88 |
| 24 | 0.05 | 1.74 | 1.80 | 1.86 | 1.94 | 2.11 | 2.13 | 2.15 | 2.18 | 2.22 | 2.25 | 2.30 | 2.36 | 2.42 | 2.51 | 2.62 | 2.78 | 3.01 | 3.40 | 4.26 |
|    | 0.01 | 2.22 | 2.33 | 2.44 | 2.58 | 2.89 | 2.93 | 2.98 | 3.03 | 3.09 | 3.17 | 3.26 | 3.36 | 3.50 | 3.67 | 3.90 | 4.22 | 4.72 | 5.61 | 7.82 |
| 25 | 0.05 | 1.72 | 1.78 | 1.84 | 1.92 | 2.09 | 2.11 | 2.14 | 2.16 | 2.20 | 2.24 | 2.28 | 2.34 | 2.40 | 2.49 | 2.60 | 2.76 | 2.99 | 3.39 | 4.24 |
|    | 0.01 | 2.18 | 2.29 | 2.40 | 2.54 | 2.85 | 2.89 | 2.94 | 2.99 | 3.06 | 3.13 | 3.22 | 3.32 | 3.46 | 3.63 | 3.85 | 4.18 | 4.68 | 5.57 | 7.77 |
| 26 | 0.05 | 1.70 | 1.76 | 1.82 | 1.90 | 2.07 | 2.09 | 2.12 | 2.15 | 2.18 | 2.22 | 2.27 | 2.32 | 2.39 | 2.47 | 2.59 | 2.74 | 2.98 | 3.37 | 4.23 |
|    | 0.01 | 2.14 | 2.25 | 2.36 | 2.50 | 2.81 | 2.86 | 2.90 | 2.96 | 3.02 | 3.09 | 3.18 | 3.29 | 3.42 | 3.59 | 3.82 | 4.14 | 4.64 | 5.53 | 7.72 |
| 27 | 0.05 | 1.68 | 1.74 | 1.81 | 1.88 | 2.06 | 2.08 | 2.10 | 2.13 | 2.17 | 2.20 | 2.25 | 2.31 | 2.37 | 2.46 | 2.57 | 2.73 | 2.96 | 3.35 | 4.21 |
|    | 0.01 | 2.11 | 2.22 | 2.33 | 2.47 | 2.78 | 2.82 | 2.87 | 2.93 | 2.99 | 3.06 | 3.15 | 3.26 | 3.39 | 3.56 | 3.78 | 4.11 | 4.60 | 5.49 | 7.68 |
| 28 | 0.05 | 1.66 | 1.73 | 1.79 | 1.87 | 2.04 | 2.06 | 2.09 | 2.12 | 2.15 | 2.19 | 2.24 | 2.29 | 2.36 | 2.45 | 2.56 | 2.71 | 2.95 | 3.34 | 4.20 |
|    | 0.01 | 2.08 | 2.19 | 2.30 | 2.44 | 2.75 | 2.79 | 2.84 | 2.90 | 2.96 | 3.03 | 3.12 | 3.23 | 3.36 | 3.53 | 3.75 | 4.07 | 4.57 | 5.45 | 7.64 |
| 29 | 0.05 | 1.65 | 1.71 | 1.77 | 1.85 | 2.03 | 2.05 | 2.08 | 2.10 | 2.14 | 2.18 | 2.22 | 2.28 | 2.35 | 2.43 | 2.55 | 2.70 | 2.93 | 3.33 | 4.18 |
|    | 0.01 | 2.05 | 2.16 | 2.27 | 2.41 | 2.73 | 2.77 | 2.81 | 2.87 | 2.93 | 3.00 | 3.09 | 3.20 | 3.33 | 3.50 | 3.73 | 4.04 | 4.54 | 5.42 | 7.60 |
| 30 | 0.05 | 1.63 | 1.70 | 1.76 | 1.84 | 2.01 | 2.04 | 2.06 | 2.09 | 2.13 | 2.16 | 2.21 | 2.27 | 2.33 | 2.42 | 2.53 | 2.69 | 2.92 | 3.32 | 4.17 |
|    | 0.01 | 2.02 | 2.13 | 2.25 | 2.39 | 2.70 | 2.74 | 2.79 | 2.84 | 2.91 | 2.98 | 3.07 | 3.17 | 3.30 | 3.47 | 3.70 | 4.02 | 4.51 | 5.39 | 7.56 |
| 31 | 0.05 | 1.62 | 1.68 | 1.75 | 1.83 | 2.00 | 2.03 | 2.05 | 2.08 | 2.11 | 2.15 | 2.20 | 2.25 | 2.32 | 2.41 | 2.52 | 2.68 | 2.91 | 3.30 | 4.16 |
|    | 0.01 | 1.99 | 2.11 | 2.22 | 2.36 | 2.68 | 2.72 | 2.77 | 2.82 | 2.88 | 2.96 | 3.04 | 3.15 | 3.28 | 3.45 | 3.67 | 3.99 | 4.48 | 5.36 | 7.53 |
| 32 | 0.05 | 1.60 | 1.67 | 1.74 | 1.82 | 1.99 | 2.01 | 2.04 | 2.07 | 2.10 | 2.14 | 2.19 | 2.24 | 2.31 | 2.40 | 2.51 | 2.67 | 2.90 | 3.29 | 4.15 |
|    | 0.01 | 1.97 | 2.08 | 2.20 | 2.34 | 2.65 | 2.70 | 2.74 | 2.80 | 2.86 | 2.93 | 3.02 | 3.13 | 3.26 | 3.43 | 3.65 | 3.97 | 4.46 | 5.34 | 7.50 |
| 33 | 0.05 | 1.59 | 1.66 | 1.72 | 1.81 | 1.98 | 2.00 | 2.03 | 2.06 | 2.09 | 2.13 | 2.18 | 2.23 | 2.30 | 2.39 | 2.50 | 2.66 | 2.89 | 3.28 | 4.14 |
|    | 0.01 | 1.95 | 2.06 | 2.18 | 2.32 | 2.64 | 2.68 | 2.72 | 2.78 | 2.84 | 2.91 | 3.00 | 3.11 | 3.24 | 3.41 | 3.63 | 3.95 | 4.44 | 5.31 | 7.47 |
| 34 | 0.05 | 1.58 | 1.65 | 1.71 | 1.80 | 1.97 | 1.99 | 2.02 | 2.05 | 2.08 | 2.12 | 2.17 | 2.23 | 2.29 | 2.38 | 2.49 | 2.65 | 2.88 | 3.28 | 4.13 |
|    | 0.01 | 1.92 | 2.04 | 2.16 | 2.30 | 2.61 | 2.66 | 2.70 | 2.76 | 2.82 | 2.89 | 2.98 | 3.09 | 3.22 | 3.39 | 3.61 | 3.93 | 4.42 | 5.29 | 7.44 |
| 35 | 0.05 | 1.57 | 1.63 | 1.70 | 1.79 | 1.96 | 1.99 | 2.01 | 2.04 | 2.07 | 2.11 | 2.16 | 2.22 | 2.29 | 2.37 | 2.49 | 2.64 | 2.87 | 3.27 | 4.12 |
|    | 0.01 | 1.90 | 2.02 | 2.14 | 2.28 | 2.60 | 2.64 | 2.69 | 2.74 | 2.80 | 2.88 | 2.96 | 3.07 | 3.20 | 3.37 | 3.59 | 3.91 | 4.40 | 5.27 | 7.42 |
| 36 | 0.05 | 1.56 | 1.62 | 1.69 | 1.78 | 1.95 | 1.98 | 2.00 | 2.03 | 2.07 | 2.11 | 2.15 | 2.21 | 2.28 | 2.36 | 2.48 | 2.63 | 2.87 | 3.26 | 4.11 |
|    | 0.01 | 1.89 | 2.00 | 2.12 | 2.26 | 2.58 | 2.62 | 2.67 | 2.72 | 2.79 | 2.86 | 2.95 | 3.05 | 3.18 | 3.35 | 3.57 | 3.89 | 4.38 | 5.25 | 7.40 |
| 38 | 0.05 | 1.54 | 1.61 | 1.68 | 1.76 | 1.94 | 1.96 | 1.99 | 2.02 | 2.05 | 2.09 | 2.14 | 2.19 | 2.26 | 2.35 | 2.46 | 2.62 | 2.85 | 3.24 | 4.10 |
|    | 0.01 | 1.85 | 1.97 | 2.09 | 2.23 | 2.55 | 2.59 | 2.64 | 2.69 | 2.75 | 2.83 | 2.92 | 3.02 | 3.15 | 3.32 | 3.54 | 3.86 | 4.34 | 5.21 | 7.35 |
| 40 | 0.05 | 1.52 | 1.59 | 1.66 | 1.74 | 1.92 | 1.95 | 1.97 | 2.00 | 2.04 | 2.08 | 2.12 | 2.18 | 2.25 | 2.34 | 2.45 | 2.61 | 2.84 | 3.23 | 4.08 |
|    | 0.01 | 1.82 | 1.94 | 2.06 | 2.20 | 2.52 | 2.56 | 2.61 | 2.66 | 2.73 | 2.80 | 2.89 | 2.99 | 3.12 | 3.29 | 3.51 | 3.83 | 4.31 | 5.18 | 7.31 |
| 42 | 0.05 | 1.50 | 1.57 | 1.65 | 1.73 | 1.91 | 1.94 | 1.96 | 1.99 | 2.03 | 2.06 | 2.11 | 2.17 | 2.24 | 2.32 | 2.44 | 2.59 | 2.83 | 3.22 | 4.07 |
|    | 0.01 | 1.79 | 1.91 | 2.03 | 2.18 | 2.50 | 2.54 | 2.59 | 2.64 | 2.70 | 2.78 | 2.86 | 2.97 | 3.10 | 3.27 | 3.49 | 3.80 | 4.29 | 5.15 | 7.28 |

**Degrees of Freedom for Denominator**

# Table B.10 (Continued)

| df (denom) | α | 1 | 2 | 3 | 4 | 5 | 6 | 7 | 8 | 9 | 10 | 11 | 12 | 13 | 14 | 15 | 30 | 50 | 100 | 1000 |
|---|---|---|---|---|---|---|---|---|---|---|---|---|---|---|---|---|---|---|---|---|
| 44 | 0.05 | 4.06 | 3.21 | 2.82 | 2.58 | 2.43 | 2.31 | 2.23 | 2.16 | 2.10 | 2.05 | 2.01 | 1.98 | 1.95 | 1.92 | 1.90 | 1.72 | 1.63 | 1.56 | 1.49 |
|  | 0.01 | 7.25 | 5.12 | 4.26 | 3.78 | 3.47 | 3.24 | 3.08 | 2.95 | 2.84 | 2.75 | 2.68 | 2.62 | 2.56 | 2.52 | 2.47 | 2.15 | 2.01 | 1.89 | 1.76 |
| 46 | 0.05 | 4.05 | 3.20 | 2.81 | 2.57 | 2.42 | 2.30 | 2.22 | 2.15 | 2.09 | 2.04 | 2.00 | 1.97 | 1.94 | 1.91 | 1.89 | 1.71 | 1.62 | 1.55 | 1.47 |
|  | 0.01 | 7.22 | 5.10 | 4.24 | 3.76 | 3.44 | 3.22 | 3.06 | 2.93 | 2.82 | 2.73 | 2.66 | 2.60 | 2.54 | 2.50 | 2.45 | 2.13 | 1.99 | 1.86 | 1.74 |
| 48 | 0.05 | 4.04 | 3.19 | 2.80 | 2.57 | 2.41 | 2.29 | 2.21 | 2.14 | 2.08 | 2.03 | 1.99 | 1.96 | 1.93 | 1.90 | 1.88 | 1.70 | 1.61 | 1.54 | 1.46 |
|  | 0.01 | 7.19 | 5.08 | 4.22 | 3.74 | 3.43 | 3.20 | 3.04 | 2.91 | 2.80 | 2.71 | 2.64 | 2.58 | 2.53 | 2.48 | 2.44 | 2.12 | 1.97 | 1.84 | 1.72 |
| 50 | 0.05 | 4.03 | 3.18 | 2.79 | 2.56 | 2.40 | 2.29 | 2.20 | 2.13 | 2.07 | 2.03 | 1.99 | 1.95 | 1.92 | 1.89 | 1.87 | 1.69 | 1.60 | 1.52 | 1.45 |
|  | 0.01 | 7.17 | 5.06 | 4.20 | 3.72 | 3.41 | 3.19 | 3.02 | 2.89 | 2.78 | 2.70 | 2.63 | 2.56 | 2.51 | 2.46 | 2.42 | 2.10 | 1.95 | 1.82 | 1.70 |
| 55 | 0.05 | 4.02 | 3.16 | 2.77 | 2.54 | 2.38 | 2.27 | 2.18 | 2.11 | 2.06 | 2.01 | 1.97 | 1.93 | 1.90 | 1.88 | 1.85 | 1.67 | 1.58 | 1.50 | 1.42 |
|  | 0.01 | 7.12 | 5.01 | 4.16 | 3.68 | 3.37 | 3.15 | 2.98 | 2.85 | 2.75 | 2.66 | 2.59 | 2.53 | 2.47 | 2.42 | 2.38 | 2.06 | 1.91 | 1.78 | 1.65 |
| 60 | 0.05 | 4.00 | 3.15 | 2.76 | 2.53 | 2.37 | 2.25 | 2.17 | 2.10 | 2.04 | 1.99 | 1.95 | 1.92 | 1.89 | 1.86 | 1.84 | 1.65 | 1.56 | 1.48 | 1.40 |
|  | 0.01 | 7.08 | 4.98 | 4.13 | 3.65 | 3.34 | 3.12 | 2.95 | 2.82 | 2.72 | 2.63 | 2.56 | 2.50 | 2.44 | 2.39 | 2.35 | 2.03 | 1.88 | 1.75 | 1.62 |
| 65 | 0.05 | 3.99 | 3.14 | 2.75 | 2.51 | 2.36 | 2.24 | 2.15 | 2.08 | 2.03 | 1.98 | 1.94 | 1.90 | 1.87 | 1.85 | 1.82 | 1.63 | 1.54 | 1.46 | 1.38 |
|  | 0.01 | 7.04 | 4.95 | 4.10 | 3.62 | 3.31 | 3.09 | 2.93 | 2.80 | 2.69 | 2.61 | 2.53 | 2.47 | 2.42 | 2.37 | 2.33 | 2.00 | 1.85 | 1.72 | 1.59 |
| 70 | 0.05 | 3.98 | 3.13 | 2.74 | 2.50 | 2.35 | 2.23 | 2.14 | 2.07 | 2.02 | 1.97 | 1.93 | 1.89 | 1.86 | 1.84 | 1.81 | 1.62 | 1.53 | 1.45 | 1.36 |
|  | 0.01 | 7.01 | 4.92 | 4.07 | 3.60 | 3.29 | 3.07 | 2.91 | 2.78 | 2.67 | 2.59 | 2.51 | 2.45 | 2.40 | 2.35 | 2.31 | 1.98 | 1.83 | 1.70 | 1.56 |
| 80 | 0.05 | 3.96 | 3.11 | 2.72 | 2.49 | 2.33 | 2.21 | 2.13 | 2.06 | 2.00 | 1.95 | 1.91 | 1.88 | 1.84 | 1.82 | 1.79 | 1.60 | 1.51 | 1.43 | 1.34 |
|  | 0.01 | 6.96 | 4.88 | 4.04 | 3.56 | 3.26 | 3.04 | 2.87 | 2.74 | 2.64 | 2.55 | 2.48 | 2.42 | 2.36 | 2.31 | 2.27 | 1.94 | 1.79 | 1.65 | 1.51 |
| 100 | 0.05 | 3.94 | 3.09 | 2.70 | 2.46 | 2.31 | 2.19 | 2.10 | 2.03 | 1.97 | 1.93 | 1.89 | 1.85 | 1.82 | 1.79 | 1.77 | 1.57 | 1.48 | 1.39 | 1.30 |
|  | 0.01 | 6.90 | 4.82 | 3.98 | 3.51 | 3.21 | 2.99 | 2.82 | 2.69 | 2.59 | 2.50 | 2.43 | 2.37 | 2.31 | 2.27 | 2.22 | 1.89 | 1.74 | 1.60 | 1.45 |
| 125 | 0.05 | 3.92 | 3.07 | 2.68 | 2.44 | 2.29 | 2.17 | 2.08 | 2.01 | 1.96 | 1.91 | 1.87 | 1.83 | 1.80 | 1.77 | 1.75 | 1.55 | 1.45 | 1.36 | 1.26 |
|  | 0.01 | 6.84 | 4.78 | 3.94 | 3.47 | 3.17 | 2.95 | 2.79 | 2.66 | 2.55 | 2.47 | 2.39 | 2.33 | 2.28 | 2.23 | 2.19 | 1.85 | 1.69 | 1.55 | 1.39 |
| 150 | 0.05 | 3.90 | 3.06 | 2.66 | 2.43 | 2.27 | 2.16 | 2.07 | 2.00 | 1.94 | 1.89 | 1.85 | 1.82 | 1.79 | 1.76 | 1.73 | 1.54 | 1.44 | 1.34 | 1.24 |
|  | 0.01 | 6.81 | 4.75 | 3.91 | 3.45 | 3.14 | 2.92 | 2.76 | 2.63 | 2.53 | 2.44 | 2.37 | 2.31 | 2.25 | 2.20 | 2.16 | 1.83 | 1.66 | 1.52 | 1.35 |
| 200 | 0.05 | 3.89 | 3.04 | 2.65 | 2.42 | 2.26 | 2.14 | 2.06 | 1.98 | 1.93 | 1.88 | 1.84 | 1.80 | 1.77 | 1.74 | 1.72 | 1.52 | 1.41 | 1.32 | 1.21 |
|  | 0.01 | 6.76 | 4.71 | 3.88 | 3.41 | 3.11 | 2.89 | 2.73 | 2.60 | 2.50 | 2.41 | 2.34 | 2.27 | 2.22 | 2.17 | 2.13 | 1.79 | 1.63 | 1.48 | 1.30 |
| 400 | 0.05 | 3.86 | 3.02 | 2.63 | 2.39 | 2.24 | 2.12 | 2.03 | 1.96 | 1.90 | 1.85 | 1.81 | 1.78 | 1.74 | 1.72 | 1.69 | 1.49 | 1.38 | 1.28 | 1.15 |
|  | 0.01 | 6.70 | 4.66 | 3.83 | 3.37 | 3.06 | 2.85 | 2.68 | 2.56 | 2.45 | 2.37 | 2.29 | 2.23 | 2.17 | 2.13 | 2.08 | 1.75 | 1.58 | 1.42 | 1.22 |
| 1000 | 0.05 | 3.85 | 3.00 | 2.61 | 2.38 | 2.22 | 2.11 | 2.02 | 1.95 | 1.89 | 1.84 | 1.80 | 1.76 | 1.73 | 1.70 | 1.68 | 1.47 | 1.36 | 1.26 | 1.11 |
|  | 0.01 | 6.66 | 4.63 | 3.80 | 3.34 | 3.04 | 2.82 | 2.66 | 2.53 | 2.43 | 2.34 | 2.27 | 2.20 | 2.15 | 2.10 | 2.06 | 1.72 | 1.54 | 1.38 | 1.16 |

Degrees of Freedom for Numerator

Degrees of Freedom for Denominator

# Table B.11: Critical Values for the $F_{max}$ Test

## Using Table B.11

To use this table, divide the largest variance by the smallest variance to create $F_{max}$. The column labeled $n$ represents the number of subjects in each group. If the sample sizes for the two groups are not equal, determine the average $n$ and round up. The other columns of numbers represent the number of treatment conditions in the study. If the observed value of $F_{max}$ is less than the tabled value, then you may assume that the variances are homogeneous: $\sigma_{smallest} = \sigma_{largest}$.

---

### Example

A researcher conducted a study with six groups. The largest variance was 20 and the smallest variance was 10, with 15 participants in each group. $F_{max} = 2.00$. The critical value of $F_{max} = 4.70$, $\alpha = .05$. Therefore, we do *not* reject the hypothesis that the variances are equivalent. The data do not appear to violate the requirement that there be homogeneity of variance for the ANOVA.

---

## Table B.11

| $n$ | $\alpha$ | Number of Variances in Study | | | | | | | | |
| | | 2 | 3 | 4 | 5 | 6 | 7 | 8 | 9 | 10 |
|---|---|---|---|---|---|---|---|---|---|---|
| 4 | .05 | 9.60 | 15.5 | 20.6 | 25.2 | 29.5 | 33.6 | 37.5 | 41.4 | 44.6 |
| | .01 | 23.2 | 37.0 | 49.0 | 59.0 | 69.0 | 79.0 | 89.0 | 97.0 | 106.0 |
| 5 | .05 | 7.2 | 10.8 | 13.7 | 16.3 | 18.7 | 20.8 | 22.9 | 24.7 | 26.5 |
| | .01 | 14.9 | 22.0 | 28.0 | 33.0 | 38.0 | 42.0 | 46.0 | 50.0 | 54.0 |
| 6 | .05 | 5.8 | 8.4 | 10.4 | 12.1 | 13.7 | 15.0 | 16.3 | 17.5 | 18.6 |
| | .01 | 11.1 | 15.5 | 19.1 | 22.0 | 25.0 | 27.0 | 30.0 | 32.0 | 34.0 |
| 7 | .05 | 5.0 | 6.9 | 8.4 | 9.7 | 10.8 | 11.8 | 12.7 | 13.5 | 14.3 |
| | .01 | 8.9 | 12.1 | 14.5 | 16.5 | 18.4 | 20.0 | 22.0 | 23.0 | 24.0 |
| 8 | .05 | 4.4 | 6.0 | 7.2 | 8.1 | 9.0 | 9.8 | 10.5 | 11.1 | 11.7 |
| | .01 | 7.5 | 9.9 | 11.7 | 13.2 | 14.5 | 15.8 | 16.9 | 17.9 | 18.9 |
| 9 | .05 | 4.0 | 5.3 | 6.3 | 7.1 | 7.8 | 8.4 | 8.9 | 9.5 | 9.9 |
| | .01 | 6.5 | 8.5 | 9.9 | 11.1 | 12.1 | 13.1 | 13.9 | 14.7 | 15.3 |
| 10 | .05 | 3.7 | 4.9 | 5.7 | 6.3 | 6.9 | 7.4 | 7.9 | 8.3 | 8.7 |
| | .01 | 5.9 | 7.4 | 8.6 | 9.6 | 10.4 | 11.1 | 11.8 | 12.4 | 12.9 |
| 12 | .05 | 3.3 | 4.2 | 4.8 | 5.3 | 5.7 | 6.1 | 6.4 | 6.7 | 7.0 |
| | .01 | 4.9 | 6.1 | 6.9 | 7.6 | 8.2 | 8.7 | 9.1 | 9.5 | 9.9 |
| 15 | .05 | 2.7 | 3.5 | 4.0 | 4.4 | 4.7 | 4.9 | 5.2 | 5.4 | 5.6 |
| | .01 | 4.1 | 4.9 | 5.5 | 6.0 | 6.4 | 6.7 | 7.1 | 7.3 | 7.5 |
| 20 | .05 | 2.5 | 2.9 | 3.3 | 3.5 | 3.7 | 3.9 | 4.1 | 4.2 | 4.4 |
| | .01 | 3.3 | 3.8 | 4.3 | 4.6 | 4.9 | 5.1 | 5.3 | 5.5 | 5.6 |

(*Continued*)

# Table B.11

| $n$ | $\alpha$ | Number of Variances in Study | | | | | | | | |
|---|---|---|---|---|---|---|---|---|---|---|
| | | 2 | 3 | 4 | 5 | 6 | 7 | 8 | 9 | 10 |
| 30 | .05 | 2.1 | 2.4 | 2.6 | 2.8 | 2.9 | 3.0 | 3.1 | 3.2 | 3.3 |
| | .01 | 2.6 | 3.0 | 3.3 | 3.4 | 3.6 | 3.7 | 3.8 | 3.9 | 4.0 |
| 60 | .05 | 1.7 | 1.9 | 1.9 | 2.0 | 2.1 | 2.2 | 2.2 | 2.3 | 2.3 |
| | .01 | 2.0 | 2.2 | 2.3 | 2.4 | 2.4 | 2.5 | 2.5 | 2.6 | 2.6 |
| $\infty$ | .05 | 1.0 | 1.0 | 1.0 | 1.0 | 1.0 | 1.0 | 1.0 | 1.0 | 1.0 |
| | .01 | 1.0 | 1.0 | 1.0 | 1.0 | 1.0 | 1.0 | 1.0 | 1.0 | 1.0 |

## Table B.12: Critical Values for the Studentized Range Test

### Using Table B.12

This table contains the critical values developed by Tukey for his HSD test. To use the table, you will need the degrees of freedom for the within-groups term in the ANOVA summary table and the number of means to be compared by the HSD test.

---

### Example

A researcher conducted a study with four groups. The degrees of freedom denominator (*df* for the within-groups factor) are 12. Using Table B.12:

$$q_{critical} = 3.62, \alpha = .10$$
$$q_{critical} = 4.20, \alpha = .05$$
$$q_{critical} = 5.50, \alpha = .01$$

# Table B.12

|  | α | \multicolumn{17}{c}{Number of Means in Set} |
|---|---|---|

| df | α | 2 | 3 | 4 | 5 | 6 | 7 | 8 | 9 | 10 | 11 | 12 | 13 | 14 | 15 | 16 | 17 | 18 |
|---|---|---|---|---|---|---|---|---|---|---|---|---|---|---|---|---|---|---|
| 1 | .10 | 8.93 | 13.40 | 16.40 | 18.50 | 20.20 | 21.50 | 22.60 | 23.60 | 24.50 | 25.20 | 25.90 | 26.50 | 27.10 | 27.60 | 28.10 | 28.50 | 29.00 |
|   | .05 | 18.00 | 27.00 | 32.80 | 37.10 | 40.40 | 43.10 | 45.40 | 47.40 | 49.10 | 50.60 | 52.00 | 53.20 | 54.30 | 55.40 | 56.30 | 57.20 | 58.00 |
|   | .01 | 90.00 | 135.0 | 164.00 | 186.00 | 202.00 | 216.00 | 227.00 | 237.00 | 246.00 | 253.00 | 260.00 | 266.00 | 272.00 | 277.00 | 282.00 | 286.00 | 290.00 |
| 2 | .10 | 4.13 | 5.73 | 6.78 | 7.54 | 8.14 | 8.63 | 9.05 | 9.41 | 9.73 | 10.00 | 10.30 | 10.50 | 10.70 | 10.90 | 11.10 | 11.20 | 11.40 |
|   | .05 | 6.09 | 8.30 | 9.80 | 10.90 | 11.70 | 12.40 | 13.00 | 13.50 | 14.00 | 14.40 | 14.70 | 15.10 | 15.40 | 15.70 | 15.90 | 16.10 | 16.40 |
|   | .01 | 14.00 | 19.00 | 22.30 | 24.70 | 26.60 | 28.20 | 29.50 | 30.70 | 31.70 | 32.60 | 33.40 | 34.10 | 34.80 | 35.40 | 36.00 | 36.50 | 37.00 |
| 3 | .10 | 3.33 | 4.47 | 5.20 | 5.74 | 6.16 | 6.51 | 6.81 | 7.06 | 7.29 | 7.49 | 7.67 | 7.83 | 7.98 | 8.12 | 8.25 | 8.37 | 8.78 |
|   | .05 | 4.50 | 5.91 | 6.82 | 7.50 | 8.04 | 8.48 | 8.85 | 9.18 | 9.46 | 9.72 | 9.95 | 10.20 | 10.40 | 10.50 | 10.70 | 10.80 | 11.00 |
|   | .01 | 8.26 | 10.60 | 12.20 | 13.30 | 14.20 | 15.00 | 15.60 | 16.20 | 16.70 | 17.10 | 17.50 | 17.90 | 18.20 | 18.50 | 18.80 | 19.10 | 19.30 |
| 4 | .10 | 3.01 | 3.98 | 4.59 | 5.04 | 5.39 | 5.69 | 5.93 | 6.14 | 6.33 | 6.50 | 6.65 | 6.78 | 6.91 | 7.03 | 7.13 | 7.23 | 7.33 |
|   | .05 | 3.93 | 5.04 | 5.76 | 6.29 | 6.71 | 7.05 | 7.35 | 7.60 | 7.83 | 8.03 | 8.21 | 8.37 | 8.52 | 8.66 | 8.79 | 8.91 | 9.03 |
|   | .01 | 6.51 | 8.12 | 9.17 | 9.96 | 10.60 | 11.10 | 11.50 | 11.90 | 12.30 | 12.60 | 12.80 | 13.10 | 13.30 | 13.50 | 13.70 | 13.90 | 14.10 |
| 5 | .10 | 2.85 | 3.72 | 4.26 | 4.66 | 4.98 | 5.24 | 5.44 | 5.65 | 5.82 | 5.97 | 6.10 | 6.22 | 6.34 | 6.44 | 6.54 | 6.63 | 6.71 |
|   | .05 | 3.64 | 4.60 | 5.22 | 5.67 | 6.03 | 6.33 | 6.58 | 6.80 | 6.99 | 7.17 | 7.32 | 7.47 | 7.60 | 7.72 | 7.83 | 7.93 | 8.03 |
|   | .01 | 5.70 | 6.97 | 7.80 | 8.42 | 8.91 | 9.32 | 9.67 | 9.97 | 10.20 | 10.50 | 10.70 | 10.90 | 11.10 | 11.20 | 11.40 | 11.60 | 11.70 |
| 6 | .10 | 2.75 | 3.56 | 4.07 | 4.44 | 4.73 | 4.97 | 5.17 | 5.34 | 5.50 | 5.64 | 5.76 | 5.88 | 5.98 | 6.08 | 6.16 | 6.25 | 6.33 |
|   | .05 | 3.46 | 4.34 | 4.90 | 5.31 | 5.63 | 5.89 | 6.12 | 6.32 | 6.49 | 6.65 | 6.79 | 6.92 | 7.03 | 7.14 | 7.24 | 7.34 | 7.43 |
|   | .01 | 5.24 | 6.33 | 7.03 | 7.56 | 7.97 | 8.32 | 8.61 | 8.87 | 9.10 | 9.30 | 9.49 | 9.65 | 9.81 | 9.95 | 10.10 | 10.20 | 10.30 |
| 7 | .10 | 2.68 | 3.45 | 3.93 | 4.28 | 4.56 | 4.78 | 4.97 | 5.14 | 5.28 | 5.41 | 5.53 | 5.64 | 5.74 | 5.83 | 5.91 | 5.99 | 6.06 |
|   | .05 | 3.34 | 4.16 | 4.69 | 5.06 | 5.36 | 5.61 | 5.82 | 6.00 | 6.16 | 6.30 | 6.43 | 6.55 | 6.66 | 6.76 | 6.85 | 6.94 | 7.02 |
|   | .01 | 4.95 | 5.92 | 6.54 | 7.01 | 7.37 | 7.68 | 7.94 | 8.17 | 8.37 | 8.55 | 8.71 | 8.86 | 9.00 | 9.12 | 9.24 | 9.35 | 9.46 |
| 8 | .10 | 2.63 | 3.37 | 3.83 | 4.17 | 4.43 | 4.65 | 4.83 | 4.99 | 5.13 | 5.25 | 5.36 | 5.46 | 5.56 | 5.64 | 5.74 | 5.83 | 5.87 |
|   | .05 | 3.26 | 4.04 | 4.53 | 4.89 | 5.17 | 5.40 | 5.60 | 5.77 | 5.92 | 6.05 | 6.18 | 6.29 | 6.39 | 6.48 | 6.57 | 6.65 | 6.73 |
|   | .01 | 4.74 | 5.63 | 6.20 | 6.63 | 6.96 | 7.24 | 7.47 | 7.68 | 7.78 | 8.03 | 8.18 | 8.31 | 8.44 | 8.55 | 8.66 | 8.76 | 8.85 |

Degrees of Freedom for Denominator

(Continued)

# Table B.12

| | | | | | | | | | Number of Means in Set | | | | | | | | | |
|---|---|---|---|---|---|---|---|---|---|---|---|---|---|---|---|---|---|---|
| df | α | 2 | 3 | 4 | 5 | 6 | 7 | 8 | 9 | 10 | 11 | 12 | 13 | 14 | 15 | 16 | 17 | 18 |
| 9 | .10 | 2.59 | 3.32 | 3.76 | 4.08 | 4.34 | 4.55 | 4.72 | 4.87 | 5.01 | 5.13 | 5.23 | 5.33 | 5.42 | 5.51 | 5.58 | 5.66 | 5.72 |
| | .05 | 3.20 | 3.95 | 4.42 | 4.76 | 5.02 | 5.24 | 5.43 | 5.60 | 5.74 | 5.87 | 5.98 | 6.09 | 6.19 | 6.28 | 6.36 | 6.44 | 6.51 |
| | .01 | 4.60 | 5.43 | 5.96 | 6.35 | 6.66 | 6.91 | 7.13 | 7.32 | 7.49 | 7.65 | 7.78 | 7.91 | 8.03 | 8.13 | 8.23 | 8.33 | 8.41 |
| 10 | .10 | 2.56 | 3.28 | 3.70 | 4.02 | 4.26 | 4.47 | 4.64 | 4.78 | 4.91 | 5.03 | 5.13 | 5.23 | 5.32 | 5.40 | 5.47 | 5.54 | 5.61 |
| | .05 | 3.15 | 3.88 | 4.33 | 4.65 | 4.91 | 5.12 | 5.30 | 5.46 | 5.60 | 5.72 | 5.83 | 5.93 | 6.03 | 6.11 | 6.19 | 6.27 | 6.34 |
| | .01 | 4.48 | 5.27 | 5.77 | 6.14 | 6.43 | 6.67 | 6.87 | 7.05 | 7.21 | 7.36 | 7.48 | 7.60 | 7.71 | 7.81 | 7.91 | 8.00 | 8.08 |
| 11 | .10 | 2.54 | 3.23 | 3.66 | 3.97 | 4.21 | 4.40 | 4.57 | 4.71 | 4.84 | 4.95 | 5.05 | 5.15 | 5.23 | 5.31 | 5.38 | 5.45 | 5.51 |
| | .05 | 3.11 | 3.82 | 4.26 | 4.57 | 4.82 | 5.03 | 5.20 | 5.35 | 5.49 | 5.61 | 5.71 | 5.81 | 5.90 | 5.99 | 6.06 | 6.18 | 6.20 |
| | .01 | 4.39 | 5.14 | 5.62 | 5.97 | 6.25 | 6.48 | 6.67 | 6.84 | 6.99 | 7.13 | 7.26 | 7.36 | 7.46 | 7.56 | 7.65 | 7.73 | 7.81 |
| 12 | .10 | 2.52 | 3.20 | 3.62 | 3.92 | 4.16 | 4.35 | 4.51 | 4.65 | 4.78 | 4.89 | 4.99 | 5.08 | 5.16 | 5.24 | 5.31 | 5.37 | 5.44 |
| | .05 | 3.08 | 3.77 | 4.20 | 4.51 | 4.75 | 4.95 | 5.12 | 5.27 | 5.40 | 5.51 | 5.62 | 5.71 | 5.80 | 5.88 | 5.95 | 6.02 | 6.09 |
| | .01 | 4.32 | 5.04 | 5.50 | 5.84 | 6.10 | 6.32 | 6.51 | 6.67 | 6.81 | 6.94 | 7.06 | 7.17 | 7.26 | 7.36 | 7.44 | 7.52 | 7.50 |
| 13 | .10 | 2.51 | 3.18 | 3.59 | 3.89 | 4.12 | 4.31 | 4.46 | 4.60 | 4.72 | 4.83 | 4.93 | 5.02 | 5.10 | 5.18 | 5.25 | 5.31 | 5.37 |
| | .05 | 3.06 | 3.73 | 4.15 | 4.45 | 4.69 | 4.88 | 5.05 | 5.19 | 5.32 | 5.43 | 5.53 | 5.63 | 5.71 | 5.79 | 5.86 | 5.93 | 6.00 |
| | .01 | 4.26 | 4.96 | 5.40 | 5.73 | 5.98 | 6.19 | 6.37 | 6.53 | 6.67 | 6.79 | 6.90 | 7.01 | 7.10 | 7.19 | 7.27 | 7.37 | 7.42 |
| 14 | .10 | 2.99 | 3.16 | 3.56 | 3.83 | 4.08 | 4.27 | 4.42 | 4.56 | 4.68 | 4.79 | 4.88 | 4.97 | 5.05 | 5.12 | 5.19 | 5.26 | 5.32 |
| | .05 | 3.03 | 3.70 | 4.11 | 4.41 | 4.64 | 4.83 | 4.99 | 5.13 | 5.25 | 5.36 | 5.46 | 5.55 | 5.64 | 5.72 | 5.79 | 5.85 | 5.92 |
| | .01 | 4.21 | 4.89 | 5.32 | 5.63 | 5.88 | 6.08 | 6.26 | 6.41 | 6.54 | 6.66 | 6.77 | 6.87 | 6.96 | 7.05 | 7.13 | 7.20 | 7.27 |
| 16 | .10 | 2.47 | 3.12 | 3.52 | 3.80 | 4.03 | 4.21 | 4.36 | 4.49 | 4.61 | 4.71 | 4.81 | 4.89 | 4.97 | 5.04 | 5.11 | 5.17 | 5.23 |
| | .05 | 3.00 | 3.65 | 4.05 | 4.33 | 4.56 | 4.74 | 4.90 | 5.03 | 5.15 | 5.26 | 5.35 | 5.44 | 5.52 | 5.59 | 5.66 | 5.73 | 5.79 |
| | .01 | 4.13 | 4.78 | 5.19 | 5.49 | 5.72 | 5.92 | 6.08 | 6.22 | 6.35 | 6.46 | 6.56 | 6.66 | 6.74 | 6.82 | 6.90 | 6.97 | 7.03 |
| 18 | .10 | 2.45 | 3.10 | 3.49 | 3.77 | 3.98 | 4.16 | 4.31 | 4.44 | 4.55 | 4.66 | 4.75 | 4.83 | 4.91 | 4.98 | 5.04 | 5.10 | 5.16 |
| | .05 | 2.97 | 3.61 | 4.00 | 4.28 | 4.49 | 4.67 | 4.82 | 4.96 | 5.07 | 5.17 | 5.27 | 5.35 | 5.43 | 5.50 | 5.57 | 5.63 | 5.69 |
| | .01 | 4.07 | 4.70 | 5.09 | 5.38 | 5.60 | 5.79 | 5.94 | 6.08 | 6.20 | 6.31 | 6.41 | 6.50 | 6.58 | 6.65 | 6.73 | 6.79 | 6.85 |
| 20 | .10 | 2.44 | 3.08 | 3.46 | 3.74 | 3.95 | 4.12 | 4.27 | 4.40 | 4.51 | 4.61 | 4.70 | 4.78 | 4.86 | 4.92 | 4.99 | 5.05 | 5.10 |
| | .05 | 2.95 | 3.58 | 3.96 | 4.23 | 4.45 | 4.62 | 4.77 | 4.90 | 5.01 | 5.11 | 5.20 | 5.28 | 5.36 | 5.43 | 5.49 | 5.55 | 5.61 |
| | .01 | 4.02 | 4.64 | 5.02 | 5.29 | 5.51 | 5.69 | 5.84 | 5.97 | 6.09 | 6.19 | 6.29 | 6.37 | 6.45 | 6.52 | 6.59 | 6.65 | 6.71 |
| 24 | .10 | 2.42 | 3.05 | 3.42 | 3.69 | 3.9 | 4.07 | 4.21 | 4.34 | 4.45 | 4.54 | 4.63 | 4.71 | 4.78 | 4.85 | 4.91 | 4.97 | 5.02 |
| | .05 | 2.92 | 3.53 | 3.9 | 4.17 | 4.37 | 4.54 | 4.68 | 4.81 | 4.92 | 5.01 | 5.1 | 5.18 | 5.25 | 5.32 | 5.38 | 5.44 | 5.49 |
| | .01 | 3.96 | 4.54 | 4.91 | 5.17 | 5.37 | 5.54 | 5.69 | 5.81 | 5.92 | 6.02 | 6.11 | 6.19 | 6.26 | 6.33 | 6.39 | 6.45 | 6.51 |

Degrees of Freedom for Denominator

| | | | | | | | | | | | | | | | | | | |
|---|---|---|---|---|---|---|---|---|---|---|---|---|---|---|---|---|---|---|
| | .10 | 2.4 | 3.02 | 3.39 | 3.65 | 3.85 | 4.02 | 4.16 | 4.28 | 4.38 | 4.47 | 4.56 | 4.64 | 4.71 | 4.77 | 4.83 | 4.89 | 4.94 |
| **30** | .05 | 2.89 | 3.49 | 3.84 | 4.1 | 4.3 | 4.46 | 4.6 | 4.72 | 4.83 | 4.92 | 5 | 5.08 | 5.15 | 5.21 | 5.27 | 5.33 | 5.38 |
| | .01 | 3.89 | 4.45 | 4.8 | 5.05 | 5.24 | 5.4 | 5.54 | 5.56 | 5.76 | 5.85 | 5.93 | 6.01 | 6.08 | 6.14 | 6.2 | 6.26 | 6.31 |
| | .10 | 2.38 | 2.99 | 3.35 | 3.61 | 3.8 | 3.96 | 4.1 | 4.22 | 4.32 | 4.41 | 4.49 | 4.56 | 4.63 | 4.7 | 4.75 | 4.81 | 4.86 |
| **40** | .05 | 2.86 | 3.44 | 3.79 | 4.04 | 4.23 | 4.39 | 4.52 | 4.63 | 4.74 | 4.82 | 4.91 | 4.98 | 5.05 | 5.11 | 5.16 | 5.22 | 5.27 |
| | .01 | 3.82 | 4.37 | 4.7 | 4.93 | 5.11 | 5.27 | 5.39 | 5.5 | 5.6 | 5.69 | 5.77 | 5.84 | 5.9 | 5.96 | 6.02 | 6.07 | 6.11 |
| | .10 | 2.36 | 2.96 | 3.31 | 3.56 | 3.76 | 3.91 | 4.04 | 4.16 | 4.26 | 4.34 | 4.42 | 4.49 | 4.56 | 4.62 | 4.68 | 4.73 | 4.78 |
| **60** | .05 | 2.83 | 3.4 | 3.74 | 3.98 | 4.16 | 4.31 | 4.44 | 4.55 | 4.65 | 4.73 | 4.81 | 4.88 | 4.94 | 5 | 5.06 | 5.11 | 5.15 |
| | .01 | 3.76 | 4.28 | 4.6 | 4.82 | 4.99 | 5.13 | 5.25 | 5.36 | 5.45 | 5.53 | 5.6 | 5.67 | 5.73 | 5.79 | 5.84 | 5.89 | 5.93 |
| | .10 | 2.34 | 2.93 | 3.28 | 3.52 | 3.71 | 3.86 | 3.99 | 4.1 | 4.19 | 4.28 | 4.35 | 4.42 | 4.49 | 4.59 | 4.6 | 4.65 | 4.69 |
| **120** | .05 | 2.8 | 3.36 | 3.69 | 3.92 | 4.1 | 4.24 | 4.36 | 4.48 | 4.56 | 4.64 | 4.72 | 4.78 | 4.84 | 4.9 | 4.95 | 5 | 5.04 |
| | .01 | 3.7 | 4.2 | 4.5 | 4.71 | 4.87 | 5.01 | 5.12 | 5.21 | 5.3 | 5.38 | 5.44 | 5.51 | 5.56 | 5.61 | 5.66 | 5.71 | 5.75 |

## Table B.13: Power of ANOVA

### Using Table B.13

The values in this table help you determine the optimal sample size for an analysis of variance given the anticipated effect size and $\alpha$-level.

---

### Example: Single-Factor Design

A researcher wishes to conduct a single-factor design with three levels of the independent variable. How many participants will the researcher require in each treatment condition to have power equal to $1 - \beta = .80$ when the effect size is moderate, $f = .25$ and $\alpha = .05$? In this example, $df_N = 2$. According to this table, $1 - \beta = .83$ when there are 55 participants in each treatment condition.

---

### Example: Factorial Design

A researcher designed a $3 \times 4$ factorial study. How many participants should the researcher use in each treatment condition to have power equal to $1 - \beta = .80$? Also assume that the effect size is moderate, $f = .25$.

First, determine the degrees of freedom for each effect in the ANOVA:

$$df_A = 2 = (3 - 1) \quad j = \text{levels of Factor A}$$
$$df_B = 3 = (4 - 1) \quad k = \text{levels of Factor B}$$
$$df_{AB} = 6 = (3 - 1)(4 - 1)$$

Next, adjust the degrees of freedom using the following equation. For this example, assume that the sample size is 10:

$$n''_{effect} = \frac{jk(n_{ij} - 1)}{df_{effect} + 1} + 1$$

| | $df_N$ | | Adjusted Sample Size | Rounded[*] Sample Size | Estimated Power |
|---|---|---|---|---|---|
| Factor A | 2 | $n'' = \dfrac{12(10-1)}{2+1} + 1$ | $n' = 37$ | $n' = 40$ | $1 - \beta \approx .68$ |
| Factor B | 3 | $n' = \dfrac{12(10-1)}{3+1} + 1$ | $n' = 28$ | $n' = 30$ | $1 - \beta \approx .61$ |
| Factor AB | 6 | $n' = \dfrac{12(10-1)}{6+1} + 1$ | $n' = 16.429$ | $n' = 16$ | $1 - \beta \approx .45$ |

[*] The adjusted sample size has been rounded to match the closest values in the power tables.

Note that for effect sizes in this type of analysis,

$$f = .10 = \text{``small''} \quad f = .25 = \text{``medium''} \quad f = .40 = \text{``large''}$$

# Table B.13

| n | $F_c$ | $\alpha = .05$ $df_N = 1$ Effect Size, $f$ | | | | $F_c$ | $\alpha = .05$ $df_N = 2$ Effect Size, $f$ | | | | $F_c$ | $\alpha = .05$ $df_N = 3$ Effect Size, $f$ | | | |
|---|---|---|---|---|---|---|---|---|---|---|---|---|---|---|---|
| | | .10 | .25 | .40 | .55 | | .10 | .25 | .40 | .55 | | .10 | .25 | .40 | .55 |
| 10 | 4.414 | .08 | .19 | .40 | .65 | 3.354 | .10 | .22 | .46 | .72 | 2.866 | .12 | .26 | .52 | .79 |
| 11 | 4.351 | .08 | .21 | .43 | .70 | 3.316 | .10 | .24 | .50 | .77 | 2.839 | .11 | .27 | .56 | .83 |
| 12 | 4.301 | .08 | .22 | .47 | .74 | 3.285 | .10 | .25 | .53 | .81 | 2.816 | .11 | .29 | .60 | .87 |
| 13 | 4.260 | .08 | .23 | .50 | .78 | 3.259 | .10 | .27 | .57 | .85 | 2.798 | .11 | .31 | .64 | .90 |
| 14 | 4.225 | .09 | .25 | .53 | .81 | 3.238 | .10 | .28 | .60 | .88 | 2.783 | .12 | .32 | .67 | .92 |
| 15 | 4.196 | .09 | .26 | .56 | .84 | 3.220 | .10 | .30 | .64 | .90 | 2.769 | .12 | .34 | .71 | .94 |
| 16 | 4.171 | .09 | .28 | .59 | .87 | 3.204 | .10 | .32 | .67 | .92 | 2.758 | .12 | .36 | .74 | .96 |
| 17 | 4.149 | .09 | .29 | .62 | .89 | 3.191 | .10 | .33 | .70 | .94 | 2.748 | .12 | .38 | .77 | .97 |
| 18 | 4.130 | .09 | .30 | .65 | .91 | 3.179 | .11 | .35 | .73 | .95 | 2.739 | .12 | .39 | .79 | .98 |
| 19 | 4.113 | .10 | .32 | .68 | .92 | 3.168 | .11 | .36 | .75 | .96 | 2.732 | .12 | .41 | .82 | .98 |
| 20 | 4.098 | .10 | .33 | .70 | .94 | 3.159 | .11 | .38 | .78 | .97 | 2.725 | .12 | .43 | .84 | .99 |
| 21 | 4.085 | .10 | .35 | .72 | .95 | 3.150 | .11 | .40 | .80 | .98 | 2.719 | .12 | .45 | .86 | .99 |
| 22 | 4.073 | .10 | .36 | .75 | .96 | 3.143 | .11 | .41 | .82 | .98 | 2.713 | .13 | .47 | .88 | .99 |
| 23 | 4.062 | .10 | .37 | .77 | .97 | 3.136 | .12 | .43 | .84 | .99 | 2.708 | .13 | .49 | .90 | .99 |
| 24 | 4.052 | .10 | .39 | .79 | .97 | 3.130 | .12 | .44 | .86 | .99 | 2.704 | .13 | .50 | .91 | .99 |
| 25 | 4.043 | .11 | .40 | .80 | .98 | 3.124 | .12 | .46 | .87 | .99 | 2.699 | .13 | .52 | .92 | .99 |
| 26 | 4.034 | .11 | .42 | .82 | .98 | 3.119 | .12 | .48 | .89 | .99 | 2.696 | .13 | .54 | .93 | .99 |
| 27 | 4.027 | .11 | .43 | .84 | .99 | 3.114 | .12 | .49 | .90 | .99 | 2.692 | .14 | .56 | .94 | .99 |
| 28 | 4.020 | .11 | .44 | .85 | .99 | 3.109 | .13 | .51 | .91 | .99 | 2.689 | .14 | .57 | .95 | .99 |
| 29 | 4.013 | .11 | .46 | .86 | .99 | 3.105 | .13 | .52 | .92 | .99 | 2.686 | .14 | .59 | .96 | .99 |
| 30 | 4.007 | .12 | .47 | .88 | .99 | 3.101 | .13 | .54 | .93 | .99 | 2.683 | .14 | .61 | .97 | .99 |
| 31 | 4.001 | .12 | .48 | .89 | .99 | 3.098 | .13 | .55 | .94 | .99 | 2.680 | .15 | .62 | .97 | .99 |
| 32 | 3.996 | .12 | .50 | .90 | .99 | 3.094 | .13 | .57 | .95 | .99 | 2.678 | .15 | .64 | .98 | .99 |
| 33 | 3.991 | .12 | .51 | .91 | .99 | 3.091 | .14 | .58 | .96 | .99 | 2.675 | .15 | .65 | .98 | .99 |
| 34 | 3.986 | .13 | .52 | .92 | .99 | 3.088 | .14 | .60 | .96 | .99 | 2.673 | .15 | .67 | .98 | .99 |
| 35 | 3.982 | .13 | .54 | .93 | .99 | 3.085 | .14 | .61 | .97 | .99 | 2.671 | .15 | .68 | .99 | .99 |
| 36 | 3.978 | .13 | .55 | .93 | .99 | 3.083 | .14 | .62 | .97 | .99 | 2.669 | .16 | .70 | .99 | .99 |
| 37 | 3.974 | .13 | .56 | .94 | .99 | 3.080 | .14 | .64 | .98 | .99 | 2.667 | .16 | .71 | .99 | .99 |
| 38 | 3.970 | .13 | .57 | .95 | .99 | 3.078 | .15 | .65 | .98 | .99 | 2.666 | .16 | .72 | .99 | .99 |
| 39 | 3.967 | .14 | .59 | .95 | .99 | 3.076 | .15 | .66 | .98 | .99 | 2.664 | .17 | .74 | .99 | .99 |
| 40 | 3.963 | .14 | .60 | .96 | .99 | 3.074 | .15 | .68 | .98 | .99 | 2.663 | .17 | .75 | .99 | .99 |
| 45 | 3.949 | .15 | .65 | .98 | .99 | 3.065 | .16 | .73 | .99 | .99 | 2.656 | .18 | .81 | .99 | .99 |
| 50 | 3.938 | .16 | .70 | .99 | .99 | 3.058 | .18 | .78 | .99 | .99 | 2.651 | .20 | .85 | .99 | .99 |
| 55 | 3.929 | .17 | .75 | .99 | .99 | 3.052 | .19 | .83 | .99 | .99 | 2.646 | .21 | .89 | .99 | .99 |
| 60 | 3.921 | .18 | .79 | .99 | .99 | 3.047 | .20 | .86 | .99 | .99 | 2.643 | .22 | .92 | .99 | .99 |
| 70 | 3.910 | .21 | .85 | .99 | .99 | 3.040 | .23 | .92 | .99 | .99 | 2.637 | .26 | .96 | .99 | .99 |
| 80 | 3.901 | .23 | .90 | .99 | .99 | 3.034 | .26 | .95 | .99 | .99 | 2.633 | .29 | .98 | .99 | .99 |
| 90 | 3.894 | .25 | .93 | .99 | .99 | 3.030 | .28 | .97 | .99 | .99 | 2.630 | .32 | .99 | .99 | .99 |
| 100 | 3.889 | .28 | .96 | .99 | .99 | 3.026 | .31 | .99 | .99 | .99 | 2.627 | .35 | .99 | .99 | .99 |
| 110 | 3.884 | .30 | .97 | .99 | .99 | 3.023 | .34 | .99 | .99 | .99 | 2.625 | .38 | .99 | .99 | .99 |
| 120 | 3.881 | .32 | .98 | .99 | .99 | 3.021 | .37 | .99 | .99 | .99 | 2.624 | .41 | .99 | .99 | .99 |
| 130 | 3.878 | .35 | .99 | .99 | .99 | 3.019 | .39 | .99 | .99 | .99 | 2.622 | .45 | .99 | .99 | .99 |
| 140 | 3.875 | .37 | .99 | .99 | .99 | 3.017 | .42 | .99 | .99 | .99 | 2.621 | .48 | .99 | .99 | .99 |
| 150 | 3.873 | .39 | .99 | .99 | .99 | 3.016 | .45 | .99 | .99 | .99 | 2.620 | .51 | .99 | .99 | .99 |

(Continued)

# Table B.13 (Continued)

| n | $F_c$ | α = .05 $df_N = 1$ Effect Size, $f$ .10 | .25 | .40 | .55 | $F_c$ | α = .05 $df_N = 2$ Effect Size, $f$ .10 | .25 | .40 | .55 | $F_c$ | α = .05 $df_N = 3$ Effect Size, $f$ .10 | .25 | .40 | .55 |
|---|---|---|---|---|---|---|---|---|---|---|---|---|---|---|---|
| 160 | 3.871 | .42 | .99 | .99 | .99 | 3.015 | .47 | .99 | .99 | .99 | 2.619 | .54 | .99 | .99 | .99 |
| 170 | 3.869 | .44 | .99 | .99 | .99 | 3.014 | .50 | .99 | .99 | .99 | 2.618 | .57 | .99 | .99 | .99 |
| 180 | 3.868 | .46 | .99 | .99 | .99 | 3.013 | .53 | .99 | .99 | .99 | 2.617 | .60 | .99 | .99 | .99 |
| 190 | 3.866 | .48 | .99 | .99 | .99 | 3.012 | .55 | .99 | .99 | .99 | 2.617 | .62 | .99 | .99 | .99 |
| 200 | 3.865 | .50 | .99 | .99 | .99 | 3.011 | .58 | .99 | .99 | .99 | 2.616 | .65 | .99 | .99 | .99 |
| 300 | 3.857 | .69 | .99 | .99 | .99 | 3.006 | .78 | .99 | .99 | .99 | 2.612 | .85 | .99 | .99 | .99 |
| 10 | 2.579 | .13 | .29 | .57 | .83 | 2.386 | .14 | .32 | .61 | .87 | 2.246 | .16 | .34 | .65 | .89 |
| 11 | 2.557 | .13 | .31 | .61 | .87 | 2.368 | .14 | .33 | .66 | .90 | 2.231 | .15 | .36 | .69 | .93 |
| 12 | 2.540 | .13 | .32 | .65 | .91 | 2.354 | .14 | .35 | .70 | .93 | 2.219 | .15 | .38 | .74 | .95 |
| 13 | 2.525 | .13 | .34 | .69 | .93 | 2.342 | .14 | .37 | .74 | .95 | 2.209 | .15 | .40 | .77 | .97 |
| 14 | 2.513 | .13 | .36 | .73 | .95 | 2.332 | .14 | .39 | .77 | .97 | 2.200 | .15 | .42 | .81 | .98 |
| 15 | 2.503 | .13 | .38 | .76 | .96 | 2.323 | .14 | .42 | .80 | .98 | 2.193 | .15 | .45 | .84 | .99 |
| 16 | 2.494 | .13 | .40 | .79 | .97 | 2.316 | .14 | .44 | .83 | .99 | 2.186 | .15 | .47 | .87 | .99 |
| 17 | 2.486 | .13 | .42 | .82 | .98 | 2.309 | .14 | .46 | .86 | .99 | 2.181 | .15 | .49 | .89 | .99 |
| 18 | 2.479 | .13 | .44 | .84 | .99 | 2.303 | .14 | .48 | .88 | .99 | 2.176 | .15 | .51 | .91 | .99 |
| 19 | 2.473 | .13 | .46 | .87 | .99 | 2.298 | .14 | .50 | .90 | .99 | 2.171 | .16 | .54 | .93 | .99 |
| 20 | 2.467 | .13 | .48 | .89 | .99 | 2.294 | .15 | .52 | .92 | .99 | 2.167 | .16 | .56 | .94 | .99 |
| 21 | 2.463 | .14 | .50 | .90 | .99 | 2.290 | .15 | .54 | .93 | .99 | 2.164 | .16 | .58 | .95 | .99 |
| 22 | 2.458 | .14 | .52 | .92 | .99 | 2.286 | .15 | .56 | .95 | .99 | 2.161 | .16 | .60 | .96 | .99 |
| 23 | 2.454 | .14 | .54 | .93 | .99 | 2.283 | .15 | .58 | .96 | .99 | 2.158 | .16 | .62 | .97 | .99 |
| 24 | 2.451 | .14 | .56 | .94 | .99 | 2.280 | .15 | .60 | .96 | .99 | 2.155 | .17 | .65 | .98 | .99 |
| 25 | 2.447 | .14 | .58 | .95 | .99 | 2.277 | .16 | .62 | .97 | .99 | 2.153 | .17 | .67 | .98 | .99 |
| 26 | 2.444 | .15 | .59 | .96 | .99 | 2.274 | .16 | .64 | .98 | .99 | 2.151 | .17 | .69 | .99 | .99 |
| 27 | 2.441 | .15 | .61 | .97 | .99 | 2.272 | .16 | .66 | .98 | .99 | 2.149 | .17 | .70 | .99 | .99 |
| 28 | 2.439 | .15 | .63 | .97 | .99 | 2.270 | .16 | .68 | .99 | .99 | 2.147 | .18 | .72 | .99 | .99 |
| 29 | 2.436 | .15 | .65 | .98 | .99 | 2.268 | .17 | .70 | .99 | .99 | 2.145 | .18 | .74 | .99 | .99 |
| 30 | 2.434 | .16 | .66 | .98 | .99 | 2.266 | .17 | .72 | .99 | .99 | 2.143 | .18 | .76 | .99 | .99 |
| 31 | 2.432 | .16 | .68 | .99 | .99 | 2.264 | .17 | .73 | .99 | .99 | 2.142 | .18 | .77 | .99 | .99 |
| 32 | 2.430 | .16 | .70 | .99 | .99 | 2.263 | .17 | .75 | .99 | .99 | 2.141 | .19 | .79 | .99 | .99 |
| 33 | 2.428 | .16 | .71 | .99 | .99 | 2.261 | .18 | .76 | .99 | .99 | 2.139 | .19 | .80 | .99 | .99 |
| 34 | 2.426 | .17 | .73 | .99 | .99 | 2.260 | .18 | .78 | .99 | .99 | 2.138 | .19 | .82 | .99 | .99 |
| 35 | 2.425 | .17 | .74 | .99 | .99 | 2.258 | .18 | .79 | .99 | .99 | 2.137 | .20 | .83 | .99 | .99 |
| 36 | 2.423 | .17 | .76 | .99 | .99 | 2.257 | .19 | .80 | .99 | .99 | 2.136 | .20 | .84 | .99 | .99 |
| 37 | 2.422 | .17 | .77 | .99 | .99 | 2.256 | .19 | .82 | .99 | .99 | 2.135 | .20 | .85 | .99 | .99 |
| 38 | 2.420 | .18 | .78 | .99 | .99 | 2.255 | .19 | .83 | .99 | .99 | 2.134 | .21 | .87 | .99 | .99 |
| 39 | 2.419 | .18 | .80 | .99 | .99 | 2.254 | .20 | .84 | .99 | .99 | 2.133 | .21 | .88 | .99 | .99 |
| 40 | 2.418 | .18 | .81 | .99 | .99 | 2.253 | .20 | .85 | .99 | .99 | 2.132 | .21 | .89 | .99 | .99 |
| 45 | 2.413 | .20 | .86 | .99 | .99 | 2.248 | .22 | .90 | .99 | .99 | 2.128 | .23 | .93 | .99 | .99 |
| 50 | 2.408 | .21 | .90 | .99 | .99 | 2.245 | .23 | .93 | .99 | .99 | 2.125 | .25 | .95 | .99 | .99 |
| 55 | 2.405 | .23 | .93 | .99 | .99 | 2.242 | .25 | .96 | .99 | .99 | 2.123 | .27 | .97 | .99 | .99 |
| 60 | 2.402 | .25 | .95 | .99 | .99 | 2.239 | .27 | .97 | .99 | .99 | 2.121 | .29 | .98 | .99 | .99 |
| 70 | 2.398 | .28 | .98 | .99 | .99 | 2.236 | .31 | .99 | .99 | .99 | 2.117 | .33 | .99 | .99 | .99 |
| 80 | 2.395 | .32 | .99 | .99 | .99 | 2.233 | .35 | .99 | .99 | .99 | 2.115 | .38 | .99 | .99 | .99 |
| 90 | 2.392 | .35 | .99 | .99 | .99 | 2.231 | .39 | .99 | .99 | .99 | 2.113 | .42 | .99 | .99 | .99 |

# Table B.13  (Continued)

| n | $F_c$ | α = .05 $df_N = 1$ Effect Size, $f$ | | | | $F_c$ | α = .05 $df_N = 2$ Effect Size, $f$ | | | | $F_c$ | α = .05 $df_N = 3$ Effect Size, $f$ | | | |
|---|---|---|---|---|---|---|---|---|---|---|---|---|---|---|---|
| | | .10 | .25 | .40 | .55 | | .10 | .25 | .40 | .55 | | .10 | .25 | .40 | .55 |
| 100 | 2.390 | .39 | .99 | .99 | .99 | 2.229 | .43 | .99 | .99 | .99 | 2.112 | .46 | .99 | .99 | .99 |
| 110 | 2.388 | .43 | .99 | .99 | .99 | 2.228 | .47 | .99 | .99 | .99 | 2.110 | .51 | .99 | .99 | .99 |
| 120 | 2.387 | .46 | .99 | .99 | .99 | 2.227 | .51 | .99 | .99 | .99 | 2.109 | .55 | .99 | .99 | .99 |
| 130 | 2.386 | .50 | .99 | .99 | .99 | 2.226 | .54 | .99 | .99 | .99 | 2.109 | .59 | .99 | .99 | .99 |
| 140 | 2.385 | .53 | .99 | .99 | .99 | 2.225 | .58 | .99 | .99 | .99 | 2.108 | .63 | .99 | .99 | .99 |
| 150 | 2.384 | .57 | .99 | .99 | .99 | 2.224 | .62 | .99 | .99 | .99 | 2.107 | .66 | .99 | .99 | .99 |
| 160 | 2.383 | .60 | .99 | .99 | .99 | 2.223 | .65 | .99 | .99 | .99 | 2.107 | .70 | .99 | .99 | .99 |
| 170 | 2.382 | .63 | .99 | .99 | .99 | 2.223 | .68 | .99 | .99 | .99 | 2.106 | .73 | .99 | .99 | .99 |
| 180 | 2.382 | .66 | .99 | .99 | .99 | 2.222 | .71 | .99 | .99 | .99 | 2.106 | .76 | .99 | .99 | .99 |
| 190 | 2.381 | .69 | .99 | .99 | .99 | 2.222 | .74 | .99 | .99 | .99 | 2.105 | .79 | .99 | .99 | .99 |
| 200 | 2.381 | .71 | .99 | .99 | .99 | 2.222 | .77 | .99 | .99 | .99 | 2.105 | .81 | .99 | .99 | .99 |
| 300 | 2.378 | .90 | .99 | .99 | .99 | 2.219 | .93 | .99 | .99 | .99 | 2.103 | .96 | .99 | .99 | .99 |
| 10 | 8.285 | .02 | .07 | .19 | .38 | 5.488 | .03 | .10 | .25 | .48 | 4.377 | .04 | .12 | .30 | .57 |
| 11 | 8.096 | .02 | .08 | .21 | .42 | 5.390 | .03 | .10 | .27 | .53 | 4.313 | .04 | .13 | .34 | .63 |
| 12 | 7.945 | .02 | .09 | .23 | .47 | 5.312 | .03 | .11 | .30 | .59 | 4.261 | .04 | .14 | .37 | .68 |
| 13 | 7.823 | .03 | .09 | .26 | .52 | 5.248 | .03 | .12 | .33 | .64 | 4.218 | .04 | .15 | .41 | .73 |
| 14 | 7.721 | .03 | .10 | .28 | .56 | 5.194 | .03 | .13 | .36 | .68 | 4.182 | .04 | .16 | .44 | .78 |
| 15 | 7.636 | .03 | .11 | .31 | .60 | 5.149 | .03 | .14 | .39 | .72 | 4.152 | .04 | .17 | .48 | .81 |
| 16 | 7.562 | .03 | .11 | .33 | .64 | 5.110 | .03 | .15 | .42 | .76 | 4.126 | .04 | .18 | .51 | .85 |
| 17 | 7.499 | .03 | .12 | .36 | .68 | 5.077 | .03 | .16 | .45 | .80 | 4.103 | .04 | .19 | .55 | .88 |
| 18 | 7.444 | .03 | .13 | .38 | .71 | 5.047 | .04 | .16 | .49 | .83 | 4.083 | .04 | .20 | .58 | .90 |
| 19 | 7.396 | .03 | .14 | .41 | .75 | 5.021 | .04 | .18 | .52 | .86 | 4.066 | .04 | .22 | .61 | .92 |
| 20 | 7.353 | .03 | .15 | .43 | .78 | 4.998 | .04 | .19 | .54 | .88 | 4.050 | .04 | .23 | .64 | .94 |
| 21 | 7.314 | .03 | .15 | .46 | .80 | 4.977 | .04 | .20 | .57 | .90 | 4.036 | .04 | .24 | .67 | .95 |
| 22 | 7.280 | .03 | .16 | .48 | .83 | 4.959 | .04 | .21 | .60 | .92 | 4.024 | .04 | .25 | .70 | .96 |
| 23 | 7.248 | .03 | .17 | .51 | .85 | 4.942 | .04 | .22 | .63 | .93 | 4.012 | .05 | .27 | .73 | .97 |
| 24 | 7.220 | .03 | .18 | .53 | .87 | 4.927 | .04 | .23 | .66 | .95 | 4.002 | .05 | .28 | .75 | .98 |
| 25 | 7.194 | .03 | .19 | .56 | .89 | 4.913 | .04 | .24 | .68 | .96 | 3.992 | .05 | .30 | .78 | .98 |
| 26 | 7.171 | .03 | .20 | .58 | .90 | 4.900 | .04 | .25 | .70 | .96 | 3.984 | .05 | .31 | .80 | .99 |
| 27 | 7.149 | .03 | .21 | .60 | .92 | 4.888 | .04 | .26 | .73 | .97 | 3.976 | .05 | .33 | .82 | .99 |
| 28 | 7.129 | .04 | .22 | .62 | .93 | 4.877 | .04 | .28 | .75 | .98 | 3.968 | .05 | .34 | .84 | .99 |
| 29 | 7.110 | .04 | .23 | .65 | .94 | 4.867 | .04 | .29 | .77 | .98 | 3.961 | .05 | .35 | .86 | 1.00 |
| 30 | 7.093 | .04 | .24 | .67 | .95 | 4.858 | .04 | .30 | .79 | .99 | 3.955 | .05 | .37 | .87 | 1.00 |
| 31 | 7.077 | .04 | .25 | .69 | .96 | 4.849 | .04 | .31 | .81 | .99 | 3.949 | .05 | .38 | .89 | 1.00 |
| 32 | 7.062 | .04 | .26 | .71 | .96 | 4.841 | .05 | .33 | .82 | .99 | 3.944 | .05 | .40 | .90 | 1.00 |
| 33 | 7.048 | .04 | .27 | .72 | .97 | 4.833 | .05 | .34 | .84 | .99 | 3.938 | .05 | .41 | .91 | 1.00 |
| 34 | 7.035 | .04 | .28 | .74 | .97 | 4.826 | .05 | .35 | .86 | 1.00 | 3.934 | .05 | .43 | .92 | 1.00 |
| 35 | 7.023 | .04 | .29 | .76 | .98 | 4.819 | .05 | .36 | .87 | 1.00 | 3.929 | .06 | .44 | .93 | 1.00 |
| 36 | 7.011 | .04 | .30 | .77 | .98 | 4.813 | .05 | .38 | .88 | 1.00 | 3.925 | .06 | .46 | .94 | 1.00 |
| 37 | 7.000 | .04 | .31 | .79 | .98 | 4.807 | .05 | .39 | .89 | 1.00 | 3.921 | .06 | .47 | .95 | 1.00 |
| 38 | 6.990 | .04 | .32 | .80 | .99 | 4.802 | .05 | .40 | .90 | 1.00 | 3.917 | .06 | .49 | .96 | 1.00 |
| 39 | 6.981 | .04 | .33 | .82 | .99 | 4.796 | .05 | .42 | .91 | 1.00 | 3.913 | .06 | .50 | .96 | 1.00 |
| 40 | 6.971 | .05 | .34 | .83 | .99 | 4.791 | .05 | .43 | .92 | 1.00 | 3.910 | .06 | .52 | .97 | 1.00 |

*(Continued)*

# Table B.13 (Continued)

| n | $F_c$ | .10 | .25 | .40 | .55 | $F_c$ | .10 | .25 | .40 | .55 | $F_c$ | .10 | .25 | .40 | .55 |
|---|---|---|---|---|---|---|---|---|---|---|---|---|---|---|---|
| | | α = .05 $df_N = 1$ Effect Size, $f$ | | | | | α = .05 $df_N = 2$ Effect Size, $f$ | | | | | α = .05 $df_N = 3$ Effect Size, $f$ | | | |
| 45 | 6.932 | .05 | .39 | .88 | 1.00 | 4.770 | .06 | .49 | .96 | 1.00 | 3.895 | .07 | .59 | .99 | 1.00 |
| 50 | 6.901 | .06 | .44 | .92 | 1.00 | 4.753 | .06 | .55 | .98 | 1.00 | 3.883 | .07 | .66 | .99 | 1.00 |
| 55 | 6.876 | .06 | .49 | .95 | 1.00 | 4.739 | .07 | .61 | .99 | 1.00 | 3.874 | .08 | .72 | 1.00 | 1.00 |
| 60 | 6.855 | .07 | .54 | .97 | 1.00 | 4.727 | .08 | .67 | .99 | 1.00 | 3.866 | .09 | .77 | 1.00 | 1.00 |
| 70 | 6.822 | .08 | .63 | .99 | 1.00 | 4.709 | .09 | .76 | 1.00 | 1.00 | 3.853 | .11 | .85 | 1.00 | 1.00 |
| 80 | 6.798 | .09 | .71 | 1.00 | 1.00 | 4.696 | .10 | .83 | 1.00 | 1.00 | 3.844 | .12 | .91 | 1.00 | 1.00 |
| 90 | 6.779 | .10 | .78 | 1.00 | 1.00 | 4.686 | .12 | .89 | 1.00 | 1.00 | 3.837 | .14 | .95 | 1.00 | 1.00 |
| 100 | 6.765 | .11 | .83 | 1.00 | 1.00 | 4.677 | .14 | .93 | 1.00 | 1.00 | 3.831 | .16 | .97 | 1.00 | 1.00 |
| 110 | 6.753 | .13 | .88 | 1.00 | 1.00 | 4.671 | .15 | .95 | 1.00 | 1.00 | 3.827 | .18 | .99 | 1.00 | 1.00 |
| 120 | 6.743 | .14 | .91 | 1.00 | 1.00 | 4.665 | .17 | .97 | 1.00 | 1.00 | 3.823 | .21 | .99 | 1.00 | 1.00 |
| 130 | 6.734 | .15 | .94 | 1.00 | 1.00 | 4.660 | .19 | .98 | 1.00 | 1.00 | 3.820 | .23 | 1.00 | 1.00 | 1.00 |
| 140 | 6.727 | .17 | .96 | 1.00 | 1.00 | 4.656 | .21 | .99 | 1.00 | 1.00 | 3.817 | .25 | 1.00 | 1.00 | 1.00 |
| 150 | 6.721 | .18 | .97 | 1.00 | 1.00 | 4.653 | .23 | .99 | 1.00 | 1.00 | 3.815 | .28 | 1.00 | 1.00 | 1.00 |
| 160 | 6.715 | .20 | .98 | 1.00 | 1.00 | 4.650 | .25 | 1.00 | 1.00 | 1.00 | 3.813 | .30 | 1.00 | 1.00 | 1.00 |
| 170 | 6.710 | .21 | .99 | 1.00 | 1.00 | 4.647 | .27 | 1.00 | 1.00 | 1.00 | 3.811 | .33 | 1.00 | 1.00 | 1.00 |
| 180 | 6.706 | .23 | .99 | 1.00 | 1.00 | 4.645 | .29 | 1.00 | 1.00 | 1.00 | 3.809 | .35 | 1.00 | 1.00 | 1.00 |
| 190 | 6.702 | .25 | .99 | 1.00 | 1.00 | 4.643 | .31 | 1.00 | 1.00 | 1.00 | 3.808 | .38 | 1.00 | 1.00 | 1.00 |
| 200 | 6.699 | .26 | 1.00 | 1.00 | 1.00 | 4.641 | .33 | 1.00 | 1.00 | 1.00 | 3.806 | .40 | 1.00 | 1.00 | 1.00 |
| 300 | 6.677 | .43 | 1.00 | 1.00 | 1.00 | 4.629 | .54 | 1.00 | 1.00 | 1.00 | 3.798 | .65 | 1.00 | 1.00 | 1.00 |
| 10 | 3.767 | .05 | .15 | .36 | .65 | 3.377 | .06 | .17 | .41 | .71 | 3.103 | .07 | .19 | .45 | .76 |
| 11 | 3.720 | .05 | .16 | .40 | .71 | 3.339 | .06 | .18 | .45 | .76 | 3.071 | .07 | .20 | .50 | .81 |
| 12 | 3.681 | .05 | .17 | .43 | .76 | 3.308 | .06 | .19 | .49 | .81 | 3.046 | .07 | .22 | .54 | .85 |
| 13 | 3.649 | .05 | .18 | .47 | .80 | 3.283 | .06 | .20 | .53 | .85 | 3.024 | .07 | .23 | .58 | .89 |
| 14 | 3.622 | .05 | .19 | .51 | .84 | 3.261 | .06 | .22 | .57 | .89 | 3.007 | .07 | .25 | .62 | .92 |
| 15 | 3.600 | .05 | .20 | .55 | .87 | 3.243 | .06 | .23 | .61 | .91 | 2.992 | .07 | .26 | .67 | .94 |
| 16 | 3.580 | .05 | .21 | .59 | .90 | 3.228 | .06 | .25 | .65 | .94 | 2.979 | .07 | .28 | .70 | .96 |
| 17 | 3.563 | .05 | .23 | .62 | .93 | 3.214 | .06 | .26 | .69 | .95 | 2.967 | .06 | .30 | .74 | .97 |
| 18 | 3.548 | .05 | .24 | .66 | .94 | 3.202 | .06 | .28 | .72 | .97 | 2.957 | .06 | .31 | .77 | .98 |
| 19 | 3.535 | .05 | .26 | .69 | .96 | 3.191 | .06 | .29 | .75 | .98 | 2.948 | .06 | .33 | .80 | .99 |
| 20 | 3.523 | .05 | .27 | .72 | .97 | 3.182 | .06 | .31 | .78 | .98 | 2.940 | .07 | .35 | .83 | .99 |
| 21 | 3.513 | .05 | .29 | .75 | .98 | 3.174 | .06 | .33 | .81 | .99 | 2.933 | .07 | .37 | .86 | .99 |
| 22 | 3.503 | .05 | .30 | .78 | .98 | 3.166 | .06 | .35 | .84 | .99 | 2.927 | .07 | .39 | .88 | .99 |
| 23 | 3.495 | .05 | .32 | .80 | .99 | 3.159 | .06 | .36 | .86 | .99 | 2.921 | .07 | .41 | .90 | .99 |
| 24 | 3.487 | .05 | .33 | .83 | .99 | 3.153 | .06 | .38 | .88 | .99 | 2.916 | .07 | .43 | .91 | .99 |
| 25 | 3.480 | .05 | .35 | .85 | .99 | 3.147 | .06 | .40 | .90 | .99 | 2.911 | .07 | .45 | .93 | .99 |
| 26 | 3.473 | .05 | .37 | .87 | .99 | 3.142 | .06 | .42 | .91 | .99 | 2.907 | .07 | .47 | .94 | .99 |
| 27 | 3.467 | .06 | .38 | .88 | .99 | 3.137 | .06 | .44 | .93 | .99 | 2.902 | .07 | .49 | .95 | .99 |
| 28 | 3.461 | .06 | .40 | .90 | .99 | 3.132 | .06 | .46 | .94 | .99 | 2.899 | .07 | .51 | .96 | .99 |
| 29 | 3.456 | .06 | .42 | .91 | .99 | 3.128 | .06 | .48 | .95 | .99 | 2.895 | .07 | .53 | .97 | .99 |
| 30 | 3.451 | .06 | .43 | .93 | .99 | 3.124 | .07 | .49 | .96 | .99 | 2.892 | .07 | .55 | .97 | .99 |
| 31 | 3.447 | .06 | .45 | .94 | .99 | 3.120 | .07 | .51 | .96 | .99 | 2.889 | .07 | .57 | .98 | .99 |
| 32 | 3.443 | .06 | .47 | .95 | .99 | 3.117 | .07 | .53 | .97 | .99 | 2.886 | .08 | .59 | .98 | .99 |
| 33 | 3.439 | .06 | .48 | .95 | .99 | 3.114 | .07 | .55 | .98 | .99 | 2.883 | .08 | .61 | .99 | .99 |

(Continued)

# Table B.13 (Continued)

| n | $F_c$ | $\alpha = .05$ $df_N = 1$ Effect Size, $f$ .10 | .25 | .40 | .55 | $F_c$ | $\alpha = .05$ $df_N = 2$ Effect Size, $f$ .10 | .25 | .40 | .55 | $F_c$ | $\alpha = .05$ $df_N = 3$ Effect Size, $f$ .10 | .25 | .40 | .55 |
|---|---|---|---|---|---|---|---|---|---|---|---|---|---|---|---|
| 34 | 3.435 | .06 | .50 | .96 | .99 | 3.111 | .07 | .57 | .98 | .99 | 2.881 | .08 | .62 | .99 | .99 |
| 35 | 3.431 | .06 | .52 | .97 | .99 | 3.108 | .07 | .58 | .98 | .99 | 2.878 | .08 | .64 | .99 | .99 |
| 36 | 3.428 | .07 | .53 | .97 | .99 | 3.105 | .07 | .60 | .99 | .99 | 2.876 | .08 | .66 | .99 | .99 |
| 37 | 3.425 | .07 | .55 | .98 | .99 | 3.103 | .07 | .62 | .99 | .99 | 2.874 | .08 | .68 | .99 | .99 |
| 38 | 3.422 | .07 | .57 | .98 | .99 | 3.101 | .08 | .64 | .99 | .99 | 2.872 | .08 | .69 | .99 | .99 |
| 39 | 3.419 | .07 | .58 | .98 | .99 | 3.098 | .08 | .65 | .99 | .99 | 2.870 | .09 | .71 | .99 | .99 |
| 40 | 3.417 | .07 | .60 | .99 | .99 | 3.096 | .08 | .67 | .99 | .99 | 2.869 | .09 | .73 | .99 | .99 |
| 45 | 3.406 | .08 | .67 | .99 | .99 | 3.087 | .09 | .74 | .99 | .99 | 2.861 | .10 | .80 | .99 | .99 |
| 50 | 3.397 | .09 | .74 | .99 | .99 | 3.080 | .10 | .80 | .99 | .99 | 2.855 | .11 | .85 | .99 | .99 |
| 55 | 3.389 | .09 | .80 | .99 | .99 | 3.074 | .11 | .86 | .99 | .99 | 2.850 | .12 | .90 | .99 | .99 |
| 60 | 3.383 | .10 | .84 | .99 | .99 | 3.069 | .12 | .90 | .99 | .99 | 2.846 | .13 | .93 | .99 | .99 |
| 70 | 3.374 | .12 | .91 | .99 | .99 | 3.062 | .14 | .95 | .99 | .99 | 2.839 | .16 | .97 | .99 | .99 |
| 80 | 3.367 | .14 | .95 | .99 | .99 | 3.056 | .16 | .98 | .99 | .99 | 2.835 | .18 | .99 | .99 | .99 |
| 90 | 3.362 | .17 | .98 | .99 | .99 | 3.052 | .19 | .99 | .99 | .99 | 2.831 | .21 | .99 | .99 | .99 |
| 100 | 3.357 | .19 | .99 | .99 | .99 | 3.048 | .22 | .99 | .99 | .99 | 2.828 | .25 | .99 | .99 | .99 |
| 110 | 3.354 | .22 | .99 | .99 | .99 | 3.045 | .25 | .99 | .99 | .99 | 2.826 | .28 | .99 | .99 | .99 |
| 120 | 3.351 | .24 | .99 | .99 | .99 | 3.043 | .28 | .99 | .99 | .99 | 2.824 | .32 | .99 | .99 | .99 |
| 130 | 3.348 | .27 | .99 | .99 | .99 | 3.041 | .31 | .99 | .99 | .99 | 2.822 | .35 | .99 | .99 | .99 |
| 140 | 3.346 | .30 | .99 | .99 | .99 | 3.039 | .34 | .99 | .99 | .99 | 2.820 | .39 | .99 | .99 | .99 |
| 150 | 3.344 | .33 | .99 | .99 | .99 | 3.038 | .38 | .99 | .99 | .99 | 2.819 | .43 | .99 | .99 | .99 |
| 160 | 3.343 | .36 | .99 | .99 | .99 | 3.036 | .41 | .99 | .99 | .99 | 2.818 | .46 | .99 | .99 | .99 |
| 170 | 3.341 | .39 | .99 | .99 | .99 | 3.035 | .44 | .99 | .99 | .99 | 2.817 | .50 | .99 | .99 | .99 |
| 180 | 3.340 | .42 | .99 | .99 | .99 | 3.034 | .48 | .99 | .99 | .99 | 2.816 | .53 | .99 | .99 | .99 |
| 190 | 3.339 | .45 | .99 | .99 | .99 | 3.033 | .51 | .99 | .99 | .99 | 2.816 | .57 | .99 | .99 | .99 |
| 200 | 3.338 | .48 | .99 | .99 | .99 | 3.033 | .54 | .99 | .99 | .99 | 2.815 | .60 | .99 | .99 | .99 |
| 300 | 3.332 | .73 | .99 | .99 | .99 | 3.027 | .80 | .99 | .99 | .99 | 2.811 | .86 | .99 | .99 | .99 |

## Table B.14: Critical Values for Chi-Squared

### Using Table B.14

For any given $df$, the table shows the values of $\chi^2_{critical}$ corresponding to various levels of probability. The $\chi^2_{observed}$ is statistically significant at a given level when it is equal to or greater than the value shown in the table.

The following are methods for determining the degrees of freedom for different types of the $\chi^2$ test:

*Goodness-of-fit test: $df = k - 1$* where $k$ represents the number of categories.

*Test of independence: $df = (r - 1)(c - 1)$* where $r$ and $c$ represent the number of rows and columns.

# Examples

$\alpha = .05 \quad df = 30$
$\chi^2_{critical} = 43.773$   If $\chi^2_{observed} \leq \chi^2_{critical}$, then reject $H_0$

# Table B.14

| df | $\alpha = 0.995$ | $\alpha = 0.99$ | $\alpha = 0.975$ | $\alpha = 0.95$ | $\alpha = 0.05$ | $\alpha = 0.025$ | $\alpha = 0.01$ | $\alpha = 0.005$ |
|----|---------|--------|---------|--------|--------|---------|--------|---------|
| 1 | 0.000 | 0.000 | 0.001 | 0.004 | 3.841 | 5.024 | 6.635 | 7.879 |
| 2 | 0.010 | 0.020 | 0.051 | 0.103 | 5.991 | 7.378 | 9.210 | 10.597 |
| 3 | 0.072 | 0.115 | 0.216 | 0.352 | 7.815 | 9.348 | 11.345 | 12.838 |
| 4 | 0.207 | 0.297 | 0.484 | 0.711 | 9.488 | 11.143 | 13.277 | 14.860 |
| 5 | 0.412 | 0.554 | 0.831 | 1.145 | 11.070 | 12.832 | 15.086 | 16.750 |
| 6 | 0.676 | 0.872 | 1.237 | 1.635 | 12.592 | 14.449 | 16.812 | 18.548 |
| 7 | 0.989 | 1.239 | 1.690 | 2.167 | 14.067 | 16.013 | 18.475 | 20.278 |
| 8 | 1.344 | 1.647 | 2.180 | 2.733 | 15.507 | 17.535 | 20.090 | 21.955 |
| 9 | 1.735 | 2.088 | 2.700 | 3.325 | 16.919 | 19.023 | 21.666 | 23.589 |
| 10 | 2.156 | 2.558 | 3.247 | 3.940 | 18.307 | 20.483 | 23.209 | 25.188 |
| 11 | 2.603 | 3.053 | 3.816 | 4.575 | 19.675 | 21.920 | 24.725 | 26.757 |
| 12 | 3.074 | 3.571 | 4.404 | 5.226 | 21.026 | 23.337 | 26.217 | 28.300 |
| 13 | 3.565 | 4.107 | 5.009 | 5.892 | 22.362 | 24.736 | 27.688 | 29.819 |
| 14 | 4.075 | 4.660 | 5.629 | 6.571 | 23.685 | 26.119 | 29.141 | 31.319 |
| 15 | 4.601 | 5.229 | 6.262 | 7.261 | 24.996 | 27.488 | 30.578 | 32.801 |
| 16 | 5.142 | 5.812 | 6.908 | 7.962 | 26.296 | 28.845 | 32.000 | 34.267 |
| 17 | 5.697 | 6.408 | 7.564 | 8.672 | 27.587 | 30.191 | 33.409 | 35.718 |
| 18 | 6.265 | 7.015 | 8.231 | 9.390 | 28.869 | 31.526 | 34.805 | 37.156 |
| 19 | 6.844 | 7.633 | 8.907 | 10.117 | 30.144 | 32.852 | 36.191 | 38.582 |
| 20 | 7.434 | 8.260 | 9.591 | 10.851 | 31.410 | 34.170 | 37.566 | 39.997 |
| 21 | 8.034 | 8.897 | 10.283 | 11.591 | 32.671 | 35.479 | 38.932 | 41.401 |
| 22 | 8.643 | 9.542 | 10.982 | 12.338 | 33.924 | 36.781 | 40.289 | 42.796 |
| 23 | 9.260 | 10.196 | 11.689 | 13.091 | 35.172 | 38.076 | 41.638 | 44.181 |
| 24 | 9.886 | 10.856 | 12.401 | 13.848 | 36.415 | 39.364 | 42.980 | 45.558 |
| 25 | 10.520 | 11.524 | 13.120 | 14.611 | 37.652 | 40.646 | 44.314 | 46.928 |
| 26 | 11.160 | 12.198 | 13.844 | 15.379 | 38.885 | 41.923 | 45.642 | 48.290 |
| 27 | 11.808 | 12.878 | 14.573 | 16.151 | 40.113 | 43.195 | 46.963 | 49.645 |
| 28 | 12.461 | 13.565 | 15.308 | 16.928 | 41.337 | 44.461 | 48.278 | 50.994 |
| 29 | 13.121 | 14.256 | 16.047 | 17.708 | 42.557 | 45.722 | 49.588 | 52.335 |
| 30 | 13.787 | 14.953 | 16.791 | 18.493 | 43.773 | 46.979 | 50.892 | 53.672 |
| 31 | 14.458 | 15.655 | 17.539 | 19.281 | 44.985 | 48.232 | 52.191 | 55.002 |
| 32 | 15.134 | 16.362 | 18.291 | 20.072 | 46.194 | 49.480 | 53.486 | 56.328 |
| 33 | 15.815 | 17.073 | 19.047 | 20.867 | 47.400 | 50.725 | 54.775 | 57.648 |
| 34 | 16.501 | 17.789 | 19.806 | 21.664 | 48.602 | 51.966 | 56.061 | 58.964 |

(*Continued*)

# Table B.14  (Continued)

| df | $\alpha = 0.995$ | $\alpha = 0.99$ | $\alpha = 0.975$ | $\alpha = 0.95$ | $\alpha = 0.05$ | $\alpha = 0.025$ | $\alpha = 0.01$ | $\alpha = 0.005$ |
|---|---|---|---|---|---|---|---|---|
| 35 | 17.192 | 18.509 | 20.569 | 22.465 | 49.802 | 53.203 | 57.342 | 60.275 |
| 36 | 17.887 | 19.233 | 21.336 | 23.269 | 50.998 | 54.437 | 58.619 | 61.581 |
| 37 | 18.586 | 19.960 | 22.106 | 24.075 | 52.192 | 55.668 | 59.893 | 62.883 |
| 38 | 19.289 | 20.691 | 22.878 | 24.884 | 53.384 | 56.895 | 61.162 | 64.181 |
| 39 | 19.996 | 21.426 | 23.654 | 25.695 | 54.572 | 58.120 | 62.428 | 65.475 |
| 40 | 20.707 | 22.164 | 24.433 | 26.509 | 55.758 | 59.342 | 63.691 | 66.766 |
| 50 | 27.991 | 29.707 | 32.357 | 34.764 | 67.505 | 71.420 | 76.154 | 79.490 |
| 60 | 35.534 | 37.485 | 40.482 | 43.188 | 79.082 | 83.298 | 88.379 | 91.952 |
| 70 | 43.275 | 45.442 | 48.758 | 51.739 | 90.531 | 95.023 | 100.425 | 104.215 |
| 80 | 51.172 | 53.540 | 57.153 | 60.391 | 101.879 | 106.629 | 112.329 | 116.321 |
| 90 | 59.196 | 61.754 | 65.647 | 69.126 | 113.145 | 118.136 | 124.116 | 128.299 |
| 100 | 67.328 | 70.065 | 74.222 | 77.929 | 124.342 | 129.561 | 135.807 | 140.170 |

## Table B.15: Critical Values for Mann-Whitney $U$-Test

### Using Table B.15

This table provides the critical values for the Mann-Whitney $U$-test. Note that when calculating this statistic, you can determine the value of $U$ and $U'$. When calculating $U$, its value must be less than or equal to the tabled value to be considered statistically significant at the level of $\alpha$ selected. When calculating $U'$, its value must be greater than or equal to the tabled value to be considered statistically significant at the level of $\alpha$ selected.

# Table B.15

Critical Values for U and U′ for a Directional Test at α = .005 or a Nondirectional Test at α = .01

**To reject the null hypothesis for the two sample sizes, *U* must be equal to or less than** the smaller of the tabled values and U′ must be equal to **or greater than** the larger of the tabled values.

Each cell shows the smaller tabled value (U) over the larger tabled value (U′), as *U / U′*.

**N1**

| N2 | 1 | 2 | 3 | 4 | 5 | 6 | 7 | 8 | 9 | 10 | 11 | 12 | 13 | 14 | 15 | 16 | 17 | 18 | 19 | 20 |
|---|---|---|---|---|---|---|---|---|---|---|---|---|---|---|---|---|---|---|---|---|
| 1 | – | – | – | – | – | – | – | – | – | – | – | – | – | – | – | – | – | – | – | – |
| 2 | – | – | – | – | – | – | – | – | – | – | – | – | – | – | – | – | – | – | 0/38 | 0/40 |
| 3 | – | – | – | – | – | – | – | – | 0/27 | 0/30 | 0/33 | 1/35 | 1/38 | 1/41 | 2/43 | 2/46 | 2/49 | 2/52 | 3/54 | 3/57 |
| 4 | – | – | – | – | – | 0/24 | 0/28 | 1/31 | 1/35 | 2/38 | 2/42 | 3/45 | 3/49 | 4/52 | 5/55 | 5/59 | 6/62 | 6/66 | 7/69 | 8/72 |
| 5 | – | – | – | – | 0/25 | 1/29 | 1/34 | 2/38 | 3/42 | 4/46 | 5/50 | 6/54 | 7/58 | 7/63 | 8/67 | 9/71 | 10/75 | 11/79 | 12/83 | 13/87 |
| 6 | – | – | – | 0/24 | 1/29 | 2/34 | 3/39 | 4/44 | 5/49 | 6/54 | 7/59 | 9/63 | 10/68 | 11/73 | 12/78 | 13/83 | 15/87 | 16/92 | 17/97 | 18/102 |
| 7 | – | – | – | 0/28 | 1/34 | 3/39 | 4/45 | 6/50 | 7/56 | 9/61 | 10/67 | 12/72 | 13/78 | 15/83 | 16/89 | 18/94 | 19/100 | 21/105 | 22/111 | 24/116 |
| 8 | – | – | – | 1/31 | 2/38 | 4/44 | 6/50 | 7/57 | 9/63 | 11/69 | 13/75 | 15/81 | 17/87 | 18/94 | 20/100 | 22/106 | 24/112 | 26/118 | 28/124 | 30/130 |
| 9 | – | – | 0/27 | 1/35 | 3/42 | 5/49 | 7/56 | 9/63 | 11/70 | 13/77 | 16/83 | 18/90 | 20/97 | 22/104 | 24/111 | 27/117 | 29/124 | 31/131 | 33/138 | 36/144 |
| 10 | – | – | 0/30 | 2/38 | 4/46 | 6/54 | 9/61 | 11/69 | 13/77 | 16/84 | 18/92 | 21/99 | 24/106 | 26/114 | 29/121 | 31/129 | 34/136 | 37/143 | 39/151 | 42/158 |
| 11 | – | – | 0/33 | 2/42 | 5/50 | 7/59 | 10/67 | 13/75 | 16/83 | 18/92 | 21/100 | 24/108 | 27/116 | 30/124 | 33/132 | 36/140 | 39/148 | 42/156 | 45/164 | 48/172 |
| 12 | – | – | 1/35 | 3/45 | 6/54 | 9/63 | 12/72 | 15/81 | 18/90 | 21/99 | 24/108 | 27/117 | 31/125 | 34/134 | 37/143 | 41/151 | 44/160 | 47/169 | 51/177 | 54/186 |
| 13 | – | – | 1/38 | 3/49 | 7/58 | 10/68 | 13/78 | 17/87 | 20/97 | 24/106 | 27/116 | 31/125 | 34/125 | 38/144 | 42/153 | 45/163 | 49/172 | 53/181 | 56/191 | 60/200 |
| 14 | – | – | 1/41 | 4/52 | 7/63 | 11/73 | 15/83 | 18/94 | 22/104 | 26/114 | 30/124 | 34/134 | 38/144 | 42/154 | 46/164 | 50/174 | 54/184 | 58/194 | 63/203 | 67/213 |
| 15 | – | – | 2/43 | 5/55 | 8/67 | 12/78 | 16/89 | 20/100 | 24/111 | 29/121 | 33/132 | 37/143 | 42/153 | 46/164 | 51/174 | 55/185 | 60/195 | 64/206 | 69/216 | 73/227 |
| 16 | – | – | 2/46 | 5/59 | 9/71 | 13/83 | 18/94 | 22/106 | 27/117 | 31/129 | 36/140 | 41/151 | 45/163 | 50/174 | 55/185 | 60/196 | 65/207 | 70/218 | 74/230 | 79/241 |
| 17 | – | – | 2/49 | 6/62 | 10/75 | 15/87 | 19/100 | 24/112 | 29/124 | 34/148 | 39/148 | 44/160 | 49/172 | 54/184 | 60/195 | 65/207 | 70/219 | 75/231 | 81/242 | 86/254 |
| 18 | – | – | 2/52 | 6/66 | 11/79 | 16/92 | 21/105 | 26/118 | 31/131 | 37/143 | 42/156 | 47/169 | 53/181 | 58/194 | 64/206 | 70/218 | 75/231 | 81/243 | 87/255 | 92/268 |
| 19 | – | 0/38 | 3/54 | 7/69 | 12/83 | 17/97 | 22/111 | 28/124 | 33/138 | 39/151 | 45/164 | 51/177 | 56/191 | 63/203 | 69/216 | 74/230 | 81/242 | 87/255 | 93/268 | 99/281 |
| 20 | – | 0/40 | 3/57 | 8/72 | 13/87 | 18/102 | 24/116 | 30/130 | 36/144 | 42/158 | 48/172 | 54/186 | 60/200 | 67/213 | 73/227 | 79/241 | 86/254 | 92/268 | 99/281 | 105/295 |

# Table B.15 (Continued)

**Critical Values for U and U′ for a Directional Test at α = .01 or a Nondirectional Test at α = .02**

To reject the null hypothesis for the two sample sizes, *U* must be equal to or less than the smaller of the tabled values and U′ must be equal to **or greater than** the larger of the tabled values.

Each cell shows two values (smaller value / larger value). *N1* is given across the top; *N2* down the side.

| N2 \ N1 | 1 | 2 | 3 | 4 | 5 | 6 | 7 | 8 | 9 | 10 | 11 | 12 | 13 | 14 | 15 | 16 | 17 | 18 | 19 | 20 |
|---|---|---|---|---|---|---|---|---|---|---|---|---|---|---|---|---|---|---|---|---|
| 1 | – | – | – | – | – | – | – | – | – | – | – | – | – | – | – | – | – | – | – | – |
| 2 | – | – | – | – | – | – | – | – | – | – | – | – | 0/26 | 0/28 | 0/30 | 0/32 | 0/34 | 0/36 | 1/37 | 1/39 |
| 3 | – | – | – | – | – | – | 0/21 | 0/24 | 1/26 | 1/29 | 1/32 | 2/34 | 2/37 | 2/40 | 3/42 | 3/45 | 4/47 | 4/50 | 4/52 | 5/55 |
| 4 | – | – | – | – | 0/20 | 1/23 | 1/27 | 2/30 | 3/33 | 3/37 | 4/40 | 5/43 | 5/47 | 6/50 | 7/53 | 7/57 | 8/60 | 9/63 | 9/67 | 10/70 |
| 5 | – | – | – | 0/20 | 1/24 | 2/28 | 3/32 | 4/36 | 5/40 | 6/44 | 7/48 | 8/52 | 9/56 | 10/60 | 11/64 | 12/68 | 13/72 | 14/76 | 15/80 | 16/84 |
| 6 | – | – | – | 1/23 | 2/28 | 3/33 | 4/38 | 6/42 | 7/47 | 8/52 | 9/57 | 11/61 | 12/66 | 13/71 | 15/75 | 16/80 | 18/84 | 19/89 | 20/94 | 22/98 |
| 7 | – | – | 0/21 | 1/27 | 3/32 | 4/38 | 6/43 | 7/49 | 9/54 | 11/59 | 12/65 | 14/70 | 16/75 | 17/81 | 19/86 | 21/91 | 23/96 | 24/102 | 26/107 | 28/112 |
| 8 | – | – | 0/24 | 2/30 | 4/36 | 6/42 | 7/49 | 9/55 | 11/61 | 13/67 | 15/73 | 17/79 | 20/84 | 22/90 | 24/96 | 26/102 | 28/108 | 30/114 | 32/120 | 34/126 |
| 9 | – | – | 1/26 | 3/33 | 5/40 | 7/47 | 9/54 | 11/61 | 14/67 | 16/74 | 18/81 | 21/87 | 23/94 | 26/100 | 28/107 | 31/113 | 33/120 | 36/126 | 38/133 | 40/140 |
| 10 | – | – | 1/29 | 3/37 | 6/44 | 8/52 | 11/59 | 13/67 | 16/74 | 19/81 | 22/88 | 24/96 | 27/103 | 30/110 | 33/117 | 36/124 | 38/132 | 41/139 | 44/146 | 47/153 |
| 11 | – | – | 1/32 | 4/40 | 7/48 | 9/57 | 12/65 | 15/73 | 18/81 | 22/88 | 25/96 | 28/104 | 31/112 | 34/120 | 37/128 | 41/135 | 44/143 | 47/151 | 50/159 | 53/167 |
| 12 | – | – | 2/34 | 5/43 | 8/52 | 11/61 | 14/70 | 17/79 | 21/87 | 24/96 | 28/104 | 31/113 | 35/121 | 38/130 | 42/138 | 46/146 | 49/155 | 53/163 | 56/172 | 60/180 |
| 13 | – | 0/26 | 2/37 | 5/47 | 9/56 | 12/66 | 16/75 | 20/84 | 23/94 | 27/103 | 31/112 | 35/121 | 39/130 | 43/139 | 47/148 | 51/157 | 55/166 | 59/175 | 63/184 | 67/193 |
| 14 | – | 0/28 | 2/40 | 6/50 | 10/60 | 13/71 | 17/81 | 22/90 | 26/100 | 30/110 | 34/120 | 38/130 | 43/139 | 47/149 | 51/159 | 56/168 | 60/178 | 65/187 | 69/197 | 73/207 |
| 15 | – | 0/30 | 3/42 | 7/53 | 11/64 | 15/75 | 19/86 | 24/96 | 28/107 | 33/117 | 37/128 | 42/138 | 47/148 | 51/159 | 56/169 | 61/179 | 66/189 | 70/200 | 75/210 | 80/220 |
| 16 | – | 0/32 | 3/45 | 7/57 | 12/68 | 16/80 | 21/91 | 26/102 | 31/113 | 36/124 | 41/135 | 46/146 | 51/157 | 56/168 | 61/179 | 66/190 | 71/201 | 76/212 | 82/222 | 87/233 |
| 17 | – | 0/34 | 4/47 | 8/60 | 13/72 | 18/84 | 23/96 | 28/108 | 33/120 | 38/132 | 44/143 | 49/155 | 55/166 | 60/178 | 66/189 | 71/201 | 77/212 | 82/224 | 88/234 | 93/247 |
| 18 | – | 0/36 | 4/50 | 9/63 | 14/76 | 19/89 | 24/102 | 30/114 | 36/126 | 41/139 | 47/151 | 53/163 | 59/175 | 65/187 | 70/200 | 76/212 | 82/224 | 88/236 | 94/248 | 100/260 |
| 19 | – | 1/37 | 4/53 | 9/67 | 15/80 | 20/94 | 26/107 | 32/120 | 38/133 | 44/146 | 50/159 | 56/172 | 63/184 | 69/197 | 75/210 | 82/222 | 88/235 | 94/248 | 101/260 | 107/273 |
| 20 | – | 1/39 | 5/55 | 10/70 | 16/84 | 22/98 | 28/112 | 34/126 | 40/140 | 47/153 | 53/167 | 60/180 | 67/193 | 73/207 | 80/220 | 87/233 | 93/247 | 100/260 | 107/273 | 114/286 |

# Table B.15 (Continued)

**Critical Values for U and U′ for a Directional Test at α = .025 or a Nondirectional Test at α = .05**

**To reject the null hypothesis for the two sample sizes, *U* must be equal to or less than** the smaller of the tabled values and U′ must be equal to **or greater than** the larger of the tabled values.

Each cell lists two values: the upper value is U and the lower value is U′.

*N1* across columns; *N2* down rows.

| N2 \ N1 | 1 | 2 | 3 | 4 | 5 | 6 | 7 | 8 | 9 | 10 | 11 | 12 | 13 | 14 | 15 | 16 | 17 | 18 | 19 | 20 |
|---|---|---|---|---|---|---|---|---|---|---|---|---|---|---|---|---|---|---|---|---|
| 1 | – | – | – | – | – | – | – | – | – | – | – | – | – | – | – | – | – | – | – | – |
| 2 | – | – | – | – | – | – | – | 0 16 | 0 18 | 0 20 | 0 22 | 1 23 | 1 25 | 1 27 | 1 29 | 1 31 | 2 32 | 2 34 | 2 36 | 2 38 |
| 3 | – | – | – | – | 0 15 | 1 17 | 1 20 | 2 22 | 2 25 | 3 27 | 3 30 | 4 32 | 4 35 | 5 37 | 5 40 | 6 42 | 6 45 | 7 47 | 7 50 | 8 52 |
| 4 | – | – | – | 0 16 | 1 19 | 2 22 | 3 25 | 4 28 | 4 32 | 5 35 | 6 38 | 7 41 | 8 44 | 9 47 | 10 50 | 11 53 | 11 57 | 12 60 | 13 63 | 13 67 |
| 5 | – | – | 0 15 | 1 19 | 2 23 | 3 27 | 5 30 | 6 34 | 7 38 | 8 42 | 9 46 | 11 49 | 12 53 | 13 57 | 14 61 | 15 65 | 17 68 | 18 72 | 19 76 | 20 80 |
| 6 | – | – | 1 17 | 2 22 | 3 27 | 5 31 | 6 36 | 8 40 | 10 44 | 11 49 | 13 53 | 14 58 | 16 62 | 17 67 | 19 71 | 21 75 | 22 80 | 24 84 | 25 89 | 27 93 |
| 7 | – | – | 1 20 | 3 25 | 5 30 | 6 36 | 8 41 | 10 46 | 12 51 | 14 56 | 16 61 | 18 66 | 20 71 | 22 76 | 24 81 | 26 86 | 28 91 | 30 96 | 32 101 | 34 106 |
| 8 | – | 0 16 | 2 22 | 4 28 | 6 34 | 8 40 | 10 46 | 13 51 | 15 57 | 17 63 | 19 69 | 22 74 | 24 80 | 26 86 | 29 91 | 31 97 | 34 102 | 36 108 | 38 111 | 41 119 |
| 9 | – | 0 18 | 2 25 | 4 32 | 7 38 | 10 44 | 12 51 | 15 57 | 17 64 | 20 70 | 23 76 | 26 82 | 28 89 | 31 95 | 34 101 | 37 107 | 39 114 | 42 120 | 45 126 | 48 132 |
| 10 | – | 0 20 | 3 27 | 5 35 | 8 42 | 11 49 | 14 56 | 17 63 | 20 70 | 23 77 | 26 84 | 29 91 | 33 97 | 36 104 | 39 111 | 42 118 | 45 125 | 48 132 | 52 138 | 55 145 |
| 11 | – | 0 22 | 3 30 | 6 38 | 9 46 | 13 53 | 16 61 | 19 69 | 23 76 | 26 84 | 30 91 | 33 99 | 37 106 | 40 114 | 44 121 | 47 129 | 51 136 | 55 143 | 58 151 | 62 158 |
| 12 | – | 1 23 | 4 32 | 7 41 | 11 49 | 14 58 | 18 66 | 22 74 | 26 82 | 29 91 | 33 99 | 37 107 | 41 115 | 45 123 | 49 131 | 53 139 | 57 147 | 61 155 | 65 163 | 69 171 |
| 13 | – | 1 25 | 4 35 | 8 44 | 12 53 | 16 62 | 20 71 | 24 80 | 28 89 | 33 97 | 37 106 | 41 115 | 45 124 | 50 132 | 54 141 | 59 149 | 63 158 | 67 167 | 72 175 | 76 184 |
| 14 | – | 1 27 | 5 37 | 9 47 | 13 51 | 17 67 | 22 76 | 26 86 | 31 95 | 36 104 | 40 114 | 45 123 | 50 132 | 55 141 | 59 151 | 64 160 | 67 171 | 74 178 | 78 188 | 83 197 |
| 15 | – | 1 29 | 5 40 | 10 50 | 14 61 | 19 71 | 24 81 | 29 91 | 34 101 | 39 111 | 44 121 | 49 131 | 54 141 | 59 151 | 64 161 | 70 170 | 75 180 | 80 190 | 85 200 | 90 210 |
| 16 | – | 1 31 | 6 42 | 11 53 | 15 65 | 21 75 | 26 86 | 31 97 | 37 107 | 42 118 | 47 129 | 53 139 | 59 149 | 64 160 | 70 170 | 75 181 | 81 191 | 86 202 | 92 212 | 98 222 |
| 17 | – | 2 32 | 6 45 | 11 57 | 17 68 | 22 80 | 28 91 | 34 102 | 39 114 | 45 125 | 51 136 | 57 147 | 63 158 | 67 171 | 75 180 | 81 191 | 87 202 | 93 213 | 99 224 | 105 235 |
| 18 | – | 2 34 | 7 47 | 12 60 | 18 72 | 24 84 | 30 96 | 36 108 | 42 120 | 48 132 | 55 143 | 61 155 | 67 167 | 74 178 | 80 190 | 86 202 | 93 213 | 99 225 | 106 236 | 112 248 |
| 19 | – | 2 36 | 7 50 | 13 63 | 19 76 | 25 89 | 32 101 | 38 114 | 45 126 | 52 138 | 58 151 | 65 163 | 72 175 | 78 188 | 85 200 | 92 212 | 99 224 | 106 236 | 113 248 | 119 261 |
| 20 | – | 2 38 | 8 52 | 13 67 | 20 80 | 27 93 | 34 106 | 41 119 | 48 132 | 55 145 | 62 158 | 69 171 | 76 184 | 83 197 | 90 210 | 98 222 | 105 235 | 112 248 | 119 261 | 127 273 |

# Table B.15 (Continued)

**Critical Values for U and U′ for a Directional Test at $\alpha =.05$ or a Nondirectional Test at $\alpha =.10$**

**To reject the null hypothesis for the two sample sizes, $U$ must be equal to or less than** the smaller of the tabled values and U′ must be equal to **or greater than** the larger of the tabled values.

Each cell shows the smaller critical value (top) over the larger critical value (bottom): U / U′.

|  | N1=1 | 2 | 3 | 4 | 5 | 6 | 7 | 8 | 9 | 10 | 11 | 12 | 13 | 14 | 15 | 16 | 17 | 18 | 19 | 20 |
|---|---|---|---|---|---|---|---|---|---|---|---|---|---|---|---|---|---|---|---|---|
| **N2=1** | - | - | - | - | - | - | - | - | - | - | - | - | - | - | - | - | - | - | 0/19 | 0/20 |
| **2** | - | - | - | - | 0/10 | 0/12 | 0/14 | 1/15 | 1/17 | 1/19 | 1/21 | 2/22 | 2/24 | 2/26 | 3/27 | 3/29 | 3/31 | 4/32 | 4/34 | 4/36 |
| **3** | - | - | 0/9 | 0/12 | 1/14 | 2/16 | 2/19 | 3/21 | 3/24 | 4/26 | 5/28 | 5/31 | 6/33 | 7/35 | 7/38 | 8/40 | 9/42 | 9/45 | 10/47 | 11/49 |
| **4** | - | - | 0/12 | 1/15 | 2/18 | 3/21 | 4/24 | 5/27 | 6/30 | 7/33 | 8/36 | 9/39 | 10/42 | 11/45 | 12/48 | 14/50 | 15/53 | 16/56 | 17/59 | 18/62 |
| **5** | - | 0/10 | 1/14 | 2/18 | 4/21 | 5/25 | 6/29 | 8/32 | 9/36 | 11/39 | 12/43 | 13/47 | 15/50 | 16/54 | 18/57 | 19/61 | 20/65 | 22/68 | 23/72 | 25/75 |
| **6** | - | 0/12 | 2/16 | 3/21 | 5/25 | 7/29 | 8/34 | 10/38 | 12/42 | 14/46 | 16/50 | 17/55 | 19/59 | 21/63 | 23/67 | 25/71 | 26/76 | 28/80 | 30/84 | 32/88 |
| **7** | - | 0/14 | 2/19 | 4/24 | 6/29 | 8/34 | 11/38 | 13/43 | 15/48 | 17/53 | 19/58 | 21/63 | 24/67 | 26/72 | 28/77 | 30/82 | 33/86 | 35/91 | 37/96 | 39/101 |
| **8** | - | 1/15 | 3/21 | 5/27 | 8/32 | 10/38 | 13/43 | 15/49 | 18/54 | 20/60 | 23/65 | 26/70 | 28/76 | 31/81 | 33/87 | 36/92 | 39/97 | 41/103 | 44/108 | 47/113 |
| **9** | - | 1/17 | 3/24 | 6/30 | 9/36 | 12/42 | 15/48 | 18/54 | 21/60 | 24/66 | 27/72 | 30/78 | 33/84 | 36/90 | 39/96 | 42/102 | 45/108 | 48/114 | 51/120 | 54/126 |
| **10** | - | 1/19 | 4/26 | 7/33 | 11/39 | 14/46 | 17/53 | 20/60 | 24/66 | 27/73 | 31/79 | 34/86 | 37/93 | 41/99 | 44/106 | 48/112 | 51/119 | 55/125 | 58/132 | 62/138 |
| **11** | - | 1/21 | 5/28 | 8/36 | 12/43 | 16/50 | 19/58 | 23/65 | 27/72 | 31/79 | 34/87 | 38/94 | 42/101 | 46/108 | 50/115 | 54/122 | 57/130 | 61/137 | 65/144 | 69/151 |
| **12** | - | 2/22 | 5/31 | 9/39 | 13/47 | 17/55 | 21/63 | 26/70 | 30/78 | 34/86 | 38/94 | 42/102 | 47/109 | 51/117 | 55/125 | 60/132 | 64/140 | 68/148 | 72/156 | 77/163 |
| **13** | - | 2/24 | 6/33 | 10/42 | 15/50 | 19/59 | 24/67 | 28/76 | 33/84 | 37/93 | 42/101 | 47/109 | 51/118 | 56/126 | 61/134 | 65/143 | 70/151 | 75/159 | 80/167 | 84/176 |
| **14** | - | 2/26 | 7/35 | 11/45 | 16/54 | 21/63 | 26/72 | 31/81 | 36/90 | 41/99 | 46/108 | 51/117 | 56/126 | 61/135 | 66/144 | 71/153 | 77/161 | 82/170 | 87/179 | 92/188 |
| **15** | - | 3/27 | 7/38 | 12/48 | 18/57 | 23/67 | 28/77 | 33/87 | 39/96 | 44/106 | 50/115 | 55/125 | 61/134 | 66/144 | 72/153 | 77/163 | 83/172 | 88/182 | 94/191 | 100/200 |
| **16** | - | 3/29 | 8/40 | 14/50 | 19/61 | 25/71 | 30/82 | 36/92 | 42/102 | 48/112 | 54/122 | 60/132 | 65/143 | 71/153 | 77/163 | 83/173 | 89/183 | 95/193 | 101/203 | 107/213 |
| **17** | - | 3/31 | 9/42 | 15/53 | 20/65 | 26/76 | 33/86 | 39/97 | 45/108 | 51/119 | 57/130 | 64/140 | 70/151 | 77/161 | 83/172 | 89/183 | 96/193 | 102/204 | 109/214 | 115/225 |
| **18** | - | 4/32 | 9/45 | 16/56 | 22/68 | 28/80 | 35/91 | 41/103 | 48/114 | 55/123 | 61/137 | 68/148 | 75/159 | 82/170 | 88/182 | 95/193 | 102/204 | 109/215 | 116/226 | 123/237 |
| **19** | - | 4/34 | 10/47 | 17/59 | 23/72 | 30/84 | 37/96 | 44/108 | 51/120 | 58/132 | 65/144 | 72/156 | 80/167 | 87/179 | 94/191 | 101/203 | 109/214 | 116/226 | 123/238 | 130/250 |
| **20** | 0/20 | 4/36 | 11/49 | 18/62 | 25/75 | 32/88 | 39/101 | 47/113 | 54/126 | 62/138 | 69/151 | 77/163 | 84/176 | 92/188 | 100/200 | 107/213 | 115/225 | 123/237 | 130/250 | 138/262 |

# Appendix C
## Answers to Knowledge Check Questions

### Chapter 1

1. Your essay should show that the questions that psychologists ask can be answered using research methods.

2. Authors of novels use their personal experiences and beliefs about human nature to create their stories. Although entertaining and often enlightening, the novelist's perspective is not the same thing as a psychologist's perspective. A psychologist will attempt to describe and explain human nature by referring to the results of scientific research. In some cases, a novelist and a psychologist may disagree on what motivates people to act as they do. The novelist may base his or her beliefs on personal experience and traditional beliefs about human motives. The psychologist will attempt to appeal to observable facts and the results of research that examine human motives.

3. Belief of the "in the zone" or "in a slump" phenomena is an example of Bacon's Idol of the Tribe. People have a tendency to assume that there is a pattern for or a logical explanation for random events. The statistician challenges this perception by showing that there is no pattern in an athlete's performance. The example also illustrates Bacon's Idol of the Theatre. Many people claim that being in the zone is a real phenomenon and treat it as a real phenomenon. This belief may be enhanced when an athlete says something like, "I've been playing really well because I am in the zone."

4. This example illustrates the Idol of the Cave because your friend used personal experience to reach the conclusion. Because your friend is a mechanic, he or she sees only cars that need service and may not consider that there are many cars that do not need service.

5. Both would agree that psychology is a science because we can use objective and empirical methods to study behavior.

6. Introspection means to examine your thoughts and mental processes. Watson objected to introspection because we cannot use public verification to confirm your introspection.

7. Piaget used methodological behaviorism because he used children's behavior to infer how they solved problems.

8. Just because a person claims that facilitated communication works does not mean that it works. There may be other explanations for the phenomenon that require empirical verification.

9. (a) Empirical analysis: The researchers observed the client's behavior. The researchers examined whether the client accurately described the picture he or she had seen. (b) Public verification: The researchers showed the children pictures and recorded the children's responses. Any researcher can repeat the study to determine whether the results will confirm the results. (c) Systematic observation: The researchers showed the facilitator and the child many different pictures of many different objects. For some trials, the researcher showed the facilitator and child the same picture. On other trials, the researcher showed the facilitator different pictures. (d) Control of the environment: The researcher presented the pictures to the facilitator and the child at the same time, but in such a way that neither the facilitator nor the child could see what the other person saw.

10. Testimonials are not reliable sources of information. By using empirical methods, we can independently verify whether the person is psychic.

11. The explanation of the results is a pseudoexplanation because there is no way to independently evaluate the existence of "negative energy." In addition, the explanation for negative energy depends on the results of the study. Why did the person fail the task? Because of the negative energy. How do we know that there was negative energy? Because the person failed the test.

12. Empirical analysis is the process of learning through observation and experimentation and quantifying observations. Public verification requires that we conduct research that others can repeat and specifically that everyone can observe the variables we examine. The systematic observation criterion requires us to make our observations under various conditions or settings. Control of environment refers to our ability to conduct our research under consistent conditions.

13. The psychologist would have to define contentment by describing observable behaviors that he or she believes relate to this mental state.

14. The therapist's reaction is an example of a pseudoexplanation. Why did the therapy not work for this child? Because the child did not want to change. How do we know that the child did not want to change? Because the child was still aggressive. To break this circular explanation, the therapist must objectively determine which children want to change their behavior and then provide the treatment. If we can correctly predict how the children will respond to the therapy, then we can conclude that their motivation affects the success of the therapy.

15. Public verification is important for all the sciences, including psychology, because it allows any researcher to verify the results of any experiment or statement about a phenomenon.

16. This response could be another example of a pseudoexplanation because the official used the effect to define the cause. We would need to use an independent test of antisocial personality to confirm the accuracy of the claim.

17. Psychology would not be a science if there were no measurement. Without measurement, there can be no public verification or systematic observation.

## Chapter 2

We will not supply the answers to the Knowledge Check questions in Chapter 2. As we noted in the chapter, ethics is the process of examining how one uses moral principles to reach a decision as to whether a behavior is right or wrong. We wrote these Knowledge Check questions in the hope that they would spark some serious debate about the appropriateness of various research projects. To use these questions effectively, you should carefully contemplate the moral implications of the research projects. You may find it useful and informative to compare your reactions to the reactions of other students and your instructor.

## Chapter 3

1. A theory is a general statement that describes a specific phenomenon. By contrast, a hypothesis is a specific statement or prediction concerning the relation between two variables.

2. (a) This is a statement of opinion, not a hypothesis. There is no attempt to define the meaning of "not good." Therefore, we do not know what behaviors in children to observe. (b) This is a statement of opinion, not a hypothesis. The statement claims that there should be a change in children's behavior but no indication of the effects of these changes. (c) This statement sounds more like a theory than a hypothesis. We can use this statement to infer the relation between variables. For example, we can predict that the intelligence of children will correlate with the intelligence of their parents. (d) This statement is a theory. We can use it to create hypotheses. (e) This statement is a hypothesis because it identifies the independent variable (the ambiguity of the situation), the dependent variable (the degree of conformity), and the relation between the variables. (f) This statement is a hypothesis because it identifies the independent variable (self-esteem), the dependent variable (volunteerism), and the relation between the variables.

3.  (a) There is a positive correlation between a student's expected grades and his or her evaluation of the instructor. (b) The student's expected grade. (c) This is a subject variable. (d) The student's evaluation of the instructor.

4.  (a) Experts will more accurately re-create the real-game examples than the novices. There will be no difference between novices and experts for the random arrangement of chess pieces.
    (i)    The chess-playing ability of the participants (experts versus novices). The pattern of chess pieces (real-game versus random).
    (ii)   Chess playing ability is a subject variable. The pattern of chess pieces is a manipulated variable.
    (iii)  The participant's ability to recall the arrangement of the chess pieces.

5.  (a) There is a correlation between the empathy and self-monitoring variables. Men and women will have different levels of empathy. Men and women will have different levels of self-monitoring.
    (i)    The participant's sex and the results on the tests are the independent variables.
    (ii)   All the variables are subject variables.
    (iii)  If Carlos wishes to explain self-monitoring using the empathy measure, then self-monitoring is the dependent variable. For the second hypothesis, empathy is the dependent variable. For the third hypothesis, self-monitoring is the dependent variable.

6.  (a) The feedback that Rebecca uses causes participants to spend more time on the impossible-to-solve items.
    (i)    The feedback that Rebecca gave the participants.
    (ii)   The feedback is a manipulated variable.
    (iii)  The time the participants spent on the impossible-to-solve problems.

7.  The population may well be the current generation of college students. The sampled population was students at their institution.

8.  Because Schimmelphenig and Sibicky wanted to examine the relation between the MSS and the evaluations of the leaders, they did not need to use random sampling. The researchers would agree, however, that their data should be interpreted with caution and that the effect should be replicated using other populations.

9 & 10.  The scores on the MSS are an independent variable. Schimmelphenig and Sibicky used the results to classify people into one of two groups, low sexism versus high sexism. In addition, level of sexism is a subject variable. Sexism is a characteristic of the participants. A second independent variable was the sex of the leader in the vignette. Some participants read about a male leader, whereas the others read about a female leader. The type of vignette was a manipulated variable because the researcher could determine whether a

participant read one type of vignette or the other. The dependent variable was the participant's rating of the leader in the vignette.

11. Scores on the MSS are interval at best. (i) The 0 is an arbitrary measure of sexism. (ii) The sex of the leader is a nominal scale.

12. The researchers used the cover story to ensure that the participants would take the research seriously; thus they attempted to make the purpose of the questionnaire sound plausible. Sexism is a construct that we cannot directly observe; it is an attitude. In addition, we use the construct to make predictions and explanations about behavior. Because we cannot directly observe sexism, we need to develop tests to measure it.

13. The score on the MSS is the operational definition of sexism.

14. That people who scored high on the sexism scale also gave female leaders lower marks is consistent with the concept of sexism.

# Chapter 4

1. No data are invalid until someone interprets them. The data may support some types of inference or conclusion but not support other conclusions. For example, we may find that the data will generalize to one population but not other populations. Similarly, the data may allow us to infer that two populations are different from each other but not to infer that the independent variable causes the dependent variable.

2. No. If the researcher cannot assume cause and effect, then he or she cannot infer the same cause-and-effect relation in the population.

3. Carryover effect: The first test may influence performance on the second test. Students may remember the questions from the first test that are similar to the questions on the second test. In addition, the first test may have allowed students to learn how to take a multiple-choice test.

   Selection bias: The students enrolled in this course may not represent the typical college student with respect to prior knowledge of the topic or motivation to learn. Mortality: Many students may withdraw from the course during the term. Therefore, the students taking the final exam are not representative of students enrolled in the typical course. Ceiling/floor effect: If the test is too easy or too difficult, then the instructor will not be able to differentiate among student performance. Ambiguity of cause: Any improvement in knowledge may reflect that the students took a course and had nothing to do with the method of instruction. There is no way to rule out alternative explanations for the improvement.

4. The researcher has evidence that changes in physiological reaction are related to lying. However, the researcher should proceed with caution when generalizing the results to other populations. For

example, college students may not be representative of persons accused of a crime. Therefore, the researcher should attempt to replicate the study with other populations and different circumstances for lying.

5. The date of publication does not automatically invalidate the data. The student needs to determine whether the phenomenon of short-term memory could be affected by changes in culture and other environmental events. Short-term memory appears to be a relatively stable phenomenon. Therefore, the results are still relevant. The interpretation of the data may be different, however, given changes in theoretical perspective.

6. The hypothesis one wishes to test will determine the research method one uses. For example, researchers wishing to show cause and effect will select a true experiment. By contrast, researchers wishing to show a correlation among variables will use a correlational design.

7. The control group allows us to observe participants' behavior in the absence of the independent experiment. If participants in the treatment and control group experience all aspects of the experiment except the independent variable, then we can account for alternative explanations such as maturation, regression toward the mean, carry-over effects, and related threats to internal validity.

8. Random assignment helps to ensure that the groups are equivalent for all factors other than the presence of the independent variable. Therefore, if we find differences among the groups, we are in a better position to infer cause and effect.

9. Although smoking may cause the health problem, the correlation design does not rule out the third variable problem. Women who smoke may know less about health issues and therefore not seek prenatal and regular medical treatment for their children.

10. (1)(i) Independent variable: Sex of the person offering help. Dependent variable: Probability that a person will offer help. (ii) Men are more altruistic than women. (iii) This is an intact group design as the sex is a subject variable. (iv) Because this is an intact-group design, we cannot offer cause-and-effect interpretations of the data. There is also a glaring problem with the study. Women may be less willing to help in this particular situation for reasons unrelated to their propensity to offer help. Therefore, this may not be a fair test of altruism. (v) It is possible that the location of the study will influence the results. For example, the rates of altruism in a rural community may be different from a larger urban area. (vi) There is no single best answer. Your answer should comment on the use of other measures of altruism and methods of ensuring that the conditions of the study are well defined.

   (2)(i) Independent variable: Class standing of student. Dependent variable: Student's evaluation of the freshman seminar. (ii) Seniors will appreciate the seminar more than freshmen. (iii) The researcher used an intact-groups design. (iv) There are several problems with the conclusion reached by the researcher. First, the statement, "the majority of the students endorsed the statement, 'I enjoyed my freshman seminar'" does not address the question regarding a change in the students' opinion of the course. Second, many students may have withdrawn from the college. Therefore, the data may not represent all the students who had enrolled in the seminar. Finally, the researcher concluded that the seminar helped the students make the transition to college. The researcher, however, has not defined what it means to make a transition to college. Therefore, the data do not support this conclusion. (v) We would want to poll all students who had completed the course both at the end of the course and after four years. Specifically, we would need to contact current seniors as well as students who withdrew from the college. We would also want to ensure that the researcher limits his or her comments to changes in student opinion of the course, not its effectiveness. (vi) There is no single best answer. Your answer should address the problems you identified in the study. (3)(i) Independent variable: Sales training course. Dependent variable: Sales of the trainees. (ii) The sales training course will cause the students to be better salespeople. (iii) The researcher can use a true experiment for this study. (iv) There is no control group. Therefore, we do not know whether the improvement in sales is due to the training or that new staff are successful independent of the training. (v) If the people participating in the study are representative of the people employed as sales representatives, then there may be few problems with external validity as long as we improve the research design. (vi) There is no single best answer. Your answer should address the problems you identified in the study.

## Chapter 5

There are no Knowledge Check questions for Chapter 5.

## Chapter 6

1. Several researchers claim that listening to music by Mozart can enhance one's performance on specific components of an intelligence test. The current research is inconsistent, however. Several researchers claim to have evidence of the Mozart effect, whereas others have not been able to replicate the effect.

2. Steele et al. decided to test a prediction based on the research by Rauscher et al. (1993). Specifically, they predicted that if the Mozart effect enhances spatial reasoning tasks, then listening to Mozart's music should enhance the participant's ability to complete the backwards digit span task.

3. Steele et al. developed their hypothesis by examining the previous research that examined the Mozart effect.

4. The researchers want to answer the question "Does listening to Mozart improve performance on measures of intelligence?" They specifically selected the backwards digit span task because it measures cognitive skills related to spatial and temporal reasoning. If the Mozart effect works, then the participant's performance on the backwards digit span task should improve after having listened to Mozart's music.

5. This is a true experiment because Steele et al. randomly assigned the participants to separate treatment conditions. In addition, there are treatment and control conditions.

6. The independent variable is the stimulus condition (music, rain, and silence) presented to the participant before completing the backwards digit span task. The dependent variable was the performance on the digit span task.

7. The music condition is the treatment condition that should produce the Mozart effect. The rain and silence conditions are control groups. The rain condition presents sound to the participant. The silence condition is a second control group and allows us to determine the participant's performance under "normal" conditions.

8. All the stimuli were presented on a tape recorder. This ensures that each participant experienced the same events and sounds. In addition, the order of the three stimulus conditions was randomized using the Latin square design. The counterbalancing design controls for practice effects.

9. Steele et al. believed, based on previous research, that the backwards digit span test measured a cognitive function that should be enhanced by the Mozart effect.

10. Steele et al. did not find evidence of the Mozart effect. The data indicate that performance on the dependent variable was equivalent for the three stimulus groups.

11. Steele et al. wanted to examine alternative explanations of the data. The "Order of Task" analysis indicated that the participant's performance did improve over time, but not as a function of the stimulus condition. Similarly, the "First Stimulus" analysis indicated that the order of the conditions did not affect the data.

12. The current data appear to confirm previous research that has not replicated the Mozart effect.

13. The silence condition is a true control condition because it represents the absence of any sound. Therefore, one cannot determine the baseline for performance.

14. Steele et al. have not resolved the inconsistencies in the Mozart effect. Their results do raise questions concerning the validity of the effect, but they have not explained the inconsistency in the results. If more researchers fail to produce the Mozart effect, however, the general

conclusion will be that the Mozart effect is an oddity and not a real phenomenon.

15. This was an important statement. Many use the existence of the Mozart effect to justify the expense of a music curriculum. Although learning about music is rewarding, we should be cautious about how we justify why students must study music. If the Mozart effect does not exist, then it is inconsistent to say that exposure to music in a curriculum improves intelligence.

# Chapter 7

1. The selection of anecdotal evidence is haphazard and biased. Scientific sampling allows all elements of the population to be represented.

2. Personal experience represents anecdotal evidence. Each of us has different life experiences that may lead us to different conclusions.

3. The common feature of all methods is that they produce a representative sample. In random sampling we select, at random, individuals from the population. For sequential sampling, we select each $k$th person from a list. For stratified sampling, we identify subgroups in the population and then sample from each of these groups. For cluster sampling, we identify natural clustering of groups and then randomly select these groups.

4. (a) Anne is using a convenience sampling procedure. (b) The three friends are not representative of all students who have enrolled in the professor's courses.

5. (a) The data may be biased. (b) Using one week of sampling may not accurately represent the student's study behavior. There may be natural variation in students' workload during the semester. For example, the week before midterm and final exams may be more demanding than other weeks.

6. (a) There is a built-in selection bias for both courses. The composition course will probably enroll only first-year students. The chemistry course will probably enroll only science majors. (b) The composition course may be more representative of all first-year students if we can assume that the course is equally open to all first-year students.

7. There are two problems with this sample. First, only people who subscribe to the magazine could respond. Second, we do not know whether the people who responded truly represent the readership of the magazine. Therefore, the size of the sample is immaterial. Larger samples are not a solution to bias in the sampling procedure.

8. He or she could use several methods. The most simple is to identify city blocks of the residential areas of the city. The researcher can then randomly select blocks and people who live within these blocks. This method is a form of cluster sampling. Another would be to obtain a

current list of all known addresses (perhaps from the city's tax office or water-service office) and then select each $k$th address.

9. Use cluster sampling. Select churches that represent the different denominations and then ask the appropriate religious leader of the church to distribute the questionnaire at an event where many from the congregation will be present.

10. This is an accurate statement. A convenience sample is little better than anecdotal evidence because the data are collected in a haphazard manner and may not be representative of the population.

11. Sampling distributions represent the distribution of sample statistics, such as the mean, that are generated when creating samples from a distribution. The sample distribution represents the individual scores for a single sample.

12. According to the Central Limit Theorem, the distribution of sample means will be normally distributed especially as sample size increases. Specifically, the size of $\sigma$ and $n$ will influence the shape of the sampling distribution.

13. Each of these will be equivalent to each other. The $M$ is an unbiased estimate of $\mu$. According to the Central Limit Theorem, $\mu_M$ will equal $\mu$.

14. Each of these will be equivalent to each other. The $SD$ is an unbiased estimate of $\sigma$. According to the Central Limit Theorem, $\sigma_M = \sigma/\sqrt{n}$.

15. (a) The natural variation among subjects, $\sigma$. (b) Sampling error, $\sigma_M$.

16. It appears that the researcher used a combination of sampling methods. The selection of the cities is a form of cluster sampling. The researchers selected these cities as representative of large metropolitan areas. In addition, there appears to be a component of stratified sampling as the cities represent different geographic regions in the country. Although an inference on our part, the researcher probably selected representative high schools within each city, another form of cluster sampling. Once they selected a school, the researchers could have then randomly sampled students from each school. To ensure a representative sample, they may have used stratified sampling within each school.

17. If the researcher used true random sampling and if the sampling frame is accurate, then the sample should be representative of the population. The Central Limit Theorem predicts that the sample mean should be representative of the population mean.

18. True probability sampling would be difficult in this situation because there may be no way to identify members of the population. Specifically, there is no suitable sampling frame that identifies cocaine abusers. Therefore, the researcher would have to use convenience or snowball sampling techniques. For convenience sampling, the researcher may choose to select people who frequent areas where

cocaine abuse is known to occur. Similarly, the researcher could use people who have been arrested for cocaine use or who are seeking cocaine treatment. The researcher could also use snowball sampling by asking known cocaine users to identify other users of the drug.

19. There may be several problems with the data. We do not know whether the alumni's records are accurate. The alumni office may have lost track of its less-successful graduates and have accurate records of alumni who earn a large income. Even if the alumni records are accurate, many of the alumni might not have agreed to complete the questionnaire. Therefore, we may have reason to suspect that the data are biased.

20. Increasing sample size has no effect on the bias of the sampling procedure. Increasing sample size will merely reduce the standard error of the mean.

# Chapter 8

1. Psychologists invent tests and measurements to help them understand the relation among variables. In some cases, the test may measure a "real" thing such as height, weight, or some other construct that is tangible. Many other constructs, such as personality or intelligence, are not tangible. The problem of reification occurs when we assume that any test measures a tangible construct when it does not.

2. "Mystique of quantity" means that people infer too much information from a few numbers. In many ways, the mystique of quantity is related to the reification problem.

3. Both constructs are related because they refer to conditions where people make inferences from measurements that cannot be supported.

4. Researchers use the terms *intelligence, personality*, and *anxiety* to help them explain the relation among several variables. We use these constructs to help us explain and predict different behavior. Therefore, these words are inventions that help us understand complex behavioral phenomena. By contrast, many people use these terms to describe enduring and tangible aspects of a person. For example, a person may claim that a friend has an extroverted personality. This use of the word suggests that there is a tangible part of the person that is extroverted. By contrast, a researcher would say that the person's behaviors and attributions can be classified as extroverted for the purpose of predicting how a person will behave in a specific situation.

5. The goal of any science is to examine the relation among variables. For all empirical studies, the researcher uses some form of hypothesis that describes the predicted relation between the independent and the

dependent variable. To test the accuracy of the hypothesis, the researcher must collect objective data. Without measurement there will be no data. Without data, the hypothesis will remain an untested speculation.

6. The goal of measurement is to collect data. We use measurement to determine what information to collect and to convert the bits of information into an objective and empirical form. All measurement is objective and standardized. Objective measurement implies that the data are not biased and that the data accurately represent the construct being measured. Standardized measurement implies that we use the same procedures consistently. As a consequence, we can directly compare different things measured with the same procedures.

7. Operational definitions are essential because they allow us to determine how we convert our observations to numbers.

8. (a) An advantage of the personal interview is that the interviewer may be able to spend time with the participant to put him or her at ease and encourage the person to answer honestly. The researcher can also ask follow-up questions to obtain more information about the person's views. The disadvantages of this technique are that it may be time consuming, and the person conducting the interview will have to be well trained to collect the data. A self-administered questionnaire may be easier and less time consuming to administer. The researcher will have to spend considerable time ensuring that the questions do not bias the participant's responses. Many people may lie about their attitudes. Therefore, the wording of the questions should be selected with care.

9. Both scales allow the researcher to assess the preference for various items. For the Likert format, we present the participants with one specific statement and then provide a format of potential responses. By contrast, for the Guttman format, we present a series of statements arranged in a meaningful sequence and then ask the participants to endorse the statement with which they agree.

10. A face-to-face interview might allow the researcher to develop a rapport with the participant that might be more difficult to do over the telephone. At the same time, the reviewer can respond to facial cues and reword the question or ask follow-up questions. The telephone interview may be far more cost effective because neither the researcher nor the participant must travel to complete the interview.

11. The researcher may get much data by posting the questionnaire on a web page, but there is no way to control who answers the questions. We would be suspicious of the representativeness of the data.

12. Pretesting allows you to ensure that the participants will understand the questions and response formats that you provide. In addition, the pretesting will allow you to determine whether there are any

objectionable questions that may reduce a participant's willingness to complete the questionnaire.

13. Yes, a researcher can use closed-response questions in a face-to-face interview. Nevertheless, this technique seems to miss the opportunity of allowing the participant to elaborate on his or her answer. Perhaps both could be used—a closed-ended question with the opportunity to elaborate.

14. The researcher could use a face-to-face interview, a mailed survey, or a survey administered to an identified group of people. The face-to-face interview and the identified group may produce higher levels of compliance with the request for information. The face-to-face interview may be expensive to conduct, and finding groups of people willing to complete a questionnaire may be difficult. The mailed survey is relatively inexpensive, but includes the risk of a low rate of compliance.

15. Closed-response questions are relatively easy to answer and score and do not require much time from the participant. There may be cases, however, when additional comments from the participant will be useful. Therefore, open-ended questions allow the participant to offer detailed comments that may produce useful information not captured by a closed-response question. Open-ended questions can be difficult to score, however, and many participants might not be willing to take the time to respond fully.

16. $\alpha = 0.02; z\alpha = 2.326; n' = 3382.$

|  | N | $n'$ |
|---|---|---|
| (a) | 1,000 | 772 |
| (b) | 5,000 | 2930 |
| (c) | 25,000 | 3027 |
| (d) | 50,000 | 3189 |

17. Dr. Blume needs to reassess how he trained the observers and how they go about making their judgments. It appears that there is considerable disagreement among the reviewers.

18. (a) You would probably select shows known to be popular among children. Therefore, one way to select the shows is to pick the shows most often watched by children. Another option would be to use cluster sampling and randomly select shows broadcast during the hours that children are most likely to watch television. (b) & (c) There is no single correct way to answer these questions. Your definition should be objective and allow you to quantify your observations. (d) Frequency would probably be the best technique for this case as you want to record the number of times the acts occur. In addition, both aggressive and altruistic acts do not require much time to complete.

19.

|  | Aggressive | Altruistic | Other | Totals |
|---|---|---|---|---|
| **Aggressive** | 121 | 13 | 57 | 191 |
| **Altruistic** | 3 | 67 | 45 | 115 |
| **Other** | 12 | 10 | 93 | 115 |
| **Totals** | 136 | 90 | 195 | 421 |

$$P_A = \frac{\Sigma O_{ii}}{T} = \frac{121 + 67 + 93}{421} = \frac{281}{421} = .6675$$

$$P_C = \frac{\Sigma R_i C_i}{T^2} = \frac{(136 \times 191) + (90 \times 115) + (195 \times 115)}{421^2} = \frac{58751}{177241} = .3315$$

$$\kappa = \frac{P_A - P_C}{1 - P_C} = \frac{.6675 - .3315}{1 - .3315} = \frac{.3360}{.6685} = .5026$$

$$\kappa = .50$$

20. As we reviewed in the chapter on ethics, there are several ethical issues to consider, including: (a) *Informed consent*—the participant must volunteer to participate and should be free to withdraw from the interview at any time. In addition, the participant should understand the nature of the questions before beginning the interview process. (b) *Confidentiality*—the researcher must ensure that the responses provided by the participant will remain confidential and anonymous. (c) *Respect the dignity of the participant*—we must ensure that the questions we ask do not harm the person and that there is a reasonable scientific merit to asking the questions.

21. If the behavior is in a clearly public space and the researcher does not interact with the individuals, then there may be no need to inform the individuals that you are recording their behavior. If the recorded behavior occurs in a private area, and if the researcher interacts with the participant, then the researcher will need to obtain the participant's consent to record the situation.

# Chapter 9

1.

A. (a) *Independent variable:* Assertiveness counseling. *Dependent variable:* Participant's assertiveness as measured by the test. (b) Assertiveness counseling causes participants to become more assertive. (c) The researcher can use a true experiment for this study. (d) There is no control group. Therefore, we cannot infer cause and effect. For example, the researcher used only the people who scored low on the assertiveness test. Consequently, the improvements could represent regression toward the mean. Similarly, the improvements could represent maturation or a carryover effect. (e) We would need to know more information about the people included in the study to determine the types of inferences we can make to various populations. (f) There is no single best answer. Your answer should comment on the use of a control group and definition of the population to whom we wish the data to apply.

B. (a) *Independent variable:* Study technique. *Dependent variable:* Grades on the exam. (b) Elaborated rehearsal improves retention of academic material. (c) The researcher used a true experiment for this study. (d) There is a confounding variable. The amount of time a person studied is correlated with the type of studying they did. Specifically, the elaborated rehearsal requirement meant that the students spent more time thinking about the material. (e) If the students in the study are representative of college-age students, then there may be few problems with external validity as long as we improve the research design. (f) There is no single best answer. Your answer should address the problems you identified in the study. Specifically, the researcher needs to control the amount of time the students spend studying.

C. (a) *Independent variable:* The presence of lying. We would assume that the researcher wants to determine the absence or presence of deception. *Dependent variable:* Performance of lie detector test. (b) The lie detector test allows one to detect deception. (c) There is no research design as the researcher used only one group. (d) There are many problems with this research, primarily that there is no control group in the study. The researcher needs to include a group of participants who did not receive the money. In addition, it appears that the researcher scored the lie detector tests. Therefore, we need to question his objectivity in evaluating the data. (e) We need to question whether the situation and the participants represent the situations experienced where a lie detector is used to determine guilt. (f) There is no single best answer. Your answer should address the problems you identified in the study. Specifically, the researcher needs to include a control group as well as a double-blind procedure.

D. (a) *Independent variable:* The effects of a pornographic film. *Dependent variable:* Average length of electrical shocks given. (b) Watching pornography increases aggression. (c) There is no research design as the researcher used only one group. (d) There are many problems with this research, primarily that there is no control group in the study. The researcher needs to include a group of participants who did not watch the movie. The researcher could use control groups that had participants watch equal-length films of different content to ensure that content of the pornographic film influenced the level of aggression. Finally, there is no clear rationale for using only men in the study. (e) The researcher needs to resolve the problems with internal validity before examining problems of external validity. In addition, the researcher needs to define the population to allow us to determine whether college men are representative of the population. (f) There is no single best answer. Your answer should address the problems you identified in the study. Specifically, the researcher needs to include sufficient control groups to examine the relation between the two variables.

2. Memory Recall Study

Men and women will differ in the number of positive memories recalled.

$$H_0: \mu_M = \mu_W \quad H_1: \mu_M = \mu_W$$

Men and women will differ in the number of negative memories recalled.

$$H_0: \mu_M = \mu_W \quad H_1: \mu_M = \mu_W$$

Men and women will differ in the average score of the Life Satisfaction Scale.

$$H_0: \mu_M = \mu_W \quad H_1: \mu_M = \mu_W$$

Essay writing and attitudes: Writing an essay will change one's attitude about a 5% increase in tuition. Students in the control group will have a different attitude than students in the experimental group.

$$H_0: \mu_C = \mu_E \quad H_1: \mu_C = \mu_E$$

3. Memory Recall Study

**Positive Memories**

$$d_2 = \frac{10.4667 - 8.4000}{\sqrt{\dfrac{4.5522 + 3.1142}{2}}}, \quad d_2 = \frac{2.0667}{1.9579}, \quad d_2 = 1.056$$

**Negative Memories**

$$d_2 = \frac{7.2000 - 5.5333}{\sqrt{\dfrac{4.1714 + 3.1237}{2}}}, \quad d_2 = \frac{1.6667}{1.9099}, \quad d_2 = 0.8727$$

**Satisfaction with Life Scale**

$$d_2 = \frac{6.1333 - 5.3333}{\sqrt{\dfrac{4.2667 + 4.0954}{2}}}, \quad d_2 = \frac{0.8000}{2.0448}, \quad d_2 = 0.3912$$

Essay writing and attitudes

$$d_2 = \frac{9.50 - 13.0}{\sqrt{\dfrac{5.17 + 4.66}{2}}}, \quad d_2 = \frac{-3.50}{4.915}, \quad d_2 = -0.712$$

4. For each data set, committing a Type I error means that we reject the null hypothesis when we should not. In the study examining the sex differences, we would assume that there is a difference between men and women when there is no such difference. By contrast, committing a Type II error means that we fail to reject the null hypothesis when we should reject it. For example, in the study examining the effects of essay writing, a Type II error would mean that we ignore the effect that writing has on attitude change.

One could argue that for all these studies, a Type II error is the greater problem in that the researcher wants to examine the relation between two variables. Ignoring this effect may mean that an important insight to human behavior will be missed. The consequence of a Type I error will be that the researcher is temporarily misled to believe that there is a meaningful relation among the variables. If the null hypothesis is correct, then the researcher and others will have a difficult time replicating the results.

# Chapter 10

1. The correlation coefficient converts the original scores to standardized or z-scores. Therefore, the coefficient converts the scores into the same scale before determining the relation between the variables.

2. The absolute value of the correlation coefficient indicates the strength of the relation between the two variables. An alternative method is to convert the correlation coefficient, $r$, to the coefficient of determination, $r^2$. The larger the coefficient of determination, the greater the relation between the two variables.

3. The only conclusion is that grades and study time are correlated. Because we cannot require a random group of students to study and another group to not study, we cannot rule out alternative explanations.

4. (a) Because of a small sample, she could have obtained a small correlation by chance. (b) The relation between the two variables

is not well defined by a straight line. (c) It is possible that the sampling procedure produced a truncation in the range of potential scores. (d) There may be no meaningful relation between the two variables.

5. Devin has a problem with his sampling procedure. We can assume that only bright students are admitted to the college. Consequently, there is a truncated-range problem. Variance of test scores for these students will be much less than the full range of test scores of all high school graduates who take the test.

6. Weight is probably a far more stable characteristic than personality.

7. Both allow us to determine the degree to which two rates agree with each other.

8. The internal consistency of a test. Higher scores of coefficient alpha indicate greater agreement among the individual test items.

9. The items in this test do not measure the same construct. It is possible that the items measure different constructs.

10. Increase the length of the test and ensure that the items measure the same construct.

11. These forms of validity help us ensure that the test measures what it is supposed to measure (convergent validity) and does not measure different constructs (discriminant validity).

12. According to the regression-to-the-mean phenomenon, we would expect that their scores would be lower the second time we tested them.

# Chapter 11

1. (a) The difference between the means will reflect the difference between the two populations, if any, and the effects of random sampling error. (b) The researcher cannot assume that the difference between the means represents anything more than random sampling error. The researcher needs to examine the standard error of the difference between means to evaluate the data. Using Student's $t$-ratio, the researcher can compare the difference between means to the standard error of the difference between means. If the $t$-ratio is sufficiently large, the researcher can reject the null hypothesis that the two population means are equivalent. (c) Decreases in the standard error will increase the absolute magnitude of the $t$-ratio. Increases in the standard error will decrease the absolute value of the $t$-ratio.

2. $H_0: \mu_1 \leq \mu_2$: No, the alternative hypothesis predicts that $H_1: \mu_1 > \mu_2$.
   $H_0: \mu_1 \geq \mu_2$: Yes, if the $t$-ratio is sufficiently large. The alternative hypothesis predicts that $H_1: \mu_1 < \mu_2$.

3. If the researcher wants to confirm a theory or a prediction, then he or she should make the prediction based on the theory, not a preliminary review of the data.

4. Researchers select inferential statistics based on the research design and research hypothesis they created and on the characteristics of the data.

5. Deciding whether to reject the null hypothesis is a value judgment, and the researcher must consider the consequences of committing either a Type I or a Type II error. Rudner argued that these consequences should direct the criteria for rejecting the null hypothesis.

6. The researcher would have to show that the independent variable preceded the dependent variable and that all alternative explanations have been ruled out.

7. (a) *False.* Although the researcher may reject the null hypothesis, the decision was an inference. Therefore, there is always a probability that the null hypothesis is correct and the researcher made a Type I error. All the researcher can do is assume that there is reasonable evidence to tentatively reject the null hypothesis and accept the alternative hypothesis. (b) *False.* We have no way of objectively determining the probability that $H_0$ is true. (c) *False.* The only inference we can draw from $p$ is that if the null hypothesis is a correct statement, then the probability of the outcome is $p < .01$. (d) *False.* The only inference we can draw from $p$ is the probability of data is $p < .01$ if the null hypothesis is a correct statement. (e) *False.* This statement is an inference of power. We cannot use the size of $p$ to determine the degree to which the results will be replicated with further research. (f) *True.*

8. (a) Because the probabilities are identical, we can infer that Mark's experiment had the greater power. He was able to detect a statistically significant effect with fewer participants. (b) The greater power may be due to the selection of levels of the independent variable, the reliability and accuracy of the measure used to quantify the dependent variable, the homogeneity of participants, or a combination of these factors.

9. $\alpha = .05$—two-tailed: $n = 400$ or 800 participants total.
$\alpha = .05$—one-tailed: $n = 300$ or 600 participants total.

10. Khalil needs to determine whether there are other levels of the independent variables that will increase the difference between the groups. He also needs to determine whether there are better ways to measure the dependent variable that are more reliable and precise. For example, the researcher might be able to increase power by collecting more observations from each participant. Finally, Khalil should determine whether there are ways to make the groups more homogeneous.

# Chapter 12

1. There are a couple advantages. First, the $F$-ratio is a single test that simultaneously examines the differences among the groups. Therefore, the researcher avoids the problem associated with an inflated Type I error rate created by multiple comparisons of sample means using the $t$-ratio. Second, the ANOVA allows the researcher to examine the relation that exists between the independent and dependent variables.

2. The researcher can assume a cause-and-effect relation if the researcher used random assignment to place participants into the treatment conditions, used a control group, and is able to discount or rule out alternative explanations.

3. The between-group variance represents the difference among the means of the groups. This variation represents the effect of the independent variable and the effect of random error. The treatment variance represents the specific effects of the independent variable.

4. The mean is 0 because we assume that the effects of error are random.

5. For a control group, $\alpha_j = 0$ because the research does not expose the participants to the independent variable.

6. a. *False.* The $F$-ratio is a comparison of the size of the between-groups variance to the within-groups variance. A large $F$-ratio merely indicates the between-groups variance is larger than the within-groups variance.

   b. *True.* As $\varepsilon_{ij}$ increases, the $MS_{within}$ also increases. All else being equal, the $F$-ratio will increase as well.

   c. *False.* No measure of variance can be less than 0.

   d. *False.* We can never prove the null hypothesis to be a correct statement. The independent variable may influence the dependent variable; however, the low power of the research design failed to allow us to detect the effect.

   e. *False.* In a true experiment the researcher controls the levels of the independent variable.

   f. *True.* See answer 5.

   g. *False.* This is false if the null hypothesis is a true statement.

7. The researcher will require approximately 18 participants per group.

8. All else being equal, any decrease in $MS_{within}$ will result in a larger $F$-ratio.

9. The ANOVA is an omnibus test because it simultaneously compares the differences among all the group means.

10. Both tests compare the difference between means. The $t$-ratio compares the difference between two group means. The $F$-ratio compares the difference among two or more means.

# Chapter 13

1.

|       | $a_1$          | $a_2$          |                 |
|-------|----------------|----------------|-----------------|
| $b_1$ | $M_{11} = 2$   | $M_{21} = 3$   | $M_{b1} = 2.5$  |
| $b_2$ | $M_{12} = 3$   | $M_{22} = 4$   | $M_{b2} = 3.5$  |
|       | $M_{a1} = 2.5$ | $M_{a2} = 3.5$ | $\bar{M} = 3.0$ |

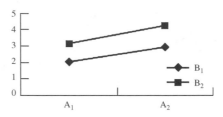

There appears to be main effects for Factors A and B, but no evidence of an interaction.

2.

|       | $a_1$          | $a_2$          |                 |
|-------|----------------|----------------|-----------------|
| $b_1$ | $M_{11} = 4$   | $M_{21} = 6$   | $M_{b1} = 5$    |
| $b_2$ | $M_{12} = 5$   | $M_{22} = 3$   | $M_{b2} = 4$    |
|       | $M_{a1} = 4.5$ | $M_{a2} = 4.5$ | $\bar{M} = 4.5$ |

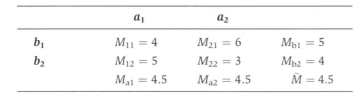

There appears to be a main effect for Factor B but not Factor A. In addition, there appears to be an interaction.

3.

|       | $a_1$        | $a_2$        |                 |
|-------|--------------|--------------|-----------------|
| $b_1$ | $M_{11} = 4$ | $M_{21} = 2$ | $M_{b1} = 3$    |
| $b_2$ | $M_{12} = 2$ | $M_{22} = 4$ | $M_{b2} = 3$    |
|       | $M_{a1} = 3$ | $M_{a2} = 3$ | $\bar{M} = 3$   |

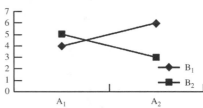

There are no main effects, but there is an interaction of the two factors.

4.

|       | $a_1$        | $a_2$        |                 |
|-------|--------------|--------------|-----------------|
| $b_1$ | $M_{11} = 5$ | $M_{21} = 9$ | $M_{b1} = 7$    |
| $b_2$ | $M_{12} = 3$ | $M_{22} = 5$ | $M_{b2} = 4$    |
|       | $M_{a1} = 4$ | $M_{a1} = 7$ | $\bar{M} = 5.5$ |

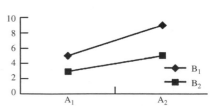

There appears to be significant main effects for both factors and the interaction.

5. a.

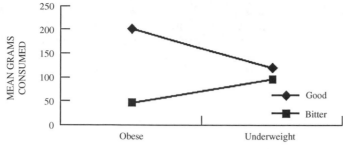

b. There appears to be an interaction between the weight of the participant and the amount of ice cream consumed. Had the researchers not included the weight variable, then it would appear the people ate the same amount of good- and bitter-tasting ice cream. The data indicate that obese participants were greatly influenced by the taste of the ice cream.

6. a.

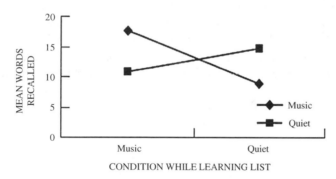

b. These data indicate an important interaction that could not be found using single-variable studies. The study indicates that people perform best when tested under the same conditions under which they learned the material.

7. The $SS_{total}$ would remain the same because the researcher is examining the same set of data. The $SS_{within}$ would become smaller, however, because some of the variance will be subsumed within the effect of the newly identified independent variable and the interaction of the two variables.

8. The lack of a statistically significant main effect does not mean that the independent variable has no effect on the dependent variable. One must examine the interaction to determine whether there is an important interplay between the two independent variables used in the research.

9. The individual cell means represent the effects of the main effects as well as the interaction of the two independent variables.

10. The two-variable ANOVA may be more powerful because the researcher includes a second independent variable in the research design. The second variable, and its interaction with the other independent variable, may reduce the size of the within-groups variance.

# Chapter 14

1. The matched-groups and repeated-measures designs are special forms of the correlated groups design. For both techniques, we identify a subject variable that can contribute to the total variability of the scores. Using matched-groups design, we group people together who share common features and then randomly assign them to different treatment conditions. This procedure ensures that the participants in the groups are highly correlated. Using the repeated-measures design, we test the same participants under different treatment conditions or on several occasions. By identifying a significant source of variance related to the difference among the participants, we can reduce the size of the within-group variance and more readily detect a difference among the group means.

2. In a matched-participants design, we group participants into similar levels based on a criterion measure and then assign the participants to the treatment conditions. In a repeated-measures design, we test the same participants under more than one condition.

3. *Contrast:* The participant reacts to the changes in the research conditions. *Fatigue:* The participants become bored or tired due to their participation in the study. *Adaptation:* The participants become used to the experiment and do not respond as they would if they were tested once. *Learning:* The participant's skill at the task increases. *Pretest sensitization:* The first measurement of the participant's behavior changes his or her perception of the purpose of the research.

4. There are several control conditions. The first control requires that we measure the participants' behavior on two occasions but not expose them to the treatment condition. This control allows us to examine how people's behavior will change over time if they do not experience the treatment. A second control condition requires us to expose the participants to the treatment and the follow-up measure, but use no pretest measure. This control allows us to examine the consequences of a treatment independent of any carryover effect. The last control group receives the posttest only. This control condition acts as the classic control group as the participants do not experience the effects of the treatment or the carryover effect.

5. Each person is his or her control because they will be tested in the control condition as well as the treatment condition. Therefore, we can use the ANOVA to determine how much of the change in

the scores was due to the independent variable and how much was due to the differences among the participants.

6. A correlated-groups ANOVA will increase power because the within-groups variance will be decreased by the variance due to the differences among the participants.

7. Researchers use these techniques when there is a significant threat of a carryover effect and the researcher wishes to use a repeated-measures design to increase power.

8. If the matching variable contributes to the within-groups variance, then this design along with the corresponding ANOVA will reduce estimates of random variance.

9. & 10. Both the matched-groups design and the yoked-control design are similar in that we want to have a high correlation between the participants in the two groups. Indeed, both research designs are special forms for the correlated-groups design. The difference between the methods is how we create the groups. For the matched-groups design we pretest our participants using a test and then pair participants who have similar scores. We then take each member of the pair and randomly assign them to either the treatment or control groups. For the yoked-control condition, we randomly assign pairs of participants to the experimental and control groups. We then arrange for the participant in the control group to have the exact same sequence of experiences as the participant in the experimental group. Researchers use the yoked-control design when the behavior of the participant affects the sequence of events in the study.

11. For an independent-groups design, each participant's behavior is independent of other participants' behavior. The participant is tested under only one treatment condition. In a correlated-groups design, the participant is tested under several situations (e.g., a repeated-measures design) or the researcher uses a matched-groups design.

# Chapter 15

1. The ABAB meets the requirements of a true experiment. The "A" phases of the design represent the control condition when the independent variable is absent. The "B" phase represents the presence of the independent variable. Therefore, the researcher can observe the relation between the independent and dependent variable by adding and removing the intervention. In addition, the researcher has direct control over the presentation of the intervention.

2. (a) In both cases, the researcher has control over the independent variable (the researcher can determine when the participants receive the treatment). Furthermore, the researcher includes a control condition that represents the absence of the critical variable. (b) Both researchers selected the participants from the same subject pool.

Therefore, the concerns regarding the external validity about the generality of the findings are the same for the two studies.

3. In the conventional true experiment, we must withhold the treatment from all the participants in the control group. Depending on the length of the experiment, this may mean that the participants will suffer the depression while others are receiving what the researcher believes to be a useful treatment. By contrast, the multiple-baseline procedures use a shorter baseline and ensure that all the participants receive the treatment.

4. The instructor could place all the students on a baseline (no homework) and routinely test their knowledge of the material. As the semester passes, the instructor would begin to ask some students to complete homework assignments. The data should indicate that knowledge of the material will increase once a student begins to complete the homework.

5. The primary difference between the two is the time-frame used to study the changes in behavior. Longitudinal research designs tend to span long times measured in weeks, months, or years. Both are similar in that the researcher wants to examine how the passage of time influences changes in behavior.

6. The primary purpose of survival analysis is to examine the time it takes for a specific event to occur in a person's life. For example, a researcher may be interested in the risk of relapse of patients who have just completed a drug and alcohol rehabilitation program.

7. Both techniques include a baseline procedure and monitor behavior after the intervention begins. In both cases, the onset of the intervention can be staggered.

## Chapter 16

1. The primary purpose of the statistic is to examine the difference between observed and expected scores. If the $\chi^2$ statistic is sufficiently large, we can assume that the frequencies in the categories are not the result of chance factors. The goodness-of-fit test examines the frequency of observations along one dimension. The test of independence examines the observations for two variables.

2. The data are not nominal. The number of bar presses is a ratio scale (there is an absolute 0). Consequently, the researcher needs to use a different statistical test such as the ANOVA.

3. Although the study is interesting, we must wonder whether the memories are independent of one another. For example, will a subject's memory of his or her father influence the memory of the mother? Because the memories may not be independent, the $\chi^2$ test may not be valid.

4.

| Goal | 1965 | 1998 | $\frac{(O_i - E_i)^2}{E_i}$ |
|------|------|------|------|
| $a$ | 15 | 8 | 3.2667 |
| $b$ | 53 | 48 | 0.4717 |
| $c$ | 25 | 57 | 40.9600 |
| $d$ | 27 | 47 | 14.8148 |
|  | 120 | 160 | 59.5132 |

$$\chi^2(N = 280, 3) = 59.5132, p < .05$$

5.

| Program | $O$ | $E$ | $\frac{(O_i - E_i)^2}{E_i}$ |
|---------|-----|-----|------|
| 1 | 12 | 12.5714 | 0.0260 |
| 2 | 23 | 12.5714 | 8.6510 |
| 3 | 8 | 12.5714 | 1.6623 |
| 4 | 7 | 12.5714 | 2.4692 |
| 5 | 15 | 12.5714 | 0.4692 |
| 6 | 5 | 12.5714 | 4.5601 |
| 7 | 18 | 12.5714 | 2.3442 |
|  | 88 | 88.0000 | 20.1818 |

$$\chi^2(N = 88, 7) = 20.1818, \ p < .05$$

6.

|  | Condition A | Condition B | Row Total |
|--|-------------|-------------|-----------|
| Helped | $O_{11} = 75$<br>$E_{11} = \dfrac{115 \times 120}{240}$<br>$E_{11} = 57.5$ | $O_{12} = 45$<br>$E_{12} = \dfrac{125 \times 120}{240}$<br>$E_{12} = 62.5$ | $R_1 = 120$ |
| No help | $O_{21} = 40$<br>$E_{21} = \dfrac{115 \times 120}{240}$<br>$E_{21} = 57.5$ | $O_{22} = 80$<br>$E_{22} = \dfrac{125 \times 120}{240}$<br>$E_{22} = 62.5$ | $R_2 = 120$ |
| Column Total | $C_1 = 115$ | $C_2 = 125$ | $T = 240$ |

$$\chi^2 = \frac{(75 - 57.5)^2}{57.5} + \frac{(45 - 62.5)^2}{62.5} + \frac{(40 - 57.5)^2}{57.5} + \frac{(80 - 62.5)^2}{62.5}$$

$$\chi^2 = 5.3261 + 4.9000 + 5.3261 + 4.9000$$

$$\chi^2 = (N = 240, 1) = 20.45, \ p < .05$$

7.
$$\chi^2 = \frac{(|25 - 30| - 1)^2}{25 + 30} = 0.2909 \quad z = \sqrt{0.2909} = 0.5394$$

The differences are not statistically significant.

8.

|   | Male | Female | Row Total |
|---|------|--------|-----------|
| + | $O_{11} = 28$ $E_{11} = \dfrac{126 \times 58}{300}$ $E_{11} = 24.36$ | $O_{12} = 30$ $E_{12} = \dfrac{174 \times 58}{300}$ $E_{12} = 33.64$ | $R_1 = 58$ |
| − | $O_{21} = 98$ $E_{21} = \dfrac{126 \times 242}{300}$ $E_{21} = 101.64$ | $O_{22} = 144$ $E_{22} = \dfrac{174 \times 242}{300}$ $E_{22} = 140.36$ | $R_2 = 242$ |
| Column Total | $C_1 = 126$ | $C_2 = 174$ | $T = 300$ |

$$\chi^2 = \frac{(28 - 24.36)^2}{24.36} + \frac{(98 - 101.64)^2}{101.64} + \frac{(30 - 33.64)^2}{33.64} + \frac{(144 - 140.36)^2}{140.36}$$
$$\chi^2 = (N = 240, 1) = 1.163, p > .05$$

According to these results we cannot reject the null hypothesis. Therefore, we must assume that we do not have data to indicate that there is a relation between one's sex and risk for binge drinking.

9.

|   | Letter | Phone call | Nothing | Row Total |
|---|--------|-----------|---------|-----------|
| Compliance | $O_{11} = 44$ $E_{11} = 44.33$ $\hat{e}_{11} = -0.08$ | $O_{12} = 68$ $E_{12} = 44.33$ $\hat{e}_{12} = 5.84$ | $O_{13} = 21$ $E_{12} = 44.33$ $\hat{e}_{13} = -5.73$ | $R_1 = 133$ |
| No compliance | $O_{11} = 56$ $E_{21} = 55.67$ $\hat{e}_{21} = 0.08$ | $O_{12} = 32$ $E_{22} = 55.67$ $\hat{e}_{22} = -5.84$ | $O_{13} = 79$ $E_{23} = 55.67$ $\hat{e}_{23} = 5.73$ | $R_2 = 167$ |
| Column Total | $C_1 = 100$ | $C_2 = 100$ | $C_3 = 100$ | $T = 300$ |

$$\chi^2 = (N = 300, 2) = 44.762, p < .05$$

It is clear from the $\chi^2$ test that there is a significant relation between presurvey contact and subsequent compliance. Examining the adjusted residuals, it is clear that the phone call had the greatest impact on increasing compliance.

# Chapter 17

1. "Mom, qualitative research tends to focus more on rich detail of a particular phenomenon instead of relying solely on numbers and statistics as quantitative research does. A mixed-methods design involves the use of both numbers/statistics and gathering data rich in detail in order to obtain the most comprehensive explanation of a phenomenon."

2. a. A possible research plan is to administer patient satisfaction surveys, at the time of checkout, that they can complete in privacy and return by mail using a prestamped envelope to assure anonymity of responses and increase the patient response rate. The surveys should consist of open-ended satisfaction questions, a write-in comment section, as well as questions with a Likert scale response format (1 = very unsatisfied, 7 = very satisfied).

   b. A possible research plan to assess employee satisfaction at an oil refinery using a mixed-methods design is to collect satisfaction information in one-on-one interviews with employees if time permits, examine current and previous turnover rates at the refinery, conduct one-on-one employee exit interviews if possible, and mail exit/satisfaction interviews to employees who left the company within the past six months. The exit/satisfaction surveys would consist of open-ended and Likert scale response formats (1 = very unsatisfied, 7 = very satisfied).

   c. A possible research plan to examine the impact of work on children in families where both parents work full-time is to administer surveys consisting of both Likert scale questions as well as open-ended format to both the child and the parents, if possible. It would also be necessary to collect information pertaining to the number of hours each parent works in a typical week, the type of work hours involved (8 A.M.–5 P.M.; night shift), the number of academic or leisure activities that the child participates in during and outside of school, the current and past grade point average (GPA) of the child, as well as the number of the child's school absences.

   d. A possible research plan to assess the benefits and costs associated with religious involvement on marital satisfaction is to create a set of questions to administer to each marriage partner separately as well as together in an interview situation. In addition, it is necessary to collect information pertaining to the number of days per week each partner attends church and the number of hours spent involved in church-related activities per week/month. It would be helpful to collect the same information using the same format from married couples of the same age and socioeconomic status as those used in the religious community.

3. Some of the most important pros of using quantitative methods are the ability to statistically analyze the information and establish a very accurate view of relationships between variables and, in some situations, cause and effect. Cons associated with quantitative methods are that they simply mathematically state that there is a relationship between two variables and they lack the ability to richly describe the relationship and provide a deeper understanding of the phenomenon.

   An important pro of qualitative methods is that they provide a way to explore new phenomenon in a descriptive manner in order to uncover underlying reasons for relationships and causality that may later be found in quantitative research strategies. In contrast, a con to the qualitative research method is that the information is more difficult to statistically support and the findings are generally not favored to be reported alone in the scientific world.

   New technology such as the Internet and e-mail is making it much more accessible for research participants to respond to survey formats, questionnaires, and interviews that incorporate a mixed-methods approach so that scientists can enjoy the pros of both methods while reaching new heights in sample sizes. New editions of statistical-analysis packages are also making it easier for researchers to code qualitative data and support their findings with numbers.

4. These examples should be generated based on your specific interests, so we are choosing not to provide you with a guideline so that you may explore your research interests independently. Be sure to consult with your professor to ensure that you are on the right track with your responses and ideas.

5. Your responses to this activity will depend on the speech of choice. Be sure to reference the information in the chapter pertaining to content analysis and be sure that you and your partner agree on the process and content. Consult with your professor to ensure that you are on the right track with your responses and ideas.

6. If time were to permit, an alternative qualitative and mixed-methods technique that these researchers could integrate into this study that would add something to what they already accomplished could be to ask the participants to indicate on the mail-in questionnaire whether they would be willing to be contacted to participate in further research regarding the study. If participants were to agree to be contacted, then each one could be asked to participate in a brief interview on campus, conducted by a primary researcher or one of the trained graduate students, that consisted of quantitative scale, intensity, and frequency questions. This opportunity would also allow the researchers to obtain more detail on the stressful incidents that were reported and any other research measure to descriptively support the quantitative data.

# Appendix A

| Xa1 | za1 | Percentile | Xa2 | za2 | Percentile |
|-----|-----|------------|-----|-----|------------|
| 26 | 1.2 | 88.5 | 11 | −1.2 | 11.5 |
| 23 | 0.6 | 72.6 | 29 | 0.6 | 72.6 |
| 17 | −0.6 | 27.4 | 17 | −0.6 | 27.4 |
| 29 | 1.8 | 96.4 | 41 | 1.8 | 96.4 |
| 22 | 0.4 | 65.5 | 27 | 0.4 | 65.5 |
| 19 | −0.2 | 42.1 | 25 | 0.2 | 57.9 |
| 11 | −1.8 | 3.6 | 5 | −1.8 | 3.6 |
| 20 | 0.0 | 50.0 | 23 | 0.0 | 50.0 |
| 18 | −0.4 | 34.5 | 19 | −0.4 | 34.5 |
| 15 | −1.0 | 15.9 | 33 | 1.0 | 84.1 |

(a) $\Sigma X_{a1} = 200$, $\Sigma X_{a2} = 230$

(b) $\Sigma X_{a1}^2 = 4{,}250$, $\Sigma X_{a2}^2 = 6{,}290$

(c) $(\Sigma X_{a1})^2 = 40{,}000$, $(\Sigma X_{a2})^2 = 52{,}900$

(d) $Mdn_{a1} = 19.5$, $Mdn_{a2} = 24$

(e) $M_{a1} = 20.0$, $M_{a2} = 23$

(f) $S_{a1}^2 = 25$, $S_{a2}^2 = 100$

(g) $s_{a1} = 5$, $s_{a2} = 10$

(h) $VAR_{u1} = 27.78$, $VAR_{a2} = 111.111$

(i) $SD_{a1} = 5.27$, $SD_{a2} = 10.54$

(j) See table

(k) See table

# Author Index

# Subject Index